MASS MEDIA
AND THE
SUPREME COURT
The Legacy of the Warren Years

MASS MEDIA
AND THE
SUPREME COURT
The Legacy of the Warren Years

FOURTH EDITION

EDITED, WITH COMMENTARIES

AND SPECIAL NOTES, BY

KENNETH S. DEVOL, Ph.D.

Professor of Journalism

California State University, Northridge

COMMUNICATION ARTS BOOKS

HASTINGS HOUSE
MAMARONECK, NEW YORK

For Nicole Erin Devol

Library of Congress Cataloging in Publication Data
Main entry under title:
Mass media and the Supreme Court.
    Excerpts from opinions of the Supreme Court, with concurrences and dissents, and articles from various journals of law and mass communication.
    Includes index.
    1. Press law—United States—Cases.   2. Telecommunica-tion—Law and legislation—United States—Cases.
3. Liberty of the press—United States—Cases.
I. Devol, Kenneth S.   II. United States. Supreme Court.
III. Series.   IV. Series: Communication arts books.
KF2750.A7M37 1982   343.73'099 82-6242
ISBN 0-8038-9305-1   347.30399   AACR2

Published simultaneously in Canada by
Saunders of Toronto, Ltd., Markham, Ontario

Printed in the United States of America

Designed by Al Lichtenberg

10 9 8 7 6 5 4 3 2 1

CONTENTS

PREFACE

A newly aroused interest in the Supreme Court emerged during the 1960s—and continued into the 1990s—largely because of the Justices' willingness to speak out on a series of First Amendment questions. With the democratic concept of majority rule as a foundation, the Warren Court turned its attention to the protection of minority rights, and included among these was freedom of expression—freedom to profess unorthodox and unpopular views. The Warren Court, and later the Burger and Rehnquist courts, undertook questions of obscenity, motion picture censorship, libel, right of privacy and trial by television—questions largely ignored prior to the 16 years of the Warren era. This new legal activism increases the importance of the Court to those interested in the mass media, political science, sociology and other disciplines devoted to the changing patterns of our social fabric.

Constitutional law is not static. It is ever-evolving, ever-changing. It is significant, therefore, that excerpts from major concurrences and dissents are included. A Justice's dissent today may later become a majority view. The great issues of the First Amendment deserve more than a mere recounting of name, date and definition. Indeed, some of the issues—obscenity is one—have escaped adequate legal definition in spite of all of our trying.

It might be helpful to the reader to note certain limits drawn by the editor. No attempt was made to review cases dealing with freedom of speech or assembly *per se*. Only questions concerning the mass media were included. Nor were cases included which deal primarily with business aspects of the media, such as anti-trust violations. Deletions in the opinions and articles were made only where indicated by ellipses, except for certain footnotes, case citations, and other occasional references which, in the view of the editor, tend to impede reading for the nonlawyer. Major citations remain in the text and appear in the table of cases. More detailed citations may be found in the casebooks.

The editor, of course, is deeply indebted to those authors and publishing houses which allowed the use of material already under copyright. These interpretations of the Court's role added immeasurably to the value of this volume. Full credit is given to these scholars and publishers in footnotes which accompany the beginning of each article.

Legal opinions are stereotyped as being verbose, ponderous and boring. While this may be true more often than not, the pens of our leading jurists have recorded expressions of great power and wisdom. It is hoped that some of these moments have been captured in this volume of readings, along with some of the drama, the struggles of mind and matter which confronted these Justices over the years.

K.S.D.

June, 1990   Northridge, California

TABLE OF CASES

MASS MEDIA
AND THE
SUPREME COURT
The Legacy of the Warren Years

CHAPTER 1

THE JUSTICES AND
THE FIRST AMENDMENT

"Congress shall make no law," says the First Amendment to the Constitution of the United States, ". . . abridging the freedom of speech, or of the press. . . ." The framers of the Constitution did not interpret "freedom," leaving that task for the courts. At first reading, the statement appears to be clear. It says "no law." This is the firm interpretation placed upon it by "absolutists" of the United States Supreme Court, who in the Warren Court included Justices Black and Douglas. Yet the history of the Court's interpretation of the First Amendment is far from absolute. Whereas the first Ten Amendments to the Constitution, the Bill of Rights, were written to end uncertainty, several of those amendments have been encased in controversy which has tended to harden in recent years. Such fundamental concepts as free speech and press, fair trial, the right to keep and bear arms, separation of church and state, the right to dissent, self-incrimination, protection against illegal searches and seizures, and due process of law all have come under increasing public scrutiny.

The adoption of the first Ten Amendments was to put at ease those who noted that the original Constitution contained no guarantee of "human" or "natural" rights. This opposition was strong enough to present a clear threat to the ratification of the larger document. The Bill of Rights, then, was adopted by the First Congress and ratified by the states in order to set aside the fears of those who foresaw a return to the more autocratic English approach to government. Even though Constitutions of most of the 13 states contained individual rights guarantees, the adoption by the Congress of these same guarantees at the federal level insured ratification of the national Constitution.

But ratification did not end debate over the First Amendment's wording. Following Jefferson's lead, some urged that the freedoms mentioned in the First Amendment should be considered "natural human rights." Others talked in terms of "liberty versus license," i.e. in terms of degree. The Supreme Court prior to the

1930s *suspended free speech and press if the expressions constituted a "reasonable tendency" to endanger society. Restraints in the 1930s were limited to only those expressions which created a "clear and present danger" to society.*

This same period saw the revival of the historic concept of "prior" or "previous restraint." The Court with the landmark Near case of 1931 attempted to define freedom of the press as prohibiting government from restraining a publication prior to its distribution unless it was determined that the contents of that publication constituted a "clear and present danger" to society or that the expression did not fall within the bounds of First Amendment protection. In the years that followed, Justices have echoed the view that the goal of the framers of the First Amendment was indeed to guard against "prior restraint" by government, but they have disagreed as to when exceptions to this rule are constitutionally valid. More recently, the Court has been more inclined to consider the rights of the individual weighed against the rights of society, i.e. the "balancing interests" concept. And, of course, the Court has continued to rule that the First Amendment is not absolute and that certain expressions by their very nature do not fall within its protection, e.g. obscenity. Each of these theories—"prior restraint," "human rights," "liberty vs. license," "reasonable tendency," "clear and present danger," "balancing interests" —has had "its day in court."

Historians usually look at the development of the United States in terms of presidential administrations. Yet decisions rendered by the Supreme Court often surpass administrative programs in their impact on the American scene. Active, literate Justices, such as Warren, Marshall, Holmes, Brandeis, Hughes, Frankfurter, Brennan, and Black, all have woven into the democratic fabric significant and lasting patterns. Without these men and their less familiar colleagues the United States would be a far different nation. Perhaps only a handful of presidents have influenced public life more than these Supreme Court Justices.

The 16 years of the Warren Court, 1953–69, have been termed the most dynamic since the 34-year tenure of Chief Justice Marshall in the early 1800s. The Court set national patterns and standards for race relations, representative government, freedom of the press and civil rights, including treatment of criminal suspects. In these decisions and others, the Warren Court changed the direction of national life.

Chief Justice Earl Warren, a former three-term governor and attorney general of California, was appointed to the bench by President Eisenhower following the death of Chief Justice Vinson. The following year he wrote the Court's opinion in its unanimous decision ordering desegregation of public schools, Brown v. Board of Education. Separate but equal, he wrote, cannot be tolerated in public education. This decision, in 1954, has been heralded as the beginning of the civil rights movement as a national commitment. The decision which the Chief Justice himself has said was most important during his tenure was the "one man, one vote" decision on legislative reapportionment.

But for all of its landmark decisions, the Court during Chief Justice Warren's tenure was one of the most divided and controversial in history. There were several non-majority decisions (some involving the media, e.g. Estes). The nation has not accepted nor has it implemented without foot-dragging many of the Court's major pronouncements (e.g. desegregation), has risen up in disbelief at some (e.g. outlawing required prayer and Bible reading in public schools), has expressed anger at others (e.g. setting higher standards for treatment of criminal suspects), and has experienced frustration due to still others (e.g. limiting obscenity prosecutions generally to hard-core pornography).

It has been charged that the major weakness of the Warren Court was its impreciseness, thereby causing confusion and frustration among the lower courts and police, as well as the general public, and its lack of what Justice Frankfurter called "judicial restraint." But the Court's lack of "judicial restraint" is applauded by the Court's supporters, who also are legion.

A criticism aimed specifically at Chief Justice Warren was that he was more a statesman than a jurist. He bonded the Court, it is claimed, more by personal warmth than by judicial logic. But this may have been the precise reason he was appointed to the bench and almost certainly was a factor in his appointment to head the President's Commission investigating the assassination of President Kennedy. Still, Senators fumed publicly, law enforcement officers complained, and ultra-right wing groups erected "Impeach Earl Warren" signs along America's highways. The criticism—and the praise—also seems to stem more from political or personal philosophy than from constitutional or legal grounds.

Another problem of the Warren Court was the huge work load it had accepted. The case volume had tripled since the days of the Hughes Court. Many areas, such as invasion of privacy, previously left to the states, became Supreme Court issues. Others, such as the relationship of motion pictures to the First Amendment and desegregation of public schools, were reversals of earlier decisions. Still others reflected an attempt to come to grips with major questions ignored or just touched upon previously, such as with libel and obscenity.

The era of Chief Justice Warren—some claim that it should not be labeled the "Warren Court" but the "Black Court" because of the great influence of the liberal Justice Hugo Black—came to an end with the close of the term in summer of 1969. But the departure of the Chief Justice alone did not close the era. Justice Black, usually considered the leader of the liberal wing, was 83 at the time of Chief Justice Warren's retirement. Justice Douglas was 70 and in troublesome health, as was Justice Harlan, also 70. The close of the era also saw the first black to assume a seat on the high court, Justice Thurgood Marshall, former Solicitor General, appointed two years before Chief Justice Warren's retirement.

Some have noted a move toward more conservative opinions as the era closed. Certainly, Justice Black had disappointed some of his supporters with several mid-1960 decisions. Also, the Court was under heavy fire from politicians who had counted their letters from home and found much criticism of some of the Court's major decisions. Indeed, some polls indicated that the public in 1969 failed to support the Court in its efforts, and public support of the Court is necessary to offset political pressures forthcoming from the Congress and the White House. Yet this support appeared to wane in the 1960s.

Symbolic of this unrest was Chief Justice Warren's announced retirement. President Johnson nominated Justice Abe Fortas, appointed to an Associate Justice seat in 1965, as Chief Justice Warren's successor. This nomination was immediately criticized by conservative members of the Senate, which must confirm presidential nominations to the bench. In public hearings, Justice Fortas was subjected to unprecedented questioning and confrontation. In face of mounting criticism, his nomination was withdrawn.

At issue were his voting record while sitting on the bench, his apparent liberalism countering a national conservative trend, his friendship with the then lame-duck President, and his constitutional philosophy. The seeds of a controversial Warren Court were bearing bitter fruit for his chosen successor. But the withdrawal of Justice Fortas's nomination as Chief Justice did not silence his critics nor the critics of the Court. In the closing months of the Warren Court, following disclosure of what some described as a conflict of interest and questionable business associations, Justice Fortas resigned from the Court. The Warren Court at its termination in June 1969, then, saw only eight of its nine chairs occupied.

Chief Justice Warren's last official act was to introduce his successor, Chief Justice Warren Burger, a widely known judge of the U.S. Court of Appeals who was nominated by President Nixon and swiftly confirmed by the Senate. The next year Justice Harry Blackmun, a long-time friend of the new Chief Justice, was confirmed for the Fortas seat following rejection of two of President Nixon's nominees, Judges Haynsworth and Carswell. And the year after that, in 1971, two additional seats became vacant with the death of Justice Black and the retirement of Justice Harlan. The former, who had served for 34 years, was considered one of the great judicial philosophers in the history of the Court and was its leading spokesman for judicial activism. Justice Harlan served for 16 years as the leading spokesman for judicial restraint. He and Black, the best of personal friends, were at opposite ends of the judicial spectrum during the Warren years. If Justice Black's focus was on the rights of the individual, Justice Harlan most often tended to look toward the needs of the larger society.

So it was that in his first term of office, President Nixon had been given the opportunity to fill four of the nine Supreme Court seats. To fill the Black and Harlan seats he selected Justices Lewis F. Powell, Jr., of Virginia, a former president of the American Bar Association, and William H. Rehnquist, a former Supreme Court clerk and Justice Department lawyer. Both can be described as scholars and judicial conservatives. And with those four appointments, the Warren era of "judicial activism" was replaced by a tone of restraint. The dissents would come not from the eloquent pleadings of Justice Harlan nor his mentor Justice Frankfurter, but from Justices Douglas, Brennan and Marshall, the remaining activists of the Warren Court.

Chief Justice Warren died in 1974 at the age of 83, and the following New Year's Eve Justice Douglas suffered a stroke which left his left side paralyzed. He underwent extensive therapy during the following months and made occasional appearances at the Supreme Court Building to hear oral arguments and to partici-

pate in the Court's work, though such activity was confined to a wheelchair and was physically exhausting and painful. Unable to continue, the 77-year-old spokesman for civil libertarianism and for the judicial activism necessary to achieve those ends, resigned within the year, ending 36 years on the High Court, longer than any previous Justice. Mr. Nixon, by this time, of course, had resigned the presidency in the wake of Watergate and had been succeeded by Gerald Ford, who, in an ironic twist of history, was to name a successor to the man against whom he had led an impeachment drive as a leader in the House of Representatives. Mr. Ford's nominee was John Paul Stevens, a judge of the U.S. Court of Appeals. His nomination was widely applauded, for Judge Stevens was considered a man of judicial thoroughness, scholarship, and integrity. Confirmation of the moderate-to-conservative judge came prior to the close of 1975. This left only Justices Brennan and Marshall—with frequent assists from Justice Stewart—remaining from the activist core which directed the Court during the Warren era.

No vacancies occurred during the four-year presidency of Jimmy Carter, making him the first President in 100 years to be denied an appointment to the Supreme Court. His successor, Ronald Reagan, promised during the campaign that one of his first appointees would be a woman. No woman to that time had served as a Justice on the High Court. The opportunity came sooner than most predicted when, just months after Mr. Reagan's inauguration, Justice Stewart announced his intention to step down. The President's nominee was Sandra Day O'Connor, a Stanford Law School classmate of Justice Rehnquist and a former member of the Arizona Senate and the Arizona Court of Appeals. She was confirmed 99–0 by the Senate in time for the October term of 1981. The departure of Justice Stewart caused additional concern among journalists, for he was a strong supporter of First Amendment rights for the press. The absence of another of the Warren Court First Amendment activists surely would be felt.

President Reagan was given the opportunity to appoint a second Justice in 1986 with the resignation of Chief Justice Burger, who at age 78 stepped down after 17 years of administering the High Court. Named to become the nation's 16th Chief Justice was Associate Justice Rehnquist. To fill the Rehnquist vacancy, Mr. Reagan nominated Antonin Scalia, 50, who served on the U.S. Court of Appeals (D.C. Circuit). He had been a "leading contender" for such an opening because of his excellent credentials and his ideological conservatism, which the Administration found in concert with its own. In addition, Justice Scalia, a former law professor at the universities of Virginia, Georgetown, Stanford and Chicago, was known for his intellect, his charm and his significant persuasive powers. A year later, in a surprise announcement, Justice Lewis Powell announced his retirement from the Court. One of the most thoughtful and respected members of the bench, Justice Powell had played an independent, centrist role in many recent rulings, and his stepping down was seen by conservatives as a chance for the President to cement the shift to the right that was evolving. President Nixon had named four Justices to the High Court. This would be President Reagan's third seat to fill. His nominee was Judge Robert Bork of the Circuit Court of Appeals in Washington, D.C. Bork was known as one who would bring an unwavering conservative agenda to the Court. His nomination was immediately attacked by those who had hoped for a less strident appointee. Following televised, often-bitter, hearings before the Senate Judiciary Committee, which fascinated the media and the nation at large, Judge Bork's nomination was rejected. A second nominee withdrew amid controversy over his background and judicial experience—or, more accurately, lack thereof. President Reagan then called on Judge Anthony M. Kennedy of the 9th Circuit Court of Appeals in California, who had written more than 400 opinions during his 12 years on the 9th Circuit and had a reputation as a strong conservative. His experience suggested that he would bring to the Court a greater openness than either of the two previous nominees. He was confirmed unanimously by the Senate and took his seat in February of 1988. With these appointments, the Court became more ideologically committed and more effectively administered than during Chief Justice Burger's years. The nation's press, however, viewed these appointments with concern, fearing further erosion of the First Amendment liberalism of the Warren days, which had ended nearly two decades earlier.

The tradition of an active, forceful Court did not begin with Chief Justice Warren. It was instituted by Chief Justice John Marshall, the fourth appointed to lead the High Court. He was named in 1801 by President John Adams and served during 34 of the most fateful years in American history. These years were filled with political struggle, threat of impeachment and, in the end, victory for the Marshall viewpoint. At stake, for example, was the concept of a strong federal government. Jefferson, one of the Court's leading adversaries, believed in a "weak" federal judiciary and in stronger state responsibility. Chief Justice Marshall argued for a strong federal system. Historians note that if the Marshall concept had lost, the Constitution might have become a weak document, somewhat similar to the Articles of Confederation. Chief Justice Marshall, for his role in strengthening the document, has been called the "Second Father of the Constitution."

The Marshall Court, then, helped establish a strong federal system, under which federal power must outweigh that of the states in time of direct conflict. Chief Justice Marshall also firmly established in Marbury v. Madison, *decided two years after his appointment, the right of "judicial review," i.e. the right of the Court to review laws enacted by the legislative branch and to pass on their constitutionality. There is nothing in the Constitution which gives this power to the Supreme Court, yet this principle is accepted today as fundamental.* Marbury v. Madison *made Supreme Court opinions the "law of the land" and insured balancing strengths among the three branches of government, legislative, executive and judicial. It guaranteed that proper "checks and balances" would be available.*

Chief Justice Marshall assumed his chair at a time when the Court was suffering from weakness, disrespect and uncertainty. The three Chief Justices before him, for example, served a total of only nine years. One, Justice Rutledge, was appointed by President Washington, but was not confirmed by the Senate.

Chief Justice Marshall had little formal schooling, but enjoyed extensive political experience in the Virginia Legislature, in the Congress and as Secretary of

State. He and Madison led the debate in Virginia for ratification of the new U.S. Constitution. But this same strength and determination which led him to insure the strong federal legal system, judicial review, and checks and balances among the three branches of government also led to his unpopularity among many leading politicians of the day and to threats of his impeachment. Similar controversies were to surround active Chief Justices in the future, including Chief Justices Hughes and Warren. But before they were to enter the public arena, another era developed which was to introduce the philosophy of two Associate Justices, Holmes and Brandeis.

Oliver Wendell Holmes, Jr., is best remembered for his enunciation of the "clear and present danger" concept. He said that the First Amendment, which establishes freedom of the press, was to prevent "previous restraint" upon the press and that no such governmental prohibition on publication should take place without there being a "clear and present danger" to society. This concept was introduced in Schenck v. United States, 249 U.S. 47 (1919), in the following opinion:

SCHENCK V. UNITED STATES
249 U.S. 47 (1919)

JUSTICE HOLMES *delivered the opinion of the Court.*

This is an indictment in three counts. The first charges a conspiracy to violate the Espionage Act of June 15, 1917, . . . by causing and attempting to cause insubordination, etc., in the military and naval forces of the United States, and to obstruct the recruiting and enlistment service of the United States, when the United States was at war with the German Empire; to wit, that the defendant willfully conspired to have printed and circulated to men who had been called and accepted for military service under the Act of May 18, 1917, a document set forth and alleged to be calculated to cause such insubordination and obstruction. The court alleges overt acts in pursuance of the conspiracy, ending in the distribution of the document set forth. The second count alleges a conspiracy to commit an offense against the United States; to wit, to use the mails for the transmission of matter declared to be non-mailable by title 12, section 2, of the Act of June 15, 1917, to wit, the above-mentioned document, with an averment of the same overt acts. The third count charges an unlawful use of the mails for the transmission of the same matter and otherwise as above. The defendants were found guilty on all the counts. They set up the First Amendment to the Constitution, forbidding Congress to make any law abridging the freedom of speech or of the press, and, bringing the case here on that ground, have argued some other points also of which we must dispose.

It is argued that the evidence, if admissible, was not sufficient to prove that the defendant Schenck was concerned in sending the documents. According to the testimony Schenck said he was general secretary of the Socialist party and had charge of the Socialist headquarters from which the documents were sent. He identified a book found there as the minutes of the executive committee of the party. The book showed a resolution of August 13, 1917, that 15,000 leaflets should be printed on the other side of one of them in use, to be mailed to men who had passed exemption boards, and for distribution. Schenck personally attended to the printing. . . . He said that he had about fifteen or sixteen thousand printed. There were files of the circular in question in the inner office which he said were printed on the other side of the one-sided circular and were there for distribution. Other copies were proved to have been sent through the mails to drafted men. Without going into confirmatory details that were proved, no reasonable man could doubt that the defendant Schenck was largely instrumental in sending the circulars about. . . .

The document in question, upon its first printed side, recited the 1st section of the 13th Amendment, said that the idea embodied in it was violated by the Conscription Act, and that a conscript is little better than a convict. In impassioned language it intimated that conscription was despotism in its worst form and a monstrous wrong against humanity, in the interest of Wall Street's chosen few. It said: "Do not submit to intimidation," but in form at least confined itself to peaceful measures, such as a petition for the repeal of the act. The other and later printed side of the sheet was headed, "Assert Your Rights." It stated reasons for alleging that anyone violated the Constitution when he refused to recognize "your right to assert your opposition to the draft," and went on: "If you do not assert and support your rights, you are helping to deny or disparage rights which it is the solemn duty of all citizens and residents of the United States to retain." It described the arguments on the other side as coming from cunning politicians and mercenary capitalist press, and even silent consent to the Conscription Law as helping to support an infamous conspiracy. It denied the power to send our citizens away to foreign shores to shoot up the people of other lands, and added that words could not express the condemnation such cold-blooded ruthlessness deserves, etc., etc., winding up, "You must do your share to maintain, support, and uphold the rights of the people of this country." Of course the document would not have been sent unless it had been intended to have some effect, and we do not see what effect it could be expected to have upon persons subject to the draft except to influence them to obstruct the carrying of it out. The defendants do not deny that the jury might find against them on this point.

But it is said, suppose that that was the tendency of this circular, it is protected by the First Amendment to the Constitution. Two of the strongest expressions are said to be quoted respectively from well-known public men. It well may be that the prohibition of laws abridging the freedom of speech is not confined to previous restraints, although to prevent them may have been the main purpose, as intimated in *Patterson v. Colorado*. We admit that in many places and in ordinary times the defendants, in saying all that was said in the circular, would have been within their constitutional rights. But the character of every act depends upon the circumstances in which it is done. The most stringent protection of free speech would not protect a man in falsely shouting fire in a theater, and causing a panic. It does not even protect a man from an injunction against uttering words that may have all the effect of force. The question in every case is whether the words used are used in such circumstances and are of such a nature as to create a clear and present danger that they will bring about the substantive evils that Congress has a right to prevent. It is a question of proximity and degree. When a nation is at war many things that might be said in time of peace are such a hindrance to its effort that their utterance will not be endured so long as men fight, and that no court could regard them as protected by any constitutional right. It seems to be admitted that if an actual obstruction of the recruiting service were proved, liability for words that produced that effect might be enforced. The Statute of 1917, in sec. 4, punishes conspiracies to obstruct as well as actual obstruction. If the act (speaking, or circulating a paper), its tendency and the intent with which it is done, are the same, we perceive no ground for saying that success alone warrants making the act a crime. . . .

     *   *   *

The question of the degree of Justice Holmes' civil libertarianism has continued to today. Much of the legislation he supported was done to improve social conditions, but generally he was not considered a "reformer." His liberalism was more intellectual than political, possibly. Nonetheless, his pronouncements pointed the way for future libertarians.

Appointed to the Court in 1902 and serving for 29 years, Justice Holmes saw law as developing along with society and not as a stagnant pronouncement based on platitudes and absolutes. He attempted to consider the broad picture of society as a whole. His ringing phrases have caused him to be called as much a philosopher as a jurist, and his strong dissents—some of which later were to become majority opinions—have caused him to be known as the "Great Dissenter." While he was not a Chief Justice, he and his colleague, Justice Brandeis, the first Jew to be named to the Court, cut as influential a path as the Court has ever seen.

It was not, however, until the Court sat under Chief Justice Charles Evans Hughes that the Holmes-Brandeis concept of "clear and present danger" was accepted as the legal test relating to censorship of unpopular ideas. Chief Justice Hughes served for 11 years beginning in 1930 and was a firm supporter of civil liberties, a view reflected in the decisions of his Court. The major freedom of expression decisions came as reactions to prior restraint by government. The landmark Near decision in 1931 held that prior restraint as a tool of suppression by government was to be eliminated in all but the most extreme cases. The Grosjean decision in 1936 removed from government the privilege of "taxing to destroy" a newspaper. And in the 1938 Lovell decision, the Court held circulation to be an integral part of freedom of the press. The final significant contribution of the Hughes Court to freedom of expression came in 1941 with the decision in Bridges. There it applied the "clear and present danger" principle to out-of-court contempt cases.

These major decisions gave new significance and clarity to First Amendment phrases. But the 1930s were not solely a time of debate within the chamber. The High Court came under increasing attack by supporters of President Franklin D.

Roosevelt, who saw the Court as standing in the way of progress urgently needed to fulfill the promise of the New Deal. The Hughes Court had held many of the President's reforms unconstitutional. In 1937 President Roosevelt sent to the Congress a judicial reorganization proposal which, among other things, would have allowed the President to appoint additional Supreme Court Justices when those on the bench reached the age of 70 and chose not to retire. The total number of Supreme Court Justices, under the proposal, could not exceed 15. This led to the hotly debated "Supreme Court packing" charge. The President felt that older Justices had too narrow a view of social needs and were unable to adapt to the changing times and requirements of a nation in distress. Opponents charged the administration with "tampering" with the balance-of-power concept and with political interference of the Court's function. The bill was defeated, but within seven years death and retirement left only two non-Roosevelt appointees on the bench.

Chief Justice Hughes, a former governor of New York, was first appointed to the bench as Associate Justice in 1910, but he resigned to run for the presidency in 1916, losing narrowly to Woodrow Wilson. He was appointed Chief Justice in 1930 following more than a decade of public service. He was considered to be the greatest Chief Justice since Chief Justice Marshall. Historians will tell us whether this label will continue to stand under the impact of Chief Justice Warren. Certainly, both were embroiled in controversy, both were dedicated to human liberties, both were active leaders and both developed strong political foes.

The evolving status and definition of "clear and present danger," which had been debated by the Court for more than 30 years, reached a major plateau in 1951 with a 6–2 decision to uphold the conviction under the Smith Act of Eugene Dennis and ten others on charges of conspiracy to teach and advocate the overthrow of the United States government by force and violence. Dennis v. United States. The plateau was somewhat of a pragmatic compromise between the Holmes-Brandeis "clear and present danger" principle and the "dangerous tendency" concept followed in Gitlow. Added was the principle of balancing various interests.

It should be noted that the petitioners were convicted for conspiracy and advocacy, not with actual violence nor with an overt attempt to overthrow the government, and that the decision came during the Korean conflict that threatened to spread to a wider war. The majority held that the state cannot be expected to withhold preventative action until the actual moment of the putsch and that obstructions to free speech and press might be necessary in order to prevent an even greater evil to society.

The decision, in effect, allows legislatures the freedom to act against probable danger, but not by indiscriminate trampling of the rights of the individual. There was no real consensus of the Court (five separate opinions written by the eight Justices taking part). However, a generally accepted sliding scale incorporating "gravity" or "probable danger" was applied to the "clear and present danger" test, though it is not universally accepted that the Court really rejected the Holmes-Brandeis concept. In addition to the importance of the case itself and the acceptance *of a more pragmatic approach to the problem of seditious utterances, the five opinions give keen insights into the philosophic conflicts in which the Court finds itself when dealing with free speech and press.*

DENNIS V. UNITED STATES
341 U.S. 494 (1951)

CHIEF JUSTICE VINSON *announced the judgment of the Court and an opinion in which Justice Reed, Justice Burton and Justice Minton join.*

. . . No important case involving free speech was decided by this Court prior to *Schenck v. United States*. Indeed, the summary treatment accorded an argument based upon an individual's claim that the First Amendment protected certain utterances indicates that the Court at earlier dates placed no unique emphasis upon that right. It was not until the classic dictum of Justice Holmes in the *Schenck* case that speech *per se* received that emphasis in a majority opinion. . . .

Nothing is more certain in modern society than the principle that there are no absolutes, that a name, a phrase, a standard has meaning only when associated with the considerations which gave birth to the nomenclature. . . .

In this case we are squarely presented with the application of the "clear and present danger" test, and must decide what that phrase imports. . . .

Obviously, the words cannot mean that before the Government may act, it must wait until the *putsch* is about to be executed, the plans have been laid and the signal is awaited. If Government is aware that a group aiming at its overthrow is attempting to indoctrinate its members and to commit them to a course whereby they will strike when the leaders feel the circumstances permit, action by the Government is required. The argument that there is no need for Government to concern itself, for Government is strong, it possesses ample powers to put down a rebellion, it may defeat the revolution with ease needs no answer. For that is not the question. Certainly an attempt to overthrow the Government by force, even though doomed from the outset because of inadequate numbers of power of the revolutionists, is a sufficient evil for Congress to prevent. . . .

Chief Judge Learned Hand, writing for the majority below, interpreted the phrase as follows: "In each case [courts] must ask whether the gravity of the 'evil,' discounted by its improbability, justifies such invasion of free speech as is necessary to avoid the danger." We adopt this statement of the rule. As articulated by Chief Judge Hand, it is as succinct and inclusive as any other we might devise at this time. It takes into consideration those factors which we deem relevant, and relates their significances. More we cannot expect from words. . . .

JUSTICE FRANKFURTER, *concurring in affirmance of the judgment.*

. . . The language of the First Amendment is to be read not as barren words found in a dictionary but as symbols of historic experience illumined by the presuppositions of those who employed them. Not what words did Madison and Hamilton use, but what was it in their minds which they conveyed? . . .

JUSTICE BLACK, *dissenting.*

. . . These petitioners were not charged with an attempt to overthrow the Government. They were not charged with overt acts of any kind designed to overthrow the Government. They were not even charged with saying anything or writing anything designed to overthrow the Government. The charge was that they agreed to assemble and to talk and publish certain ideas at a later date: The indictment is that they conspired to organize the Communist Party and to use speech or newspapers and other publications in the future to teach and advocate the forcible overthrow of the Government. No matter how it is worded, this is a virulent form of prior censorship of speech and press, which I believe the First Amendment forbids. . . .

So long as this Court exercises the power of judicial review of legislation, I cannot agree that the First Amendment permits us to sustain laws suppressing freedom of speech and press on the basis of Congress' or our own notions of mere "reasonableness." Such a doctrine waters down the First Amendment so that it amounts to little more than an admonition to Congress. The Amendment as so construed is not likely to protect any but those "safe" or orthodox views which rarely need its protection. . . .

JUSTICE DOUGLAS, *dissenting.*

. . . So far as the present record is concerned, what petitioners did was to organize people to teach and themselves teach the Marxist-Leninist doctrine contained chiefly in four books: *Foundations of Leninism* by Stalin (1924), *The Communist Manifesto* by Marx and Engels (1848), *State and Revolution* by Lenin (1917), *History of the Communist Party of the Soviet Union* (B) (1939).

Those books are to Soviet Communism what *Mein Kampf* was to Nazism. If they are understood, the ugliness of Communism is revealed, its deceit and cunning are exposed, the nature of its activities becomes apparent, and the chances of its success less likely. That is not, of course, the reason why petitioners chose these books for their classrooms. They are fervent Communists to whom these volumes are gospel. They preached the creed with the hope that some day it would be acted upon.

The opinion of the Court does not outlaw these texts nor condemn them to the fire, as the Communists do literature offensive to their creed. But if the books themselves are not outlawed, if they can lawfully remain on library shelves, by what reasoning does their use in a classroom become a crime? It would not be a crime under the Act to introduce these books to a class, though that would be teaching what the creed of violent overthrow of the government is. The Act, as construed, requires the element of intent—that those who teach the creed believe in it. The crime then depends not on what is taught but on who the teacher is. That is to make freedom of speech turn not on *what is said*, but on the intent with which it is said. Once we start down that road we enter territory dangerous to the liberties of every citizen. . . .

*   *   *

While much of the press was lamenting what it perceived to be the Burger Court's chipping away at the foundations of the First Amendment set in place by the Warren Court in the more traditional news areas such as libel and newsgathering (see Chapters 9 and 3), the Burger Court in the middle 1970s took an expansive approach to the First Amendment in the area of what is called "commercial speech." While it is true that the 1964 New York Times v. Sullivan *libel case involved advertising of civil rights arguments (Chapter 9) and the* Bigelow v. Virginia *decision of a decade later expanded freedom of expression in advertising of social issues or social services (Chapter 5), it was not until 1976 and the* Virginia State Board of Pharmacy v. Virginia Citizen's Consumer Council *case that the Supreme Court faced head-on the issue of overturning the* Valentine v. Chrestensen *decision of 1942, which denied First Amendment protection to commercial advertising. The question in* Virginia Pharmacy *dealt with a state prohibition against the advertising of prescription drug prices. In a 7–1 decision (Justice Rehnquist being the lone dissenter), the Court held that advertising and commercial speech often are as important in our society as political speech—even more so to the ill, the aged and the poor. The free enterprise concept also was emphasized. While the Court indicated that false, misleading or deceptive advertising would not qualify for this new constitutional protection, the move to grant First Amendment rights to commercial speech was a significant expansion of First Amendment philosophy.*

VIRGINIA STATE BOARD OF PHARMACY
V.
VIRGINIA CITIZEN'S CONSUMER COUNCIL
425 U.S. 748 (1976)

JUSTICE BLACKMUN *delivered the opinion of the Court.*

The plaintiff-appellees in this case attack, as violative of the First and Four-teenth Amendments, that portion of [the] Va. Code which provides that a pharmacist licensed in Virginia is guilty of unprofessional conduct if he "publishes, advertises or promotes, directly or indirectly, in any manner whatsoever, any amount, price, fee, premium, discount, rebate or credit terms . . . for any drugs which may be dispensed only by prescription." . . .

The . . . attack on the statute is one made not by one directly subject to its prohibition, that is, a pharmacist, but by prescription drug consumers who claim that they would greatly benefit if the prohibition were lifted and advertising freely allowed. The plaintiffs are an individual Virginia resident who suffers from diseases that require her to take prescription drugs on a daily basis, and two non-profit organizations. Their claim is that the First Amendment entitles the user of prescription drugs to receive information that pharmacists wish to communicate to them through advertising and other promotional means, concerning the prices of such drugs.

Certainly that information may be of value. Drug prices in Virginia, for both prescription and nonprescription items, strikingly vary from outlet to outlet even within the same locality. It is stipulated, for example, that . . . in the Newport News-Hampton area the cost of tetracycline ranges from $1.20 to $9.00, a difference of 650%.

The question first arises whether, even assuming that First Amendment protection attaches to the flow of drug price information, it is a protection enjoyed by the appellees as recipients of the information, and not solely, if at all, by the advertisers themselves who seek to disseminate that information.

Freedom of speech presupposes a willing speaker. But where a speaker exists, as is the case here, the protection afforded is to the communication, to its source and to its recipients both. This is clear from the decided cases. In *Lamont v. Postmaster General*, the Court upheld the First Amendment rights of citizens to receive political publications sent from abroad. More recently, in *Kleindienst v. Mandel*, we acknowledged that this Court has referred to a First Amendment right to "receive information and ideas," and that freedom of speech " 'necessarily protects the right to receive.' ". . . If there is a right to advertise, there is a reciprocal right to receive the advertising, and it may be asserted by these appellees.

The appellants contend that the advertisement of prescription drug prices is outside the protection of the First Amendment because it is "commercial speech." There can be no question that in past decisions the Court has given some indication that commercial speech is unprotected. In *Valentine v. Chrestensen*, the Court upheld a New York statute that prohibited the distribution of any "handbill, circular . . . or other advertising matter whatsoever in or upon any street." The Court concluded that, although the First Amendment would forbid the banning of all communication by handbill in the public thoroughfares, it imposed "no such restraint on government as respects purely commercial advertising." Further support for a "commercial speech" exception to the First Amendment may perhaps be found in *Breard v. Alexandria*, where the Court upheld a conviction for violation of an ordinance prohibiting door-to-door solicitation of magazine subscriptions. The Court reasoned: "The selling . . . brings into the transaction a commercial feature," and it distinguished *Martin v. Struthers*, where it had reversed a conviction for door-to-door distribution of leaflets publicizing a religious meeting, as a case involving "no element of the commercial." Moreover, the Court several times has stressed that communications to which First Amendment protection was given were *not* "purely commercial." *New York Times Co. v. Sullivan*. . . .

Last Term, in *Bigelow v. Virginia*, the notion of unprotected "commercial speech" all but passed from the scene. We reversed a conviction for violation of a Virginia statute that made the circulation of any publication to encourage or promote the processing of an abortion in Virginia a misdemeanor. The defendant had published in his newspaper the availability of abortions in New York. The advertisement in question, in addition to announcing that abortions were legal in New York, offered the services of a referral agency in that State. We rejected the contention that the publication was unprotected because it was commercial. *Chrestensen's* continued validity was questioned. . . .

Here, in contrast, the question whether there is a First Amendment exception for "commercial speech" is squarely before us. Our pharmacist does not wish to editorialize on any subject, cultural, philosophical, or political. He does not wish to report any particularly newsworthy fact, or to make generalized observations even about commercial matters. The "idea" he wishes to communicate is simply this: "I will sell you the X prescription drug at the Y price." Our question, then, is whether this communication is wholly outside the protection of the First Amendment.

We begin with several propositions that already are settled or beyond serious dispute. It is clear, for example, that speech does not lose its First Amendment protection because money is spent to project it, as in a paid advertisement of one form or another. *New York Times Co. v. Sullivan.* Speech likewise is protected even though it is carried in a form that is "sold" for profit, *Smith v. California* (books); *Joseph Burstyn, Inc. v. Wilson* (motion pictures). . . . As to the particular consumer's interest in the free flow of commercial information, that interest may be as keen, if not keener by far, than his interest in the day's most urgent political debate. Appellees' case in this respect is a convincing one. Those whom the suppression of prescription drug price information hits the hardest are the poor, the sick, and particularly the aged. A disproportionate amount of their income tends to be spent on prescription drugs; yet they are the least able to learn, by shopping from pharmacist to pharmacist, where their scarce dollars are best spent. When drug prices vary as strikingly as they do, information as to who is charging what becomes more than a convenience. It could mean the alleviation of physical pain or the enjoyment of basic necessities. . . .

In concluding that commercial speech, like other varieties, is protected, we of course do not hold that it can never be regulated in any way. Some forms of commercial speech regulation are surely permissible. We mention a few only to make clear that they are not before us and therefore are not foreclosed by this case.

There is no claim, for example, that the prohibition on prescription drug price advertising is a mere time, place, and manner restriction. We have often approved restrictions of that kind provided that they are justified without reference to the content of the regulated speech, that they serve a significant governmental interest, and that in so doing they leave open ample alternative channels for communication of the information. Whatever may be the proper bounds of time, place, and manner restrictions on commercial speech, they are plainly exceeded by this Virginia statute, which singles out speech of a particular content and seeks to prevent its dissemination completely.

Nor is there any claim that prescription drug price advertisements are forbidden because they are false or misleading in any way. Untruthful speech, commercial or otherwise, has never been protected for its own sake. Obviously, much commercial speech is not provably false, or even wholly false, but only deceptive or misleading. We foresee no obstacle to a State's dealing effectively with this problem. The First Amendment, as we construe it today, does not prohibit the State from insuring that the stream of commercial information flow cleanly as well as freely. . . .

What is at issue is whether a State may completely suppress the dissemination of concededly truthful information about entirely lawful activity, fearful of that information's effect upon its disseminators and its recipients. Reserving other questions, we conclude that the answer to this one is in the negative. . . .

JUSTICE REHNQUIST, *dissenting*.

. . . The statute . . . only forbids *pharmacists* to publish this price information. There is no prohibition against a consumer group, such as appellees, collecting and publishing comparative price information as to various pharmacies in an area. Indeed they have done as much in their briefs in this case. Yet, though appellees could both receive and publish the information in question the Court finds that they have standing to protest that pharmacists are not allowed to advertise. Thus, contrary to the assertion of the Court, appellees are not asserting their "right to receive information" at all but rather the right of some third party to publish. . . .

There are undoubted difficulties with an effort to draw a bright line between "commercial speech" on the one hand and "protected speech" on the other, and the Court does better to face up to these difficulties than to attempt to hide them under labels. In this case, however, the Court has unfortunately substituted for the wavering line previously thought to exist between commercial speech and protected speech a no more satisfactory line of its own—that between "truthful" commercial speech, on the one hand, and that which is "false and misleading" on the other. . . .

. . . It is undoubtedly arguable that many people in the country regard the choice of shampoo as just as important as who may be elected to local, state, or national political office, but that does not automatically bring information about competing shampoos within the protection of the First Amendment. . . .

*   *   *

The Court, relying heavily on the Virginia Pharmacy *decision, threw out a year later another law which forbade another type of advertising—the placing of "for sale" signs in one's front yard.* Linmark Associates v. Willingboro. *A New Jersey community had banned the use of such signs in hopes of preventing "block busting," i.e. the flight of white residents who sell their homes "in panic" when they fear a significant influx of minority families into their neighborhoods. The Court in a 8–0 decision (Justice Rehnquist did not participate) noted that while community stabil-*

ity is a valid concern and the goals of such laws indeed may be laudable, the First Amendment cannot condone such prohibitions on commercial speech.

Later that same year, the Court also struck down rules which prohibited lawyers from advertising. Bates v. Arizona State Bar. *This 5–4 decision reinforced the concept of the right to disseminate truthful and appropriate commercial information. Though the decision was narrow in its scope, it has been significant in its impact on the professions of law and medicine, among others.*

A further expansion of the commercial speech doctrine came a year later, in 1978, in the decision of First National Bank of Boston v. Bellotti. *The question here was whether the state could prohibit corporations from spending corporate funds to advertise for or against ballot measures which did not significantly affect the corporation's business. The decision was 5–4, but if this concept continues its expansion into other areas of state control of commercial speech (political campaign spending, for example), it could have as much impact on our society as any decision handed down during the decade.*

Some forms of communication, of course, have long been ruled as falling outside constitutional protection. Sedition is one (see Schenck and Dennis, covered earlier), and obscenity is another (see Chapters 6 and 7). But given the tight restrictions the courts have placed on government attempts to censor obscene material, "borderline" publications, such as child pornography and depictions of violence against women, raise complex issues for both legislators and judges. Can sexually oriented material, if deemed harmful to societal interests, be banned if it is not legally obscene?

The Supreme Court answered the first question in 1982 in New York v. Ferber. *Justice White, writing for the Court, removed child pornography from First Amendment protection on the condition that the statutes be carefully drawn, so as not to infringe on protected material. There were no dissenting Justices, though some expressed concern about where such broadening state powers might lead. But White noted a "compelling need" for society to protect the physical and psychological needs of minors and noted that such special protection had been granted to minors earlier by the Court in both media and nonmedia cases. (See* Ginsberg v. New York *in Chapter 7.)*

The issue of depictions of violence against women reached the political arena by the middle 1980s. In 1984 the Indianapolis City Council approved an ordinance that defined violent pornography against women as a form of sexual discrimination and, as such, a violation of women's civil rights. It sanctioned civil suits and authorized the city to halt such "discriminatory practices" by banning offending books or magazines. Minneapolis, Los Angeles and other cities either passed or considered similar ordinances to counter what many believe to be a growing danger to society generally and to women specifically. But as with most government attempts to restrict First Amendment freedoms, there was little consensus. Women's groups split on the issue, as did civil libertarians.

The Indianapolis ordinance was ruled unconstitutional by the U.S. District

Court when challenged by the Indiana Civil Liberties Union. The Supreme Court in early 1986 declined to hear the case by a 6–3 vote, with Justices Burger, Rehnquist and O'Connor making up the minority. The Minneapolis ordinance was vetoed by the mayor.

But despite vetoes and challenges to constitutionality, the issue had been raised in cities across the country. It should be noted, too, that the Supreme Court in Pittsburgh Press v. Pittsburgh Commission on Human Relations *had already given support to the principle that First Amendment rights may have to be set aside if they conflict with civil rights goals established by the Congress. (See Chapter 2.) The question of censoring or allowing civil damage suits against publications which depict violence against women, then, will surely be heard from again as issues are clarified and solutions are refined.*

NEW YORK V. FERBER
458 U.S. 747 (1982)

JUSTICE WHITE *delivered the opinion of the Court.*

At issue in this case is the constitutionality of a New York criminal statute which prohibits persons from knowingly promoting sexual performances by children under the age of 16 by distributing material which depicts such performances.

In recent years, the exploitive use of children in the production of pornography has become a serious national problem. The federal government and forty-seven States have sought to combat the problem with statutes specifically directed at the production of child pornography. At least half of such statutes do not require that the materials produced be legally obscene. Thirty-five States and the United States Congress have also passed legislation prohibiting the distribution of such materials; twenty States prohibit the distribution of material depicting children engaged in sexual conduct without requiring that the material be legally obscene. . . .

First. It is evident beyond the need for elaboration that a state's interest in "safeguarding the physical and psychological well-being of a minor" is "compelling." *Globe Newspapers v. Superior Court.*

"A democratic society rests, for its continuance, upon the healthy well-rounded growth of young people into full maturity as citizens." *Prince v. Massachusetts.* . . . In *Ginsberg v. New York,* we sustained a New York law protecting children from exposure to nonobscene literature. Most recently, we held that the government's interest in the "well-being of its youth" justified special treatment of indecent broadcasting received by adults as well as children. *FCC v. Pacifica Foundation.*

The prevention of sexual exploitation and abuse of children constitutes a government objective of surpassing importance. . . .

Second. The distribution of photographs and films depicting sexual activity by juveniles is intrinsically related to the sexual abuse of children in at least two ways. First, the materials produced are a permanent record of the children's participation and the harm to the child is exacerbated by their circulation. Second, the distribution network for child pornography must be closed if the production of material which requires the sexual exploitation of children is to be effectively controlled. Indeed, there is no serious contention that the legislature was unjustified in believing that it is difficult, if not impossible, to halt the exploitation of children by pursuing only those who produce the photographs and movies. . . .

Third. The advertising and selling of child pornography provides an economic motive for, and is thus an integral part of, the production of such materials, an activity illegal throughout the nation. "It rarely has been suggested that the constitutional freedom for speech and press extends its immunity to speech or writing used as an integral part of conduct in violation of a valid criminal statute." *Giboney v. Empire Storage & Ice Co.* . . .

Fourth. The value of permitting live performances and photographic reproductions of children engaged in lewd sexual conduct is exceedingly modest, if not *de minimis.* We consider it unlikely that visual depictions of children performing sexual acts or lewdly exhibiting their genitals would often constitute an important and necessary part of a literary performance or scientific or educational work. As the trial court in this case observed, if it were necessary for literary or artistic value, a person over the statutory age who perhaps looked younger could be utilized. Simulation outside of the prohibition of the statute could provide another alternative. Nor is there is any question here of censoring a particular literary theme or portrayal of sexual activity. The First Amendment interest is limited to that of rendering the portrayal somewhat more "realistic" by utilizing or photographing children.

Fifth. Recognizing and classifying child pornography as a category of material outside the protection of the First Amendment is not incompatible with our earlier decisions. "The question whether speech is, or is not protected by the First Amendment often depends on the content of the speech." *Young v. American Mini Theatres.*

JUSTICE STEVENS, *concurring in the judgment.*

. . . A holding that respondent may be punished for selling these two films does not require us to conclude that other users of these very films, or that other motion pictures containing similar scenes, are beyond the pale of constitutional protection. Thus, the exhibition of these films before a legislative committee studying a proposed amendment to a state law, or before a group of research scientists studying human behavior, could not, in my opinion, be made a crime. Moreover, it is at least conceivable that a serious work of art, a documentary on behavioral problems, or a medical or psychiatric teaching device, might include a scene from one of these films and, when viewed as a whole in a proper setting, be entitled to constitutional protection. The question whether a specific act of communication is protected by the First Amendment always requires some consideration of both its content and its context. . . .

*   *   *

But in 1986, in one of the last and surely one of the most unusual decisions of the Burger era, the Court by another 5–4 vote appeared to slow the expansion of commercial speech rights by holding that a Puerto Rico statute which prohibited the advertising of legalized casino gambling was a valid restriction of commercial speech and, as such, did not violate the Constitution. Posadas de Puerto Rico Associates v. Tourism Company of Puerto Rico. *Associate Justice Rehnquist wrote the opinion of the Court, reflecting again his strong states rights position. He was joined by Justices Burger, White, Powell and O'Connor. The oddity here was twofold: first, the prohibition applies only to advertising aimed at residents, and not at tourists either inside or outside Puerto Rico; second, it allowed the banning of advertising of a legal activity.*

This latter point was not lost on the Congress, which at the time was holding hearings on proposals to ban all cigarette advertising and promotion. Smoking, of course, may be compared to casino gambling in that it is a legal activity, yet evidence has pointed to its harmful effects. The Court, therefore, gave encouragement to antismoking groups by suggesting that even though the activity itself might be legal, the advertising of that activity could be prohibited if there were a substantial government interest in doing so. We haven't heard the last of this one yet.

POSADAS DE PUERTO RICO V. TOURISM CO.
478 U.S. 328 (1986)

JUSTICE REHNQUIST *delivered the opinion of the Court.*

. . . The particular kind of commercial speech at issue here, namely, advertising of casino gambling aimed at the residents of Puerto Rico, concerns a lawful activity and is not misleading or fraudulent, at least in the abstract. . . . The [government's] interest at stake in this case, as determined by the Superior Court, is the reduction of demand for casino gambling by the residents of Puerto Rico. Appellant acknowledged the existence of this interest in its February 24, 1982, letter to the Tourism Company. The Tourism Company's brief before this Court explains the legislature's belief that "[e]xcessive casino gambling among local residents . . . would produce serious harmful effects on the health, safety and welfare of the Puerto Rican citizens, such as the disruption of moral and cultural patterns, the increase in local crime, the fostering of prostitution, the development of corruption, and the infiltration of organized crime." These are some of the very same concerns, of course, that have motivated the vast majority of the 50 States to prohibit casino gambling. We have no difficulty in concluding that the Puerto Rico

Legislature's interest in the health, safety and welfare of its citizens constitutes a "substantial" governmental interest.

. . . [An] analysis basically involve[s] a consideration of the "fit" between the legislature's ends and the means chosen to accomplish those ends. [It] asks the question whether the challenged restrictions on commercial speech "directly advance" the government's asserted interest. In the instant case, the answer to this question is clearly "yes." The Puerto Rico Legislature obviously believed, when it enacted the advertising restrictions at issue here, that advertising of casino gambling aimed at the residents of Puerto Rico would serve to increase the demand for the product advertised. We think the legislature's belief is a reasonable one, and the fact that appellant has chosen to litigate this case all the way to this Court indicates that appellant shares the legislature's view. . . .

Appellant argues, however, that the challenged advertising restrictions are underinclusive because other kinds of gambling such as horse racing, cockfighting, and the lottery may be advertised to the residents of Puerto Rico. Appellant's argument is misplaced for two reasons. First, whether other kinds of gambling are advertised in Puerto Rico or not, the restrictions on advertising of casino gambling "directly advance" the legislature's interest in reducing demand for games of chance. Second, the legislature's interest, as previously identified, is not necessarily to reduce demand for all games of chance, but to reduce demand for casino gambling. According to the Superior Court, horse racing, cockfighting, "picas," or small games of chance at fiestas, and the lottery "have been traditionally part of the Puerto Rican's roots," so that "the legislator could have been more flexible than in authorizing more sophisticated games which are not so widely sponsored by the people." In other words, the legislature felt that for Puerto Ricans the risks associated with casino gambling were significantly greater than those associated with the more traditional kinds of gambling in Puerto Rico. In our view, the legislature's separate classification of casino gambling, for purposes of the advertising ban, satisfies the . . . analysis.

We also think it clear beyond peradventure that the challenged statute and regulations . . . are no more extensive than necessary to serve the government's interest. The narrowing constructions of the advertising restrictions announced by the Superior Court ensure that the restrictions will not affect advertising of casino gambling aimed at tourists, but will apply only to such advertising when aimed at the residents of Puerto Rico. . . . Appellant contends, however, that the First Amendment requires the Puerto Rico Legislature to reduce demand for casino gambling among the residents of Puerto Rico not by suppressing commercial speech that might *encourage* such gambling, but by promulgating additional speech designed to *discourage* it. We reject this contention. We think it is up to the legislature to decide whether or not such a "counterspeech" policy would be as effective in reducing the demand for casino gambling as a restriction on advertising. The legislature could conclude, as it apparently did here, that residents of Puerto Rico are already aware of the risks of casino gambling, yet would nevertheless be induced by widespread advertising to engage in such potentially harmful conduct. . . .

In short, we conclude that the statute and regulations at issue in this case, as construed by the Superior Court, pass muster. . . . We therefore hold that the Supreme Court of Puerto Rico properly rejected appellant's First Amendment claim.

JUSTICE BRENNAN, *with whom Justice Marshall and Justice Blackmun join, dissenting.*

It is well settled that the First Amendment protects commercial speech from unwarranted governmental regulation. . . .

I see no reason why commercial speech should be afforded less protection than other types of speech where, as here, the government seeks to suppress commercial speech in order to deprive consumers of accurate information concerning lawful activity. . . . However, no differences between commercial and other kinds of speech justify protecting commercial speech less extensively where, as here, the government seeks to manipulate private behavior by depriving citizens of truthful information concerning lawful activities. . . .

. . . Under our commercial speech precedents, Puerto Rico constitutionally may restrict truthful speech concerning lawful activity only if its interest in doing so is substantial, if the restrictions directly advance the Commonwealth's asserted interest and if the restrictions are no more extensive than necessary to advance that interest. . . . While tipping its hat to these standards, the Court does little more than defer to what it perceives to be the determination by Puerto Rico's legislature that a ban on casino advertising aimed at residents is reasonable. The Court totally ignores the fact that commercial speech is entitled to substantial First Amendment protection, giving the government unprecedented authority to eviscerate constitutionally protected expression.

JUSTICE STEVENS, *with whom Justice Marshall and Justice Blackmun join, dissenting.*

The Court concludes that "the greater power to completely ban casino gambling necessarily includes the lesser power to ban advertising of casino gambling." Whether a State may ban all advertising of an activity that it permits but could prohibit—such as gambling, prostitution, or the consumption of marijuana or liquor—is an elegant question of constitutional law. It is not, however, appropriate to address that question in this case because Puerto Rico's rather bizarre restraints on speech are so plainly forbidden by the First Amendment.

Puerto Rico does not simply "ban advertising of casino gambling." Rather, Puerto Rico blatantly discriminates in its punishment of speech depending on the publication, audience, and words employed. Moreover, the prohibitions, as now construed by the Puerto Rico courts, establish a regime of prior restraint and articulate a standard that is hopelessly vague and unpredictable.

With respect to the publisher, in stark, unabashed language, the Superior Court's construction favors certain identifiable publications and disfavors others. If the publication (or medium) is from outside Puerto Rico, it is very favored indeed. . . . If the publication is native to Puerto Rico, however—the *San Juan Star,* for instance—it is subject to a far more rigid system of restraints and controls regarding the manner in which a certain form of speech (casino ads) may be carried in its pages. Unless the Court is prepared to uphold an Illinois regulation of speech that subjects *The New York Times* to one standard and *The Chicago Tribune* to another, I do not understand why it is willing to uphold a Puerto Rico regulation that applies one standard to *The New York Times* and another to the *San Juan Star.*

With respect to the audience, the newly construed regulations plainly discriminate in terms of the intended listener or reader. Casino advertising must be "addressed to tourists." It must not "invite the residents of Puerto Rico to visit the casino." The regulation thus poses what might be viewed as a reverse Privileges and Immunities problem: Puerto Rico's residents are singled out for disfavored treatment in comparison to all other Americans. But nothing so fancy is required to recognize the obvious First Amendment problem in this kind of audience discrimination. I cannot imagine that this Court would uphold an Illinois regulation that forbade advertising "addressed" to Illinois residents while allowing the same advertiser to communicate his message to visitors and commuters; we should be no more willing to uphold a Puerto Rico regulation that forbids advertising "addressed" to Puerto Rico residents. . . .

*   *   *

An interesting free speech case that demonstrates the approach of the Justices to the First Amendment was Prune Yard v. Robins. *The Supreme Court since the* Lovell v. Griffin *decision of 1938 (see Chapter 2) generally had granted broad rights to distribute constitutionally protected literature and had invalidated legislative attempts to thwart any free flow of information important to our society. But it had balked at agreeing to the premise that the Constitution allows this distribution to take place in privately owned shopping centers over the objection of the owners.* Lloyd v. Tanner. *The California Supreme Court ruled in 1979 that the state constitution was more expansive than the Federal document in allowing such access to private property and that it prohibited the owners of the Prune Yard shopping center near San Jose from excluding a group of young persons who were circulating petitions and handing out literature within the confines of the popular, open-air mall. The Prune Yard owners appealed to the United States Supreme Court, which in 1980 unanimously upheld the California decision. The case is important to media law students for several reasons, not the least of which is in what it may foretell for future media cases, such as placement of newsracks or the sale of certain literature in bookstores within malls. Indeed, only months after* Prune Yard *had come down, there were additional suits in California seeking access to private or "semi-private" property areas, such as condominium developments, by newspapers and shoppers which previously had been banned. E.g.* Laguna News Post v. Golden West Publishing. *A second importance is found in the clarity of the federalism example exhibited by the Supreme Court, a concept which is becoming more important as the Court's conservative coalescence is becoming more pronounced under the leadership of Justice Rehnquist, who wrote the opinion in* Prune Yard. *This case was, if you will, a "states rights" case. The Court in* Prune Yard *did not overturn its previous* Lloyd *decision, but indicated merely that states may give their citizens greater speech and press rights under their own constitutions than does the Federal government give under the Federal Constitution and, in this case, that such an allowance did not violate any constitutional right of the Prune Yard owners.*

*   *   *

The success of the Court in fulfilling the promise of the First Amendment is debatable at best. Within a decade after the adoption of the Bill of Rights, the Congress passed the first in a series of laws to restrict speech and writing, the Alien and Sedition Acts of 1798. These short-lived laws were passed much to the anguish of citizens who forecast a return to "sovereign rule" from which they had intended to divorce themselves. The acts imposed fines and imprisonment on persons who wrote or spoke in a manner so as to arouse discontent with the government. The basic question then—and to this day—is whether the framers of the First Amendment meant to guarantee to the citizens the absolute right to comment upon and to criticize their government, i.e. whether the framers meant "no law" in a literal and absolute sense. Does the Constitution protect all speech or just "approved" speech? This debate is the history of the Supreme Court in its role as interpreter of the First Amendment.

In civil cases, such as libel and invasion of privacy, the Warren Court noted that the purpose of free speech and press guarantees of the First Amendment and applied to the states by the Fourteenth Amendment (Gitlow v. New York) is to encourage open and diverse debate as necessary to any political or social change desired by a free society. The debate, the Supreme Court has ruled, may be robust, unpopular, diverse, unpleasant, caustic, sharp, and even untruthful. Only compelling interests by the state, therefore, have been accepted by the Court when questions of restricted public debate have come before it.

The pull and tug of judicial philosophy must be expected to continue unless one adopts the "absolutist" theory, i.e. that the "no law" wording of the First Amendment means just that—"no law." But this has not been the prevailing view. So, the tone of the nine-member panel can be expected to vary with the decades, with the events of the day, with presidential appointments and with changes within the Justices themselves.

The continuing struggle for freedom of expression is neither new nor easy. An early victim was Socrates, who was condemned to death in 399 B.C. for speaking the truth as he saw it.

Freedom of expression to a democratic form of government is not a mere luxury, but a necessity. Democracy to move forward demands informed criticism. Answers to the complex problems facing free nations today are to be found in the great public debates, both spoken and written—debates that invite the tests of reflection and rebuttal.

Truth is not always found in the majority view. Indeed, much social legislation now governing the nation was first proposed by those in the minority. And many First Amendment freedoms enjoyed in this nation today were born in Supreme Court dissents of decades past.

The Supreme Court is "apolitical" in that the Justices, appointed for life, are not responsible to the electorate. But there are four built-in methods for checking the power of the Court, though three of these have rarely been used.

First, the Senate may reject a presidential Supreme Court nomination. The first such challenge—a successful one—came in 1795 with the rejection of Justice Rutledge, a former Associate Justice who had been nominated as Chief Justice by President Washington. More recent challenges by members of the Senate have been aimed at Justice Brandeis, the first Jew to sit with the High Court, and Justice Fortas, Associate Justice nominated by President Johnson to succeed Chief Justice Warren, a nomination which was later withdrawn, and rejections of three Presidential nominees—two of President Nixon and one of President Reagan.

Second, a Justice may be impeached. However, no Supreme Court Justice has been removed from the bench through impeachment and conviction.

Third, the Court's actions may be checked by amendment to the Constitution. The Supreme Court, for example, held the graduated income tax to be unconstitutional, a ruling which was overturned by the passage of the Sixteenth Amendment. More recently the Court refused to strike down a poll tax only to be reversed by the passage of the Twenty-fourth Amendment. But the same "check power," it should be noted, has dangers as well. It is possible, for example, to amend the Constitution to include second-class citizenship for racial or religious minorities or to alter or dilute the role of the Court itself.

Finally, Supreme Court decisions may be overturned by later decisions of the Court itself, as was the case with public school segregation and First Amendment protection for motion pictures. The framers of the Constitution wrote in generalities. They stated principles and pointed to goals rather than to specifics. They were wise enough to prepare for unforeseen technological and social changes. So they wrote in terms of "due process" and "equal protection under the law," both imprecise terms which necessarily demand social and political interpretation. It should not come as a surprise, then, that changing times require changing interpretations by the Justices.

Because the Constitution "is" what the Justices say it is, the Court is considered by many to be the most powerful group in the world. The greatest restraining influence remains the restraint of the Justices themselves. Still, the Supreme Court cannot create. As Justice Frankfurter noted, the Court acts merely as a "brake" on others' actions. It probes into government, but does not have the responsibility to govern. It merely says "yes" or "no"—and even then only when asked to do so.

The following chapters undoubtedly will raise as many questions as they will answer, but such is the plight of all learning. And it is from these unanswered questions that new ideas are born and new solutions honed.

Much unfinished First Amendment business remains before the Supreme Court. One such item is the growing debate surrounding "freedom of information."

Does freedom of the press imply a public's "right to know"? Freedom of speech and press is of little value to a democracy if the media are deprived of data to transmit to a waiting electorate.

Also, the Court has spoken only haltingly on several basic media problems including a workable definition of obscenity, cable television restrictions, licensing of motion pictures and limits of allowable defamation and of privacy, to name but a few. Administrative problems also face future Courts. The sharp rise in the caseload is one, the reliance on a "book-by-book" definition of obscenity another.

But the overriding First Amendment challenge in these times of world and national conflict is for this nation to guarantee to its citizens the freedom of expression intended by the Constitution. Who but the Supreme Court can guarantee this freedom? Will it be guarded by the politicians—the government in power? Can it be maintained by the media or by the people themselves? And, finally, who but the Court will guard the guardian?

THE SUPREME COURT AND THE PRESS

BY JOHN P. MACKENZIE*

The conventional wisdom about the relationship between the Warren Court and the news media runs something like this: With a few exceptions, the press corps is populated by persons with only a superficial understanding of the Court, its processes, and the values with which it deals. The Court has poured out pages of legal learning, but its reasoning has been largely ignored by a result-oriented news industry interested only in the superficial aspects of the Court's work. The Court can trace much of its "bad press," its "poor image," to the often sloppy and inaccurate work of news gatherers operating in mindless deadline competition. The competition to be first with the story has been the chief obstacle in these critical years to a better public understanding of the Court and of our liberties and laws.

The difficulty with this characterization is that it contains just enough truth to appear reasonably complete. This picture of the press, because it is plausible, unfortunately may actually mask difficulties that lie deeper both in the structure of complex news media and in the Court's practices as they affect both the media and the general public—difficulties which, if recognized, may provide some opportunities for better understanding of the Court. If the Warren Court has received an especially bad press, there is blame enough to go around for it; the Court and the press should each accept shares of the blame, but within each institution the blame must be reallocated.

If the ultimate history of the Warren Court includes a judgment that the press has been unfair to the institution, this surely ought to be labeled as ingratitude of the highest order. *New York Times Co. v. Sullivan* and its progeny have carved out press freedoms to print news without fear of libel judgments under standards more generous and permissive to the fourth estate than the standards set by responsible newspapers for themselves. It is well that the Court has done so, and it is especially appropriate in a period when executive officials and political candidates have expressed mounting hostility toward the news media. Not only ideas, but men dealing in ideas and words, need breathing space to survive. These great First Amendment decisions contemplated that judges, like other public men, would suffer considerable personal abuse and that they must be rugged enough to take most of it, but the Court surely did not mean to invite press treatment of itself that was unfair as well as highly critical.

* John P. MacKenzie. "The Warren Court and the Press." *Michigan Law Review*, Vol. 67, No. 2 (December 1968), p. 303. Reprinted with permission of the author, a former Supreme Court reporter for the *Washington Post* and later a member of the Editorial Board of the *New York Times*.

Before discussing what the Court and the press have done to injure each other, it is worth noting that each has thrived somewhat on the developing relationships of the past decade and a half. By any definition of that elusive concept known as "news," an activist and innovative Supreme Court makes news and thus provides grist for the press. In turn, to an increasing degree, the press has been expanding its resources to cope with the flow of judicial news. Thus, the media have been giving the Court more exposure to the public.

It must be stated, however, that the relationships between press and Court have been complex and difficult. Some of the problems are built into the systems of both institutions. The Court begins as a mystery, and the reporter or editor who fails to appreciate the fact that certain things about the Supreme Court will remain unknowable and consequently unprintable simply does not understand the situation. The Court's decisions are the start of an argument more often than they are the final, definitive word on a given subject. Opinions often are written in such a way that they mask the difficulties of a case rather than illuminate them. New decisions frequently cannot be reconciled with prior rulings because "policy considerations, not always apparent on the surface, are powerful agents of decision."

Certainly not all the turmoil of the conference room spills over into the delivery of opinions. Secrecy at several levels both protects and obscures the Court and its work. The process of marshalling a Court, of compromise, of submerging dissents and concurrences, or of bringing them about, can only be imagined or deduced by the contemporary chronicler of the Court; history lags decades behind with its revelations of the Court's inner workings. This is not to say that newsmen need be privy to the Court's inner dealings, helpful as that might be, to describe its decisions accurately and well. But I would suggest that murky decision-reporting may be the reporting of murky decisions as well as the murky reporting of decisions.

The handling of petitions for certiorari—a process replete with elements of subjectivity and perhaps even arbitrariness—eludes the attempts of newsmen to fathom, much less to communicate to the general public, the sense of what the Court is doing. Certiorari action is the antithesis of what the Opinion of the Court is supposed to represent: a reasoned judicial action reasonably explained. Yet when the Court does speak through opinions, the press is frequently found lacking both in capacity for understanding and capacity for handling the material. Precious newspaper space, when it is available, often is wasted on trivia at the expense of reporting a decision's principal message and impact. Newspapers often fail to adjust to the abnormally large volume of material produced on a "decision day," or to the task of reporting the widespread implications of a landmark decision.

Some of the demands made by the flow of Supreme Court news are beyond the capabilities of all newspapers; some are beyond the capacities of all but the newspapers most dedicated to complete coverage of the institution. For example, the actions of the last two Mondays of the October 1963 term consume all of Volume 378 of the United States Reports. The decisions and orders of June 12, 1967, the final day of that term, are printed in Volume 388, which exceeds 580 pages. Many of these decisions have remained under advisement until the end of a term precisely because of their difficulty and complexity, elements that frequently correlate with newsworthiness. Many of them are sufficiently interesting to warrant substantial newspaper coverage, which often includes printing their full texts or excerpts. Many decisions generate, or should generate, "side-bar" or feature stories of their own on the same day. Supreme Court stories compete with each other for available column space, and all the Court news of a given day must in turn compete with all the other news from everywhere else in the world.

Between the Court and the press stands perhaps the most primitive arrangement in the entire communications industry for access to an important source of news material and distribution of the information generated by that source. On days of decision delivery, two dozen newsmen and newswomen gather in the press room on the ground floor of the Supreme Court Building to receive opinions in page proof form as they are delivered orally in the courtroom one floor above. Each Justice's contribution is passed out one opinion at a time, so that if there are, for example, several separate opinions in a cluster of three related cases, the news reporter will not be able to tell what has happened until he has assembled his entire bundle of opinions one by one.

Upstairs in the courtroom, at a row of desks between the high bench and the counsel's podium, sit six newsmen (several more are seated elsewhere in the audience), three of whom represent the Associated Press, United Press International, and the Dow-Jones financial ticker. As opinions are delivered orally, Court messengers deliver printed copies to the six desks. The two wire service reporters send their copies through pneumatic tubes to fellow workers waiting in cubicles below. The AP reporter there, aided by an assistant, types out his stories and dictates them over the telephone to a stenographer at the office of the service's Washington bureau. The UPI reporter does essentially the same thing, but hands his copy to a teletype operator for direct transmission to the bureau office for editing. Reporters for the major afternoon newspapers must devise methods of their own for getting copy to their main offices. Reporters for morning papers do not have "all day" to perform the same tasks, but they have a much easier time of it at the moment of decision delivery. For example, they need not resort to the device used by their more time-pressed colleagues—that of preparing "canned" stories about petitions for certiorari that are released automatically when the Court announces its action granting or denying review. Such articles are prepared so that they can be transmitted with the insertion or change of a few words depending on the Court's order.

The Court's clerical and semiclerical workings pose problems of their own. In the day-to-day coverage of the Supreme Court the reporter may encounter secrecy at every stage, not all of it necessary to the independent performance of the judicial function. There may be secret pleadings, of which one minor but colorful example will suffice. On December 4, 1967, the Court denied review to two topless, and by definition newsworthy, young ladies from Los Angeles, whose petition claimed First Amendment protection for their chosen form of expression. The ladies sought relief from the toils of prosecution by means of a petition for a writ of habeas corpus—a remedy that was intriguing in itself—but had been spurned by the lower courts. Unbeknownst to the press, which was inclined to take the petition at face value, the Court was in receipt of a letter, actually a responsive pleading, notifying the Justices that the defendants were pursuing normal appellate remedies at the same time. This information made their petition much less urgent and it might well have chilled the press interest in the case as well as the Court's. Only Justice Douglas noted his vote in favor of review. The letter was lodged in a correspondence file, a fact which this reporter learned by accident after his and other news stories about the case had been printed.

There also may be secret correspondence which does not amount to a pleading but which nevertheless may shape the outcome of a case or materially affect the writing of an opinion. In *Rees v. Peyton*, a court-appointed attorney in a capital case communicated to the Court by letter the fact that his client wanted to dismiss his petition, a suicidal step which counsel was understandably resisting. Again, the communication was placed in a correspondence file apart from the remainder of the record. A request to see the correspondence was denied by the Clerk's office, initially on grounds that it might invade the lawyer-client relationship and later on no grounds at all. At length the letter was released. Similarly, it might be noted that the celebrated communication from J. Edgar Hoover, Director of the Federal Bureau of Investigation, regarding FBI interrogation practices—one which figured importantly in the Chief Justice's opinion in *Miranda v. Arizona*—has not been made public despite requests for access to it.

There may also be secret exhibits, such as the one requested from the bench by the Chief Justice in *Giles v. Maryland*, which may prove decisive in a case. There may even be secret petitions for certiorari in a controversy not involving national security; this occurred recently in a bitterly fought domestic relations case from Maryland. And, although the Court's press room is supposed to have available all briefs that are filed, the word "filed" is a term of art meaning "accepted for filing with the Court." This excludes many papers which the Justices see, including many amicus curiae briefs lodged with the Court pending its disposition of a motion for leave to file when one or both parties has objected to the filing. The "deferred appendix" method authorized by the 1967 revisions in the Supreme Court's rules means that more major briefs will be formally on file with the Court in proof form; however, the briefs, while available for inspection if the fact of filing is known to the news reporter, do not become available generally until later when printed copies are delivered to the Court.

In what way, then, have these ingredients—the nature of the Court's work, the lack of capacity on the part of the press, and the Court's own administrative habits—combined to influence the public's view of the Supreme Court? Examples abound in which the principal cause of public confusion must be laid to one or another of these elements. The examples are to be found primarily in the areas of deepest controversy: race relations, use of confessions in criminal cases, reapportionment, obscenity, and religion.

In the area of the Warren Court's central achievement, the promotion of equal treatment for racial minorities, the Court must take some share of the blame for the bad press it received. One source of difficulty was the famous footnote 11 in *Brown v. Board of Education*, which cited "modern authority" as to the state of psychological knowledge about the detrimental effects of state-imposed segregated education. The importance of the gratuitous footnote was emphasized out of all proportion by segregationists, and at least by hindsight it seems to have been inevitable that this should be so. The press contributed to the difficulty not so much by misreporting the opinion as by failing to muster the depth of understanding to place the footnote in perspective by comparing "modern authority" with the amateur sociology used by the nineteenth century Court.

In the field of criminal law, another area in which the Warren Court has made headlines, one may again see the difficulty of attributing blame. As with civil rights, it is virtually certain that most members of the general public literally know about the Supreme Court's work in this area only what they have read in the newspapers, heard on the radio, or seen on television. Mixed though the picture may be, it has become clear at least to this writer that press misinterpretation of *Escobedo*, *Miranda*, and *Wade*, to name several of the most controversial decisions, has not been the fault of the "regular" reporters at the Supreme Court, whether writers for wire services or daily newspapers. These decisions probably were reported more accurately under the deadline pressure of decision day than they have been reported since that time.

In *Escobedo*, for example, it was widely and correctly reported at the time of decision that the suspect's incriminating statements had been ruled inadmissible because he had been denied access to counsel who had already been retained and who was figuratively beating on the interrogation room door while the petitioner was being questioned in disregard of his express wish to consult his lawyer. Since his release from the murder charge against him, Danny Escobedo has been embroiled with the law many times; finally, in 1968, he was convicted on federal criminal charges. Yet, in most of the news accounts about the later life of Danny Escobedo, the Court's initial decision has been described as one which threw out his confession on grounds that police refused to let him see "*a laywer.*" *Miranda* may have mooted the distinction, at least for trials starting after June 13, 1966, but surely the fact that Escobedo was denied permission to consult a previously retained attorney makes a difference to an evaluation of the situation that confronted the now-notorious petitioner. Given the actual factual setting, the ruling seems less based on a "technicality" or excessive solicitude for a criminal.

Fairness demands acknowledgment that writers of subsequent news reports dealing with any Supreme Court decision may themselves be working under considerable deadline pressure, and usually they suffer from the added handicap of not having immediate access to the written texts of the Court's opinions. An after-dinner speaker may opine that the Supreme Court would throw out the confession of a man who walked up to a policeman on a street corner and told him of a crime he had just committed. The speaker might also say, as indeed members of the United States Senate were fond of saying during the battle over the nomination of

Justice Fortas to replace Chief Justice Warren, that the Court "has made it impossible to prohibit or punish the showing of indecent movies to children." What does the reporter do when confronted by such statements while on an otherwise routine assignment to cover the speech? His only source of help may be the newspaper's legal correspondent, if there is one and if he is sufficiently knowledgeable in such matters; the legal correspondent may be able to furnish information for a brief statement in the story, telling, for the benefit of the uninformed reader, what the Court actually did or said. . . .

The failure of communications, so at odds with the Court's necessary function as a constitutional teacher, had worthy origins. The school desegregation cases would doubtless have been excoriated by segregationists no matter what form of words the Court had chosen, and segregationist officials clearly would have defied the rulings just as vigorously. Perhaps *Brown v. Board of Education*, besides being a catalyst for other constitutional breakthroughs, set the pattern for the Warren Court's judicial conduct in the face of conservative hostility. The Court sent the message out that segregation was unlawful; the message came back that unlawfulness would persist in parts of the land; and the Court became determined to do whatever justice it could on its own. Similarly, in the criminal law field, Earl Warren and some of his colleagues ultimately expressed doubts that the Court could issue a constitutional exclusionary rule that would be effective in actual police practice; however, they undertook to lay down the rules anyway, although quite possibly the Justices were conditioned to some disappointment about the level of compliance.

Under Chief Justice Warren significant advances were made in the techniques of communicating the Court's work to the public, although the advances were outstripped by events. Starting soon after *Brown*, the press at its best began to reach new levels of competence. The Court made the press' job a bit easier by meeting at ten a.m. instead of at noon. The Association of American Law Schools began a helpful program of issuing background memoranda for the press on major cases which had been argued before the Court. The Court also began to space out the delivery of some of its opinions. Some often-mentioned experiments were not tried, however—most notably the proposal to supply the press with opinions a few hours in advance of delivery in order to give reporters time to compose more careful articles. Apparently the deterrent has been fear that some decisions, especially important economic ones, might be compromised by early release no matter what precautions were taken by the short-handed Court staff. The experiment should be tried anyway, if necessary with the specific exclusion of such economic cases. In the future, the Court must also seriously consider some *rapprochement* with television and re-examination of its ban on cameras in the courtroom. Television will certainly not invest money, manpower, and air time to cover a subject that will not reward the medium pictorially, and more and more Americans seem to receive all or most of their news over that medium.

During his confirmation hearings, Justice Fortas offered in broad outline a mixture of proposals for study of many of these problems. He mentioned the already-accomplished revision of the "Decision Monday" procedure and noted that the burden on the press had been relieved somewhat but perhaps could be relieved more. He suggested expanding the Association of American Law Schools' project (now supported by the American Bar Foundation), which supplies helpful memoranda about most of the argued cases to the press at the time of argument, to the post-decision phase of the Court's work. He also recommended that statistical information be compiled for newsmen; as an example of a little-reported fact, he cited the results of a survey showing that 92 or 93 per cent of all criminal cases presented to the Court for review during the October 1967 term had been rejected. He commended the formation of an organization of practitioners before the Court. And, he suggested coming to grips with the pressing problems of radio and television coverage.

. . . The cornerstone for constructing any improvements is that the Supreme Court must be an open institution—as open as is truly consistent with proper adjudication and as open as the democratic society the Warren Court sought so earnestly to fashion.

"UNINHIBITED, ROBUST, AND WIDE-OPEN"—
A NOTE ON FREE SPEECH AND THE WARREN COURT

By Harry Kalven, Jr. *

There are several ways to give at the outset, in quick summary, an overall impression of the Warren Court in the area of the First Amendment. The quotation in the title can for many reasons be taken as its trademark. The quotation comes, of course, from a statement about public debate made in the Court's preeminent decision, *New York Times v. Sullivan*, and it carries echoes of Alexander Meiklejohn. We have, according to Justice Brennan, "a profound national commitment to the principle that debate on public issues should be uninhibited, robust, and wide-open. . . ." What catches the eye is the daring, unconventional selection of adjectives. These words capture the special quality of the Court's stance toward First Amendment issues. They express the gusto and enthusiasm with which the Court has tackled such issues. They indicate an awareness that heresy is robust; that counterstatement on public issues, if it is to be vital and perform its function, may not always be polite. And, most significantly, they express a desire to make a fresh statement about the principles of free speech rather than simply repeat the classic phrases of Holmes in *Abrams* and Brandeis in *Whitney*. The Court is interested enough to be minting contemporary epigrams—to be making it its own.

For a further impression of the Court's work in the First Amendment field, we might turn to the 1959 case involving *Lady Chatterley's Lover* in movie form, *Kingsley Pictures Corp. v. Regents*. Chiefly because of an inability to agree on precisely how the court below had disposed of the case, the Supreme Court, although unanimous in reversing, found it necessary to produce six separate opinions. Of particular interest for the moment is Justice Stewart's opinion: he read the court below as banning the movie because it had dealt too sympathetically with adultery. In meeting this objection he was moved to restate the basic principle with notable freshness:

> It is contended that the State's action was justified because the motion picture attractively portrays a relationship which is contrary to the moral standards, the religious precepts, and the legal code of its citizenry. This argument misconceives what it is that the Constitution protects. Its guarantee is not confined to the expression of ideas that are conventional or shared by a

* Harry Kalven, Jr. " 'Uninhibited, Robust, and Wide-open'—A Note on Free Speech and The Warren Court." *Michigan Law Review*, Vol. 67 (December 1968), p. 289. Used with permission of the author, a professor of law at the University of Chicago.

majority. It protects advocacy of the opinion that adultery may sometimes be proper no less than advocacy of socialism or the single tax. And in the realm of ideas it protects expression which is eloquent no less than that which is unconvincing.

Again what strikes the special note is not just the firm grasp of the basic principle but the gallantry, if you will, of its restatement. It is easier to champion freedom for the thought we hate than for the thought that embarrasses.

Yet another way of reducing to quick summary the special quality of this Court with regard to First Amendment issues is to compare the opinions in *Curtis Publishing Company v. Butts*, decided in 1967, with the opinion in *Debs v. United States*. The *Debs* case was decided March 10, 1919, exactly one week after *Schenck* had launched the clear-and-present-danger formula. In an opinion by Justice Holmes, the Court affirmed Debs' conviction (carrying a ten-year prison sentence) for attempting to incite insubordination, disloyalty, mutiny, and refusal of duty in the armed forces and for attempting to obstruct the recruiting and enlistment service of the United States in violation of the Espionage Act of 1917. The overt conduct of Debs consisted solely in making a public speech to a general adult audience in Canton, Ohio. At the time he was a major national political figure, and in 1920 he was to run as the Socialist candidate for President from prison and receive over 900,000 votes.

The speech itself, which is summarized in Justice Holmes' opinion, involved a criticism of war in general and World War I in particular from a Socialist point of view. It asserted, for example, that "the master class has always declared the war and the subject class has always fought the battles. . . ." It expressed sympathy for several others already convicted for their opposition to the war, saying that "if they were guilty so was he." It appears that most of the speech was devoted to Socialist themes apart from the war, and it concluded with the exhortation: "Don't worry about the charge of treason to your masters; but be concerned about the treason that involves yourselves." During the trial Debs addressed the jury himself and stated: "I have been accused of obstructing the war. I admit it. Gentlemen, I abhor war. I would oppose the war if I stood alone."

The Court disposed of the case in a perfunctory two-page opinion, treating as the chief question whether a jury could find that "one purpose of the speech, whether incidental or not does not matter, was to oppose not only war in general but this war, and that the opposition was so expressed that its natural and intended effect would be to obstruct recruiting." The First Amendment defense exacted only the following sentence from Justice Holmes: "The chief defenses upon which the defendant seemed willing to rely were the denial that we have dealt with and that based upon the First Amendment to the Constitution, disposed of in *Schenck v. United States*. . . ." The decision was unanimous and without any comment from Justice Brandeis.

Let us now jump a half century to *Butts*. At issue there was a judgment under state law in a libel action brought by a noted football coach against a national magazine for an article which in effect accused him of "fixing" a college football game by giving his team's secrets in advance of the game to the opposing coach. The case produced an elaborate outpouring of opinions and an intricate pattern of votes in the five-to-four decision affirming the judgment. All Justices agreed that since Butts was a public figure, the reporting of his activities was in the public domain and therefore the state libel law was subject to the discipline of the First Amendment. The Justices divided over what level of privilege the defendant publisher must be given to satisfy the constitutional concern with freedom of speech. Three separate positions were expressed: Justices Black and Douglas would have granted an absolute or unqualified privilege not defeasible by any showing of malice. At the other extreme, Justice Harlan, joined by Justices Clark, Fortas, and Stewart, held the privilege defeated by a showing of "highly unreasonable conduct constituting an extreme departure from the standards of investigation and reporting ordinarily adhered to by responsible journalists." The middle ground was occupied by Justices Brennan, White, and the Chief Justice, who would have adhered to the standards set forth in New York Times and thus would have held the privilege defeasible by actual malice—defined as "knowing falsehood or reckless disregard for truth." Out of this unpromising and apparently trivial factual context came deeply felt essays on freedom of speech by Justices Harlan, Black, and the Chief Justice. In wondering about all this on another occasion, I observed:

> This is perhaps the fitting moment to pause to marvel at the pattern of the Court's argument on this issue. The Court was divided 5 to 4 on whether the constitutional standard for the conditional privilege of those who libel public figures is that it be defeasible only upon a showing of reckless disregard for truth or merely on a showing of an extreme departure from professional newspaper standards! Further it was understood that the chief significance of the standard relates simply to how jury instructions will be worded. Yet this nuance triggered a major debate in the court on the theory of free speech. [1967 Sup. Ct. Rev. 267]

And in speculating on why these issues held such extraordinary power to move the Supreme Court—after noting that in the sequence of cases following New York Times the Court had located a novel and difficult issue involving "public speech interlaced with comments on individuals"—I could only add: "Second, it shows once again—and it is a splendid thing—that all members of this Court care deeply about free speech values and their proper handling by law. Only a concerned Court would have worked so hard on such a problem."

The difference between Debs and Butts is a measure of how much the Court's approach to free speech has changed over the years since World War I. And it is a difference, it will be noted, in result, in theory, in style, and, above all, in concern.

But even as one acknowledges the deep concern of this Court for the First Amendment, there is need to pause at the outset for a perplexity and an irony. The perplexity is one that must have troubled all the contributors to this Symposium: What exactly is one referring to when he speaks of the Warren Court? Are we simply using the Chief Justiceship as a device to mark off a span of years? Would it have been any more arbitrary to talk of the work of the Court from, say, 1958 to 1964? If we find some distinctive traits in that work, as both friends and critics of the Court are so readily prone to do in the First Amendment area, to whom are we ascribing them? To some durable *team* of Justices? To the special influence of the Chief? The Court's roster during the Warren years has included some seventeen Justices, and the "Warren Court" has for varying periods of time numbered among its members Justices Minton, Burton, Clark, Whittaker, Reed, Jackson, Goldberg, and Frankfurter. Perhaps we should adapt the old Greek conundrum and ask if we can comment on the same Court twice.

I would hesitate to adopt the alternative and say that what unifies the topic is the distinctive influence of the Chief Justice on the Court's response to the First Amendment. This would require not only that we find a distinctive pattern of decisions, but that we connect it up somehow to the chairmanship of the Chief—which seems to me to attribute excessive power to that office.

But perhaps I am being too solemn about it all. There has indeed been a kind of First Amendment team: Black and Douglas have been on the Court during the entire tenure of the Chief Justice. Brennan and Harlan were appointed in 1956, and Stewart in 1958. And it is the analysis and response of these six Justices to the First Amendment that I have chiefly in mind in considering the Warren Court's reaction to free speech issues. At least we match here the rough unity of topic provided, say, by talk of the greatness of the New York Yankees in the middle 1920s.

. . . The wretched controversy over the Fortas appointment was interpreted widely as an attack more on the Court as a whole than on Justice Fortas. The Senate was presumably providing its own commentary on the work of the Warren Court. And for our immediate purposes, it is striking how much of the Senate's concern was with the work of the Court in the First Amendment area. There is a temptation to brood over the gap which appears to have been created between the First Amendment values the Court has championed and those the public, or a considerable segment of the public, will tolerate. Is there, then, a *political* limit on the meaning of the First Amendment? Two offsetting considerations should, in any event, be noted. The Senate's free-speech grievances related almost exclusively, so far as I could tell, to the decisions on obscenity and did not put in issue the striking work of the Court in other areas of First Amendment concern. Further, such a gap between public and judicial attitudes may be a healthy sign. The tradition has never been that freedom of speech was a value to be left to majority vote; indeed, that may be the whole point of the First Amendment and of judicial review under it.

I

At the Museum of Science and Industry in Chicago there is a chart which occupies a long wall and which graphs over time the changes in human technology. The time span is some 50,000 years, and the introduction of each technological advance—from the first crude stone used as a tool for digging to today's latest electronic or space age wonders—is entered on the graph. The result is a stunning visual impression of the acceleration of cultural inheritance. Man has made more major technical advances in the past 100 years than in the previous 49,900!

There is a general analogy here to the making of law. Invention seems to breed invention, and precedent breeds more precedent. But I cite the Museum wall to make a specific point about the Warren Court. If one were to imagine a comparable scheme charting the incidence of First Amendment cases from 1791 to date, the parallel would be striking indeed; we would get a proper sense of the accelerated accumulation of First Amendment precedents in the past fifteen years. The point is, I think, a neutral one. It goes for the moment not to the quality of the Court's answers but to its willingness to confront First Amendment questions at an unprecedented rate. The result is that a great part of the law, and a greater part of what is of interest today to the teacher or commentator, is the work of the Warren Court.

Even the quickest survey makes the point. All of the constitutional decisions on obscenity have come from this Court, starting with *Roth* in 1957; if one is interested in law and obscenity he will perforce find himself studying essentially the work of the Warren Court. Similarly, the constitutional law on libel has—with the exception of *Beauharnais* in 1952—come from this Court, starting with *New York Times* in 1964. . . .

There is perhaps one other way of putting into perspective how much the Warren Court has enriched the constitutional doctrine of freedom of speech, press, and assembly. It is to compare the classic book in the field, Chafee's *Free Speech in the United States*, first published in 1920 and republished in elaborated form in 1941, with the current corpus of law. A book today performing the function of Chafee's volume would look notably different, deal to a considerable degree with different principles, and confront to a considerable extent different problems. If the analytic density of the Chafee book were to be maintained, the contemporary treatment would surely require two volumes; and the second volume would be devoted to the work of the Warren Court.

II

It is not feasible within the compass of this Article to attempt a systematic review of the results the Court has achieved in the various areas of First Amendment law. I should prefer, therefore, to check off briefly some of the new *ideas* the Court has introduced into the field.

New York Times may have effected a major alteration in official thinking about free speech. To begin with, the Court introduced the attractive notion that the First Amendment has a "central meaning" and thus suggested the possibility of a "core" theory of free speech. The central meaning suggested in *Times* appears to be the notion that seditious libel is not actionable.

It must be admitted that the promise of radical rethinking of the theory and rationale of the First Amendment which this invites has not as yet been judicially pursued. The Court has been careful, however, to preserve the status of *New York*

Times as a key precedent. The Court has also made visible a new kind of problem in *Times* and its sequelae: the question of whether falsity in fact as contrasted with falsity in doctrine is entitled to any protection. This problem arises when discussion of issues in the public domain is interlaced with statements of fact about particular individuals. The issue is whether in protecting the individual's interest in reputation or privacy we will give him a veto power over the general discussion. This was the problem in *Times* itself and again in *Time Inc. v. Hill, Butts,* and *Associated Press v. Walker;* it looms as a large issue since much public discussion appears to have this mixed quality. The dilemma is a difficult one, but the Court has confronted it and, to my mind, has made real progress toward a satisfactory solution.

Perhaps equally important is the abrogation of outmoded ideas by the Court; the most significant step here, I suggest, has been the great reduction in the status and prestige of the clear-and-present-danger test. Immediately prior to the advent of the Warren Court, this test had a considerable claim as *the* criterion of the constitutionality of an exercise of governmental authority over communication. In limited areas the test may still be alive, but it has been conspicuous by its absence from opinions in the last decade. Since the test—whatever sense it may have made in the limited context in which it originated—is clumsy and artificial when expanded into a general criterion of permissible speech, the decline in its fortunes under the Warren Court seems to be an intellectual gain.

Another major conceptual contribution of the Warren Court has been development of the idea of self-censorship. A regulation of communication may run afoul of the Constitution not because it is aimed directly at free speech, but because in operation it may trigger a set of behavioral consequences which amount in effect to people censoring themselves in order to avoid trouble with the law. The idea has appeared in several cases, and, while the Court has not yet addressed a major opinion to it, it has all the earmarks of a seminal concept. The cases have varied in contexts from *Speiser v. Randall,* to *Smith v. California,* to *Time Inc. v. Hill.* In *Speiser* the Court invalidated a state statute requiring affidavits of non-Communist affiliation as a condition for a tax exemption. The vice was a subtle one: as the Court understood the state procedure, the affidavit was not conclusive; thus the burden of proof of nonsubversion was left on the applicant. The Court stated:

> The vice of the present procedure is that, where the particular speech falls close to the line separating the lawful and the unlawful, the possibility of mistaken factfinding—inherent in all litigation—will create the danger that the legitimate utterance will be penalized. The man who knows that he must bring forth proof and persuade another of the lawfulness of his conduct necessarily must steer far wider of the unlawful zone than if the State must bear these burdens.

In *Smith* the Court confronted an ordinance imposing strict criminal liability on the sellers of obscene books. Again, the Court found the vice in the chain of consequences such regulation might engender:

By dispensing with any requirement of knowledge of the contents of the book on the part of the seller, the ordinance tends to impose a severe limitation on the public's access to constitutionally protected matter. For if the bookseller is criminally liable without knowledge of the contents, and the ordinance fulfills its purpose, he will tend to restrict the books he sells to those he has inspected; and thus the State will have imposed a restriction upon the distribution of constitutionally protected as well as obscene literature. . . . The bookseller's self-censorship, compelled by the State, would be a censorship affecting the whole public, hardly less virulent for being privately administered.

Finally, in the context of tort liability for "false light" privacy, the Court in *Hill* conceptualized the problem as one of triggering self-censorship; it thus would give the publisher a conditional privilege defeasible only by actual malice:

We create grave risk of serious impairment of the indispensable service of a free press in a free society if we saddle the press with the impossible burden of verifying to a certainty the facts associated in a news article with a person's name, picture or portrait, particularly as related to nondefamatory matter. Even negligence would be a most elusive standard especially when the content of the speech itself affords no warning of prospective harm to another through falsity. . . . Fear of large verdicts in damage suits for innocent or merely negligent misstatement, even the fear of expense involved in their defense, must inevitably cause publishers "to steer . . . wider of the unlawful zone. . . ."

The Court is thus in command of a versatile concept which represents, I think, a fascinating addition to the vocabulary of First Amendment doctrine. It should perhaps be acknowledged that the opinions in all three cases were written by Justice Brennan.

One other potentially powerful idea of the Warren Court should be noted: the principle that strict economy of means is required when communication is regulated. It is not enough that the end be legitimate; the means must not be wasteful of First Amendment values. The seeds of this notion first appeared in *Schneider v. New Jersey*, decided in 1939, which invalidated a prohibition against distributing leaflets where the governmental objective was to prevent littering the streets. But the idea was given its fullest expression by the Warren Court in *Shelton v. Tucker*, which voided a state statute requiring each school teacher as a condition of employment to file annually an affidavit listing every organization to which he had belonged or contributed in the preceding five years. The Court found that, although the state had a legitimate interest in the organizational commitments of its teachers, the statute gratuitously overshot its target. Justice Stewart stated the principle this way:

In a series of decisions this Court has held that, even though the governmental purpose be legitimate and substantial, that purpose cannot be pursued by means that broadly stifle fundamental personal liberties when the end can more narrowly be achieved. The breadth of legislative abridgment must be viewed in the light of less drastic means for achieving the same basic purpose.

It remains to be seen whether this principle, too, will be seminal. There is more than a suggestion in it of a preferred-position thesis. Legislation regulating communication may not be presumptively unconstitutional today, but under the economy principle it will not be entitled to, In Holmes' phrase, "a penumbra" of legislative convenience.

III

The momentum of the Warren Court in other areas of constitutional law has been the source of sustained controversy and criticism. Without attempting to assess the merits of such criticism in general, I should like to explore whether in the special area of free speech the Court's work is subject to similar disapproval.

It has frequently been objected that the Court has moved too fast and in giant steps rather than with the gradual deliberation appropriate to the judicial process, that its opinions have often displayed inadequate craftsmanship, that it has failed to confront the issues and to rationalize its results with appropriate rigor. However, if we consider for a moment the work of the Court in two important areas—obscenity and the scope of the power of congressional investigating committees—these criticisms do not appear warranted. To be sure there had been, as we noted, no constitutional decisions whatsoever on the obscenity issue prior to 1957. But that was simply because such cases had not come before the Court; there was no general consensus that such regulation was constitutional. In fact, there had long been recognized a tension between obscenity regulation and the First Amendment. It is enough to cite the widespread praise of Judge Woolsey's decision and opinion in the *Ulysses* case to document the tension generally seen between the regulation of obscenity and the reach of the First Amendment; by the time the Supreme Court entered the field in the *Roth* case, judges in other courts had explicitly noted the constitutional shadows.

Moreover, in *Roth* the Court *upheld* the constitutionality of the obscenity regulation involved. In doing so, however, it recognized and attempted to define the constitutional limitations on such regulation. While in the past decade an unusual number of obscenity cases have reached the Supreme Court, the sequence of resulting decisions can fairly be characterized as involving the gradual resolution of limited and closely related problems on a case-by-case basis. Thus, *Kingsley Pictures* resolved the problems of thematic obscenity; *Butler v. Michigan* resolved the problems of regulation of general literature distribution keyed to what is suitable for children; and *Smith* dealt with permissible regulation of booksellers. Moreover, *Manual Enterprises v. Day* added the element of "patent offensiveness" to the constitutional definition of obscenity, and *Jacobellis v. Ohio* attached the element of "utterly without redeeming significance." If there has been a jarring note, it has come not in accelerating the liberation of arts and letters from obscenity censorship, but rather from the sudden move in the opposite direction in *Ginzburg v. United States* by adding the perplexing "pandering" element to the constitutional test.

It is true that the Court has been conspicuous within itself as to how to handle obscenity cases. It is possible to detect at least six different doctrinal positions among the nine Justices. But this is due, I would suggest, to the intrinsic awkwardness of the problem rather than to a judicial failure to take the cases seriously or to face the issues squarely. In any event, the Court cannot be criticized for rushing past existing precedent in order to abolish censorship altogether. . . .

We noted at the start that the topic of the Warren Court is an oblique, elusive one. Surely it would be easier to discuss straight away the substantive issues the Court has dealt with rather than to probe for some pattern of positions distinctive to the personality of this particular Court. Nevertheless, as we also said at the outset, there does seem to be a special trademark to this Court's work in the area of freedom of speech, press, and assembly. There is a zest for these problems and a creative touch in working with them. It has been noted that there are overtones of Alexander Meiklejohn in the Court's idiom. It may, therefore, not be inappropriate to turn to Mr. Meiklejohn for a final comment. Speaking of the principle of the First Amendment, he once said: "We must think for it as well as fight for it." The Warren Court in its enriching gloss on the amendment over the past fifteen years has done a good deal to help us do both.

LITIGIOUS AGE GIVES RISE TO MEDIA LAW

By C. David Rambo*

A multitude of challenges to press rights coupled with government's pervasive presence in most aspects of American business have touched off an increasing need among newspapers for legal assistance.

From this has evolved the field of media law, whose practitioners are part of a new elite called on to help apply and preserve the First Amendment.

"I've been in the business 25 years," says Kuyk Logan, managing editor of *The Houston Post*, "and I'm spending more time with attorneys than I ever have."

"Fifteen years ago there really wasn't any concentrated expertise in the field," says noted media lawyer James C. Goodale, former general counsel of *The New York Times*. "Since that time, there has developed a so-called mass communications lawyer or press lawyer."

There is no formal association of media attorneys and no firm count of their number. But observers agree the cadre is growing. One indicator is registration figures of the annual media law seminar in New York City sponsored by Practising Law Institute. Goodale, program chairman, says the event drew an average 75 participants in its first and second years. The ninth annual seminar scheduled Nov. 19–20 is expected to attract 250–300 communications lawyers.

Another indicator is the 1977 founding of *Media Law Reporter*, published by the Bureau of National Affairs Inc. and now virtually required reading in the communications law camp. Designed especially for media attorneys, the publication reprints press law decisions, and reports on significant regulatory developments. Circulation has climbed to about 1,150 from an initial 300 subscribers, says Managing Editor Cynthia J. Bolbach.

One of the biggest reasons for the growth of media law is "the increasing litigiousness of our society," observes James D. Spaniolo, general counsel of *The Miami Herald*.

"The public seems willing to attack all establishments," says Richard M. Schmidt, Jr., general counsel of the American Society of Newspaper Editors. "Years back, when someone went to the hospital and died after an illness, it was considered to be the will of God, and that was it. But now the first thing they seem to do is say, 'Can we sue?'"

In addition to libel and privacy matters, media lawyers are dealing with a

* From C. David Rambo. "Litigious Age Gives Rise to Media Law." *presstime*, Vol. 3, No. 11 (November 1981), p. 4. Reprinted by permission from *presstime*, the journal of the American Newspaper Publishers Association. The author is a *presstime* staff writer.

sharp rise in questions about reporter privilege, gag orders, courtroom closures, subpoenas of journalists, access to public records and meetings, newsroom searches and other First Amendment issues. Many are "creatures of the last 10 years," notes Bruce W. Sanford, an attorney whose clients include the Society of Professional Journalists, Sigma Delta Chi.

Many lawyers are spending much time just keeping their press clients informed of the latest legal developments. "There's a lot of activity popping all over the place," says Robert C. Lobdell, vice president and general counsel of the *Los Angeles Times*. "A lawyer simply has to keep his publishers and editors, and the business staff for that matter, aware and up to date on what the law is."

Much of the heightened activity stems from the courts. And while most media lawyers agree there has been an increase in the number of cases and troublesome outcomes, they don't always agree on the reasons.

Court opinions adverse to the press are a byproduct of "a long-term institutional conflict going on between the judicial system and the press," says lawyer-journalist Jack C. Landau, director of The Reporters Committee for Freedom of the Press.

ANPA General Counsel Arthur B. Hanson strongly disagrees. He says that "courts"—meaning judges in general and the U.S. Supreme Court under Chief Justice Warren E. Burger in particular—are not "anti-press."

"Some of the greatest affirmations of press freedoms in the 20th century" have come from the Burger court, agrees Sanford.

Hanson contends that the cause of the increased court activity involving the press—especially libel cases—is attributable in large part to careless reporters and editors.

Schmidt says he would agree there was a "post-Watergate syndrome" characterized by a crop of investigative reporters "who were willing to rush to print with anything." But he says "the pendulum has swung back, and I think we're going into more careful reporting and more careful editing." . . .

Regardless of where the lawyers keep offices, editors and attorneys alike say successful relationships depend on firm ground rules. Each side must know the other's responsibilities to avoid "a big philosophical pretzel twist," Lobdell observes.

Most important, many editors and lawyers agree, is that editors and publishers—not the lawyers—make editorial decisions. "I want them to let me know where I stand and how much risk is involved in running this story," explains James P. Gannon, executive editor of the *Des Moines Register and Tribune*. "They'll say, 'Here's the law, here's the situation, here's what's happened in other cases.' " Then Gannon will decide what to do.

"It's a very sophisticated relationship," observes Goodale. The job of the media attorney, he says, should be "to figure out how to get the story published," not quashed. "Some lawyers are good at it, and some lawyers are terrible at it." Probably the worst are "straight-line, corporate lawyers who don't know how to deal with publications," he says.

Ken Paulson, assistant managing editor of *The Courier-News* in Bridgewater, N.J., and the holder of a law degree, adds that some lawyers unfamiliar with the mission of the newsroom could take the attitude, "Look, this story's going to cause a lot of trouble if you publish. On the other hand, if you don't publish, all you lose is eight inches of copy.' . . . Well, it's a lot more than eight inches of copy to a newspaper editor."

Those sentiments are echoed by Mike Kautsch, a lawyer and former investigative reporter at *The Atlanta Journal* and now assistant professor of journalism at the University of Kansas. He says he knows of instances in which stories have been "modified and even gutted" by the handiwork of lawyers insensitive to the editorial process.

He even fears that lawyers could "usurp the editorial role and become the final arbiter."

To that fear [R. Scott] Whiteside of the *Kansas City Star* and *Times* adds the danger that editors might, over time, allow them to do just that. If attorneys are readily available, editors may start to abdicate their responsibilities by saying, " 'The lawyer approved it, and it's OK to run it.' "

Another strain on the newspaper-attorney relationship can occur when the lawyer is a prominent one and the subject of highly publicized news stories.

A recent example involves Chicago libel expert Don H. Reuben, who counts among his clients the *Chicago Tribune* and John Cardinal Cody, the Roman Catholic prelate whom the rival *Sun-Times* reported is under investigation for allegedly diverting church funds to a longtime friend.

Tribune Editor and Executive Vice President James D. Squires says Reuben's involvement makes no difference in the *Tribune's* coverage of the volatile affair. However, he concedes that "anytime the newspaper lawyer is a prominent one who represents people who are in the news . . . there is always the problem of the *appearance* of a problem."

For his part, Reuben says he has "been in this situation 100 times," and the "real way to keep it pure is for (a newspaper's counsel) to be a Trappist monk." . . .

As legal issues, particularly free press/fair trial issues, multiplied in the '70s, ANPA formed a Press-Bar Relations Committee and a joint ANPA/ABA Task Force to promote understanding between the media and the bar.

Among other groups beefing up their legal work:

● SPJ,SDX in 1978 was spending "$1,000 of our budget money on legal, and now we're spending pretty close to $80,000 (per year)," says President Howard Graves. It has stepped up efforts on Capitol Hill and in filing friend-of-the-court briefs, and this year hired Sanford as its first general counsel.

● ASNE's spending on freedom-of-information efforts "has increased at least ten-fold" since 1968 when Schmidt became general counsel, he says. The society has filed more friend-of-the-court briefs, heightened its monitoring of legislation on the federal and state levels, and has expanded its campaigns to inform editors of developments in the legal and government arena.

● The National Newspaper Association, representing primarily small daily and weekly newspapers, historically has emphasized legal and government affairs via lobbying in Washington. New President George J. Measer wants to increase those efforts.

• The Reporters Committee was started in 1970 by a handful of journalists concerned about attacks on press freedoms. Currently it has about 4,500 paying sponsors, a staff of four lawyers and nine law school interns. The committee collects information and court decisions on a broad range of legal issues, testifies before Congress and submits court briefs on behalf of the press, and publishes the bi-monthly magazine *News Media and the Law*.

Other tools of this growing trade include the 23-year-old Freedom of Information Center at the University of Missouri, which serves as a repository for information on First Amendment cases, the new Libel Defense Center which reports on developments in libel and privacy and *Media Law Reporter*.

Another byproduct of the rise in media law is the increase in the number of journalists with law degrees. "We are finding that more and more people we interview for general newspaper jobs have a law degree," says [Chris] Waddle of the *Kansas City Times*. "We've got lawyers all over the place."

Paulson of *The Courier-News* says his law degree helps him be a better journalist. "There are so many parallels between the law and journalism," he explains. "It's essentially taking a great many facts and boiling them into an understandable form."

Paulson explains he always wanted to work as a newspaper journalist but a "frozen job market" prevented him from landing a job after graduating from college in 1975. He then went to law school "to get some expertise to improve my marketability." It worked.

But few law school graduates who are former reporters return to their beat, observes Professor Marc A. Franklin of Stanford University Law School. . . .

But whether as general counsel or publisher, in-house counsel or outside retainee, superstar in front of the Supreme Court or small-town attorney fighting a local marshal's warrant, the media lawyer has carved a large niche in an increasingly complex business.

No one is predicting that role will do anything but expand.

CHAPTER 2

PRIOR RESTRAINT

A *fundamental difference between the system of government employed in the United States and that of many other countries is found in the Supreme Court's interpretation of constitutional prohibition against government censorship,* i.e. *against restraint prior to publication. Autocratic rulers historically have stifled dissent by requiring government approval through licensing or prepublication review of all broadcasts, books and periodicals. The United States Supreme Court has affirmed that "whatever a man publishes, he publishes at his peril," but at the same time the Court has banished any system of "prior restraint" or "previous restraint" in all but extreme cases. The Court has continued to hold that the First Amendment is not absolute and that under certain circumstances pre-publication restraint may be justified, but these cases usually have been restricted to film censorship, obscenity (both covered in later chapters) or sedition.*

The Court has not stood still for thinly veiled attempts of various state and local legislative bodies to restrict the press through passage of certain nefarious laws, such as anti-litter legislation, prejudicial taxation schemes or "public nuisance" ordinances. Any law which tends to restrict constitutionally protected expressions must be accompanied by strict safeguards against misuse, the Court has ruled. These safeguards against prior restraint, however, in no way conflict with the possibility of punishment or legal redress subsequent to publicction.

Such guarantees of freedom were not always the case in this country. The first newspaper to be published in America, Benjamin Harris's Public Occurrences, *was suspended after its first issue appeared in 1690 when the colonial Governor found contents not to his liking. He issued a statement declaring that the publication had been printed without authority, that it was not to be circulated and that all such future publications were to secure a license before going to press. Nearly half a century later, in the 1730s John Peter Zenger was jailed and tried for seditious libel after a series of attacks on a colonial Governor in his* New York Weekly Journal. *His trial—and acquittal—resulted in the first major victory for freedom of the press in the American colonies. The case, because of its many technical peculiarities, had more symbolic than legal precedence. Still it was heralded as the tide of the future by those opposed to "establishment" rule of the colonies.*

The landmark case dealing with "prior restraint" came in 1931 with Near v. Minnesota (283 U.S. 697), which came six years after the Court ruled that the free speech and press principles of the First Amendment applied to the states through the Fourteenth Amendment (Gitlow v. New York). *Sidestepping the "clear and present danger" question, the Supreme Court focused instead on "prior restraint," a principle which had not been defined by the Court. Near, publisher of the* Saturday Press, *challenged a Minnesota law which authorized abatement as a public nuisance of publications deemed "malicious, scandalous, and defamatory." Near appealed that such action would violate the Fourteenth Amendment in that it would deny him freedom to publish without due process of law. Chief Justice Hughes, who spoke for the 5–4 majority, agreed, terming the Minnesota statute suppression rather than punishment. He further noted that other avenues of legal redress, e.g. libel action, still were open to those who sought to punish the publisher for alleged wrongdoing. In his publication, Near had severely attacked public officials and had alleged dishonesty and racketeering. Pre-publication censorship, the Court ruled, clearly was not philosophically compatible with the First Amendment.*

NEAR V. MINNESOTA
283 U.S. 697 (1931)

CHIEF JUSTICE HUGHES *delivered the opinion of the Court.*

. . . This statute, for the suppression as a public nuisance of a newspaper or periodical, is unusual, if not unique, and raises questions of grave importance transcending the local interests involved in the particular action. It is no longer open to doubt that the liberty of the press and of speech is within the liberty safeguarded by the due process clause of the 14th Amendment from invasion by state action. . . . The limits of this sovereign power must always be determined with appropriate regard to the particular subject of its exercise. . . .

First. The statute is not aimed at the redress of individual or private wrongs. Remedies for libel remain available and unaffected. . . .

Second. The statute is directed not simply at the circulation of scandalous and defamatory statements with regard to private citizens, but at the continued publication by newspapers and periodicals of charges against public officers of corruption, malfeasance in office, or serious neglect of duty. . . .

Third. The object of the statute is not punishment, in the ordinary sense, but suppression of the offending newspaper or periodical. The reason for the enactment, as the state court has said, is that prosecution to enforce penal statutes for libel do not result in "efficient repression or suppression of the evils of scandal." . . .

Under this statute, a publisher of a newspaper or periodical, undertaking to conduct a campaign to expose and to censure official derelictions, and devoting his publication principally to that purpose, must face not simply the possibility of a verdict against him in a suit or prosecution for libel, but a determination that his newspaper or periodical is a public nuisance to be abated, and that this abatement and suppression will follow unless he is prepared with legal evidence to prove the truth of the charges and also to satisfy the court that, in addition to being true, the matter was published with good motives and for justifiable ends.

This suppression is accomplished by enjoining publication and that restraint is the object and effect of the statute.

Fourth. The statute not only operates to suppress the offending newspaper or periodical but to put the publisher under an effective censorship. When a newspaper or periodical is found to be "malicious, scandalous and defamatory," and is suppressed as such, resumption of publication is punishable as a contempt of court by fine or imprisonment. . . .

If we cut through mere details of procedure, the operation and effect of the statute in substance is that public authorities may bring the owner or publisher of the newspaper or periodical before a judge upon a charge of conducting a business of publishing scandalous and defamatory matter—in particular that the matter consists of charges against public officers of official dereliction—and unless the owner or publisher is able and disposed to bring competent evidence to satisfy the judge that the charges are true and are published with good motives and for justifiable ends, his newspaper or periodical is suppressed and further publication is made punishable as a contempt. This is of the essence of censorship. . . .

The statute in question cannot be justified by reason of the fact that the publisher is permitted to show, before injunction issues, that the matter published is true and is published with good motives and for justifiable ends. If such a statute, authorizing suppression and injunction on such a basis, is constitutionally valid, it would be equally permissible for the legislature to provide that at any time the publisher of any newspaper could be brought before a court, or even an administrative officer (as the constitutional protection may not be regarded as resting on mere procedural details) and required to produce proof of the truth of his publication, or of what he intended to publish, and of his motives, or stand enjoined. . . . The recognition of authority to impose previous restraint upon publication in order to protect the community against the circulation of charges of misconduct, and especially of official misconduct, necessarily would carry with it the admission of the authority of the censor against which the constitutional barrier was erected. . . .

Equally unavailing is the insistence that the statute is designed to prevent the circulation of scandal which tends to disturb the public peace and to provoke assaults and the commission of crime. Charges of reprehensible conduct, and in particular of official malfeasance, unquestionably create a public scandal, but the theory of the constitutional guaranty is that even a more serious public evil would be caused by authority to prevent publication. . . .

For these reasons we hold the statute, so far as it authorized the proceedings in this action . . . to be an infringement of the liberty of the press guaranteed by the Fourteenth Amendment. We should add that this decision rests upon the operation and effect of the statute, without regard to the question of the truth of the charges contained in the particular periodical. . . .

*   *   *

Five years after Near, *the Court struck down what it held to be an unreasonable and inequitable tax on newspapers, but at the same time held that newspapers were not immune from fair taxation to support normal governmental functions.* Grosjean v. American Press. *At issue was a 1934 Louisiana tax of two per cent placed on all newspapers and magazines with weekly circulations of more than 20,000. The tax has been described as retaliatory against those publications which were opposed to the actions of Huey Long. A unanimous Supreme Court held the tax to be discriminatory, unusual and a means of control and, therefore, invalid. "Normal" taxation to support government services was not ruled out, however. The Court in* Grosjean *relied upon* Near, *but interpreted the First Amendment's free press philosophy as more encompassing than simply "prior restraint."*

The Court also ruled that constitutional guarantees of freedom of the press included the right to distribute a publication as well as freedom to print it. Lovell v. Griffin. . . . *Similarly, the Court held in* Martin v. Struthers *that the citizen has a right to receive printed matter. Circulation, said the Court, is essential to the concept of publishing.*

In Lovell, *the Court looked at an ordinance of the City of Griffin, Ga., which prohibited the distribution of circulars, advertising or literature of any type unless written permission was first obtained from the city manager. This prohibition was challenged under the First and Fourteenth Amendments as abridging free press guarantees. Chief Justice Hughes, in a strongly worded opinion for the 8–0 majority, agreed. He noted the importance of pamphlets in the history of the nation and held, significantly, that free press guarantees included circulation and were not intended solely for newspapers, but for pamphlets and leaflets as well.*

LOVELL V. GRIFFIN
303 U.S. 444 (1938)

CHIEF JUSTICE HUGHES *delivered the opinion of the Court.*

. . . Freedom of speech and freedom of the press, which are protected by the First Amendment from infringement by Congress, are among the fundamental personal rights and liberties which are protected by the Fourteenth Amendment from invasion by state action. It is also well settled that municipal ordinances adopted under state authority constitute state action and are within the prohibition of the amendment.

The ordinance in its broad sweep prohibits the distribution of "circulars, handbooks, advertising, or literature of any kind." It manifestly applies to pamphlets, magazines and periodicals. The evidence against appellant was that she distributed a certain pamphlet and a magazine called the "Golden Age." Whether in actual administration the ordinance is applied, as apparently it could be, to newspapers does not appear. The City Manager testified that "everyone applies to me for a license to distribute literature in this City. None of these people (including defendant) secured a permit from me to distribute literature in the City of Griffin." The ordinance is not limited to "literature" that is obscene or offensive to public morals or that advocates unlawful conduct. There is no suggestion that the pamphlet and magazine distributed in the instant case were of that character. The ordinance embraces "literature" in the widest sense.

The ordinance is comprehensive with respect to the method of distribution. It covers every sort of circulation "either by hand or otherwise." There is thus no restriction in its application with respect to time or place. It is not limited to ways which might be regarded as inconsistent with the maintenance of public order, or as involving disorderly conduct, the molestation of the inhabitants, or the misuse or littering of the streets. The ordinance prohibits the distribution of literature of any kind at any time, at any place, and in any manner without a permit from the City Manager.

We think that the ordinance is invalid on its face. Whatever the motive which induced its adoption, its character is such that it strikes at the very foundation of the freedom of the press by subjecting it to license and censorship. The struggle for the freedom of the press was primarily directed against the power of the licensor. It was against that power that John Milton directed his assault by his "Appeal for the Liberty of Unlicensed Printing." And the liberty of the press became initially a right to publish *without* a license what formerly could be published only *with* one.". . .

The liberty of the press is not confined to newspapers and periodicals. It necessarily embraces pamphlets and leaflets. These indeed have been historic weapons in the defense of liberty, as the pamphlets of Thomas Paine and others in our own history abundantly attest. The press in its historic connotation comprehends every sort of publication which affords a vehicle of information and opinion. What we have had recent occasion to say with respect to the vital importance of protecting this essential liberty from every sort of infringement need not be repeated.

The ordinance cannot be saved because it relates to distribution and not to publication. "Liberty of circulating is as essential to that freedom as liberty of publishing; indeed, without the circulation, the publication would be of little value." *Ex Parte Jackson.* . . .

* * *

The question of prohibiting election editorials on election day came before the Warren Court on appeal from James E. Mills, editor of the Birmingham (Ala.) Post-Herald. *He had been convicted under Alabama law for a 1962 election-day editorial urging voters to abandon the city's commissioner form of government in favor of a mayor-council plan. The change was approved. At issue were the principles of freedom of speech and press and the state's police power to set standards of conduct for orderly elections. The Court in a 1966 decision held the Alabama law to be unconstitutional.*

MILLS V. ALABAMA
384 U.S. 214 (1966)

JUSTICE BLACK *delivered the opinion of the Court.*

The question squarely presented here is whether a State, consistently with the United States Constitution, can make it a crime for the editor of a daily newspaper to write and publish an editorial *on election day* urging people to vote a certain way on issues submitted to them. . . .

. . . The First Amendment, which applies to the States through the Fourteenth, prohibits laws "abridging the freedom of speech, or of the press." The question here is whether it abridges freedom of the press for a State to punish a newspaper editor for doing no more than publishing an editorial on election day urging people to vote a particular way in the election. We should point out at once that this question in no way involves the extent of a State's power to regulate conduct in and around the polls in order to maintain peace, order and decorum there. The sole reason for the charge that Mills violated the law is that he wrote and published an editorial on election day which urged Birmingham voters to cast their votes in favor of changing their form of government.

Whatever differences may exist about interpretations of the First Amendment, there is practically universal agreement that a major purpose of that Amendment was to protect the free discussion of governmental affairs. This of course includes discussions of candidates, structures and forms of government, the manner in which government is operated or should be operated, and all such matters relating to political processes. The Constitution specifically selected the press, which includes not only newspapers, books, and magazines, but also humble leaflets and circulars, to play an important role in the discussion of public affairs. Thus the press serves and was designed to serve as a powerful antidote to any abuses of power by governmental officials and as a constitutionally chosen means for keeping officials elected by the people responsible to all the people whom they were selected to serve. Suppression of the right of the press to praise or criticize governmental agents and to clamor and contend for or against change, which is all that this editorial did, muzzles one of the very agencies the Framers of our Constitution thoughtfully and deliberately selected to improve our society and keep it free. The Alabama Corrupt Practices Act by providing criminal penalties for publishing editorials such as the one here silences the press at a time when it can be most effective. It is difficult to conceive of a more obvious and flagrant abridgment of the constitutionally guaranteed freedom of the press.

. . . The state statute leaves people free to hurl their campaign charges up to the last minute of the day before election. The law held valid by the Alabama Supreme Court then goes on to make it a crime to answer those "last minute" charges on election day, the only time they can be effectively answered. Because the law prevents any adequate reply to these charges, it is wholly ineffective in protecting the electorate "from confusive last-minute charges and countercharges." We hold that no test of reasonableness can save a state law from invalidation as a violation of the First Amendment when the law makes it a crime for a newspaper editor to do no more than urge people to vote one way or another in a publicly held election. . . .

*   *   *

In what some believe to be the most serious threat to a free press in decades, the Justice Department brought suit in June of 1971 to halt publication by the New York Times—and later the Washington Post *and other newspapers—of the "Pentagon Papers," secret government documents detailing the history of the U.S. involvement in the Vietnam War. The* New York Times *published three installments, but suspended a fourth when the Federal Court at the request of the government issued a temporary order halting further publication of the material.* New York Times *attorney and Yale Law Professor Alexander M. Bickel claimed that successful efforts by the government to restrain newspapers prior to publication had never happened before in the history of the Republic. It was, he said, a classic case of censorship. The government claimed threats to the national security. The newspaper denied such threats and claimed that a free, democratic society is best served by the public's right to know, that embarrassment to the Pentagon—not national security—was the real reason behind the injunctive action, and that such restraints prior to publication are repugnant to the national interest and the Constitution. Separate Federal Courts of Appeal decided differently in the two early cases brought to them. In New York, the* Times *was given permission to resume publication of the series, but only those portions deemed by the government not detrimental to national security. In Washington, the* Post *was given permission to resume full publication. The question went immediately to the Supreme Court, which was about to adjourn for the summer recess.*

The Supreme Court heard oral arguments June 26, 1971, in an unusual Saturday session and announced its decision just four days later and 15 days after the injunction was first ordered against the Times. *In a 6–3 decision, the Justices rejected the Government's claim that the national security would be imperiled by publication of the documents. The order freeing the newspapers to print the documents in full was given in a brief, unsigned opinion. Each Justice, then, added a separate opinion. Dissenting were Chief Justice Burger and Justices Blackmun and Harlan, all of whom were critical of the speed with which they were called upon to reach a judgment.*

The action of the Court disappointed both sides. The Government, of course, lost its bid to keep the documents secret. In addition, Congress had begun hearings into possible revisions of the procedures used in classification of materials allegedly sensitive to national security. But the media were disappointed also, for the division of the Court, as revealed by the nine separate opinions, held out the possibility that prior restraint by the Government at some future time would be acceptable to a majority of the Justices. The opinion did not close the door on prior restraint, as some had hoped it would. Indeed, the Government was successful—if only temporarily—in its first known attempt at "censorship through injunction." Still, the message was clear: the First Amendment demands that with any attempt at prior restraint by government, the burden of proving grave danger to the nation would be a heavy burden indeed. The Near *principle stood the test, though questions remained as to the effect the decision would have on future similar actions by government or the media.*

The unsigned opinion appears in its entirety, followed by edited versions of each of the nine Justices' separate opinions.

NEW YORK TIMES V. UNITED STATES

UNITED STATES V. WASHINGTON POST
403 U.S. 713 (1971)

PER CURIAM.

We granted certiorari in these cases in which the United States seeks to enjoin the *New York Times* and the *Washington Post* from publishing the contents of a classified study entitled "History of U.S. Decision-Making Process on Vietnam Policy."

"Any system of prior restraints of expression comes to this court bearing a heavy presumption against its constitutional validity." *Bantan Books, Inc. v. Sullivan,* 372 U.S. 58, 70 (1963); see also *Near v. Minnesota,* 283 U.S. 697 (1931). The Government "thus carries a heavy burden of showing justification for the enforcement of such restraint." *Organization for a Better Austin v. Keefe* (1971). The District Court for the Southern District of New York in the *New York Times* case and the District Court for the District of Columbia and the Court of Appeals for the District of Columbia Circuit in the *Washington Post* case held that the Government had not met that burden. We agree.

The judgment of the Court of Appeals for the District of Columbia Circuit is therefore affirmed. The order of the Court of Appeals for the Second Circuit is reversed and the case is remanded with directions to enter a judgment affirming the judgment of the District Court for the Southern District of New York. The stays entered June 25, 1971, by the court are vacated. The mandates shall issue forthwith.

So ordered.

JUSTICE BLACK, *with whom Justice Douglas joins, concurring.*

. . . I believe that every moment's continuance of the injunction against these newspapers amounts to a flagrant, indefensible and continuing violation of the First Amendment. . . . In my view it is unfortunate that some of my brethren are apparently willing to hold that the publication of news may sometimes be enjoined. Such a holding would make a shambles of the First Amendment. . . .

. . . Now, for the first time in the 182 years since the founding of the Republic, the Federal Courts are asked to hold that the First Amendment does not mean what it says, but rather means that the Government can halt the publication of current news of vital importance to the people of this country.

In seeking injunctions against these newspapers and in its presentation to the Court, the Executive Branch seems to have forgotten the essential purpose and history of the First Amendment. When the Constitution was adopted, many people strongly opposed it because the document contained no Bill of Rights to safeguard certain basic freedoms. They especially feared that the new powers granted to a central government might be interpreted to permit the Government to curtail freedom of religion, press, assembly and speech. In response to an overwhelming public clamor, James Madison offered a series of amendments to satisfy citizens that these great liberties would remain safe and beyond the power of government to abridge. . . . The amendments were offered to curtail and restrict the general powers granted to the Executive, Legislative, and Judicial Branches two years before in the original Constitution. The Bill of Rights changed the original Constitution into a new charter under which no branch of government could abridge the people's freedoms of press, speech, religion and assembly. Yet the Solicitor General argues and some members of the Court appear to agree that the general powers of the Government adopted in the original Constitution should be interpreted to limit and restrict the specific and emphatic guarantees of the Bill of Rights adopted later. I can imagine no greater perversion of history. . . .

. . . The press was to serve the governed, not the governors. The Government's power to censor the press was abolished so that the press would remain forever free to censure the Government. The press was protected so that it could bare the secrets of government and inform the people. Only a free and unrestrained press can effectively expose deception in government. And paramount among the responsibilities of a free press is the duty to prevent any part of the government from deceiving the people and sending them off to distant lands to die of foreign fevers and foreign shot and shell. In my view, far from deserving condemnation for their courageous reporting, the *New York Times,* the *Washington Post* and other newspapers should be commended for serving the purpose that the Founding Fathers saw so clearly. In revealing the workings of government that led to the Vietnam war, the newspapers nobly did precisely that which the Founders hoped and trusted they would do. . . .

JUSTICE DOUGLAS, *with whom Justice Black joins, concurring.*

. . . It should be noted at the outset that the First Amendment provides that "Congress shall make no law . . . abridging the freedom of speech or of the press." That leaves, in my view, no room for governmental restraint on the press.

There is, moreover, no statute barring the publication by the press of the material which the *Times* and *Post* seek to use. . . .

Thus Congress has been faithful to the command of the First Amendment in this area. . . .

These disclosures may have a serious impact. But that is no basis for sanctioning a previous restraint on the press. . . .

The dominant purpose of the First Amendment was to prohibit the widespread practice of governmental suppression of embarrassing information. It is common knowledge that the First Amendment was adopted against the widespread use of the common law seditious libel to punish the dissemination of material that is embarrassing to the powers-that-be. . . . The present cases will, I think, go down in history as the most dramatic illustration of that principle. A debate of large proportions goes on in the nation over our posture in Vietnam. That debate antedated the disclosure of the contents of the present documents. The latter are highly relevant to the debate in progress.

Secrecy in government is fundamentally anti-democratic, perpetuating bureaucratic errors. Open debate and discussion of public issues are vital to our national health. On public questions there should be "open and robust debate." . . .

JUSTICE BRENNAN, *concurring.*

. . . So far as I can determine, never before has the United States sought to enjoin a newspaper from publishing information in its possession. . . .

The error which has pervaded these cases from the outset was the granting of any injunctive relief whatsoever, interim or otherwise. The entire thrust of the government's claim throughout these cases has been that publication of the material sought to be enjoined "could," or "might," or "may" prejudice the national interest in various ways. But the First Amendment tolerates absolutely no prior judicial restraints of the press predicated upon surmise or conjecture that untoward consequences may result. Our cases, it is true, have indicated that there is a single, extremely narrow class of cases in which the First Amendment's ban on prior judicial restraint may be overridden. Our cases have thus far indicated that such cases may arise only when the nation "is at war," *Schenck v. United States* 249 U.S. 47, 52 (1919), during which times "no one would question but that a government might prevent actual obstruction to its recruiting service or the publication of the sailing dates of transports or the number and location of troops." *Near v. Minnesota*, 283 U.S. 697, 716 (1931). Even if the present world situation were assumed to be tantamount to a time of war, or if the power of presently available armaments would justify even in peacetime the suppression of information that would set in

motion a nuclear holocaust, in neither of these actions has the government presented or even alleged that publication of items from or based upon the material at
issue would cause the happening of an event of that nature. . . . In no event may
mere conclusions be sufficient: for if the Executive Branch seeks judicial aid in
preventing publication, it must inevitably submit the basis upon which that aid is
sought to scrutiny by the judiciary. And therefore, every restraint issued in this case,
whatever its form, has violated the First Amendment—and none the less so because
that restraint was justified as necessary to afford the Court an opportunity to
examine the claim more thoroughly. Unless and until the government has clearly
made out its case, the First Amendment commands that no injunction may issue.

JUSTICE STEWART, *with whom Justice White joins, concurring.*

   . . . In the absence of the governmental checks and balances present in other
areas of our national life, the only effective restraint upon executive policy and
power in the areas of national defense and international affairs may lie in an
enlightened citizenry—in an informed and critical public opinion which alone
can here protect the values of democratic government. For this reason, it is perhaps
here that a press that is alert, aware, and free most vitally serves the basic purpose of
the First Amendment. For without an informed and free press there cannot be an
enlightened people.
   Yet it is elementary that the successful conduct of international diplomacy and
the maintenance of an effective national defense require both confidentiality and
secrecy. Other nations can hardly deal with this nation in an atmosphere of mutual
trust unless they can be assured that their confidences will be kept. . . . In the area
of basic national defense the frequent need for absolute secrecy is, of course, self-
evident.
   I think there can be but one answer to this dilemma, if dilemma it be. The
responsibility must be where the power is. If the Constitution gives the Executive a
large degree of unshared power in the conduct of foreign affairs and the maintenance of our national defense, then under the Constitution the Executive must
have the largely unshared duty to determine and preserve the degree of internal
security necessary to exercise that power successfully. It is an awesome responsibility, requiring judgment and wisdom of a high order. I should suppose that
moral, political, and practical consideration would dictate that a very first principle
of that wisdom would be an insistence upon avoiding secrecy for its own sake.
   For when everything is classified, then nothing is classified, and the system
becomes one to be disregarded by the cynical or the careless, and to be manipu-
lated by those intent on self-protection or self-promotion. I should suppose, in
short, that the hallmark of a truly effective internal security system would be the
maximum possible disclosure, recognizing that secrecy can best be preserved only
when credibility is truly maintained. . . .

JUSTICE WHITE, *with whom Justice Stewart joins, concurring.*

   I concur in today's judgments, but only because of the concededly extraordinary protection against prior restraints enjoyed by the press under our constitutional system. I do not say that in no circumstances would the First Amendment permit an injunction against publishing information about Government plans or operations. Nor, after examining the materials the Government characterizes as the most sensitive and destructive, can I deny that revelation of these documents will do substantial damage to public interests. Indeed, I am confident that their disclosure will have the result. But I nevertheless agree that the United States has not satisfied the very heavy burden which it must meet to warrant an injunction against publication in these cases, at least in the absence of express and appropriately limited congressional authorization for prior restraints in circumstances such as these.

The Government's position is simply stated: the responsibility of the Executive for the conduct of the foreign affairs and for the security of the nation is so basic that the President is entitled to an injunction against publication of a newspaper story whenever he can convince a court that the information to be revealed threatens "grave and irreparable" injury to the public interest; and the injunction should issue whether or not the material to be published is classified, whether or not publication would be lawful under relevant criminal statutes enacted by Congress and regardless of the circumstances by which the newspaper came into possession of the information.

At least in the absence of legislation by Congress, based on its own investigations and findings, I am quite unable to agree that the inherent powers of the Executive and the courts reach so far as to authorize remedies having such sweeping potential for inhibiting publications by the press. . . .

JUSTICE MARSHALL, concurring.

. . . The issue is whether this court or the Congress has the power to make law. . . .

. . . It may be more convenient for the Executive if it need only convince a judge to prohibit conduct rather than to ask the Congress to pass a law and it may be more convenient to enforce a contempt order than seek a criminal conviction in a jury trial. Moreover, it may be considered politically wise to get a court to share the responsibility for arresting those who the Executive has probable cause to believe are violating the law. But convenience and political considerations of the moment do not justify a basic departure from the principles of our system of government.

In this case we are not faced with a situation where Congress has failed to provide the Executive with broad power to protect the nation from disclosure of damaging state secrets. Congress has on several occasions given extensive consideration to the problem of protecting the military and strategic secrets of the United States. This consideration has resulted in the enactment of statutes making it a crime to receive, disclose, communicate, withhold, and publish certain documents, photographs, instruments, appliances and information. . . .

Thus it would seem that in order for this Court to issue an injunction it would require a showing that such an injunction would enhance the already existing power of the government to act. . . . Here there has been no attempt to make such a showing. The Solicitor General does not even mention in his brief whether the Government considers there to be probable cause to believe a crime has been committed or whether there is a conspiracy to commit future crimes. . . .

Even if it is determined that the Government could not in good faith bring criminal prosecutions against the *New York Times* and the *Washington Post*, it is clear that Congress has specifically rejected passing legislation that would have clearly given the President the power he seeks here and made the current activities of the newspapers unlawful. When Congress specifically declines to make conduct unlawful it is not for this Court to redecide those issues—to overrule Congress. . . .

CHIEF JUSTICE BURGER, *dissenting.*

So clear are the constitutional limitations on prior restraint against expression, that from the time of *Near v. Minnesota* . . . (1931) until recently in *Organization for a Better Austin v. Keefe* (1971), we have had little occasion to be concerned with cases involving prior restraints against news reporting on matters of public interest. There is, therefore, little variation among the members of the Court in terms of resistance to prior restraints against publication. Adherence to this basic constitutional principle, however, does not make this case a simple one. In this case, the imperative of a free and unfettered press comes into collision with another imperative, the effective functioning of a complex modern government and specifically the effective exercise of certain constitutional powers of the Executive. Only those who view the First Amendment as an absolute in all circumstances—a view I respect, but reject—can find such a case as this to be simple or easy. . . .

. . . A great issue of this kind should be tried in a judicial atmosphere conducive to thoughtful, reflective deliberation, especially when haste, in terms of hours, is unwarranted in the light of the long period the *Times*, by its own choice, deferred publication.

It is not disputed that the *Times* has had unauthorized possession of the documents for three to four months, during which it has had its expert analysts studying them, presumably digesting them and preparing the material for publication. During all of this time, the *Times*, presumably in its capacity as trustee of the public's "right-to-know," has held up publication for purposes it considered proper and thus public knowledge was delayed. No doubt this was for a good reason; the analysis of 7,000 pages of complex material drawn from a vastly greater volume of material would inevitably take time and the writing of good news stories takes time. But why should the United States Government, from whom this information was illegally acquired by someone, along with all the counsel, trial judges and appellate judges be placed under needless pressure? . . .

Would it have been unreasonable, since the newspaper could anticipate the Government's objections to release of secret material, to give the Government an opportunity to review the entire collection and determine whether agreement could be reached on publication? . . .

With such an approach—one that great newspapers have in the past practiced and stated editorially to be the duty of an honorable press—the newspapers and Government might well have narrowed the area of disagreement as to what was and was not publishable, leaving the remainder to be resolved in orderly litigation if necessary. To me it is hardly believable that a newspaper long regarded as a great institution in American life would fail to perform one of the basic and simple duties of every citizen with respect to the discovery or possession of stolen property or secret government documents. That duty, I had thought—perhaps naively—was to report forthwith, to responsible public officers. This duty rests on taxi drivers, justices and the *New York Times*. If the action of the judges up to now has been correct, that result is sheer happenstance. . . .

JUSTICE HARLAN, *with whom the Chief Justice and Justice Blackmun join, dissenting.*

. . . With all respect, I consider that the court has been almost irresponsibly feverish in dealing with these cases. . . .

This frenzied train of events took place in the name of the presumption against prior restraints created by the First Amendment. Due regard for the extraordinarily important and difficult questions involved in these litigations should have led the Court to shun such a precipitate timetable. . . .

These are difficult questions of fact, of law, and of judgment; the potential consequences of erroneous decision are enormous. The time which has been available to us, to the lower courts, and to the parties has been wholly inadequate for giving these cases the kind of consideration they deserve. . . .

Forced as I am to reach the merits of these cases, I dissent from the opinion and judgments of the Court. Within the severe limitations imposed by the time constraints under which I have been required to operate, I can only state my reasons in telescoped form, even though in different circumstances I would have felt constrained to deal with the cases in the fuller sweep indicated above. . . .

. . . It is plain to me that the scope of the judicial function in passing upon the activities of the Executive Branch of the Government in the field of foreign affairs is very narrowly restricted. This view is, I think, dictated by the concept of separation of powers upon which our constitutional systems rests. . . .

JUSTICE BLACKMUN.

. . . At this point the focus is on only the comparatively few documents specified by the Government as critical. So far as the other material—vast in amount—is concerned, let it be published and published forthwith if the newspapers, once the strain is gone and the sensationalism is eased, still feel the urge to do so.

But we are concerned here with the few documents specified from the 47 volumes. . . .

The *New York Times* clandestinely devoted a period of three months examining the 47 volumes that came into its unauthorized possession. Once it had begun publication of material from those volumes, the New York case now before us emerged. It immediately assumed, and ever since has maintained, a frenetic pace and character. Seemingly, once publication started, the material could not be made public fast enough. Seemingly from then on, every deferral or delay, by restraint or otherwise, was abhorrent and was to be deemed violative of the First Amendment and of the public's "right immediately to know." Yet that newspaper stood before us at oral argument and professed criticism of the Government for not lodging its protest earlier than by a Monday telegram following the initial Sunday publication.

The District of Columbia case is much the same.

. . . The country would be none the worse off were the cases tried quickly, to be sure, but in the customary and properly deliberative manner. The most recent of the material, it is said, dates no later than 1968, already about three years ago, and the *Times* itself took three months to formulate its plan of procedure and, thus, deprived its public for that period.

The First Amendment, after all, is only one part of an entire Constitution. Article II of the great document vests in the Executive Branch primary power over the conduct of foreign affairs and places in that branch the responsibility for the nation's safety. Each provision of the Constitution is important, and I cannot subscribe to a doctrine of unlimited absolutism for the First Amendment at the cost of downgrading other provisions. . . .

. . . What is needed here is a weighing, upon properly developed standards, of the broad right of the press to print and of the very narrow right of the government to prevent. Such standards are not yet developed. The parties here are in disagreement as to what those standards should be. But even the newspapers concede that there are situations where restraint is in order and is constitutional. . . .

I therefore would remand these cases to be developed expeditiously, of course, but on a schedule permitting the orderly presentation of evidence from both sides, with the use of discovery, if necessary, as authorized by the rules, and with the preparation of briefs, oral argument and court opinions of a quality better than has been seen to this point. . . .

I strongly urge, and sincerely hope, that these two newspapers will be fully aware of their ultimate responsibilities to the United States of America . . . I hope that damage already has not been done. If, however, damage has been done, and if, with the Court's action today, these newspapers proceed to publish the critical documents and there results therefrom "the death of soldiers, the destruction of alliances, the greatly increased difficulty of negotiation with our enemies, the inability of our diplomats to negotiate," to which list I might add the factors of prolongation of the war and of further delay in the freeing of United States prisoners, then the nation's people will know where the responsibility for these sad consequences rests.

*　　*　　*

Two decisions following the Pentagon Papers ruling made it clear—if further clarity were needed—that the Supreme Court does not view the First Amendment as an absolute prohibition against prior restraint. The first came in 1972 when the Court refused to hear the appeal in United States v. Marchetti. *The second came a year later in* Pittsburgh Press v. Pittsburgh Commission on Human Relations. *In the former, Victor Marchetti, a former Central Intelligence Agency employee, had sought to publish along with co-author John D. Marks, a former State Department official, a book titled* The CIA and the Cult of Intelligence. *Upon hearing of the intention to submit a manuscript to the Knopf publishing firm, the CIA obtained an injunction to force the submission of the manuscript to the CIA first for approval. Clouding the issue was a secrecy agreement Marchetti made when he joined the CIA in 1955 in which he promised not to divulge any CIA secrets without specific approval from the agency. Government lawyers, then, argued that this was not a First Amendment issue, but merely one of contractual agreements. The U.S. District Court ruled for the government, a ruling upheld by the Court of Appeals, though the three-judge appellate panel softened the restraint a bit by limiting the CIA censorship to only those portions of the manuscript which contained classified material. The 1972 Supreme Court refusal to hear the case allowed the Appeals Court decision to stand. Subsequent court action, however, resulted in a significant reduction in the amount of material censored by the CIA as demands for proof of classification were required. The original deletion list of 339 sections of the book was reduced finally to 25, and the book reached the bookstores in 1974 with those deletions indicated. Two later CIA cases,* Snepp *and* Agee, *are discussed in Chapter 3 because they did not address prior restraint per se.*

In the Pittsburgh Press *decision of 1973, the Supreme Court ruled 5–4 that it was not a violation of the First Amendment for the Pittsburgh Commission on Human Relations to order the newspaper to stop printing help-wanted advertisements which were segregated by sex. The Court's majority attempted to differentiate between commercial advertising, such as the help-wanted ads under question, and advertising which espouses issues of important public issues, such as was found in the* New York Times v. Sullivan *case, discussed in Chapter 9. (See also Chapter 5, "Public Access to the Media.") The thrust behind the suit, of course, was the Fourteenth Amendment and the social movement toward equal opportunity in employment. The effect of the ruling, however, was to place a direct restraint on what the press may publish. Apparently, if an advertiser or publisher wishes to discriminate in an ad for a commercial product, that message loses its First Amendment protection. Justice Stewart, in a strong dissent, argued that the decision tells a newspaper "in advance what it can print and what it cannot. . . . It approves a government order dictating to a publisher in advance how he must arrange the layout of pages in his newspaper." Also dissenting was the unusual and interesting combination of Chief Justice Burger and Associate Justices Blackmun and Douglas.*

PITTSBURGH PRESS V. PITTSBURGH COMMISSION ON HUMAN RELATIONS
413 U.S. 376 (1973)

JUSTICE POWELL *delivered the opinion of the Court.*

The Human Relations Ordinance of the City of Pittsburgh (the Ordinance) has been construed below by the courts of Pennsylvania as forbidding newspapers to carry "help-wanted" advertisements in sex-designated columns except where the employer or advertiser is free to make hiring or employment referral decisions on the basis of sex. We are called upon to decide whether the Ordinance as so construed violates the freedoms of speech and of the press guaranteed by the First and Fourteenth Amendments. This issue is a sensitive one, and a full understanding of the context in which it arises is critical to its resolution. . . .

There is little need to reiterate that the freedoms of speech and of the press rank among our most cherished liberties. As Mr. Justice Black put it: "In the First Amendment the Founding Fathers gave the free press the protection it must have to fulfill its essential role in our democracy." *New York Times Co. v. United States.* . . .

But no suggestion is made in this case that the Ordinance was passed with any purpose of muzzling or curbing the press. Nor does Pittsburgh Press argue that the Ordinance threatens its financial viability or impairs in any significant way its ability to publish and distribute its newspaper. In any event, such a contention would not be supported by the record.

In a limited way, however, the Ordinance as construed does affect the makeup of the help-wanted section of the newspaper. Under the modified order, Pittsburgh Press will be required to abandon its present policy of providing sex-designated columns and allowing advertisers to select the columns in which their help-wanted advertisements will be placed. . . .

Under some circumstances, at least, a newspaper's editorial judgments in connection with an advertisement take on the character of the advertisement and, in those cases, the scope of the newspaper's First Amendment protection may be affected by the content of the advertisement. In the context of a libelous advertisement, for example, this Court has held that the First Amendment does not shield a newspaper from punishment for libel when with actual malice it publishes a falsely defamatory advertisement. Assuming the requisite state of mind, then, nothing in a newspaper's editorial decision to accept an advertisement changes the character of the falsely defamatory statements. The newspaper may not defend a libel suit on the ground that the falsely defamatory statements are not its own. . . .

. . . Discrimination in employment is not only commercial activity, it is *illegal* commercial activity under the Ordinance. We have no doubt that a newspaper constitutionally could be forbidden to publish a want ad proposing a sale of narcotics or soliciting prostitutes. Nor would the result be different if the nature of the transaction were indicated by placement under columns captioned "Narcotics for Sale" and "Prostitutes Wanted" rather than stated within the four corners of the advertisement.

The illegality in this case may be less overt, but we see no difference in principle here. . . .

. . . The Commission and the courts below concluded that the practice of placing want ads for non-exempt employment in sex-designated columns did indeed "aid" employers to indicate illegal sex preferences. The advertisements, as embroidered by their placement, signaled that the advertisers were likely to show an illegal sex preference in their hiring decisions. . . .

CHIEF JUSTICE BURGER, *dissenting.*

Despite the Court's efforts to decide only the narrow question presented in this case, the holding represents, for me, a disturbing enlargement of the "commercial speech" doctrine, *Valentine v. Chrestensen* and a serious encroachment on the freedom of press guaranteed by the First Amendment. It also launches the courts on what I perceive to be a treacherous path of defining what layout and organizational decisions of newspapers are "sufficiently associated" with the "commercial" parts of the papers as to be constitutionally unprotected and therefore subject to governmental regulation. Assuming, *arguendo,* that the First Amendment permits the States to place restrictions on the content of commercial advertisements, I would not enlarge that power to reach the layout and organizational decisions of a newspaper. . . .

. . . I believe the First Amendment freedom of press includes the right of a newspaper to arrange the content of its paper, whether it be news editorials, or advertising, as it sees fit. In the final analysis, the readers are the ultimate "controllers" no matter what excesses are indulged in by even a flamboyant or venal press; that it often takes a long time for these influences to bear fruit is inherent in our system.

JUSTICE STEWART, *with whom Justice Douglas joins, dissenting.*

I have no doubt that it is within the police power of the city of Pittsburgh to prohibit discrimination in private employment on the basis of race, color, religion, ancestry, national origin, place of birth, or sex. I do not doubt, either, that in enforcing such a policy the city may prohibit employers from indicating any such discrimination when they make known the availability of employment opportunities. But neither of those propositions resolves the question before us in this case.

That question, to put it simply, is whether any government agency—local, state, or federal—can tell a newspaper in advance what it can print and what it cannot. Under the First and Fourteenth Amendments I think no government agency in this Nation has any such power. . . .

So far as I know, this is the first case in this or any other American court that permits a government agency to enter a composing room of a newspaper and dictate to the publisher the layout and makeup of the newspaper's pages. This is the first such case, but I fear it may not be the last. The camel's nose is in the tent. . . .

So long as Members of this Court view the First Amendment as no more than a set of "values" to be balanced against other "values," that Amendment will remain in grave jeopardy. . . .

It is said that the goal of the Pittsburgh ordinance is a laudable one, and so indeed it is. But, in the words of Mr. Justice Brandeis, "Experience should teach us to be most on our guard to protect liberty when the Government's purposes are beneficent. Men born to freedom are naturally alert to repel invasion of their liberty by evil-minded rulers. The greatest dangers to liberty lurk in insidious encroachment by men of zeal, well-meaning but without understanding." *Olmstead v. United States.* . . .

Those who think the First Amendment can and should be subordinated to other socially desirable interests will hail today's decision. But I find it frightening. For I believe the constitutional guarantee of a free press is more than precatory. I believe it is a clear command that government must never be allowed to lay its heavy editorial hand on any newspaper in this country.

✳   ✳   ✳

Because the Pentagon Papers decision dealt with information obtained surreptitiously, there remained the question of laws which prohibit publication of facts from the public records. A significant decision on this question was handed down in 1975, Cox Broadcasting Corp. v. Cohn. A Georgia law made it a misdemeanor to publish or broadcast names of rape victims. The father of one such victim instituted an invasion-of-privacy suit following broadcast of his daughter's name over station WSB-TV in Atlanta. Her name was revealed only after it was used in open court during the trial of her accused attackers. A complicating factor was that the victim had died following the attack, thereby eliminating one of the motivating elements in enacting such laws, i.e. to protect the victim from future embarrassment or harassment. The Supreme Court in an 8–1 decision threw out the invasion-of-privacy suit and, apparently, voided the Georgia law and similar laws in other states. The First and Fourteenth Amendments, wrote Justice White for the majority, "command nothing less than that the States may not impose sanctions for the publication of truthful information contained in official court records open to public inspection." Dissenting was Justice Rehnquist, who argued that the Supreme Court should not have entered the case in the first place. The Court declined to expand its ruling to include any truthful information, no matter how embarrassing or how obtained, as had been requested by Cox Broadcasting. The Court acknowledged a "zone of privacy" which states may enact to protect for their citizens and answered only the narrow question of the publication of factual information obtained in the public records. It left for another day, then, the broader question. The implications of this decision are important also to the law of privacy, covered in Chapter 10, and to newsgathering, which is covered in Chapter 3.

COX BROADCASTING CORP. V. COHN
420 U.S. 469 (1975)

JUSTICE WHITE *delivered the opinion of the Court.*

The issue before us in this case is whether consistently with the First and Fourteenth Amendments a State may extend a cause of action for damages for invasion of privacy caused by the publication of the name of a deceased rape victim which was publicly revealed in connection with the prosecution of the crime.

In August 1971, appellee's 17-year-old daughter was the victim of a rape and did not survive the incident. Six youths were soon indicted for murder and rape. Although there was substantial press coverage of the crime and of subsequent developments, the identity of the victim was not disclosed pending trial, perhaps because [State law] makes it a misdemeanor to publish or broadcast the name or identity of a rape victim. In April 1972, some eight months later, the six defendants appeared in court. Five pled guilty to rape or attempted rape, the charge of murder having been dropped. The guilty pleas were accepted by the court, and the trial of the defendant pleading not guilty was set for a later date.

In the course of the proceedings that day, appellant Wassell, a reporter covering the incident for his employer, learned the name of the victim from an examination of the indictments which were made available for his inspection in the courtroom. That the name of the victim appears in the indictments and that the indictments were public records available for inspection are not disputed. Later that day, Wassell broadcast over the facilities of station WSB-TV, a television station owned by appellant Cox Broadcasting Corporation, a news report concerning the court proceedings. The report named the victim of the crime and was repeated the following day.

In May 1972, appellee brought an action for money damages against appellants, . . . claiming that his right to privacy had been invaded by the television broadcasts giving the name of his deceased daughter. Appellants admitted the broadcasts but claimed that they were privileged under both state law and the First and Fourteenth Amendments. The trial court, rejecting appellants' constitutional claims and holding that the Georgia statute gave a civil remedy to those injured by its violation, granted summary judgment to appellee as to liability, with the determination of damages to await trial by jury. . . .

Georgia stoutly defends both [its State law] and the State's common law privacy action challenged here. Her claims are not without force, for powerful arguments can be made, and have been made, that however it may be ultimately defined, there *is* a zone of privacy surrounding every individual, a zone within which the State may protect him from intrusion by the press, with all its attendant publicity. Indeed, the central thesis of the root article by Warren and Brandeis, "The Right of Privacy," 4 *Harv. L. Rev.* 193, 196 (1890), was that the press was overstepping its prerogatives by publishing essentially private information and that there should be a remedy for the alleged abuses. . . .

Thus even the prevailing law of invasion of privacy generally recognizes that the interests in privacy fade when the information involved already appears on the public record. The conclusion is compelling when viewed in terms of the First and Fourteenth Amendments and in light of the public interest in a vigorous press. The Georgia cause of action for invasion of privacy through public disclosure of the name of a rape victim imposes sanctions on pure expression—the content of a publication—and not conduct or a combination of speech and nonspeech elements that might otherwise be open to regulation or prohibition. See *United States v. O'Brien.* The publication of truthful information available on the public record contains none of the indicia of those limited categories of expression, such as "fighting" words, which "are no essential part of any exposition of ideas, and are of such slight social value as a step to truth that any benefit that may be derived from them is clearly outweighed by the social interest in order and morality." *Chaplinsky v. New Hampshire.*

By placing the information in the public domain on official court records, the State must be presumed to have concluded that the public interest was thereby being served. Public records by their very nature are of interest to those concerned with the administration of government, and a public benefit is performed by the reporting of the true contents of the records by the media. The freedom of the press to publish that information appears to us to be of critical importance to our type of government in which the citizenry is the final judge of the proper conduct of public business. In preserving that form of government the First and Fourteenth Amendments command nothing less than that the States may not impose sanctions for the publication of truthful information contained in official court records open to public inspection.

We are reluctant to embark on a course that would make public records generally available to the media but forbid their publication if offensive to the sensibilities of the supposed reasonable man. Such a rule would make it very difficult for the press to inform their readers about the public business and yet stay within the law. The rule would invite timidity and self-censorship and very likely lead to the suppression of many items that would otherwise be put into print and that should be made available to the public. At the very least, the First and Fourteenth Amendments will not allow exposing the press to liability for truthfully publishing information released to the public in official court records. If there are privacy interests to be protected in judicial proceedings, the States must respond by means which avoid public documentation or other exposure of private information. Their political institutions must weigh the interests in privacy with the interests of the public to know and of the press to publish. Once true information is disclosed in public court documents open to public inspection, the press cannot be sanctioned for publishing it. In this instance as in others reliance must rest upon the judgment of those who decide what to publish or broadcast. See *Miami Herald Publishing Co. v. Tornillo.*

Appellant Wassell based his televised report upon notes taken during the court proceedings and obtained the name of the victim from the indictments handed to him at his request during a recess in the hearing. Appellee has not contended that the name was obtained in an improper fashion or that it was not on an official court document open to public inspection. Under these circumstances, the protection of freedom of the press provided by the First and Fourteenth Amendments bars the State of Georgia from making appellants' broadcast the basis of civil liability.

Reversed.

*   *   *

In what appeared to be a landmark extension of the Near, New York Times and Cox Broadcasting philosophies, a unanimous Supreme Court in 1976 ruled that trial judges cannot keep the press from reporting what transpires in open criminal courts unless there is firm evidence that such publication would almost certainly result in the denial of a fair trial. Mere speculation is not enough. Nebraska Press Assn. v. Stuart. Judges were admonished to seek other means of ensuring fairness, such as postponing the trial or changing its location. Since the Dr. Sam Sheppard decision of 1966, there has been increasing use of "gag" or "protective" orders in which judges order the press not to report what is said in court. As in the New York Times decision, the majority of Justices did not rule out prior restraint in all cases, but said that any such restraint would carry with it a heavy burden of proof. Indeed, three of the Justices—Brennan, Marshall and Stewart—would have gone further by banning totally any judicial censorship. And two others—Justices Stevens and White—hinted that if the broader issue were squarely confronted, they might well side with those who favor an absolute ban on judges' "gag orders." So, the message to trial judges seemed to be clear, even though an absolute ban was not forthcoming.

The Nebraska Press Assn. case involved an open preliminary hearing in which witnesses told of a confession by Erwin Charles Simants that he murdered six members of a Nebraska farm family. It was this testimony that the trial judge ordered not published, an order sustained by the State courts, but overturned by the U.S. Supreme Court. Since the key constitutional issue was one of basic prior restraint by the judiciary, the question is treated here rather than in Chapters 11 and 12, which deal with fair trial. Other judge-imposed restrictions are covered in Newsgathering, Chapter 3, which follows.

NEBRASKA PRESS ASSN. V. STUART
427 U.S. 539 (1976)

CHIEF JUSTICE BURGER delivered the opinion of the Court.

. . . [Past] cases demonstrate that pretrial publicity—even pervasive, adverse publicity—does not inevitably lead to an unfair trial. . . .

A prior restraint . . . has an immediate and irreversible sanction. If it can be said that a threat of criminal or civil sanctions after publication "chills" speech, prior restraint "freezes" it at least for the time.

The damage can be particularly great when the prior restraint falls upon the communication of news and commentary on current events. Truthful reports of public judicial proceedings have been afforded special protection against subsequent punishment. For the same reasons the protection against prior restraint should have particular force as applied to reporting of criminal proceedings, whether the crime in question is a single isolated act or a pattern of criminal conduct. . . . The extraordinary protections afforded by the First Amendment carry with them something in the nature of a fiduciary duty to exercise the protected rights responsibly—a duty widely acknowledged but not always observed by editors and publishers. It is not asking too much to suggest that those who exercise First Amendment rights in newspapers or broadcasting enterprises direct some effort to protect the rights of an accused to a fair trial by unbiased jurors. . . .

. . . [I]t is . . . clear that the barriers to prior restraint remain high unless we are to abandon what the Court has said for nearly a quarter of our national existence and implied throughout all of it. . . .

JUSTICE BRENNAN, *with whom Justice Stewart and Justice Marshall concur, concurring in the judgment.*

. . . Commentary and reporting on the criminal justice system is at the core of First Amendment values, for the operation and integrity of that system is of crucial import to citizens concerned with the administration of Government. Secrecy of judicial action can only breed ignorance and distrust of courts and suspicion concerning the competence and impartiality of judges; free and robust reporting, criticism, and debate can contribute to public understanding of the rule of law and to comprehension of the functioning of the entire criminal judicial system, as well as improve the quality of that system by subjecting it to the cleansing effects of exposure and public accountability. . . .

A judge importuned to issue a prior restraint in the pretrial context will be unable to predict the manner in which the potentially prejudicial information would be published, the frequency with which it would be repeated or the emphasis it would be given, the context in which or purpose for which it would be reported, the scope of the audience that would be exposed to the information, or the impact, evaluated in terms of current standards for assessing juror impartiality, the information would have on that audience. These considerations would render speculative the prospective impact on a fair trail of reporting even an alleged confession or other information "strongly implicative" of the accused. . . .

. . . Recognition of any judicial authority to impose prior restraints on the basis of harm to the Sixth Amendment rights of particular defendants, especially since that harm must remain speculative, will thus inevitably interject judges at all levels into censorship roles that are simply inappropriate and impermissible under the First Amendment. Indeed, the potential for arbitrary and excessive judicial utilization of any such power would be exacerbated by the fact that judges and committing magistrates might in some cases be determining the propriety of publishing information that reflects on their competence, integrity or general performance on the bench. . . .

. . . To hold that courts cannot impose any prior restraints on the reporting of or commentary upon information revealed in open court proceedings, disclosed in public documents, or divulged by other sources with respect to the criminal justice system is not, I must emphasize, to countenance the sacrifice of precious Sixth Amendment rights on the altar of the First Amendment. For although there may in some instances be tension between uninhibited and robust reporting by the press and fair trials for criminal defendants, judges possess adequate tools short of injunctions against reporting for relieving that tension. To be sure, these alternatives may require greater sensitivity and effort on the part of judges conducting criminal trials than would the stifling of publicity through the simple expedient of issuing a restrictive order on the press, but that sensitivity and effort is required in order to ensure the full enjoyment and proper accommodation of both First and Sixth Amendment rights. . . .

*   *   *

In a significant prior restraint decision—perhaps the major "victory" for the press in an otherwise "disastrous" 1978–79 period—a 7–0 Supreme Court held that newspapers, or other citizens, could not be criminally prosecuted for publishing accurate information obtained from secret judicial proceedings. Landmark Communications v. Virginia. *The press had sought a broader ruling, one that would have banned criminal prosecution for publication of any accurate story dealing with public activities of any public official, but the Court did not go that far. A Norfolk newspaper, the* Virginian-Pilot, *was indicted for disclosing, in violation of state law, that a judge, whom the paper named, was being investigated by a state commission. The paper was found guilty and was fined $500. The Supreme Court, in overturning the conviction on First Amendment grounds, did not deny states the right to penalize those who "leak" or steal secret government documents, but held, in effect, that once such information is in the hands of the press, the press generally is free to report that information without penalty, if it does so accurately. Note the similarities between this case and* Cox Broadcasting, *covered earlier. Also, this First Amendment concept is reinforced in* Smith v. Daily Mail, *a newsgathering case covered in Chapter 3. Justices Brennan and Powell did not participate in the* Landmark *decision. Justice Brennan was recovering from an operation during the times of oral arguments, and Justice Powell, a Virginian, was thought to see a conflict of interests because of personal or business affiliations with participants in the case. Formal explanations for nonparticipation in a case normally are not forthcoming.*

LANDMARK COMMUNICATIONS V. VIRGINIA
435 U.S. 829 (1978)

CHIEF JUSTICE BURGER *delivered the opinion of the Court.*

The question presented on this appeal is whether the Commonwealth of Virginia may subject persons, including newspapers, to criminal sanctions for divulging information regarding proceedings before a state judicial review commission which is authorized to hear complaints as to judges' disability or misconduct, when such proceedings are declared confidential by the State Constitution and statutes.

On October 4, 1975, *The Virginian Pilot*, a Landmark newspaper, published an article which accurately reported on a pending inquiry by the Virginia Judicial Inquiry and Review Commission and identified the state judge whose conduct was being investigated. . . .

The narrow and limited question presented then is whether the First Amendment permits the criminal punishment of third persons who are strangers to the inquiry, including news media, for divulging or publishing truthful information regarding confidential proceedings of the Judicial Inquiry and Review Commission. We are not here concerned with the possible applicability of the statute to one who secures the information by illegal means and thereafter divulges it. We do not have before us any constitutional challenge to a State's power to keep the Commission's proceedings confidential or to punish participants for breach of this mandate. Nor does Landmark argue for any constitutionally compelled right of access for the press to those proceedings. Finally as the Supreme Court of Virginia held, and appellant does not dispute, the challenged statute does not constitute a prior restraint or attempt by the State to censor the news media.

Landmark urges as the dispositive answer to the question presented that truthful reporting about public officials in connection with their public duties is always insulated from the imposition of criminal sanctions by the First Amendment. . . .

The operation of the Virginia Commission, no less than the operation of the judicial system itself, is a matter of public interest, necessarily engaging the attention of the news media. The article published by Landmark provided accurate factual information about a legislatively authorized inquiry pending before the Judicial Inquiry Commission, and in so doing clearly served those interests in public scrutiny and discussion of governmental affairs which the First Amendment was adopted to protect.

The Commonwealth concedes that "[w]ithout question the First Amendment seeks to protect the freedom of the press to report and to criticize judicial conduct," but it argues that such protection does not extend to the publication of information "which by Constitutional mandate is to be confidential.". . .

The Commonwealth also focuses on what it perceives to be the pernicious effects of public discussion of Commission proceedings to support its argument. It contends that the public interest is not served by discussion of unfounded allegations of misconduct which defames honest judges and serves only to demean the administration of justice. The functioning of the Commission itself is also claimed to be impeded by premature disclosure of the complainant, witnesses, and the judge under investigation. . . .

It can be assumed for purposes of decision that confidentiality of Commission proceedings serves legitimate state interests. The question, however, is whether these interests are sufficient to justify the encroachment on First Amendment guarantees which the imposition of criminal sanctions entails with respect to nonparticipants such as Landmark. The Commonwealth has offered little more than assertion and conjecture to support its claim that without criminal sanctions the objectives of the statutory scheme would be seriously undermined. . . .

Moreover, neither the Commonwealth's interest in protecting the reputation of its judges, nor in maintaining the institutional integrity of its courts is sufficient to justify the subsequent punishment of speech at issue here, even on the assumption that criminal sanctions do in fact enhance the guarantee of confidentiality. Admittedly, the State has an interest in protecting the good repute of its judges, like that of all other public officials. Our prior cases have firmly established, however, that injury to official reputation is an insufficient reason "for repressing speech that would otherwise be free," *New York Times v. Sullivan.* . . .

The Supreme Court of Virginia relied on the clear and present danger test in rejecting Landmark's claim. We question the relevance of that standard here; moreover we cannot accept the mechanical application of the test which led that court to its conclusion. Mr. Justice Holmes' test was never intended "to express a technical legal doctrine or to convey a formula for adjudicating cases." *Pennekamp v. Florida.* Properly applied, the test requires a court to make its own inquiry into the imminence and magnitude of the danger said to flow from the particular utterance and then to balance the character of the evil, as well as its likelihood, against the need for free and unfettered expression. The possibility that other measures will serve the State's interests should also be weighed. . . .

In a series of cases raising the question of whether the contempt power could be used to punish out of court comments concerning pending cases or grand jury investigations, this Court has consistently rejected the argument that such commentary constituted a clear and present danger to the administration of justice. What emerges from these cases is the "working principle that the substantive evil must be extremely serious and the degree of imminence extremely high before utterances can be punished," *Bridges v. California*, and that a "solidity of evidence," *Pennekamp v. Florida, supra*, is necessary to make the requisite showing of imminence. "The danger must not be remote or even probable; it must immediately imperil." *Craig v. Harney.*

The efforts of the Supreme Court of Virginia to distinguish those cases from this case are unpersuasive. . . .

＊   ＊   ＊

The question of whether a city can ban billboards was answered—sort of—by
the Supreme Court in 1981. In Metromedia v. San Diego, a severely divided Court
held 6–3 that the city ordinance as written was prior restraint, at least insofar as its
implications to political messages were concerned. The decision, which reversed a
California Supreme Court ruling, appeared to leave the way open, however, for
legislative bodies to ban some types of billboards or to attempt to draw more
narrowly defined prohibitions. Still, it was a victory, if only temporary, for the
billboard industry and for those who supported it in this case, including the
American Civil Liberties Union and the American Newspaper Publishers Association.

A second municipal ordinance relative to advertising, though not dealing with
the traditional mass media per se, reached the Supreme Court the next year and was
decided in 1984. It involved a Los Angeles ordinance that banned political posters
from public property, such as utility poles and street signs. City Council v. Taxpayers for Vincent. The 9th Circuit Court of Appeals had ruled that such a ban was
a violation of political free speech, but the Supreme Court disagreed. In a 6–3
ruling it said that cities had a legitimate public interest in removing "visual clutter"
and potential safety hazards from their public property. Other forms of distributing
political messages were available to local candidates, the Court said, and it was not
shown that candidate Robert Vincent had been discriminated against in the
administration of the ordinance. Dissenting were Justices Blackmun, Brennan and
Marshall. Justice Brennan stated that small posters are an economical and practical
way of reaching a localized audience, such as one for a city council seat. Mass
media, including radio, television and large daily newspapers—such as the Los
Angeles Times, in this case—were too expensive and wasteful, since the message
would also go to hundreds of thousands of persons who could not vote for the
candidate because they were in other council districts. The court majority disagreed,
however, suggesting other economical ways of reaching the voter, such as parades and
speeches. The Court also pointed out that the decision did not ban such posters but
merely supported the city's attempts to restrict their locations—a reasonable exercise, the Court said, of government power.

In Metromedia, legal maneuvering between the city of San Diego and the
industry had been going on for nearly a decade by the time the Court handed down
its opinion. Towns and cities across the country had been watching with interest.
Even though it threw out San Diego's ordinance as unconstitutional restraint on
speech, some clues were offered by the Justices as to what might be acceptable
billboard limitations. Only two Justices, Brennan and Blackmun, indicated that
any ban on billboards would be unconstitutional prior restraint. Another four,
however, White, Stewart, Marshall and Powell, in forming the Court's nucleus,
appeared to take exception to the ban primarily because it applied to all types of
speech—political as well as commercial. One might assume, on the basis of reading
those Justices' opinions, that some would approve a ban that allowed ample freedom

for political messages. The three dissenters, Burger, Rehnquist and Stevens, argued that the ordinance should stand as written—banning nearly all off-site billboards. They focused heavily on the concept of federalism and on the right of the city to regulate its own affairs. The question of whether billboards per se are to be given full First Amendment privileges will have to wait for another day, for another ordinance, and for another appeal. While it might appear obvious that the Court would approve limitations on billboards if such limitations applied only to commercial messages, the Court in recent years has granted commercial speech greater latitude, not less. See Chapters 1 and 5. And, of course, Justices Stewart and Burger have been replaced. Finally, it can be said that the Court, by its division, did little to assist the public in understanding where the First Amendment fits into a city's attempts to control the quality of its environment. This question, as important as it is to free speech, to the media, to the environment, and to the economy, is far from settled.

METROMEDIA V. SAN DIEGO
453 U.S. 490 (1981)

JUSTICE WHITE *announced the judgment of the Court and delivered an opinion in which Justice Stewart, Justice Marshall and Justice Powell join.*

This case involves the validity of an ordinance of the city of San Diego, Cal., imposing substantial prohibitions on the erection of outdoor advertising displays within the city.

Stating that its purpose was "to eliminate hazards to pedestrians and motorists brought about by distracting sign displays" and "to preserve and improve the appearance of the City," San Diego enacted an ordinance to prohibit "outdoor advertising display signs." The California Supreme Court subsequently defined the term "advertising display sign" as "a rigidly assembled sign, display, or device permanently affixed to the ground or permanently attached to a building or other inherently permanent structure constituting, or used for the display of, a commercial or other advertisement to the public." "Advertising display signs" include any sign that "directs attention to a product, service or activity, event, person, institution or business."

The ordinance provides two kinds of exceptions to the general prohibition: on-site signs and signs falling within 12 specified categories. . . .

Billboards, . . . like other media of communication, combine communicative and noncommunicative aspects. As with other media, the government has legitimate interests in controlling the noncommunicative aspects of the medium, *Kovacs v. Cooper, supra,* but the First and Fourteenth Amendments foreclose a similar interest in controlling the communicative aspects. Because regulation of the noncommunicative aspects of a medium often impinges to some degree on the communicative aspects, it has been necessary for the courts to reconcile the government's regulatory interests with the individual's right to expression. "[A] court may not escape the task of assessing the First Amendment interest at stake and weighing it against the public interest allegedly served by the regulation." *Linmark Associates, Inc. v. Willingboro,* quoting *Bigelow v. Virginia.* Performance of this task requires a particularized inquiry into the nature of the conflicting interests at stake here, beginning with a precise appraisal of the character of the ordinance as it affects communication.

As construed by the California Supreme Court, the ordinance restricts the use of certain kinds of outdoor signs. That restriction is defined in two ways: first, by reference to the structural characteristics of the sign; second, by reference to the content, or message, of the sign. Thus, the regulation only applies to a "permanent structure constituting, or used for the display of, a commercial or other advertisement to the public." Within that class, the only permitted signs are those (1) identifying the premises on which the sign is located, or its owner or occupant, or advertising the goods produced or services rendered on such property and (2) those within one of the specified exemptions to the general prohibition, such as temporary political campaign signs. To determine if any billboard is prohibited by the ordinance, one must determine how it is constructed, where it is located, and what message it carries.

Thus, under the ordinance (1) a sign advertising goods or services available on the property where the sign is located is allowed; (2) a sign on a building or other property advertising goods or services produced or offered elsewhere is barred; (3) noncommercial advertising, unless within one of the specific exceptions, is everywhere prohibited. The occupant of property may advertise his own goods or services; he may not advertise the goods or services of others, nor may he display most noncommercial messages. . . .

It is nevertheless argued that the city denigrates its interest in traffic safety and beauty and defeats its own case by permitting on-site advertising and other specified signs. Appellants question whether the distinction between on-site and off-site advertising on the same property is justifiable in terms of either esthetics or traffic safety. The ordinance permits the occupant of property to use billboards located on that property to advertise goods and services offered at that location; identical billboards, equally distracting and unattractive, that advertise goods or services available elsewhere are prohibited even if permitting the latter would not multiply the number of billboards. . . .

The fact that the city may value commercial messages relating to on-site goods and services more than it values commercial communications relating to off-site goods and services does not justify prohibiting an occupant from displaying its own ideas or those of others. . . .

JUSTICE BRENNAN, *with whom Justice Blackmun joins, concurring in the judgment.*

. . . I have little doubt that some jurisdictions will easily carry the burden of proving the substantiality of their interest in aesthetics. For example, the parties acknowledge that a historical community such as Williamsburg, Va. should be able to prove that its interests in aesthetics and historical authenticity are sufficiently important that the First Amendment value attached to billboards must yield. And I would be surprised if the Federal Government had much trouble making the argument that billboards could be entirely banned in Yellowstone National Park, where their very existence would so obviously be inconsistent with the surrounding landscape. I express no view on whether San Diego or other large urban areas will be able to meet the burden. But San Diego failed to do so here, and for that reason I would strike down its ordinance. . . .

The plurality apparently reads the on-site premises exception as limited solely to commercial speech. I find no such limitation in the ordinance. . . . As I read the ordinance, the content of the sign depends strictly on the identity of the owner or occupant of the premises. If the occupant is a commercial enterprise, the substance of a permissible identifying sign would be commercial. If the occupant is an enterprise usually associated with noncommercial speech, the substance of the identifying sign would be noncommercial. Just as a supermarket or barbershop could identify itself by name, so too could a political campaign headquarters or a public interest group. I would also presume that, if a barbershop could advertise haircuts, a political campaign headquarters could advertise "Vote for Brown," or "Vote for Proposition 13."

More importantly, I cannot agree with the plurality's view that an ordinance totally banning commercial billboards but allowing noncommercial billboards would be constitutional. For me, such an ordinance raises First Amendment problems at least as serious as those raised by a total ban, for it gives city officials the right—before approving a billboard—to determine whether the proposed message is "commercial" or "noncommercial.". . . Because making such determinations would entail a substantial exercise of discretion by city's officials, it presents a real danger of curtailing noncommercial speech in the guise of regulating commercial speech. . . .

CHIEF JUSTICE BURGER, *dissenting.*

Today the Court takes an extraordinary—even a bizarre—step by severely limiting the power of a city to act on risks it perceives to traffic safety and the environment posed by large, permanent billboards. Those joining the plurality opinion invalidate a city's effort to minimize these traffic hazards and eyesores simply because, in exercising rational legislative judgment, it has chosen to permit a narrow class of signs that serve special needs.

Relying on simplistic platitudes about content, subject matter, and the dearth of other means to communicate, the billboard industry attempts to escape the real and growing problems every municipality faces in protecting safety and preserving the environment in an urban area. The Court's disposition of the serious issues involved exhibits insensitivity to the impact of these billboards on those who must live with them and the delicacy of the legislative judgments involved in regulating them. American cities desiring to mitigate the dangers mentioned must, as a matter of *federal constitutional law*, elect between two unsatisfactory options: (a) allowing all "noncommercial" signs, no matter how many, how dangerous, or how damaging to the environment; or (b) forbidding signs altogether. Indeed, lurking in the recesses of today's opinions is a not-so-veiled threat that the second option, too, may soon be withdrawn. . . .

San Diego adopted its ordinance to eradicate what it perceives—and what it has a right to perceive—as ugly and dangerous eyesores thrust upon its citizens. This was done with two objectives in mind: the disfigurement of the surroundings and the elimination of the danger posed by these large, eye-catching signs that divert the attention of motorists. The plurality acknowledges—as they must—that promoting traffic safety and preserving scenic beauty "are substantial governmental goals." But, having acknowledged the legitimacy of local governmental authority, the plurality largely ignores it. . . .

The messages conveyed on San Diego billboards—whether commercial, political, social, or religious—are not inseparable from the billboards that carry them. These same messages can reach an equally large audience through a variety of other media: newspapers, television, radio, magazines, direct mail, pamphlets, etc. True, these other methods may not be so "eye-catching"—or so cheap—as billboards, but there has been no suggestion that billboards heretofore have advanced any particular viewpoint or issue disproportionately to advertising generally. Thus, the ideas billboard advertisers have been presenting are not *relatively* disadvantaged vis-à-vis the messages of those who heretofore have chosen other methods of spreading their views. It borders on the frivolous to suggest that the San Diego ordinance infringes on freedom of expression, given the wide range of alternative means available. . . .

*   *   *

Another conflict between the right to distribute a message and "environmental clutter" faced the Court in 1988. Lakewood v. Plain Dealer Publishing Co. At issue here were not billboards, but newsracks. The city of Lakewood, Ohio, had passed an ordinance requiring that newspaper vending machines receive permits, be insured, meet certain design standards and otherwise comply with "reasonable" requirements to be determined by the mayor. The Circuit Court of Appeals ruled the ordinance unconstitutional because of the wide latitude it gave the mayor in making determinations of compliance. The Supreme Court affirmed by a 4–3 vote. Justice Brennan, writing for the Court, noted the dangers of unrestrained licensing requirements involving the media. See Lovell v. Griffin and Grosjean v. American Press Co. The Court, however, did not rule out time, place and manner restrictions. Indeed, the Court in the past has held that such restrictions are acceptable if they are reasonable, content neutral and intrusive only to the extent necessary to accomplish the legitimate goals of the community. "Unbridled discretion" on the part of government to control newspaper distribution, however, could not be tolerated under the Constitution.

The freedom of the open marketplace, however, does not necessarily apply to the schoolroom. Hazelwood School District v. Kuhlmeier. *An educational setting, the Justices ruled in 1988, is not a "public forum" and, therefore, school authorities may control content of student-produced campus newspapers if those publications are part of the school curriculum. The debate focused on who the "publisher" of a high school newspaper is, whether editorial decisions made by school authorities constitute "censorship" or are merely "publisher" discretion, whether a school setting is a public forum, and whether the First Amendment affords student newspapers press freedoms similar to those found by newspapers in the real world. The 5–3 vote of the Supreme Court supported the school district and principal. It drew a distinction between this case and its 1969 decision in* Tinker v. Des Moines School District, *the so-called "black armband case." In that case student protesters wore black armbands to protest United States involvement in the Vietnam war. The Court drew a distinction between the non-curricular, individual "symbolic speech" of* Tinker, *and the school (i.e. government) supported product of the school's journalism class. The high school principal had removed two pages of the school publication,* Spectrum, *featuring articles by and interviews with students, which dealt with teenage pregnancy and the effect of divorce on children. Even though the interviews were anonymous, the principal expressed concern over possible identification of those involved and their privacy.*

Educators generally fumed their disapproval, while the nation's newspapers, interestingly, generally supported the Court's finding, resurrecting the old saw that "freedom of the press belongs to the person who owns it," in this case the school board. It should be pointed out that the impact clearly was limited to the public schools, and was not extended to college or university newspapers. While it is possible that the Court could make that extension at some future time, that possibility seems remote.

HAZELWOOD SCHOOL DISTRICT V. KUHLMEIER
484 U.S. 260 (1988)

JUSTICE WHITE *delivered the opinion of the Court in which Justices Rehnquist, Stevens, O'Connor, and Scalia joined.*

. . . Students in the public schools do not "shed their constitutional rights to freedom of speech or expression at the schoolhouse gate." . . . They cannot be punished merely for expressing their personal views on the school premises— whether "in the cafeteria, or on the playing field, or on the campus during the authorized hours." . . . unless school authorities have reason to believe that such expression will "substantially interfere with the work of the school or impinge upon the rights of other students." . . .

We deal first with the question whether *Spectrum* may appropriately be characterized as a forum for public expression. The public schools do not possess all of the attributes of streets, parks, and other traditional public forums that "time out of mind, have been used for purposes of assembly, communicating thoughts between citizens, and discussing public questions." . . . Hence, school facilities may be deemed to be public forums only if school authorities have "by policy or by practice" opened those facilities "for indiscriminate use by the general public," *Perry Education Assn. v. Perry Local Educators' Assn.* . . .

The policy of school officials toward *Spectrum* . . . provided that "[s]chool sponsored publications are developed within the adopted curriculum and its educational implications in regular classroom activities." The Hazelwood East Curriculum Guide described the Journalism II course as a "laboratory situation in which the students publish the school newspaper applying skills they have learned in Journalism I." The lessons that were to be learned from the Journalism II course, according to the Curriculum Guide, included development of journalistic skills under deadline pressure, "the legal, moral, and ethical restrictions imposed upon journalists within the school community," and "responsibility and acceptance of criticism for articles of opinion." Journalism II was taught by a faculty member during regular class hours. Students received grades and academic credit for their performance in the course. . . .

The question whether the First Amendment requires a school to tolerate particular student speech—the question that we addressed in *Tinker*—is different from the question whether the First Amendment requires a school affirmatively to promote particular student speech. The former question addresses educators' ability to silence a student's personal expression that happens to occur on the school premises. The latter question concerns educators' authority over school-sponsored publications, theatrical productions, and other expressive activities that students, parents, and members of the public might reasonably perceive to bear the imprimatur of the school. These activities may fairly be characterized as part of the school curriculum, whether or not they occur in a traditional classroom setting, so long as they are supervised by faculty members and designed to impart particular knowledge or skills to student participants and audiences.

Educators are entitled to exercise greater control over this second form of student expression to assure that participants learn whatever lessons the activity is designed to teach, that readers or listeners are not exposed to material that may be inappropriate for their level of maturity, and that the views of the individual speaker are not erroneously attributed to the school. Hence, a school may in its capacity as publisher of a school newspaper or producer of a school play "disassociate itself," . . . not only from speech that would "substantially interfere with [its] work . . . or impinge upon the rights of other students," *Tinker*, but also from speech that is, for example, ungrammatical, poorly written, inadequately researched, biased or prejudiced, vulgar or profane, or unsuitable for immature audiences. A school must be able to set high standards for the student speech that is disseminated under its auspices—standards that may be higher than those demanded by some newspaper publishers or theatrical producers in the "real" world—and may refuse to disseminate student speech that does not meet those standards. In addition, a school must be able to take into account the emotional maturity of the intended audience in determining whether to disseminate student speech on potentially sensitive topics, which might range from the existence of Santa Claus in an elementary school setting to the particulars of teenage sexual activity in a high school setting. A school must also retain the authority to refuse to sponsor student speech that might reasonably be perceived to advocate drug or alcohol use, irresponsible sex, or conduct otherwise inconsistent with "the shared values of a civilized social order," or to associate the school with any position other than neutrality on matters of political controversy. Otherwise, the schools would be unduly constrained from fulfilling their role as "a principal instrument in awakening the child to cultural values, in preparing him for later professional training, and in helping him to adjust normally to his environment." *Brown v. Board of Education. . . .*

JUSTICE BRENNAN, *with whom Justice Marshall and Justice Blackmun join, dissenting.*

When the young men and women of Hazelwood East High School registered for Journalism II, they expected a civics lesson. *Spectrum*, the newspaper they were to publish, "was not just a class exercise in which students learned to prepare papers and hone writing skills, it was a . . . forum established to give students an opportunity to express their views while gaining an appreciation of their rights and responsibilities under the First Amendment to the United States Constitution. . . .

Public education serves vital national interests in preparing the Nation's youth for life in our increasingly complex society and for the duties of citizenship in our democratic Republic. . . . The public school conveys to our young the information and tools required not merely to survive in, but to contribute to, civilized society. It also inculcates in tomorrow's leaders the "fundamental values necessary to the maintenance of a democratic political system." . . .

The sole concomitant of school sponsorship that might conceivably justify the distinction that the Court draws between sponsored and nonsponsored student expression is the risk "that the views of the individual speaker [might be] erroneously attributed to the school." Of course, the risk of erroneous attribution inheres in any student expression, including "personal expression" that, like the Tinker's armbands, "happens to occur on the school premises." Nevertheless, the majority is certainly correct that indicia of school sponsorship increase the likelihood of such attribution, and that state educators may therefore have a legitimate interest in dissociating themselves from student speech.

But "[e]ven though the governmental purpose be legitimate and substantial, that purpose cannot be pursued by means that broadly stifle fundamental personal liberties when the end can be more narrowly achieved." Dissociative means short of censorship are available to the school. It could, for example, require the student activity to publish a disclaimer, such as the "Statement of Policy" that *Spectrum* published each school year announcing that "[a]ll . . . editorials appearing in this newspaper reflect the opinions of the *Spectrum* staff, which are not necessarily shared by the administrators or faculty of Hazelwood East," or it could simply issue its own response clarifying the official position on the matter and explaining why the student position is wrong. Yet, without so much as acknowledging the less oppressive alternatives, the Court approves of brutal censorship. . . .

The young men and women of Hazelwood East expected a civics lesson, but not the one the Court teaches them today.

FREE AT LAST, AT LEAST

By Jack C. Landau*

[June 30th, 1971] at 2:30 P.M., Chief Justice Warren E. Burger looked up at the crowded Supreme Court chamber and delivered the Court's opinion in the cases of *The New York Times Co. v. the United States*, and the *United States v. The Washington Post Co.* By a vote of 6-to-3, the Supreme Court dissolved restraining orders against the *Times* and the *Post* which had prohibited them from further publication of the "Top Secret" 7,000-page, 47-volume "History of U.S. Decision Making Process on Vietnam Policy."

The *Times* and the *Post* immediately announced that their partially stilled presses would roll again. The Boston *Globe* flashed the decision to an assistant editor waiting inside the vault of The First National Bank of Boston where the documents had been stored by agreement with a Boston Federal Court.

The decision was, as both the *Times* and the *Post* reported in their news stories, a "historic" victory. In the 182 years of this republic, no President (and President Nixon had personally approved the law suits) had possessed the political audacity or constitutional temerity to ask the courts to silence a newspaper; nor had any federal court, at the request of the government or any other person, issued a prepublication censorship ban against an established news publication.

For the time being, that great First Amendment tradition had been reaffirmed, although, under the circumstances, somewhat tenuously.

The decision was greeted with "complete joy and delight" by Arthur Ochs Sulzberger, the publisher of the *Times* which ran an accompanying editorial claiming a "ringing victory for freedom under law."

Mrs. Katharine Graham, the publisher of the *Post*, was considerably more restrained—"We are terribly gratified by the result"—as was the *Post*'s accompanying editorial entitled "Free—At Last" which pointed out: "There is not much comfort, let alone clear cut law, to be found in yesterday's outcome."

Within the next week, as the emotional heat of victory receded into the cool light of reason, more and more publications, such as *Newsweek* and *The Wall Street Journal*, were saying—quite correctly—that the *Times/Post* ruling was narrow, limited and vague. Far from making the press "stronger" than before—as the *Times*' lawyer, Alexander Bickel, claimed—the traditional interpretation of freedom of the press was probably weakened by the whole affair.

* From Jack C. Landau. "Free at Last, at Least." *The Quill*, Vol. 59, No. 8 (August, 1971), p. 7. Used with permission of *The Quill*, published by the Society of Professional Journalists. The author is former editor-in-chief of *The News Media and the Law*, published by the Reporters Committee for Freedom of the Press.

After all, the Nixon Administration had succeeded with action in an endeavor which no previous government had even dared to suggest. It had silenced four of the most respected newspapers in the nation: The *Times* for 15 days, the *Post* for 11 days, the *Globe* for 8 days and the St. Louis *Post Dispatch* for 4 days. It had used the threat of a law suit to induce the *Christian Science Monitor* to voluntarily censor itself. And, despite the firmest constitutional traditions against prepublication censorship, it had convinced a majority of five judges of the influential U.S. Court of Appeals in New York City and three Supreme Court justices that the bans should be extended even longer.

Balanced against this unprecedented series of government victories, the Supreme Court issued the following "historic" four-sentence ruling:

"(1) Any system of prior restraints of expression comes to this Court bearing a heavy presumption against its constitutional validity.

"(2) The government 'thus carries a heavy burden of showing justification for the enforcement of such a restraint.'

"(3) The District Court for the Southern District of New York in The New York *Times* case and the District Court . . . and the Court of Appeals for the District of Columbia Circuit in The Washington *Post* case held that the government had not met that burden.

"(4) We agree."

That's all. There is none of the famed Supreme Court rhetoric upholding "the most treasured traditions of a free society," nor any stinging condemnations of government censorship.

More importantly, in terms of legal precedent, there is no disapproval of the original restraining order against the *Times* issued on June 15th; no criticism of the extensive in-chambers secret hearings from which the public and the press were excluded; no constitutional standard for what the "burden" of proof should have been for the government; no discussion of the facts upon which the government based its case—and thus no guidelines for editors, judges and lawyers who may be faced with similar problems in the future.

In short, the opinion says only that the government failed to carry its (undefined) "burden" of proof that the (undefined) national security would be (undefined) endangered on the specific facts in this case: facts which are forever sealed in secret briefs and secret transcripts of closed hearings in judges' chambers.

The decision cited only three prior cases, of which the most famous is the 1931 ruling in *Near v. Minnesota*. The *Near* case stands for a dual proposition: that "liberty of the press . . . has meant, principally, although not exclusively, immunity from previous restraints or censorship"; and also that the First Amendment protection "is not absolutely unlimited" because it may be infringed upon "if the security of the community" is threatened—exactly what the government claimed and the *Times/Post* challenged, which is how the whole case started in the first place. Thus, even the Supreme Court case citations are a circular enigma.

Any further aid and comfort which the press may obtain from the *Times/Post* case comes from the six majority concurring opinions.

Two justices, Hugo L. Black and William O. Douglas, restated their "absolutist" position that the First Amendment bars prepublication censorship under all circumstances.

Two justices, William J. Brennan, Jr. and Thurgood Marshall, said that the government had not presented sufficient evidence on June 15th to justify even the initial ban against the *Times*.

Two justices, Byron White and Potter Stewart, the so-called "swing vote" justices, said that the total evidence presented by the government in four previous hearings (two District Courts and two Courts of Appeals) showed that the information was of "substantial damage to public interests" but did not pose a "grave and immediate" danger to the national security.

The three dissenting justices were more consistent. They complained that the "feverish" pace of the litigation deprived the Supreme Court of sufficient time to carefully weigh the issues. They would have sent the cases back for further hearings in the lower courts. They were Chief Justice Burger and Justices John M. Harlan and Harry C. Blackmun.

Perhaps a more helpful way to understand the diverse opinions in the case is to synthesize the nine separate opinions by issues:

• Did the government present enough evidence on June 15th to justify the initial ban against the *Times*? yes, 4-to-4 (1 unsure).

• Did the government present enough evidence after hearings in the District Courts and Courts of Appeals to justify a long-term ban against the *Times* and the *Post*? no, 6-to-3.

• Could Congress pass legislation giving the courts the power to censor newspapers, at least temporarily, under circumstances similar to the *Times/Post* case? yes, 6-to-2 (1 unsure).

• Could the Court, in the *Times/Post* case, permanently ban the Pentagon Papers if the government had presented enough evidence to show a "grave," "immediate," and "direct" threat to the national security? yes, 7-to-2.

It is fairly safe to assume that there will be no duplication of the *Times/Post* case in the near future, with 7,000 pages of classified documents falling into the hands of the press.

But that improbability hardly means that the *Times/Post* decision will have no practical effect on the press in the future.

First: Both the *Times* and the *Post* in their editorials called for improved procedures within the Executive branch to assure—to some greater degree—that the "top secret" stamp is not placed willy-nilly on millions of unimportant documents from SALT talk outlines to the National Security Council luncheon menu.

This may mean that the press will have access to more government information. But there is also a danger. A "secret" classification is within the sole discretion of the Pentagon, State Department and other executive agencies. It is a self-serving declaration by the Executive branch that publication of the document will endanger the national security, a declaration that the *Times* and *Post* contested and rebutted.

The government, even under improved procedures, should be forced to prove in court on a document-by-document basis that the information is so damaging as to justify censorship. No editor should delegate to the Executive branch what he may and may not print without at least an adversary hearing in a court.

Second: Pursuant to the suggestions of three justices, there may be a congressional law authorizing the federal courts to issue short restraining orders any time a rubber-stamped "secret" document is to be published.

This would pose the same type of constitutional problems as the *Times/Post* case, except the press would be fighting the legislative rather than the executive branch.

One proponent for this type of law was Mr. Bickel who told the Supreme Court, during the oral arguments: "I would wish that Congress took a look at the . . . Espionage Acts and cleaned them up so that we could have statutes that are clearly applicable . . ."

To which Justice Douglas commented: "That is a very strange argument for the *Times* to be making. The Congress can make all this illegal by passing laws."

There is a strong tradition in constitutional law, strongly championed by the late Felix Frankfurter, that Congress has somewhat more power to temporarily limit individual rights than the President alone.

In the *Times/Post* case, the President was asserting his "inherent power" under the Constitution to protect the national security, separate and apart from congressional authorization to seek a censorship ban (an authorization, by the way, which Congress specifically rejected when it passed the Espionage Acts).

Third: The government may indict *New York Times* reporter Neil Sheehan and those reporters on seven other newspapers who might have conspired to illegally obtain the government documents. Any such prosecutions, like the indictment against Dr. Daniel Ellsberg, would probably be brought under a section of the Espionage Act which makes it a crime to conspire to "willfully communicate" documents "relating to the national defense" if the documents are obtained from a person having "unauthorized possession."

Executives of the *Times* and *Post* have said privately that their reporters did not participate in any unauthorized removals of the documents. Furthermore, there is a major constitutional case—now pending before the Supreme Court—on whether it is a violation of the First Amendment to force a reporter to disclose his sources. [*Branzburg v. Hayes*, decided in 1972.] In addition, one section of the Act appears to say that the document has to be communicated with intent "to believe (it) could be used to the injury of the United States or to the advantage of any foreign nation."

Under any circumstances, it will be difficult to prove that the *Times* and the *Post* published the articles to injure the nation. As the *Times'* bureau chief, Max Frankel, said on the NBC News broadcast: "The fact is, that nobody, not in the government and not in the press, can play God and is omniscient enough to know what the consequences of truth are . . ."

In the *Times/Post* opinion, five justices pointed to the criminal laws as alternatives to censorship. Even with such an invitation, one fact seems clear: the criminal cases against the reporters would be such close questions legally that a decision to indict would be a purely discretionary political determination by the Attorney General.

Fourth: It is entirely probable that a newspaper may obtain a limited amount of secret information, such as the SALT talks strategy, and that government would again attempt to ban publication.

What would probably happen would be a total replay of the *Times/Post* litigation with a short restraining order, a secret trial, an appeal and a Supreme Court appeal. The danger here is that the SALT talk story may not be an historical document where a short delay in publication poses no problems to the public's right to know about its government. The whole value of its publication may be lost in a one-week delay.

Another real possibility is that the principles of the *Times/Post* case could encourage restraining orders at the state and local level.

Suppose, for example, that Washington, D.C. has a tense racial situation and the *Post* has a picture of a white policeman brutally beating a pregnant, blind Negro nurse. The city government goes into court and alleges that publication of the picture would cause a riot—a danger to the "security" of the city.

It must be remembered that the grandfather exemption doctrine, authorizing prepublication censorship, is Justice Holmes' famous statement permitting a suspension of free speech if there is a "clear and present danger" to society: "The most stringent protection of free speech would not protect a man in falsely shouting fire in a crowded theatre and causing a panic." And he wasn't talking about a theater attended by SALT talk negotiators. He was describing the general doctrine by which any government—federal, state or local—has a right to protect itself from dire disorder.

In our racial tension example, it seems likely that a judge would at least briefly restrain the *Post* from publishing the picture, just as courts have banned political demonstrations which posed threats to communities.

Much of the problem in the *Times* portion of the case is that the *Times* seemed to treat the proceedings more like a leisurely, scholarly debate at the Yale Law School, where Mr. Bickel teaches, than like an outrageous and illegal gagging of a great newspaper.

By refusing to appeal the original four-day ban on the *Times*, he conceded that the New York court was freezing the "status quo"—when the "status quo" in fact was the unfettered right to publish which would have been maintained by no injunction.

Perhaps the most remarkable incident in the whole affair took place Friday morning, three days after the ban was imposed, when Mr. Bickel argued that the *Times* was now "irreparably injured" in an intolerable manner—not because of the injunction alone, but because the *Post* had started publishing the documents.

"It seems to us," said Mr. Bickel, "that the radical change in the situation . . . is the readers of the *New York Times* alone in this country are deprived of this story.

This is a degree of irreparable damage which varies, is different . . . altogether from the situation that confronted your Honor on Tuesday last when you granted the temporary restraining order."

From this argument, one may deduce that the *Times'* lawyer was claiming that a critical factor in freedom of the press may not be the inherent right of each newspaper to publish, but may depend upon whether the competition can match the story.

It is important to remember that precise situation on June 15th. The government came to court alleging danger to the national security but without a single, solitary fact to back up that statement. There was no allegation that, for example, "Document A-007 would ruin prisoner exchange negotiations," or that "Document B-007 would disclose the key to a code"—nothing but the conclusory statements of Pentagon and State Department officials about the national security when the State Department had not even found its copy of the study.

And here comes Mr. Bickel armed with the great constitutional tradition against prepublication censorship. He sympathizes with the government's position that it needs several days' time to familiarize itself with the facts in the seven-million word study. Therefore, he does not demand an immediate trial within 24 hours to elicit the facts showing a national security threat; nor appeals when the judge, without any facts, silences the *Times* for one, two, three, four days; nor asks the judge to certify immediately the restraining order on appeal under a special rule which permits injunction appeals when "there is substantial ground for differences of opinion" on the prevailing law; nor claims that the injunction is constitutionally void and advises the *Times* to publish anyway and ultimately risks being held in contempt of court—a risk which was only recently taken by one of the *Times'* own reporters, Earl Caldwell, when he refused to turn over his notes to a federal grand jury in San Francisco; and by CBS President Frank Stanton when he refused to give the House Interstate and Foreign Commerce Committee out-takes of "The Selling of the Pentagon."

Judge Gerhardt Gessell, who took only eight hours in refusing to enjoin the *Post*, emphasized that time was of the essence and that the right to publish was so precious that no one can "measure the effects of even a momentary delay."

Compare this statement with Mr. Bickel's refusal to be rushed, or as he told the Supreme Court approvingly: "There is no evidence I know of that Judge (Murray) Gurfein rushed the proceedings" by his four-day delay. To which one might inquire: "And why not?"

Stated more dramatically: Suppose the *Times* had printed 1,000 test-run copies of the newspaper including the Pentagon Papers and then, in conformity complain, don't be surprised if the judge tells you to calm down. After all, how can your First Amendment rights be damaged by a temporary restraining order when a similar order did not pose an "irreparable injury" to the New York *Times*—that is, not until the *Post* got hold of the story.

And if you want to avoid the whole affair, take the advice of a Boston *Globe* editor who said that the courts will never be able to censor you if you "dump it all at once." Today, that still may be the best answer.

FREEDOM OF SPEECH AS I SEE IT

BY ZECHARIAH CHAFEE, JR.*

Speech should be fruitful as well as free. Our experience introduces this qualification into the classical argument of Milton and John Stuart Mill, that only through open discussion is truth discovered and spread. In their simpler times, they thought it enough to remove legal obstacles like the censorship and sedition prosecutions. Mill assumed that if men were only left alone, their reasoning powers would eventually impel them to choose the best ideas and the wisest course of action. To us this policy is too exclusively negative. For example what is the use of telling an unpopular speaker that he will incur no criminal penalties by his proposed address, so long as every hall owner in the city declines to rent him space for his meeting and there are no vacant lots available? There should be municipal auditoriums, school houses out of school hours, church forums, parks in summer, all open to thresh out every question of public importance, with just as few restrictions as possible, for otherwise the subjects that most need to be discussed will be the very subjects that will be ruled out as unsuitable for discussion.

We must do more than remove the discouragements to open discussion. We must exert ourselves to supply active encouragements.

Physical space and lack of interference alone will not make discussion fruitful. We must take affirmative steps to improve the methods by which discussion is carried on. Of late years the argument of Milton and Mill has been questioned, because truth does not seem to emerge from a controversy in the automatic way their logic would lead us to expect. For one thing, reason is less praised nowadays than a century ago; instead, emotions conscious and unconscious are commonly said to dominate the conduct of men. Is it any longer possible to discover truth amidst the clashing blares of advertisements, loud speakers, gigantic billboards, party programs, propaganda of a hundred kinds? To sift the truth from all these half truths seems to demand a statistical investigation beyond the limits of anybody's time and money. So some modern thinkers despairingly conclude that the great mass of voters cannot be trusted to detect the fallacies in emotional arguments by Communists and hence must be prevented from hearing them. Even the intellectuals don't seem to do much better in reaching Truth by conflicting arguments. For example, take controversies between professors. They talk and talk, and at the end each sticks to his initial position. On which side does Truth stand? We still do not know. Then too, the emergencies seem greater and more pressing than of yore. We

---

* From Zechariah Chafee, Jr. "Freedom of Speech as I See It Today." *Journalism Quarterly,* Vol. 18 (June 1941), p. 158. Used with permission of the *Journalism Quarterly.* The author was a professor of law at Harvard University.

are less willing to await the outcome of prolonged verbal contests. Perhaps Truth will win in the long run; but in the long run, as Walter Lippmann says, we shall all be dead—and perhaps not peacefully in our beds either. Debating is only fiddling while Rome burns. Away with all this talk, let's have action—now.

Nevertheless, the main argument of Milton and Mill still holds good. All that this disappointment means is that friction is a much bigger drag on the progress of Truth than they supposed. Efforts to lessen the friction are essential to the success of freedom of speech. It is a problem, not for law, but for education in the wide sense that includes more than schools and youngsters. The conflict of oral evidence and arguments can be made increasingly profitable by wise improvements in technique. . . . Journalists and other writers value accuracy of facts far more than formerly—we can expect even more from them in future. None of us can get rid of our emotions, but we can learn to drive them in harness. As for blazing propaganda on both sides, young Americans can be trained to keep alive the gumption which comes down to us from Colonial farmers; this will make them distrust all men who conceal greed or a lust for power behind any flag, whether red or red-white-and-blue.

Reason is more imperfect than we used to believe. Yet it still remains the best guide we have, better than our emotions, better even than patriotism, better than any single human guide, however exalted his position.

A second point deserves renewed emphasis. The effect of suppression extends far beyond the agitators actually put in jail, far beyond the pamphlets physically destroyed. A favorite argument against free speech is that the men who are thus conspicuously silenced had little to say that was worth hearing. Concede for the moment that the public would suffer no serious loss if every Communist leaflet were burned or if some prominent pacifist were imprisoned, as perhaps he might be under the loose language of the unprecedented federal sedition law passed last spring, for discouraging drafted men by his talk about plowing every fourth boy under. Even so, my contention is that the pertinacious orators and writers who get hauled up are merely extremist spokesmen for a mass of more thoughtful and more retiring men and women, who share in varying degrees the same critical attitude toward prevailing policies and institutions. When you put the hot-heads in jail, these cooler people don't get arrested—they just keep quiet. And so we lose things they could tell us, which would be very advantageous for the future course of the nation. Once the prosecutions begin, then the hush-hush begins too. Discussion becomes one-sided and artificial. Questions that need to be threshed out don't get threshed out. . . .

The Supreme Court, though much more anxious to support liberty of speech than it was twenty years ago, can do nothing to keep discussion open during an emergency. Cases of suppression will get to Washington long after the emergency is over. What counts is what the local United States judges do. Still more important is the attitude of the prosecutors and police, because they can stifle free speech by breaking up meetings by arrests and confiscating pamphlets, and then not bothering to bring many persons to trial. Above all, the maintenance of open discussion depends on all of you, on the great body of unofficial citizens. If a community does not respect liberty for unpopular ideas, it can easily drive such ideas underground by persistent discouragement and sneers, by social ostracism, by boycotts of newspapers and magazines, by refusal to rent halls, by objections to the use of municipal auditorium and school houses, by discharging teachers and professors and journalists, by mobs and threats of lynching. On the other hand an atmosphere of open and unimpeded controversy may be made as fully a part of the life of a community as any other American tradition. The law plays only a small part in either suppression or freedom. In the long run the public gets just as much freedom of speech as it really wants.

This brings me to my final argument for freedom of speech. It creates the happiest kind of country. It is the best way to make men and women love their country. Mill says:

> A state which dwarfs its men, in order that they may be more docile instruments in its hands even for beneficial purposes, will find that with small men no great thing can really be accomplished.

And Arthur Garfield Hays tells the story of a liberated slave who met his former master on the street. The master asked, "Are you as well off as before you were free?" The Negro admitted that his clothes were frayed, his house leaked, and his meals were nothing like the food on the old plantation. "Well, wouldn't you rather be a slave again?" "No, massa. There's a sort of a looseness about this here freedom that I likes."

Doubtless it was an inspiring sight to see the Piazza Venezia in Rome full of well-drilled blackshirts in serried ranks cheering Mussolini or to watch Nuremberg thronged with hundreds of thousands of Nazis raising their arms in perfect unison at the first glimpse of Hitler. In contrast our easy-going crowds seem sloppy and purposeless, going hither and thither about their own tasks and amusements. But we do not have the other side of the picture—when every knock on the door may mean that the father of the family is to be dragged off to a concentration camp from which no word returns; great newspapers reduced to mere echoes of the master's voice; the professorships of universities that once led the world filled as we fill third-class postmasterships; the devoted love of young men and women broken up by racial hatreds; the exiles; the boycotts; and what is perhaps worst of all, those who conform to the will of the men in power in order to avoid financial ruin or worse, and yet, even while holding their jobs, live days and nights in the uneasy fear of calamity and the shameful consciousness that they have had to sell out their minds and souls. Once commit ourselves to the ideal of enforced national unanimity, and all this logically and easily follows.

Behind the dozens of sedition bills in Congress last session, behind teachers' oaths and compulsory flag salutes, is a desire to make our citizens loyal to their government. Loyalty is a beautiful idea, but you cannot create it by compulsion and force. A government is at bottom the officials who carry it on, legislators and prosecutors, school superintendents and police. If it is composed of legislators who pass short-sighted sedition laws by overwhelming majorities, of narrow-minded school superintendents who oust thoughtful teachers of American history and eight-year-old children whose rooted religious convictions prevent them from sharing in a brief ceremony, a government of snoopers and spies and secret police, how can you expect love and loyalty? You make men love their government and country by giving them the kind of government and the kind of country that inspire respect and love, a country that is free and unafraid, that lets the discontented talk in order to learn the causes for their discontent and end those causes, that refuse to impel men to spy on their neighbors, that protects its citizens vigorously from harmful acts while it leaves the remedies for objectionable ideas to counter-argument and time.

Plutarch's *Lives* were the favorite reading of men who framed and ratified our Constitution. There they found the story of Timoleon who saved his native city of Syracuse from the Carthaginian tyrants. In later years young hot-heads used to get up in the public assembly and abuse Timoleon as an old fossil. His friends urged him just to say the word, and they would soon silence his detractors. But Timoleon insisted on letting the vituperative youngsters have their say. "He had taken all the extreme pains and labor he had done, and had passed so many dangers, in order that every citizen and inhabitant of Syracuse might frankly use the liberty of their laws. He thanked the gods that they had granted him the thing he had so oft requested of them in his prayers, which was, that he might some day see the Syracusans have full power and liberty to say what they pleased."

It is such a spirit that makes us love the United States of America. With all the shortcomings of economic organization, with all the narrowness and ignorance of politicians, we know that we are still immeasurably freer than we should be in Italy, Germany or Russia to say what we think and write what we believe and do what we want. "There's a looseness about this here freedom that I likes."

Let us not in our anxiety to protect ourselves from foreign tyrants imitate some of their worst acts, and sacrifice in the process of national defense the very liberties which we are defending.

CHAPTER 3

NEWSGATHERING

A *major debate of the 1970s was whether the Burger Court—called "Nixon's revenge" by some—was actually anti-press, as many were claiming, or was merely protecting the integrity of the national Constitution and of common law principles, as others argued. The furor which erupted on editorial pages across the nation was a result primarily of a series of newsgathering decisions which began early that decade. Two fundamental and significant issues were at stake. First was whether the First Amendment grants special privileges to the established press by virtue of its traditional "watchdog" role or whether the press enjoys only those constitutional rights enjoyed by all citizens. Second was whether the right of access to information was an integral part of the First Amendment. The press lost on both counts. As the opinions in this chapter indicate, the Supreme Court has taken the position, first, that press rights under the Constitution generally are no greater than those enjoyed by all citizens, and, second, that there is nothing in the Constitution which insists that the press—or any group, for that matter—be granted access to information it may want. The reaction of the media as the decade wore on and as this series of decisions was handed down was persistent, vociferous and predictable. This reaction—some say overreaction—reached a level by the late 1970s that could no longer be ignored. One important response came from Justice Brennan in a speech at Rutgers University. That speech appears later in this chapter.*

The reason that this reaction was so heated was that nearly all of the news-gathering cases in the '70s "went against" the press, which saw its role as "watch-dog" being eroded by the highest court in the land. It lost case after case, as lower courts picked up the cue from the Supreme Court and responded in kind at the state and local levels. The peak in this decade of media anguish probably came in 1979 with the Supreme Court's ruling in Gannett v. DePasquale, *which allowed closure of pretrial hearings and which the press saw as a prelude to secret trials. There were exceptions to this apparent anti-press stand, of course. One could point to* Smith v.

Daily Mail. *But generally, starting with the* Branzburg *decision of 1972, the Supreme Court gave the press a decade it would just as soon forget.*

Four major points should be made prior to looking into the opinions themselves. First, the Burger Court was firm in its position that, with few exceptions, whatever information the press possesses it may publish or broadcast, if such publication is accurate. This, presumably, could be called a "pro-press" position. See Smith *again, plus* Cox Broadcasting v. Cohn, Landmark Communications v. Virginia *and* Nebraska Press Association v. Stuart.

Second, this right to publish or broadcast information already in hand does not suggest that there is a collateral right of access to information. Common law does not support the premise that newsgathering is per se *an integral part of the freedom of the press. In addition, while there is a strong tradition of open government in this country, statute books are full of exceptions to this openness, and the courts have done little to overturn those statutes.*

Third, it should be emphasized that the Justices have not "banned" the press in these instances. They have indicated merely that under the Constitution they can find no special access to information or special privilege for the press. If legislators, for example, wish to grant privileges such as shield laws to reporters, they apparently may do so. And, if the Congress wishes to amend—or to abolish, for that matter— the Federal Freedom of Information Act, it may do so. Indeed, one of the debates during the years of President Reagan's administration was over proposed amendments to the FOI Act which the press felt would further hamper the newsgathering process. These decisions of the Supreme Court, then, should be read as supporting the familiar theme of federalism rather than one of advocating secrecy.

Finally, it should be mentioned that while the press has applauded the Warren Court for its strong First Amendment stands—with justification—and has criticized the Burger Court for what it sees as a chipping away at those First Amendment foundations, the Warren Court did not attempt to answer the difficult questions posed in this chapter, those questions involving newsgathering and whether access to information is essential to the effectiveness of the First Amendment. One can only speculate what the Warren Court would have done with these issues. The Burger Court grappled with them, and the outcome was not what the media had hoped for.

If there is a single, important theme to come from the following opinions, then, it would appear to be that the reporter, in general, has no greater rights by virtue of his or her role as journalist than does any other interested citizen, unless those special privileges are granted under state or Federal statute. The media, after all, are not the only "watchdogs" protecting the public welfare. Indeed, some would say that the press has not been the best of "watchdogs" when compared with other public interest groups such as, say, the Ralph Nader organization or Common Cause. Certainly, the media's use of the FOI Act has been disappointing, and they entered the areas of consumer protection and environmental concerns late. Also, how does one define "journalist"? Should one have to be a salaried staff member to obtain certain constitutional privileges? What of freelance writers? Should they have less access to information merely because they prefer the freedom of working for themselves? And should you or I, as concerned citizens, have less access to the information we need to function intelligently in a democracy than does a reporter? Should we have to rely solely on "the press" (however that is defined) to tell us the information we need? What can be found in the Constitution to support such a distinction? The Constitution is a delicate document which requires sensitive interpretation. With every decision of the Court, some segment of our society makes known its unhappiness. But that is the fate of the Court as its nine individuals struggle to reach accommodation with the times, with the historic words they interpret, with their colleagues, and with themselves. The ultimate challenge is not, as many in the media would have us believe, the "right to know." Democracy does not demand that all of us know everything about everything else or everything about everybody. The challenge is to determine what is important or appropriate for us to know so that we can better function as a free society. The question, then, centers around not just the "right to know," but the "right to know what, about whom, and when." Answers to those questions require a balancing of the various interests involved, those of the individuals and the larger society, as well as those of the press. Where does legitimate newsgathering end and "prying" begin? Or invasion of privacy? Or obstruction of justice? And where is the line that separates responsible journalism from titillation or sensationalism? The "right to know" is a popular battlecry among members of the media, but without greater specificity and definition, it is one without much substance and without much support from the Supreme Court, common law or the Constitution.

This new question of First Amendment definition of media privilege surfaced in the early 1970s. There is little disagreement among journalists that subpoena action has a serious "chilling effect" on reporters as they attempt to perform their "watchdog" functions over government and that widespread support of these subpoenas by the courts would be disastrous to the public's right to know. The first such action to gain national attention came with a Federal Grand Jury subpoena of New York Times reporter Earl Caldwell in an attempt to force him to reveal his sources of information for stories dealing with the Black Panther organization. By 1974, half of the states had "shield laws" which are aimed at protecting newsmen from being forced to reveal their sources of news, but there was no such Federal law. The U.S. Supreme Court by a 5–4 margin held that the First Amendment does not automatically give journalists the right to refuse such judicial orders. The decision was handed down along with two others, Branzburg v. Hayes and In re Pappas. It should be noted that there are subtle differences among the three. Caldwell refused to appear or testify before a Federal Grand Jury relative to information he had gathered from other persons. Branzburg of the Louisville Courier-Journal refused to answer Grand Jury questions about drug law violations he had personally observed. Pappas, a television reporter, had visited a Black Panther organization headquarters, but refused to tell a Grand Jury what he had seen there. Caldwell was supported in the lower courts, but the U.S. Supreme Court rejected the arguments of all three of the journalists.

BRANZBURG V. HAYES

IN RE PAPPAS

U.S. V. CALDWELL

408 U.S. 665 (1972)

JUSTICE WHITE *delivered the opinion of the Court.*

. . . The sole issue before us is the obligation of reporters to respond to grand jury subpoenas as other citizens do and to answer questions relevant to an investigation into the commission of crime. Citizens generally are not constitutionally immune from grand jury subpoenas; and neither the First Amendment nor other constitutional provision protects the average citizen from disclosing to a grand jury information that he has received in confidence. The claim is, however, that reporters are exempt from these obligations because if forced to respond to subpoenas and identify their sources or disclose other confidences, their informants will refuse or be reluctant to furnish newsworthy information in the future. This asserted burden on newsgathering is said to make compelled testimony from newsmen constitutionally suspect and require a privileged position for them.

It is clear that the First Amendment does not invalidate every incidental burdening of the press that may result from the enforcement of civil or criminal statutes of general applicability. Under prior cases, otherwise valid laws serving substantial public interests may be enforced against the press as against others, despite the possible burden that may be imposed. The Court has emphasized that "[t]he publisher of a newspaper has no special immunity from the application of general laws. He has no special privilege to invade the rights and liberties of others." *Associated Press v. NLRB.*

It has generally been held that the First Amendment does not guarantee the press a constitutional right of special access to information not available to the public generally. In *Zemel v. Rusk,* for example, the Court sustained the Government's refusal to validate passports to Cuba even though that restriction "rendered less than wholly free the flow of information concerning that country." The ban on travel was held constitutional, for "[t]he right to speak and publish does not carry with it the unrestrained right to gather information."

Despite the fact that newsgathering may be hampered, the press is regularly excluded from grand jury proceedings, our own conferences, the meetings of other official bodies gathered in executive session, and the meetings of private organizations. Newsmen have no constitutional right of access to the scenes of crime or disaster when the general public is excluded, and they may be prohibited from attending or publishing information about trials if such restrictions are necessary to assure a defendant a fair trial before an impartial tribunal. In *Sheppard v. Maxwell*, for example, the Court reversed a state court conviction where the trial court failed to adopt "stricter rules governing the use of the courtroom by newsmen as Sheppard's counsel requested," neglected to insulate witnesses from the press, and made no "effort to control the release of leads, information, and gossip to the press by police officers, witnesses, and the counsel for both sides." "[T]he trial court might well have proscribed extrajudicial statements by any lawyer, party, witness, or court official which divulged prejudicial matters."

It is thus not surprising that the great weight of authority is that newsmen are not exempt from the normal duty of appearing before a grand jury and answering questions relevant to a criminal investigation. At common law, courts consistently refused to recognize the existence of any privilege authorizing a newsman to refuse to reveal confidential information to a grand jury. . . .

A number of states have provided newsmen a statutory privilege of varying breadth, but the majority have not done so, and none has been provided by federal statute. Until now the only testimonial privilege for unofficial witnesses that is rooted in the federal Constitution is the Fifth Amendment privilege against compelled self-incrimination. We are asked to create another by interpreting the First Amendment to grant newsmen a testimonial privilege that other citizens do not enjoy. This we decline to do. . . .

The argument that the flow of news will be diminished by compelling reporters to aid the grand jury in a criminal investigation is not irrational, nor are the records before us silent on the matter. But we remain unclear how often and to what extent informers are actually deterred from furnishing information when newsmen are forced to testify before a grand jury. The available data indicate that some newsmen rely a great deal on confidential sources and that some informants are particularly sensitive to the threat of exposure and may be silenced if it is held by this Court that, ordinarily, newsmen must testify pursuant to subpoenas, but the evidence fails to demonstrate that there would be a significant constriction of the flow of news to the public if this Court reaffirms the prior common law and constitutional rule regarding the testimonial obligations of newsmen. Estimates of the inhibiting effect of such subpoenas on the willingness of informants to make disclosures to newsmen are widely divergent and to a great extent speculative. It would be difficult to canvass the views of the informants themselves; surveys of reporters on this topic are chiefly opinions of predicted informant behavior and must be viewed in the light of the professional self-interest of the interviewees.

Reliance by the press on confidential informants does not mean that all such sources will in fact dry up because of the later possible appearance of the newsman before a grand jury. The reporter may never be called and if he objects to testifying, the prosecution may not insist. Also, the relationship of many informants to the press is a symbiotic one which is unlikely to be greatly inhibited by the threat of subpoena: quite often, such informants are members of a minority political or cultural group which relies heavily on the media to propagate its views, publicize its aims, and magnify its exposure to the public. Moreover, grand juries characteristically conduct secret proceedings, and law enforcement officers are themselves experienced in dealing with informers and have their own methods for protecting them without interference with the effective administration of justice. There is little before us indicating that informants whose interest in avoiding exposure is that it may threaten job security, personal safety, or peace of mind, would in fact be in a worse position, or would think they would be, if they risked placing their trust in public officials as well as reporters. We doubt if the informer who prefers anonymity but is sincerely interested in furnishing evidence of crime will always or very often be deterred by the prospect of dealing with those public authorities characteristically charged with the duty to protect the public interest as well as his.

Accepting the fact, however, that an undetermined number of informants not themselves implicated in crime will nevertheless, for whatever reason, refuse to talk to newsmen if they fear identification by a reporter in an official investigation, we cannot accept the argument that the public interest in possible future news about crime from undisclosed, unverified sources must take precedence over the public interest in pursuing and prosecuting those crimes reported to the press by informants and in thus deterring the commission of such crimes in the future. . . .

We are admonished that refusal to provide a First Amendment reporter's privilege will undermine the freedom of the press to collect and disseminate news. But this is not the lesson history teaches us. As noted previously, the common law recognized no such privilege, and the constitutional argument was not even asserted until 1958. From the beginning of our country the press has operated without constitutional protection for press informants, and the press has flourished. The existing constitutional rules have not been a serious obstacle to either the development or retention of confidential news sources by the press.

It is said that currently press subpoenas have multiplied, that mutual distrust and tension between press and officialdom have increased, that reporting styles have changed, and that there is now more need for confidential sources, particularly where the press seeks news about minority cultural and political groups or dissident organizations suspicious of the law and public officials. These developments, even if true, are treacherous grounds for a far-reaching interpretation of the First Amendment fastening a nationwide rule on courts, grand juries, and prosecuting officials everywhere. . . .

. . . The administration of a constitutional newsman's privilege would present practical and conceptual difficulties of a high order. Sooner or later, it would be necessary to define those categories of newsmen who qualified for the privilege, a questionable procedure in light of the traditional doctrine that liberty of the press is the right of the lonely pamphleteer who uses carbon paper or a mimeograph just as much as of the large metropolitan publisher who utilizes the latest photocomposition methods. Freedom of the press is a "fundamental personal right" which "is not confined to newspapers and periodicals. It necessarily embraces pamphlets and leaflets. . . . The press in its historic connotation comprehends every sort of publication which affords a vehicle of information and opinion." *Lovell v. City of*

Griffin. The informative function asserted by representatives of the organized press in the present cases is also performed by lecturers, political pollsters, novelists, academic researchers, and dramatists. Almost any author may quite accurately assert that he is contributing to the flow of information to the public, that he relies on confidential sources of information, and that these sources will be silenced if he is forced to make disclosures before a grand jury.

At the federal level, Congress has freedom to determine whether a statutory newsman's privilege is necessary and desirable and to fashion standards and rules as narrow or broad as deemed necessary to address the evil discerned and, equally important, to refashion those rules as experience from time to time may dictate. There is also merit in leaving state legislatures free, within First Amendment limits, to fashion their own standards in light of the conditions and problems with respect to the relations between law enforcement officials and press in their own areas. It goes without saying, of course, that we are powerless to erect any bar to state courts responding in their own way and construing their own constitutions so as to recognize a newsman's privilege, either qualified or absolute.

In addition, there is much force in the pragmatic view that the press has at its disposal powerful mechanisms of communication and is far from helpless to protect itself from harassment or substantial harm. Furthermore, if what the newsmen urged in these cases is true—that law enforcement cannot hope to gain and may suffer from subpoenaing newsmen before grand juries—prosecutors will be loath to risk so much for so little. . . .

Finally, as we have earlier indicated, newsgathering is not without its First Amendment protections, and grand jury investigations if instituted or conducted other than in good faith, would pose wholly different issues for resolution under the First Amendment. Official harassment of the press undertaken not for purposes of law enforcement but to disrupt a reporter's relationship with his news sources would have no justification. Grand juries are subject to judicial control and subpoenas to motions to quash. We do not expect courts will forget that grand juries must operate within the limits of the First Amendment as well as the Fifth. . . .

JUSTICE POWELL, *concurring.*

. . . As indicated in the concluding portion of the opinion, the Court states that no harassment of newsmen will be tolerated. If a newsman believes that the grand jury investigation is not being conducted in good faith he is not without remedy. Indeed, if the newsman is called upon to give information bearing only a remote and tenuous relationship to the subject of the investigation, or if he has some other reason to believe that his testimony implicates confidential source relationships without a legitimate need of law enforcement, he will have access to the Court on a motion to quash and an appropriate protective order may be entered. The asserted claim to privilege should be judged on its facts by the striking of a proper balance between freedom of the press and the obligation of all citizens to give relevant testimony with respect to criminal conduct. The balance of these vital constitutional and societal interests on a case-by-case basis accords with the tried and traditional way of adjudicating such questions.

In short, the courts will be available to newsmen under circumstances where legitimate First Amendment interests require protection.

JUSTICE DOUGLAS, *dissenting.*

. . . The starting point for decision pretty well marks the range within which the end result lies. The *New York Times*, whose reporting functions are at issue here, takes the amazing position that First Amendment rights are to be balanced against other needs or conveniences of government. My belief is that all of the "balancing" was done by those who wrote the Bill of Rights. By casting the First Amendment in absolute terms, they repudiated the timid, watered-down, emasculated versions of the First Amendment which both the Government and the *New York Times* advance in the case.

Today's decision is more than a clog upon newsgathering. It is a signal to publishers and editors that they should exercise caution in how they use whatever information they can obtain. Without immunity they may be summoned to account for their criticism. Entrenched officers have been quick to crash their powers down upon unfriendly commentators.

The intrusion of government into this domain is symptomatic of the disease of this society. As the years pass the power of government becomes more and more pervasive. It is a power to suffocate both people and causes. Those in power, whatever their politics, want only to perpetuate it. Now that the fences of the law and the tradition that has protected the press are broken down the people are the victims. The First Amendment, as I read it, was designed precisely to prevent that tragedy.

JUSTICE STEWART, *with whom Justice Brennan and Justice Marshall join, dissenting.*

. . . It is obvious that informants are necessary to the newsgathering process as we know it today. If it is to perform its constitutional mission, the press must do far more than merely print public statements or publish prepared handouts. Familiarity with the people and circumstances involved in the myriad background activities that result in the final product called "news" is vital to complete and responsible journalism, unless the press is to be a captive mouthpiece of "newsmakers."

It is equally obvious that the promise of confidentiality may be a necessary prerequisite to a productive relationship between a newsman and his informants. An officeholder may fear his superior; a member of the bureaucracy, his associates; a dissident, the scorn of majority opinion. All may have information valuable to the public discourse, yet each may be willing to relate that information only in confidence to a reporter whom he trusts, either because of excessive caution or because of a reasonable fear of reprisals or censure for unorthodox views. The First

Amendment concern must not be with the motives of any particular news source, but rather with the conditions in which informants of all shades of the spectrum may make information available through the press to the public. . . .

Finally, and most important, when governmental officials possess an unchecked power to compel newsmen to disclose information received in confidence, sources will clearly be deterred from giving information, and reporters will clearly be deterred from publishing it, because uncertainty about exercise of the power will lead to "self-censorship." The uncertainty arises, of course, because the judiciary has traditionally imposed virtually no limitations on the grand jury's broad investigatory powers.

After today's decision, the potential informant can never be sure that his identity or off-the-record communications will not subsequently be revealed through the compelled testimony of a newsman. A public spirited person inside government, who is not implicated in any crime, will now be fearful of revealing corruption or other governmental wrongdoing, because he will now know he can subsequently be identified by use of compulsory process. The potential source must, therefore, choose between risking exposure by giving information or avoiding the risk by remaining silent.

The reporter must speculate about whether contact with a controversial source or publication of controversial material will lead to a subpoena. In the event of a subpoena, under today's decision, the newsman will know that he must choose between being punished for contempt if he refuses to testify, or violating his profession's ethics and impairing his resourcefulness as a reporter if he discloses confidential information. . . .

*   *   *

A major confrontation between the subpoena powers of the Federal Government and freedom of the press occurred early in 1971, this time involving the Congress rather than the courts. A House subcommittee headed by Rep. Staggers subpoenaed CBS notes and "outtakes" involved in the production of the network documentary "The Selling of the Pentagon." Outtakes are materials gathered in connection with the production of the program, but not actually used over the air. They include unused film and tape. The documentary presented evidence that the Defense Department was spending tens of millions of dollars in public relations allocations each year solely to "sell" the Vietnam war to the public and that news coming out of the Pentagon was so tightly controlled that the military was easily able to hide its mistakes. CBS President Frank Stanton declined to make notes and outtakes available to the subcommittee, claiming congressional harassment and incompatibility with the First Amendment. The charges made in the documentary were not the focal point of the subpoena. At issue were news judgments and editing which were alleged to have resulted in distortion. Dr. Stanton pointed out that since the Federal Government licenses broadcasters, such subpoena actions, if allowed to stand, would have a particularly "chilling effect" upon broadcast journalism. Following his appearance before the subcommittee and his refusal to supply notes and outtakes, Dr. Stanton was threatened by Chairman Staggers with contempt of Congress. Dr. Stanton earlier had stated that he would take the question to the Supreme Court if necessary. The Congress, however, rejected the contempt move.

The use of a subpoena is one path of action law enforcement authorities may take to get information they believe they need from a journalist who does not voluntarily wish to cooperate. That was the path sustained by the Supreme Court in Branzburg. Another is to search the newsroom for the needed information through possession of a warrant issued by a magistrate. The constitutionality of such a search was questioned in Zurcher v. Stanford Daily. And just as Branzburg had denied a special privilege to the press to turn away from a subpoena, Zurcher denied that there exists under the First Amendment any special privilege by which the news media could deny legally authorized searches. Zurcher was thought by journalists to have an even greater "chilling effect" on newsgathering than did Branzburg. It is important to note that neither the newspaper nor the students were accused of illegal acts.

The 5–3 decision by the Supreme Court that all citizens must respond to these "third party" or "innocent party" searches—journalists included—brought more than a dozen bills before the Congress aimed at correcting what was perceived to be a major threat to press freedom. What emerged was a new Federal law signed by President Carter in 1980 which forbade newsroom searches with five major exceptions. Search warrants for newsrooms can be issued (1) if the journalist is suspected of criminal wrongdoing in connection with the material sought, (2) if immediate search is likely to prevent death or personal injury, (3) if national security or classified documents are involved, (4) if there is reason to believe that the material sought would be altered or destroyed during the additional time it would take to subpoena the material, or (5) if a subpoena has been issued but has failed to produce the material sought, if all other reasonable avenues for gaining the material have failed or if further delay would threaten the "interests of justice."

One reason for the strong media and legislative reaction lies in the difference between a subpoena and a search warrant. The issuance of a subpoena allows time to consult counsel and to appeal prior to having the material become available to investigators. A newsroom search, however, offers no such time. The officers appear with the warrant and gain immediate access to the files. Also, the search cannot help but allow officers to rummage through confidential material neither sought nor relevant to the investigation at hand. A search, by its very nature, requires a sorting of material, most—or perhaps all—of which is irrelevant, but which might be of interest to authorities. These might include investigative stories which, for example, involve highly placed political figures—or even the police themselves.

Still, the Court again took the position that such special press rights do not flow from the First Amendment, but must be granted by the legislative branch, if they are to be granted at all. The Congress could not come to agreement on the question of allowing the media a privilege to deny subpoenas following Branzburg, but did grant special privilege to refuse "third party" searches following Zurcher.

ZURCHER V. STANFORD DAILY
436 U.S. 547 (1978)

JUSTICE WHITE *delivered the opinion of the Court.*

The terms of the Fourth Amendment, applicable to the States by virtue of the Fourteenth Amendment, are familiar:

> "The right of the people to be secure in their persons, houses, papers, and effects, against unreasonable searches and seizures, shall not be violated, and no Warrants shall issue, but upon probable cause, supported by Oath or affirmation, and particularly describing the place to be searched, and the persons or things to be seized."

As heretofore understood, the Amendment has not been a barrier to warrants to search property on which there is probable cause to believe that fruits, instrumentalities, or evidence of crime is located, whether or not the owner or possessor of the premises to be searched is himself reasonably suspected of complicity in the crime being investigated. We are now asked to reconstrue the Fourth Amendment and to hold for the first time that when the place to be searched is occupied by a person not then a suspect, a warrant to search for criminal objects and evidence reasonably believed to be located there should not issue except in the most unusual circumstances [—a so-called third-party search—] and that except in such circumstances, a subpoena must be relied upon to recover the objects or evidence sought.

Late in the day on Friday, April 9, 1971, officers of the Palo Alto Police Department and of the Santa Clara County Sheriff's Department responded to a call from the director of the Stanford University Hospital requesting the removal of a large group of demonstrators who had seized the hospital's administrative offices and occupied them since the previous afternoon. After several futile efforts to persuade the demonstrators to leave peacefully, more drastic measures were employed. The demonstrators had barricaded the doors at both ends of a hall adjacent to the administrative offices. The police chose to force their way in at the west end of the corridor. As they did so, a group of demonstrators emerged through the doors at the east end and, armed with sticks and clubs, attacked the group of nine police officers stationed there. One officer was knocked to the floor and struck repeatedly on the head; another suffered a broken shoulder. All nine were injured. There were no police photographers at the east doors, and most bystanders and reporters were on the west side. The officers themselves were able to identify only two of their assailants, but one of them did see at least one person photographing the assault at the east doors.

On Sunday, April 11, a special edition of the *Stanford Daily (Daily)*, a student newspaper published at Stanford University, carried articles and photographs devoted to the hospital protest and the violent clash between demonstrators and police. The photographs carried the byline of a *Daily* staff member and indicated that he had been at the east end of the hospital hallway where he could have photographed the assault on the nine officers. The next day, the Santa Clara County District Attorney's Office secured a warrant from the municipal court for an immediate search of the *Daily's* offices for negatives, film and pictures showing the events and occurrences at the hospital on the evening of April 9. The warrant issued on a finding of "just, probable and reasonable cause for believing that: Negatives and photographs and films, evidence material and relevant to the identification of the perpetrators of felonies, to wit, Battery on a Peace Officer, and Assault with a Deadly Weapon, will be located [on the premises of the *Daily*]." The warrant affidavit contained no allegation or indication that members of the *Daily* staff were in any way involved in unlawful acts at the hospital.

The search pursuant to the warrant was conducted later that day by four police officers and took place in the presence of some members of the *Daily* staff. The *Daily's* photographic laboratories, filing cabinets, desks, and waste paper baskets were searched. Locked drawers and rooms were not opened. The officers apparently had opportunity to read notes and correspondence during the search; but contrary to claims of the staff, the officers denied that they had exceeded the limits of the warrant. They had not been advised by the staff that the areas they were searching contained confidential materials. The search revealed only the photographs that had already been published on April 11, and no materials were removed from the *Daily's* office.

A month later the *Daily* and various members of its staff, respondents here, brought a civil action in the United States District Court for the Northern District of California seeking declaratory and injunctive relief . . . against the police officers who conducted the search, the chief of police, the district attorney and one of his deputies, and the judge who had issued the warrant. The complaint alleged that the search of the *Daily's* office had deprived respondents under color of state law of rights secured to them by the First, Fourth, and Fourteenth Amendments of the United States Constitution. . . .

The issue here is how the Fourth Amendment is to be construed and applied to the "third party" search, the recurring situation where state authorities have probable cause to believe that fruits, instrumentalities, or other evidence of crime is located on identified property but do not then have probable cause to believe that the owner or possessor of the property is himself implicated in the crime that has occurred or is occurring. . . .

. . . Search warrants are not directed at persons; they authorize the search of "places" and the seizure of "things," and as a constitutional matter they need not even name the person from whom the things will be seized. *United States v. Kahn.* . . .

The critical element in a reasonable search is not that the owner of the property is suspected of crime but that there is reasonable cause to believe that the specific "things" to be searched for and seized are located on the property to which entry is sought. In *Carroll v. U.S.* . . .

. . . [I]t is untenable to conclude that property may not be searched unless its occupant is reasonably suspected of crime and is subject to arrest. And if those considered free of criminal involvement may nevertheless be searched or inspected under civil statutes, it is difficult to understand why the Fourth Amendment would prevent entry onto their property to recover evidence of a crime not committed by them but by others. As we understand the structure and language of the Fourth Amendment and our cases expounding it, valid warrants to search property may be issued when it is satisfactorily demonstrated to the magistrate that fruits, instrumentalities, or evidence of crime is located on the premises. The Fourth Amendment has itself struck the balance between privacy and public need, and there is no occasion or justification for a court to revise the Amendment and strike a new balance by denying the search warrant in the circumstances present here and by insisting that the investigation proceed by subpoena, whether on the theory that the latter is a less intrusive alternative, or otherwise. . . .

The District Court held, and respondents assert here, that whatever may be true of third-party searches generally, where the third party is a newspaper, there are additional factors derived from the First Amendment that justify a nearly *per se* rule forbidding the search warrant and permitting only the subpoena. The general submission is that searches of newspaper offices for evidence of crime reasonably believed to be on the premises will seriously threaten the ability of the press to gather, analyze, and disseminate news. This is said to be true for several reasons: first, searches will be physically disruptive to such an extent that timely publication will be impeded. Second, confidential sources of information will dry up, and the press will also lose opportunities to cover various events because of fears of the participants that press files will be readily available to the authorities. Third, reporters will be deterred from recording and preserving their recollections for future use if such information is subject to seizure. Fourth, the processing of news and its dissemination will be chilled by the prospects that searches will disclose internal editorial deliberations. Fifth, the press will resort to self-censorship to conceal its possession of information of potential interest to the police. . . .

. . . Aware of the long struggle between Crown and press and desiring to curb unjustified official intrusions, the Framers took the enormously important step of subjecting searches to the test of reasonableness and to the general rule requiring search warrants issued by neutral magistrates. They nevertheless did not forbid warrants where the press was involved, did not require special showings that subpoenas would be impractical, and did not insist that the owner of the place to be searched, if connected with the press, must be shown to be implicated in the offense being investigated. . . . Properly administered, the preconditions for a warrant—probable cause, specificity with respect to the place to be searched and the things to be seized, and overall reasonableness—should afford sufficient protection against the harms that are assertedly threatened by warrants for searching newspaper offices.

There is no reason to believe, for example, that magistrates cannot guard against searches of the type, scope, and intrusiveness that would actually interfere with the timely publication of a newspaper. Nor, if the requirements of specificity and reasonableness are properly applied, policed, and observed, will there be any occasion or opportunity for officers to rummage at large in newspaper files or to intrude into or to deter normal editorial and publication decisions. The warrant issued in this case authorized nothing of this sort. Nor are we convinced, anymore than we were in *Branzburg v. Hayes*, that confidential sources will disappear and that the press will suppress news because of fears of warranted searches. Whatever incremental effect there may be in this regard if search warrants, as well as subpoenas, are permissible in proper circumstances, it does not make a constitutional difference in our judgment. . . .

JUSTICE POWELL, *concurring.*

. . . If the Framers had believed that the press was entitled to a special procedure, not available to others, when government authorities required evidence in its possession, one would have expected the terms of the Fourth Amendment to reflect that belief. As the opinion of the Court points out, the struggle from which the Fourth Amendment emerged was that between Crown and press. The Framers were painfully aware of that history, and their response to it was the Fourth Amendment. Hence, there is every reason to believe that the usual procedures contemplated by the Fourth Amendment do indeed apply to the press, as to every other person.

This is not to say that a warrant which would be sufficient to support the search of an apartment or an automobile necessarily would be reasonable in supporting the search of a newspaper office. As the Court's opinion makes clear, the magistrate must judge the reasonableness of every warrant in light of circumstances of the particular case, carefully considering the description of the evidence sought, the situation of the premises, and the position and interests of the owner or occupant. While there is no justification for the establishment of a separate Fourth Amendment procedure for the press, a magistrate asked to issue a warrant for the search of press offices can and should take cognizance of the independent values protected by the First Amendment. . . .

JUSTICE STEWART, *with whom Justice Marshall joins, dissenting.*

. . . It seems to me self-evident that police searches of newspaper offices burden the freedom of the press. The most immediate and obvious First Amendment injury caused by such a visitation by the police is physical disruption of the operation of the newspaper. Policemen occupying a newsroom and searching it thoroughly for what may be an extended period of time will inevitably interrupt its normal operations, and thus impair or even temporarily prevent the process of newsgathering, writing, editing, and publishing. By contrast, a subpoena would afford the newspaper itself an opportunity to locate whatever material might be requested and produce it.

But there is another and more serious burden on a free press imposed by an unannounced police search of a newspaper office: the possibility of disclosure of information received from confidential sources, or of the identity of the sources themselves. Protection of those sources is necessary to ensure that the press can fulfill its constitutionally designated function of informing the public, because important information can often be obtained only by an assurance that the source will not be revealed. . . .

Today the Court does not question the existence of this constitutional protection, but says only that it is not "convinced . . . that confidential sources will disappear and that the press will suppress news because of fears of warranted searches." This facile conclusion seems to me to ignore common experience. It requires no blind leap of faith to understand that a person who gives information to a journalist only on condition that his identity will not be revealed will be less likely to give that information if he knows that, despite the journalist's assurance, his identity may in fact be disclosed. And it cannot be denied that confidential information may be exposed to the eyes of police officers who execute a search warrant by rummaging through the files, cabinets, desks and wastebaskets of a newsroom. Since the indisputable effect of such searches will thus be to prevent a newsman from being able to promise confidentiality to his potential sources, it seems obvious to me that a journalist's access to information, and thus the public's, will thereby be impaired.

A search warrant allows police officers to ransack the files of a newspaper, reading each and every document until they have found the one named in the warrant, while a subpoena would permit the newspaper itself to produce only the specific documents requested. A search, unlike a subpoena, will therefore lead to the needless exposure of confidential information completely unrelated to the purpose of the investigation. The knowledge that police officers can make an unannounced raid on a newsroom is thus bound to have a deterrent effect on the availability of confidential news sources. The end result, wholly inimical to the First Amendment, will be a diminishing flow of potentially important information to the public. . . .

It is well to recall the actual circumstances of this case. The application for a warrant showed only that there was reason to believe that photographic evidence of assaults on the police would be found in the offices of the *Stanford Daily*. There was no emergency need to protect life or property by an immediate search. The evidence sought was not contraband, but material obtained by the *Daily* in the normal exercise of its journalistic function. Neither the *Daily* nor any member of its staff was suspected of criminal activity. And there was no showing the *Daily* would not respond to a subpoena commanding production of the photographs, or that for any other reason a subpoena could not be obtained. Surely, then, a subpoena would have been just as effective as a police raid in obtaining the production of the material sought by the Santa Clara County District Attorney. . . .

The decisions of this Court establish that a prior adversary judicial hearing is generally required to assess in advance any threatened invasion of First Amendment liberty. A search by police officers affords no timely opportunity for such a hearing, since a search warrant is ordinarily issued *ex parte* upon the affidavit of a policeman or prosecutor. There is no opportunity to challenge the necessity for the search until after it has occurred and the constitutional protection of the newspaper has been irretrievably invaded.

On the other hand, a subpoena would allow a newspaper, through a motion to quash, an opportunity for an adversary hearing. . . . If in the present case, the *Stanford Daily* had been served with a subpoena, it would have had an opportunity to demonstrate to the court what the police ultimately found to be true—that the evidence sought did not exist. The legitimate needs of government thus would have been served without infringing the freedom of the press. . . .

* * *

Though not involving advertising directly, another 1978 decision dealing with media access proved to be a setback for the media. It involved President Nixon and the famous White House tapes. Four years earlier, the Supreme Court had ordered the President to comply with a subpoena from the Watergate special prosecutor by handing over the tapes so that they might be used in the Watergate trial. United States v. Nixon. *During that trial, broadcasters approached Judge John Sirica in hopes of obtaining copies of 22 hours of tapes played to the jury in open court for their own broadcast and commercial purposes, such as sale of copies to the general public. They argued, of course, that those segments had been heard at the trial and were now part of the public record. As such, they said, they should be made fully available to the public, not just through transcripts in printed form. Judge Sirica denied their request, but the Court of Appeals reversed, noting the public nature of the material. The Supreme Court, however, disagreed.* Nixon v. Warner Communications. *Justice Powell, writing for the majority in a 7–2 decision, balanced the competing interests of those involved and acknowledged the uniqueness of the situation in coming down on the side of the President's attorneys. He also noted that neither the First Amendment nor the Sixth Amendment requires release of this specific audio technology to the press, restating the Court's often-held position that, generally, the press is guaranteed no greater rights to information on the public record than those which are granted to the general public.*

The press continued to seek Supreme Court sanction of special privileges under the First Amendment when acting in its newsgathering role. One important, yet tightly controlled, source of news is the prison system and those individuals held under its supervision. Two 1974 decisions had involved reporters who sought to interview prisoners while incarcerated in state and Federal institutions. Pell v. Procunier *and* Saxbe v. Washington Post. *The Court held that prison regulations or warden decisions which ban in-person interviews between reporters and inmates did not violate the First Amendment rights of either group. Justice Stewart spoke for the majority in both cases, 6–3 in Pell and 5–4 in Saxbe. Cited were problems of rehabilitation, institutional security and the availability of alternate means of communication. Also mentioned in the opinion was the* Branzburg *philosophy that the First Amendment does not give the press a constitutional right—special access, in this case—which is not available to the general public.*

Four years later, a similar conclusion was reached in Houchins v. KQED. *The*

San Francisco television station sought access to the Santa Rita County jail following an inmate suicide in 1975. Reports of the suicide investigation suggested that jail conditions were particularly poor. KQED wanted entry to inspect the facilities and to take pictures, a request denied by Sheriff Houchins. He indicated, however, that the press was welcome to join others during a public tour. He argued that other means could be found by the press to properly perform its newsgathering role. These might include letters and telephone calls to inmates and interviews with specific, willing inmates and with those who have visited prisoners. The station argued for access-to-news rights under the First Amendment, but lost by a 4–3 plurality. Justices Blackmun and Marshall did not participate. The importance of the KQED decision is in the emphasis it gives to earlier decisions of the 1970s. Chief Justice Burger echoed the now-familiar theme that the media have a right to gather news from any source by legal means, but that this newsgathering right does not "compel others—private persons or governments—to supply information."

HOUCHINS V. KQED
438 U.S. 1 (1978)

CHIEF JUSTICE BURGER *announced the judgment of the Court and delivered an opinion, in which Justice White and Justice Rehnquist joined.*

The question presented is whether the news media have a constitutional right of access to a county jail, over and above that of other persons, to interview inmates and make sound recordings, films, and photographs for publication and broadcasting by newspapers, radio and television.

Petitioner Houchins, as Sheriff of Alameda County, Cal., controls all access to the Alameda County Jail at Santa Rita. Respondent KQED operates licensed television and radio broadcasting stations which have frequently reported newsworthy events relating to penal institutions in the San Francisco Bay Area. On March 31, 1975, KQED reported the suicide of a prisoner in the Greystone portion of the Santa Rita Jail. The report included a statement by a psychiatrist that the conditions at the Greystone facility were responsible for the illnesses of his patient-prisoners there, and a statement from petitioner denying that prison conditions were responsible for the prisoners' illnesses.

KQED requested permission to inspect and take pictures within the Greystone facility. After permission was refused, KQED and the Alameda and Oakland Branches of the National Association for the Advancement of Colored People (NAACP) filed suit. . . . They alleged that petitioner had violated the First Amendment by refusing to permit media access and failing to provide any effective means by which the public could be informed of conditions prevailing in the Greystone facility or learn of the prisoners' grievances. Public access to such information was essential, they asserted, in order for NAACP members to participate in the public debate on jail conditions in Alameda County. They further asserted that television coverage of the conditions in the cells and facilities was the most effective way of informing the public of prison conditions.

The complaint requested a preliminary and permanent injunction to prevent petitioner from "excluding KQED news personnel from the Greystone cells and Santa Rita facilities and generally preventing full and accurate news coverage of the conditions prevailing therein.". . .

In support of the request for a preliminary injunction, respondents presented testimony and affidavits stating that other penal complexes had permitted media interviews of inmates and substantial media access without experiencing significant security or administrative problems. They contended that the monthly public tours at Santa Rita failed to provide adequate access to the jail for two reasons: (a) once the scheduled tours had been filled, media representatives who had not signed up for them had no access and were unable to cover newsworthy events at the jail; (b) the prohibition on photography and tape recordings, the exclusion of portions of the jail from the tours, and the practice of keeping inmates generally removed from view substantially reduced the usefulness of the tours to the media. . . .

Petitioner filed an affidavit noting the various means by which information concerning the jail could reach the public. Attached to the affidavit were the current prison mail, visitation and phone call regulations. The regulations allowed inmates to send an unlimited number of letters to judges, attorneys, elected officials, the Attorney General, petitioner, jail officials or probation officers, all of which could be sealed prior to mailing. Other letters were subject to inspection for contraband but the regulations provided that no inmate mail would be read.

With few exceptions, all persons, including representatives of the media, who knew a prisoner could visit him. Media reporters could interview inmates awaiting trial with the consent of the inmate, his attorney, the district attorney and the court. . . .

We can agree with many of the respondents' generalized assertions; conditions in jails and prisons are clearly matters "of great public importance." *Pell v. Procunier.* Penal facilities are public institutions which require large amounts of public funds, and their mission is crucial in our criminal justice system. Each person placed in prison becomes, in effect, a ward of the state for whom society assumes broad responsibility. It is equally true that with greater information, the public can more intelligently form opinions about prison conditions. Beyond question, the role of the media is important; acting as the "eyes and ears" of the public, they can be a powerful and constructive force, contributing to remedial action in the conduct of public business. They have served that function since the beginning of the Republic, but like all other components of our society media representatives are subject to limits.

The media are not a substitute for or an adjunct of government, and like the courts, they are "ill-equipped" to deal with problems of prison administration. We must not confuse the role of the media with that of government; each has special, crucial functions each complementing—and sometimes conflicting with—the other.

The public importance of conditions in penal facilities and the media's role of providing information afford no basis for reading into the Constitution a right of the public or the media to enter these institutions, with camera equipment, and take moving and still pictures of inmates for broadcast purposes. This Court has never intimated a First Amendment guarantee of a right of access to all sources of information within government control. . . .

. . . There is an undoubted right to gather news "from any source by means within the law," but that affords no basis for the claim that the First Amendment compels others—private persons or governments—to supply information. . . .

A number of alternatives are available to prevent problems in penal facilities from escaping public attention. The early penal reform movements in this country and England gained impetus as a result of reports from citizens and visiting committees who volunteered or received commissions to visit penal institutions and make reports. Citizen task forces and prison visitation committees continue to play an important role in keeping the public informed on deficiencies of prison systems and need for reforms. Grand juries, with the potent subpoena power—not available to the media—traditionally concern themselves with conditions in public institutions; a prosecutor or judge may initiate similar inquiries and the legislative power embraces an arsenal of weapons for inquiry relating to tax supported institutions. In each case, these public bodies are generally compelled to publish their findings, and if they default, the power of the media is always available to generate public pressure for disclosure. . . .

Neither the First Amendment nor Fourteenth Amendment mandates a right of access to government information or sources of information within the government's control. Under our holdings in *Pell* and *Saxbe*, until the political branches decree otherwise, as they are free to do, the media has no special right of access to the Alameda County Jail different from or greater than that accorded the public generally. . . .

JUSTICE STEVENS, *with whom Justice Brennan and Justice Powell join, dissenting.*

. . . The evidence revealed the inadequacy of the tours as a means of obtaining information about the inmates and their conditions of confinement for transmission to the public. The tours failed to enter certain areas of the jail. They afforded no opportunity to photograph conditions within the facility, and the photographs which the County offered for sale to tour visitors omitted certain jail characteristics, such as catwalks above the cells from which guards can observe the inmates. The tours provided no opportunity to question randomly encountered inmates about jail conditions. Indeed, to the extent possible inmates were kept out of sight during the tour, preventing the tour visitors from obtaining a realistic picture of the conditions of confinement within the jail. In addition, the fixed scheduling of the tours prevented coverage of newsworthy events at the jail.

Of most importance, all of the remaining tours were completely booked and there was no assurance that any tour would be conducted after December of 1975.

The District Court found that KQED had no access to the jail and that the broad restraints on access were not required by legitimate penological interests. . . .

In this case, the record demonstrates that both the public and the press had been consistently denied any access to the inner portions of the Santa Rita jail, that there had been excessive censorship of inmate correspondence, and that there was no valid justification for these broad restraints on the flow of information. . . .

*   *   *

The 1970s were not entirely bleak for the press. As the decade was ending, the Supreme Court announced an important newsgathering decision involving the publication of information ascertained legally and published accurately. Smith v. Daily Mail. *A West Virginia statute made it a crime for a newspaper, without approval of the juvenile court, to publish the name of any youth charged as a juvenile offender. The Court, in an 8–0 decision, held the law to be unconstitutional. Justice Powell took no part in the 1979 decision. The statute had been used to indict five journalists from the* Charleston Gazette *and the* Daily Mail, *which had named a 14-year-old boy held in the fatal shooting of a school classmate. The name was obtained merely by asking witnesses and others at the scene to identify the boy. Chief Justice Burger, writing for the majority, noted that the accounts were obtained legally, were truthful and were not in conflict with more urgent state interests. The conclusion supports earlier decisions in* Cox Broadcasting, Nebraska Press Association *and* Landmark. *(See Chapter 2.) Together, these decisions appear to form a foundation which allows the press to publish accurately matters of public concern which it has in its possession and which supports the newsgathering function of the media.*

SMITH V. DAILY MAIL
443 U.S. 97 (1979)

CHIEF JUSTICE BURGER *delivered the opinion of the Court.*

We granted certiorari to consider whether a West Virginia statute violates the First and Fourteenth Amendments of the United States Constitution by making it a crime for a newspaper to publish, without the written approval of the juvenile court, the name of any youth charged as a juvenile offender. . . .

On February 9, 1978, a 15-year-old student was shot and killed at Hayes Junior High School in St. Albans, W. Va., a small community located about 13 miles outside of Charleston, W. Va. The alleged assailant, a 14-year-old classmate, was identified by seven different eye witnesses and was arrested by police soon after the incident.

The Charleston *Daily Mail* and the Charleston *Daily Gazette*, respondents here, learned of the shooting by monitoring routinely the police band radio frequency; they immediately dispatched reporters and photographers to the Junior High School. The reporters for both papers obtained the name of the alleged assailant simply by asking various witnesses, the police and an assistant prosecuting attorney who were at the school.

The staffs of both newspapers prepared articles for publication about the incident. The *Daily Mail's* first article appeared in its February 9 afternoon edition. The article did not mention the alleged attacker's name. The editorial decision to omit the name was made because of the statutory prohibition against publication, without prior court approval.

The *Daily Gazette* made a contrary editorial decision and published the juvenile's name and picture in an article about the shooting that appeared in the February 10 morning edition of the paper. In addition, the name of the alleged juvenile attacker was broadcast over at least three different radio stations on February 9 and 10. Since the information had become public knowledge, the *Daily Mail* decided to include the juvenile's name in an article in its afternoon paper on February 10.

On March 1, an indictment against the respondents was returned by a grand jury. The indictment alleged that each knowingly published the name of a youth involved in a juvenile proceeding in violation of W. Va. Code. . . .

Our recent decisions demonstrate that state action to punish the publication of truthful information seldom can satisfy constitutional standards. . . .

None of these opinions directly controls this case; however, all suggest strongly that if a newspaper lawfully obtains truthful information about a matter of public significance then state officials may not constitutionally punish publication of the information, absent a need to further a state interest of the highest order. These cases involved situations where the government itself provided or made possible press access to the information. That factor is not controlling. Here respondents relied upon routine newspaper reporting techniques to ascertain the identity of the alleged assailant. A free press cannot be made to rely solely upon the sufferance of government to supply it with information. If the information is lawfully obtained, as it was here, the state may not punish its publication except when necessary to further an interest more substantial than is present here.

The sole interest advanced by the State to justify its criminal statute is to protect the anonymity of the juvenile offender. It is asserted that confidentiality will further his rehabilitation because publication of the name may encourage further antisocial conduct and also may cause the juvenile to lose future employment or suffer other consequences for this single offense. . . .

Our holding in this case is narrow. There is no issue before us of unlawful press access to confidential judicial proceedings; there is no issue here of privacy or prejudicial pretrial publicity. At issue is simply the power of a state to punish the truthful publication of an alleged juvenile delinquent's name lawfully obtained by a newspaper. The asserted state interest cannot justify the statute's imposition of criminal sanctions on this type of publication. Accordingly, the judgment of the West Virginia Supreme Court of Appeals is

Affirmed.

*   *   *

The question of whether courts might require a journalist to reveal his or her thoughts and "inter-office" communications was answered in 1979. The preparation of the television program "60 Minutes" was central to a libel suit brought by an admittedly public figure, Lt. Col. Anthony Herbert. Herbert v. Lando. Public figures in libel actions must establish that the medium published or broadcast the defamation either knowing it was false or with reckless disregard of its truth or falsity. See Chapter 9. Herbert in 1973 sued producer Barry Lando and reporter Mike Wallace for libel following a "60 Minutes" telecast which he claimed falsely portrayed him as a liar. The military's role in the Vietnam war was at issue. Herbert's claim was that, being a public figure, he was given no opportunity to establish the necessary degree of fault, i.e. malice, on the part of the "60 Minutes" staff unless he could question them about their thoughts and newsroom discussions as they prepared the broadcast. Lando declined to answer several questions about putting the show together—questions which Herbert felt were vital to his case if he were to be given a chance to seek redress for the alleged defamation. Lando's response focused on the importance of newsroom confidentiality and its privilege under the First Amendment. The Supreme Court sided with Herbert by a 6–3 vote. Justices Brennan, Marshall and Stewart dissented.

While features of this case differ significantly from those of the 1972 Branzburg question, weight is added to the argument that the First Amendment provides no privilege of confidentiality to journalists in the preparation of their stories—either from having to reveal confidential sources, as in Branzburg, or newsroom discussion, as in the present case. Trial courts almost certainly will require plaintiffs to demonstrate that such testimony is essential to their cases and to the administration of justice. Still, the fear that one's thoughts and discussions with newsroom colleagues in gathering and preparing a story might be ordered to be revealed by a libel suit cannot help but "chill" the freedom of such thought and discussion. Reporters and editors should be aware that they apparently will find little sympathy from the highest court in the land if trial courts find that revelation of those thoughts and communications are essential to the administration of justice.

HERBERT V. LANDO
441 U.S. 153 (1979)

JUSTICE WHITE *delivered the opinion of the Court.*

By virtue of the First and Fourteenth Amendments, neither the Federal nor a State Government may make any law "abridging the freedom of speech, or of the press. . . ." . . . [W]e are urged to hold for the first time that when a member of the press is alleged to have circulated damaging falsehoods and is sued for injury to the plaintiff's reputation, the plaintiff is barred from inquiring into the editorial processes of those responsible for the publication, even though the inquiry would produce evidence material to the proof of a critical element of his cause of action.

Petitioner, Anthony Herbert, is a retired Army officer who had extended war-time service in Vietnam and who received widespread media attention in 1969–1970 when he accused his superior officers of covering up reports of atrocities and other war crimes. Three years later, on February 4, 1973, respondent Columbia Broadcasting System, Inc. (CBS), broadcast [on the popular "60 Minutes" program] a report on petitioner and his accusations. The program was produced and edited by respondent Barry Lando and was narrated by respondent Mike Wallace. Lando later published a related article in *Atlantic Monthly* magazine. Herbert then sued Lando, Wallace, CBS, and *Atlantic Monthly* for defamation. In his complaint, Herbert alleged that the program and article falsely and maliciously portrayed him as a liar and a person who had made war-crimes charges to explain his relief from command, and he requested substantial damages for injury to his reputation and to the literary value of a book he had just published recounting his experiences.

Although his cause of action arose under New York State defamation law, Herbert conceded that because he was a "public figure" the First and Fourteenth Amendments precluded recovery absent proof that respondents had published a damaging falsehood "with 'actual malice'—that is, with knowledge that it was false or with reckless disregard of whether it was false or not." This was the holding of *New York Times v. Sullivan*, with respect to alleged libels of public officials, and extended to "public figures" by *Curtis Publishing Co. v. Butts*. Under this rule, absent knowing falsehood, liability requires proof of reckless disregard for truth, that is, that the defendant "in fact entertained serious doubts as to the truth of his publication." *St. Amant v. Thompson*. . . .

. . . [T]he District Court ruled that because the defendant's state of mind was of "central importance" to the issue of malice in the case, it was obvious that the questions were relevant and "entirely appropriate to Herbert's efforts to discover whether Lando had any reason to doubt the veracity of certain of his sources, or, equally significant, to prefer the veracity of one source over another.". . .

A divided [appeals] panel reversed the District Court. . . .

. . . *New York Times* and its progeny made it essential to proving liability that plaintiffs focus on the conduct and state of mind of the defendant. To be liable, the alleged defamer of public officials or of public figures must know or have reason to suspect that his publication is false. In other cases proof of some kind of fault, negligence perhaps, is essential to recovery. Inevitably, unless liability is to be completely foreclosed, the thoughts and editorial processes of the alleged defamer would be open to examination. . . .

Furthermore, long before *New York Times* was decided, certain qualified privileges had developed to protect a publisher from liability for libel unless the publication was made with malice. Malice was defined in numerous ways, but in general depended upon a showing that the defendant acted with improper motive. This showing in turn hinged upon the intent of purpose with which the publication was made, the belief of the defendant in the truth of his statement, or upon the ill will which the defendant might have borne towards the defendant.

Courts have traditionally admitted any direct or indirect evidence relevant to the state of mind of the defendant and necessary to defeat a conditional privilege or enhance damages. The rules are applicable to the press and to other defendants alike, and it is evident that the courts across the country have long been accepting evidence going to the editorial processes of the media without encountering constitutional objections. . . .

. . . .[I]n the 15 years since *New York Times*, the doctrine announced by that case, which represented a major development and which was widely perceived as essentially protective of press freedoms, has been repeatedly affirmed as the appropriate First Amendment standard applicable in libel actions brought by public officials and public figures. At the same time, however, the Court has reiterated its conviction—reflected in the laws of defamation of all of the States—that the individual's interest in his reputation is also a basic concern.

We are thus being asked to modify firmly established constitutional doctrine by placing beyond the plaintiffs reach a range of direct evidence relevant to proving knowing or reckless falsehood by the publisher of an alleged libel, elements that are critical to plaintiffs such as Herbert. The case for making this modification is by no means clear and convincing, and we decline to accept it.

Furthermore, the outer boundaries of the editorial privilege now urged are difficult to perceive. The opinions below did not state, and respondents do not explain, precisely when the editorial process begins and when it ends. Moreover, although we are told that respondent Lando was willing to testify as to what he "knew" and what he had "learned" from his interviews, as opposed to what he "believed," it is not at all clear why the suggested editorial privilege would not cover knowledge as well as belief about the veracity of published reports. It is worth noting here that the privilege as asserted by respondents would also immunize from inquiry the internal communications occurring during the editorial process and thus place beyond reach what the defendant participants learned or knew as the result of such collegiate conversations or exchanges. If damaging admissions to colleagues are to be barred from evidence, would a reporter's admissions made to third parties not participating in the editorial process also be immune from inquiry? . . .

. . . The President does not have an absolute privilege against disclosure of materials subpoenaed for a judicial proceeding. *United States v. Nixon.* In so holding, we found that although the President has a powerful interest in confidentiality of communications between himself and his advisers, that interest must yield to a demonstrated specific need for evidence. . . .

*   *   *

Justice is administered not only at trials, but through a variety of hearings and conferences. It has been estimated that more than 90 percent of all criminal cases are settled, one way or another, at preliminary hearing stages, thereby negating the need for a trial itself. The press, therefore, sees as urgent its freedom to attend such hearings as it performs its traditional "watchdog" role. Most citizens learn about the effectiveness of the judicial branch of government only through the media. So, it was with great shock and anger that the media learned that the Supreme Court would allow closing of these pre-trial hearings in cases where the judge believes prejudicial publicity is a threat to a fair trial and exclusion of the public and the press is necessary to the administration of justice. In such cases, the Court said, the rights of the public and the press are secondary. A balancing must be considered. The violent reaction of the press to the 5–4 decision was not without justification. There appeared to be considerable confusion among the Justices as to what Gannett *really meant. In his opinion of the Court, for example, Justice Stewart suggested that the Sixth Amendment extended to the accused, and not to the public or the press. The extension of this reasoning would allow closed trials also. In addition, Justice Stewart's opinion repeatedly referred to "trials" when pre-trial hearings were under consideration. Attempts by some of the Justices to "clarify" the Court's position in* Gannett *did little to soothe the media. See, for example, the speech by Justice Brennan in this chapter. The specter of secret trials was too imminent to ignore. Indeed, trial judges around the country began closing trials as well as preliminary hearings. The furor lasted until the* Richmond Newspapers *decision one year later, but even that, presumably, did not alter the position of the Court insofar as pre-trial hearings were concerned. Joining Justice Stewart to make the majority in* Gannett *were Justices Burger, Powell, Rehnquist and Stevens.*

GANNETT V. DePASQUALE
443 U.S. 368 (1979)

JUSTICE STEWART *delivered the opinion of the Court.*

The question presented in this case is whether members of the public have an independent constitutional right to insist upon access to a pretrial judicial proceeding, even though the accused, the prosecutor and the trial judge all have agreed to the closure of that proceeding in order to assure a fair trial. . . .

This Court has long recognized that adverse publicity can endanger the ability of a defendant to receive a fair trial. To safeguard the due process rights of the accused, a trial judge has an affirmative constitutional duty to minimize the effects of prejudicial pretrial publicity. And because of the Constitution's pervasive concern for these due process rights, a trial judge may surely take protective measures even when they are not strictly and inescapably necessary.

Publicity concerning pretrial suppression hearings such as the one involved in the present case poses special risks of unfairness. The whole purpose of such hearings is to screen out unreliable or illegally obtained evidence and insure that this evidence does not become known to the jury. Publicity concerning the proceedings at a pretrial hearing, however, could influence public opinion against a defendant and inform potential jurors of inculpatory information wholly inadmissible at the actual trial.

The danger of publicity concerning pretrial suppression hearings is particularly acute, because it may be difficult to measure with any degree of certainty the effects of such publicity on the fairness of the trial. After the commencement of the trial itself, inadmissible prejudicial information about a defendant can be kept from a jury by a variety of means. When such information is publicized during a pre-trial proceeding, however, it may never be altogether kept from potential jurors. Closure of pretrial proceedings is often one of the most effective methods that a trial judge can employ to attempt to insure that the fairness of a trial will not be jeopardized by the dissemination of such information throughout the community before the trial itself has even begun. . . .

The Sixth Amendment, applicable to the States through the Fourteenth, surrounds a criminal trial with guarantees such as the rights to notice, confrontation, and compulsory process that have as their overriding purpose the protection of the accused from prosecutorial and judicial abuses. Among the guarantees that the Amendment provides to a person charged with the commission of a criminal offense, and to him alone, is the "right to a speedy and public trial, by an impartial jury." The Constitution nowhere mentions any right of access to a criminal trial on the part of the public; its guarantee, like the others enumerated, is personal to the accused. . . .

Closed pretrial proceedings have been a familiar part of the judicial landscape in this country. . . . The original New York Field Code of Criminal Procedure published in 1850, for example, provided that pretrial hearings should be closed to the public "upon the request of a defendant.". . .

For these reasons, we hold that members of the public have no constitutional right under the Sixth and Fourteenth Amendments to attend criminal trials. . . .

*   *   *

The first two years of the 1980s saw two more Supreme Court decisions unfriendly to the press. While neither involved newsgathering per se, both demonstrated the Court's support for the government's attempts to enjoin disclosures by disgruntled employees, in these cases, former employees of the Central Intelligence Agency. Earlier, the Court had refused to hear an appeal in the case of Victor Marchetti, also a former CIA agent, who saw the Court sanction the censorship of parts of his book. (See Chapter 1.) In 1980, the case of Frank Snepp was decided. He also published criticism of the CIA, but without first submitting the manuscript to the agency for review, as required by the contract required of all CIA employees. Snepp v. United States. The following year, the Court decided against Philip Agee, who published a book which went beyond Snepp's in that it revealed classified material. Haig v. Agee.

Some significant differences in these cases should be pointed out. Marchetti submitted his book to the agency, as called for in his CIA employment agreement, so the argument in the courts focused on which passages, if any, were classified. Snepp did not submit his manuscript to the CIA for review, but it contained no classified information. The government, in fact, did not even contend at the trial that secret information had been revealed, but sued only for breach of contract. The judge ruled that the CIA's contract with Snepp had, indeed, been violated and, as penalty, ordered that all of Snepp's royalties be paid to the CIA. The Supreme Court sustained the judge's ruling without oral arguments and in a per curiam opinion. Justices Stevens, Brennan and Marshall dissented. Agee, on the other hand, did reveal classified information, some of which was alleged to have brought harm to individuals within the agency and to their families, as well as to the nation's foreign policy. One method used by Agee to discredit the agency was to reveal the names of CIA agents working overseas.

The importance of these decisions to newsgathering is found in the Court's support of the government in its attempts to control criticism. First, there was clear prior restraint in the Marchetti case. Second is the requirement by the CIA of an agreement of secrecy and of censorial rights between itself and its employees and former employees. One must acknowledge the need of such requirements in organizations charged with maintaining an overseas spy network. But one can also envision the spread of such contractual requirements to other government jobs, some perhaps vital to the nation's security, but others not so. Third, of course, was the Supreme Court's allowing of sanctions of various forms against writers who were critical of the government. It is clear that the Supreme Court has given broad powers to the government when claims of national security are made or when government contracts are violated.

SNEPP V. UNITED STATES
444 U.S. 507 (1980)

PER CURIAM

. . . Based on his experiences as a CIA agent, Snepp published a book about certain CIA activities in South Vietnam. Snepp published the account without submitting it to the Agency for prepublication review. As an express condition of his employment with the CIA in 1968, however, Snepp had executed an agreement promising that he would "not . . . publish . . . any information or material relating to the Agency, its activities or intelligence activities generally, either during or after the term of [his] employment . . . without specific prior approval of the Agency." The promise was an integral part of Snepp's concurrent undertaking "not to disclose any classified information relating to the Agency without proper authorization."

Thus, Snepp had pledged not to divulge *classified* information and not to publish *any* information without prepublication clearance. The Government brought this suit to enforce Snepp's agreement. It sought a declaration that Snepp had breached the contract, an injunction requiring Snepp to submit future writings for prepublication review, and an order imposing a constructive trust for the Government's benefit on all profits that Snepp might earn from publishing the book in violation of his fiduciary obligations to the Agency. . . .

Snepp's employment with the CIA involved an extremely high degree of trust. In the opening sentence of the agreement that he signed, Snepp explicitly recognized that he was entering a trust relationship. The trust agreement specifically imposed the obligation not to publish *any* information relating to the Agency without submitting the information for clearance. Snepp stipulated at trial that— after undertaking this obligation—he had been "assigned to various positions of trust" and that he had been granted "frequent access to classified information, including information regarding intelligence sources and methods." Snepp published his book about CIA activities on the basis of this background and exposure. He deliberately and surreptitiously violated his obligation to submit all material for prepublication review. Thus, he exposed the classified information with which he had been entrusted to the risk of disclosure.

Whether Snepp violated his trust does not depend upon whether his book actually contained classified information. The Government does not deny—as a general principle—Snepp's right to publish unclassified information. Nor does it contend—at this stage of the litigation—that Snepp's book contains classified material. The Government simply claims that, in light of the special trust reposed in him and the agreement that he signed, Snepp should have given the CIA an opportunity to determine whether the material he proposed to publish would compromise classified information or sources. Neither of the Government's concessions undercuts its claim that Snepp's failure to submit to prepublication review was a breach of his trust. . . .

The Government could not pursue the only remedy that the Court of Appeals left it without losing the benefit of the bargain it seeks to enforce. Proof of the tortious conduct necessary to sustain an award of punitive damages might force the Government to disclose some of the very confidences that Snepp promised to protect. The trial of such a suit, before a jury if the defendant so elects, would subject the CIA and its officials to probing discovery into the Agency's highly confidential affairs. Rarely would the Government run this risk. In a letter introduced at Snepp's trial, former CIA Director Colby noted the analogous problem in criminal cases. Existing law, he stated, "requires the revelation in open court of confirming or additional information of such a nature that the potential damage to the national security precludes prosecution." When the Government cannot secure its remedy without unacceptable risks, it has no remedy at all. . . .

. . . If the agent secures prepublication clearance, he can publish with no fear of liability. If the agent publishes unreviewed material in violation of his fiduciary and contractual obligation, the trust remedy simply requires him to disgorge the benefits of his faithlessness. Since the remedy is swift and sure, it is tailored to deter those who would place sensitive information at risk. And since the remedy reaches only funds attributable to the breach, it cannot saddle the former agent with exemplary damages out of all proportion to his gain. . . .

JUSTICE STEVENS, *with whom Justice Brennan and Justice Marshall join, dissenting.*

. . . In this case Snepp admittedly breached his duty to submit the manuscript of his book, *Decent Interval,* to the CIA for prepublication review. However, the Government has conceded that the book contains no classified, nonpublic material. Thus, by definition, the interest in confidentiality that Snepp's contract was designed to protect has not been compromised. Nevertheless, the Court today grants the Government unprecedented and drastic relief in the form of a constructive trust over the profits derived by Snepp from the sale of the book. Because that remedy is not authorized by any applicable law and because it is most inappropriate for the Court to dispose of this novel issue summarily on the Government's conditional cross-petition for certiorari, I respectfully dissent. . . .

The uninhibited character of today's exercise in lawmaking is highlighted by the Court's disregard of two venerable principles that favor a more conservative approach to this case.

First, for centuries the English-speaking judiciary refused to grant equitable relief unless the plaintiff could show that his remedy at law was inadequate. Without waiting for an opportunity to appraise the adequacy of the punitive damage remedy in this case, the Court has jumped to the conclusion that equitable relief is necessary.

Second, and of greater importance, the Court seems unaware of the fact that its drastic new remedy has been fashioned to enforce a species of prior restraint on a citizen's right to criticize his government. Inherent in this prior restraint is the risk that the reviewing agency will misuse its authority to delay the publication of a critical work or to persuade an author to modify the contents of his work beyond the demands of secrecy. The character of the covenant as a prior restraint on free speech surely imposes an especially heavy burden on the censor to justify the remedy it seeks. It would take more than the Court has written to persuade me that that burden has been met.

I respectfully dissent.

＊   ＊   ＊

As noted above, the case of Philip Agee had elements not found in the Snepp case. The Court, by 7–2, decided in favor of the government, but because Agee was a United States citizen living in West Germany, the United States had little control over his public pronouncements or his royalties. The government, however, chose to exercise one power it did have. It lifted Agee's passport. That decision came after then-Secretary of State Cyrus Vance heard reports that Agee had been invited to sit on a tribunal to hear the case against the 52 Americans being held hostage in Iran.

The Supreme Court had allowed passports to be invalidated in the past, e.g. Zemel v. Rusk. Still, journalists across the nation saw danger in this latest exercise of government power, despite their distaste for Agee's revealing the names of CIA agents working in foreign countries. The decision apparently gives the government broad power to deny its citizens, including reporters, a right to travel abroad— essential to newsgathering—when national security is used as the basis for such denial. It might be suggested that the Agee decision was founded more on punishment of Agee or prevention of international embarrassment to the United States than it did on national security. Agee, presumably, was saying in West Germany all that he could say in Iran. By 1981, the year the decision came down, Alexander Haig had succeeded Vance as Secretary of State, hence the name of Haig as appellant in the opinion.

A Massachusetts law that mandated the closing of rape or other sexual assault trials when juvenile victims were testifying was declared unconstitutional by the Supreme Court in 1982. Globe Newspapers v. Superior Court. *While such closures might indeed be appropriate, the 6–3 majority held that such decisions were best made by the trial judge on a case-by-case basis, not by legislative fiat. The ruling was narrow, focusing on the mandatory nature of the statute, which automatically excluded the press and public. Such decisions must be left to the judge, Justice Brennan wrote for the majority. Justices Burger, Rehnquist and Stevens dissented. The Court's ruling emphasized the responsibility of the trial judge as reflected in earlier cases, such as* Cox Broadcasting, Gannett *(covered earlier in this chapter),* Richmond Newspapers *(Chapter 11) and* Chandler *(Chapter 12). However, that responsibility must be exercised with discretion.*

GLOBE NEWSPAPERS V. SUPERIOR COURT
457 U.S. 596 (1982)

JUSTICE BRENNAN *delivered the opinion of the Court.*

. . . Massachusetts General Laws, as construed by the Massachusetts Supreme Judicial Court, require trial judges, at trials for specified sexual offenses involving a victim under the age of 18, to exclude the press and general public from the courtroom during the testimony of that victim. The question presented is whether the statute thus construed violates the First Amendment as applied to the States through the Fourteenth Amendment.

The case began when appellant, Globe Newspaper Co. (Globe), unsuccessfully attempted to gain access to a rape trial conducted in the Superior Court for the County of Norfolk, Commonwealth of Massachusetts. The criminal defendant in that trial had been charged with the forcible rape and forced unnatural rape of three girls who were minors at the time of trial—two sixteen years of age and one seventeen. In April 1979, during hearings on several preliminary motions, the trial judge ordered the courtroom closed. . . . The defendant immediately objected to that exclusion order, and the prosecution stated for purposes of the record that the order was issued on the court's "own motion and not at the request of the Commonwealth.". . .

The state interests asserted to support [the law], though articulated in various ways, are reducible to two: the protection of minor victims of sex crimes from further trauma and embarrassment; and the encouragement of such victims to come forward and testify in a truthful and credible manner. We consider these interests in turn.

We agree with respondent that the first interest—safe-guarding the physical and psychological well-being of a minor is a compelling one. But as compelling as that interest is, it does not justify a *mandatory* closure rule, for it is clear that the circumstances of the particular case may affect the significance of the interest. A trial court can determine on a case-by-case basis whether closure is necessary to protect the welfare of a minor victim. Among the factors to be weighed are the minor victim's age, psychological maturity, and understanding, the nature of the crime, the desires of the victim and the interests of parents and relatives. [The law,] in contrast, requires closure even if the victim does not seek the exclusion of the press and general public, and would not suffer injury by their presence. In the case before us, for example, the names of the minor victims were already in the public record, and the record indicates that the victims may have been willing to testify despite the presence of the press. If the trial court had been permitted to exercise its discretion, closure might well have been deemed unnecessary. . . .

Nor can [the law] be justified on the basis of the Commonwealth's second asserted interest—the encouragement of minor victims of sex crimes to come forward and provide accurate testimony. The Commonwealth has offered no empirical support for the claim that the rule of automatic closure . . . will lead to an increase in the number of minor sex victims coming forward and cooperating with state authorities. Not only is the claim speculative in empirical terms, but it is also open to serious question as a matter of logic and common sense. Although [the law] bars the press and general public from the courtroom during the testimony of minor sex victims, the press is not denied access to the transcript, court personnel, or any other possible source that could provide an account of the minor victim's testimony. Thus [it] cannot prevent the press from publicizing the substance of a minor victim's testimony, as well as his or her identity. If the Commonwealth's interest in encouraging minor victims to come forward depends on keeping such matters secret, [it] hardly advances that interest in an effective manner. And even if [the law] effectively advanced the State's interest, it is doubtful that the interest would be sufficient to overcome the constitutional attack, for that same interest could be relied on to support an array of mandatory-closure rules designed to encourage victims to come forward: surely it cannot be suggested that minor victims of sex crimes are the *only* crime victims who, because of publicity attendant to criminal trials, are reluctant to come forward and testify. The State's argument based on this interest therefore proves too much and runs contrary to the very foundation of the right of access recognized in *Richmond Newspapers*: namely, "that a presumption of openness inheres in the very nature of a criminal trial under our system of justice."

CHIEF JUSTICE BURGER, *with whom Justice Rehnquist joins, dissenting.*

Historically our Society has gone to great lengths to protect minors *charged* with crime, particularly by prohibiting the release of the names of offenders, barring the press and public from juvenile proceedings, and sealing the records of those proceedings. Yet today the Court holds unconstitutional a state statute designed to protect not the *accused*, but the minor *victims* of sex crimes. In doing so, it advances a disturbing paradox. Although states are permitted, for example, to mandate the closure of all proceedings in order to protect a 17-year-old charged with rape, they are not permitted to require the closing of part of criminal proceedings in order to protect an innocent child who has been raped or otherwise sexually abused. . . .

Neither the purpose of the law nor its effect is primarily to deny the press or public access to information; the verbatim transcript is made available to the public and the media and may be used without limit. We therefore need only examine whether the restrictions imposed are reasonable and whether the interests of the Commonwealth override the very limited incidental effects of the law on First Amendment rights. . . .

. . . There is no basis whatever for this cavalier disregard of the reality of human experience. It makes no sense to criticize the Commonwealth for its failure to offer empirical data in support of its rule; only by allowing state experimentation may such empirical evidence be produced. "It is one of the happy incidents of the federal system that a State may, if its citizens choose, serve as a laboratory, and try novel social and economic experiments without risk to the rest of the country." *New State Ice Co. v. Liebmann.* . . .

The Commonwealth's interests are clearly furthered by the mandatory nature of the closure statute. Certainly if the law were discretionary, most judges would exercise that discretion soundly and would avoid unnecessary harm to the child, but victims and their families are entitled to assurance of such protection. The legislature did not act irrationally in deciding not to leave the closure determination to the idiosyncracies of individual judges subject to the pressures available to the media. The victim might very well experience considerable distress prior to the court appearance, wondering, in the absence of such statutory protection, whether public testimony will be required. The mere possibility of public testimony may cause parents and children to decide not to report these heinous crimes. If, as psychologists report, the courtroom experience in such cases is almost as traumatic as the crime itself, a state certainly should be able to take whatever reasonable steps it believes are necessary to reduce that trauma. Furthermore, we cannot expect victims and their parents to be aware of all of the nuances of state law; a person who sees newspaper, or perhaps even television, reports of a minor victim's testimony may very well be deterred from reporting a crime on the belief that public testimony will be required. It is within the power of the state to provide for mandatory closure to alleviate such understandable fears and encourage the reporting of such crimes.

*   *   *

The mid-1980s saw three significant Supreme Court decisions that seemed to depart from the earlier Gannett *suggestion of limited access to the courts. By 1987, then, it appeared that despite* Gannett, *access of the press and the public to the nation's courtrooms was guaranteed in all but the most extreme cases. The first of this trio,* Press-Enterprise v. Superior Court, *dealt with* voir dire *proceedings, the questioning of potential jurors before the actual start of the trial. Without dissent, the Court said that the Riverside, California trial judge erred in excluding the press and public from all but three days of a six-week* voir dire. *The case involved a rape-murder. The newspaper had sought a transcript of the closed pretrial proceeding after the suspect had been found guilty and sentenced to death. In its ruling the Supreme Court in effect extended the 1980* Richmond Newspapers *decision involving public trials to include pretrial hearings as well. (See Chapter 11.) Upon occasion, the Court acknowledged, there may be an "overriding interest" to exclude the public and to seal parts of the transcripts, but those times should be rare and, when they do occur, the burden of justifying those closures falls on the judge. The presumption, Chief Justice Burger said for the Court, is on openness.*

PRESS-ENTERPRISE V. SUPERIOR COURT
464 U.S. 501 (1984)

CHIEF JUSTICE BURGER *delivered the opinion of the court.*

We granted certiorari to decide whether the guarantees of open public proceedings in criminal trials cover proceedings for the *voir dire* examination of potential jurors.

The presumption of openness may be overcome only by an overriding interest based on findings that closure is essential to preserve higher values and is narrowly tailored to serve that interest. The interest is to be articulated along with findings specific enough that a reviewing court can determine whether the closure order was properly entered. We now turn to whether the presumption of openness has been rebutted in this case.

Although three days of *voir dire* in this case were open to the public, *six weeks* of the proceedings were closed, and media requests for the transcript were denied. The Superior Court asserted two interests in support of its closure order and orders denying a transcript: the right of the defendant to a fair trial, and the right to privacy of the prospective jurors, for any whose "special experiences in sensitive areas . . . do not appear to be appropriate for public discussion."

Of course the right of an accused to fundamental fairness in the jury selection process is a compelling interest. But the California court's conclusion that Sixth Amendment and privacy interests were sufficient to warrant prolonged closure was unsupported by findings showing that an open proceeding in fact threatened those interests; hence it is not possible to conclude that closure was warranted. Even with findings adequate to support closure, the trial court's orders denying access to *voir dire* testimony failed to consider whether alternatives were available to protect the interests of the prospective jurors that the trial court's orders sought to guard. Absent consideration of alternatives to closure, the trial court could not constitutionally close the *voir dire.*

The jury selection process may, in some circumstances, give rise to a compelling interest of a prospective juror when interrogation touches on deeply personal matters that person has legitimate reasons for keeping out of the public domain. The trial involved testimony concerning an alleged rape of a teenage girl. Some questions may have been appropriate to prospective jurors that would give rise to legitimate privacy interests of those persons. For example, a prospective juror might privately inform the judge that she, or a member of her family, had been raped but had declined to seek prosecution because of the embarrassment and emotional trauma from the very disclosure of the episode. The privacy interests of such a prospective juror must be balanced against the historic values we have discussed and the need for openness of the process.

To preserve fairness and at the same time protect legitimate privacy, a trial judge must at all times maintain control of the process of jury selection and should inform the array of prospective jurors, once the general nature of sensitive questions is made known to them, that those individuals believing public questioning will prove damaging because of embarrassment, may properly request an opportunity to present the problem to the judge *in camera* but with counsel present and on the record. . . .

*　　　*　　　*

The second case of the three, Waller v. Georgia, *came four months after* Press-Enterprise *and involved a suppression hearing. The question, similar to that of* Press-Enterprise, *was whether the right to a public trial extends to certain pretrial courtroom activities. The defendants were charged with racketeering. Justice Powell, writing for a unanimous Court, said that such hearings often are as important as the trials and might be the only proceedings available to the public in a given case— such as when a suspect pleads guilty and eliminates the need for a trial. As in* Press-Enterprise, *suppression hearings can be closed if there is an "overriding" need to do so, but again the emphasis was on the presumption of openness. While there are differences between* Waller *and* Gannett—*the prosecution sought the closure in* Waller *over the objections of the defendants, for example—*Waller *appeared to be another "clarification" of the confusing* Gannett *opinion and was welcomed by the news media.*

WALLER V. GEORGIA
467 U.S. 39 (1984)

JUSTICE POWELL *delivered the opinion of the Court.*

This case requires us to decide the extent to which a hearing on a motion to suppress evidence may be closed to the public over the objection of the defendant consistently with the Sixth and Fourteenth Amendment right to a public trial. . . .

On June 21, 1982, a jury was empaneled and then excused while the court heard the closure and suppression motions. The prosecutor argued that the suppression hearing should be closed because under the Georgia wiretap statute "[a]ny publication" of information obtained under a wiretap warrant that was not "necessary and essential" would cause the information to be inadmissible as evidence. The prosecutor stated that the evidence derived in the wiretaps would "involve" some persons who were indicted but were not then on trial, and some persons who were not then indicted. He said that if published in open court, the evidence "[might] very well be tainted." The trial court agreed. . . . Over objection, the court ordered the suppression hearing closed to all persons other than witnesses, court personnel, the parties, and the lawyers.

The suppression hearing lasted seven days. The parties do not dispute that less than two-and-one-half hours were devoted to playing tapes of intercepted telephone conversations. The intercepted conversations that were played included some persons who were not then on trial, but no one who had not been named in the indictment; one person who had not been indicted was mentioned in the recorded calls. The remainder of the hearing concerned such matters as the procedures used. . . .

This case presents three questions: First, does the accused's Sixth Amendment right to a public trial extend to a suppression hearing conducted prior to the presentation of evidence to the jury? Second, if so, was the right violated here? Third, if so, what is the appropriate remedy?

This Court has not recently considered the extent of the accused's right under the Sixth Amendment to insist upon a public trial, and has never considered the extent to which that right extends beyond the actual proof at trial. We are not, however, without relevant precedents. In several recent cases, the Court found that the press and public have a qualified First Amendment right to attend a criminal trial. We also have extended that right not only to the trial as such but also to the *voir dire* proceeding in which the jury is selected. Moreover, in an earlier case in this line, *Gannett Co. v. DePasquale,* we considered whether this right extends to a pretrial suppression hearing. While the Court's opinion did not reach the question, a majority of the Justices concluded that the public had a qualified constitutional right to attend such hearings.

In each of these cases the Court has made clear that the right to an open trial may give way in certain cases to other rights or interests, such as the defendant's right to a fair trial or the government's interest in inhibiting disclosure of sensitive information. Such circumstances will be rare, however, and the balance of interests must be struck with special care. . . .

Applying these tests to the case at bar, we find the closure of the entire suppression hearing plainly was unjustified. Under *Press-Enterprise*, the party seeking to close the hearing must advance an overriding interest that is likely to be prejudiced, the closure must be no broader than necessary to protect that interest, the trial court must consider reasonable alternatives to closing the proceeding, and it must make findings adequate to support the closure. . . .

. . . As a result, the trial court's findings were broad and general, and did not purport to justify closure of the entire hearing. The court did not consider alternatives to immediate closure of the entire hearing: directing the government to provide more detail about its need for closure, *in camera* if necessary, and closing only those parts of the hearing that jeopardized the interests advanced. As it turned out, of course, the closure was far more extensive than necessary. The tapes lasted only two-and-one-half hours of the seven-day hearing, and few of them mentioned or involved parties not then before the court. . . .

*　　*　　*

Perhaps the most important of this trio of closed pretrial hearing cases again involved the Riverside Press-Enterprise *in California. This 1986 case, called "Press-Enterprise II" to distinguish it from the 1984 case, involved the closing of a 41-day preliminary hearing for Robert Diaz, a nurse charged with killing twelve elderly hospital patients. The California court had ruled that there was no constitutional right of access to pretrial proceedings and that the state law which allowed such hearings to be closed when "necessary" allowed closure if a defendant could show a "reasonable likelihood of prejudice." Chief Justice Burger wrote for the majority in this case as he did for* Press-Enterprise I, *but Justices Rehnquist and Stevens dissented this time. In California, preliminary hearings have evolved into "near trials," the Supreme Court noted. Because of this, these hearings often are the "final and most important" events in a criminal justice procedure.*

The Chief Justice had long been a student of history. He resigned his Court seat in 1986 to chair full-time the 1987 bicentennial celebration of the signing of the Constitution. In his Press-Enterprise II *opinion, he devotes some time to the historical significance of open trials and to our English heritage. It would appear, then, that in the last media opinion he was to write for the Court, he came down on the side of the press, which is somewhat ironic, given the hostility of the press toward the 17 years of the Burger Court generally and the Chief Justice particularly. Of course, after the Warren Court era of activism, few justices probably could have "pleased" the press as much as did the "team" of Warren, Black, Douglas, Stewart, Fortas, Goldberg and the two still on the Court when Burger resigned, Justices Brennan and Marshall.*

PRESS-ENTERPRISE V. SUPERIOR COURT
478 U.S. 1 (1986)

CHIEF JUSTICE BURGER *delivered the opinion of the Court.*

We granted certiorari to decide whether petitioner has a First Amendment right of access to transcripts of a preliminary hearing growing out of a criminal prosecution. . . .

The right to an open public trial is a shared right of the accused and the public, the common concern being the assurance of fairness. Only recently, in *Waller v. Georgia*, for example, we considered whether the defendant's Sixth Amendment right to an open trial prevented the closure of a suppression hearing over the defendant's objection. We noted that the First Amendment right of access would in most instances attach to such proceedings and that "the explicit Sixth Amendment right of the accused is no less protective of a public trial than the implicit First Amendment right of the press and public." When the defendant objects to the closure of a suppression hearing, therefore, the hearing must be open unless the party seeking to close the hearing advances an overriding interest that is likely to be prejudiced.

Here, unlike *Waller*, the right asserted is not the defendant's Sixth Amendment right to a public trial since the defendant requested a *closed* preliminary hearing. Instead, the right asserted here is that of the public under the First Amendment. The California Supreme Court concluded that the First Amendment was not implicated because the proceeding was not a criminal trial, but a preliminary hearing. However, the First Amendment question cannot be resolved solely on the label we give the event, *i.e.*, "trial" or otherwise, particularly where the preliminary hearing functions much like a full scale trial.

In cases dealing with the claim of a First Amendment right of access to criminal proceedings, our decisions have emphasized two complementary considerations. First, because a " 'tradition of accessibility implies the favorable judgment of experience,' " we have considered whether the place and process has historically been open to the press and general public.

In *Press-Enterprise I*, for example, we observed "that, since the development of trial by jury, the process of selection of jurors has presumptively been a public process with exceptions only for good cause shown." In *Richmond Newspapers*, we reviewed some of the early history of England's open trials from the day when a 'trial was much like a "town meeting." In the days before the Norman Conquest, criminal cases were brought before "moots," a collection of the freemen in the community. The public trial, "one of the essential qualities of a court of justice" in England, was recognized early on in the colonies. There were risks, of course, inherent in such a "town meeting" trial—the risk that it might become a gathering moved by emotions or passions growing from the nature of a crime; a "lynch mob" ambience is hardly conducive to calm, reasoned decisionmaking based on evidence. Plainly the modern trial with jurors open to interrogation for possible bias is a far cry from the "town meeting trial" of ancient English practice. Yet even our modern procedural protections have their origin in the ancient common law principle which provided, not for closed proceedings, but rather for rules of conduct for those who attend trials.

Second, in this setting the Court has traditionally considered whether public access plays a significant positive role in the functioning of the particular process in question. Although many governmental processes operate best under public scrutiny, it takes little imagination to recognize that there are some kinds of government operations that would be totally frustrated if conducted openly. . . .

The considerations that led the Court to apply the First Amendment right of access to criminal trials in *Richmond Newspapers* and *Globe* and the selection of jurors in *Press-Enterprise I* lead us to conclude that the right of access applies to preliminary hearings as conducted in California.

First, there has been a tradition of accessibility to preliminary hearings of the type conducted in California. Although grand jury proceedings have traditionally been closed to the public and the accused, preliminary hearings conducted before neutral and detached magistrates have been open to the public. Long ago in the celebrated trial of Aaron Burr for treason, for example, with Chief Justice Marshall sitting as trial judge, the probable cause hearing was held in the Hall of the House of Delegates in Virginia, the court room being too small to accommodate the crush of interested citizens. From *Burr* until the present day, the near uniform practice of state and federal courts has been to conduct preliminary hearings in open court. As we noted in *Gannett*, several states following the original New York Field Code of Criminal Procedure published in 1850 have allowed preliminary hearings to be closed on the motion of the accused. But even in these states the proceedings are presumptively open to the public and are closed only for cause shown. Open preliminary hearings, therefore, have been accorded " 'the favorable judgment of experience.' "

The second question is whether public access to preliminary hearings as they are conducted in California plays a particularly significant positive role in the actual functioning of the process. We have already determined in *Richmond Newspapers*, *Globe*, and *Press-Enterprise I* that public access to criminal trials and the selection of jurors is essential to the proper functioning of the criminal justice system. California preliminary hearings are sufficiently like a trial to justify the same conclusion.

In California, to bring a felon to trial, the prosecutor has a choice of securing a grand jury indictment or a finding of probable cause following a preliminary hearing. Even when the accused has been indicted by a grand jury, however, he has an absolute right to an elaborate preliminary hearing before a neutral magistrate. The accused has the right to personally appear at the hearing, to be represented by counsel, to cross-examine hostile witnesses, to present exculpatory evidence, and to exclude illegally obtained evidence. If the magistrate determines that probable cause exists, the accused is bound over for trial; such a finding leads to a guilty plea in the majority of cases.

It is true that unlike a criminal trial, the California preliminary hearing cannot result in the conviction of the accused, and the adjudication is before a magistrate or other judicial officer without a jury. But these features, standing alone, do not make public access any less essential to the proper functioning of the proceedings in the overall criminal justice process. Because of its extensive scope, the preliminary hearing is often the final and most important in the criminal proceeding. As the California Supreme Court stated in *San Jose Mercury-News v. Municipal Court*, the preliminary hearing in many cases provides "the sole occasion for public observation of the criminal justice system. . . ."

We therefore conclude that the qualified First Amendment right of access to criminal proceedings applies to preliminary hearings as they are conducted in California.

Since a qualified First Amendment right of access attaches to preliminary hearings in California . . . , the proceedings cannot be closed unless specific, on the record findings are made demonstrating that "closure is essential to preserve higher values and is narrowly tailored to serve that interest." If the interest asserted is the right of the accused to a fair trial, the preliminary hearing shall be closed only if specific findings are made demonstrating that, first, there is a substantial probability that the defendant's right to a fair trial will be prejudiced by publicity that closure would prevent and, second, reasonable alternatives to closure cannot adequately protect the defendant's fair trial rights. . . .

JUSTICE STEVENS, *with whom Justice Rehnquist joins as to Part II, dissenting.*

. . . [It] has always been apparent that the freedom to obtain information that the Government has a legitimate interest in not disclosing is far narrower than the freedom to disseminate information, which is "virtually absolute" in most contexts. In this case, the risk of prejudice to the defendant's right to a fair trial is perfectly obvious. For me, that risk is far more significant than the countervailing interest in publishing the transcript of the preliminary hearing sooner rather than later. The interest in prompt publication—in my view—is no greater than the interest in prompt publication of grand jury transcripts. As explained more fully below, we have always recognized the legitimacy of the governmental interest in the secrecy of grand jury proceedings, and I am unpersuaded that the difference between such proceedings and the rather elaborate procedure for determining probable cause that California has adopted strengthens the First Amendment claim to access asserted in this case. . . .

By abjuring strict reliance on history and emphasizing the broad value of openness, the Court tacitly recognizes the importance of public access to government proceedings generally. Regrettably, the Court has taken seriously the stated requirement that the sealing of a transcript be justified by a "compelling" or "overriding" governmental interest and that the closure order be "narrowly tailored to serve that interest."

. . . A requirement of some legitimate reason for closure in this case requires an affirmance. The constitutionally-grounded fair trial interests of the accused if he is bound over for trial, and the reputational interests of the accused if he is not, provide a substantial reason for delaying access to the transcript for at least the short time before trial. By taking its own verbal formulation seriously, the Court reverses—without comment or explanation or any attempt at reconciliation—the holding in *Gannett* that a "reasonable probability of prejudice" is enough to overcome the First Amendment right of access to a preliminary proceeding. It is unfortunate that the Court neglects this opportunity to fit the result in this case into the body of precedent dealing with access rights generally. I fear that today's decision will simply further unsettle the law in this area.

I respectfully dissent.

THE PRESS AND THE COURTS

By William J. Brennan, Jr. *

I begin with the premise that there exists a fundamental and necessary interdependence of the Court and the press. The press needs the Court, if only for the simple reason that the Court is the ultimate guardian of the constitutional rights that support the press. And the Court has a concomitant need for the press, because through the press the Court receives the tacit and accumulated experience of the Nation, and because the judgments of the Court ought also to instruct and to inspire—the Court needs the medium of the press to fulfill this task.

This partnership of the Court and the press is not unique; it is merely exemplary of the function that the press serves in our society. As money is to the economy, so the press is to our political culture: it is the medium of circulation. It is the currency through which the knowledge of recent events is exchanged; the coin by which *public* discussion may be purchased.

This analogy, of course, cannot be pressed too far. Unlike a medium of circulation, which receives the passive valuation of others, the press is active, shaping and defining the very arena in which events assume their public character. In this the press performs a tripartite role. It chooses which events it will publicize; it disseminates, to a greater or lesser extent, selected information about these events; and it adopts toward these events attitudes which are often instrumental in forming public opinion.

These functions are of manifest importance for the political life of the Nation. A democracy depends upon the existence of a *public* life and culture, and in a country of some 220 million, this would scarcely be possible without the press. I believe now, and have always believed, that, insofar as the First Amendment shields the wellsprings of our democracy, it also provides protection for the press in the exercise of these functions, for, as I said in an opinion for the Court many years ago: the guarantees of the First Amendment "are not for the benefit of the press so much as for the benefit of all of us. A broadly defined freedom of the press assures the maintenance of our political system and an open society." *Time, Inc. v. Hill.*

In recent years the press has taken vigorous exception to decisions of the Court circumscribing the protections the First Amendment extends to the press in the exercise of these functions. I have dissented from many of these opinions as

---

* From an address delivered Oct. 17, 1979, at the dedication of the Samuel I. Newhouse Law Center, Rutgers University. Used with permission of the author, an Associate Justice of the Supreme Court of the United States.

hampering, if not shackling the press' performance of its crucial role in helping maintain our open society, and have no intention of standing here today to defend them. And I of course fully support the right and duty of the press to express its dissatisfaction with opinions of the Court with which it disagrees. I am concerned, however, that in the heat of the controversy the press may be misapprehending the fundamental issues at stake, and may consequently fail in its important task of illuminating these issues for the Court and the public.

The violence of the controversy cannot be explained merely by the fact that the Court has ruled adversely to the press' interests. While the argument that the ability of the press to function has suffered grievous and unjustified damage may have merit in some cases, in others the vehemence of the press' reaction has been out of all proportion to the injury suffered. The source of the press' particular bitterness can, I believe, be identified. It stems from the confusion of two distinct models of the role of the press in our society that claim the protection of the First Amendment.

Under one model—which I call the "speech" model—the press requires and is accorded the absolute protection of the First Amendment. In the other model—I call it the "structural" model—the press' interests may conflict with other societal interests and adjustment of the conflict on occasion favors the competing claim.

The "speech" model is familiar. It is as comfortable as a pair of old shoes, and the press, in its present conflict with the Court, most often slips into the language and rhetorical stance with which this model is associated even when only the "structural" model is at issue. According to this traditional "speech" model, the primary purpose of the First Amendment is more or less absolutely to prohibit any interference with freedom of expression. The press is seen as the public spokesman *par excellence*. Indeed, this model sometimes depicts the press as simply a collection of individuals who wish to speak out and broadly disseminate their views. This model draws its considerable power—I emphasize—from the abiding commitment we all feel to the right of self-expression, and, so far as it goes, this model commands the widest consensus. In the past two years, for example, the Court has twice unanimously struck down state statutes which prohibited the press from speaking out on certain subjects, and the Court has firmly rejected judicial attempts to muzzle press publication through prior restraints. The "speech" model thus readily lends itself to the heady rhetoric of absolutism.

The "speech" model, however, has its limitations. It is a mistake to suppose that the First Amendment protects *only* self-expression, only the right to speak out. I believe that the First Amendment in addition fosters the values of democratic self-government. In the words of Professor Zechariah Chafee, "[t]he First Amendment protects . . . a social interest in the attainment of truth, so that the country may not only adopt the wisest course of action but carry it out in the wisest way." The Amendment therefore also forbids the government from interfering with the communicative processes through which we citizens exercise and prepare to exercise our rights of self-government. The individual right to speak out, even millions of such rights aggregated together, will not sufficiently protect these social interests. It is in recognition of this fact that the Court has referred to "the circulation of information to which *the public is entitled* in virtue of the constitutional guarantees." *Grosjean v. American Press Co.* (emphasis supplied).

Another way of saying this is that the First Amendment protects the structure of communications necessary for the existence of our democracy. This insight suggests the second model to describe the role of the press in our society. This second model is structural in nature. It focuses on the relationship of the press to the communicative functions required by our democratic beliefs. To the extent the press makes these functions possible, this model requires that it receive the protection of the First Amendment. A good example is the press' role in providing and circulating the information necessary for informed public discussion. To the extent the press, or, for that matter, to the extent that any institution uniquely performs this role, it should receive unique First Amendment protection.

This "structural" model of the press has several important implications. It significantly extends the umbrella of the press' constitutional protections. The press is not only shielded when it speaks out, but when it performs all the myriad tasks necessary for it to gather and disseminate the news. As you can easily see, the stretch of this protection is theoretically endless. Any imposition of any kind on the press will in some measure affect its ability to perform protected functions. Therefore this model requires a Court to weigh the effects of the imposition against the social interests which are served by the imposition. This inquiry is impersonal, almost sociological in nature. But it does not fit comfortably with the absolutist rhetoric associated with the first model of the press I have discussed. For here, I repeat, the Court must weigh the effects of the imposition inhibiting press access against the social interests served by the imposition.

The decisions that have aroused the sharpest controversy between the Court and the press have been those decisions in which the Court has tried to wrestle with the constitutional implications of this structural model of the press. For example, the reporters in *Branzburg v. Hayes* argued that if they were compelled to reveal confidential sources or notes before a Grand Jury, their ability to gather the news would be impaired. The case did not involve any substantive restrictions on press publications. The contention of the press was simply that reporters must be excused from duties imposed on all other citizens because the fulfillment of those duties would impair the press' ability to support the structure of communications protected by the First Amendment. In its decision, the Court acknowledged that First Amendment interests were involved in the process of news gathering, but concluded that these interests were outweighed by society's interest in the enforcement of the criminal law.

Similarly, in *Zurcher v. Stanford Daily*, a student newspaper contended that its offices could not be searched, as is usually the case, upon the issuance of a valid search warrant, but that a subpoena which would give the newspaper the opportunity to contest the search in advance was necessary. Again, the issue was not any restriction on what the newspaper could actually say, but rather whether special procedures were necessary to protect the press' ability to gather and publish the news. Once again, the Court held that whatever First Amendment interests were implicated were outweighed by society's interest in law enforcement.

Both these cases struck vehement, if not violent reactions from the press. About *Zurcher,* for example, the President of the American Newspaper Publishers Association stated that the opinion "puts a sledge hammer in the hands of those who would batter the American people's First Amendment rights." Unfortunately, the resulting controversy generated more heat than light, and the reason, I think, is that the press, in order to strengthen its rhetorical position, insisted on treating these cases exactly as if they involved only the traditional model of the press as public spokesman. The *Washington Star,* for example, argued that "it matters all too little whether abridgment takes the obvious forms of suppression and censorship, or the casual rummaging of a newspaper office on a search warrant."

Of course, as I have been trying to make clear, it matters a great deal whether the press is abridged because restrictions are imposed on what it may say, or whether the press is abridged because its ability to gather the news or otherwise perform communicative functions necessary for a democracy is impaired. The two different situations stem from two distinct constitutional models of the press in our society, and require two distinct forms of analysis. The strong, absolutist rhetoric appropriate to the first model is only obfuscatory with respect to the second. The tendency of the press to confuse these two models has, in my opinion, been at the root of much of the recent acrimony in press-Court relations. The press has reacted as if its role as a public spokesman were being restricted, and, as a consequence, it has on occasion overreacted.

Perhaps the clearest example is the recent case of *Herbert v. Lando.* The *Herbert* case was a lineal descendent of the decision of *New York Times Co. v. Sullivan. Sullivan* held that a public official could not successfully sue a media defendant for libel unless he could demonstrate that the alleged defamatory publication was issued with "actual malice," that is with knowing or reckless disregard of the truth. Subsequent decisions extended this holding to public figures, like Colonel Herbert, and made clear that actual malice turned on the media defendant's "subjective awareness of probable falsity." *Gertz v. Robert Welch, Inc.* The theory of *Sullivan* was that if the media were liable for large damage judgments for the publication of false defamatory information, the resulting inhibitions might undermine the robust public discussion so essential to a democracy. If a journalist knew that he was publishing defamatory falsehood, however, the First Amendment would offer him no protection.

The *Herbert* case raised the question whether a public-figure plaintiff could in discovery ask a defendant journalist about his state of mind when publishing the alleged defamatory falsehood. Now it is clear that a journalist's state of mind is relevant to his "subjective awareness of probable falsity," and thus to the issue of actual malice. And traditionally a plaintiff is entitled to discovery on all relevant issues. Privileges are rare and strictly construed. Nevertheless, the press argued that it could not perform its functions under the First Amendment unless a special "editorial" privilege were created to shield it from such inquiries.

The Court rejected this argument, and the result was a virtually unprecedented outpouring of scathing criticism. One paper said that the decision was an example of the Court following "its anti-press course into what can only be called an Orwellian domain," while the managing editor of the *St. Louis Post-Dispatch* stated that the opinion "has the potential of totally inhibiting the press to a degree seldom seen outside a dictatorial or fascist country."

I dissented in part in *Herbert*, but I can say with some degree of confidence that the decision deserved a more considered response on the part of the press than it received. The injury done the press was simply not of the magnitude to justify the resulting firestorm of acrimonious criticism. In its rush to cudgel the Court, the press acted as if the decision imposed restrictions on what the press could say, as though the actual malice standard of *Sullivan* were overruled. In fact two newspapers actually erroneously characterized the opinion as holding that truth would no longer be an absolute defense to libel suits, while several others appeared to read the opinion as reverting to the old common-law definition of "malice" as ill will. Putting aside, however, such unfortunate examples of inaccurate reporting, the deepest source of the press' outrage was I think well captured by William Leonard, president of CBS news. Mr. Leonard said that *Herbert* denied constitutional protection to "the journalist's most precious possession—his mind, his thoughts and his editorial judgment."

I understand and sympathize with Mr. Leonard's concern. Being asked about one's state of mind can be a demeaning and unpleasant experience. Nevertheless, the inquiry into a defendant's state of mind, into his intent, is one of the most common procedures in the law. Almost all crimes require that some element of the defendant's intent be established, as do all intentional torts, such as trespass, assault, or conversion. State of mind can also be relevant to questions of fraud, mistake, and recklessness. And, in the area of libel, it would scarcely be fair to say that a plaintiff can only recover if he establishes intentional falsehood and at the same time to say that he cannot inquire into a defendant's intentions.

But in its outrage against the *Herbert* decision, the press unfortunately misapprehended the role model of the press involved. To it the decision was simply a "George Orwellian invasion of the mind," which meant, as Jack Landau, director of the Reporters Committee for Freedom of the Press put it, that "the press will soon have lost the last constitutional shred of its editorial privacy and independence from the government." The true role model involved can be ignored, however, only on the assumption that a journalist's state of mind is somehow special, and cannot be impinged for any purpose. It is important to note that this assumption gathers its rhetorical basis from the model of the press as public spokesman. For when a citizen speaks publically he *is* special, and, with only rare and stringent exceptions, what he says cannot be restricted for any purpose. But, as I have made clear, this is not the model of the press at issue in *Herbert*. The decision does not affect the actual malice standard set out in *Sullivan*. Instead the question raised by *Herbert* is whether the press' ability to perform the communicative functions required by our democratic society would be significantly impaired if an editorial privilege were not created.

Note that this is a difficult and factual question by sharp or sensational rhetoric. In my view reporters will not cease to publish because they are later asked about their state of mind. On the other hand, predecisional communications among editors may well be curtailed if they may later be used as evidence in libel suits. Since a democracy requires an informed and accurate press, and since predecisional editorial communications contribute to informed and accurate editorial judgments, I would have held that such communications should receive a qualified privilege. I say a *qualified* privilege because even the executive privilege bestowed upon the President of the United States so that he may receive the informed and unimpeded advice of his aides, is, as the case of *United States v. Nixon*, makes clear, a qualified privilege.

A majority of my colleagues rejected my position because it believed that the accuracy of resulting publications would not be impaired if predecisional editorial communications were revealed. This is a matter of judgment, about which reasonable men may differ. It is also, at least in form, an empirical question, upon which the lessons of later experience may be persuasively brought to bear. If the press wishes to play a part in this process, it must carefully distinguish the basis on which its constitutional claim is based, and it must tailor its arguments and its rhetoric accordingly. This may involve a certain loss of innocence, a certain recognition that the press, like other institutions, must accommodate a variety of important social interests. But the sad complexity of our society makes this inevitable, and there is no alternative but a shrill and impotent isolation.

These are hard words, but there is much at stake, not the least of which is the ability of the press to resume its sure voice as a reliable conscience of this Nation. Last Term there were decisions of the Supreme Court justifying far more concern than *Herbert v. Lando* and about which the press was uniquely qualified to speak. Yet the credibility of the press was impaired by the excesses of its reactions to *Lando*. An example is the case of *Gannett Co., Inc. v. DePasquale* [See Chapter 3.] in which the Court, in a 5–4 vote, held that members of the public had no constitutional right under the Sixth and Fourteenth Amendments to attend pretrial hearings in a criminal case.

Gannett involves the Sixth rather than the First Amendment and so does not fit into either of the two models I have sketched out. The case concerns the right of the public, not merely of the press, and at its heart is interpretation of the kind of government we have set for ourselves in our Constitution. The question is whether that government will be visible to the people, who are its authors. *Gannett* holds that judges, as officers of that government, may in certain circumstances remove themselves from public view and perhaps also holds that they can make this decision without even considering the interests of the people. I believe that the

Farmers did not conceive such a government, and that they had in mind the truth precisely captured several generations later by Lord Acton: "Everything secret degenerates, even the administration of justice."

Any damage by the Court's decision in *Gannett* can of course be undone through legislative enactments, should a concerned citizenry so demand. [See *Richmond Newspapers v. Virginia*, Chapter 11.] The clear voice of the press, however, is an essential part of any such enterprise, especially about a subject that bears so closely on press' business. The press did, I am happy to note, intelligently and searchingly criticize the *Gannett* decision. It was distinctly noted that the decision was "much more than another controversial 'press case,' " but was in fact "a decision about the relationship of the public to the judicial process." *N.Y. Times.* The point I wish to stress, however, is that the impact of the press' quite correct reaction was undercut by the unjustified violence of its previous responses to *Herbert v. Lando* and other such cases involving the structural model of the press. This fact was cogently noted by Anthony Lewis in his [July 5, 1979] column in the *New York Times:*

> The press . . . should forswear absolutes. The reiterated claim of recent years that its freedom has no limits has done the press no good. If the press began recognizing that these are difficult issues, involving more than one interest, it could more effectively criticize the facile simplicities of a Gannett decision.

I think Mr. Lewis is correct. And I say this with some urgency, for the integrity of the press must be preserved, not only for cases like *Gannett*, where the press puts forward the claims of the public, but even for cases like *Zurcher*, where the press puts forward its own structural claims. For the application of the First Amendment is far from certain in the as yet uncharted domains foreshadowed by the structural model of the press. The Court needs help in scouting these dim areas in which the shield of the Amendment is put forward not to guard the personal right to speak, but to protect social functions of impersonal dimensions. The press can and must assist the Court in mustering proper legal conclusions from the accumulated experience of the Nation. But the press can be of assistance only if bitterness does not cloud its vision, nor self-righteousness its judgment.

CHAPTER **4**

GOVERNMENT
REGULATION

The unique nature of broadcasting brings with it problems which do not concern the print media. First is the newness of the industry and its lack of legal precedent. Second, there are rapidly changing developments which alter the very core of electronic journalism, e.g. cable television (or CATV) and FM radio. Third, there is limited access to the broadcasting band, thereby requiring control of available airwaves. Fourth, there are interstate and internal problems resulting from the fact that broadcast signals cannot be controlled at state or national borders. Finally, there is the overriding philosophy in this country that the airwaves belong to the people and that commercial broadcasters are to use these "public properties" only in the public interest.

Early experiments in broadcasting began prior to World War I and increased rapidly following the Armistice. This growth was uncontrolled and led to broadcasting chaos involving overlapping signals and battles over location on the radio dial. The emerging industry soon asked for Federal assistance in establishing ground rules for broadcasters. The result was the Radio Act of 1927 in which the Congress authorized a five-man commission to regulate forms of radio communication. It was established under this Act that the airwaves were to remain public in nature and that licenses would be granted to private parties to broadcast in the "public interest, convenience, or necessity." This commission in 1934 was given added responsibility and renamed the Federal Communications Commission.

The entry of television in the 1920s signalled new problems for the Commission. World War II held up development of commercial television, but the growth of the television industry in the last quarter century probably has been greater than any in the history of industrial development. Though the FCC took steps to encourage independent stations and to control networks, the networks became paramount, just as they did in the development of radio. Coaxial cable and microwave relay resulted in coast-to-coast broadcasting by 1951.

A decade before Chief Justice Warren donned his robes, the Supreme Court received its first major broadcasting case. National Broadcasting Co. v. United States, 319 U.S. 190 (1943). *In its decision, the Court held that denial of a broadcasting license by the FCC did not violate First Amendment guarantees of free speech.*

NATIONAL BROADCASTING CO. V. UNITED STATES
319 U.S. 190 (1943)

JUSTICE FRANKFURTER *delivered the opinion of the Court.*

. . . We come . . . to an appeal to the First Amendment. The Regulations, even if valid in all other respects, must fall because they abridge, say the appellants, their right of free speech. If that be so, it would follow that every person whose application for a license to operate a station is denied by the Commission is thereby denied his constitutional right of free speech. Freedom of utterance is abridged to many who wish to use the limited facilities of radio. Unlike other modes of expression, radio inherently is not available to all. That is its unique characteristic, and that is why, unlike other modes of expression, it is subject to governmental regulation. Because it cannot be used by all, some who wish to use it must be denied. But Congress did not authorize the Commission to choose among applicants upon the basis of their political, economic or social views, or upon any other capricious basis. If it did, or if the Commission by these Regulations proposed a choice among applicants upon some such basis, the issue before us would be wholly different. The question here is simply whether the Commission, by announcing that it will refuse licenses to persons who engage in specified network practices (a basis for choice which we hold is comprehended within the statutory criterion of "public interest"), is thereby denying such persons the constitutional right of free speech. The right of free speech does not include, however, the right to use facilities of radio without a license. The licensing system established by Congress in the Communications Act of 1934 was a proper exercise of its power over commerce. The standard it provided for the licensing of stations was the "public interest, convenience, or necessity." Denial of a station license on that ground, if valid under the Act, is not a denial of free speech. . . .

*   *   *

During the 16-year period of the Warren Court, legal questions regarding broadcasting began to increase just as they did in other types of public expression. With Chief Justice Warren writing the majority opinion, the Court in 1954 held that the popular "give away" programs did not constitute a lottery. Federal Communications Commission v. American Broadcasting Co. *Eleven years later, the Chief Justice again spoke for the Court, which ruled in a much publicized case that television commercial tests generally must show what they purport to show.* Federal Trade Commission v. Colgate-Palmolive Co.

As the Warren Court entered its final years, the broadcasting industry came under increasing pressure from the FCC, the Federal Trade Commission and the Congress. Proposals to place greater restrictions on broadcasters were introduced from various elements of public life. Among these proposals, aimed primarily at television, were those to restrict news reporting and programming, to investigate ownership practices and license renewal policies, to study the effects of televised violence, to ban cigarette advertising, to institute penalties for false and misleading advertising, and to consider the licensing of networks. Clearly, influential segments of society felt that television self-regulation was weak and largely ineffectual.

At the same time, the FCC signaled the possibility of a new era of activism in the public interest. The Commission required anti-smoking messages and later called for an outright ban on cigarette commercials on television. It also authorized a nation-wide system of pay (or subscription) television, launched a broad study of media ownership patterns, toughened fairness doctrine policies, limited network control of prime-time programming, and revoked the license of a major broadcaster (WHDH, Boston).

The Commission itself did not escape criticism during this turbulent period. It was chastised in 1969 for its renewal of the license to station WLBT, Jackson, Miss., a station accused of racial prejudice in its broadcasting policies. The question of the renewal was taken to court and, in a significant decision, the U.S. Court of Appeals vacated the license, implying broadly expanded powers in the public's attempts to challenge licensing decisions. The judge who wrote the unanimous three-man Appellate Court opinion was, significantly, to be Chief Justice Warren's successor, Chief Justice Warren Burger.

The Congress traditionally has held that the widest possible dissemination of information is in the best interest of an open, democratic society. This is reflected in its establishment of post offices and post roads and in its authorization of lower postal rates to publications through second-class mailing permits. However, the right to use the postal facilities may be denied to those who circulate matters deemed harmful to the general public or matter not constitutionally protected, i.e. obscene or seditious material.

President Washington argued for the establishment of an efficient postal service as necessary to democratic government. There were fears, however, that a strong federal postal branch would result in government surveillance and possible control of content of the mail. The Continental Congress in 1775 named the renowned publisher and statesman Benjamin Franklin America's first Postmaster General. It was common for colonial postmasters also to be publishers.

In 1782 the Continental Congress prohibited the inspection of sealed mail, such as first class letters. This inspection was undertaken in early colonial days as a means of ascertaining disloyalty to the king. Nearly a century later, in 1878, the Supreme Court in Ex parte Jackson *ruled that freedom of the press has little meaning without freedom to distribute, but that inspection of unsealed printed matter, such as newspapers, did not interfere with this freedom.*

Justice Holmes once said an adequate postal distribution service is as important to free written expression as a tongue is to free speech. While newspapers, books, magazines and educational material all may be mailed at reduced rates, this privilege has resulted in censorial practices by various postmasters. The warnings of colonialists who feared that federal postal service would result in government interference of mail were fully realized with the rise of Anthony Comstock, who waged through the Post Office the nation's most nefarious one-man anti-obscenity campaign. Postmasters in the mid-1800s ruled on postal acceptability of printed matter submitted to the Post Office for mailing. In 1913 the Supreme Court in Lewis Publishing Co. v. Morgan, *authorized the Post Office Department to uphold standards set by the Congress in granting second-class permits.*

In Milwaukee Publishing Co. v. Burleson *the Court upheld refusal of postal services under the Espionage Act of 1917, but more importantly the case furnished an opportunity for strong dissents by Justices Brandeis and Holmes, whose views were to become the majority view in* Hannegan v. Esquire *a quarter of a century later. 327 U.S. 146 (1946). The censorial rights of the postmaster were terminated with the landmark* Hannegan *decision. Postmaster General Hannegan had acted to revoke the second-class permit of* Esquire Magazine *as "morally improper" and not devoted to the public good. He cited as his authority the Postal Classification Act of 1879. The Court, Justice Douglas voicing the 8–0 opinion, disagreed.*

HANNEGAN V. ESQUIRE
327 U.S. 146 (1946)

JUSTICE DOUGLAS *delivered the opinion of the Court.*

Congress has made obscene material nonmailable, and has applied criminal sanctions for the enforcement of that policy. It has divided mailable matter into four classes, periodical publications constituting the second-class. And it has specified four conditions upon which a publication shall be admitted to the second-class. The Fourth condition, which is the only one relevant here, provides:

> Except as otherwise provided by law, the conditions upon which a publication shall be admitted to the second-class are as follows . . . Fourth. It must be originated and published for the dissemination of information of a public character, or devoted to literature, the sciences, arts, or some special industry, and having a legitimate list of subscribers. Nothing herein contained shall be so construed as to admit to the second-class rate regular publications designed primarily for advertising purposes, or for free circulation, or for circulation at nominal rates.

Respondent is the publisher of *Esquire Magazine,* a monthly periodical which was granted a second-class permit in 1933. In 1943 . . . a citation was issued to respondent by the . . . Postmaster General . . . to show cause why that permit should not be suspended or revoked. A hearing was held before a board designated by the then Postmaster General. The board recommended that the permit not be revoked. Petitioner's predecessor took a different view. He did not find that *Esquire Magazine* contained obscene material and therefore was nonmailable. He revoked its second-class permit because he found that it did not comply with the Fourth condition. The gist of his holding is contained in the following excerpt from his opinion:

> The plain language of this statute does not assume a publication must in fact be 'obscene' within the intendment of the postal obscenity statutes before it can be found not to be 'originated and published for the dissemination of information of a public character, or devoted to literature, the sciences, arts, or some special industry.'
>
> Writings and pictures may be indecent, vulgar, and risque and still not be obscene in a technical sense. Such writings and pictures may be in that obscure and treacherous borderland zone where the average person hesitates to find them technically obscene, but still may see ample proof that they are morally improper and not for the public welfare and the public good. When such writings or pictures occur in isolated instances their dangerous tendencies and malignant qualities may be considered of lesser importance.
>
> When, however, they become a dominant and systematic feature they most certainly cannot be said to be for the public good, and a publication which uses them in that manner is not making the 'special contribution to the public welfare' which Congress intended by the Fourth condition.
>
> A publication to enjoy these unique mail privileges and special preferences is bound to do more than refrain from disseminating material which is obscene or bordering on the obscene. It is under a positive duty to contribute to the public good and the public welfare. . . .

The issues of *Esquire Magazine* under attack are those for January to November inclusive of 1943. The material complained of embraces in bulk only a small percentage of those issues. Regular features of the magazine (called "The Magazine for Men") include articles on topics of current interest, short stories, sports articles or stories, short articles by men prominent in various fields of activities, articles about men prominent in the news, a book review department headed by the late William Lyon Phelps, a theatrical department headed by George Jean Nathan, a department devoted to lively arts by Gilbert Seldes, a department devoted to men's clothing, and pictoral features, including war action paintings, color photographs of dogs and water colors or etchings of game birds and reproductions of famous paintings, prints and drawings. There was very little in these features which was challenged. But petitioner's predecessor found that the objectionable items, though a small percentage of the total bulk, were regular recurrent features which gave the magazine its dominant tone or characteristic. These include jokes, cartoons, pictures, articles, and poems. They were said to reflect the smoking-room type of humor, featuring, in the main, sex. Some witnesses found the challenged items highly objectionable, calling them salacious and indecent. Others thought they were only racy and risque. Some condemned them as being merely in poor taste. Other witnesses could find no objection to them.

An examination of the items makes plain, we think, that the controversy is not whether the magazine publishes "information of a public character" or is devoted to "literature" or to the "arts." It is whether the contents are "good" or "bad." To uphold the order of revocation would, therefore, grant the Postmaster General a power of censorship. Such a power is so abhorrent to our traditions that a purpose to grant it should not be easily inferred. . . .

The policy of Congress has been clear. It has been to encourage the distribution of periodicals which disseminated "information of a public character" or which were devoted to "literature, the sciences, arts, or some special industry," because it was thought that those publications as a class contributed to the public good. The standards prescribed in the Fourth condition have been criticized, but not on the ground that they provide for censorship. As stated by the Postal Commission of 1911:

> The original object in placing on second-class matter a rate far below that on any other class of mail was to encourage the dissemination of news and current literature of educational value. This object has been only in part attained. The low rate has helped to stimulate an enormous mass of periodicals, many of which are of little utility for the cause of popular education. Others are of excellent quality, but the experience of the post office has shown the impossibility of making a satisfactory test based upon literary or educational values. To attempt to do so would be to set up a censorship of the press. Of necessity the words of the statute—"devoted to literature, the sciences, arts, or some special industry"—must have a broad interpretation.

We may assume that Congress has a broad power of classification and need not open second-class mail to publications of all types. The categories of publications entitled to that classification have indeed varied through the years. And the Court held in *Ex parte Jackson* that Congress could constitutionally make it a crime to send fraudulent or obscene material through the mails. But grave constitutional questions are immediately raised once it is said that the use of the mails is a privilege which may be extended or withheld on any grounds whatsoever. See the dissents of Mr. Justice Brandeis and Mr. Justice Holmes in *United States ex rel. Milwaukee S.D. Pub. Co. v. Burleson.* Under that view the second-class rate could be granted on condition that certain economic or political ideas not be disseminated. The provisions of the Fourth condition would have to be far more explicit for us to assume that Congress made such a radical departure from our traditions and undertook to clothe the Postmaster General with the power to supervise the tastes of the reading public of the country.

It is plain, as we have said, that the favorable second-class rates were granted periodicals meeting the requirements of the Fourth condition, so that the public good might be served through a dissemination of the class of periodicals described. But that is a far cry from assuming that Congress had any idea that each applicant for the second-class rate must convince the Postmaster General that his publication positively contributes to the public good or public welfare. Under our system of government there is an accommodation for the widest varieties of tastes and ideas. What is good literature, what has educational value, what is refined public information, what is good art, varies with individuals as it does from one generation to another. There doubtless would be a contrariety of views concerning Cervantes' *Don Quixote*, Shakespeare's *Venus and Adonis*, or Zola's *Nana*. But a requirement that literature or art conform to some norm prescribed by an official smacks of an ideology foreign to our system. The basic values implicit in the requirements of the Fourth condition can be served only by uncensored distribution of literature. From the multitude of competing offerings the public will pick and choose. What seems to one to be trash may have for others fleeting or even enduring values. But to withdraw the second-class rate from this publication today because its contents seemed to one official not good for the public would sanction withdrawal of the second-class rate tomorrow from another periodical whose social or economic views seemed harmful to another official. The validity of the obscenity laws is recognition that the mails may not be used to satisfy all tastes, no matter how perverted. But Congress has left the Postmaster General with no power to prescribe standards for the literature or the art which a mailable periodical disseminates. . . .

* * *

Rulings of the Warren Court in the 1960s further extended First Amendment guarantees of distribution through the United States mails. In 1962 the Court overruled the Postmaster, who had refused to accept magazines he himself had judged to be obscene (Manual Enterprises v. Day) *and three years later overturned Post Office practices of delaying unsealed mail from overseas* (Lamont v. Postmaster General).

In the Manual Enterprises *case, Postmaster General Day declared nonmailable certain magazines consisting largely of nude and seminude photographs of male models. The magazine also included photographers' names and addresses and advertisements telling how additional such material might be obtained. The Warren Court by a 6–1 majority declined to support the Postmaster General, but, despite the sizable majority, could not reach a consensus as to the reasons for their decision. Of importance to the study of postal censorship was the concurrence of Justice Brennan, who was joined by Chief Justice Warren and Justice Douglas. Their position was that the Postmaster is not given the authority to decide arbitrarily which publications are obscene and, therefore, nonmailable. A second element is of great importance to the general discussion of literary obscenity. See Chapters 6 and 7. Justice Harlan, joined by Justice Stewart, submitted an additional test to the "prurient interest" criterion of Roth. See Chapter 6. A work must be "patently offensive," they maintained, in order for it to be judged obscene. Even though there was no strong consensus by the Court, it appears clear that the Justices gave greater latitude to freedom of the press by further restricting attempts at governmental censorship.*

In the Lamont decision, the Warren Court in 1965 decided in two cases that it was unconstitutional for postal officials to delay delivery of alleged Communist propaganda as authorized by a 1962 statute. Under the law, addressees, after being informed that the Post Office was holding unsealed matter deemed to be Communist propaganda, would have to specifically request that postal officials forward the matter being detained. It was charged that the Post Office compiled lists of those who requested the alleged propaganda and routinely made these lists available to other government agencies, such as the House Committee on Un-American Activities. The Court by an 8–0 vote held that the act was an unconstitutional infringement on free speech and press.

The steady trend since Hannegan, the landmark case in postal censorship, has been to restrict the powers of the postmaster in deciding what matter is nonmailable and what matter should be denied second-class postal privileges, which are essential to wide periodical circulation. This trend carried through the Warren Court and the 1980s. Other important mail cases, Ginzburg v. United States and United States v. Reidel, are more directly concerned with the Supreme Court's attitude toward obscenity per se and are covered in Chapter 7.

LAMONT V. POSTMASTER GENERAL

FIXA V. HEILBERG
381 U.S. 301 (1965)

JUSTICE DOUGLAS *delivered the opinion of the Court.*

. . . The statute contains an exemption from its provisions for mail addressed to government agencies and educational institutions, or officials thereof, and for mail sent pursuant to a reciprocal cultural international agreement.

To implement the statute the Post Office maintains 10 or 11 screening points through which is routed all unsealed mail from the designated foreign countries. At these points the nonexempt mail is examined by Customs authorities. When it is determined that a piece of mail is "communist political propaganda," the addressee is mailed a notice identifying the mail being detained and advising that it will be destroyed unless the addressee requests delivery by returning an attached reply card within 20 days. . . .

We conclude that the Act as construed and applied is unconstitutional because it requires an official act (*viz.*, returning the reply card) as a limitation on the unfettered exercise of the addressee's First Amendment rights. As stated by Mr. Justice Holmes in *Milwaukee Pub. Co. v. Burleson* (dissenting): "The United States may give up the Post Office when it sees fit, but while it carries it on the use of the mails is almost as much a part of free speech as the right to use our tongues.". . .

. . . We do not have here, any more than we had in *Hannegan v. Esquire, Inc.*, any question concerning the extent to which Congress may classify the mail and fix the charges for its carriage. Nor do we reach the question whether the standard here applied could pass constitutional muster. Nor do we deal with the right of Customs to inspect material from abroad for contraband. We rest on the narrow ground that the addressee in order to receive his mail must request in writing that it be delivered. This amounts in our judgment to an unconstitutional abridgment of the addressee's First Amendment rights. The addressee carries an affirmative obligation which we do not think the Government may impose on him. This requirement is almost certain to have a deterrent effect, especially as respects those who have sensitive positions. Their livelihood may be dependent on a security clearance. Public officials, like schoolteachers who have no tenure, might think they would invite disaster if they read what the Federal Government says contains the seeds of treason. Apart from them, any addressee is likely to feel some inhibition in sending for literature which federal officials have condemned as "communist political propaganda." The regime of this Act is at war with the "uninhibited, robust, and wide-open" debate and discussion that are contemplated by the First Amendment. *New York Times Co. v. Sullivan.* . . .

JUSTICE BRENNAN, *with whom Justice Goldberg joins, concurring.*

. . . It is true that the First Amendment contains no specific guarantee of access to publications. However, the protection of the Bill of Rights goes beyond the specific guarantees to protect from Congressional abridgment those equally fundamental personal rights necessary to make the express guarantees fully meaningful.

I think the right to receive publications is such a fundamental right. The dissemination of ideas can accomplish nothing if otherwise willing addressees are not free to receive and consider them. It would be a barren marketplace of ideas that had only sellers and no buyers. . . .

*   *   *

A key element in the federal government's anti-obscenity drive of the late 1960s was the Federal Anti-Pandering Act, which was passed by the Congress in 1967 to take effect in 1968 and which was ruled upon by the post-Warren Court of 1970. It allowed persons to stop firms from continuing to send through the mails "pandering advertisements" which the recipients consider "erotically arousing or sexually provocative." When persons received such advertisements, they were to inform the Post Office, which, in turn, was to notify the sender to remove that person's name from his mailing lists. Three characteristics of the law should be emphasized. First, only unsolicited advertisements were involved. The law did not include, for example, magazines or other material desired by the addressee. Second, the addressee was to be the sole judge as to the "erotically arousing or sexually provocative" qualities of the advertisement. And third, action to stop the sending of the materials was to be initiated by the addressee, not the government.

Chief Justice Burger, writing for a unanimous Court in Rowan v. Post Office Dept., 397 U.S. 728 (1970), *described the law as a new element in one's right of privacy. In challenging the law, mailers and publishers claimed their freedoms of speech, press, and distribution were being denied. The Chief Justice's answer was that "the asserted right of the mailer . . . stops at the outer boundary of every person's domain." A three-judge federal district court in Los Angeles had previously held the law constitutional. The Supreme Court agreed. Congress had acted in response to parents and others who had claimed their homes were being deluged with advertisements for sexual material they found offensive. The Post Office had said that by 1970, complaints of such material being received through the mails had risen to more than 250,000 per year.*

ROWAN V. POST OFFICE DEPT.
397 U.S. 728 (1970)

CHIEF JUSTICE BURGER *delivered the opinion of the Court.*

. . . The essence of appellants' argument is that the statute violates their constitutional right to communicate. One sentence in appellants' brief perhaps characterizes their entire position:

> The freedom to communicate orally and by the written word and, indeed, in every manner whatsoever is imperative to a free and sane society.

Without doubt the public postal system is an indispensable adjunct of every civilized society and communication is imperative to a healthy social order. But the right of every person "to be let alone" must be placed in the scales with the right of others to communicate.

In today's complex society we are inescapably captive audiences for many purposes, but a sufficient measure of individual autonomy must survive to permit every householder to exercise control over unwanted mail. To make the householder the exclusive and final judge of what will cross his threshold undoubtedly has the effect of impeding the flow of ideas, information and arguments which, ideally, he should receive and consider. Today's merchandising methods, the plethora of mass mailings subsidized by low postal rates, and the growth of the sale of large mailing lists as an industry in itself have changed the mailman from a carrier of primarily private communications, as he was in a more leisurely day, and has made him an adjunct of the mass mailer who sends unsolicited and often unwanted mail into every home. It places no strain on the doctrine of judicial notice to observe that whether measured by pieces or pounds, Everyman's mail today is made up overwhelmingly of material he did not seek from persons he does not know. And all too often it is matter he finds offensive.

In *Martin v. Struthers*, Mr. Justice Black, for the Court, while supporting the "[f]reedom to distribute information to every citizen," acknowledged a limitation in terms of leaving "with the homeowner himself" the power to decide "whether distributors of literature may lawfully call at a home." Weighing the highly important right to communicate, but without trying to determine where it fits into constitutional imperatives, against the very basic right to be free from sights, sounds and tangible matter we do not want, it seems to us that a mailer's right to communicate must stop at the mailbox of an unreceptive addressee.

The Court has traditionally respected the right of a householder to bar, by order or notice, solicitors, hawkers, and peddlers from his property. In this case the mailer's right to communicate is circumscribed only by an affirmative act of the addressee giving notice that he wishes no further mailings from that mailer.

To hold less would tend to license a form of trespass and would make hardly more sense than to say that a radio or television viewer may not twist the dial to cut off an offensive or boring communication and thus bar its entering his home. Nothing in the Constitution compels us to listen to or view any unwanted communication, whatever its merit; we see no basis for according the printed word or pictures a different or more preferred status because they are sent by mail. The ancient concept that "a man's home is his castle" into which "not even the king may enter" has lost none of its vitality, and none of the recognized exceptions includes any right to communicate offensively with another.

Both the absoluteness of the citizen's right under sec. 4009 and its finality are essential; what may not be provocative to one person may well be to another. In operative effect the power of the householder under the statute is unlimited; he or she may prohibit the mailing of a dry goods catalog because he objects to the contents—or indeed the text of the language touting the merchandise. Congress provided this sweeping power not only to protect privacy but to avoid possible constitutional questions that might arise from vesting the power to make any discretionary evaluation of the material in a governmental official.

In effect, Congress has erected a wall—or more accurately permits a citizen to erect a wall—that no advertiser may penetrate without his acquiescence. The continuing operative effect of a mailing ban once imposed presents no constitutional obstacles; the citizen cannot be put to the burden of determining on repeated occasions whether the offending mailer has altered his material so as to make it acceptable. Nor should the householder be at risk that offensive material come into the hands of his children before it can be stopped.

We therefore categorically reject the argument that a vendor has a right under the Constitution or otherwise to send unwanted material into the home of another. If this prohibition operates to impede the flow of even valid ideas, the answer is that no one has a right to press even "good" ideas on an unwilling recipient. That we are often "captives" outside the sanctuary of the home and subject to objectionable speech and other sound does not mean we must be captives everywhere. The asserted right of a mailer, we repeat, stops at the outer boundary of every person's domain. . . .

*   *   *

Eight months after upholding the government's case in Rowan, *the Supreme Court unanimously rejected as unconstitutional the administration's use of two other laws which had been used by the Post Office to block what it termed the flow of pornographic matter through the mails.* Blount v. Rizzi, 400 U.S. 410 (1971). *One allowed the Post Office to deny mail and money orders to persons who, through administrative hearings, were deemed to be dealing in obscene matter. The other allowed for the discontinuance of mail delivery to these same persons while the proceedings were under way.*

The opinion, by Justice Brennan, relied heavily on a 1965 film case, Freedman v. Maryland, *in which the Court established that the First Amendment (1) requires swift review by the courts, rather than simply hearings by governmental agencies in questions of obscenity, and (2) places the heavy burden of proof on the government rather than on the accused. The Mail Box, run by Tony Rizzi of Los Angeles, distributed so-called "girlie magazines," alleged by the Post Office to be obscene. The Book Bin was a distribution firm in Atlanta. In these two cases, three-judge federal courts ruled separately that the postal regulations in question lacked constitutional safeguards. The Supreme Court, deciding both cases together, agreed. Justice Black, long an advocate of the "absolutist" position relative to the First Amendment, concurred in the result, but did not join in the opinion.*

Another postal regulation aimed at obscenity was passed by the Congress in 1970 as part of the Postal Reorganization Act. It became effective in February of 1971. Several questions as to the constitutionality of the law have been raised. Shortly after the effective date, a Los Angeles federal judge issued a temporary restraining order to prohibit the Post Office from enforcing the new regulations.

The 1970 law allows citizens who do not wish to receive "sexually oriented" material to place their names on a list maintained by the Post Office. Publishers and mailers of "sexually oriented" material must purchase these lists and subsequent monthly supplements. Mailings of "sexually oriented" matter to those on the lists would carry a heavy penalty for the mailer.

One of the constitutional problems, of course, is in trying to determine what type of material is legally "sexually oriented." See Ginzburg. *Another is the supposed "chilling effect" such lists have on those in government or other sensitive jobs. See* Lamont. *Differences should be noted between this law and the 1967 law upheld by the Court in* Rowan. *The more recent law restrains the mailer prior to any distribution and calls upon him to make legal, definitive judgments in classifying his material. The 1967 law, on the other hand, requires the recipient to make the judgment as to what is offensive to him personally after he has had an opportunity to inspect the material sent to him from a publishing house. The Court, almost certainly, will have to decide whether these differences, and others, place significant restraints on constitutionally protected expression.*

The Supreme Court has responded to at least one aspect of the 1970 congressional package dealing with distribution of sexual information. In a 1983 ruling, it said that a law banning the mailing of unsolicited information about contraceptives violates First Amendment rights of free speech. Bolger v. Youngs Drug Products Corp. It was a disappointment to the Reagan Administration, which had supported the ban. The case was brought to the courts by Youngs, manufacturer of Trojan prophylactics. Youngs had been warned by the U.S. Postal Service that it could not use the mails to distribute informational advertisements about Trojans. The main arguments in support of the ban were that some recipients would find the material offensive and that some would fall into the hands of teenagers without knowledge or consent of their parents. Justice Marshall, writing for the 8–0 Court, noted that there was a pressing need for birth control information, that teenagers learn about contraceptives from their school health classes, that such information is now readily available in various popular magazines, that condoms are openly displayed on drug store shelves, that the "short journey from the mail box to the trash can" is not too great a burden for those who find such ads objectionable, and that under the Rowan decision of 13 years earlier, persons may go to the post office to demand that companies remove their names from the mailing lists of certain materials they find sexually offensive. The Court thereby continued to extend commercial speech rights under the Constitution. (But see Posadas, handed down later, in Chapter 1.)

Control of broadcast content by the Federal Communications Commission, however, was supported in a major 1978 decision, FCC v. Pacifica. At issue was a 12-minute satirical monologue on language entitled "Filthy Words" by comedian George Carlin which was played on radio station WBAI-FM, the Pacifica outlet in New York. The 5–4 decision suggested that the FCC was warranted in acting against a broadcaster who plays "indecent"—though admittedly not obscene—matter during times young listeners would likely be in the audience. A distinction was made between "censoring" material in advance and "reviewing" content of programs after they were broadcast as a regular part of evaluating the performance of license holders. The Court's opinion, written by Justice Stevens, did not draw parameters around what might be considered "indecent." Dissenting were Justices Stewart, Brennan, White and Marshall. Broadcasters generally have expressed concern over the "chill" such decisions have on selection of material. Are broadcasts, they wonder, to reflect only that which is appropriate for children? It is important to note (1) the lack of guidance from the Court on just what is and what is not "indecent," (2) the fact that on-air warnings about the language used in the monologue did not deter the Court's majority, and (3) the action by the FCC resulted from a single complaint filed by a father driving with his son while listening to the car radio.

FCC V. PACIFICA FOUNDATION
438 U.S. 726 (1978)

JUSTICE STEVENS *delivered the opinion of the Court.*

This case requires that we decide whether the Federal Communications Commission has any power to regulate a radio broadcast that is indecent but not obscene.

A satiric humorist named George Carlin recorded a 12-minute monologue entitled "Filthy Words" before a live audience in a California theater. He began by referring to his thoughts about the "words you couldn't say on the public, ah, airwaves, um, the ones you definitely wouldn't say, ever." He proceeded to list those words and repeat them over and over again in a variety of colloquialisms. The transcript of the recording indicates frequent laughter from the audience.

At about 2 o'clock in the afternoon on Tuesday, October 30, 1973, a New York radio station owned by respondent, Pacifica Foundation, broadcast the "Filthy Words" monologue. A few weeks later a man, who stated that he had heard the broadcast while driving with his young son, wrote a letter complaining to the Commission. He stated that, although he could perhaps understand the "record's being sold for private use, I certainly cannot understand the broadcast of same over the air that, supposedly, you control."

The complaint was forwarded to the station for comment. In its response, Pacifica explained that the monologue had been played during a program about contemporary society's attitude toward language and that immediately before its broadcast listeners had been advised that it included "sensitive language which might be regarded as offensive to some." Pacifica characterized George Carlin as "a significant social satirist" who "like Twain and Sahl before him, examines the language of ordinary people. . . . Carlin is not mouthing obscenities, he is merely using words to satirize as harmless and essentially silly our attitudes towards those words." Pacifica states that it was not aware of any other complaints about the broadcast.

The Commission did not impose formal sanctions, but it did state that the order would be "associated with the station's license file, and in the event that subsequent complaints are received, the Commission will then decide whether it should utilize any of the available sanctions it has been granted by Congress.". . .

The relevant statutory questions are whether the Commission's action is forbidden "censorship" within the meaning of 47 U.S.C. sec. 326 and whether speech that concededly is not obscene may be restricted as "indecent.". . .

The prohibition against censorship unequivocally denies the Commission any power to edit proposed broadcasts in advance and to excise material considered inappropriate for the airwaves. The prohibition, however, has never been construed to deny the Commission the power to review the content of completed broadcasts in the performance of its regulatory duties. . . .

The only other statutory question presented by this case is whether the afternoon broadcast of the "Filthy Words" monologue was indecent within the meaning of sec. 1464. . . .

The plain language of the statute does not support Pacifica's argument. The words "obscene, indecent, or profane" are written in the disjunctive, implying that each has a separate meaning. . . .

. . . [O]ur review is limited to the question whether the Commission has the authority to proscribe this particular broadcast. . . .

It is true that the Commission's order may lead some broadcasters to censor themselves. At most, however, the Commission's definition of indecency will deter only the broadcasting of patently offensive references to excretory and sexual organs and activities. While some of these references may be protected, they surely lie at the periphery of First Amendment concern.

When the issue is narrowed to the facts of this case, the question is whether the First Amendment denies government any power to restrict the public broadcast of indecent language in any circumstances. For if the government has any such power, this was an appropriate occasion for its exercise.

The words of the Carlin monologue are unquestionably "speech" within the meaning of the First Amendment. It is equally clear that the Commission's objections to the broadcast were based in part on its content. The order must therefore fall if, as Pacifica argues, the First Amendment prohibits all governmental regulation that depends on the content of speech. Our past cases demonstrate, however, that no such absolute rule is mandated by the Constitution. . . .

The question of this case is whether a broadcast of patently offensive words dealing with sex and excretion may be regulated because of its content. Obscene materials have been denied the protection of the First Amendment because their content is so offensive to contemporary moral standards. *Roth v. United States.* . . .

Although these words ordinarily lack literary, political, or scientific value, they are not entirely outside the protection of the First Amendment. Some uses of even the most offensive words are unquestionably protected. Indeed, we may assume, *arguendo*, that this monologue would be protected in other contexts. Nonetheless, the constitutional protection accorded to a communication containing such patently offensive sexual and excretory language need not be the same in every context. It is a characteristic of speech such as this that both its capacity to offend and its "social value," to use Mr. Justice Murphy's term, vary with the circumstances. Words that are commonplace in one setting are shocking in another. To paraphrase Mr. Justice Harlan, one occasion's lyric is another's vulgarity. *Cohen v. California.*

In this case it is undisputed that the content of Pacifica's broadcast was "vulgar," "offensive," and "shocking." Because content of that character is not entitled to absolute constitutional protection under all circumstances, we must consider its context in order to determine whether the Commission's action was constitutionally permissible.

We have long recognized that each medium of expression presents special First Amendment problems. *Joseph Burstyn, Inc. v. Wilson.* And of all forms of communication, it is broadcasting that has received the most limited First Amendment protection. . . .

. . . First, the broadcast media have established a uniquely pervasive presence in the lives of all Americans. Patently offensive, indecent material presented over the airwaves confronts the citizen, not only in public, but also in the privacy of the home, where the individual's right to be let alone plainly outweighs the First Amendment rights of an intruder. *Rowan v. Post Office Department.* Because the broadcast audience is constantly tuning in and out, prior warnings cannot completely protect the listener or viewer from unexpected program content. To say that one may avoid further offense by turning off the radio when he hears indecent language is like saying that the remedy for an assault is to run away after the first blow. One may hang up on an indecent phone call, but the option does not give the caller a constitutional immunity or avoid a harm that has already taken place.

Second, broadcasting is uniquely accessible to children, even those too young to read. Although Cohen's written message might have been incomprehensible to a first grader, Pacifica's broadcast could have enlarged a child's vocabulary in an instant. Other forms of offensive expression may be withheld from the young without restricting the expression at its source. Bookstores and motion picture theaters, for example, may be prohibited from making indecent material available to children. We held in *Ginsberg v. New York* that the government's interest in the "well being of its youth" and in supporting "parents' claim to authority in their own household" justified the regulation of otherwise protected expression. The ease with which children may obtain access to broadcast material, coupled with the concerns recognized in *Ginsberg,* amply justify special treatment of indecent broadcasting.

It is appropriate, in conclusion, to emphasize the narrowness of our holding. This case does not involve a two-way radio conversation between a cab driver and a dispatcher, or a telecast of an Elizabethan comedy. We have not decided that an occasional expletive in either setting would justify any sanction or, indeed, that this broadcast would justify a criminal prosecution. The Commission's decision rested entirely on a nuisance rationale under which context is all-important. The concept requires consideration of a host of variables. The time of day was emphasized by the Commission. The content of the program in which the language is used will also affect the composition of the audience, and differences between radio, television, and perhaps closed circuit transmissions, may also be relevant. As Mr. Justice Sutherland wrote, a "nuisance may be merely a right thing in the wrong place— like a pig in the parlor instead of the barnyard." *Euclid v. Ambler Realty Co.* We simply hold that when the Commission finds that a pig has entered the parlor, the exercise of its regulatory power does not depend on proof that the pig is obscene.

The judgment of the Court of Appeals is reversed.

JUSTICE POWELL, *with whom Justice Blackmun joins, concurring.*

. . . The Commission's holding does not prevent willing adults from purchasing Carlin's record, from attending his performances, or, indeed, from reading the transcript reprinted as an appendix to the Court's opinion. On its face, it does not prevent respondent from broadcasting the monologue during late evening hours when fewer children are likely to be in the audience, nor from broadcasting discussions of the contemporary use of language at any time during the day. The Commission's holding, and certainly the Court's holding today, does not speak to cases involving the isolated use of a potentially offensive word in the course of a radio broadcast, as distinguished from the verbal shock treatment administered by respondent here. . . .

. . . [H]owever, . . . I do not subscribe to the theory that the Justices of this Court are free generally to decide on the basis of its content which speech protected by the First Amendment is most "valuable" and hence deserving of the most protection, and which is less "valuable" and hence deserving of less protection. In my view, the result in this case does not turn on whether Carlin's monologue, viewed as a whole, or the words that comprise it, have more or less "value" than a candidate's campaign speech. This is a judgment for each person to make, not one for the judges to impose upon him.

The result turns instead on the unique characteristics of the broadcast media, combined with society's right to protect its children from speech generally agreed to be inappropriate for their years, and with the interest of unwilling adults in not being assaulted by such offensive speech in their homes. . . .

JUSTICE BRENNAN, *with whom Justice Marshall joins, dissenting.*

. . . I find the Court's misapplication of fundamental First Amendment principles so patent, and its attempt to impose *its* notions of propriety on the whole of the American people so misguided, that I am unable to remain silent.

For the second time in two years, see *Young v. American Mini Theatres*, the Court refuses to embrace the notion, completely antithetical to basic First Amendment values, that the degree of protection the First Amendment affords protected speech varies with the social value ascribed to that speech by five Members of this Court. Moreover, as do all parties, all Members of the Court agree that the Carlin monologue aired by Station WBAI does not fall within one of the categories of speech, such as "fighting words," *Chaplinsky v. New Hampshire*, or obscenity, *Roth v. United States*, that is totally without First Amendment protection. . . .

. . . Yet despite the Court's refusal to create a sliding scale of First Amendment protection calibrated to this Court's perception of the worth of a communication's content, and despite our unanimous agreement that the Carlin monologue is protected speech, a majority of the Court nevertheless finds that, on the facts of this case, the FCC is not constitutionally barred from imposing sanctions on Pacifica for its airing of the Carlin monologue. This majority apparently believes that the

FCC's disapproval of Pacifica's afternoon broadcast of Carlin's "Dirty Words" recording is a permissible time, place, and manner regulation. . . .

. . . Whatever the minimal discomfort suffered by a listener who inadvertently tunes into a program he finds offensive during the brief interval before he can simply extend his arm and switch stations or flick the "off" button, it is surely worth the candle to preserve the broadcaster's right to send, and the right of those interested to receive, a message entitled to full First Amendment protection. To reach a contrary balance, as does the Court, is clearly, to follow Mr. Justice Stevens' reliance on animal metaphors, "to burn the house to roast the pig."

The Court's balance, of necessity, fails to accord proper weight to the interests of listeners who wish to hear broadcasts the FCC deems offensive. It permits majoritarian tastes completely to preclude a protected message from entering the homes of a receptive, unoffended minority. No decision of this Court supports such a result. Where the individuals comprising the offended majority may freely choose to reject the material being offered, we have never found their privacy interests of such moment to warrant the suppression of speech on privacy grounds. . . .

Because the Carlin monologue is obviously not an erotic appeal to the prurient interests of children, the Court, for the first time, allows the government to prevent minors from gaining access to materials that are not obscene, and are therefore protected, as to them. . . .

. . . As surprising as it may be to individual Members of this Court, some parents may actually find Mr. Carlin's unabashed attitude towards the seven "dirty words" healthy, and deem it desirable to expose their children to the manner in which Mr. Carlin defuses the taboo surrounding the words. Such parents may constitute a minority of the American public, but the absence of great numbers willing to exercise the right to raise their children in this fashion does not alter the right's nature or its existence. Only the Court's regrettable decision does that. . . .

Today's decision will . . . have its greatest impact on broadcasters desiring to reach, and listening audiences comprised of, persons who do not share the Court's view as to which words or expressions are acceptable and who, for a variety of reasons, including a conscious desire to flout majoritarian conventions, express themselves using words that may be regarded as offensive by those from different socioeconomic backgrounds. In this context, the Court's decision may be seen for what, in the broader perspective, it really is: another of the dominant culture's inevitable efforts to force those groups who do not share its mores to conform to its way of thinking, acting, and speaking. . . .

JUSTICE STEWART, *with whom Justice Brennan, Justice White, and Justice Marshall join, dissenting.*

. . . I would hold . . . that Congress intended, by using the word "indecent" in [the statute] to prohibit nothing more than obscene speech. Under that reading of the statute, the Commission's order in this case was not authorized, and on that basis I would affirm the judgment of the Court of Appeals.

*   *   *

Also in 1978, the Court in an 8–0 decision again supported the FCC in its regulatory role. The Commission had prohibited future joint ownership of newspaper and broadcasting combinations within the same community and also divestiture of certain existing combinations. FCC v. National Citizens Committee for Broadcasting. The NCCB, while supporting the thrust of the FCC move, brought the action hoping the Court would require divestiture of all existing combinations, not just those singled out by the FCC. The Supreme Court, in an opinion by Justice Marshall, opted for the balancing of interests in siding with the FCC.

As we entered the decade of the '80s and with the election of President Reagan, the move to deregulate the broadcasting industry was hastened. (See also Chapter 5, which follows.) The FCC recommended changes in the Communications Act which, among other things, would repeal the Equal Time Provision, which broadcasters have been opposing for years. Those recommendations went to the Congress for consideration. In the meantime, the FCC was relaxing its own internal procedures and requirements for radio licenses. For example, "ascertainment"—the requirement of community opinion and need surveys—was dropped as were policies of reviewing the radio time devoted to news and public affairs and to advertising. Cable also was being deregulated as it was expanding.

The Supreme Court also was adding to the deregulation movement during this period. In a 1984 decision, the Court held that public radio and television stations could not be barred from editorializing. FCC v. League of Women Voters. In another of the Burger Court's 5–4 splits, Justice Brennan, writing for the majority, said that the importance of being "fully and broadly" informed on matters of public concern is paramount and that the laws which prohibit noncommercial stations receiving public funds from delivering editorials had to give way to this greater need. The law was challenged by the Pacifica Foundation and the League of Women Voters. Joining Justice Brennan to make up the majority were Justices Blackmun, Marshall, Powell and O'Connor.

The significance of these moves, along with those which certainly will come from the FCC and the Congress in the 1990s, will not be known soon. And the question remains of television's place in deregulation and what effect it will have on content and viewer reaction.

The legality of private, noncommercial video recording in the home was the subject of a 1984 ruling by the Supreme Court. Sony v. Universal City Studios. In a severely divided 5–4 ruling, the Court held that such use is not an infringement of copyright, thereby reversing a ruling of the Ninth Circuit Court of Appeals. Justice Stevens focused not on constitutional questions, but on the copyright law, the "fair use" aspects of that law and the "time-shifting" advantages of VCRs, which were being installed in millions of the nation's homes each year. He did, however, invite Congress to re-examine the law in light of this popular new technology, an invitation the Congress accepted.

The case had been closely followed because of its enormous financial and *philosophical impact on the entertainment industry and the fact that it involved several industry giants—Sony, Universal Studios and Walt Disney Productions. Joining Justice Stevens in the majority was an interesting combination of Justice White, conservative Justices Burger and O'Connor, and liberal Justice Brennan. Dissenting were Justices Blackmun, Marshall, Powell and Rehnquist.*

SONY CORP. V. UNIVERSAL CITY STUDIOS
464 U.S. 417 (1984)

JUSTICE STEVENS *delivered the opinion of the Court.*

Petitioners manufacture and sell home video tape recorders. Respondents own the copyrights on some of the television programs that are broadcast on the public airwaves. Some members of the general public use video tape recorders sold by petitioners to record some of these broadcasts, as well as a large number of other broadcasts. The question presented is whether the sale of petitioners' copying equipment to the general public violates any of the rights conferred upon respondents by the Copyright Act. . . .

The respondents and Sony both conducted surveys of the way the Betamax machine was used by several hundred owners during a sample period in 1978. Although there were some differences in the surveys, they both showed that the primary use of the machine for most owners was "time-shifting,"—the practice of recording a program to view it once at a later time, and thereafter erasing it. Time-shifting enables viewers to see programs they otherwise would miss because they are not at home, are occupied with other tasks, or are viewing a program on another station at the time of a broadcast that they desire to watch. Both surveys also showed, however, that a substantial number of interviewees had accumulated libraries of tapes. Sony's survey indicated that over 80% of the interviewees watched at least as much regular television as they had before owning a Betamax. Respondents offered no evidence of decreased television viewing by Betamax owners. . . .

The lengthy trial of the case in the District Court concerned the private, home use of VTR's for recording programs broadcast on the public airwaves without charge to the viewer. No issue concerning the transfer of tapes to other persons, the use of home-recorded tapes for public performances, or the copying of programs transmitted on pay or cable television systems was raised. . . .

The District Court concluded that noncommercial home use recording of material broadcast over the public airwaves was a fair use of copyrighted works and did not constitute copyright infringement. It emphasized the fact that the material was broadcast free to the public at large, the noncommercial character of the use, and the private character of the activity conducted entirely within the home. Moreover, the court found that the purpose of this use served the public interest in increasing access to television programming, an interest that "is consistent with the First Amendment policy of providing the fullest possible access to information through the public airwaves. *Columbia Broadcasting System, Inc. v. Democratic National Committee.* Even when an entire copyrighted work was recorded, the District Court regarded the copying as fair use "because there is no accompanying reduction in the market for 'plaintiff's original work.' " *Ibid.*

As an independent ground of decision, the District Court also concluded that Sony could not be held liable as a contributory infringer even if the home use of a VTR was considered an infringing use. The District Court noted that Sony had no direct involvement with any Betamax purchasers who recorded copyrighted works off the air. Sony's advertising was silent on the subject of possible copyright infringement, but its instruction booklet contained the following statement:

> "Television programs, films, videotapes and other materials may be copyrighted. Unauthorized recording of such material may be contrary to the provisions of the United States copyright laws." *Id.* . . .

As the text of the Constitution makes plain, it is Congress that has been assigned the task of defining the scope of the limited monopoly that should be granted to authors or to inventors in order to give the public appropriate access to their work product. Because this task involves a difficult balance between the interests of authors and inventors in the control and exploitation of their writings and discoveries on the one hand, and society's competing interest in the free flow of ideas, information, and commerce on the other hand, our patent and copyright statutes have been amended repeatedly.

From its beginning, the law of copyright has developed in response to significant changes in technology. Indeed, it was the invention of a new form of copying equipment—the printing press—that gave rise to the original need for copyright protection. Repeatedly, as new developments have occurred in this country, it has been the Congress that has fashioned the new rules that new technology made necessary. Thus, long before the enactment of the Copyright Act of 1909, it was settled that the protection given to copyrights is wholly statutory. The remedies for infringement "are only those prescribed by Congress." *Thompson v. Hubbard.*

The judiciary's reluctance to expand the protections afforded by the copyright without explicit legislative guidance is a recurring theme.

When these factors are all weighed in the "equitable rule of reason" balance, we must conclude that this record amply supports the District Court's conclusion that home time-shifting is fair use. In light of the findings of the District Court regarding the state of the empirical data, it is clear that the Court of Appeals erred in holding that the statute as presently written bars such conduct.

In summary, the record and findings of the District Court lead us to two conclusions. First, Sony demonstrated a significant likelihood that substantial numbers of copyright holders who license their works for broadcast on free television would not object to having their broadcasts time-shifted by private viewers. And second, respondents failed to demonstrate that time-shifting would cause any likelihood of nonminimal harm to the potential market for, or the value of, their copyrighted works. The Betamax is, therefore, capable of substantial noninfringing uses. Sony's sale of such equipment to the general public does not constitute contributory infringement of respondent's copyrights. . . .

One may search the Copyright Act in vain for any sign that the elected representatives of the millions of people who watch television every day have made it unlawful to copy a program for later viewing at home, or have enacted a flat prohibition against the sale of machines that make such copying possible.

It may well be that Congress will take a fresh look at this new technology, just as it so often has examined other innovations in the past. But it is not our job to apply laws that have not yet been written. Applying the copyright statute, as it now reads, to the facts as they have been developed in this case, the judgment of the Court of Appeals must be reversed.

It is so ordered.

JUSTICE BLACKMUN, *with whom Justice Marshall, Justice Powell, and Justice Rehnquist join, dissenting.*

. . . The doctrine of fair use has been called, with some justification, "the most troublesome in the whole law of copyright." Although courts have constructed lists of factors to be considered in determining whether a particular use is fair, no fixed criteria have emerged by which that determination can be made. This Court thus far has provided no guidance; although fair use issues have come here twice, on each occasion the Court was equally divided and no opinion was forthcoming.

Nor did Congress provide definitive rules when it codified the fair use doctrine in the 1976 Act; it simply incorporated a list of factors "to be considered": the "purpose and character of the use," the "nature of the copyrighted work," the "amount and substantiality of the portion used," and, perhaps the most important, the "effect of the use upon the *potential* market for or value of the copyrighted work" (emphasis supplied). No particular weight, however, was assigned to any of these, and the list was not intended to be exclusive. The House and Senate Reports explain that sec. 107 does no more than give "statutory recognition" to the fair use doctrine; it was intended "to restate the present judicial doctrine of fair use, not to change, narrow, or enlarge it in any way."

Despite this absence of clear standards, the fair use doctrine plays a crucial role in the law of copyright. The purpose of copyright protection, in the words of the Constitution, is to "promote the Progress of Science and useful Arts." Copyright is based on the belief that by granting authors the exclusive rights to reproduce their works, they are given an incentive to create, and that "encouragement of individual effort by personal gain is the best way to advance public welfare through the talents of authors and inventors in 'Science and the useful Arts.' " The monopoly created by copyright thus rewards the individual author in order to benefit the public.

There are situations, nevertheless, in which strict enforcement of this monopoly would inhibit the very "Progress of Science and useful Arts" that copyright is intended to promote. An obvious example is the researcher or scholar whose own work depends on the ability to refer to and to quote the work of prior scholars. Obviously, no author could create a new work if he were first required to repeat the research of every author who had gone before him. The scholar, like the ordinary user, of course could be left to bargain with each copyright owner for permission to quote from or refer to prior works. But there is a crucial difference between the scholar and the ordinary user. When the ordinary user decides that the owner's price is too high, and forgoes use of the work, only the individual is the loser. When the scholar forgoes the use of a prior work, not only does his own work suffer, but the public is deprived of his contribution to knowledge. The scholar's work, in other words, produces external benefits from which everyone profits. In such a case, the fair use doctrine acts as a form of subsidy—albeit at the first author's expense—to permit the second author to make limited use of the first author's work for the public good. . . .

The making of a videotape recording for home viewing is an ordinary rather than a productive use of the Studios' copyrighted works. The District Court found that "Betamax owners use the copy for the same purpose as the original. They add nothing of their own."

. . . Courts should move with caution, however, in depriving authors of protection from unproductive "ordinary" uses. . . . Although such a use may seem harmless when viewed in isolation, "[i]solated instances of minor infringements, when multiplied many times, become in the aggregate a major inroad on copyright that must be prevented."

I therefore conclude that, at least when the proposed use is an unproductive one, a copyright owner need prove only a *potential* for harm to the market for or the value of the copyrighted work. . . .

*   *   *

Another copyright decision involving the "fair use" principle was handed down by the Court the following year. Harper & Row v. Nation Enterprises. *It is a decision which should be of particular interest to reporters and editors who quote from material when copyright protection might be an issue. In 1977, former President Gerald Ford contracted with Harper & Row to publish his memoirs, including elements of the Nixon pardon. Magazine rights were sold to* Time. *Shortly before the* Time *article was to run,* The Nation *obtained an unauthorized copy of the manuscript and published extensive excerpts from it. In a 6–3 decision, the Court held that such publication was not "fair use."* The Nation *had claimed that the newsworthiness of the account qualified under the "fair use" privilege. The Court disagreed. Writing for the majority was Justice O'Connor. Dissenting were Justices Brennan, Marshall and White.*

HARPER & ROW V. NATION
471 U.S. 539 (1985)

JUSTICE O'CONNOR *delivered the opinion of the Court.*

This case requires us to consider to what extent the "fair use" provision of the Copyright Revision Act of 1976, 17 U.S.C. sec. 107 (hereinafter the Copyright Act), sanctions the unauthorized use of quotations from a public figure's unpublished manuscript. In March 1979, an undisclosed source provided *The Nation* magazine with the unpublished manuscript of A *Time to Heal: The Autobiography of Gerald R. Ford*. Working directly from the purloined manuscript, an editor of *The Nation* produced a short piece entitled "The Ford Memoirs—Behind the Nixon Pardon." The piece was timed to "scoop" an article scheduled shortly to appear in *Time* magazine. *Time* had agreed to purchase the exclusive right to print prepublication excerpts from the copyright holders, Harper & Row Publishers, Inc. (hereinafter Harper & Row) and Reader's Digest Association, Inc. (hereinafter Reader's Digest). As a result of *The Nation* article, *Time* canceled its agreement. Petitioners brought a successful copyright action against *The Nation*. On appeal, the Second Circuit reversed the lower court's finding of infringement, holding that *The Nation's* act was sanctioned as a "fair use" of the copyrighted material. We granted certiorari, and we now reverse. . . .

. . . [Victor Navasky, editor of *The Nation*,] hastily put together what he believed was "a real hot news story" composed of quotes, paraphrases and facts drawn exclusively from the manuscript. Mr. Navasky attempted no independent commentary, research or criticism, in part because of the need for speed if he was to "make news" by "publish[ing] in advance of publication of the Ford book." The 2,250 word article, reprinted in the Appendix to this opinion, appeared on April 3, 1979. As a result of *The Nation's* article, *Time* canceled its piece and refused to pay the remaining $12,500. . . .

The District Court rejected respondents' argument that *The Nation's* piece was a "fair use" sanctioned by the Act. Though billed as "hot news," the article contained no new facts. The magazine had "published its article for profit," taking "the heart" of "a soon-to-be-published" work. This unauthorized use "caused the *Time* agreement to be aborted and thus diminished the value of the copyright." . . .

[T]he *Nation* has admitted to lifting verbatim quotes of the author's original language totalling between 300 and 400 words and constituting some 13% of *The Nation* article. In using generous verbatim excerpts of Mr. Ford's unpublished manuscript to lend authenticity to its account of the forthcoming memoirs, *The Nation* effectively arrogated to itself the right of first publication, an important marketable subsidiary right. For the reasons set forth below, we find that this use of the copyrighted manuscript, even stripped to the verbatim quotes conceded by *The*

Nation to be copyrightable expression, was not a fair use within the meaning of the Copyright Act.

Fair use was traditionally defined as "a privilege in others than the owner of the copyright to use the copyrighted material in a reasonable manner without his consent." H. Ball. . . .

Fair use is a mixed question of law and fact. . . . The four factors identified by Congress as especially relevant in determining whether the use was fair are: (1) the purpose and character of the use; (2) the nature of the copyrighted work; (3) the substantiality of the portion used in relation to the copyrighted work as a whole; (4) the effect on the potential market for or value of the copyrighted work. We address each one separately. . . .

. . . In arguing that the purpose of news reporting is not purely commercial, *The Nation* misses the point entirely. The crux of the profit/nonprofit distinction is not whether the sole motive of the use is monetary gain but whether the user stands to profit from exploitation of the copyrighted material without paying the customary price. . . .

In evaluating character and purpose we cannot ignore *The Nation's* stated purpose of scooping the forthcoming hardcover and *Time* abstracts. *The Nation's* use had not merely the incidental effect but the *intended purpose* of supplanting the copyright holder's commercially valuable right of first publication. . . . Also relevant to the "character" of the use is "the propriety of the defendant's conduct." "Fair use presupposes 'good faith' and 'fair dealing.' " The trial court found that *The Nation* knowingly exploited a purloined manuscript. Unlike the typical claim of fair use, *The Nation* cannot offer up even the fiction of consent as justification. Like its competitor newsweekly, it was free to bid for the right of abstracting excerpts from *A Time to Heal*. Fair use "distinguishes between 'a true scholar and a chiseler who infringes a work for personal profit.' "

Second, the Act directs attention to the nature of the copyrighted work. A *Time to Heal* may be characterized as an unpublished historical narrative or autobiography. The law generally recognizes a greater need to disseminate factual works than works of fiction or fantasy. . . . Some of the briefer quotes from the memoir are arguably necessary adequately to convey the facts; for example, Mr. Ford's characterization of the White House tapes as the "smoking gun" is perhaps so integral to the idea expressed as to be inseparable from it. But *The Nation* did not stop at isolated phrases and instead excerpted subjective descriptions and portraits of public figures whose power lies in the author's individualized expression. Such use, focusing on the most expressive elements of the work, exceeds that necessary to disseminate the facts.

The fact that a work is unpublished is a critical element of its "nature." Our prior discussion establishes that the scope of fair use is narrower with respect to unpublished works. While even substantial quotations might qualify as fair use in a review of a published work or a news account of a speech that had been delivered to the public or disseminated to the press, . . . the author's right to control the first public appearance of his expression weighs against such use of the work before its release. The right of first publication encompasses not only the choice whether to publish at all, but also the choices when, where and in what form first to publish a work.

In the case of Mr. Ford's manuscript, the copyright holders' interest in confidentiality is irrefutable; the copyright holders had entered into a contractual undertaking to "keep the manuscript confidential" and required that all those to whom the manuscript was shown also "sign an agreement to keep the manuscript confidential." While the copyright holders' contract with *Time* required *Time* to submit its proposed article seven days before publication, *The Nation's* clandestine publication afforded no such opportunity for creative or quality control. It was hastily patched together and contained "a number of inaccuracies." A use that so clearly infringes the copyright holder's interests in confidentiality and creative control is difficult to characterize as "fair."

Next, the Act directs us to examine the amount and substantiality of the portion used in relation to the copyrighted work as a whole. . . .

Stripped to the verbatim quotes, the direct takings from the unpublished manuscript constitute at least 13% of the infringing article. . . . *The Nation* article is structured around the quoted excerpts which serve as its dramatic focal points. . . .

Finally, the Act focuses on "the effect of the use upon the potential market for or value of the copyrighted work." This last factor is undoubtedly the single most important element of fair use. . . . "Fair use, when properly applied, is limited to copying by others which does not materially impair the marketability of the work which is copied." Nimmer. . . . Rarely will a case of copyright infringement present such clear-cut evidence of actual damage. Petitioners assured *Time* that there would be no other authorized publication of *any* portion of the unpublished manuscript prior to April 23, 1979. *Any* publication of material from chapters 1 and 3 would permit *Time* to renegotiate its final payment. . . .

More important, to negate fair use one need only show that if the challenged use "should become widespread, it would adversely affect the *potential* market for the copyrighted work." *Sony Corp. v. Universal City Studios, Inc.* . . .

JUSTICE BRENNAN, *with whom Justice White and Justice Marshall join, dissenting.*

. . . [I]nfringement of copyright must be based on a taking of literary form, as opposed to the ideas or information contained in a copyrighted work. Deciding whether an infringing appropriation of literary form has occurred is difficult for at least two reasons. First, the distinction between literary form and information or ideas is often elusive in practice. Second, infringement must be based on a *substantial* appropriation of literary form. This determination is equally challenging. Not surprisingly, the test for infringement has defied precise formulation. In general, though, the inquiry proceeds along two axes: *how closely* has the second author tracked the first author's particular language and structure of presentation; and *how much* of the first author's language and structure has the second author appropriated. . . .

The article does not mimic Mr. Ford's structure. The information *The Nation* presents is drawn from scattered sections of the Ford work and does not appear in the sequence in which Mr. Ford presented it. Some of *The Nation's* discussion of the pardon does roughly track the order in which the Ford manuscript presents information about the pardon. With respect to this similarity, however, Mr. Ford has done no more than present the facts chronologically and cannot claim infringement when a subsequent author similarly presents the facts of history in a chronological manner. Also, it is difficult to suggest that a 2000-word article could bodily appropriate the structure of a 200,000-word book. Most of what Mr. Ford created, and most of the history he recounted, was simply not represented in *The Nation's* article.

When *The Nation* was not quoting Mr. Ford, therefore, its efforts to convey the historical information in the Ford manuscript did not so closely and substantially track Mr. Ford's language and structure as to constitute an appropriation of literary form. . . .

The Nation's purpose in quoting 300 words of the Ford manuscript was, as the Court acknowledges, news reporting. The Ford work contained information about important events of recent history. Two principals, Mr. Ford and General Alexander Haig, were at the time of *The Nation's* publication in 1979 widely thought to be candidates for the Presidency. That *The Nation* objectively reported the information in the Ford manuscript without independent commentary in no way diminishes the conclusion that it was reporting news. A typical news story differs from an editorial precisely in that it presents newsworthy information in a straightforward and unelaborated manner. Nor does the source of the information render *The Nation's* article any less a news report. Often books and manuscripts, solicited and unsolicited, are the subject matter of news reports. Frequently the manuscripts are unpublished at the time of the news report.

Section 107 lists news reporting as a prime example of fair use of another's expression. Like criticism and all other purposes Congress explicitly approved in sec. 107, news reporting informs the public; the language of sec. 107 makes clear that Congress saw the spread of knowledge and information as the strongest justification for a properly limited appropriation of expression. The Court of Appeals was therefore correct to conclude that the purpose of *The Nation's* use— dissemination of the information contained in the quotations of Mr. Ford's work— furthered the public interest. In light of the explicit congressional endorsement in sec. 107, the purpose for which Ford's literary form was borrowed strongly favors a finding of fair use.

The Court concedes the validity of the news reporting purpose, but then quickly offsets it against three purportedly countervailing considerations. First, the Court asserts that because *The Nation* publishes for profit, its publication of the

Ford quotes is a presumptively unfair commercial use. Second, the Court claims that *The Nation's* stated desire to create a 'news event' signalled an illegitimate purpose of supplanting the copyright owner's right of first publication. . . .

. . . A news business earns its reputation, and therefore its readership, through consistent prompt publication of news—and often through "scooping" rivals. . . . The record suggests only that *The Nation* sought to be the first to reveal the information in the Ford manuscript. *The Nation's* stated purpose of scooping the competition should under those circumstances have no negative bearing on the claim of fair use. Indeed the Court's reliance on this factor would seem to amount to little more than distaste for the standard journalistic practice of seeking to be the first to publish news. . . .

BROADCAST JOURNALISM: AT THE
CROSSROADS OF FREEDOM

By William S. Paley*

. . . [O]ne of the great battles that broadcast journalism has been fighting in this country, since its beginning in the late 1920s, has been to establish the principle that a free press must be inclusive if it is to serve its common purpose in a free society. This means recognition that journalism transmitted over the air should not, for that reason, be inhibited by government, any more than the print media should be, from informing the people, from contributing and stimulating informed discussion among them and from helping to enable them to take the action essential to effective self-government.

The fight for this recognition—and it is a battle we in broadcasting are still fighting—has not been easy. In the first place, broadcast stations are licensed by the Federal government. Originally, this was for technical reasons—to avoid chaos in the use of the airwaves—a fact that has often been forgotten. There was also believed to be a quantitative factor involved—"the scarcity principle," which, as I shall point out later, has turned out to be more theoretical than real. This centered on the technical fact that there had to be, in the spectrum, some limit on the number of broadcasting stations, whereas there was no technical limit on the number of newspapers that could be printed. As it turned out, economic realities came to be more limiting in newspaper publishing than technical realities did in broadcasting.

In the actual evolution of broadcasting as an information medium, however, I think that most broadcasters were far less concerned with theoretic considerations than with a respect for its sheer strength as a medium. Consequently, we saw it as our clear responsibility to protect the public from the misuse of broadcasting as a result either of government interference or pressure or of possible selfish or biased interests of broadcasters themselves. At CBS—and I think generally throughout broadcasting—the principles of fairness in dealing with news and public affairs— as well as other guidelines to assure responsible broadcasting in this area—were voluntarily and painstakingly arrived at and put into practice. At the same time it was—and remains—our firm conviction that what constitutes fairness should be determined by those responsible for the operations of the media and not by a

---

* From an address by William S. Paley, Founder and Chairman, CBS, Inc., delivered at the dedication of the Newhouse Communications Center, Syracuse University, May 31, 1974. Used with permission of CBS.

governmental agency policing them and imposing upon them its own definitions and its own arbitrary rulings.

The long and continuing struggle of broadcast journalism to assert and maintain its position as part of the free press has centered very largely on this issue: whether defining and resolving problems of fairness should be left, under the principles of the First Amendment, to broadcasters, who are answerable to their audiences, vulnerable to their competitors and exposed to constant public criticism, or whether it should be left to a government agency to determine these matters.

Historically, the Fairness Doctrine was not formally enunciated as a policy of the Federal Communications Commission until 1949, when it was adopted as part of an FCC report upholding the right of broadcast licensees to editorialize. The purpose of the Fairness Doctrine was to insure that the exercise of the right to editorialize did not lead to rampant bias on the air. The new policy was designed not to repress the expression of opinion but on the contrary to stimulate a multiplicity of opinions. Despite its good intentions, however, the Fairness Doctrine had implicit dangers in that it conferred upon a government agency the power to judge a news organization's performance. In recent years, this danger has become real as the FCC began considering complaints on a broadcast-by-broadcast basis, almost line-by-line and minute-by-minute. One station, for example, was ruled unfair because the FCC found that, on one news program, "approximately 425 lines were devoted to expression of views opposing the legalization of casino gambling whereas approximately 115 lines were devoted to the proponent's views." Inevitably, such super-editing by a government agency has become a vexing symbol of broadcasting's second-class citizenship in journalism. Misapplication of the principle became a springboard for attack on the media by various government officials for purposes unrelated to the original concept of fairness. Such attacks, if they had not been resisted, would long since have led to the weakening of broadcasting as an arm of the free press and have destroyed its ability to function as an effective tool of democratic life and growth. In recent years the symptoms of broadcast journalism's second-class status have become so clear as to reveal how the Fairness Doctrine can be used as a device to influence the content of news and public affairs broadcasting.

This is not a matter of seeing ghosts lurking in every corner. Consider some of the actions and trends emerging in just the past five years, to restrict or condition the freedom of broadcasting to operate fully and freely in the public interest—as the press always has—undirected by judicial commands, unhampered by bureaucratic reviews, unchallenged by administrative probings and unthreatened by executive reprisals.

In 1969 the Supreme Court decided that the FCC had the power under the Fairness Doctrine to promulgate its so-called "personal attack" rules, which require broadcasters to follow automatic notification and requirements for time to reply whenever the "honesty, character, integrity" of a person or group is questioned. While certain news broadcasts are exempt from the rules, First Amendment values are, nevertheless, compromised when a governmental commission becomes the final arbitrator of journalistic fairness and can prescribe the remedy. Recent events demonstrate the fundamental danger of lodging with a governmental commission—however well intentioned it may be—the power to review and penalize broadcasters as a result of a finding that a particular news broadcast was "unfair."

Already attempts have been made to extend the principle to entertainment and advertising. To cite a recent example in entertainment, perhaps one of the most distinguished dramas ever presented on television, "The Autobiography of Miss Jane Pittman," the story of a former slave, was the subject of a complaint demanding time on the grounds that it put whites in an unfavorable light—a complaint which the FCC wisely rejected. In commercials, some complaints under the Fairness Doctrine have assumed the militant guise of "counteradvertising." Unsatisfied with broad-gauged existing restraints on deceptive advertising, they would demand that, under the Fairness Doctrine, free time be provided opponents of a company or a product or service on the vaguest grounds conceivable. The implications of this are clear: it could, by reducing broadcasting as an effective advertising medium, so endanger its economic viability as to reduce its effectiveness in all other respects, including its journalistic role. . . .

The intrusion of the government into the content and style of broadcast journalism has led to an open season of attacks upon the basic principle of the free press: namely, that what is published—whether on the printed page or over the air—is best left to those doing the publishing and any judgment as to its interest and value is best left to the people reading, hearing or seeing it.

Few Presidential administrations, in my experience, have been consistently pleased with the press: all want to be constantly approved and admired. But that is not the function of the press, and previous administrations, though often displeased with the press, did not seek to undermine or punish it. The startling fact of the [Nixon] Administration is that, virtually from its inception, it [had] launched a systematic effort to discredit both the objectives and the conduct of those journalists whose treatment of the news it disapproves. None of the news media has been immune to verbal onslaughts from the White House; but broadcast journalism, in particular, has been subjected to unprecedented direct threats to inhibit, weaken and disable it. Even though not all these threats have been actually put into practice and none have succeeded in their motives, they are nevertheless shocking and frightening in their implications. They have been directed at impugning the integrity of able and respected reporters; at setting up monitoring systems, whose findings were to determine whether agencies of the Federal government could be used to investigate and intimidate the offending media; also at splitting networks from their affiliates by threatening non-renewal of the latter's licenses; and at weakening the economic basis of costly broadcast news operations by clumsy appeals to advertisers to boycott networks and stations which fail to report the news as the White House sees it.

As the history of this continuous campaign to undermine broadcast journalism has unfolded, the inescapable impression emerges that there are those in positions of power and trust who are, from all appearances, against a free press—and that they are against it, not just because they *think* it will distort some facts, but also because they *know* that it will disclose others.

So I say, with all the strength at my command, that the time has now come to eliminate entirely the Fairness Doctrine from government rule books or statutes. In spite of the fact that the FCC has shown moderation in putting it to use, the very fact that the Fairness Doctrine confers on a government agency the power to sit in judgment over news broadcasts makes it a tempting device for use by any administration in power to influence the content of broadcast journalism.

Meanwhile, broadcast journalism is continuing to carry out its mission of honest, thorough and responsible reporting. It continues to rate high in the public confidence. And there is surfacing a growing sense that the Fairness Doctrine has outlived its usefulness. Broadly recognized as the leading constitutional authority in the United States Senate, Sam Ervin has characterized the enforced fairness concept as "a fickle affront to the First Amendment" and strongly urged an inquiry "to consider how to move broadcasting out of the Government control. . . ." In a landmark 7–2 decision last year, the Supreme Court emphatically rejected the contentions of those who would impose even more restrictive obligations on broadcasters. It declared, "The question here is not whether there is to be discussion of controversial issues of public importance on the broadcast media, but rather who shall determine what issues are to be discussed by whom, and when. . . . For better or worse, editing is what editors are for; and editing is selection and choice of materials," and it goes on: "If we must choose whether editorial decisions are to be made in the free judgment of individual broadcasters, or imposed by bureaucratic fiat, the choice must be for freedom." The Chairman of the FCC, Richard Wiley, has indicated his receptiveness to studying the suspending of the Fairness Doctrine in areas where there are a sufficient number of licenses. And Senator Pastore, Chairman of the Senate Subcommittee on Communications, has taken an open-minded view in announcing his proposal to hold hearings to reexamine the policy.

In addition to the offense done the freedom of broadcast journalism by fairness enforced by government, the arithmetic of the communications field today offers convincing evidence that the scarcity principle has no validity as grounds for enforced fairness. On the contrary, it calls for clear and outright repeal of the Doctrine. A sparseness of broadcast outlets, as compared to daily newspapers, no longer exists. As a matter of fact, the situation is inverted. When the regulatory powers over broadcasting were first enacted in 1927, there were 677 broadcasting stations in the United States and 1,949 daily newspapers. Today there are 8,434 broadcasting stations and 1,774 daily newspapers. The multiplicity of voices heard over these stations—two-thirds of which have no network affiliation—far exceeds that provided by any mass medium at any time in our history. The vast majority of news and public affairs broadcasts originates with the thousands of local stations, whether or not they have network affiliations. Americans spend, in an average week, 555 million hours watching television news broadcasts. Of these hours, 394 million are spent on locally produced news and 161 million hours on network news broadcasts. In radio the ratio of locally produced to network produced news is overwhelming, all but a small fraction is local.

There is, furthermore, a very little overlapping of control of broadcast stations by newspapers: 19 percent of the 934 television stations are owned by newspapers, and 7 percent of the 7,500 radio stations. And there are just as many national television networks as there are wire services or national general news weeklies. In addition, of course, broadcast journalism must compete for public confidence with all the newspapers, as well as monthly, quarterly, biweekly and weekly periodicals, also books and newsletters, and educational, civic, professional, and other meetings. All of these add to the giant mix that conveys, appraises or interprets information and presents and discusses issues. The possibility of any major news source consistently distorting or misusing its function in the face of all these other competing forces for enlightenment is virtually non-existent. This pluralism constitutes the strongest safeguard that a free society can have against abuses of freedom of the press.

A free people just does not tolerate persistent bias if it has such a wide range of free choices. And never in the history of communications has a medium been as wholly susceptible to watch-dogging by the entire population. A further check on the overall fairness of broadcast journalism is that it is consistently and universally subjected to review and criticism. Every major newspaper in the United States reports every day on how broadcasting is doing its job and who is doing it—often faulting us, occasionally praising us, but never ignoring us. Most general interest magazines add their comments and criticisms every week and every month. A hundred and thirty-four publications—daily, weekly, monthly and quarterly—deal exclusively or to a major extent with broadcasting; and their circulation runs into millions. Letters from private citizens, running into thousands every week, clearly indicate that the public consider themselves our real supervisors and do not hesitate to let us know how well or how fairly they think we're carrying out our jobs. At CBS News—as I am sure at other broadcast news organizations—we have carefully thought out guidelines, continuous reviews of our work and formal procedures to make certain that we are doing it responsibly. And the fact is that we seem to be doing it well. Independently run public opinion polls at regular intervals question the American people as to the degree of their confidence in broadcast journalism. The last such poll revealed that the largest number by far, 56 percent, considered broadcasting the most believable news media of all.

In a free society, this pluralism, this watchfulness and this competition among literally hundreds of news sources for public confidence constitute the forces that are the true judges of broadcasting's fairness and should be the only ones. Government should simply—as a matter of asserted national policy consistent with what I believe to be the spirit of the First Amendment—repudiate the Fairness Doctrine and specifically immunize news and public affairs broadcasting from any form of governmental oversight or supervision whatsoever.

Twenty years ago—almost to the day—I had occasion to address myself to the freedom and responsibility of broadcasters. I said then, "Some people may question the desirability of placing in the hands of the broadcaster this important element of control. To this point I would say that undoubtedly there may be abuses, as there are in other media. But I for one have enough faith in the vitality of the democratic process, in the intelligence of the American people and in the freshness of the competitive climate to believe that the goodwill and the determined intent of broadcasters to be fair, coupled with the powerful voice of the people, will provide far better protection against abuse than any other form of control."

Nothing during the past 20 years has led me to change my mind or to qualify those words.

If there is any risk—and there is—in this belief that, to quote Jefferson's words, ". . . the people . . . may safely be trusted to hear everything true and false, and to form a correct judgment between them"—and there is a risk—then it is the risk basic and continuous in any free society. But it has been the verdict of our forebears and the experience of ourselves that a free society is not the safest way of life: it is only the best.

AMERICAN TELEVISION: PURVEYOR OF DAYDREAMS

BY MARTIN ESSLIN AND MILLICENT DILLON*

Television as it now exists in the U.S. has created a unique historical situation, says Martin Esslin, internationally known drama critic and professor of drama at Stanford in *The Age of Television* (*The Portable Stanford*, 136 pp. $5.85 paper). "For the first time the least intellectually developed segment of society is dictating the intellectual level of society's chief medium of information and communication." Esslin analyzes and criticizes American television as an outsider, a European-born British citizen who was the head of BBC radio drama for 13 years until his retirement six years ago. "I don't want to appear to be an arrogant European intellectual, feeling superior, because I don't feel superior. I am concerned about America; I feel it's the world's hope," he said in a recent campus interview.

To Esslin television presents a danger with long-term consequences that are political, economic, cultural, and psychological. At the same time, he asserts, the very character of television tends to trivialize the danger. The dramatic nature of television, Esslin writes, induces a schizophrenic state of mind, blunting the distinction between the real and fictional. "The viewer who from his grandstand seat at the TV window sees wars, acts of terrorism, murders, and executions—reality turned into thrilling entertainment—is kept in a schizophrenic state of mind the reverse of that produced by soap operas and series, which are fictions perceived not only as fictions but also, at the same time, as realities that are more real events in the real world." In his analysis of television as a medium that is essentially dramatic, Esslin points out that soap operas and series operate at the level of "communal daydreams." "TV reflects the collective unconscious of the American people, reflects it rather than trying to come to grips with it. And it reflects it at the lowest level of intellectual life and the lowest level of psychic life," Esslin says.

Conversely, TV news itself loses claim to objectivity, as it too becomes only another program shaped to titillate and excite the viewer in dramatic terms. Citing the takeover of the American embassy in Iran, Esslin notes that in television "the perpetrators of these actions find an almost ideal field for publicizing themselves, especially when the moment for the final assault or hostage exchange arrives, and everything is in place and can be fully and minutely shown on the TV screen. In

* From "American Television: Purveyor of Daydreams that Transmute Reality." *The Stanford Observer*, Vol. 16, No. 1 (October 1981). Used with permission of *The Stanford Observer*, Harry Press, editor. The article was based on an interview by writer Millicent Dillon. Esslin is Professor of Drama at Stanford University and former head of BBC radio drama.

the end the terrorists might be said to be actually working for television by providing the thrills and the violence that enable the news shows to compete with fictional thrillers and an endless stream of often sadomasochistic drama. Here, then, the nature of television as an entertainment medium actually dictates the development of events in the real world." In this process, Esslin suggests, for the viewer the entire political process becomes less real, utterly remote, and beyond the influence of individual participation.

The present commercial structure of American television, pandering to the lowest common denominator, has solidified this process. "A very large industry which makes enormous capital investments is devoted to making the population more stupid and to demeaning their sensibilities, thereby undoing the effects of education itself." According to Esslin, everyone in the U.S. acts as if the present commercial structure were God-given, but in fact the development of that structure was a matter of chance economic and social and political factors at the time of the birth of the broadcasting industry. "The most terrifying thing is the almost universal acceptance in this country of the situation as it is. And it is very curious that no one has taken the trouble to look at how this problem has been solved in other countries."

In Britain, he points out, completely different situations arose, in large part because of the effect of one man, Lord John Reith, the first general manager of the BBC. Reith invented a new kind of public body: an organization established by the state but independent of it in its daily operation, and financed directly by its users through the license fee. The corporation is controlled by a board of governors who are appointed by the Queen for five-year terms. The Royal Charter forbids the BBC to raise any money by advertising.

The argument that government financing results in government control is a specious one to Esslin. In his 15 years as director of BBC drama—for radio and TV—he remembers one occasion when a play had to be referred to the director of BBC. "The one time I remember was in connection with a play by Harold Pinter that was scheduled to be put on at the Aldrich Theater. At that time the censors could still challenge the language of a play. There was one line in the play in which a character used a then unacceptable word. The word changed. Pinter said, 'I won't change it.' I read about this in the paper and asked Pinter if he'd like the play done on radio. 'Only if the word is left in,' he said. I rang up the Director-General. 'I've got this problem,' I told him. The Director-General asked to see the play and two days later returned it to me with a note that it was okay, that the words were essential to the artistic integrity of the play. So I broadcast it the way it was written. No Heavens fell upon me. I think I got one letter of protest."

Esslin acknowledges, however, that in his position at BBC he did go to great lengths not to expose children to extreme violence or pornography. "But it was the kind of consideration any editor must give to his material. Finally it's a matter of searching one's own conscience."

Esslin's strongest attack in his book is devoted to children's programming on TV. "Children's cartoons are scandalous, terribly ugly, badly drawn, and terribly brutal—and they are embedded in advertisements for junk food." Again, he insists, it's a matter of the profit motive. "Now mind you," he says, "I'm not against the capitalist system; in fact I'm a great supporter of it, since I've seen the way Eastern European countries have worked out. But what I am arguing for is the necessity for choice, for the end of the dictatorship of the majority. The point is that in England there is an alternative channel. One channel is set up for mass appeal. The other is not. "On BBC 2 it's possible to say, 'I'd like to do this program. I think it won't get more than five percent of the viewers. But even five percent is two and a half million people. That's a helluva lot of people. And think what it would be in the U.S."

"In theory," writes Esslin, "the United States already has a mixed system. However, in practice, The Public Broadcasting Service has no stable financial base and has not yet succeeded in building up a network that can effectively and on an equal basis compete with the commercial system—equal in the sense of providing as full and well-balanced a service, complete with news, documentaries, drama, arts programs, etc., as do public service networks in other countries. "The solution to the problem clearly lies in finding an acceptable basis for the financing of such a full public broadcasting system. If, as usually argued, the license fee system so widely used and so fully accepted in Europe would be politically unacceptable in the U.S., alternative means of funding could be found. A small tax on all TV sets, for example, would yield substantial annual revenues. . . . Or there could be a special tax on the profits of the commercial networks to go to the public system. Any of these methods of financing would be preferable to a direct government grant that has to be budgeted annually, which subjects public television service to direct political pressure."

Esslin concludes by saying, "The absence of an adequately funded public television service in the U.S. in an age when other nations are in a position to make much fuller use of the positive potential of so powerful a medium amounts to no less than a national tragedy. "Surely the essence of a democracy lies in its ability to change conditions that have been recognized as immoral, harmful, or degrading. The wasteland of television is not an unalterable feature of the American land-scape. It is man-made and therefore not beyond the range of determined social and political action."

CHAPTER **5**

PUBLIC ACCESS
TO THE MASS MEDIA

A question of the public's right of access to the mass media received two significant stimulants in the late 1960s. The first was a 1967 article in the Harvard Law Review *by Jerome A. Barron, Professor of Law at George Washington University, who became the best known spokesman for the position favoring guaranteed public access to the media. The second was a 1969 Supreme Court decision,* Red Lion Broadcasting Co. v. The FCC, *in which the Court without dissent strongly supported the FCC's "fairness doctrine." Speculation immediately followed that such a concept might, indeed, be applied also to the print media. But the Justices five years later in* Miami Herald v. Tornillo *unanimously declined to expand their broadcast "right of reply" requirement to newspapers, pointing to conditions which distinguish the two media.*

In the Red Lion *decision, the last media decision to be handed down by the Warren Court, two significant principles regarding First Amendment freedoms and the broadcaster were announced. First, the Court held that the unique nature of broadcasting requires standards of First Amendment interpretation different from those applied to the print media. This, in effect, extended to broadcasting the Court's 1961* Times Film *principle, which applied separate standards of freedom of expression to motion pictures. The Radio Television News Directors Association and many individual broadcasters had argued for several years that free speech standards be applied uniformly to all media, electronic and print. The court rejected that appeal. Second, and reflecting the principle mentioned above, the Court ruled that enforcement of the FCC's fairness doctrine does not violate First Amendment guarantees of the broadcaster. The thrust of the First Amendment, the Court said, is aimed at protecting the listening and viewing citizen rather than the licensed broadcaster. The fairness doctrine requires that when a person is attacked on radio or television he must be given an opportunity to reply. The decision was 7–0. Justice Douglas did not take part because of absence during oral arguments, and Justice*

Fortas' resignation earlier that spring left the Court with one vacant seat at the time of the decision. Two years later, in June of 1971, the FCC announced its intention to review the fairness doctrine and asked interested persons to submit statements. The Commission dropped the doctrine in the 1980s. Congress attempted to make the fairness doctrine a part of Federal law, but the bill was vetoed by President Reagan.

RED LION BROADCASTING CO. V. FEDERAL COMMUNICATIONS COMMISSION

UNITED STATES V. RADIO TELEVISION NEWS DIRECTORS ASSN. 395 U.S. 367 (1969)

JUSTICE WHITE *delivered the opinion of the Court.*

. . . *Red Lion* involves the application of the fairness doctrine to a particular broadcast, and *RTNDA* arises as an action to review the FCC's 1967 promulgation of the personal attack and political editorializing regulations, which were laid down after the *Red Lion* litigation had begun.

. . . The Red Lion Broadcasting Company is licensed to operate a Pennsylvania radio station, WGCB. On November 27, 1964, WGCB carried a 15-minute broadcast by Reverend Billy James Hargis as part of a "Christian Crusade" series. A book by Fred J. Cook entitled *Goldwater—Extremist on the Right* was discussed by Hargis, who said that Cook had been fired by a newspaper for fabricating false charges against city officials; that Cook had then worked for a Communist-affiliated publication; that he had defended Alger Hiss and attacked J. Edgar Hoover and the Central Intelligence Agency; and that he had now written a "book to smear and destroy Barry Goldwater." When Cook heard of the broadcast he concluded that he had been personally attacked and demanded free reply time, which the station refused. After an exchange of letters among Cook, Red Lion, and the FCC, the FCC declared that the Hargis broadcast constituted a personal attack on Cook; that Red Lion had failed to meet its obligation under the fairness doctrine. . . .

The [RTNDA] broadcasters challenge the fairness doctrine and its specific manifestations in the personal attack and political editorial rules on conventional First Amendment grounds, alleging that the rules abridge their freedom of speech and press. Their contention is that the First Amendment protects their desire to use their allotted frequencies continuously to broadcast whatever they choose, and to exclude whomever they choose from ever using that frequency. No man may be prevented from saying or publishing what he thinks, or from refusing in his speech or other utterances to give equal weight to the views of his opponents. This right, they say, applies equally to broadcasters.

Although broadcasting is clearly a medium affected by a First Amendment interest, *United States v. Paramount Pictures, Inc.*, differences in the characteristics of new media justify differences in the First Amendment standards applied to them. *Joseph Burstyn, Inc. v. Wilson.* For example, the ability of new technology to produce sounds more raucous than those of the human voice justifies restrictions on the sound level, and on the hours and places of use, of sound trucks so long as the restrictions are reasonable and applied without discrimination. *Kovacs v. Cooper.*

Just as the Government may limit the use of sound amplifying equipment potentially so noisy that it drowns out civilized private speech, so may the Government limit the use of broadcast equipment. The right of free speech of a broadcaster, the user of a sound truck, or any other individual does not embrace a right to snuff out the free speech of others. *Associated Press v. United States.*

. . . Because of the scarcity of radio frequencies, the Government is permitted to put restraints on licensees in favor of others whose views should be expressed on this unique medium. But the people as a whole retain their interest in free speech by radio and their collective right to have the medium function consistently with the ends and purposes of the First Amendment. It is the right of the viewers and listeners, not the right of the broadcasters, which is paramount. It is the purpose of the First Amendment to preserve an uninhibited marketplace of ideas in which truth will ultimately prevail, rather than to countenance monopolization of that market, whether it be by the Government itself or a private licensee. . . . It is the right of the public to receive suitable access to social, political, esthetic, moral, and other ideas and experiences which is crucial here. . . .

In terms of constitutional principle, and as enforced sharing of a scarce resource, the personal attack and political editorial rules are indistinguishable from the equal-time provision of sec. 315, a specific enactment of Congress requiring stations to set aside reply time under specified circumstances and to which the fairness doctrine and these constituent regulations are important complements. That provision, which has been part of the law since 1927, Radio Act of 1927, has been held valid by this Court as an obligation of the licensee relieving him of any power in any way to prevent or censor the broadcast, and thus insulating him from liability for defamation. The constitutionality of the statute under the First Amendment was unquestioned.

Nor can we say that it is inconsistent with the First Amendment goal of producing an informed public capable of conducting its own affairs to require a broadcaster to permit answers to personal attacks occurring in the course of discussing controversial issues, or to require that the political opponents of those endorsed by the station be given a chance to communicate with the public. Otherwise, station owners and a few networks would have unfettered power to make time available only to the highest bidders, to communicate only their own views on public issues, people and candidates, and to permit on the air only those with whom they agreed. There is no sanctuary in the First Amendment for unlimited private censorship operating in a medium not open to all. . . .

In view of the prevalence of scarcity of broadcast frequencies, the Government's role in allocating those frequencies, and the legitimate claims of those unable without governmental assistance to gain access to those frequencies for expression of their views, we hold the regulations and ruling at issue here are both authorized by statute and constitutional. The judgment of the Court of Appeals in *Red Lion* is affirmed and that in *RTNDA* reversed and the causes remanded for proceedings consistent with this opinion.

*   *   *

A series of four major decisions relative to the First Amendment and access to the media by those who sought to advertise surfaced in 1973 with the complex CBS v. Democratic National Committee *decision, handed down along with* FCC v. Business Executives' Move for a Vietnam Peace. *In the following two years the Court dealt with political ads on a public transportation line and abortion ads in a newspaper, both of which follow. Rejected by the Court in* CBS v. DNC *was the argument that the First Amendment and the public nature of broadcasting compel broadcasters to accept advertising on issues of public importance. The Justices wrote five separate opinions attempting to explain their various views in siding with the broadcasters, who had argued that they should retain control over the commercials they air. Seven Justices generally favored the judgment of the Court, but would concur with only parts of Chief Justice Burger's opinion. Dissenting were Justices Brennan and Marshall. The question had received extensive debate because of the potential impact on broadcasting generally, the broader question of guaranteed access to the media by various interested groups, and the political nature of the two groups seeking access in these particular cases—one a major political party and the other an anti-war organization.*

CBS V. DEMOCRATIC NATIONAL COMMITTEE

BUSINESS EXECUTIVES' MOVE FOR A VIETNAM PEACE V. FCC
412 U.S. 94 (1973)

CHIEF JUSTICE BURGER *delivered the opinion of the Court.*

We granted the writ in these cases to consider whether a broadcast licensee's general policy of not selling advertising time to individuals or groups wishing to speak out on issues they consider important violates the Federal Communications Act of 1934 or the First Amendment.

In two orders announced the same day, the Federal Communications Commission ruled that a broadcaster who meets his public obligation to provide full and fair coverage of public issues is not required to accept editorial advertisements. A divided Court of Appeals reversed the Commission, holding that a broadcaster's fixed policy of refusing editorial advertisements violates the First Amendment; the court remanded the cases to the Commission to develop procedures and guidelines for administering a First Amendment right of access. . . .

Balancing the various First Amendment interests involved in the broadcast media and determining what best serves the public's right to be informed is a task of a great delicacy and difficulty. The process must necessarily be undertaken within the framework of the regulatory scheme that has evolved over the course of the past half-century. For during that time, Congress and its chosen administrative agency have established a delicately balanced system of regulation intended to serve the interests of all concerned. The problems of regulation are rendered more difficult because the broadcast industry is dynamic in terms of technological change; solutions adequate a decade ago are not necessarily so now, and those acceptable today may well be outmoded 10 years hence. . . . The judgment of the legislative branch cannot be ignored or undervalued simply because one segment of the broadcast constituency casts its claims under the umbrella of the First Amendment. That is not to say we "defer" to the judgment of the Congress and the Commission on a constitutional question, nor that we would hesitate to invoke the Constitution should we determine that the Commission has not fulfilled its task with appropriate sensitivity to the interests in free expression. The point is, rather, that when we face a complex problem with many hard questions and few easy answers we do well to pay careful attention to how the other branches of government have addressed the same problem. . . .

As we have seen, with the advent of radio a half century ago Congress was faced with a fundamental choice between total government ownership and control of the new medium—the choice of most other countries—or some other alternative. Long before the impact and potential of the medium was realized, Congress opted for a system of private broadcasters licensed and regulated by Government. The legislative history suggests that this choice was influenced not only by traditional attitudes toward private enterprise, but by a desire to maintain for licensees, so far as consistent with necessary regulation, a traditional journalistic role. . . .

The tensions inherent in such a regulatory structure emerge more clearly when we compare a private newspaper with a broadcast licensee. The power of a privately owned newspaper to advance its own political, social, and economic views is bounded by only two factors: first, the acceptance of a sufficient number of readers—and hence advertisers—to assure financial success; and, second, the journalistic integrity of its editors and publishers. A broadcast licensee has a large measure of journalistic freedom but not as large as that exercised by a newspaper. A licensee must balance what it might prefer to do as a private entrepreneur with what it is required to do as a "public trustee." To perform its statutory duties, the Commission must oversee without censoring. This suggests something of the difficulty and delicacy of administering the Communications Act—a function calling for flexibility and the capacity to adjust and readjust the regulatory mechanism to meet changing problems and needs.

The licensee policy challenged in this case is intimately related to the journalistic role of a licensee for which it has been given initial and primary responsibility by Congress. The licensee's policy against accepting editorial advertising cannot be examined as an abstract proposition, but must be viewed in the context of its journalistic role. It does not help to press on us the idea that editorial ads are "like" commercial ads for the licensee's policy against editorial spot ads is expressly based on a journalistic judgment that 10 to 60 second spot announcements are ill suited to intelligible and intelligent treatment of public issues; the broadcaster has chosen to provide a balanced treatment of controversial questions in a more comprehensive form. Obviously the licensee's evaluation is based on its own journalistic judgment of priorities and newsworthiness.

Moreover, the Commission has not fostered the licensee policy challenged here; it has simply declined to command particular action because it fell within the area of journalistic discretion. The Commission explicitly emphasized that "there is of course no Commission policy thwarting the sale of time to comment on public issues." The Commission's reasoning, consistent with nearly 40 years of precedent, is that so long as a licensee meets its "public trustee" obligation to provide balanced coverage of issues and events, it has broad discretion to decide how that obligation will be met. . . .

There remains for consideration the question whether the "public interest" standard of the Communications Act requires broadcasters to accept editorial advertisements or, whether, assuming governmental action, broadcasters are required to do so by reason of the First Amendment. In resolving those issues, we are guided by the "venerable principle that the construction of a statute by those charged with its execution should be followed unless there are compelling indications that it is wrong. . . ." *Red Lion.*

The Commission was justified in concluding that the public interest in providing access to the marketplace of "ideas and experiences" would scarcely be served by a system so heavily weighted in favor of the financially affluent, or those with access to wealth. Even under a first-come-first-served system, proposed by the dissenting Commissioner in these cases, the views of the affluent could well prevail over those of others, since they would have it within their power to purchase time more frequently. Moreover, there is the substantial danger, as the Court of Appeals acknowledged, that the time allotted for editorial advertising could be monopolized by those of one political persuasion. . . .

If the Fairness Doctrine were applied to editorial advertising, there is also the substantial danger that the effective operation of that doctrine would be jeopardized. To minimize financial hardship and to comply fully with its public responsibilities a broadcaster might well be forced to make regular programming time available to those holding a view different from that expressed in an editorial advertisement; indeed, BEM has suggested as much in its brief. The result would be a further erosion of the journalistic discretion of broadcasters in the coverage of public issues, and a transfer of control over the treatment of public issues from the licensees who are accountable to private individuals who are not. The public interest would no longer be "paramount" but rather subordinate to private whim especially since, under the Court of Appeals' decision, a broadcaster would be largely precluded from rejecting editorial advertisements that dealt with matters trivial or insignificant or already fairly covered by the broadcaster. . . .

Nor can we accept the Court of Appeals' view that every potential speaker is "the best judge" of what the listening public ought to hear or indeed the best judge of the merits of his or her views. All journalistic tradition and experience is to the contrary. For better or worse, editing is what editors are for; and editing is selection and choice of material. That editors—newspaper or broadcast—can and do abuse this power is beyond doubt, but that is not reason to deny the discretion Congress provided. Calculated risks of abuse are taken in order to preserve higher values. The presence of these risks is nothing new; the authors of the Bill of Rights accepted the reality that these risks were evils for which there was no acceptable remedy other than a spirit of moderation and a sense of responsibility—and civility—on the part of those who exercise the guaranteed freedoms of expression. . . .

Under a constitutionally commanded and government supervised right-of-access system urged by respondents and mandated by the Court of Appeals, the Commission would be required to oversee far more of the day-to-day operations of broadcasters' conduct, deciding such questions as whether a particular individual or group has had sufficient opportunity to present its viewpoint and whether a particular viewpoint has already been sufficiently aired. Regimenting broadcasters is too radical a therapy for the ailment respondents complain of.

Under the Fairness Doctrine the Commission's responsibility is to judge whether a licensee's overall performance indicates a sustained good faith effort to meet the public interest in being fully and fairly informed. The Commission's responsibilities under a right-of-access system would tend to draw it into a continuing case-by-case determination of who should be heard and when. . . .

The Commission is also entitled to take into account the reality that in a very real sense listeners and viewers constitute a "captive audience." The "captive" nature of the broadcast audience was recognized as early as 1924, when Commerce Secretary Hoover remarked at the Fourth National Radio Conference that "the radio listener does not have the same opinion that the reader of publications has—to ignore advertising in which he is not interested—and he may resent its invasion on his set." As the broadcast media became more pervasive in our society, the problem has become more acute. . . .

Conceivably at some future date Congress or the Commission—or the broadcasters—may devise some kind of limited right of access that is both practicable and desirable. Indeed, the Commission noted in these proceedings that the advent of cable television will afford increased opportunities for the discussion of public issues. . . .

For the present the Commission is conducting a wide-ranging study into the effectiveness of the Fairness Doctrine to see what needs to be done to improve the coverage and presentation of public issues on the broadcast media. . . .

JUSTICE DOUGLAS.

While I join the Court in reversing the judgment below, I do so for quite different reasons.

My conclusion is that the TV and radio stand in the same protected position under the First Amendment as do newspapers and magazines. The philosophy of the First Amendment requires that result, for the fear that Madison and Jefferson had of government intrusion is perhaps even more relevant to TV and radio than it is to newspapers and other like publications. . . .

JUSTICE BRENNAN, *with whom Justice Marshall concurs, dissenting.*

. . . As a practical matter, the Court's reliance on the Fairness Doctrine as an "adequate" alternative to editorial advertising seriously overestimates the ability— or willingness—of broadcasters to expose the public to the "widest possible dissemination of information from diverse and antagonistic sources." As Professor Jaffe has noted, "there is considerable possibility that the broadcaster will exercise a large amount of self-censorship and try to avoid as much controversy as he safely can." Indeed, in light of the strong interest of broadcasters in maximizing their audience, and therefore their profits, it seems almost naive to expect the majority of broadcasters to produce the variety and controversiality of material necessary to reflect a full spectrum of viewpoints. Stated simply, angry customers are not good customers and, in the commercial world of mass communications, it is simply "bad business" to espouse—or even to allow others to espouse—the heterodox or the controversial. As a result, even under the Fairness Doctrine, broadcasters generally tend to permit only established—or at least moderated—views to enter the broadcast world's "marketplace of ideas."

Moreover, the Court's reliance on the Fairness Doctrine as the *sole* means of informing the public seriously misconceives and underestimates the public's interest in receiving ideas and information directly from the advocates of those ideas without the interposition of journalistic middlemen. Under the Fairness Doctrine, broadcasters decide what issues are "important," how "fully" to cover them, and what format, time and style of coverage are "appropriate." The retention of such *absolute* control in the hands of a few government licensees is inimical to the First Amendment, for vigorous, free debate can be attained only when members of the public have at least *some* opportunity to take the initiative and editorial control into their own hands.

Our legal system reflects a belief that truth is best illuminated by a collision of genuine advocates. Under the Fairness Doctrine, however, accompanied by an absolute ban on editorial advertising, the public is compelled to rely *exclusively* on the "journalistic discretion" of broadcasters, who serve in theory as surrogate spokesmen for all sides of all issues. This separation of the advocate from the expression of his views can serve only to diminish the effectiveness of that expression. . . .

Nor is this case concerned solely with the adequacy of coverage of those views and issues which generally are recognized as "newsworthy." For also at stake is the right of the public to receive suitable access to new and generally unperceived ideas and opinions. Under the Fairness Doctrine, the broadcaster is required to present only *representative* community views and voices on controversial issues" of public importance. Thus, by definition, the Fairness Doctrine tends to perpetuate coverage of those "views and voices" that are already established, while failing to provide for exposure of the public to those "views and voices" that are novel, unorthodox or unrepresentative of prevailing opinion.

Finally, it should be noted that the Fairness Doctrine permits, indeed *requires*, broadcasters to determine for themselves which views and issues are sufficiently "important" to warrant discussion. The briefs of the broadcaster-petitioners in this case illustrate the type of "journalistic discretion" licensees now exercise in this regard. Thus, ABC suggests that it would refuse to air those views which *it* considers "scandalous" or "crackpot," while CBS would exclude those issues or opinions that are "insignificant" or "trivial." Similarly, NBC would bar speech that strays "beyond the bounds of normally accepted taste," and WTOP would protect the public from subjects that are "slight, parochial or inappropriate."

The genius of the First Amendment, however, is that it has always defined what the public ought to hear by permitting speakers to say what they wish. . . .

. . . [T]he *absolute* ban on editorial advertising seems particularly offensive because, although broadcasters refuse to sell any airtime whatever to groups or individuals wishing to speak out on controversial issues of public importance, they make such airtime readily available to those "commercial" advertisers who seek to peddle their goods and services to the public. Thus, as the system now operates, any person wishing to market a particular brand of beer, soap, toothpaste, or deodorant has direct, personal, and instantaneous access to the electronic media. He can present his own message, in his own words, in any format he selects and at a time of his own choosing. Yet a similar individual seeking to discuss war, peace, pollution, or the suffering of the poor is denied this right to speak. Instead, he is compelled to rely on the beneficence of a corporate "trustee" appointed by the Government to argue his case for him. . . .

*   *   *

The second of the access-through-advertising questions involved a candidate for state office in Ohio who sought to place his political advertising on vehicles of the public transit system of the city of Shaker Heights. Lehman v. Shaker Heights. He was refused on the basis of a policy which denied such access to political advertising. Metromedia, Inc. was the agency handling this account for the city. Henry J. Lehman argued that this refusal was a denial of his First Amendment rights as a candidate for public office, pointing to the acceptance by the transit line of commercial product advertising, the public nature of the transit system, and the importance to a democratic society of the electoral function. The Justices by a 5–4 vote, however, disagreed, though a majority could not agree on the reasons. Speaking for the plurality was Justice Blackmun, who was joined by Justices Burger, Rehnquist, and

White. Justice Douglas wrote a separate concurring opinion in which he focused on the question of the rider's right of privacy.

*   *   *

The third advertising/First Amendment decision in three years came as the Court neared its 1975 summer recess. Bigelow v. Virginia. The question here involved a state law which prohibited newspapers from running advertisements on abortion services. Jeffrey C. Bigelow, publisher of a Charlottesville weekly newspaper, was convicted under such a law. The Supreme Court held 7–2, however, that the Virginia law was unconstitutional. Such advertising, the Court held, is protected by the First Amendment because it deals with "matters of clear public interest." Justice Blackmun, writing for the majority, attempted to distinguish between the "public interest" type of advertising and that which attempts to sell commercial products only. While conceding that advertising generally can fall under more strict regulation than can non-commercial matter, the Court pointed to its landmark 1964 Times v. Sullivan decision and ruled that the mere purchase of newspaper space did not per se erase the potential for First Amendment protection. Dissenting were Justices Rehnquist and White, both of whom, incidentally, dissented also in the controversial 1973 abortion decision, Roe v. Wade.

BIGELOW V. VIRGINIA
421 U.S. 809 (1975)

JUSTICE BLACKMUN *delivered the opinion of the Court.*

An advertisement carried in appellant's newspaper led to his conviction for a violation of a Virginia statute that made it a misdemeanor, by the sale or circulation of any publication, to encourage or prompt the procuring of an abortion. The issue here is whether the editor-appellant's First Amendment rights were unconstitutionally abridged by the statute. The First Amendment, of course, is applicable to the States through the Fourteenth Amendment. *Schneider v. State.*

The *Virginia Weekly* was a newspaper published by the Virginia Weekly Associates of Charlottesville. It was issued in that city and circulated in Albemarle County, with particular focus on the campus of the University of Virginia. Appellant, Jeffrey C. Bigelow, was a director and the managing editor and responsible officer of the newspaper. . . .

It is to be observed that the advertisement announced that the Women's Pavilion of New York City would help women with unwanted pregnancies to obtain "immediate placement in accredited hospitals and clinics at low cost" and would "make all arrangements" on a "strictly confidential" basis; that it offered "information and counseling"; that it gave the organization's address and telephone numbers; and that it stated that abortions "are now legal in New York" and there "are no residency requirements." Although the advertisement did not contain the name of any licensed physician, the "placement" to which it referred was to "accredited hospitals and clinics."

On May 13 Bigelow was charged with violating Va. Code Sec. 18.1–63. The statute at that time read:

> "If any person by publication, lecture, advertisement, or by the sale or circulation of any publication, or in any other manner, encourage or prompt the procuring of abortion or miscarriage, he shall be guilty of a misdemeanor." . . .

The central assumption made by the Supreme Court of Virginia was that the First Amendment guarantees of speech and press are inapplicable to paid commercial advertisements. Our cases, however, clearly establish that speech is not stripped of First Amendment protection merely because it appears in that form, *Pittsburgh Press Co. v. Pittsburgh Comm'n on Human Relation, New York Times Co. v. Sullivan.*

The fact that the particular advertisement in appellant's newspaper had commercial aspects or reflected the advertiser's commercial interests did not negate all First Amendment guarantees. The State was not free of constitutional restraint merely because the advertisement involved sales or "solicitation," *Murdock v. Pennsylvania,* or because appellant was paid for printing it, *New York Times Co. v. Sullivan, Smith v. California,* or because appellant's motive or the motive of the advertiser may have involved financial gain, *Thomas v. Collins.* The existence of "commercial activity, in itself, is no justification for narrowing the protection of expression secured by the First Amendment." *Ginzburg v. United States.*

Although other categories of speech—such as fighting words, *Chaplinski v. New Hampshire,* or obscenity, *Roth v. United States, Miller v. California,* or libel, *Gertz v. Robert Welch, Inc.,* or incitement, *Brandenburg v. Ohio*—have been held unprotected, no contention has been made that the particular speech embraced in the advertisement in question is within any of these categories.

. . . The advertisement published in appellant's newspaper did more than simply propose a commercial transaction. It contained factual material of clear "public interest." Portions of its message, most prominently the lines "Abortions are now legal in New York. There are no residency requirements," involve the exercise of the freedom of communicating information and disseminating opinion.

Viewed in its entirety, the advertisement conveyed information of potential interest and value to a diverse audience—not only to readers possibly in need of the services offered, but also to those with a general curiosity about, or genuine interest in, the subject matter or the law of another State and its development, and to readers seeking reform in Virginia. The mere existence of the Women's Pavilion in New York City, with the possibility of its being typical of other organizations there, and the availability of the services offered, were not unnewsworthy. Also, the activity advertised pertained to constitutional interests. See *Roe v. Wade* and *Doe v. Bolton.* Thus, in this case, appellant's First Amendment interests coincided with the constitutional interests of the general public. . . .

*   *   *

And fourth, the Supreme Court in 1976 handed down a significant access decision which extended the Bigelow principle to at least some commercial product advertising. Virginia Pharmacy Board v. Virginia Citizens Consumer Council. In a 7–1 ruling, the Court declared unconstitutional a state law which banned price advertising of prescription drugs. See Chapter 1.

The following year, the Court continued to expand advertising rights under the First Amendment. By 8–0, the Justices held that a municipality's ban on "for sale" signs on front lawns of homes violated free speech guarantees. Linmark Associates v. Willingboro. The ban was instituted by the township in response to a fear of "white flight," a panic selling of homes by white owners who feared that large numbers of homes being sold in the community to minority buyers would depress their property values. In the opinion of the Court, Justice Marshall wrote that the Virginia Pharmacy decision of 1976 denied a government body such "sweeping powers."

A few weeks later, the Court handed down another advertising and access case, Carey v. Population Services International, in which the Justices ruled 7–2 that a New York law limiting advertising—and sale—of birth control devices violated the Constitution. "Compelling state interests," the majority said, must be shown if government wished to restrict speech of such societal value.

Finally, also in 1977, the Court broke with legal tradition by holding 5–4 that lawyers were free to advertise their fees, at least for more routine legal services. Bates v. State Bar of Arizona.

The following year, the Court granted First Amendment rights to banks which wished to spend funds to promote or oppose ballot measures. First National Bank v. Bellotti. The direction of the Supreme Court as it moved into the late 1980s, then, appeared to be clear—that, within certain parameters, the state would have to show a "compelling interest" before it could deny access to the advertising channels open to those who seek them, assuming the media are willing to offer time or space for sale.

In what was generally considered the most explosive First Amendment issue since the Pentagon Papers confrontation of 1971, the Supreme Court ruled in 1974 that a state may not require a newspaper to publish something it does not wish to publish. Miami Herald Publishing Co. v. Tornillo. "A newspaper," wrote Chief Justice Burger for a unanimous Court, "is more than a passive receptacle or conduit for news, comment, and advertising." A long-ignored Florida law required news-papers to offer, free of charge, equal space to candidates for public office who were criticized in their columns. This "right of reply" concept, of course, had been upheld in broadcasting in the 1969 Red Lion decision. Prof. Jerome Barron of the George Washington University Law School, long an advocate of the right-of-reply concept, represented Pat L. Tornillo, Jr., a candidate for the Florida House of Representa-tives. The Miami Herald, which had opposed Tornillo's candidacy, argued that the Florida law requiring that equal space be offered was unconstitutional because of both the cost involved, the ultimate "chilling effect" it would have on editors, and *the usurpation of the editorial function by the state. The significance of this decision can be seen in the fact that U.S. Senator John McClellan, Democrat of Arkansas, had indicated prior to the Supreme Court decision that he was prepared to introduce before the Congress a Federal "right of reply" bill if the High Court were to sustain the Florida statute. And President Nixon let it be known that the White House and the Justice Department were working on an administration version of a similar law in the event that the Court ruled such laws meet the constitutional test. Broadcasters, of course, were hoping for new signs that the Court would include radio and television in any opinion which would be favorable to the media, thereby granting First Amendment equality between the two media and reducing or eliminating the force of the fairness doctrine, which broadcasters feel violates their constitutional rights. But broadcasting was mentioned only in passing. Still, many in the electronic field saw this lack of mention as a positive sign because they believe the trend is away from guaranteed public access generally and away from the Red Lion philosophy specifically. The Court was unanimous in this 1974 decision that, for better or for worse, it was fundamental to the First Amendment that editors be free to do their own editing rather than to have the government do it for them. "A responsible press," wrote Chief Justice Burger, "is an undoubtedly desirable goal, but press responsibility is not mandated by the Constitution and like many other virtues it cannot be legislated."*

MIAMI HERALD V. TORNILLO
418 U.S. 241 (1974)

CHIEF JUSTICE BURGER *delivered the opinion of the Court.*

The issue in this case is whether a state statute granting a political candidate a right to equal space to reply to criticism and attacks on his record by a newspaper, violates the guarantees of a free press. . . .

The challenged statute creates a right of reply to press criticism of a candidate for nomination or election. The statute was enacted in 1913 and this is only the second recorded case decided under its provisions.

Appellant contends the statute is void on its face because it purports to regulate the content of a newspaper in violation of the First Amendment. Alternatively, it is urged that the statute is void for vagueness since no editor could know exactly what words would call the statute into operation. It is also contended that the statute fails to distinguish between critical comment which is and is not defamatory.

The appellee and supporting advocates of an enforceable right of access to the press vigorously argue that Government has an obligation to ensure that a wide variety of views reach the public. The contentions of access proponents will be set out in some detail. It is urged that at the time the First Amendment to the Constitution was enacted in 1791 as part of our Bill of Rights, the press was broadly representative of the people it was serving. While many of the newspapers were intensely partisan and narrow in their views, the press collectively presented a broad range of opinions to readers. Entry into publishing was inexpensive; pamphlets and books provided meaningful alternatives to the organized press for the expression of unpopular ideas and often treated events and expressed views not covered by conventional newspapers. A true marketplace of ideas existed in which there was relatively easy access to the channels of communication.

Access advocates submit that although newspapers of the present are superficially similar to those of 1791 the press of today is in reality very different from that known in the early years of our national existence. In the past half century a communications revolution has seen the introduction of radio and television into our lives, the promise of a global community through the use of communications satellites, and the spectre of a "wired" nation by means of an expanding cable television network with two-way capabilities. The printed press, it is said, has not escaped the effects of this revolution. Newspapers have become big business and there are far fewer of them to serve a larger literate population. Chains of newspapers, national newspapers, national wire and news services, and one-newspaper towns, are the dominant features of a press that has become noncompetitive and enormously powerful and influential in its capacity to manipulate popular opinion and change the course of events. Major metropolitan newspapers have collaborated to establish news services national in scope. Such national news organizations provide syndicated "interpretative reporting" as well as syndicated features and commentary, all of which can serve as part of the new school of "advocacy journalism."

The elimination of competing newspapers in most of our large cities, and the concentration of control of media that results from the only newspaper being owned by the same interests which own a television station and a radio station, are important components of this trend toward concentration of control of outlets to inform the public.

The result of these vast changes has been to place in a few hands the power to inform the American people and shape public opinion. Much of the editorial opinion and commentary that is printed is that of syndicated columnists distributed nationwide and, as a result, we are told, on national and world issues there tends to be a homogeneity of editorial opinion, commentary, and interpretative analysis. The abuses of bias and manipulative reportage are, likewise, said to be the result of the vast accommodations of unreviewable power in the modern media empires. In effect, it is claimed, the public has lost any ability to respond or to contribute in a meaningful way to the debate on issues. . . .

However much validity may be found in these arguments, at each point the implementation of a remedy such as an enforceable right of access necessarily calls for some mechanism, either governmental or consensual. If it is governmental coercion, this at once brings about a confrontation with the express provisions of the First Amendment and the judicial gloss on the amendment developed over the years.

We see that beginning with *Associated Press*, the Court has expressed sensitivity as to whether a restriction or requirement constituted the compulsion exerted by government on a newspaper to print that which it would not otherwise print. The clear implication has been that any such a compulsion to publish that which " 'reason' tells them should not be published" is unconstitutional. A responsible press is an undoubtedly desirable goal, but press responsibility is not mandated by the Constitution and like many other virtues it cannot be legislated. . . .

. . . The Florida statute operates as a command in the same sense as a statute or regulation forbidding appellant from publishing specified matter. Governmental restraint on publishing need not fall into familiar or traditional patterns to be subject to constitutional limitations on governmental powers. *Grosjean v. American Press Co.* The Florida statute exacts a penalty on the basis of the content of a newspaper. The first phase of the penalty resulting from the compelled printing of a reply is exacted in terms of the cost in printing and composing time and materials and in taking up space that could be devoted to other material the newspaper may have preferred to print. It is correct, as appellee contends, that a newspaper is not subject to the finite technological limitations of time that confront a broadcaster but it is not correct to say that, as an economic reality, a newspaper can proceed to infinite expansion of its column space to accommodate the replies that a government agency determines or a statute commands the readers should have available.

Faced with the penalties that would accrue to any newspaper that published news or commentary arguably within the reach of the right of access statute, editors might well conclude that the safe course is to avoid controversy and that, under the operation of the Florida statute, political and electoral coverage would be blunted or reduced. Government-enforced right of access inescapably "dampens the vigor and limits the variety of public debate," *New York Times Co. v. Sullivan.*

Even if a newspaper would face no additional costs to comply with a compulsory access law and would not be forced to forego publication of news or opinion by the inclusion of a reply, the Florida statute fails to clear the barriers of the First Amendment because of its intrusion into the function of editors. A newspaper is more than a passive receptacle or conduit for news, comment, and advertising. The choice of material to go into a newspaper, and the decisions made as to limitations on the size of the paper, and content, and treatment of public issues and public officials—whether fair or unfair—constitutes the exercise of editorial control and judgment. It has yet to be demonstrated how governmental regulation of this crucial process can be exercised consistent with First Amendment guarantees of a free press as they have evolved to this time. Accordingly, the judgment of the Supreme Court of Florida is reversed.

It is so ordered.

JUSTICE WHITE, *concurring.*

. . . A newspaper or magazine is not a public utility subject to "reasonable" governmental regulation in matters affecting the exercise of journalistic judgment as to what shall be printed. *Mills v. Alabama.* We have learned, and continue to learn, from what we view as the unhappy experiences of other nations where government has been allowed to meddle in the internal editorial affairs of newspapers. . . .

Of course, the press is not always accurate, or even responsible, and may not present full and fair debate on important public issues. But the balance struck by the First Amendment with respect to the press is that society must take the risk that occasionally debate on vital matters will not be comprehensive and that all viewpoints may not be expressed. The press would be unlicensed because, in Jefferson's words, "[w]here the press is free, and every man able to read, all is safe." Any other accommodation—any other system that would supplant private control of the press with the heavy hand of government intrusion—would make the government the censor of what the people may read and know. . . .

✽   ✽   ✽

The question of access to the electronic media continued into the 1980s with two major cases, one dealing with cable television and the other with broadcast. In FCC v. Midwest Video, the Court held 6–3 that the FCC cannot require cable TV operators to set aside free channels for use by private citizens or public interest groups who wish to bring differing political viewpoints before the viewers. These are the so-called "public access" channels. The FCC had claimed that cable television is akin to a common carrier, such as a public utility company. Thus, cable TV franchise holders could be required to "contribute" free time as a public service. The Court, however, in this 1979 ruling, held that such a requirement of access was beyond the authority of the FCC.

A major decision in 1981 affirmed an FCC ruling that the networks were in error when in 1979 they turned down the Carter-Mondale campaign when it sought air time for campaign purposes. CBS v. FCC. By a vote of 6–3, the Supreme Court held that the FCC was operating within its authority in ordering CBS, ABC and NBC to air the ad. The networks had declined, claiming that the December 1979 air date was too early for the 1980 presidential campaign to begin. Chief Justice Burger wrote the majority opinion, noting that the interests of the public are paramount. Justices White, Rehnquist and Stevens dissented.

CBS V. FCC

ABC V. FCC

NBC V. FCC
453 U.S. 367 (1981)

CHIEF JUSTICE BURGER *delivered the opinion of the Court.*

We granted certiorari to consider whether the Federal Communications Commission properly construed 47 U. S. C. sec. 312 (a)(7) and determined that petitioners failed to provide "reasonable access to . . . the use of a broadcasting station" as required by the statute.

On October 11, 1979, Gerald M. Rafshoon, President of the Carter-Mondale Presidential Committee, requested each of the three major television networks to provide time for a 30-minute program between 8 P.M. and 10:30 P.M. on either the 4th, 5th, 6th, or 7th of December 1979. The Committee intended to present, in conjunction with President Carter's formal announcement of his candidacy, a documentary outlining the record of his administration.

The networks declined to make the requested time available. Petitioner CBS emphasized the large number of candidates for the Republican and Democratic Presidential nominations and the potential disruption of regular programming to accommodate requests for equal treatment, but it offered to sell two 5-minute segments to the Committee, one at 10:55 P.M. on December 8 and one in the daytime. Petitioner ABC replied that it had not yet decided when it would begin selling political time for the 1980 Presidential campaign, but subsequently indicated that it would allow such sales in January 1980. Petitioner NBC, noting the number of potential requests for time from Presidential candidates, stated that it was not prepared to sell time for political programs as early as December 1979.

On October 29, 1979, the Carter-Mondale Presidential Committee filed a complaint with the Federal Communications Commission, charging that the networks had violated their obligation to provide "reasonable access" under sec. 312 (a)(7) of the Communications Act of 1934, as amended. Title 47 U. S. C. sec. 312 (a)(7) states:

> The Commission may revoke any station license or construction permit . . .
>
> (7) for willful or repeated failure to allow reasonable access to or to permit purchase of reasonable amounts of time for the use of a broadcasting station by a legally qualified candidate for Federal elective office on behalf of his candidacy.

At an open meeting on November 20, 1979, the Commission, by a 4-to-3 vote, ruled that the networks had violated [the statute] . . .

The Commission's repeated construction of [the statute] as affording an affirmative right of reasonable access to individual candidates for federal elective office comports with the statute's language and legislative history and has received congressional review. Therefore, departure from that construction is unwarranted. "Congress' failure to repeal or revise [the statute] in the face of such administrative interpretation [is] persuasive evidence that that interpretation is the one intended by Congress." *Zemel v. Rusk.*

In support of their narrow reading of [the statute] as simply a restatement of the public interest obligation, petitioners cite our decision in *CBS, Inc. v. Democratic National Committee,* which held that neither the First Amendment nor the Communications Act requires broadcasters to accept paid editorial advertisements from citizens at large. . . .

Broadcasters are free to deny the sale of air time prior to the commencement of a campaign, but once a campaign has begun, they must give reasonable and good faith attention to access requests from "legally qualified" candidates for federal elective office. Such requests must be considered on an individualized basis, and broadcasters are required to tailor their responses to accommodate, as much as reasonably possible, a candidate's stated purposes in seeking air time. In responding to access requests, however, broadcasters may also give weight to such factors as the amount of time previously sold to the candidate, the disruptive impact on regular programming, and the likelihood of requests for time by rival candidates under the equal opportunities provision of sec. 315(a). These considerations may not be invoked as pretexts for denying access; to justify a negative response, broadcasters must cite a realistic danger of substantial program disruption—perhaps caused by insufficient notice to allow adjustments in the schedule—or of an excessive number of equal time requests. Further, in order to facilitate review by the Commission, broadcasters must explain their reasons for refusing time or making a more limited counteroffer. If broadcasters take the appropriate factors into account and act reasonably and in good faith, their decisions will be entitled to deference even if the Commission's analysis would have differed in the first instance. But if broadcasters adopt "across-the-board policies" and do not attempt to respond to the individualized situation of a particular candidate, the Commission is not compelled to sustain their denial of access. . . .

The Commission has concluded that, as a threshold matter, it will independently determine whether a campaign has begun and the obligations imposed by sec. 312 (a)(7) have attached. Petitioners assert that, in undertaking such a task, the Commission becomes improperly involved in the electoral process and seriously impairs broadcaster discretion.

However, petitioners fail to recognize that the Commission does not set the starting date for a campaign. . . .

Here, the Carter-Mondale Presidential Committee sought broadcast time approximately 11 months before the 1980 Presidential election and 8 months before the Democratic national convention. In determining that a national campaign was underway at that point, the Commission stressed: (a) that 10 candidates formally had announced their intention to seek the Republican nomination, and two candidates had done so for the Democratic nomination; (b) that various states had started the delegate selection process; (c) that candidates were traveling across the country making speeches and attempting to raise funds; (d) that national campaign organizations were established and operating; (e) that the Iowa caucus would be held the following month; (f) that public officials and private groups were making endorsements; and (g) that the national print media had given campaign activities prominent coverage for almost 2 months. . . .

Nevertheless, petitioners ABC and NBC refused to sell the Carter-Mondale Presidential Committee any time in December 1979 on the ground that it was "too early in the political season." These petitioners made no counteroffers, but adopted "blanket" policies refusing access despite the admonition against such an approach. . . . Likewise, petitioner CBS, while not barring access completely, had an across-the-board policy of selling only 5-minute spots. . . .

Section 312 (a)(7) represents an effort by Congress to assure that an important resource—the airwaves—will be used in the public interest. We hold that the statutory right of access, as defined by the Commission and applied in these cases, properly balances the First Amendment rights of federal candidates, the public, and broadcasters.

The judgment of the Court of Appeals is

Affirmed.

CHAPTER 6

OBSCENITY DEFINED

Those in power historically have attempted to ban as harmful those viewpoints and expressions they find uncomfortable. This is best illustrated through the study of obscenity. Although there is no substantial body of evidence to establish a cause-and-effect relationship between exposure to erotic material and anti-social behavior, strong voices in this country have argued for more than a century that obscenity is not protected by constitutional guarantees of free speech and press. The Supreme Court has been among those voices. Conversely, there is some evidence to indicate that salacious material might tend to have the opposite effect, i.e. that it might be beneficial to society as a vicarious outlet or "escape valve." It is safe to say only that the record is not yet clear.

Critics of restrictive anti-obscenity legislation point to three other arguments which they say make such legislation almost impossible to understand or to enforce. First, even our most learned judges, legislators and philosophers cannot reach agreement as to what constitutes obscenity. Second, no other area of constitutional law is so dependent upon the temperament of the presiding judge or jury. And third, the area of obscenity is the most ill-defined body of law in American jurisprudence.

What is clear, however, is that a changing morality spread across the nation in the decades following World War II. This is reflected in advertising, motion pictures, the stage, magazines, books and personal patterns of behavior. Our forefathers were not confronted publicly with the dilemma we face today because of their puritan controls, the difficult agrarian life, lack of mass printing and distribution, low literacy rates and less leisure time, among other reasons. It is generally accepted that reading of salacious literature was accomplished in earlier times, but only by those of means, prominence and education, and without fanfare.

With the rise of the middle class and industrial technology in the mid-nineteenth century, Congress and state legislatures began to deal with censorship of alleged obscenity. The most significant of these was the famous "Comstock Law" of

1873, which meted out censorship with a heavy hand. Anthony Comstock, who had campaigned with the slogan "Books are Feeders for Brothels" (Ernst and Morris, Censorship: The Search for the Obscene, p. 30), directed his campaign at the Congress and the Post Office. Following the passage of strict anti-obscenity measures, Comstock was appointed special agent to the Post Office to assist in uncovering violations. State legislatures followed with similar restrictive laws. Meanwhile, in England, the 1868 "Hicklin rule" was enunciated by Lord Chief Justice Cockburn and was accepted both in England and the United States as the test of obscenity. A work was judged on isolated passages and on its estimated effect on the most susceptible person.

Comstock censorship and the "Hicklin test" stood until 1913, when it was challenged by publisher Mitchell Kennerly. Judge Learned Hand preferred to interpret obscenity as "the present critical point in the compromise between candor and shame at which the community may have arrived here and now." United States v. Kennerly. 209 F. 119.

The watershed case involving censorship was United States v. One Book called "Ulysses." Customs officials had denied the entry of James Joyce's novel into the United States, but Judge John M. Woolsey in a frequently quoted opinion ruled the book not obscene. He held that the test was to be based on a person with "average sex instincts," rather than the "most susceptible" person of the "Hicklin test." His views were sustained the following year in the Circuit Court of Appeals by jurists Learned and Augustus Hand. By the mid-1930s, then, books were judged as a whole, taking into consideration the average reader, the author's intent, and the relevance to the theme of the passages in question.

The first major case involving a question of obscenity to come to the Supreme Court was decided in 1948 (Winters v. New York). A bookseller had been convicted under a section of the New York Penal Law which made it a misdemeanor for anyone to sell or distribute obscene publications. Obscene publications included those "primarily made up of . . . criminal deeds of bloodshed, lust or crime." In holding the New York statute unconstitutional as too vague and indefinite, the 6–3 majority ruled that the first essential of due process is that persons of common intelligence should not be required to guess at the meaning and interpretation of a law and that they must be able to ascertain the courses of conduct they may lawfully pursue.

Following this "opening round" of obscenity tests, the Warren Court was drawn into the debate. It handed down 17 major decisions on obscenity and related censorship questions in the 16 years under Chief Justice Warren. The Roth decision of 1957 was the first attempt by the Court to define obscenity. That definition, with refinements covered in the next chapter, lasted through the Warren years and with the Miller modifications into the Rehnquist years.

In the first of two cases preliminary to the landmark Roth decision, the Warren Court emphasized that a statute must be reasonably related to the evil with which it is intended to deal. Butler v. Michigan. The Michigan Penal Code made it a misdemeanor to sell literary material which would corrupt the morals of youth or tend to incite them to violent, depraved, or immoral acts. The Court in 1957 *through Justice Frankfurter held unanimously that the statute violated the due process clause of the Fourteenth Amendment because the statute was not reasonably related to the evil with which it sought to deal. Rather, it tended to reduce the reading level of the adult population to that of a child.*

The question of the constitutionality per se of an anti-obscenity law was resolved later that same year with the Kingsley Books *decision. The appellants were convicted under a New York obscenity statute and brought to the Court the question of whether such laws were constitutional at all. Appellants did not appeal the lower court finding that the publications were in fact obscene but raised only the question of the constitutionality of the statute. The Court, by a 5–4 margin, upheld the New York law and therefore approved the concept of anti-obscenity legislation in cases where these statutes were drawn carefully and with full legal procedural safeguards. Dissenting were Justices Warren, Douglas, Brennan, and Black. The decision was announced on the same day as* Roth, *but interestingly there was no hint as to the magnitude of the landmark decision which was to follow.*

KINGSLEY BOOKS, INC. V. BROWN
354 U.S. 436 (1957)

JUSTICE FRANKFURTER *delivered the opinion of the Court.*

In an unbroken series of cases extending over a long stretch of this Court's history, it has been accepted as a postulate that "the primary requirements of decency may be enforced against obscure publications." *Near v. Minnesota.* And so our starting point is that New York can constitutionally convict appellants of keeping for sale the booklets incontestably found to be obscene. . . .

If New York chooses to subject persons who disseminate obscene "literature" to criminal prosecution and also to deal with such books as deodands of old, or both, with due regard, of course, to appropriate opportunities for the trial of the underlying issue, it is not for us to gainsay its selection of remedies. Just as *Near v. Minnesota*, one of the landmark opinions in shaping the constitutional protection of freedom of speech and of the press, left no doubts that "Liberty of speech, and of the press, is also not an absolute right," it likewise made clear that "the protection even as to previous restraint is not absolutely unlimited." To be sure, the limitation is the exception; it is to be closely confined so as to preclude what may fairly be deemed licensing or censorship. . . .

CHIEF JUSTICE WARREN, *dissenting.*

. . . This is not a criminal obscenity case. Nor is it a case ordering the destruction of materials disseminated by a person who has been convicted of an offense for doing so, as would be authorized under provisions in the laws of New York and other states. It is a case wherein the New York police, under a different state statute, located books which, in their opinion, were unfit for public use because of obscenity and then obtained a court order for their condemnation and destruction.

The majority opinion sanctions this proceeding. I would not. Unlike the criminal cases decided today, this New York law places the book on trial. There is totally lacking any standard in the statute for judging the book in context. The personal element basic to the criminal laws is entirely absent. In my judgment, the same object may have wholly different impact depending upon the setting in which it is placed. Under this statute, the setting is irrelevant.

It is the manner of use that should determine obscenity. It is the conduct of the individual that should be judged, not the quality of art or literature. To do otherwise is to impose a prior restraint and hence to violate the Constitution. Certainly in the absence of a prior judicial determination of illegal use, books, pictures and other objects of expression should not be destroyed. It savors too much of book burning.

I would reverse.

JUSTICE DOUGLAS, *with whom Justice Black concurs, dissenting.*

. . . This provision is defended on the ground that it is only a little encroachment, that a hearing must be promptly given and a finding of obscenity promptly made. But every publisher knows what awful effect a decree issued in secret can have. We tread here on First Amendment grounds. And nothing is more devastating to the rights that it guarantees than the power to restrain publication before even a hearing is held. This is prior restraint and censorship at its worst.

. . . I think every publication is a separate offense which entitles the accused to a separate trial. Juries or judges may differ in their opinions, community by community, case by case. The publisher is entitled to that leeway under our constitutional system. One is entitled to defend every utterance on its merits and not to suffer today for what he uttered yesterday. Free speech is not to be regulated like diseased cattle and impure butter. The audience (in this case the judge or the jury) that hissed yesterday may applaud today, even for the same performance. . . .

*   *   *

The most important decision to come from the Supreme Court in the area of obscenity sprang from the Roth *and* Alberts *cases, decided upon together. Never before had the Court faced so squarely the problem of trying to define obscenity. The background of the cases is relatively unimportant when weighed against the three important rules of law enunciated by Justice Brennan, speaking for the Court: (1) Obscenity is not protected by the First Amendment thereby eliminating the need to use the "clear and present danger" test; (2) the Court for the first time defined obscene material as matter "which deals with sex in a manner appealing to prurient interest," thereby separating obscenity from sex per se; and (3) the standard for judging obscenity is not by the effect of an isolated passage upon the most susceptible person, but "whether to the average person, applying contemporary community standards, the dominant theme of the material taken as a whole appeals to prurient interest," thereby laying to rest the old "Hicklin rule." The decision, as in Kingsley Books, decided the same day, was 5–4. Several refinements and augmentations were to come within the next decades, but the Court had for the first time faced the issue head-on and had attempted to hammer out a formula upon which to judge obscenity.*

ROTH V. UNITED STATES

ALBERTS V. CALIFORNIA
354 U.S. 476 (1957)

JUSTICE BRENNAN *delivered the opinion of the Court.*

The constitutionality of a criminal obscenity statute is the question in each of these cases. In *Roth*, the primary constitutional question is whether the federal obscenity statute violates the provision of the First Amendment that "Congress shall make no law . . . abridging the freedom of speech, or of the press. . . ." In *Alberts*, the primary constitutional question is whether the obscenity provisions of the California Penal Code invade the freedoms of speech and press as they may be incorporated in the liberty protected from state action of the Due Process Clause of the Fourteenth Amendment.

Other constitutional questions are: whether these statutes violate due process, because too vague to support conviction for crime; whether power to punish speech and press offensive to decency and morality is in the States alone, so that the federal obscenity statutes violates the Ninth and Tenth Amendments (raised in *Roth*); and whether Congress, by enacting the federal obscenity statute, under the power . . . to establish post offices and post roads, pre-empted the regulation of the subject matter (raised in *Alberts*).

Roth conducted a business in New York in the publication and sale of books, photographs and magazines. He used circulars and advertising matter to solicit sales. He was convicted by a jury in the District Court for the Southern District of New York upon 4 counts of a 26-count indictment charging him with mailing obscene circulars and advertising, and an obscene book, in violation of the federal obscenity statute. His conviction was affirmed by the Court of Appeals for the Second Circuit. We granted certiorari.

Alberts conducted a mail-order business from Los Angeles. He was convicted by the Judge of the Municipal Court of the Beverly Hills Judicial District (having waived a jury trial) under a misdemeanor complaint which charged him with lewdly keeping for sale obscene and indecent books, and with writing, composing and publishing an obscene advertisement of them, in violation of the California Penal Code. The conviction was affirmed by the Appellate Department of the Supreme Court of the State of California in and for the County of Los Angeles. We noted the probable jurisdiction.

The dispositive question is whether obscenity is utterance within the area of protected speech and press. Although this is the first time the question has been squarely presented to this Court, either under the First Amendment or under the Fourteenth Amendment, expressions found in numerous opinions indicate that this Court has always assumed that obscenity is not protected by the freedoms of speech and press. . . .

In light of this history it is apparent that the unconditional phrasing of the First Amendment was not intended to protect every utterance. This phrasing did not prevent this Court from concluding that libelous utterances are not within the area of constitutionally protected speech. *Beauharnais v. Illinois.* At the time of the adoption of the First Amendment, obscenity law was not as fully developed as libel law, but there is sufficiently contemporaneous evidence to show that obscenity, too, was outside the protection intended for speech and press.

The protection given speech and press was fashioned to assume unfettered interchange of ideas for the bringing about of political and social changes desired by the people. . . .

All ideas having even the slightest redeeming social importance—unorthodox ideas, controversial ideas, even ideas hateful to the prevailing climate of opinion—have the full protection of the guarantees, unless excludable because they encroach upon the limited area of more important interests. But implicit in the history of the First Amendment is the rejection of obscenity as utterly without redeeming social importance. This rejection for that reason is mirrored in the universal judgment that obscenity should be restrained, reflected in the international agreement of over 50 nations, in the obscenity laws of all of the 48 States, and in the 20 obscenity laws enacted by the Congress from 1842 to 1956. This is the same judgment expressed by this Court in *Chaplinsky v. New Hampshire:*

> . . . There are certain well-defined and narrowly limited classes of speech, the prevention and punishment of which have never been thought to raise any Constitutional problem. These include the lewd and obscene. . . . It has been well observed that such utterances are no essential part of any exposition of ideas, and are of such slight social value as a step to truth that any benefit that may be derived from them is clearly outweighed by the social interest in order and morality. . . .

We hold that obscenity is not within the area of constitutionally protected speech or press.

It is strenuously urged that these obscenity statutes offend the constitutional guarantees because they punish incitation to impure sexual thoughts, not shown to be related to any overt antisocial conduct which is or may be incited in the persons stimulated to such thoughts. . . . It is insisted that the constitutional guarantees are violated because convictions may be had without proof either that obscene material will perceptibly create a clear and present danger of antisocial conduct, or will probably induce its recipients to such conduct. But, in light of our holding that obscenity is not protected speech, the complete answer to this argument is in the holding of this Court in *Beauharnais v. Illinois:*

> Libelous utterances not being within the area of constitutionally pro-
> tected speech, it is unnecessary, either for us or for the State courts, to
> consider the issues behind the phrase 'clear and present danger.' Certainly no
> one would contend that obscene speech, for example, may be punished only
> upon a showing of such circumstances. Libel, as we have seen, is in the same
> class.

However, sex and obscenity are not synonymous. Obscene material is material which deals with sex in a manner appealing to prurient interest. The portrayal
of sex, *e.g.*, in art, literature and scientific works, is not itself sufficient reason to
deny material the constitutional protection of freedom of speech and press. Sex, a
great and mysterious motive force in human life, has indisputably been a subject of
absorbing interest to mankind through the ages; it is one of the vital problems of
human interest and public concern. As to all such problems, this Court said in
Thornhill v. Alabama:

> The freedom of speech and of the press guaranteed by the Constitution
> embraces at the least the liberty to discuss publicly and truthfully all matters of
> public concern without previous restraint or fear of subsequent punishment.
> The exigencies of the colonial period and the efforts to secure freedom from
> oppressive administration developed a broadened conception of these liberties
> as adequate to supply the public need for information and education with
> respect to the significant issues of the times. . . . Freedom of discussion, if it
> would fulfill its historic function in this nation, must embrace all issues about
> which information is needed or appropriate to enable the members of society
> to cope with the exigencies of their period.

The fundamental freedoms of speech and press have contributed greatly to the
development and well-being of our free society and are indispensable to its continued growth. Ceaseless vigilance is the watchword to prevent their erosion by
Congress or by the States. The door barring federal and state intrusion into this area
cannot be left ajar; it must be kept tightly closed and opened only the slightest crack
necessary to prevent encroachment upon more important interests. It is therefore
vital that the standards for judging obscenity safeguard the protection of freedom of
speech and press for material which does not treat sex in a manner appealing to
prurient interest.

The early leading standard of obscenity allowed material to be judged merely
by the effect of an isolated excerpt upon particularly susceptible persons. Some
American courts adopted this standard but later decisions have rejected it and
substituted this test: whether to the average person, applying contemporary community standards, the dominant theme of the material taken as a whole appeals to
prurient interest. The *Hicklin* test, judging obscenity by the effect of isolated

passages upon the most susceptible persons, might well encompass material legitimately treating with sex, and so it must be rejected as unconstitutionally restrictive of the freedoms of speech and press. On the other hand, the substituted standard provides safeguards adequate to withstand the charge of constitutional infirmity. . . .

CHIEF JUSTICE WARREN, *concurring in the result.*

I agree with the result reached by the Court in these cases, but, because we are operating in a field of expression and because broad language used here may eventually be applied to the arts and sciences and freedom of communication generally, I would limit our decision to the facts before us and to the validity of the statutes in question as applied. . . .

That there is a social problem presented by obscenity is attested by the expression of the legislatures of the 48 states as well as the Congress. To recognize the existence of a problem, however, does not require that we sustain any and all measures adopted to meet that problem. The history of the application of laws designed to suppress the obscene demonstrates convincingly that the power of government can be invoked under them against great art or literature, scientific treatises, or works exciting social controversy. Mistakes of the past prove that there is a strong countervailing interest to be considered in the freedoms guaranteed by the First and Fourteenth Amendments.

The line dividing the salacious or pornographic from literature or science is not straight and unwavering. Present laws depend largely upon the effect that the materials may have upon those who receive them. It is manifest that the same object may have a different impact, varying according to the part of the community it reached. But there is more to these cases. It is not the book that is on trial; it is a person. The conduct of the defendant is the central issue, not the obscenity of a book or picture. The nature of the materials is, of course, relevant as an attribute of the defendant's conduct, but the materials are thus placed in context from which they draw color and character. A wholly different result might be reached in a different setting.

The personal element in these cases is seen most strongly in the requirement of scienter. Under the California law, the prohibited activity must be done "willfully and lewdly." The federal statute limits the crime to acts done "knowingly." In his charge to the jury, the district judge stated that the matter must be "calculated" to corrupt or debauch. The defendants in both these cases were engaged in the business of purveying textual or graphic matter openly advertised to appeal to erotic interest of their customers. They were plainly engaged in the commercial exploitation of the morbid and shameful craving for materials with prurient effect. I believe that the State and Federal Governments can constitutionally punish such conduct. That is all that these cases present to us, and that is all we need to decide. . . .

JUSTICE HARLAN, *concurring in the result in* [Alberts] *and dissenting in* [Roth].

I regret not to be able to join the Court's opinion. I cannot do so because I find lurking beneath its disarming generalizations a number of problems which not only leave me with serious misgivings as to the future effect of today's decisions, but which also, in my view, call for different results in these two cases.

My basic difficulties with the Court's opinion are threefold. First, the opinion paints with such a broad brush that I fear it may result in a loosening of the tight reins which state and federal courts should hold upon the enforcement of obscenity statutes. Second, the Court fails to discriminate between the different factors which, in my opinion, are involved in the constitutional adjudication of state and federal obscenity cases. Third, relevant distinctions between the two obscenity statutes here involved, and the Court's own definition of "obscenity," are ignored.

In final analysis, the problem presented by these cases is how far, and on what terms, the state and federal governments have power to punish individuals for disseminating books considered to be undesirable because of their nature or supposed deleterious effect upon human conduct. . . . The Court seems to assume that "obscenity" is a peculiar genus of "speech and press," which is as distinct, recognizable, and classifiable as poison ivy is among other plants. On this basis the constitutional question before us simply becomes, as the Court says, whether "obscenity," as an abstraction, is protected by the First and Fourteenth Amendments, and the question whether a particular book may be suppressed becomes a mere matter of classification, of "fact," to be entrusted to a fact-finder and insulated from independent constitutional judgment. But surely the problem cannot be solved in such a generalized fashion. Every communication has an individuality and "value" of its own. The suppression of a particular writing or other tangible form of expression is, therefore, an individual matter, and in the nature of things every such suppression raises an individual constitutional problem, in which a reviewing court must determine for itself whether the attacked expression is suppressible within constitutional standards. Since those standards do not readily lend themselves to generalized definitions, the constitutional problem in the last analysis becomes one of particularized judgments which appellate courts must make for themselves. . . .

. . . Many juries might find that Joyce's *Ulysses* or Boccaccio's *Decameron* was obscene, and yet the conviction of a defendant for selling either book would raise, for me, the gravest constitutional problems, for no such verdict could convince me, without more, that these books are "utterly without redeeming social importance." In short, I do not understand how the Court can resolve the constitutional problems now before it without making its own independent judgment upon the character of the material upon which these convictions were based. I am very much afraid that the broad manner in which the Court has decided these cases will tend to obscure the peculiar responsibilities resting on state and federal courts in this field and encourage them to rely on easy labeling and jury verdicts as a substitute for facing up to the tough individual problems of constitutional judgment involved in every obscenity case. . . .

Quite a different situation is presented . . . where the Federal Government imposes the ban. The danger is perhaps not great if the people of one State, through their legislature, decide that *Lady Chatterley's Lover* goes so far beyond the acceptable standards of candor that it will be deemed offensive and non-sellable, for the State next door is still free to make its own choice. At least we do not have one uniform standard. But the dangers to free thought and expression are truly great if the Federal Government imposes a blanket ban over the Nation on such a book. The prerogative of the States to differ on their ideas of morality will be destroyed, the ability of States to experiment will be stunted. The fact that the people of one State cannot read some of the works of D. H. Lawrence seems to me, if not wise or desirable, at least acceptable. But that no person in the United States should be allowed to do so seems to me to be intolerable, and violative of both the letter and spirit of the First Amendment.

I judge this case, then, in view of what I think is the attenuated federal interest in this field, in view of the very real danger of deadening uniformity which can result from nation-wide federal censorship, and in view of the fact that the constitutionality of this conviction must be weighed against the First and not the Fourteenth Amendment. So viewed, I do not think that this conviction can be upheld. The petitioner was convicted under a statute which, under the judge's charge, makes it criminal to sell books which "tend to stir sexual impulses and lead to sexually impure thoughts." I cannot agree that any book which tends to stir sexual impulses and lead to sexually impure thoughts necessarily is "utterly without redeeming social importance." Not only did this charge fail to measure up to the standards which I understand the Court to approve, but as far as I can see, much of the great literature of the world could lead to conviction under such a view of the statute. Moreover, in no event do I think that the limited federal interest in this area can extend to mere "thoughts." The Federal Government has no business, whether under the postal or commerce power, to bar the sale of books because they might lead to any kind of "thoughts."

It is no answer to say, as the Court does, that obscenity is not protected speech. The point is that this statute, as here construed, defines obscenity so widely that it encompasses matters which might very well be protected speech. I do not think that the federal statute can be constitutionally construed to reach other than what the Government has termed as "hard-core" pornography. Nor do I think the statute can fairly be read as directed only at persons who are engaged in the business of catering to the prurient minded, even though their wares fall short of hard-core pornography. Such a statute would raise constitutional questions of a different order. That being so, and since in my opinion the material here involved cannot be said to be hard-core pornography, I would reverse this case with instructions to dismiss the indictment.

JUSTICE DOUGLAS, *with whom Justice Black concurs, dissenting.*

When we sustain these convictions, we make the legality of a publication turn on the purity of thought which a book or tract instills in the mind of the reader. I do not think we can approve that standard and be faithful to the command of the First

Amendment, which by its terms is a restraint on Congress and which by the Fourteenth is a restraint on the States. . . .

By these standards punishment is inflicted for thoughts provoked, not for overt acts nor antisocial conduct. This test cannot be squared with our decisions under the First Amendment. Even the ill-starred *Dennis* case conceded that speech to be punishable must have some relation to action which could be penalized by government. *Dennis v. United States.* This issue cannot be avoided by saying that obscenity is not protected by the First Amendment. The question remains, what is the constitutional test of obscenity?

The tests by which these convictions were obtained require only the arousing of sexual thoughts. Yet the arousing of sexual thoughts, and desires, happens every day in normal life in dozens of ways. Nearly 30 years ago a questionnaire sent to college and normal school women graduates asked what things were most stimulating sexually. Of 409 replies, 9 said "music"; 18 said "pictures"; 29 said "dancing"; 40 said "drama"; 95 said "books"; and 218 said "man." Alpert, "Judicial Censorship of Obscene Literature," 52 Harv L Rev 40, 73. . . .

If we were certain that impurity of sexual thoughts impelled to action, we would be on less dangerous ground in punishing the distributors of this sex literature. But it is by no means clear that obscene literature, as so defined, is a significant factor in influencing substantial deviations from the community standards.

There are a number of reasons for real and substantial doubts as to the soundness of that hypothesis. (1) Scientific studies of juvenile delinquency demonstrate that those who get into trouble, and are the greatest concern of the advocates of censorship, are far less inclined to read than those who do not become delinquent. The delinquents are generally the adventurous type, who have little use for reading and other non-active entertainment. Thus, even assuming that reading sometimes has an adverse effect upon moral conduct, the effect is not likely to be substantial, for those who are susceptible seldom read. (2) Sheldon and Eleanor Glueck, who are among the country's leading authorities on the treatment and causes of juvenile delinquency, have recently published the results of a ten-year study of its causes. They exhaustively studied approximately 90 factors and influences that might lead to or explain juvenile delinquency, but the Gluecks gave no consideration to the type of reading material, if any, read by the delinquents. This is, of course, consistent with their finding that delinquents read very little. When those who know so much about the problem of delinquency among youth—the very group about whom the advocates of censorship are most concerned—conclude that what delinquents read has so little effect upon their conduct that it is not worth investigating in an exhaustive study of causes, there is good reason for serious doubt concerning the basic hypothesis on which obscenity censorship is defended. (3) The many other influences in society that stimulate sexual desire are so much more frequent in their influence, and so much more potent in their effect, that the influence of reading is likely, at most, to be relatively insignificant in the composite of forces that lead an individual into conduct deviating from the community sex standards. The Kinsey studies show the minor degree to which literature serves as a potent sexual stimulant. . . .

The absence of dependable information on the effect of obscene literature on human conduct should make us wary. It should put us on the side of protecting society's interest in literature, except and unless it can be said that the particular publication has an impact on action that the government can control.

As noted, the trial judge in the *Roth* case charged the jury in the alternative that the federal obscenity statute outlaws literature dealing with sex which offends "the common conscience of the community." That standard is, in my view, more inimical still to freedom of expression.

The standard of what offends "the common conscience of the community" conflicts, in my judgment, with the command of the First Amendment that "Congress shall make no law . . . abridging the freedom of speech, or of the press." Certainly that standard would not be an acceptable one if religion, economics, politics or philosophy were involved. How does it become a constitutional standard when literature treating with sex is concerned?

Any test that turns on what is offensive to the community's standards is too loose, too capricious, too destructive of freedom of expression to be squared with the First Amendment. Under that test, juries can censor, suppress, and punish what they don't like, provided the matter relates to "sexual impurity" or has a tendency "to excite lustful thought." This is community censorship in one of its worst forms. It creates a regime where in the battle between the literati and the Philistines, the Philistines are certain to win. If experience in this field teaches anything, it is that "censorship of obscenity has almost always been both irrational and indiscriminate.". . .

I can understand (and at times even sympathize) with programs of civic groups and church groups to protect and defend the existing moral standards of the community. I can understand the motives of the Anthony Comstocks who would impose Victorian standards on the community. When speech alone is involved, I do not think that government, consistently with the First Amendment, can become the sponsor of any of these movements. I do not think that government, consistently with the First Amendment, can throw its weight behind one school or another. Government should be concerned with antisocial conduct, not with utterances. Thus, if the First Amendment guarantee of freedom of speech and press is to mean anything in this field, it must allow protests even against the moral code that the standard of the day sets for the community. In other words, literature should not be suppressed merely because it offends the moral code of the censor. . . .

I do not think that the problem can be resolved by the Court's statement that "obscenity is not expression protected by the First Amendment." With the exception of *Beauharnais v. Illinois*, none of our cases has resolved problems of free speech and free press by placing any form of expression beyond the pale of the absolute prohibition of the First Amendment. Unlike the law of libel, wrongfully relied on in *Beauharnais*, there is no special historical evidence that literature dealing with sex was intended to be treated in a special manner by those who drafted the First Amendment. . . . I reject too the implication that problems of freedom of speech and of the press are to be resolved by weighing against the values of free expression, the judgment of the Court that a particular form of the expression has "no redeeming social importance." The First Amendment, its prohibition in terms absolute, was designed to preclude courts as well as legislatures from weighing the values of speech against silence. The First Amendment puts free speech in the preferred position. . . .

I would give the broad sweep of the First Amendment full support. I have the same confidence in the ability of our people to reject noxious literature as I have in their capacity to sort out the true from the false in theology, economics, politics, or any other field.

*   *   *

Despite Roth, *distribution of a variety of sexually explicit—though perhaps not legally obscene—films, books and magazines continues. Attempts to differentiate between the legally obscene and the artistically erotic has taken an enormous amount of the Court's time. Efforts at censorship are, after all, issues of basic First Amendment freedom. And this difficulty of definition has caused a major dilemma for politicians who seek to impose on the media either their own standards or those of irate voters back home. One solution, of course, would be to show that a clear and present danger to society exists—a causal relationship between salacious material and anti-social or violent behavior of those persons exposed to such material, for example. Two major national commissions looked into this question. The first was appointed by President Johnson and reported to President Nixon in 1970; the second was named by Attorney General Edwin Meese and reported its findings in 1986.*

The Nixon Commission relied heavily on research and original investigation. The outcome was widely awaited, for it was the first such national effort in this country. But senators and members of Congress who found its conclusions not to their liking urged President Nixon to reject its findings out of hand—which he did, while noting that he had not read the report and did not intend to. So much for reliance on evidence in attempting to understand our social problems.

The second commission was suspect from the outset because of the stated bias of the Reagan administration, the backgrounds of those chosen to serve as commissioners, the methodology used, and the limited time and funding given to the project. The report of the Meese Commission, as it was known, was predictable. Interestingly, its recommendations were disappointing to conservatives, for little guidance on how to solve the problem was forthcoming. Nor did it escape critics that the chair, Henry Hudson, a former county prosecutor who achieved notoriety for his crackdown on "adult" bookstores in Virginia, said afterward that if the Commission had relied on scientific data for its findings, its work would be "inconclusive." A final irony, captured by press photographers of the day, was that Mr. Meese accepted the report in Washington standing in front of a statue of a bare-breasted female figure symbolizing justice. What follows, then, are excerpts from the 1970 Commission report and a brief article discussing the Meese Commission effort.

OBSCENITY: RECOMMENDATIONS
OF THE PRESIDENT'S COMMISSION*

I. Non-legislative Recommendations

The Commission believes that much of the "problem" regarding materials which depict explicit sexual activity stems from the inability or reluctance of people in our society to be open and direct in dealing with sexual matters. This most often manifests itself in the inhibition of talking openly and directly about sex. Professionals use highly technical language when they discuss sex; others of us escape by using euphemisms—or by not talking about sex at all. Direct and open conversation about sex between parent and child is too rare in our society.

Failure to talk openly and directly about sex has several consequences. It overemphasizes sex, gives it a magical non-natural quality, making it more attractive and fascinating. It diverts the expression of sexual interest out of more legitimate channels, into less legitimate channels. Such failure makes teaching children and adolescents to become fully and adequately functioning sexual adults a more difficult task. And it clogs legitimate channels for transmitting sexual information and forces people to use clandestine and unreliable sources.

The Commission believes that interest in sex is normal, healthy, good. Interest in sex begins very early in life and continues throughout the life cycle although the strength of this interest varies from stage to stage. With the onset of puberty, physiological and hormonal changes occur which both quicken interest and make the individual more responsive to sexual interest. The individual needs information about sex in order to understand himself, place his new experiences in a proper context, and cope with his new feelings.

The basic institutions of marriage and the family are built in our society primarily on sexual attraction, love, and sexual expression. These institutions can function successfully only to the extent that they have a healthy base. Thus the very foundation of our society rests upon healthy sexual attitudes grounded in appropriate and accurate sexual information.

Sexual information is so important and so necessary that if people cannot obtain it openly and directly from legitimate sources and through accurate and legitimate channels, they will seek it through whatever channels and sources are available. Clandestine sources may not only be inaccurate but may also be distorted and provide a warped context.

The Commission believes that accurate, appropriate sex information provided openly and directly through legitimate channels and from reliable sources in healthy contexts can compete successfully with potentially distorted, warped,

---

* From the Report of the Commission on Obscenity and Pornography. Washington, D.C.: Government Printing Office, 1970, at p. 47.

inaccurate, and unreliable information from clandestine, illegitimate sources; and it believes that the attitudes and orientations toward sex produced by the open communication of appropriate sex information from reliable sources through legitimate channels will be normal and healthy, providing a solid foundation for the basic institutions of our society. . . .

II. LEGISLATIVE RECOMMENDATIONS

On the basis of its findings, the Commission makes the following legislative recommendations. The disagreements of particular Commissioners with aspects of the Commission's legislative recommendations are noted below, where the recommendations are discussed in detail. Commissioners Link, Hill, and Keating have filed a joint dissenting statement. In addition, Commissioners Keating and Link have submitted separate remarks. Commissioners Larsen and Wolfgang have filed statements explaining their dissent from certain Commission recommendations. A number of other Commissioners have filed short separate statements.

In general outline, the Commission recommends that federal, state, and local legislation should not seek to interfere with the right of adults who wish to do so to read, obtain, or view explicit sexual materials. On the other hand, we recommend legislative regulations upon the sale of sexual materials to young persons who do not have the consent of their parents, and we also recommend legislation to protect persons from having sexual materials thrust upon them without their consent through the mails or through open public display.

The Commission's specific legislative recommendations and the reasons underlying these recommendations are as follows:

A. *Statutes Relating to Adults*

The Commission recommends that federal, state, and local legislation prohibiting the sale, exhibition, or distribution of sexual materials to consenting adults should be repealed. Twelve of the 17 participating members of the Commission join in this recommendation. Two additional Commissioners subscribe to the bulk of the Commission's Report, but do not believe that the evidence presented at this time is sufficient to warrant the repeal of all prohibitions upon what adults may obtain. Three Commissioners dissent from the recommendation to repeal adult legislation and would retain existing laws prohibiting the dissemination of obscene materials to adults.

The Commission believes that there is no warrant for continued governmental interference with the full freedom of adults to read, obtain or view whatever such material they wish. Our conclusion is based upon the following considerations:

1. Extensive empirical investigation, both by the Commission and by others, provides no evidence that exposure to or use of explicit sexual materials play a significant role in the causation of social or individual harms such as crime, delinquency, sexual or nonsexual deviancy or severe emotional disturbances. This research and its results are described in detail in the Report of the Effects Panel of the Commission and are summarized above in the Overview of Commission

findings. Empirical investigation thus supports the opinion of a substantial majority of persons professionally engaged in the treatment of deviancy, delinquency and antisocial behavior, that exposure to sexually explicit materials has no harmful causal role in these areas.

Studies show that a number of factors, such as disorganized family relationships and unfavorable peer influences, are intimately related to harmful sexual behavior or adverse character development. Exposure to sexually explicit materials, however, cannot be counted as among these determinative factors. Despite the existence of widespread legal prohibitions upon the dissemination of such materials, exposure to them appears to be a usual and harmless part of the process of growing up in our society and a frequent and nondamaging occurrence among adults. Indeed, a few Commission studies indicate that a possible distinction between sexual offenders and other people, with regard to experience with explicit sexual materials, is that sex offenders have seen markedly *less* of such materials while maturing.

This is not to say that exposure to explicit sexual materials has no effect upon human behavior. A prominent effect of exposure to sexual materials is that persons tend to talk more about sex as a result of seeing such materials. In addition, many persons become temporarily sexually aroused upon viewing explicit sexual materials and the frequency of their sexual activity may, in consequence, increase for short periods. Such behavior, however, is the type of sexual activity already established as usual activity for the particular individual.

In sum, empirical research designed to clarify the questions has found no evidence to date that exposure to explicit sexual materials plays a significant role in the causation of delinquent or criminal behavior among youth or adults.

2. On the positive side, explicit sexual materials are sought as a source of entertainment and information by substantial numbers of American adults. At times, these materials also appear to serve to increase and facilitate constructive communication about sexual matters within marriage. The most frequent purchaser of explicit sexual materials is a college-educated, married male, in his thirties or forties, who is of above average socio-economic status. Even where materials are legally available to them, young adults and older adolescents do not constitute an important portion of the purchases of such materials.

3. Society's attempts to legislate for adults in the area of obscenity have not been successful. Present laws prohibiting the consensual sale or distribution of explicit sexual materials to adults are extremely unsatisfactory in their practical application. The Constitution permits material to be deemed "obscene" for adults only if, as a whole, it appeals to the "prurient" interest of the average person, is "patently offensive" in light of "community standards," and lacks "redeeming social value." These vague and highly subjective aesthetic, psychological and moral tests do not provide meaningful guidance for law enforcement officials, juries or courts. As a result, law is inconsistently and sometimes erroneously applied and the distinctions made by courts between prohibited and permissible materials often appear indefensible. Errors in the application of the law and

uncertainty about its scope also cause interference with the communication of constitutionally protected materials.

4. Public opinion in America does not support the imposition of legal prohibitions upon the right of adults to read or see explicit sexual materials. While a minority of Americans favors such prohibitions, a majority of the American people presently are of the view that adults should be legally able to read or see explicit sexual materials if they wish to do so.

5. The lack of consensus among Americans concerning whether explicit sexual materials should be available to adults in our society, and the significant number of adults who wish to have access to such materials, pose serious problems regarding the enforcement of legal prohibitions upon adults, even aside from the vagueness and subjectivity of present law. Consistent enforcement of even the clearest prohibitions upon consensual adult exposure to explicit sexual materials would require the expenditure of considerable law enforcement resources. In the absence of a persuasive demonstration of damage flowing from consensual exposure to such materials, there seems no justification for thus adding to the overwhelming tasks already placed upon the law enforcement system. Inconsistent enforcement of prohibitions, on the other hand, invites discriminatory action based upon considerations not directly relevant to the policy of the law. The latter alternative also breeds public disrespect for the legal process.

6. The foregoing considerations take on added significance because of the fact that adult obscenity laws deal in the realm of speech and communication. Americans deeply value the right of each individual to determine for himself what books he wishes to read and what pictures or films he wishes to see. Our traditions of free speech and press also value and protect the right of writers, publishers, and booksellers to serve the diverse interests of the public. The spirit and letter of our Constitution tell us that government should not seek to interfere with these rights unless a clear threat of harm makes that course imperative. Moreover, the possibility of the misuse of general obscenity statutes prohibiting distributions of books and films to adults constitutes a continuing threat to the free communication of ideas among Americans—one of the most important foundations of our liberties.

7. In reaching its recommendation that government should not seek to prohibit censensual distributions of sexual materials to adults, the Commission discussed several arguments which are often advanced in support of such legislation. The Commission carefully considered the view that adult legislation should be retained in order to aid in the protection of young persons from exposure to explicit sexual materials. We do not believe that the objective of protecting youth may justifiably be achieved at the expense of denying adults materials of their choice. It seems to us wholly inappropriate to adjust the level of adult communication to that considered suitable for children. Indeed, the Supreme Court has unanimously held that adult legislation premised on this basis is a clearly unconstitutional interference with liberty.

8. There is no reason to suppose that elimination of governmental prohibitions upon the sexual materials which may be made available to adults would

adversely affect the availability to the public of other books, magazines, and films. At the present time, a large range of very explicit textual and pictorial materials are available to adults without legal restrictions in many areas of the country. The size of this industry is small when compared with the overall industry in books, magazines, and motion pictures, and the business in explicit sexual materials is insignificant in comparison with other national economic enterprises. Nor is the business an especially profitable one; profit levels are, on the average, either normal as compared with other businesses or distinctly below average. The typical business entity is a relatively small entrepreneurial enterprise. The long-term consumer interest in such materials has remained relatively stable in the context of the economic growth of the nation generally, and of the media industries in particular.

9. The Commission has also taken cognizance of the concern of many people that the lawful distribution of explicit sexual materials to adults may have a deleterious effect upon the individual morality of American citizens and upon the moral climate in America as a whole. This concern appears to flow from a belief that exposure to explicit materials may cause moral confusion which, in turn, may induce antisocial or criminal behavior. As noted above, the Commission has found no evidence to support such a contention. Nor is there evidence that exposure to explicit sexual materials adversely affects character or moral attitudes regarding sex and sexual conduct.

The concern about the effect of obscenity upon morality is also expressed as a concern about the impact of sexual materials upon American values and standards. Such values and standards are currently in a process of complex change, in both sexual and nonsexual areas. The open availability of increasingly explicit sexual materials is only one of these changes. The current flux in sexual values is related to a number of powerful influences, among which are the ready availability of effective methods of contraception, changes of the role of women in our society, and the increased education and mobility of our citizens. The availability of explicit sexual materials is, the Commission believes, not one of the important influences on sexual morality.

The Commission is of the view that it is exceedingly unwise for government to attempt to legislate individual moral values and standards independent of behavior, especially by restrictions upon consensual communication. This is certainly true in the absence of a clear public mandate to do so, and our studies have revealed no such mandate in the area of obscenity.

The Commission recognizes and believes that the existence of sound moral standards is of vital importance to individuals and to society. To be effective and meaningful, however, these standards must be based upon deep personal commitment flowing from values instilled in the home, in educational and religious training, and through individual resolutions of personal confrontations with human experience. Governmental regulation of moral choice can deprive the individual of the responsibility for personal decision which is essential to the formation of genuine moral standards. Such regulation would also tend to establish an official moral orthodoxy, contrary to our most fundamental constitutional traditions.

Therefore, the Commission recommends the repeal of existing federal legislation which prohibits or interferes with consensual distribution of "obscene" materials to adults. These statutes are: 18 U.S.C. sec. 1461, 1462, 1464, and 1465; 19 U.S.C. sec. 1305; and 39 U.S.C. sec. 3006. The Commission also recommends the repeal of existing state and local legislation which may similarly prohibit the consensual sale, exhibition, or the distribution of sexual materials to adults.

B. *Statutes Relating to Young Persons*

The Commission recommends the adoption by the States of legislation set forth in the Drafts of Proposed Statutes in Section III of this Part of the Commission's Report prohibiting the commercial distribution or display for sale of certain sexual materials to young persons. Similar legislation might also be adopted, where appropriate, by local governments and by the Federal Government for application in areas, such as the District of Columbia, where it has primary jurisdiction over distributional conduct.

The Commission's recommendation of juvenile legislation is joined in by 14 members of the Commission. Two of these feel the legislation should be drawn so as to include appropriate descriptions identifying the material as being unlawful for sale to children. Three members disagree. Other members of the Commission, who generally join in its recommendation for juvenile legislation, disagree with various detailed aspects of the Commission's legislative proposal. These disagreements are noted in the following discussion.

The Commission's recommendation of juvenile legislation flows from these findings and considerations:

A primary basis for the Commission's recommendation for repeal of adult legislation is the fact that extensive empirical investigations do not indicate any causal relationship between exposure to or use of explicit sexual materials and such social or individual harms such as crime, delinquency, sexual or nonsexual deviancy, or severe emotional disturbances. The absence of empirical evidence supporting such a causal relationship also applies to the exposure of children to erotic materials. However, insufficient research is presently available on the effect of the exposure of children to sexually explicit materials to enable us to reach conclusions with the same degree of confidence as for adult exposure. Strong ethical feelings against experimentally exposing children to sexually explicit materials considerably reduced the possibility of gathering the necessary data and information regarding young persons.

In view of the limited amount of information concerning the effects of sexually explicit materials on children, other considerations have assumed primary importance in the Commission's deliberations. The Commission has been influenced, to a considerable degree, by its finding that a large majority of Americans believe that children should not be exposed to certain sexual materials. In addition, the Commission takes the view that parents should be free to make their own conclusions regarding the suitability of explicit sexual materials for their children and that it is appropriate for legislation to aid parents in controlling the access of their children to such materials during their formative years. The Commission recognizes that legislation cannot possibly isolate children from such materials entirely; it also recognizes that exposure of children to sexual materials may not only do no harm but may, in certain instances, actually facilitate much needed communication between parent and child over sexual matters. The Commission is aware, as well, of the considerable danger of creating an unnatural attraction or an enhanced interest in certain materials by making them "forbidden fruit" for young persons. The Commission believes, however, that these considerations can and should be weighed by individual parents in determining their attitudes toward the exposure of their children to sexual materials, and that legislation should aid, rather than undermine, such parental choice.

Taking account of the above considerations, the modern juvenile legislation recommended by the Commission applies only to distributions to children made without parental consent. The recommended legislation applies only to commercial distributions and exhibitions; in the very few instances where non-commercial conduct in this area creates a problem it can be dealt with under existing legal principles for the protection of young persons, such as prohibitions upon contributing to the delinquency of minors. The model legislation also prohibits displaying certain sexual materials for sale in a manner which permits children to view materials which cannot be sold to them. Two members of the Commission, who recommend legislation prohibiting sales to juveniles, do not join in recommending this regulation upon display; one member of the Commission recommends only this display provision, and does not recommend a special statute prohibiting sales to young persons.

The Commission, pursuant to Congressional direction, has given close attention to the definitions of prohibited material included in its recommended model legislation for young persons. A paramount consideration in the Commission's deliberations has been that definitions of prohibited material be as specific and explicit as possible. Such specificity aids law enforcement and facilitates and encourages voluntary adherence to law on the part of retail dealers and exhibitors while causing as little interference as possible with the proper distribution of materials to children and adults. The Commission's recommended legislation seeks to eliminate subjective definitional criteria insofar as that is possible and goes further in that regard than existing state legislation.

The Commission believes that only pictorial material should fall within prohibitions upon sale or commercial display to young persons. An attempt to define prohibited textual materials for young persons with the same degree of specificity as pictorial materials would, the Commission believes, not be advisable. Many worthwhile textual works containing considerable value for young persons, treat sex in an explicit manner and are presently available to young persons. There appears to be no satisfactory way to distinguish, through a workable legal definition, between these works and those which may be deemed inappropriate by some persons for commercial distribution to young persons. As a result, the inclusion of textual material within juvenile legislative prohibitions would pose considerable risks for dealers and distributors in determining what books might legally be sold or displayed to young persons and would thus inhibit the entire distribution of verbal materials by those dealers who do not wish to expose themselves to such risks. The speculative risk of harm to juveniles from some textual material does not justify these dangers. The Commission believes, in addition, that parental concern over the material commercially available to children most often applies to pictorial matter.

The definition recommended by the Commission for inclusion in juvenile legislation covers a range of explicit pictorial and three-dimensional depictions of sexual activity. It does not, however, apply to depictions of nudity alone, unless genital areas are exposed and emphasized. The definition is applicable only if the explicit pictorial material constitutes a dominant part of a work. An exception is provided for works of artistic or anthropological significance.

Seven Commissioners would include verbal materials within the definition of materials prohibited for sale to young persons. They would, however, also include a broad exception for such textual materials when they bear literary, historical, scientific, educational, or other similar social value for young persons.

Because of changing standards as to what material, if any, is inappropriate for sale or display to children, the Commission's model statute contains a provision requiring legislative reconsideration of the need for, and scope of, such legislation at six-year intervals.

The model statute also exempts broadcast or telecast activity from its scope. Industry self-regulation in the past has resulted in little need for governmental intervention. If a need for governmental regulation should arise, the Commission believes that such regulations would be most appropriately prepared in this specialized area through the regulating power of the Federal Communications Commission, rather than through diverse state laws.

The Commission has not fixed upon a precise age limit for inclusion in its recommended juvenile legislation, believing that such a determination is most appropriately made by the States and localities which enact such provisions in light of local standards. All States now fix the age in juvenile obscenity statutes at under 17 or under 18 years. The recommended model statute also excludes married persons, whatever their age, from the category of juveniles protected by the legislation.

The Commission considered the possibility of recommending the enactment of uniform federal legislation requiring a notice or label to be affixed to materials by their publishers, importers or manufacturers, when such materials fall within a definitional provision identical to that included within the recommended state or local model juvenile statute. Under such legislation, the required notice might be used by retail dealers and exhibitors, in jurisdictions which adopt the recommended juvenile legislation, as a guide to what material could not be sold or displayed to young persons. The Commission concluded, however, that such a federal notice or labeling provision would be unwise. So long as definitional provisions are drafted to be as specific as possible, and especially if they include only pictorial material, the Commission believes that the establishment of a federal regulatory notice system is probably unnecessary; specific definitions of pictorial material, such as the Commission recommends, should themselves enable retail dealers and exhibitors to make accurate judgments regarding the status of particular magazines and films. The Commission is also extremely reluctant to recommend imposing any federal system for labeling reading or viewing matter on the basis of its quality or content. The precedent of such required labeling would pose a serious potential threat to First Amendment liberties in other areas of communication. Labels indicating sexual content might also be used artificially to enhance the appeal of certain materials. Two Commissioners favor federally imposed labeling in order to advise dealers as clearly and accurately as possible about what material is forbidden for sale to young persons, placing the responsibility for judging whether material falls within the statute on the publisher or producer who is completely aware of its contents and who is in a position to examine each item individually. . . .

THE GREAT SMUT HUNT

By Robert Yoakum*

It is tempting to laugh off the Attorney General's Commission on Pornography. The zany field trips in search of smut, the endless and futile efforts to define pornography, the pretense that what it recommended wasn't censorship, all provided abundant material for editors, columnists, and cartoonists to ridicule the commission and its report. But while it is easy to guffaw at this federal farce scripted by Edwin Meese—who picked the eleven commission members (six of whom were anti-porn activists, another two of whom shared their views), and who named porn prosecutor Henry Hudson as its head—the comedy of errors has a darker side.

An examination of the motives that led to the formation of the commission, and of the major—albeit overlooked—victory achieved by the administration's censors shows that politics may have had as much to do with the great smut hunt as any attempt to answer the question of whether there is a causal relation between sex and violence. The administration had been looking for raw meat to satisfy the appetite of the religious right—people vexed at the Reagan administration because the Constitution has not yet been amended to permit school prayers, abolish abortion, outlaw pornography, and balance the budget.

One of the most effective members of the evangelical right was, and is, Reverend Don Wildmon, head of the National Federation for Decency in Tupelo, Mississippi, and an unofficial adviser to the Meese commission. It was Wildmon and his placard-bearing vigilantes who, even before the commission began its sessions, succeeded in purging *Playboy* and *Penthouse* from some 6,000 stores.

This past February—five months before the commission announced its findings—the commission's executive director, Alan E. Sears, took a leaf from the reverend's book. On February 11, Sears sent his now-famous, or infamous, letter to five magazine distributors and thirteen chain-store executives saying that the commission had "received testimony alleging that your company is involved in the sale or distribution of pornography. The Commission," the letter continued, "has determined that it would be appropriate to allow your company an opportunity to respond to the allegations prior to drafting its final report section on identified distributors."

There were several curious things about this letter: It was sent despite the expressed objections of several, and perhaps all, of the commission's members. Some members weren't even aware that the letter, written on Justice Department

* From Robert Yoakum. "The Great Smut Hunt." *Columbia Journalism Review*, Vol. 25, No. 3 (September/October 1986), p. 24. Used with permission of the *Columbia Journalism Review* and the author, a syndicated columnist.

stationery, had been sent until as much as a month later, when convenience-store chains began to announce that they were removing the offending magazines. The only "testimony" alleging that the targeted stores and distributors were selling pornography had been that of Reverend Wildmon down in Tupelo. Most important, Sears's letter did not point out that the "pornographic" magazines Wildmon referred to were primarily *Playboy* and *Penthouse*.

At the time, Sears's letter seemed a prodigious gaffe—and, indeed, a federal judge ordered him to rescind it. In hindsight, Sears's end run appears a shrewd bit of strategy. The commission had already informally concluded that *Playboy* and *Penthouse* were neither obscene nor unlawful. What Sears's letter accomplished was the removal of the two magazines from an additional 14,000 stores. In all its coverage of Meese's smut busters, the press overlooked a crucial fact—that *Playboy* and *Penthouse*, but particularly the former, reach hundreds of thousands of readers with political articles by some of our nation's best writers—messages that are anathema to the Reagan administration.

In a single stroke, then, Meese, Sears, or whoever, censored, not smut, but political reporting and commentary. *Playboy*'s newsstand sales have dropped 700,000 since the last change in its advertising rate base. In what other magazine will the people in those newly purified towns read, routinely, articles that sharply criticize the religious right, Reagan's policies, government censorship, the politics of the anti-abortionists, Pentagon and CIA blunders, and Justice Department injustices? Look at a tiny sampling of *Playboy* titles: "Reagan and the Revival of Racism," "Inside the New Right War Machine," "Compulsory Child-birth," "*Playboy* Interview: Fidel Castro," "Exhuming the Spooks," "Support our Boys in Nicaragua" (a satire), "Reagan's Star Wars Plan Won't Work."

The war begun by Wildmon has recently expanded. Reverend Jimmy Swaggart has launched a campaign, already successful in one convenience-store chain, to rid the shelves of *Rolling Stone*, which also runs political articles, and other rock magazines.

The U.S. is by no means the only country in which sexual and political censorship go hand in hand. Sex magazines are banned in the Soviet Union and all Eastern bloc countries, in Iran and Iraq, in South Africa and Chile and China, but are widely available in Denmark, Norway, and Sweden, where political freedoms thrive. There is obviously a lesson here, but it is one that the Reagan administration, in its eagerness to silence its critics and placate the religious right, is willing to ignore. The specific lesson for journalists is that censors are censors are censors. And a free press must stoutly oppose them whether they come garbed as commissars, clerics, or clowns.

CHAPTER **7**

OBSCENITY REDEFINED

The decades following Roth *saw attempted clarification and refinement, then growing confusion. The cases included in this chapter illustrate the point. The Court ruled that booksellers cannot be expected to have knowledge of each book on their shelves* (Smith v. California), *that strict safeguards of search and seizure must be followed* (Marcus v. Search Warrant), *and that "vigilantism" and "harassment" would not be allowed* (Bantam Books v. Sullivan).

Three cases decided upon together in 1966 resulted in further refinement. In Memoirs v. Massachusetts *it was emphasized that the work in question must be "utterly" without redeeming social importance to be judged obscene (later to be rejected in* Miller); *in* Ginzburg v. United States *the concept of "pandering" to erotic interests was introduced as a basis for an obscenity conviction; and in* Mishkin v. New York *the Court held that appealing to prurient interest of a deviant group was a basis for an obscenity conviction.*

Two years later, an additional pair of far-reaching decisions handed down together led the Court for the first time to hold that state and local legislatures may enact carefully drawn laws to protect children from purchasing literature or seeing films even though those same items would be constitutionally available to adults. Ginsberg v. New York *and* Interstate Circuit, Inc. v. Dallas.

In its last decision on obscenity, the Warren Court in the spring of its final term ruled that citizens are free to read and view within the privacy of their own homes obscene material. Stanley v. Georgia.

Cases of lesser importance or ones during this decade in which no opinions were written included granting access to the mails of a magazine designed for homosexuals (One, Inc. v. Olesen) *and one for nudists* (Sunshine Book Co. v. Summerfield), *both announced in 1958. In 1964 the Court reversed an obscenity conviction on arguments of violation of procedural safeguards and due process, but could not agree on a majority opinion despite the 7–2 reversal. A* Quantity of Books v. Kansas.

It also reversed per curiam *the obscenity judgment against Henry Miller's* Tropic of Cancer, *though again the justices could not reach unanimity as to their reasons for reversal.* Grove Press, Inc. v. Gerstein. *In 1967, the Supreme Court emphasized in a* per curiam *decision that "spicy" books and "girlie" movies are not obscene per se and, therefore, are afforded the protection of the First Amendment.* Redrup v. New York.

The more conservative Burger Court, however, took a different tack in the early and middle 1970s. Several decisions indicated a return to the definitions of "basic Roth" and a rejection of the trend liberals hoped for following the Stanley *and* Redrup *decisions. In 1971, two years after* Stanley, *the Court handed down three decisions which tended to encourage obscenity prosecutions at the state and local levels by making it more difficult for Federal courts to intervene in cases involving state obscenity laws.* Perez v. Ledesma, Dyson v. Stein, *and* Byrne v. Karalexis. *In addition, two cases decided later that year prohibited Customs and the Postal Service from being a party to the distribution of obscene matter,* Stanley *notwithstanding.* United States v. Thirty-Seven Photographs *and* United States v. Reidel.

The Court ended its 1972–73 term with a flurry of obscenity decisions— announcing five results in one day. The most significant was Miller v. California, *which established new tests for judging obscenity and which is included later in this chapter. Others that day prohibited obscene matter (1) from being transported through interstate commerce* (United States v. Orito), *(2) from being sold even though there were no illustrations* (Kaplan v. California), *(3) from being imported even for private use under the* Stanley *principle* (United States v. Twelve 200-Ft. Reels of Super 8 mm. Film), *and (4) from being shown in an adults-only theater under the* Stanley *and* Ginsberg *principles* (Paris Adult Theater I v. Slaton).

The following year, on June 24, 1974, the Supreme Court upheld the conviction of William Hamling for mailing brochures deemed to be obscene. Hamling v. United States. *The mailed advertisements promoted, with explicit pictures, a book titled* The Illustrated Presidential Report of the Commission on Obscenity and Pornography. *The text of the work was from the actual governmental report, but Hamling added photographs to illustrate what the report dealt with. A complicating factor in this case was the fact that Hamling was tried prior to the* Miller *decision, which established state or local standards as those by which to judge obscenity. The trial judge had advised the jury that national standards were to be used and had ruled inadmissible a San Diego* (where Hamling did business) *survey which indicated that a majority of local residents favored availability of the Hamling brochure.*

Finally, one year later to the day, the Supreme Court in another 5–4 decision dealt a serious blow to those who had hoped to rely on the Federal Constitution and the Federal courts to "rescue" them from state court convictions for violation of state obscenity laws. Hicks v. Miranda. *At issue was the film "Deep Throat," which had been seized as violating California obscenity laws. Rather than appeal his conviction in the state courts, theater owner Vincent Miranda instituted civil action in the*

Federal courts seeking return of the film and theater receipts and a declaration that the film was protected by the First Amendment. Justice White in the opinion of the Court admonished the Federal courts to not interfere with proper state court prosecutions. A strong dissent by Justice Stewart suggested that the decision ousted the Federal courts from their "historic role" as overseers of constitutional rights. "It is an open invitation to state officials," he wrote, "to institute state proceedings in order to defeat Federal jurisdiction. . . . Today's opinion virtually instructs state officials to answer Federal complaints with state indictments." The effect of the decision, called by some the most important of the 1974–75 term, is to instruct Federal judges to delay intervention in state prosecutions until those prosecutions have run their course. Justice Stewart feared a "race to the courthouse" by both state and Federal officials in order to establish jurisdiction. He was joined in dissenting to the Hicks ruling by Justices Brennan, Douglas, and Marshall, all of whom were holdovers from Warren Court days and all of whom dissented to the 1973 landmark Miller decision and the more recent Hamling case. If there were doubts about the Burger Court's direction relative to obscenity prosecutions, they should have been dispelled by the 1980s.

Including the pertinent decisions involving motion pictures, covered in Chapter 8, the following eleven guidelines can be used to summarize the Court's position on obscenity as the 1980s end:

1. *Obscene material intended for public use does not fall within the protection of the First Amendment.* (Kingsley Books, Roth, Miller)
2. *Sex and obscenity are not synonymous.* (Roth and Redrup)
3. *Ideas may not be proscribed merely because they may be repellent to the majority.* (Kingsley International Pictures)
4. *Possession of obscene material depicting adults within the privacy of one's own home cannot be proscribed by the state* (Stanley), *but possession of child pornography may be prohibited.* (Osborne)
5. *To be judged obscene, material must lack "serious literary, artistic, political or scientific value."* (Miller)
6. *To be judged obscene, the dominant theme of the material taken as a whole must be patently offensive* (Manual Enterprises, Miller), *must appeal to the prurient interest* (Roth, Miller) *of the average adult* (Butler, Ginsberg, Pinkus), *applying contemporary community standards* (Roth, Miller), *or must appeal to the prurient interest of a clearly defined deviant group for which it is designed.* (Mishkin)
7. *If one seeks constitutional protection for his or her work, the purveyor's promotional material must not pander to the salacious or the sexually provocative.* (Ginzburg)
8. *Swift judicial review in obscenity cases must be guaranteed* (Kingsley Books and Freedman) *and the burden of proof in film cases lies with the censor.* (Freedman)

9. *Motion pictures fall under the protection of the First Amendment* (Burstyn v. Wilson), *but because of the unique nature of the medium, special safeguards* (i.e. *licensing*) *may be imposed by the state.* (Times Film)

10. *Literature and films which are constitutionally available to adults are not necessarily constitutionally available to minors.* (Ginsberg *and* Interstate Circuit)

11. *Communities may exercise their land zoning powers to limit location of "adult entertainment" establishments* (e.g. *bookstores or motion picture theaters which distribute material of a highly erotic nature but not considered obscene under the law*) *if they do so with care and reason so as to ensure the constitutional rights or protected communications.* (Young, Schad *and* Renton)

The question of a bookseller's responsibility was before the Court in the 1959 case of Eleazar Smith, proprietor of a Los Angeles Bookstore. Smith v. California. *He was arrested under an ordinance which forbade possession for sale of obscene materials, even though the bookseller might not have knowledge of the contents of the publication in question. The Court in a unanimous decision ruled the ordinance unconstitutional. It held that one could not expect a bookseller to have detailed knowledge of all publications on his shelves, nor could he be expected to make difficult judgments as to the obscenity of each of them. Also, the Court said that this California law would tend to restrict distribution of reading matter which was protected by the Constitution and important to a free society. The bookseller, the Court held, probably would tend to restrict sales only to those volumes he felt were "safe." This reduction in the public's access to reading matter was judged unwise and unconstitutional.*

Two years later, the Court further restricted action taken by local authorities in dealing with obscenity. A Missouri Court authorized search and seizure of certain magazine stands for the purpose of confiscating copies of publications later judged to be obscene. The warrant was issued on the testimony of a single police officer who, after visiting the newsstands, had asserted the periodicals being sold were obscene. No judicial scrutiny was given prior to the search and seizure. Justice Brennan delivered the opinion for the unanimous Court, saying that the procedures employed lacked adequate safeguards to protect non-obscene material from unconstitutional confiscation. Marcus v. Search Warrant.

Similarly, the Rhode Island legislature in 1956 created a nine-person commission appointed by the governor to encourage morality in youth and to combat juvenile delinquency. One of the charges given this body was to "educate" the public relative to obscene literature and to investigate and recommend the prosecution of alleged violators of the state's obscenity statutes. The commission asked for bookseller "cooperation" in removing alleged objectionable publications. The appellants argued that this amounted to nothing more than "police harassment," intimidation, and "vigilantism." The court, in another of the continuing series of obscenity opinions read by Justice Brennan, struck down the commission's actions as a thinly veiled scheme of informal censorship. A comparison with Kingsley Books, Inc. *would be pertinent.*

BANTAM BOOKS, INC. V. SULLIVAN
372 U.S. 58 (1963)

JUSTICE BRENNAN *delivered the opinion of the Court.*

. . . Appellants are four New York publishers of paperback books which have for some time been widely distributed in Rhode Island. Max Silverstein & Sons is the exclusive wholesale distributor of appellants' publications throughout most of the State. The Commission's practice has been to notify a distributor on official Commission stationery that certain designated books or magazines distributed by him had been reviewed by the Commission and had been declared by a majority of its members to be objectionable for sale, distribution or display to youths under 18 years of age. Silverstein had received at least 35 such notices at the time this suit was brought. Among the paperback books listed by the Commission as "objection-able" were one published by appellant Dell Publishing Co., Inc. and another published by appellant Bantam Books, Inc.

The typical notice to Silverstein either solicited or thanked Silverstein, in advance, for his "cooperation" with the Commission, usually reminding Silverstein of the Commission's duty to recommend to the Attorney General prosecution of purveyors of obscenity. Copies of the lists of "objectionable" publications were circulated to local police departments, and Silverstein was so informed in the notices.

Silverstein's reaction on receipt of a notice was to take steps to stop further circulation of copies of the listed publications. He would not fill pending orders for such publications and would refuse new orders. He instructed his field men to visit his retailers and to pick up all unsold copies, and would then promptly return them to the publishers. A local police officer usually visited Silverstein shortly after Silverstein's receipt of a notice to learn what action he had taken. Silverstein was usually able to inform the officer that a specified number of the total of copies received from a publisher had been returned. According to the testimony, Silverstein acted as he did on receipt of the notice, "rather than face the possibility of some sort of a court action against ourselves, as well as the people that we supply." His "cooperation" was given to avoid becoming involved in a "court proceeding" with a "duly authorized organization.". . .

What Rhode Island has done, in fact, has been to subject the distribution of publications to a system of prior administrative restraints, since the Commission is not a judicial body and its decisions to list particular publications as objectionable do not follow judicial determinations that such publications may lawfully be banned. Any system of prior restraint of expression comes to this Court bearing a heavy presumption against its constitutional validity. . . . We have tolerated such a system only where it operated under judicial superintendence and assured an almost immediate judicial determination of the validity of the restraint. *Kingsley Books, Inc. v. Brown.* The system at bar includes no such saving features. On the contrary, its capacity for suppression of constitutionally protected publications is far in excess of that of the typical licensing scheme held constitutionally invalid by this Court. There is no provision whatever for judicial superintendence before notices issue or even for judicial review of the Commission's determinations of objectionableness. The publisher or distributor is not even entitled to notice and hearing before his publications are listed by the Commission as objectionable. Moreover, the Commission's statutory mandate is vague and uninformative, and the Commission has done nothing to make it more precise. Publications are listed as "objectionable" without further elucidation. The distributor is left to speculate whether the Commission considers his publication obscene or simply harmful to juvenile morality. For the Commission's domain is the whole of youthful morals. Finally, we note that although the Commission's supposed concern is limited to youthful readers, the "cooperation" it seeks from distributors invariably entails the complete suppression of the listed publications; adult readers are equally deprived of the opportunity to purchase the publications in the State. Cf. *Butler v. Michigan.*

The procedures of the Commission are radically deficient. They fall far short of the constitutional requirements of governmental regulation of obscenity. We hold that the system of informal censorship disclosed by this record violates the Fourteenth Amendment.

In holding that the activities disclosed on this record are constitutionally proscribed, we do not mean to suggest that private consultation between law enforcement officers and distributors prior to the institution of a judicial proceeding can never be constitutionally permissible. We do not hold that law enforcement officers must renounce all informal contacts with persons suspected of violating valid laws prohibiting obscenity. Where such consultation is genuinely undertaken with the purpose of aiding the distributor to comply with such laws and avoid prosecution under them, it need not retard the full enjoyment of First Amendment freedoms. But that is not this case. The appellees are not law enforcement officers; they do not pretend that they are qualified to give or that they attempt to give distributors only fair legal advice. Their conduct as disclosed by this record shows plainly that they went far beyond advising the distributors of their legal rights and liabilities. Their operation was in fact a scheme of state censorship effectuated by extralegal sanctions; they acted as an agency not to advise but to suppress.

JUSTICE CLARK, *concurring in the result.*

As I read the opinion of the Court, it does much fine talking about freedom of expression and much condemning of the Commission's overzealous efforts to implement the State's obscenity laws for the protection of Rhode Island's youth but, as if shearing a hog, comes up with little wool. In short, it creates the proverbial tempest in a teapot over a number of notices sent out by the Commission asking the cooperation of magazine distributors in preventing the sale of obscene literature to juveniles. . . .

In my view the Court should simply direct the Commission to abandon its delusions of grandeur and leave the issuance of "orders" to enforcement officials and "the State's criminal regulation of obscenity" to the prosecutors, who can substitute prosecution for "thinly veiled threats" in appropriate cases. . . .

JUSTICE HARLAN, *dissenting.*

The Court's opinion fails to give due consideration to what I regard as the central issue in this case—the accommodation that must be made between Rhode Island's concern with the problem of juvenile delinquency and the right of freedom of expression assured by the Fourteenth Amendment. . . .

This Rhode Island Commission was formed for the laudable purpose of combatting juvenile delinquency. While there is as yet no consensus of scientific opinion on the causal relationship between youthful reading or viewing of the "obscene" and delinquent behavior, . . . Rhode Island's approach to the problem is not without respectable support. . . . The States should have a wide range of choice in dealing with such problems, . . . and this court should not interfere with state legislative judgments on them except upon the clearest showing of unconstitutionality. . . .

*   *   *

In the first of three pronouncements on obscenity handed down on the same day, the Warren Court in a 6–3 decision tossed out a Massachusetts court obscenity judgment against the "erotic classic" Memoirs of a Woman of Pleasure, *better known as* Fanny Hill. *Those in the majority, however, could not reach agreement as to the logic that led them to overrule the lower court. The effect of the ruling, however, was to emphasize the concept that material must be "utterly without social redeeming importance" in order for it to be judged obscene, a concept later rejected in* Miller. *The Massachusetts court had held that there might be some value, but not enough to save it from being judged obscene. Illustrating the divergence with which the Court ruled in this case, Justices Brennan, Warren, and Fortas emphasized the failure of the lower court to weigh the "redeeming social importance" of the work, Justice Black held that the court was without constitutional power to limit speech or press, Justice Douglas argued that the government has no power to limit ideas, and Justice Stewart said that the work did not constitute "hard-core pornography." Dissenting were Justice Clark, who held that the book was obscene and had no conceivable social importance, Justice Harlan, who argued that the Fourteenth Amendment says only that obscenity criteria must be applied rationally as was done by the lower court, and Justice White, who held that if the state insists on treating* Memoirs *as obscene, the First Amendment does not prohibit this treatment. It is interesting to note that in* Memoirs *there are none of the "four-letter words" which usually accompany obscenity allegations. Also, it is generally held that* Fanny Hill, *written in 1749, was involved in the first test of obscenity in this country.* Commonwealth v. Holmes, 17 Mass. 335 (1821).

MEMOIRS V. MASSACHUSETTS
383 U.S. 413 (1966)

JUSTICE BRENNAN *announced the judgment of the Court and delivered an opinion in which the Chief Justice and Justice Fortas join.*

. . . The sole question before the state courts was whether *Memoirs* satisfies the test of obscenity established in *Roth v. United States.*

. . . Under this definition, as elaborated in subsequent cases, three elements must coalesce: it must be established that (a) the dominant theme of the material taken as a whole appeals to a prurient interest in sex; (b) the material is patently offensive because it affronts contemporary community standards relating to the description or representation of sexual matters; and (c) the material is utterly without redeeming social value.

The [Massachusetts] Supreme Judicial Court erred in holding that a book need not be "unqualifiedly worthless before it can be deemed obscene." A book cannot be proscribed unless it is found to be *utterly* without redeeming social value. This is so even though the book is found to possess the requisite prurient appeal and to be patently offensive. Each of the three federal constitutional criteria is to be applied independently; the social value of the book can neither be weighed against nor canceled by its prurient appeal or patent offensiveness. Hence, even on the view of the court below that *Memoirs* possessed only a modicum of social value, its judgment must be reversed as being founded on an erroneous interpretation of a federal constitutional standard. . . .

JUSTICE DOUGLAS, *concurring.*

. . . Every time an obscenity case is to be argued here, my office is flooded with letters and postal cards urging me to protect the community or the Nation by striking down the publication. The messages are often identical even down to commas and semicolons. The inference is irresistible that they were all copied from a school or church blackboard. Dozens of postal cards often are mailed from the same precinct. The drives are incessant and the pressures are great. Happily we do not bow to them. I mention them only to emphasize the lack of popular understanding of our constitutional system. Publications and utterances were made immune from majoritarian control by the First Amendment, applicable to the States by reason of the Fourteenth. No exceptions were made, not even for obscenity. The Court's contrary conclusion in *Roth*, where obscenity was found to be "outside" the First Amendment, is without justification. . . .

JUSTICE CLARK, *dissenting.*

It is with regret that I write this dissenting opinion. However, the public should know of the continuous flow of pornographic material reaching this Court and the increasing problem States have in controlling it. *Memoirs of a Woman of Pleasure,* the book involved here, is typical. I have "stomached" past cases for almost 10 years without much outcry. Though I am not known to be a purist—or a shrinking violet—this book is too much even for me. It is important that the Court has refused to declare it obscene and thus gives it further circulation. In order to give my remarks the proper setting I have been obliged to portray the book's contents, which gives me embarrassment. However, quotations from typical episodes would so debase our reports that I will not follow that course. . . .

In my view evidence of social importance is relevant to the determination of the ultimate question of obscenity. But social importance does not constitute a separate and distinct constitutional test. Such evidence must be considered together with evidence that the material in question appeals to prurient interest and is patently offensive. Accordingly, we must first turn to the book here under attack. . . .

. . . In my view, the book's repeated and unrelieved appeals to the prurient interest of the average person leave it utterly without redeeming social importance.

JUSTICE HARLAN, *dissenting.*

The central development that emerges from the aftermath of *Roth v. United States* is that no stable approach to the obscenity problem has yet been devised by this Court. Two Justices believe that the First and Fourteenth Amendments absolutely protect obscene and nonobscene material alike. Another Justice believes that neither the States nor the Federal Government may suppress any material save for "hard-core pornography.". . .

My premise is that in the area of obscenity the Constitution does not bind the States and the Federal Government in precisely the same fashion. . . .

. . . Federal suppression of allegedly obscene matter should, in my view, be constitutionally limited to that often described as "hard-core pornography.". . .

To me it is plain, for instance, that *Fanny Hill* does not fall within this class and could not be barred from the federal mails. . . .

State obscenity laws present problems of quite a different order. The varying conditions across the country, the range of views on the need and reasons for curbing obscenity, and the traditions of local self-government in matters of public welfare all favor a far more flexible attitude in defining the bounds for the States. From my standpoint, the Fourteenth Amendment requires of a State only that it apply criteria rationally related to the accepted notion of obscenity and that it reach results not wholly out of step with current American standards. . . .

JUSTICE WHITE, *dissenting.*

In my view, "social importance" is not an independent test of obscenity but is relevant only to determining the predominant prurient interest of the material, a determination which the court or the jury will make based on the material itself and all the evidence in the case, expert or otherwise.

Application of the *Roth* test, as I understand it, necessarily involves the exercise of judgment by legislatures, courts and juries. . . .

Finally, it should be remembered that if the publication and sale of *Fanny Hill* and like books are proscribed, it is not the Constitution that imposes the ban. Censure stems from a legislative act, and legislatures are constitutionally free to embrace such books whenever they wish to do so. But if a State insists in treating *Fanny Hill* as obscene and forbidding its sale, the First Amendment does not prevent it from doing so.

I would affirm the judgment below.

* * *

No obscenity decision in the 1960s created so much heated discussion as did the Ginzburg *decision, handed down on the same day as* Memoirs, supra, *and* Mishkin. *With* Ginzburg, *the Court in a 5–4 decision interjected a new element as a test for obscenity—pandering, i.e. openly advertising and appealing to erotic interests. This takes into account the intent of the author and apparently is to be applied in borderline cases. A publisher, the Court held, cannot plead "redeeming social importance" on the one hand and then blatantly emphasize the salacious on the other. Dissenters pointed out that the material mailed by Ginzburg was not judged obscene and that the Court's action was not based upon the publications, but the manner in which they were promoted. Justice Black again took his "absolutist" view of the First Amendment. Justice Douglas did likewise, and in addition, questioned advertising in general under this ruling. Justice Harlan reiterated his view that only "hard-core pornography" should be banned. And Justice Stewart denied that Ginzburg had enjoyed due process because of the new test imposed by the Court in disapproving of his "sordid business." Ginzburg had been sentenced to a five-year prison term plus $28,000 fine.*

GINZBURG V. UNITED STATES
383 U.S. 463 (1966)

JUSTICE BRENNAN *delivered the opinion of the Court.*

. . . In the cases in which this Court has decided obscenity questions since *Roth*, it has regarded the materials as sufficient in themselves for the determination of the question. In the present case, however, the prosecution charged the offense in the context of the circumstances of production, sale, and publicity and assumed that, standing alone, the publications themselves might not be obscene. We agree that the question of obscenity may include consideration of the setting in which the publications were presented as an aid to determining the question of obscenity, and assume without deciding that the prosecution could not have succeeded otherwise. . . . We view the publications against a background of commercial exploitation of erotica solely for the sake of their prurient appeal. The record in that regard amply supports the decision of the trial judge that the mailing of all three publications offended the statute.

The three publications were *Eros*, a hard-cover magazine of expensive format; *Liaison*, a bi-weekly newsletter; and *The Housewife's Handbook on Selective Promiscuity* (hereinafter the *Handbook*), a short book. The issue of *Eros* specified in the indictment, Vol. 1, No. 4, contains 15 articles and photo-essays on the subject of love, sex, and sexual relations. The specified issue of *Liaison*, Vol. 1, No. 1, contains a prefatory "Letter from the Editors" announcing its dedication to "keeping sex an art and preventing it from becoming a science." The remainder of the issue consists of digests of two articles concerning sex and sexual relations which had earlier appeared in professional journals and a report of an interview with a psychotherapist who favors the broadest license in sexual relationships. As the trial judge noted, "[w]hile the treatment is largely superficial, it is presented entirely without restraint of any kind. According to defendants' own expert, it is entirely without literary merit." The *Handbook* purports to be a sexual autobiography detailing with complete candor the author's sexual experiences from age 3 to age 36. The text includes, the prefatory and concluding sections of the book elaborate, her views on such subjects as sex education of children, laws regulating private consensual adult sexual practices, and the equality of women in sexual relationships. It was claimed at trial that women would find the book valuable, for example as a marriage manual or as an aid to the sex education of their children.

Besides testimony as to the merit of the material, there was abundant evidence to show that each of the accused publications was originated or sold as stock in trade of the sordid business of pandering—"the business of purveying textual or graphic matter openly advertised to appeal to the erotic interest of their customers." *Eros* early sought mailing privilege from the postmasters of Intercourse and Blue Ball, Pennsylvania. The trial court found the obvious, that these hamlets were chosen only for the value their names would have in furthering petitioners' efforts to sell their publications on the basis of salacious appeal; the facilities of the post offices were inadequate to handle the anticipated volume of mail, and the privileges were denied. Mailing privileges were then obtained from the postmaster of Middlesex, New Jersey. *Eros* and *Liaison* thereafter mailed several million circulars soliciting subscriptions from that post office; over 5,500 copies of the *Handbook* were mailed.

This evidence, in our view, was relevant in determining the ultimate question of "obscenity" and, in the context of this record, serves to resolve all ambiguity and doubt. The deliberate representation of petitioners' publications as erotically arousing, for example, stimulated the reader to accept them as prurient; he looks for titillation, not for saving intellectual content. Similarly, such representation would tend to force public confrontation with the potentially offensive aspects of the work; the brazenness of such an appeal heightens the offensiveness of the publications to those who are offended by such material. And the circumstances of presentation and dissemination of material are equally relevant to determining whether social importance claimed for material in the courtroom was, in the circumstances, pretense or reality—whether it was the basis upon which it was traded in the marketplace or a spurious claim for litigation purposes. Where the purveyor's sole emphasis is on the sexually provocative aspects of his publications, that fact may be decisive in the determination of obscenity. Certainly in a prosecution which, as here, does not necessarily imply suppression of the materials involved, the fact that they originate or are used as a subject of pandering is relevant to the application of the *Roth* test. . . .

It is important to stress that this analysis simply elaborates the test by which the obscenity *vel non* of the material must be judged. Where an exploitation of interests in titillation by pornography is shown with respect to material lending itself to such exploitation through pervasive treatment or description of sexual matters, such evidence may support the determination that the material is obscene even though in other contexts the material would escape such condemnation. . . .

JUSTICE BLACK, *dissenting*.

Only one stark fact emerges with clarity out of the confusing welter of opinions and thousands of words written in this and two other cases today. That fact is that Ginzburg, petitioner here, is now finally and authoritatively condemned to serve five years in prison for distributing printed material about sex which neither Ginzburg nor anyone else could possibly have known to be criminal. Since, as I have said many times, I believe the Federal Government is without any power whatever under the Constitution to put any type of burden on speech and expression of ideas of any kind (as distinguished from conduct), I agree with Part II of the dissent of my Brother Douglas in this case, and I would reverse Ginzburg's conviction on this ground alone. Even assuming, however, that the Court is correct in holding today that Congress does have power to clamp official censorship on some subjects selected by the Court in some ways approved by it, I believe that the federal obscenity statute as enacted by Congress and as enforced by the Court against Ginzburg in this case should be held invalid on two other grounds.

Criminal punishment by government, although universally recognized as a necessity in limited areas of conduct, is an exercise of one of government's most awesome and dangerous powers. Consequently, wise and good governments make all possible efforts to hedge this dangerous power by restricting it within easily identifiable boundaries. . . .

I agree with my Brother Harlan that the Court has in effect rewritten the federal obscenity statute and thereby imposed on Ginzburg standards and criteria that Congress never thought about, or if it did think about them certainly did not adopt them. Consequently, Ginzburg is, as I see it, having his conviction and sentence affirmed upon the basis of a statute amended by this Court for violation of which amended statute he was not charged in the courts below. Such an affirmance we have said violates due process. . . .

My conclusion is that certainly after the fourteen separate opinions handed down in these three cases today no person, not even the most learned judge much less a layman, is capable of knowing in advance of an ultimate decision in his particular case by this Court whether certain material comes within the area of "obscenity" as that term is confused by the Court today. For this reason even if, as appears from the result of the three cases today, this country is far along the way to a censorship of the subjects about which the people can talk or write, we need not commit further constitutional transgressions by leaving people in the dark as to what literature or what words or what symbols if distributed through the mails make a man a criminal. As bad and obnoxious as I believe governmental censorship is in a Nation that has accepted the First Amendment as its basic ideal for freedom, I am compelled to say that censorship that would stamp certain books and literature as illegal in advance of publication or conviction would in some ways be preferable to the unpredictable book-by-book censorship into which we have now drifted. . . .

JUSTICE DOUGLAS, *dissenting*.

The use of sex symbols to sell literature, today condemned by the Court, engrafts another exception on First Amendment rights that is as unwarranted as the judge-made exception concerning obscenity. This new exception condemns an advertising technique as old as history. The advertisements of our best magazines are chock-full of thighs, ankles, calves, bosoms, eyes, and hair, to draw the potential buyers' attention to lotions, tires, food, liquor, clothing, autos, and even insurance policies. The sexy advertisement neither adds nor detracts from the quality of the merchandise being offered for sale. And I do not see how it adds to or detracts one whit from the legality of the book being distributed. A book should stand on its own, irrespective of the reasons why it was written or the wiles used in selling it. I cannot imagine any promotional effort that would make chapters 7 and 8 of the *Song of Solomon* any the less or any more worthy of First Amendment protection than does its unostentatious inclusion in the average edition of the Bible. . . .

JUSTICE HARLAN, *dissenting*.

The First Amendment, in the obscenity area, no longer fully protects material on its face nonobscene, for such material must now also be examined in the light of the defendant's conduct, attitude, motives. This seems to me a mere euphemism for allowing punishment of a person who mails otherwise constitutionally protected material just because a jury or a judge may not find him or his business agreeable. Were a State to enact a "panderer" statute under its police power, I have little doubt that—subject to clear drafting to avoid attacks on vagueness and equal protection grounds—such a statute would be constitutional. Possibly the same might be true of the Federal Government acting under its postal or commerce powers. What I fear the Court has done today is in effect to write a new statute, but without the sharply focused definitions and standards necessary in such a sensitive area. Casting such a dubious gloss over a straight-forward 101-year-old statute (see 13 Stat. 507) is for me an astonishing piece of judicial improvisation. . . .

JUSTICE STEWART, *dissenting*.

The petitioner has been sentenced to five years in prison for sending through the mail copies of a magazine, a pamphlet, and a book. There was testimony at this trial that these publications possess artistic and social merit. Personally, I have a hard time discerning any. Most of the material strikes me as both vulgar and unedifying. But if the First Amendment means anything, it means that a man cannot be sent to prison merely for distributing publications which offend a judge's esthetic sensibilities, mine or any other's.

Censorship reflects a society's lack of confidence in itself. It is a hallmark of an authoritarian regime. Long ago those who wrote our First Amendment charted a different course. They believed a society can be truly strong only when it is truly free. In the realm of expression they put their faith, for better or for worse, in the enlightened choice of the people, free from the interference of a policeman's intrusive thumb or a judge's heavy hand. So it is that the Constitution protects coarse expression as well as refined, and vulgarity no less than elegance. A book worthless to me may convey something of value to my neighbor. In the free society to which our Constitution has committed us, it is for each to choose for himself. . . .

There does exist a distinct and easily identifiable class of material in which all of these elements coalesce. It is that, and that alone, which I think government may constitutionally suppress, whether by criminal or civil sanctions. I have referred to such material before as hard-core pornography, without trying further to define it. *Jacobellis v. Ohio.* . . .

The Court today appears to concede that the materials Ginzburg mailed were themselves protected by the First Amendment. But, the Court says, Ginzburg can still be sentenced to five years in prison for mailing them. Why? Because, says the Court, he was guilty of "commercial exploitation," of "pandering," and of "titillation." But Ginzburg was not charged with "commercial exploitation"; he was not charged with "pandering"; he was not charged with "titillation." Therefore, to affirm his conviction now on any of those grounds, even if otherwise valid, is to deny him due process of law. But those grounds are not, of course, otherwise valid. Neither the statute under which Ginzburg was convicted nor any other federal statute I know of makes "commercial exploitation" or "pandering" or "titillation" a criminal offense. And any criminal law that sought to do so in the terms so elusively defined by the Court would, of course, be unconstitutionally vague and therefore void. All of these matters are developed in the dissenting opinions of my Brethren, and I simply note here that I fully agree with them.

For me, however, there is another aspect of the Court's opinion in this case that is even more regrettable. Today the Court assumes the power to deny Ralph Ginzburg the protection of the First Amendment because it disapproves of his "sordid business." That is a power the Court does not possess. For the First Amendment protects us all with an even hand. It applies to Ralph Ginzburg with no less completeness and force than to G. P. Putnam's Sons. In upholding and enforcing the Bill of Rights, this Court has no power to pick or to choose. When we lose sight of that fixed star of constitutional adjudication, we lose our way. For then we forsake a government of law and are left with government by Big Brother. . . .

*   *   *

Another new dimension was invoked the same day in the case of Edward Mishkin, a New York publisher of sado-masochistic material. Mishkin v. New York. *It was claimed that Mishkin's books were of no interest to the "average person" (Roth), but were written only to certain deviant groups. Again speaking for the majority, Justice Brennan held that the "prurient interest" requirement of Roth could be met if the material in question is aimed at the prurient interest of a clearly defined deviate group, in addition to the "average person" as in Roth. In the 6–3 decision, dissents echoed previous stands: Justice Black holding that the state has no power to limit freedom of expression, Justice Douglas arguing that the First Amendment allows all ideas to be expressed, even if "offbeat," and Justice Stewart again holding that the material before the Court did not constitute "hard-core pornography."*

The inevitable question of the constitutionality of variable standards of obscenity, one standard for adults and another for children, was answered by the Warren Court in a 1968 decision, Ginsberg v. New York. *The Court held that the state has the power to "protect" its children from material deemed harmful to them—in this case four "girlie" magazines—even though this same material would be constitutionally available to adults. It was the first time the Court had upheld a censorship law designed specifically to apply to minors. Justice Brennan, writing for the 6–3 majority, acknowledged that there was no scientifically demonstrated causal relationship between the reading of salacious literature and antisocial behavior, but noted also that this relationship had not been disproved either. Justice Fortas, dissenting, chastised his colleagues for not considering the alleged obscenity of the magazines in question, and Justice Douglas, also dissenting, labeled the Court the "nation's board of censors." A similar principle in relation to motion picture classification was expressed in* Interstate Circuit, Inc. v. Dallas, *handed down the same day.*

GINSBERG V. NEW YORK
390 U.S. 629 (1968)

JUSTICE BRENNAN *delivered the opinion of the Court.*

This case presents the question of the constitutionality on its face of a New York criminal obscenity statute which prohibits the sale to minors under 17 years of age of material defined to be obscene on the basis of its appeal to them whether or not it would be obscene to adults.

Appellant and his wife operate "Sam's Stationery and Luncheonette" in Bellmore, Long Island. They have a lunch counter and, among other things, also sell magazines including some so-called "girlie" magazines. Appellant was prosecuted under two informations, each in two counts, which charged that he personally sold a 16-year-old boy two "girlie" magazines on each of two dates in October 1965, in violation of sec. 484-h of the New York Penal Law. He was tried before a judge without a jury in Nassau County District Court and was found guilty on both counts. The judge found (1) that the magazines contained pictures which depicted female "nudity" in a manner defined in subsection 1 (b), that is "the showing of . . . female . . . buttocks with less than a full opaque covering, or the showing of the female breast with less than a fully opaque covering of any portion thereof below the top of the nipple . . . ," and (2) that the pictures were "harmful to minors" in that they had, within the meaning of subsection 1 (f), ". . . that quality of . . . representation . . . of nudity . . . [which] . . . (i) predominantly appeals to the prurient, shameful or morbid interest of minors, and (ii) is patently offensive to prevailing standards in the adult community as a whole with respect to what is suitable material for minors, and (iii) is utterly without redeeming social importance for minors.". . . .

The "girlie" picture magazines involved in the sales here are not obscene for adults. *Redrup v. New York*. But sec. 484-h does not bar the appellant from stocking the magazines and selling them to persons 17 years of age or older. . . .

Appellant's attack is not that New York was without power to draw the line at age 17. Rather, his contention is the broad proposition that the scope of the constitutional freedom of expression secured to a citizen to read or see material concerned with sex cannot be made to depend upon whether the citizen is an adult or a minor. He accordingly insists that the denial to minors under 17 of access to material condemned by sec. 484-h, insofar as that material is not obscene for persons 17 years of age or older, constitutes an unconstitutional deprivation of protected liberty. . . .

The well-being of its children is of course a subject within the State's constitutional power to regulate, and, in our view, two interests justify the limitations in sec. 484-h upon the availability of sex material to minors under 17, at least if it was rational for the legislature to find that the minors' exposure to such material might be harmful. . . . Indeed, subsection 1 (f) (ii) of sec. 484-h expressly recognizes the parental role in assessing sex related material harmful to minors according "to prevailing standards in the adult community as a whole with respect to what is suitable material for minors." Moreover, the prohibition against sales to minors does not bar parents who so desire from purchasing the magazines for their children.

The State also has an independent interest in the well-being of its youth. . . . In *Prince v. Massachusetts*, this Court . . . recognized that the State has an interest "to protect the welfare of children" and to see that they are "safeguarded from abuses" which might prevent their "growth into free and independent well-developed men and citizens." The only question remaining, therefore, is whether the New York Legislature might rationally conclude, as it has, that exposure to the materials proscribed by sec. 484-h constitutes such an "abuse."

Section 484-e of the law states a legislative finding that the material condemned by sec. 484-h is "a basic factor in impairing the ethical and moral development of our youth and a clear and present danger to the people of the state." It is very doubtful that this finding expresses an accepted scientific fact. But obscenity is not protected expression and may be suppressed without a showing of the circumstances which lie behind the phrase "clear and present danger" in its application to protected speech. *Roth v. United States.* . . . [T]here is no lack of "studies" which purport to demonstrate that obscenity is or is not "a basic factor in impairing the ethical and moral development of . . . youth and a clear and present danger to the people of the state." But the growing consensus of commentators is that "[w]hile these studies all agree that a causal link has not been demonstrated, they are equally agreed that a causal link has not been disproved either." We do not demand of legislatures a "scientifically certain criteria of legislation.". . .

JUSTICE DOUGLAS, *with whom Justice Black concurs, dissenting.*

. . . The notion of censorship is founded on the belief that speech and press sometimes do harm and therefore can be regulated. I once visited a foreign nation where the regime of censorship was so strict that all I could find in the bookstalls were tracts on religion and tracts on mathematics. Today the Court determines the constitutionality of New York's law regulating the sale of literature to children on the basis of the reasonableness of the law in light of the welfare of the child. If the problem of state and federal regulation of "obscenity" is in the field of substantive due process, I see no reason to limit the legislatures to protecting children alone. The "juvenile delinquents" I have known are mostly over 50 years of age. If rationality is the measure of the validity of this law, then I can see how modern Anthony Comstocks could make out a case for "protecting" many groups in our society, not merely children.

While I find the literature and movies which come to us for clearance exceedingly dull and boring, I understand how some can and do become very excited and alarmed and think that something should be done to stop the flow. It is one thing for parents and the religious organizations to be active and involved. It is quite a different matter for the State to become implicated as a censor. As I read the First Amendment, it was designed to keep the State and the hands of all state officials off the printing presses of America and off the distribution systems for all printed literature. . . .

. . . Censors are of course propelled by their own neuroses. That is why a universally accepted definition of obscenity is impossible. Any definition is indeed highly subjective, turning on the neurosis of the censor. Those who have a deep-seated, subconscious conflict may well become either great crusaders against a particular kind of literature or avid customers of it. That, of course, is the danger of letting any group of citizens be the judges of what other people, young or old, should read. . . .

＊   ＊   ＊

In its final decision on obscenity, the Warren Court ruled that the state may not prohibit mere possession of obscene material within the privacy of one's home. "If the First Amendment means anything," wrote Justice Marshall in the opinion of the Court, "it means that a state has no business telling a man, sitting alone in his own house, what books he may read or what films he may watch. Our whole constitutional heritage rebels at the thought of giving government the power to control men's minds." He was careful, however, to distinguish between the conditions of the Stanley case and permissible state control of the distribution of obscene matter, such as was upheld in Roth and subsequent decisions. Stanley was sentenced to one year in prison for possession of obscene material, a violation of Georgia statutes. In a concurring opinion, Justices Stewart, Brennan and White departed from the majority by noting that their vote for reversal of Stanley's conviction was based on the conditions of the search of his home rather than on the private possession question. The Warren Court clearly took a final firm step in protecting one's rights under the Constitution to read or view privately whatever one wishes without interference from the state. The importance of Stanley, however, has eroded with time and new appointments to the High Court. The decision has taken on more importance in questions of privacy. Also, the Supreme Court in 1990 ruled 6-3 that child pornography does not fall within the material Stanley protects. Osborne v. Ohio. See also New York v. Ferber in Chapter 1. The dreams of those who hoped Stanley would be a springboard to new First Amendment liberalism were not to be realized.

STANLEY V. GEORGIA
394 U.S. 557 (1969)

JUSTICE MARSHALL *delivered the opinion of the Court.*

An investigation of appellant's alleged bookmaking activities led to the issuance of a search warrant for appellant's home. Under authority of this warrant, federal and state agents secured entrance. They found very little evidence of bookmaking activity, but while looking through a desk drawer in an upstairs bedroom, one of the federal agents, accompanied by a state officer, found three reels of eight-millimeter film. Using a projector and screen found in an upstairs living room, they viewed the films. The state officer concluded that they were obscene and seized them.

It is true that *Roth* does declare, seemingly without qualification, that obscenity is not protected by the First Amendment. That statement has been repeated in various forms in subsequent cases. However, neither *Roth* nor any subsequent decision of this Court dealt with the precise problem involved in the present case. *Roth* was convicted of mailing obscene circulars and advertising, and an obscene book, in violation of a federal obscenity statute. . . . None of the statements cited by the Court in *Roth* for the proposition that "this Court has always assumed that obscenity is not protected by the freedoms of speech and press" were made in the context of a statute punishing mere private possession of obscene material; the cases cited deal for the most part with use of the mails to distribute objectionable material or with some form of public distribution or dissemination. Moreover, none of this Court's decisions subsequent to *Roth* involved prosecution for private possession of obscene materials. Those cases dealt with the power of the State and Federal Governments to prohibit or regulate certain public actions taken or intended to be taken with respect to obscene matter. . . .

. . . [Appellant] is asserting the right to read or observe what he pleases—the right to satisfy his intellectual and emotional needs in the privacy of his own home. He is asserting the right to be free from state inquiry into the contents of his library. Georgia contends that appellant does not have these rights, that there are certain types of materials that the individual may not read or even possess. Georgia justifies this assertion by arguing that the films in the present case are obscene. But we think that mere categorization of these films as "obscene" is insufficient justification for such a drastic invasion of personal liberties guaranteed by the First and Fourteenth Amendments. Whatever may be the justifications for other statutes regulating obscenity, we do not think they reach into the privacy of one's own home. If the First Amendment means anything, it means that a State has no business telling a man, sitting alone in his own house, what books he may read or what films he may watch. Our whole constitutional heritage rebels at the thought of giving government the power to control men's minds.

And yet, in the face of these traditional notions of individual liberty, Georgia asserts the right to protect the individual's mind from the effects of obscenity. We are not certain that this argument amounts to anything more than the assertion that the State has the right to control the moral content of a person's thoughts. To some, this may be a noble purpose, but it is wholly inconsistent with the philosophy of the First Amendment. . . .

JUSTICE STEWART, *with whom Justice Brennan and Justice White join, concurring in the result.*

. . . To condone what happened here is to invite a government official to use a seemingly precise and legal warrant only as a ticket to get into a man's home, and, once inside, to launch forth upon unconfined searches and indiscriminate seizures as if armed with all the unbridled and illegal power of a general warrant. . . .

*   *   *

Two decisions of 1971 began to minimize the 1969 Stanley rule. Both dealt with distribution of obscene matter in light of the Stanley decision, which allowed individual citizens to possess obscene material for their private use. The first case, Thirty-Seven Photographs, *involved seizure by customs officials of allegedly obscene material publisher Milton Luros was attempting to bring into the United States from Europe. Luros claimed he wanted to use the pictures in a book describing sexual positions. The lower courts, citing Stanley, found for Luros, but the Supreme Court reversed, holding that the approval of private possession of obscene matter under Stanley did not prohibit the government from removing such material intended for commercial purposes from the normal channels of commerce. Justice White's opinion was joined by Chief Justice Burger and Justices Blackmun and Brennan. Justices Black, Douglas and Marshall dissented. Justices Harlan and*

Stewart agreed with the first part of the White opinion setting constitutionally allowable time limits for the initiation of forfeiture proceedings, but Justice Stewart emphasized that he would support the rights of an individual citizen to bring through customs obscene matter intended for personal use.

A second post-Stanley decision handed down the same day emphasized the principles outlined in the landmark 1957 Roth decision, thereby ruling out the use of the mails to deliver obscene material. Using reasoning similar to that used in Thirty-Seven Photographs, *the Supreme Court majority ruled that Stanley's approval of the possession of obscene matter for private use did not sanction the use of the channels of commerce to distribute obscene material nor did it sanction the government (i.e. the Postal Service) to be a party to such distribution. Norman Reidel had been indicted for mailing an illustrated publication, "The True Facts About Imported Pornography." The lower courts dismissed the indictment under the* Stanley *principle. A seven-man Supreme Court majority reversed. Justice White delivered the opinion of the Court. Justices Black and Douglas dissented. It was to be Justice Black's final statement on obscenity and is recalled because of his strident—yet tempered—scolding of his colleagues. He died the following September at age 85 following 34 years on the Supreme Court during which he became known as one of its great philosophers and humanists.*

UNITED STATES V. REIDEL
402 U.S. 351 (1971)

JUSTICE WHITE *delivered the opinion of the Court.*

. . . The District Court ignored both *Roth* and the express limitations on the reach of the *Stanley* decision. Relying on the statement in *Stanley* that "the Constitution protects the right to receive information and ideas . . . regardless of their social worth," the trial judge reasoned that "if a person has the right to receive and possess this material, then someone must have the right to deliver it to him.". . .

The District Court gave *Stanley* too wide a sweep. To extrapolate from Stanley's right to have a peruse obscene material in the privacy of his own home a First Amendment right in Reidel to sell it to him would effectively scuttle *Roth*, the precise result that the *Stanley* opinion abjured. Whatever the scope of the "right to receive" referred to in *Stanley*, it is not so broad as to immunize the dealings in obscenity in which Reidel engaged here—dealings which *Roth* held unprotected by the First Amendment. . . .

The personal constitutional rights of those like Stanley to possess and read obscenity in their homes and their freedom of mind and thought do not depend on whether the materials are obscene or whether obscenity is constitutionally protected. Their rights to have and view that material in private are independently saved by the Constitution.

Reidel is in a wholly different position. He has no complaints about governmental violations of his private thoughts or fantasies, but stands squarely on a claimed First Amendment right to do business in obscenity and use the mails in the process. But *Roth* has squarely placed obscenity and its distribution outside the reach of the First Amendment and they remain there today. *Stanley* did not overrule *Roth* and we decline to do so now. . . .

JUSTICE BLACK, *with whom Justice Douglas joins, dissenting.*

. . . I particularly regret to see the Court revive the doctrine of *Roth v. United States* that "obscenity" is speech for some reason unprotected by the First Amendment. As the Court's many decisions in this area demonstrate, it is extremely difficult for judges or any other citizens to agree on what is "obscene." Since the distinctions between protected speech and "obscenity" are so elusive and obscure almost every "obscenity" case involves difficult constitutional issues. After *Roth* our docket and those of other courts have constantly been crowded with cases where judges are called upon to decide whether a particular book, magazine, or movie may be banned. I have expressed before my view that I can imagine no task for which this Court of lifetime judges is less equipped to deal.

. . . Despite the proven shortcomings of *Roth*, the majority today reaffirms the validity of that dubious decision. Thus, for the foreseeable future this Court must sit as a Board of Supreme Censors, sifting through books and magazines and watching movies because some official fears they deal too explicitly with sex. I can imagine no more distasteful, useless, and time-consuming task for the members of this Court than perusing this material to determine whether it has "redeeming social value." This absurd spectacle could be avoided if we would adhere to the literal command of the First Amendment that "Congress shall make no law . . . abridging the freedom of speech, or of the press. . . ."

Since the plurality opinion offers no plausible reason to distinguish private possession of "obscenity" from importation for private use, I can only conclude that at least four members of the Court would overrule *Stanley*. Or perhaps in the future that case will be recognized as good law only when a man writes salacious books in his attic, prints them in his basement, and reads them in his living room. . . .

*　　*　　*

Not only was the Burger Court returning to Roth, *but in a June 1973 decision,* Miller v. California, *it was, by a 5–4 majority, strengthening* Roth *by firmly rejecting two mitigating concepts suggested during the Warren era. One was the "national standards" test for judging what was obscene suggested by a plurality decision in the* Jacobellis v. Ohio *film case of 1964. The Court in* Miller *was not specific relative to state-wide or local standards, discussing both state offenses and "local tastes.". . .*

Equally important in the 1973 Miller *decision was a rejection of another earlier test suggested in* Memoirs v. Massachusetts—*that to be judged obscene, the material would have to be "utterly without redeeming social value," a test extremely difficult to establish legally. In its place the Burger majority in* Miller *held that the work only must lack "serious literary, artistic, political, or scientific value," certainly easier for prosecutors to prove, though probably just as difficult to define. Because of its frequent use, this test is best known by its acronym SLAPS, for "serious literary, artistic, political, or scientific."*

Justice Brennan, the author of the Roth *opinion 16 years earlier and considered the Warren Court's "resident expert" on obscenity, dissented in* Miller *and in another case filed the same day* (Paris Adult Theatre I v. Slaton, *covered in Chapter 8). In the latter, he denounced current legal thinking relative to obscenity as well as his* Roth *philosophy, which, he said, had proven to be a failure. Douglas also scratched at new ground when, in addition to his usual "absolutist" position relative to the First Amendment, he suggested as preferable to the present chaos a constitutional amendment including some sort of national "censor" who would at least be able to offer some legal guidance to writers and artists who now must publish before any type of legal assessment is offered on the legality of what they have published and then, of course, it may be too late to avoid arrest and prosecution. Also dissenting were two other Warren Court holdovers, Justices Marshall and Stewart. The five-man majority, then, was made up of Justices Burger, Blackmun, Powell, Rehnquist (all Nixon appointees) and White (appointed by President Kennedy). Chief Justice Burger, writing for the majority, noted that not since* Roth *had a majority of the Justices been able to agree on any standard of what constituted obscene matter. Much in Burger's opinion can be compared with his earlier opinion in* Rowan *(see Chapter 4). Both emphasize invasion-of-privacy aspects inherent in unsolicited material deemed offensive by the recipient.*

It apparently was the hope of the majority in Miller *that his "new definition" of obscenity would spare the Federal courts—particularly the Supreme Court—of an increasing number of complex obscenity cases. The Court apparently was attempting to tell state and local governments that, in effect, they were free to set their own community standards of "taste and decency" and to settle their own problems. But the years immediately following* Miller *indicated that such hope was folly. The SLAPS test appeared to be as confusing and uncertain as were the Justices' earlier attempts at defining the indefinable. For example, authors, publishers, librarians, and filmmakers foresaw a nightmare of various municipalities across the nation deciding what, for that particular community, would be legally obscene. Such a movement would make national distribution all but impossible. Indeed, two film cases,* Jenkins v. Georgia *and* Erznoznik v. Jacksonville *(included in Chapter 8), dealt with that specific problem, but the Court could add little in the way of clarification to* Miller. *It appeared by the early 1990s, then, that the Burger and Rehnquist courts had continued a series of fruitless "clarifications" to* Miller *in the same way the Warren Court attempted to "clarify"* Roth. *And again, the recommendations of the President's Commission on Obscenity and Pornography (see Chapter 6) were ignored. The* Miller *decision, then, was a most significant turning point, but one which offered no help to an impossibly muddled mosaic, and was a jolting setback to those who favored a more libertarian approach to the delicate relationship between the First Amendment and literature and the arts.*

MILLER V. CALIFORNIA
413 U.S. 15 (1973)

CHIEF JUSTICE BURGER *delivered the opinion of the Court.*

This is one of a group of "obscenity-pornography" cases being reviewed by the Court in a re-examination of standards enunciated in earlier cases involving what Mr. Justice Harlan called "the intractable obscenity problem."

Appellant conducted a mass mailing campaign to advertise the sale of illustrated books, euphemistically called "adult" material. After a jury trial, he was convicted of violating California Penal Code sec. 311.2(a), a misdemeanor, by knowingly distributing obscene matter, and the Appellate Department, Superior Court of California, County of Orange, summarily affirmed the judgment without opinion. Appellant's conviction was specifically based on his conduct in causing five unsolicited advertising brochures to be sent through the mail in an envelope addressed to a restaurant in Newport Beach, California. The envelope was opened by the manager of the restaurant and his mother. They had not requested the brochures; they complained to the police.

The brochures advertise four books entitled "Intercourse," "Man-Woman," "Sex Orgies Illustrated," and "An Illustrated History of Pornography," and a film entitled "Marital Intercourse." While the brochures contain some descriptive printed material, primarily they consist of pictures and drawings very explicitly depicting men and women in groups of two or more engaging in a variety of sexual activities, with genitals often prominently displayed. . . .

Apart from the initial formulation in the *Roth* case, no majority of the Court has at any given time been able to agree on a standard to determine what constitutes obscene, pornographic material subject to regulation under the States' police power. . . .

This much has been categorically settled by the Court, that obscene material is unprotected by the First Amendment. . . . We acknowledge, however, the inherent dangers of undertaking to regulate any form of expression. State statutes designed to regulate obscene materials must be carefully limited. As a result, we now confine the permissible scope of such regulation to works which depict or describe sexual conduct. That conduct must be specifically defined by the applicable state law, as written or authoritatively construed. . . .

The basic guidelines for the trier of fact must be: (a) whether "the average person, applying contemporary community standards," would find that the work, taken as a whole, appeals to the prurient interest, (b) whether the work depicts or describes, in a patently offensive way, sexual conduct specifically defined by the applicable state law, and (c) whether the work, taken as a whole, lacks serious literary, artistic, political, or scientific value. We do not adopt as a constitutional standard the *"utterly* without redeeming social value" test of *Memoirs v. Massachusetts*; that concept has never commanded the adherence of more than three Justices at one time. . . .

We emphasize that it is not our function to propose regulatory schemes for the States. That must await their concrete legislative efforts. It is possible, however, to give a few plain examples of what a state statute could define for regulation under the second part (b) of the standard announced in this opinion:

(a) Patently offensive representations or descriptions of ultimate sexual acts, normal or perverted, actual or simulated.

(b) Patently offensive representations or descriptions of masturbation, excretory functions, and lewd exhibition of the genitals.

Sex and nudity may not be exploited without limit by films or pictures exhibited or sold in places of public accommodation any more than live sex and nudity can be exhibited or sold without limit in such public places. At a minimum, prurient, patently offensive depiction or description of sexual conduct must have serious literary, artistic, political, or scientific value to merit First Amendment protection. For example, medical books for the education of physicians and related personnel necessarily use graphic illustrations and descriptions of human anatomy. In resolving the inevitably sensitive questions of fact and law, we must continue to rely on the jury system, accompanied by the safeguards that judges, rules of evidence, presumption of innocence and other protective features provide, as we do with rape, murder and a host of other offenses against society and its individual members. . . .

Under a national Constitution, fundamental First Amendment limitations on the powers of the States do not vary from community to community, but this does not mean that there are, or should or can be, fixed, uniform national standards of precisely what appeals to the "prurient interest" or is "patently offensive." These are essentially questions of fact, and our nation is simply too big and too diverse for this Court to reasonably expect that such standards could be articulated for all 50 States in a single formulation, even assuming the prerequisite consensus exists. When triers of fact are asked to decide whether "the average person, applying contemporary community standards," would consider certain materials "prurient," it would be unrealistic to require that the answer be based on some abstract formulation. The adversary system, with lay jurors as the usual ultimate fact finders in criminal prosecutions, has historically permitted triers-of-fact to draw on the standards of their community, guided always by limiting instructions on the law. To require a State to structure obscenity proceedings around evidence of a *national* "community standard" would be an exercise in futility. . . .

It is neither realistic nor constitutionally sound to read the First Amendment as requiring that the people of Maine or Mississippi accept public depiction of conduct found tolerable in Las Vegas, or New York City. . . .

. . . One can concede that the "sexual revolution" of recent years may have had useful byproducts in striking layers of prudery from a subject long irrationally kept from needed ventilation. But it does not follow that no regulation of patently offensive "hard core" materials is needed or permissible; civilized people do not allow unregulated access to heroin because it is a derivative of medicinal morphine.

In sum we (a) reaffirm the *Roth* holding that obscene material is not protected by the First Amendment, (b) hold that such material can be regulated by the States, subject to the specific safeguards enunciated above, without a showing that the material is "*utterly* without redeeming social value," and (c) hold that obscenity is to be determined by applying "contemporary community standards," not "national standards.". . .

JUSTICE DOUGLAS, *dissenting.*

. . . Today the Court retreats from the earlier formulations of the constitutional test and undertakes to make new definitions. This effort, like the earlier ones, is earnest and well-intentioned. The difficulty is that we do not deal with constitutional terms, since "obscenity" is not mentioned in the Constitution or Bill of Rights. And the First Amendment makes no such exception from "the press" which it undertakes to protect nor, as I have said on other occasions, is an exception necessarily implied, for there was no recognized exception to the free press at the time the Bill of Rights was adopted which treated "obscene" publications differently from other types of papers, magazines, and books. So there are no constitutional guidelines for deciding what is and what is not "obscene." The Court is at large because we deal with tastes and standards of literature. . . .

Obscenity cases usually generate tremendous emotional outbursts. They have no business being in the courts. If a constitutional amendment authorized censorship, the censor would probably be an administrative agency. Then criminal prosecutions could follow if and when publishers defied the censor and sold their literature. Under that regime a publisher would know when he was on dangerous ground. Under the present regime—whether the old standards or the new ones are used—the criminal law becomes a trap. . . .

. . . Obscenity—which even we cannot define with precision—is a hodge-podge. To send men to jail for violating standards they cannot understand, construe, and apply is a monstrous thing to do in a nation dedicated to fair trials and due process. . . .

If there are to be restraints on what is obscene, then a constitutional amendment should be the way of achieving the end. There are societies where religion and mathematics are the only free segments. It would be a dark day for America if that were our destiny. But the people can make it such if they choose to write obscenity into the Constitution and define it. . . .

*   *   *

As was anticipated, the years following Miller *were filled with decisions which sought to "clarify" earlier Supreme Court obscenity rulings. Two 1977 cases illus-*

trate the point. Ward v. Illinois *dealt with a conviction based on sado-masochistic material which was not specifically banned by state statute. The Court held that obscenity laws need not describe precisely all types of sexual activity which were to be outlawed in the media. With Justice White writing for the 5–4 majority, the Court held that the Illinois law was sufficiently clear in what it attempted to deal with. Justice Stevens, on the other hand, claimed in dissent that the Court in* Ward *was abandoning "one of the cornerstones of the* Miller *test," that of limiting prosecutions to those activities specifically banned.*

Second, the Justices, also by 5–4, supported the Ginzburg *and* Hamling *concepts by ruling that juries could consider "commercial exploitation"—pandering— in deciding obscenity issues.* Splawn v. California. *Again in dissent, Justice Stevens argued that, as in* Ginzburg, *the Court was allowing convictions based upon how certain material was marketed. He was joined in dissent by Justices Brennan, Marshall and Stewart, the three "traditional" dissenters in these types of cases.*

But certainly the most significant decision to come after Miller—*and perhaps one of the most significant in the whole series of Supreme Court decisions in dealing with salacious expression—came with* Young v. American Mini Theatres. *The Court held, again by 5–4, that local police powers allowed land zoning regulations to be used to limit the locations of so-called "adult entertainment" establishments. Unlike Boston's attempts to concentrate such businesses in a central "core" (called the "combat zone" in Boston), the city of Detroit drew an ordinance which required dispersal of businesses such as "adult" bookstores and theatres. The key question was whether zoning restrictions denied First Amendment protection to constitutionally protected expression. Obscenity, per se, was not at issue. Covered in the zoning ordinance were establishments appealing to adults who sought erotic or salacious entertainment, but which presumably offered entertainment protected under the Constitution.*

Cities and counties around the nation passed similar laws following the Young *decision, but the full impact of the Court's action will take some time to develop because most of the new ordinances carried "grandfather" clauses which allowed existing businesses to remain until, say, they were sold. Still, it is an interesting approach to a vexing problem. The decision seemed to support others which allowed control of nonobscene matter such as* Times Film (*Chapter 8*) *and* Pacifica (*Chapter 4*).

YOUNG V. AMERICAN MINI THEATRES
427 U.S. 50 (1976)

JUSTICE STEVENS *delivered the opinion of the Court.*

Zoning ordinances adopted by the city of Detroit differentiate between motion picture theaters which exhibit sexually explicit "adult" movies and those which do not. The principal question presented by this case is whether that statutory classification is unconstitutional because it is based on the content of communication protected by the First Amendment.

Effective November 2, 1972, Detroit adopted the ordinances challenged in this litigation. Instead of concentrating "adult" theaters in limited zones, these ordinances require that such theaters be dispersed. Specifically, an adult theater may not be located within 1,000 feet of any two other "regulated uses" or within 500 feet of a residential area. The term "regulated uses" includes 10 different kinds of establishments in addition to adult theaters. . . .

[We] are . . . persuaded that the 1,000-foot restriction does not, in itself, create an impermissible restraint on protected communication. The city's interest in planning and regulating the use of property for commercial purposes is clearly adequate to support that kind of restriction applicable to all theaters within the city limits. In short, apart from the fact that the ordinances treat adult theaters differently from other theaters and the fact that the classification is predicated on the content of material shown in the respective theaters, the regulation of the place where such films may be exhibited does not offend the First Amendment. . . .

The question whether speech is, or is not, protected by the First Amendment often depends on the content of the speech. Thus, the line between permissible advocacy and impermissible incitation to crime or violence depends, not merely on the setting in which the speech occurs, but also on exactly what the speaker had to say. . . .

Such a line may be drawn on the basis of content without violating the government's paramount obligation of neutrality in its regulation of protected communication. For the regulation of the places where sexually explicit films may be exhibited is unaffected by whatever social, political, or philosophical message a film may be intended to communicate; whether a motion picture ridicules or characterizes one point of view or another, the effect of the ordinances is exactly the same.

Moreover, even though we recognize that the First Amendment will not tolerate the total suppression of erotic materials that have some arguably artistic value, it is manifest that society's interest in protecting this type of expression is of a wholly different, and lesser, magnitude than the interest in untrammeled political debate that inspired Voltaire's immortal comment. Whether political oratory or philosophical discussion moves us to applaud or to despise what is said, every schoolchild can understand why our duty to defend the right to speak remains the same. But few of us would march our sons and daughters off to war to preserve the citizen's right to see "Specified Sexual Activities" exhibited in the theaters of our choice. Even though the First Amendment protects communication in that area from total suppression, we hold that the State may legitimately use the content of these materials as the basis for placing them in a different classification from other motion pictures. . . .

JUSTICE POWELL, *concurring.*

Although I agree with much of what is said in the Court's opinion, . . . my approach to the resolution of this case is sufficiently different to prompt me to write separately. I view the case as presenting an example of innovative land-use regulation, implicating First Amendment concerns only incidentally and to a limited extent.

One-half century ago this Court broadly sustained the power of local municipalities to utilize the then relatively novel concept of land-use regulation in order to meet effectively the increasing encroachments of urbanization upon the quality of life of their citizens. . . .

In the intervening years zoning has become an accepted necessity in our increasingly urbanized society, and the types of zoning restrictions have taken on forms far more complex and innovative. . . .

. . . Our cases reveal . . . that the central concern of the First Amendment in this area is that there be a free flow from creator to audience of whatever message a film or a book might convey. Mr. Justice Douglas stated the core idea succinctly: "In this Nation every writer, actor, or producer, no matter what medium of expression he may use, should be freed from the censor." *Superior Films v. Department of Education.* In many instances, for example with respect to certain criminal statutes or censorship or licensing schemes, it is only the theater owner or the bookseller who can protect this interest. But the central First Amendment concern remains the need to maintain free access of the public to the expression.

In this case, there is no indication that the application of the Anti-Skid Row Ordinance to adult theaters has the effect of suppressing production of or, to any significant degree, restricting access to adult movies. . . .

The inquiry for First Amendment purposes is not concerned with economic impact; rather, it looks only to the effect of this ordinance upon freedom of expression. This prompts essentially two inquiries: (i) Does the ordinance impose any content limitation on the creators of adult movies or their ability to make them available to whom they desire, and (ii) does it restrict in any significant way the viewing of these movies by those who desire to see them? On the record in this case, these inquiries must be answered in the negative. . . .

JUSTICE STEWART, *with whom Justice Brennan, Justice Marshall, and Justice Blackmun join, dissenting.*

The Court today holds that the First and Fourteenth Amendments do not prevent the city of Detroit from using a system of prior restraints and criminal sanctions to enforce content-based restrictions on the geographic location of motion picture theaters that exhibit nonobscene but sexually oriented films. I dissent from this drastic departure from established principles of First Amendment law.

This case does not involve a simple zoning ordinance, or a content-neutral time, place, and manner restriction, or a regulation of obscene expression or other speech that is entitled to less than the full protection of the First Amendment. . . .

The fact that the "offensive" speech here may not address "important" topics—"ideas of social and political significance," in the Court's terminology—does not mean that it is less worthy of constitutional protection. "Wholly neutral futilities . . . come under the protection of free speech as fully as do Keats' poems or Donne's sermons." *Winters v. New York.* . . .

The Court must never forget that the consequences of rigorously enforcing the guarantees of the First Amendment are frequently unpleasant. Much speech that seems to be of little or no value will enter the marketplace of ideas, threatening the quality of our social discourse and, more generally, the serenity of our lives. But that is the price to be paid for constitutional freedom.

JUSTICE BLACKMUN, *with whom Justice Brennan, Justice Stewart, and Justice Marshall join, dissenting.*

I join Mr. Justice Stewart's dissent, and write separately to identify an independent ground on which, for me, the challenged ordinance is unconstitutional. That ground is vagueness.

We should put ourselves for a moment in the shoes of the motion picture exhibitor. Let us suppose that, having previously offered only a more innocuous fare, he decides to vary it by exhibiting on certain days films from a series which occasionally deals explicitly with sex. The exhibitor must determine whether this places his theater into the "adult" class prescribed by the challenged ordinance. If the theater is within that class, it must be licensed, and it may be entirely prohibited, depending on its location.

"Adult" status *vel non* depends on whether the theater is "used for presenting" films that are "distinguished or characterized by an emphasis on" certain specified activities, including sexual intercourse, or specified anatomical areas. It will be simple enough, as the operator screens films, to tell when one of these areas or activities is being depicted, but if the depiction represents only a part of the films' subject matter, I am at a loss to know how he will tell whether they are "distinguished or characterized by an emphasis" on those areas and activities. The ordinance gives him no guidance. Neither does it instruct him on how to tell whether, assuming the films in question are thus "distinguished or characterized," his theater is being "used for presenting" such films. That phrase could mean *ever* used, *often* used, or *predominantly* used, to name a few possibilities.

Let us assume the exhibitor concludes that the film series will render his showhouse an "adult" theater. He still must determine whether the operation of the theater is prohibited by virtue of there being two other "regulated uses" within 1,000 feet. His task of determining whether his own theater is "adult" is suddenly multiplied by however many neighbors he may have that arguably are within that same class. He must, in other words, know and evaluate not only his own films, but those of any competitor within 1,000 feet. And neighboring theaters are not his only worry, since the list of regulated uses also includes "adult" bookstores, "Group 'D' Cabaret[s]," sellers of alcoholic beverages for consumption on the premises, hotels, motels, pawnshops, pool halls, public lodging houses, "secondhand stores," shoeshine parlors, and "taxi dance halls." The exhibitor must master all these definitions. Some he will find very clear, of course; others less so. A neighboring bookstore is "adult," for example, if a "substantial or significant portion of its stock in trade" is "distinguished or characterized" in the same way as the films shown in an "adult" theater.

The exhibitor's compounded task of applying the statutory definitions to himself and his neighbors, furthermore, is an on-going one. At any moment he could become a violator of the ordinance because some neighbor has slipped into a "regulated use" classification. . . .

We should not be swayed in this case by the characterization of the challenged ordinance as merely a "zoning" regulation, or by the "adult" nature of the affected material. By whatever name, this ordinance prohibits the showing of certain films in certain places, imposing criminal sanctions for violation of the ban. And however distasteful we may suspect the films to be, we cannot approve their suppression without any judicial finding that they are obscene under this Court's carefully delineated and considered standards.

*   *   *

Continuing the "Miller clarifications," the Supreme Court in 1978 reversed an obscenity conviction on the grounds that the judge had erred in instructing the jury, in its determination of "community standards," to consider all in the community— including children. Pinkus v. U.S. Such an inclusion, the Supreme Court held in reversing, would significantly alter the determination of "average person" against whom the jury must compare the material under question. All others in the community, including sensitive persons, can be included in this deliberation, but not children unless there is evidence that they were intended recipients of the material. This decision would seem to support the concept of "variable standards" set down in Ginsberg v. New York. The Court's decision also accepted the "pandering" concept of Ginzburg and Splawn when the material is of a "borderline" nature. In a lone dissent, Justice Powell indicated that he found no fault with the exclusion of children, but he objected to sending the case back, arguing that the instructions to the jury in this instance constituted a harmless error.

A logical extension of the Young decision of 1976 would be to "zone out" all forms of "adult entertainment." So, it was probably inevitable that such a question would come before the Supreme Court. In 1981 the Justices handed down their decision in Schad v. Mount Ephraim. By a 7–2 vote, they ruled unconstitutional Mount Ephraim's zoning restrictions which totally banned live, nude dancing. The majority indicated that Young should not be seen as granting license to exclude from a community various constitutionally protected forms of expression, including the display of the nude human form. While the decision narrowed somewhat the freedom of communities to act under Young, it did not alter the Court's acceptance of the zoning approach to control salacious—though protected—expression.

Indeed, just five years later, the Court reinforced the use of zoning ordinances to control "adult" entertainment establishments. Renton v. Playtime. The ordinance of Renton, Washington, a city of 30,000 people near Seattle, was similar to the one accepted by the Court in Young, but it had the effect of limiting such businesses to a largely vacant, 520-acre industrial area of the city. The question, of course, was the *"reasonableness"* of what Justice Rehnquist, writing for the seven-justice majority, called a time, place and manner restriction. While the Renton case involved a movie house, it is assumed that the principle would apply as well to "adult" bookstores and other such businesses. Justices Brennan and Marshall dissented.

RENTON V. PLAYTIME
475 U.S. 41 (1986)

JUSTICE REHNQUIST *delivered the opinion of the Court.*

. . . In our view, the resolution of this case is largely dictated by our decision in *Young v. American Mini Theatres, Inc.* There, although five Members of the Court did not agree on a single rationale for the decision, we held that the city of Detroit's zoning ordinance, which prohibited locating an adult theater within 1,000 feet of any two other "regulated uses" or within 500 feet of any residential zone, did not violate the First and Fourteenth Amendments. The Renton ordinance, like the one in *American Mini Theatres*, does not ban adult theaters altogether, but merely provides that such theaters may not be located within 1,000 feet of any residential zone, single- or multiple-family dwelling, church, park, or school. The ordinance is therefore properly analyzed as a form of time, place, and manner regulation.

Describing the ordinance as a time, place, and manner regulation is, of course, only the first step in our inquiry. This Court has long held that regulations enacted for the purpose of restraining speech on the basis of its content presumptively violate the First Amendment. . . . On the other hand, so-called "content-neutral" time, place, and manner regulations are acceptable so long as they are designed to serve a substantial governmental interest and do not unreasonably limit alternative avenues of communication. . . .

At first glance, the Renton ordinance, like the ordinance in *American Mini Theatres*, does not appear to fit neatly into either the "content-based" or the "content-neutral" category. To be sure, the ordinance treats theaters that specialize in adult films differently from other kinds of theaters. Nevertheless, as the District Court concluded, the Renton ordinance is aimed not at the *content* of the films shown at "adult motion picture theatres," but rather at the *secondary effects* of such theatres on the surrounding community. . . .

In short, the Renton ordinance is completely consistent with our definition of "content-neutral" speech regulations as those that "are *justified* without reference to the content of the regulated speech." *Virginia Pharmacy Board v. Virginia Citizens Consumer Council, Inc.*

The appropriate inquiry in this case, then, is whether the Renton ordinance is designed to serve a substantial governmental interest and allows for reasonable alternative avenues of communication. . . . It is clear that the ordinance meets such a standard. As a majority of this Court recognized in *American Mini*

Theatres, a city's "interest in attempting to preserve the quality of urban life is one that must be accorded high respect.". . .

We also find no constitutional defect in the method chosen by Renton to further its substantial interests. Cities may regulate adult theaters by dispersing them, as in Detroit, or by effectively concentrating them, as in Renton. . . .

Finally, turning to the question whether the Renton ordinance allows for reasonable alternative avenues of communication, we note that the ordinance leaves some 520 acres, or more than five percent of the entire land area of Renton, open to use as adult theater sites. The District Court found, and the Court of Appeals did not dispute the finding, that the 520 acres of land consists of "[a]mple, accessible real estate," including "acreage in all stages of development from raw land to developed, industrial, warehouse, office, and shopping space that is criss-crossed by freeways, highways, and roads."

Respondents argue, however, that some of the land in question is already occupied by existing businesses, that "practically none" of the undeveloped land is currently for sale or lease, and that in general there are no "commercially viable" adult theater sites within the 520 acres left open by the Renton ordinance. The Court of Appeals accepted these arguments, concluded that the 520 acres was not truly "available" land, and therefore held that the Renton ordinance "would result in a substantial restriction" on speech.

We disagree with both the reasoning and the conclusion of the Court of Appeals. That respondents must fend for themselves in the real estate market, on an equal footing with other prospective purchasers and lessees, does not give rise to a First Amendment violation. And although we have cautioned against the enactment of zoning regulations that have "the effect of suppressing, or greatly restricting access to, lawful speech," *American Mini Theatres*, we have never suggested that the First Amendment compels the Government to ensure that adult theaters, or any other kinds of speech-related businesses for that matter, will be able to obtain sites at bargain prices. . . . In our view, the First Amendment requires only that Renton refrain from effectively denying respondents a reasonable opportunity to open and operate an adult theater within the city, and the ordinance before us easily meets this requirement.

In sum, we find that the Renton ordinance represents a valid governmental response to the "admittedly serious problems" created by adult theaters. Renton has not used "the power to zone as a pretext for suppressing expression," but rather has sought to make some areas available for adult theaters and their patrons, while at the same time preserving the quality of life in the community at large by preventing those theaters from locating in other areas. This, after all, is the essence of zoning. Here, as in *American Mini Theatres*, the city has enacted a zoning ordinance that meets these goals while also satisfying the dictates of the First Amendment. . . .

JUSTICE BRENNAN, *joined by Justice Marshall, dissenting.*

. . . The fact that adult movie theaters may cause harmful "secondary" land use effects may arguably give Renton a compelling reason to regulate such establishments; it does not mean, however, that such regulations are content-neutral. Because the ordinance imposes special restrictions on certain kinds of speech on the basis of *content*, I cannot simply accept, as the Court does, Renton's claim that the ordinance was not designed to suppress the content of adult movies. "[W]hen regulation is based on the content of speech, governmental action must be scrutinized more carefully to ensure that communication has not been prohibited 'merely because public officials disapprove the speaker's views.'" *Consolidated Edison Co.* . . .

The ordinance discriminates on its face against certain forms of speech based on content. Movie theaters specializing in "adult motion pictures" may not be located within 1,000 feet of any residential zone, single- or multiple-family dwelling, church, park, or school. Other motion picture theaters, and other forms of "adult entertainment," such as bars, massage parlors, and adult bookstores, are not subject to the same restrictions. This selective treatment strongly suggests that Renton was interested not in controlling the "secondary effects" associated with adult businesses, but in discriminating against adult theaters based on the content of the films they exhibit. The Court ignores this discriminatory treatment, declaring that Renton is free "to address the potential problems created by one particular kind of adult business," and to amend the ordinance in the future to include other adult enterprises. However, because of the First Amendment interests at stake here, this one-step-at-a-time analysis is wholly inappropriate. . . .

THE OBSCENITY QUAGMIRE

By Burt Pines*

. . . On June 30, 1973, the United States Supreme Court issued a series of rulings with the purpose of easing what the late Justice Harlan called its "intractable" obscenity problem. In the principal case decided on that day, *Miller v. California*, the Court reviewed the constitutionality of California's Penal Code Section 311. Penal Code Section 311 had been drafted in light of the decision in *Roth v. United States*. That decision seemed to require, as a precondition to a finding of obscenity, that the material in question be completely without "the slightest redeeming social importance." Penal Code Section 311 incorporated similar language in its definition of obscenity.

A principle holding of *Miller* was to substitute for the "utterly without" test the looser requirement that material could be found obscene if it "lack serious literary, artistic, political or scientific value." To help ameliorate the problem of giving publishers "fair notice" of what is obscene, the Court also required that a state obscenity statute, either by its very language or by judicial interpretation, "specifically define" the kinds of acts, if portrayed, that could lead to a finding the material was "obscene." As examples, the Court indicated that a state could prohibit the distribution of:

> (a) Patently offensive representations or descriptions of ultimate sexual acts, normal or perverted, actual or simulated.
> (b) Patently offensive representations of descriptions of masturbation, excretory functions and lewd exhibitions of the genitals.

Combined with this redefinition of the boundaries of obscenity, the Court also articulated an expanded role for local juries using "local standards" to find matter obscene.

The Court undoubtedly hoped that by making it easier for local juries to find material obscene, fewer cases would plague the Court on appeals from convictions. The Court's hope was not, however, realized. Rather than clearing up the obscenity quagmire, *Miller* only deepened it.

What happened to California's Penal Code Section 311 in the wake of *Miller* is a prime example of the incredible muddle that has been created nationwide by the Court's obscenity decisions. It should be remembered that California Penal Code Section 311 was the very statute around which the constitutional discussion

---

* From Burt Pines. "The Obscenity Quagmire." *California State Bar Journal*, Vol. 49 (November/December, 1974), p. 509. Used with permission of the *California State Bar Journal* and the author, former Los Angeles City Attorney.

in *Miller* revolved. However, no clear decision on the constitutionality of the California statute emerged from the *Miller* decision. Rather, the Supreme Court merely remanded the case to the lower state courts for reconsideration in light of its new standards for the constitutionality of state obscenity regulations.

The California Court of Appeals then decided *People v. Enskat* (in which the City Attorney's Office of Los Angeles represented the People). *Enskat* held that prior California state court decisions had supplied the elements of specificity to Penal Code Section 311 required by *Miller*. As a result, the California obscenity statute passed constitutional muster.

Since the City Attorney's Office represents one of the parties, this article is not the proper place to discuss the merits and demerits of *Enskat*. It is, however, vital to note that a federal three-judge court later disagreed with *Enskat* and issued and later reaffirmed a declaration that Section 311, even as interpreted by California state courts, did not meet *Miller's* specificity standards. Thus, California's obscenity law has been caught in a wrestling match between state and federal courts—the outcome of which may not definitely be decided for some time.

Similar post-*Miller* lower court struggles with state obscenity statutes have occurred nationwide. Furthermore, despite the Supreme Court's hope, obscenity litigation continues to occupy the Justices' time and attention. Only recently, for example, they had to overturn the finding of a local Georgia jury that the critically acclaimed film "Carnal Knowledge" was obscene. [*Jenkins v. Georgia*. See chapter 6.] The Justices were able to do so only after personally viewing the movie. The "Carnal Knowledge" opinion makes it clear that the Court will continue to be the ultimate decision-maker on the question whether material is in fact obscene. Thus, despite *Miller*, the Court continues to sit as the nation's super-censor.

The litigation and confusion in the obscenity area indicates one aspect of the consequences of using criminal sanctions to attempt to eliminate the distribution of explicit material to forewarned adults. The use of criminal sanctions in an area so open to debate means that a constitutional issue is likely to be raised in almost every case. The "Carnal Knowledge" opinion indicates that the question of obscenity as a fact is always open to defendants on appeal. Furthermore, because of the public's extensive patronage of the adult materials industry, defendants in obscenity cases seem to have no difficulty paying for the expensive legal fees necessary to raise these constitutional issues. So long as distribution of obscenity to forewarned adults is criminalized, protracted and inconclusive litigation will continue to occupy the courts.

It is not only the courts who are caught in the obscenity quagmire. Law enforcement agencies and prosecution offices, too, suffer "intractable" problems because of the current law. The experience of the Los Angeles City Attorney's Office illustrates the difficulties, from a prosecutorial viewpoint, of using criminal sanctions as a means of attempting to eliminate the adult materials industry.

A. *The Futility of Enforcement*—To understand the problems of enforcing the current obscenity laws, it is necessary to know something of the structure of the adult materials industry. Many establishments which distribute adult materials do so through a system of absentee ownership. A particular adult bookstore in Hollywood may well be owned by a California corporation whose owners and officers are Texas residents and never set foot in California.

This system of absentee ownership is a crucial factor in the frustration of obscenity law enforcement. For it is a constitutional requirement that only those persons who have knowledge of the contents, nature and character of the matter sold or displayed on the premises can be criminally charged with responsibility for its distribution. Such knowledge is exceedingly difficult, if not impossible, to establish for absentee owners. For example, in *People v. Bromberg*, the court held that knowledge of the activities of an adult movie theater was not imputed to an absentee owner solely because he was the president and sole stockholder of the controlling corporation. As a result, cases filed in the obscenity area tend to be against employees of absentee owners and not the owners themselves. Local prosecution drives against "smut" do not usually net the "big fish."

If an employee is convicted and his or her conditions of probation include abstention from further involvement in the adult materials industry, that person seeks other employment and another employee is hired. The distribution of the material continues, despite innumerable convictions of employees, because the industry is lucrative enough to bear the costs of the conviction and replacement of its employees.

Even in those rare instances where a case can be made against an owner, inordinate amounts of police investigatory time are required. The police must identify the true owner and establish somehow that the owner does have the requisite "knowledge." Alternatively, they must literally track the owner down and read him a statement as to the nature of the business his establishment carries on, thereby imputing knowledge to him.

The practical result of this is that obscenity prosecutions are, to a large extent, more shadow than substance. Despite the extensive past prosecution efforts of the Los Angeles City Attorney's Office, the adult materials industry still thrives in Los Angeles. Innumerable and endless convictions of clerks, ticket sellers and popcorn vendors do not end or markedly diminish the distribution of adult materials, but, as will be shown below, waste law enforcement and prosecution resources that could better be directed to deterring serious crimes against persons and property. All such convictions do, basically, is satisfy temporarily a desire on the part of some segments of the public to do something about "smut."

B. *Changing Public Attitudes*—Adding to the practical difficulties of obscenity law enforcement is the fact that public attitudes towards adult materials are changing. As a result, jurors are becoming more and more reluctant to convict in cases that involve distribution of materials to adults who know what they are seeing or buying.

Following the decision in *Enskat*, for example, the Los Angeles City Attorney's Office again undertook to bring obscenity cases to trial. Two cases were tried in the Fall of 1973. One took approximately a week to try and resulted in a conviction of one count, acquittal on five counts, and a hung jury on two counts, which the court subsequently dismissed. The sexual conduct depicted in each of the eight counts of the complaint was virtually identical. The second trial in 1973 involved two full length films as well as a number of advertising trailers and required a month to try. The jury convicted on only one of the two films. It acquitted on the other film and acquitted on all of the advertising trailers. These acquittals occurred despite the fact that the sexual conduct portrayed in each of the films and indeed in each of the advertising trailers was very graphic and substantially similar.

In early 1974 the Los Angeles City Attorney's Office tried the now famous film, "Behind the Green Door." Because the defendants had stipulated to their operation of the theater and to their knowledge of the nature of the film, the only issue for the jury was obscenity. The film was very graphic and very explicit. The trial consumed two and one-half weeks. The jury, after two days of deliberations, found the film not obscene, and acquitted.

Similar mixed results in obscenity prosecutions have occurred all over the country. Results in "Deep Throat" prosecutions are particularly interesting, as that film depicts graphic sexual activity for approximately 50 minutes of its 62-minute running time. In California, to the best of my knowledge, no jury has convicted a defendant under Section 311 for distributing or exhibiting "Deep Throat." Numerous attempts, however, have been made. The Los Angeles County District Attorney's Office recently dismissed charges against the film after a trial consuming several months resulted in only a hung jury. Prosecutions against distributors or exhibitors of "Deep Throat" have resulted in jury verdicts of acquittal in Downey and Ontario. Outside California, prosecutions against "Deep Throat" have also resulted in acquittals or hung juries in communities across the country as diverse as Binghamton, New York; Cincinnati, Ohio; Houston, Texas; the heart of the Bible belt, Sioux Falls, South Dakota. Prosecutors nationwide have had similar difficulty in obtaining convictions in cases involving "Behind the Green Door" and "Devil in Miss Jones."

The point of this recitation is not to argue that convictions in obscenity cases can never be obtained. They can. The point is, rather, that they are becoming far more difficult to obtain. The reason is that juries merely reflect a growing public tolerance of the right of forewarned adults to read and see what they want.

In a recent public opinion poll conducted by the respected Field polling organization and introduced into evidence by the defense in the Los Angeles trial of "Behind the Green Door," of those surveyed, 52% favored the idea of allowing forewarned adults to see whatever they wanted, so long as there were limits placed on the advertising and promotion of explicit material. Ten percent of those surveyed favored no restrictions on the availability of explicit material to adults, nor on the advertising of such material. Thus, almost two-thirds of those surveyed favored unlimited availability of explicit material for adults. Only 31% of those surveyed favored a total ban on all explicit and completely graphic depictions of sexual acts from all public availability.

C. *The Costs of an Obscenity Prosecution*—In light of the negligible effect of obscenity prosecutions and the growing public tolerance of the right of forewarned adults to see what they want, the question must be asked whether the law enforcement resources now directed to obscenity prosecutions could not be better utilized in the fight against the ever increasing menace of crimes against persons and property. The costs of prosecution are considerable. A police officer must spend at least one full day on the most simple obscenity case involving a search warrant. As previously mentioned, far more investigatory time is required in any attempt at prosecution of absentee owners of adult materials stores or movie houses. In addition, from one-half to one and one-half days' court time is required for the investigating officer's testimony if a case goes to trial.

Prosecutorial time costs include at least one-half working day in an attempt to negotiate a plea bargain, and a staggering two to five weeks to try a contested case. The judicial time involved is substantially identical. Additionally, the inevitable appeal from a conviction requires at least three days of attorney time to prepare. Overall, this office has estimated the total governmental costs for relatively typical contested obscenity prosecutions at somewhere between $10,000–$25,000 per case. Sometimes costs run much higher, as, for example, a quarter of a million dollars in the prosecution of "Deep Throat" by Los Angeles County.

Given the expense, frustration and uncertainty involved in obscenity prosecutions, it is not surprising that many prosecution offices are reexamining their value in light of the pressing need to stem the rising level of crime against persons and property. The Sacramento County District Attorney's Office has foresworn further obscenity prosecutions and is in the process of dismissing its pending case. The District Attorney there took this action because prosecuting distributors of explicit material is, in his words, "futile, frustrating and extremely costly." The San Francisco District Attorney's Office has substantially foregone further prosecutions. In Pennsylvania, the Allegheny County District Attorney has made a similar decision. Houston, Texas prosecution officials, after two lengthy trials against "Deep Throat" ended in hung juries, decided not to prosecute any further obscenity cases involving quality adult entertainment films. Overall, there is a growing national trend to reexamine the value of obscenity prosecutions in light of more pressing law enforcement needs.

Money and frustration are not the only costs of keeping the present obscenity laws on our statute books. Other, more intangible, but, nonetheless, very real costs, must also be considered.

A. *Depriving the Public of What It Wants*—One reason obscenity prosecutions are now so difficult to win is that public attitudes toward explicit adult materials have changed. This is demonstrated by the growing public patronage of such material. "Deep Throat," for example, set a Los Angeles record for any type of movie exhibited at a single theater by grossing $3.2 million dollars during an 81-week run. Three "X-rated" films, "Deep Throat," "Devil in Miss Jones" and "Last Tango in Paris," were among Los Angeles' top grossing first-run movies between October 1972 and September 1973, placing first, seventh and eighth respectively.

Obviously, viewers of explicit movies and other material are not limited to a small group of perverts.

A *New York Times* article entitled "Smut, Variously Defined, Is Booming Nationwide" states, "A check by *New York Times* correspondents in more than a dozen cities indicated that commerce in pornography today is more robust than ever despite the [*Miller*] guidelines." The article also states that beyond the obvious public acceptance of established shops and movie houses, there appears to have been a breakdown of organized resistance from church, school and community groups that traditionally have clamored for enforcement of anti-obscenity laws.

Significant costs to the legal system can result when it is made criminal to produce or distribute a product large numbers of people want. In effect, a "black market" for the material is created, which results in raising the price to consumers and allowing unsavory criminal elements to corner the distribution scheme. The publicity surrounding criminal prosecutions only places an aura of mystery and intrigue around explicit material, thereby increasing public patronage of such material. It is certainly reasonable to speculate that the financial success of "Deep Throat" was directly related to the number of prosecutions brought against its exhibitors.

Another cost is widespread disrespect and disregard for the law. An unenforceable and ineffective law gives the public the impression of erratic justice. Prohibition is a prime example of the consequences of criminalizing the distribution of a product large numbers of people want. Criminal sanctions should generally be reserved for serious conduct threatening harm to lives and property. Their use to penalize the distribution of explicit material to forewarned adults must, at best, be regarded as questionable.

B. *The Constitutional Costs*—Despite all the reams of print and legal scholarship devoted to the subject, the distinction between the obscene and non-obscene is now no clearer than when the debate began. As a result, publishers seeking to disseminate works which involve discussion of sex and society's attitudes towards it do not know if that dissemination is criminally punishable. They thus may hesitate to publish their works and perhaps may not do so altogether.

No one can measure the loss to the exchange of ideas and information in our society that results from this "chill" on free expression. The difficulty is exemplified, however, by the fact that serious and critically acclaimed films such as "Carnal Knowledge," and books like James Joyce's *Ulysses* and D. H. Lawrence's *Lady Chatterley's Lover* have at one time or another been thought "obscene" by government censors. Our society is enriched and expanded by such serious artistic endeavors. Who knows how many films were not made or books not written, for fear of obscenity prosecutions? Almost as bad, is the thought that artists are compelled to modify and shape their professional judgments around the obscenity laws. Often they must compromise their message to meet the censor's taste. Severe differences of opinion on the social value of much of today's explicit adult material exist, and equally qualified experts hold very different opinions on the merits of the same material. As the San Francisco Committee on Crime stated, "The truth of the matter is, there can be no objective test for determining what is pornography." Because the subject is so debatable, the very process of judicially distinguishing the obscene from the constitutionality protected, deters the exercise of free expression.

Another significant cost of constitutional values of the current obscenity laws is to individual privacy and freedom of choice. The Supreme Court has recognized that an individual has a constitutional right to read or see whatever he or she wants in the privacy of his or her home. Any other holding would have put government dangerously near being in the business of thought control. Large numbers of people want to purchase explicit material for their own private consumption. The Supreme Court has failed to recognize their right to do so. It is up to the legislature to recognize it.

Against all of their costs, both practical and constitutional, what benefit is there to society from the present obscenity statutes? I believe that the legitimate goals of the present obscenity legislation can be achieved by more narrowly drawn statutes, that would allow forewarned adults to read or see whatever they wish.

Some people are offended by the very idea that other people read and enjoy explicit adult material. One of the premises of our free society, however, is that people should be able to read and think without government interference. The fact that some people object to others reading or viewing explicit material is simply not a legitimate basis for legislation. The best empirical evidence available indicates that the reading or viewing of explicit material causes no harm to adults or to society. Indeed, if anything, the available evidence indicates the contrary.

Another, and more substantial basis for legislation, is the type of personal offense which occurs when explicit material is thrust upon individuals who do not wish to see it. The obverse side of the freedom to read and see is the freedom to refuse to read and see personally offensive material. It is very possible, however, to protect the right not to be offended without infringing on the right to read and see.

First, it can be made a crime to distribute "explicit" publications to individuals who are not aware of the contents of the matter they are receiving. Thus, adult bookstores and movie houses could be required to post prominent, understandable warnings, that persons entering those establishments would likely encounter material which some might find offensive.

Second, displaying explicit sexual material in a manner where it is open to view by unforewarned members of the general public can be punished. Thus, the sleaziness on our public rights of way that accompanies the distribution of explicit material could be regulated. It is important to remember, however, that any such regulations must stay within constitutional bounds. Sanctions could not, for example, apply to a sign indicating nothing more than a movie house specializes in "adult films," and naming the particular film showing at the time.

The legislation just outlined in concept is not unprecedented. It has been recommended by the President's Commission on Obscenity and Pornography and the San Francisco Committee on Crime. Its elements are present in the current law of the states of Vermont, West Virginia, Montana and New Mexico. The concept of allowing forewarned adults to read or see whatever they want has the support of major responsible public opinion leaders of the community such as the *Los Angeles Times*, KNBC-TV, Los Angeles, and KABC-TV, Los Angeles.

Apart from the problem of distribution to unforewarned adults, there is also the problem of distribution of explicit material to minors without the consent of the minor's parents. Obviously, a large part of this problem could be mitigated by adoption of the kind of measures discussed above. By containing the adult materials industry in a limited area and requiring explicit warnings of the type of matter being distributed in a particular store, parents should be far better able to regulate the kind of material their children see. In addition, however, criminal sanctions that already exist for distribution of obscene matter to minors should be retained. The important value of a parent's ability to guide and protect the development of their children as they see fit is worthy of protection by criminal sanctions. Indeed, the Supreme Court has hinted that the scope of constitutional protection for explicit material is less when what is at issue is its distribution to minors. By carefully segregating the problem of distribution of explicit material to juveniles from the completely dissimilar problem of the distribution of that material to adults, the former problem can be more effectively handled by courts and law enforcers alike. Again, the recent legislation in other states enumerated above could well provide a suitable model for California.

The present obscenity laws are unworkable, ineffective and expensive in both economic and non-economic terms. They have consumed millions of dollars of the limited resources of the criminal justice system for very little social benefit. The legislature must pull California out of this obscenity quagmire as soon as possible.

CHAPTER **8**

MOTION PICTURE

CENSORSHIP

Motion pictures as a means of mass communication are in their infancy when compared with the print media, but the film medium has grown rapidly and has demonstrated massive impact over its first half-century. The Supreme Court has noted that films have a "greater capacity for evil" than do the print media and, as such, are held in a unique position relative to First Amendment protection. It was first ruled, in a 1915 case, that motion pictures did not fall under First Amendment safeguards because they were considered diversionary entertainment only and a "business pure and simple." Mutual Film Corp. v. Ohio.

It was not until the 1950s that the Court reversed itself and firmly granted motion pictures constitutional recognition along with speech and press. Burstyn v. Wilson. *A change in the 1915 Mutual Film philosophy, however, was hinted at in 1948 when Justice Douglas in his opinion dealing with a Sherman Act question wrote, "We have no doubt that motion pictures, like newspapers and radio, are included in the press whose freedom is guaranteed by the First Amendment."* United States v. Paramount. *This was the first indication that the Court might depart from its "business only" position in* Mutual Film. *While that single statement was all the Court said at the time about films and the First Amendment, the apparent leaning of the Court did not go unnoticed by those interested in freedom of expression for motion pictures, and before long the Warren Court was to be presented with the opportunity to explain more fully the hint given by Justice Douglas in 1948.*

The philosophy of the Mutual Film *decision was finally overturned in 1952 with* Burstyn v. Wilson, *in which the Supreme Court, for the first time, firmly held that motion pictures are to be included within the protective scope of the First Amendment. It left to another day, however, the broader questions of film censorship and licensing, restricting itself only to the specific question at hand, i.e. the New York law as related to the sacrilegious. At question was the film "The Miracle," the showing of which brought cries of outrage from various religious and private pressure groups. The 9–0 decision, in addition to placing films within the First Amendment, struck a philosophic blow at those private groups which attempt to impose their beliefs on the general viewing public. While Justice Clark's opinion of the Court did note unique characteristics which set films aside from other forms of expression under constitutional protection, it held that it was not the intent of the Constitution to protect the "religious sensitivities" of some at the expense of freedom of expression.*

JOSEPH BURSTYN, INC. V. WILSON
343 U.S. 495 (1952)

JUSTICE CLARK *delivered the opinion of the Court.*

The issue here is the constitutionality, under the First and Fourteenth Amendments, of a New York statute which permits the banning of motion picture films on the grounds that they are "sacrilegious." That statute makes it unlawful "to exhibit, or to sell, lease or lend for exhibition at any place of amusement for pay or in connection with any business in the state of New York, any motion picture film or reel (with specified exceptions not relevant here), unless there is at the time in full force and effect a valid license or permit therefor of the education department. . . ."

Appellant is a corporation engaged in the business of distributing motion pictures. It owns the exclusive rights to distribute throughout the United States a film produced in Italy entitled "The Miracle." On November 30, 1950, after having examined the picture, the motion picture division of the New York education department, acting under the statute quoted above, issued to appellant a license authorizing exhibition of "The Miracle," with English subtitles, as one part of a trilogy called "Ways of Love." Thereafter, for a period of approximately eight weeks, "Ways of Love" was exhibited publicly in a motion picture theater whereby appellant received a stated percentage of the admission price.

During this period, the New York State Board of Regents, which by statute is made the head of the education department, received "hundreds of letters, telegrams, post cards, affidavits and other communications" both protesting against and defending the public exhibition of "The Miracle." The Chancellor of the Board of Regents requested three members of the Board to view the picture and to make a report to the entire Board. After viewing the film, this committee reported to the Board that in its opinion there was basis for the claim that the picture was "sacrilegious." Thereafter, on January 19, 1951, the Regents directed appellant to show cause, at a hearing to be held on January 30, why its license to show "The Miracle" should not be rescinded on that ground. Appellant appeared at his hearing, which was conducted by the same three-member committee of the Regents which had previously viewed the picture, and challenged the jurisdiction of the committee and of the Regents to proceed with the case. With the consent of the committee, various interested persons and organizations submitted to it briefs and exhibits bearing upon the merits of the picture and upon the constitutional and statutory questions involved. On February 16, 1951, the Regents, after viewing "The Miracle," determined that it was "sacrilegious" and for that reason ordered the Commissioner of Education to rescind appellant's license to exhibit the picture. The Commissioner did so. . . .

In a series of decisions beginning with *Gitlow v. New York*, this Court held that the liberty of speech and of the press which the First Amendment guarantees against abridgment by the federal government is within the liberty safeguarded by the Due Process Clause of the Fourteenth Amendment from invasion by state action. That principle has been followed and reaffirmed to the present day. . . .

The present case is the first to present squarely to us the question whether motion pictures are within the ambit of protection which the First Amendment, through the Fourteenth, secures to any form of "speech" or "the press."

It cannot be doubted that motion pictures are a significant medium for the communication of ideas. They may affect public attitudes and behavior in a variety of ways, ranging from direct espousal of a political or social doctrine to the subtle shaping of thought which characterizes all artistic expression. The importance of motion pictures as an organ of public opinion is not lessened by the fact that they are designed to entertain as well as to inform. As was said in *Winters v. New York*:

> "The line between the informing and the entertaining is too elusive for the protection of that basic right [a free press]. Everyone is familiar with instances of propaganda through fiction. What is one man's amusement, teaches another's doctrine."

It is urged that motion pictures do not fall within the First Amendment's aegis because their production, distribution, and exhibition is a large-scale business conducted for private profit. We cannot agree. That books, newspapers, and magazines are published and sold for profit does not prevent them from being a form of expression whose liberty is safeguarded by the First Amendment. We fail to see why operation for profit should have any different effect in the case of motion pictures.

It is further urged that motion pictures possess a greater capacity for evil, particularly among the youth of a community, than other modes of expression. Even if one were to accept this hypothesis, it does not follow that motion pictures should be disqualified from First Amendment protection. If there be capacity for evil it may be relevant in determining the permissible scope of community control, but it does not authorize substantially unbridled censorship such as we have here.

For the foregoing reasons, we conclude that expression by means of motion pictures is included within the free speech and the free press guarantee of the First and Fourteenth Amendments. To the extent that language in the opinion in *Mutual Film Corp. v. Industrial Commission* is out of harmony with the views here set forth, we no longer adhere to it.

To hold that liberty of expression by means of motion pictures is guaranteed by the First and Fourteenth Amendments, however, is not the end of our problem. It does not follow that the Constitution requires absolute freedom to exhibit every motion picture of every kind at all times and all places. That much is evident from the series of decisions of this Court with respect to other media of communication of ideas. Nor does it follow that motion pictures are necessarily subject to the precise rules governing any other particular method of expression. Each method tends to present its own peculiar problems. But the basic principles of freedom of speech and the press, like the First Amendment's command, do not vary. Those principles, as they have frequently been enunciated by this Court, make freedom of expression the rule. There is no justification in this case for making an exception to that rule.

The statute involved here does not seek to punish, as a past offense, speech or writing falling within the permissible scope of subsequent punishment. On the contrary, New York requires that permission to communicate ideas be obtained in advance from state officials who judge the content of the words and pictures sought to be communicated. This Court recognized many years ago that such a previous restraint is a form of infringement upon freedom of expression to be especially condemned. *Near v. Minnesota*, 283 U.S. 697. The Court there recounted the history which indicates that a major purpose of the First Amendment guarantee of a free press was to prevent prior restraints upon publication, although it was carefully pointed out that the liberty of the press is not limited to that protection. It was further stated that "the protection even as to previous restraint is not absolutely unlimited. But the limitation has been recognized only in exceptional cases." In the light of the First Amendment's history and of the *Near* decision, the State has a heavy burden to demonstrate that the limitation challenged here presents such an exceptional case.

New York's highest court says there is "nothing mysterious" about the statutory provision applied in this case: "It is simply this: that no religion, as that word is understood by the ordinary, reasonable person, shall be treated with contempt, mockery, scorn and ridicule. . . ." This is far from the kind of narrow exception to freedom of expression which a state may carve out to satisfy the adverse demands of other interests of society. In seeking to apply the broad and all-inclusive definition of "sacrilegious" given by the New York courts, the censor is set adrift upon a boundless sea amid a myriad of conflicting currents of religious views, with no charts but those provided by the most vocal and powerful orthodoxies. New York cannot vest such unlimited restraining control over motion pictures in a censor. Under such a standard the most careful and tolerant censor would find it virtually impossible to avoid favoring one religion over another, and he would be subject to an inevitable tendency to ban the expression of unpopular sentiments sacred to a religious minority. Application of the "sacrilegious" test, in these or other respects, might raise substantial questions under the First Amendment's guarantee of separate church and state with freedom of worship for all. However, from the standpoint of freedom of speech and the press, it is enough to point out that the state has no legitimate interest in protecting any or all religions from views distasteful to them which is sufficient to justify prior restraints upon the expression of those views. It is not the business of government in our nation to suppress real or imagined attacks upon a particular religious doctrine, whether they appear in publications, speeches, or motion pictures.

Since the term "sacrilegious" is the sole standard under attack here, it is not necessary for us to decide, for example, whether a state may censor motion pictures under a clearly drawn statute designed and applied to prevent the showing of obscene films. That is a very different question from the one now before us. We hold only that under the First and Fourteenth Amendments a state may not ban a film on the basis of a censor's conclusion that it is "sacrilegious.". . .

*   *   *

Film censorship through the late 1940s and into the early 1950s was based on the judgment of isolated scenes rather than on the context of the work as a whole. This approach was similar to the one used in early literary censorship. Scene-by-scene inspection often was made by state and local licensing agencies. Nakedness was limited to travelogue-like pictures of African or South Sea natives or to blurred suggestions in more commercial ventures. It was standard practice during these years to film sexually frank scenes twice, once for domestic exhibition and again for foreign showing, the latter allowing greater sexual latitude.

Following the unanimous 1952 landmark Burstyn *decision granting First Amendment protection to motion pictures, the Supreme Court began to hit hard at film censorship practices in a number of controversial areas. The Court also lifted bans against "Pinky," the interracial story of a girl who "passed for white"* (Gelling v. Texas); *two films, the American "Native Son," which dealt with racial frictions, and the French "La Ronde," which included the question of promiscuity* (Superior Films, Inc. v. Ohio); *and the French film "Game of Love," which also dealt with sex in an explicit manner* (Times Film Corp. v. Chicago). *This latter case, decided in 1957, should not be confused with a major decision of the same title handed down in 1961.*

In the 1961 Times Film *case, the Court faced the question of prior restraint per se by acknowledging the unique characteristic of motion pictures. In a heated exchange of opinions, the Court ruled 5–4 that licensing and "prior screening" requirements involving motion pictures did not violate the constitutional guarantees of free speech and press. Chief Justice Warren issued one of his strongest dissents in which he enumerated incident after incident which clearly pointed to the dangers inherent in government censorship of films. Most of his citations dealt with political and moral questions rather than with sex and obscenity and clearly left the impression that a little censorship often leads to more. Censorship of motion pictures, he concluded, was not in the best interests of a free society.*

It was left for the Warren Court of the 1960s, then, to interpret and clarify the Times Film *ruling. The Court responded by placing tight restrictions on the licensing practices rather than by overturning its 1961* Times Film *ruling. In* Freedman v. Maryland *the Court ruled that while licensing boards were constitutional, their censoring of films must be given swift judicial reviews in courts of law and that the burden of proof in these cases must lie with the censor rather than with the exhibitor. Finally, in the* Interstate Circuit *case of 1968, the final film censorship decision announced by the Warren Court, the Justices suggested they would accept state and local motion picture classification laws (e.g., "adults only") if these laws were drawn carefully.*

In all cases except those dealing with hard-core pornography, then, the Warren Court for all practical purposes eliminated film censorship for adult viewers. These decisions did not put the censor out of business, however. The Interstate Circuit and Ginsberg decisions gave new life to the few state jurisdictions which have continued to exercise prior restraint through licensing and certainly will encourage legislation establishing others. Also, the clear change in direction of the Burger Court with its conservative majority has given new life to film as well as print media censorship. The 1973 Miller decision, discussed in the previous chapter, re-defined obscenity and, therefore, is as important to films as it is to literature. And Paris Adult Theatre I v. Slaton, *handed down on the same day as* Miller, *rejected the concept that consenting adults should be allowed to voluntarily view an obscene film in a clearly marked "adult theater" if a state wished to prohibit such viewing.*

It should be pointed out here that these decisions were based on the Roth test and were focused on what the Court saw as obscene. They should not be construed as allowing carte blanche censorship of nonobscene matter, even though a given community may find the film in question highly distasteful. In 1974, for example, a unanimous Supreme Court held the serious and highly acclaimed film "Carnal Knowledge" to be a constitutionally protected work of art even though a jury in the community of Albany, Georgia, felt otherwise. Jenkins v. Georgia. And in 1975, a 6–3 vote of the Court struck down a Jacksonville, Florida, ordinance banning the showing of bare breasts and buttocks on drive-in movie screens visible from public streets. Erznoznik v. Jacksonville.

In addition, it has been argued that more restraint is practiced by nongovernment groups than by "official" censors. These censorial pressures, familiar to all producers, come from magazines and newspapers, parent-teacher organizations, civic betterment clubs and church groups, to name a few. Classification by these groups has continued or intensified in spite of—or because of—court decisions. Also, the industry itself is not without restraints. Fearing Federal control, producers in the 1930s drew a self-regulatory code for the industry. As years progressed, however, the code became less and less a force in guiding the industry. The competition of television made demands for "bolder" movies in order to "pry" audiences from their easy chairs in front of television sets. The increasing popularity of more realistic foreign films (even though customs censorship continued largely unchecked), and the rise of the American independent filmmaker also made the code more hypothetical than effective. Indeed, producers who subscribed to the code sometimes subverted the intent of the agreement by releasing "adult" films under different company names. In addition, producers sometimes found that controversy or lack of code approval were financially more beneficial than was simple code approval.

The state of New York, seven years after the Burstyn decision granting films First Amendment protection, was the scene of the first major debate for the Warren

Court regarding censorship of motion pictures. The Court was unanimous in affirming the 1952 Burstyn decision, but failed to come to grips with the fundamental question of the right of state and local governments to prescreen, license and censor films prior to their public showing. At issue here was a film version of the D. H. Lawrence novel, Lady Chatterley's Lover, a story of love between a woman of wealth and her husband's gamekeeper. The famed novel itself had had its own skirmishes with censorship. The film was refused a license until three isolated scenes were cut, these scenes judged to be "immoral." Justice Stewart wrote the opinion of the Court in which it was pointed out that a film may not be censored merely because it portrays ideas that are rejected by the majority, in this case that adultery might for some persons and under some circumstances be desirable. The Court noted that the censoring of an idea, such as was done in the immediate case, struck at the very heart of the Constitution. Justices Douglas and Black, as they had argued with literary censorship, took the position that any form of motion picture censorship violates the First and Fourteenth Amendments.

KINGSLEY INTERNATIONAL PICTURES CORP. V. REGENTS
360 U.S. 684 (1959)

JUSTICE STEWART *delivered the opinion of the Court.*

Once again the Court is required to consider the impact of New York's motion picture licensing law upon First Amendment liberties, protected by the Fourteenth Amendment from infringement by the States. . . .

What New York has done . . . is to prevent the exhibition of a motion picture because that picture advocates an idea—that adultery under certain circumstances may be proper behavior. Yet the First Amendment's basic guarantee is of freedom to advocate ideas. The State, quite simply, has thus struck at the very heart of constitutionally protected liberty.

It is contended that the State's action was justified because the motion picture attractively portrays a relationship which is contrary to the moral standards, the religious precepts, and the legal code of its citizenry. This argument misconceives what it is that the Constitution protects. Its guarantee is not confined to the expression of ideas that are conventional or shared by a majority. It protects advocacy of the opinion that adultery may sometimes be proper, no less than advocacy of socialism or the single tax. And in the realm of ideas it protects expression which is eloquent no less than that which is unconvincing. . . .

The inflexible command which the New York Court of Appeals has attributed to the State Legislature thus cuts so close to the core of constitutional freedom as to make it quite needless in this case to examine the periphery. Specifically, there is no occasion to consider the appellant's contention that the State is entirely without power to require films of any kind to be licensed prior to their exhibition. Nor need we here determine whether, despite problems peculiar to motion pictures, the controls which a State may impose upon this medium of expression are precisely coextensive with those allowable for newspapers, books, or individual speech. It is enough for the present case to reaffirm that motion pictures are within the First and Fourteenth Amendments' basic protection. *Joseph Burstyn, Inc. v. Wilson.*

JUSTICE BLACK, *concurring.*

I concur in the Court's opinion and judgment but add a few words because of concurring opinions by several Justices who rely on their appraisal of the movie "Lady Chatterley's Lover" for holding that New York cannot constitutionally bar it. Unlike them, I have not seen the picture. My view is that stated by Mr. Justice Douglas, that prior censorship of moving pictures like prior censorship of newspapers and books violates the First and Fourteenth Amendments. If despite the Constitution, however, this Nation is to embark on the dangerous road of censorship, my belief is that this Court is about the most inappropriate Supreme Board of Censors that could be found. So far as I know, judges possess no special expertise providing exceptional competency to set standards and to supervise the private morals of the Nation. In addition, the Justices of this Court seem especially unsuited to make the kind of value judgments—as to what movies are good or bad for local communities—which the concurring opinions appear to require. We are told that the only way we can decide whether a State or municipality can constitutionally bar movies is for this Court to view and appraise each movie on a case-by-case basis. Under these circumstances, every member of the Court must exercise his own judgment as to how bad a picture is, a judgment which is ultimately based at least in large part on his own standard of what is immoral. The end result of such decisions seems to me to be a purely personal determination by individual Justices as to whether a particular picture viewed is too bad to allow it to be seen by the public. Such an individualized determination cannot be guided by reasonably fixed and certain standards. Accordingly, neither States nor moving picture makers can possibly know in advance, with any fair degree of certainty, what can or cannot be done in the field of movie making and exhibiting. This uncertainty cannot easily be reconciled with the rule of law which our Constitution envisages. . . .

JUSTICE DOUGLAS, *with whom Justice Black joins, concurring.*

While I join in the opinion of the Court, I adhere to the views I expressed in *Superior Films v. Department of Education* that censorship of movies is unconstitutional, since it is a form of "previous restraint" that is as much at war with the First Amendment, made applicable to the States through the Fourteenth, as the censorship struck down in *Near v. Minnesota.* If a particular movie violates a valid law, the exhibitor can be prosecuted in the usual way. I can find in the First Amendment no room for any censor whether he is scanning an editorial, reading a news broadcast, editing a novel or a play, or previewing a movie. . . .

Happily government censorship has put down few roots in this country. The American tradition is represented by *Near v. Minnesota.* We have in the United States no counterpart of the Lord Chamberlain who is censor over England's stage.

As late as 1941 only six States had systems of censorship for movies. Chafee, *Free Speech in the United States* (1941), p. 540. That number has now been reduced to four—Kansas, Maryland, New York, and Virginia—plus a few cities. . . . And from what information is available, movie censors do not seem to be very active. Deletion of the residual part of censorship that remains would constitute the elimination of an institution that intrudes on First Amendment rights.

JUSTICE CLARK, *concurring in the result.*

. . . [A]s my Brother Harlan points out, "each time such a statute is struck down, the State is left in more confusion." This is true where broad grounds are employed leaving no indication as to what may be necessary to meet the requirements of due process. I see no grounds for confusion, however, were a statute to ban "pornographic" films, or those that "portray *acts* of sexual immorality, perversion or lewdness." If New York's statute had been so construed by its highest court I believe it would have met the requirements of due process. Instead, it placed more emphasis on what the film teaches than on what it depicts. There is where the confusion enters. For this reason, I would reverse on the authority of *Burstyn.*

*   *   *

The Court of 1961 finally faced the question of the constitutionality of motion picture censorship with a 5–4 decision that cities and states do have the right to pre-screen and to issue permits for public exhibition. At issue was the film "Don Juan," a version of the Mozart opera "Don Giovanni," which admittedly would have received a permit had one been applied for. The critical issue was one of prior restraint. The five-man majority, Justices Clark, Frankfurter, Harlan, Whittaker and Stewart, held that free speech is not absolute and that it was within the constitutional framework for Chicago to protect its citizens from the dangers of obscenity by licensing films, although warning that it was not the intent of the Court to give carte blanche *to local government censors. The decision brought heated dissents, with Chief Justice Warren's being the most memorable as he outlines past film censorship battles.*

TIMES FILM CORP. V. CHICAGO
365 U.S. 43 (1961)

JUSTICE CLARK *delivered the opinion of the Court.*

. . . We are satisfied that a justiciable controversy exists. The section of Chicago's ordinance in controversy specifically provides that a permit for the public exhibition of a motion picture must be obtained; that such "permit shall be granted only after the motion picture film for which said permit is requested has been produced at the office of the commissioner of police for examination"; that the commissioner shall refuse the permit if the picture does not meet certain standards; and that in the event of such refusal the applicant may appeal to the mayor for a *de novo* hearing and his action shall be final. Violation of the ordinance carries certain punishments. The petitioner complied with the requirements of the ordinance, save for the production of the film for examination. The claim is that this concrete and specific statutory requirement, the production of the film at the office of the Commissioner for examination, is invalid as a previous restraint on freedom of speech. In *Joseph Burstyn, Inc. v. Wilson* we held that motion pictures are included "within the free speech and free press guarantee of the First and Fourteenth Amendments." Admittedly, the challenged section of the ordinance imposes a previous restraint, and the broad justiciable issue is therefore present as to whether the ambit of constitutional protection includes complete and absolute freedom to exhibit, at least once, any and every kind of motion picture. It is that question alone which we decide. We have concluded that sec. 155–4 of Chicago's ordinance requiring the submission of films prior to their public exhibition is not, on the grounds set forth, void on its face. . . .

[T]here is not a word in the record as to the nature and content of "Don Juan." We are left entirely in the dark in this regard, as were the city officials and the other reviewing courts. Petitioner claims that the nature of the film is irrelevant, and that even if this film contains the basest type of pornography, or incitement to riot, or forceful overthrow of orderly government, it may nonetheless be shown without prior submission for examination. The challenge here is to the censor's basic authority; it does not go to any statutory standards employed by the censor or procedural requirements as to the submission of the film. . . .

Petitioner would have us hold that the public exhibition of motion pictures must be allowed under any circumstances. The State's sole remedy, it says, is the invocation of criminal process under the Illinois pornography statute, and then only after a transgression. But this position . . . is founded upon the claim of absolute privilege against prior restraint under the First Amendment—a claim without sanction in our cases. To illustrate its fallacy, we need only point to one of the "exceptional cases" which Chief Justice Hughes enumerated in *Near v. Minnesota*, namely, "the primary requirements of decency [that] may be enforced against obscene publications." Moreover, we later held specifically "that obscenity is not within the area of constitutionally protected speech or press." *Roth v. United States.* Chicago emphasizes here its duty to protect its people against the dangers of obscenity in the public exhibition of motion pictures. To this argument petitioner's only answer is that regardless of the capacity for, or extent of, such an evil, previous restraint cannot be justified. With this we cannot agree. We recognized in *Burstyn* that "capacity for evil . . . may be relevant in determining the permissible scope of community control" and that motion pictures were not "necessarily subject to the precise rules governing any other particular method of expression. Each method," we said, "tends to present its own peculiar problems."

Certainly petitioner's broadside attack does not warrant, nor could it justify on the record here, our saying that—aside from any consideration of the other "exceptional cases" mentioned in our decisions—the State is stripped of all constitutional power to prevent, in the most effective fashion, the utterance of this class of speech. It is not for this Court to limit the State in its selection of the remedy it deems most effective to cope with such a problem, absent, of course, a showing of unreasonable strictures on individual liberty resulting from its application in particular circumstances. *Kingsley Books, Inc. v. Brown.* We, of course, are not holding that city officials may be granted the power to prevent the showing of any motion picture they deem unworthy of a license. *Joseph Burstyn, Inc. v. Wilson.*

As to what may be decided when a concrete case involving a specific standard provided by this ordinance is presented, we intimate no opinion. The petitioner has not challenged all—or for that matter, any—of the ordinance's standards. Naturally we could not say that every one of the standards, including those which Illinois' highest court has found sufficient, is so vague on its face that the entire ordinance is void. At this time we say no more than this—that we are dealing with motion pictures and, even as to them, only in the context of the broadside attack presented on this record.

CHIEF JUSTICE WARREN, *with whom Justice Black, Justice Douglas and Justice Brennan join, dissenting.*

I cannot agree either with the conclusion reached by the Court or with the reasons advanced for its support. To me, this case clearly presents the question of our approval of unlimited censorship of motion pictures before exhibition through a system of administrative licensing. Moreover, the decision presents a real danger of eventual censorship for every form of communication, be it newspapers, journals, books, magazines, television, radio or public speeches. The Court purports to leave these questions for another day, but I am aware of no constitutional principle which permits us to hold that the communication of ideas through one medium may be censored while other media are immune. Of course each medium presents its own peculiar problems, but they are not of the kind which would authorize the censorship of one form of communication and not the others. I submit that in arriving at its decision the Court has interpreted our cases contrary to the intention at the time of their rendition and, in exalting the censor of motion pictures, has endangered the First and Fourteenth Amendment rights of all others engaged in the dissemination of ideas. . . .

Let it be completely clear what the Court's decision does. It gives official license to the censor, approving a grant of power to city officials to prevent the showing of any moving picture these officials deem unworthy of a license. It thus gives formal sanction to censorship in its purest and most far-reaching form, to a classical plan of licensing that, in our country, most closely approaches the English licensing laws of the seventeenth century which were commonly used to suppress dissent in the mother country and in the colonies. . . .

Perhaps today's surrender was forecast by *Kingsley Books, Inc. v. Brown.* But, that was obviously not this case, and accepting *arguendo* the correctness of that decision, I believe that it leads to a result contrary to that reached today. The statute in *Kingsley* authorized "the chief executive, or legal officer, of a municipality to invoke a 'limited injunctive remedy,' under closely defined procedural safeguards, against the sale and distribution of written and printed matter found after due trial [by a court] to be obscene. . . ." The Chicago scheme has no procedural safeguards; there is no trial of the issue before the blanket injunction against exhibition becomes effective. In *Kingsley*, the grounds for the restraint were that the written or printed matter was "obscene, lewd, lascivious, filthy, indecent, or disgusting . . . or immoral. . . ." The Chicago objective is to capture much more. The *Kingsley* statute required the existence of some cause to believe that the publication was obscene before the publication was put on trial. The Chicago ordinance requires no such showing.

The booklets enjoined from distribution in *Kingsley* were concededly obscene. There is no indication that this is true of the moving picture here. This was treated as a particularly crucial distinction. Thus, the Court has suggested that, in times of national emergency, the Government might impose a prior restraint upon "the publication of the sailing dates of transports or the number and location of troops." *Near v. Minnesota*. But, surely this is not to suggest that the Government might require that all newspapers be submitted to a censor in order to assist it in preventing such information from reaching print. Yet in this case the Court gives its blessing to the censorship of all motion pictures in order to prevent the exhibition of those it feels to be constitutionally unprotected.

The statute in *Kingsley* specified that the person sought to be enjoined was to be entitled to a trial of the issues within one day after joinder and a decision was to be rendered by the court within two days of the conclusion of the trial. The Chicago plan makes no provision for prompt judicial determination. In *Kingsley*, the person enjoined had available the defense that the written or printed matter was not obscene if an attempt was made to punish him for disobedience of the injunction. The Chicago ordinance admits no defense in a prosecution for failure to procure a license other than that the motion picture was submitted to the censor and a license was obtained.

Finally, the Court in *Kingsley* painstakingly attempted to establish that that statute, in its effective operation, was no more a previous restraint on, or interference with, the liberty of speech and press than a statute imposing criminal punishment for the publication of pornography. In each situation, it contended, the publication may have passed into the hands of the public. Of course, this argument is inadmissible in this case and the Court does not purport to advance it. . . .

A revelation of the extent to which censorship has recently been used in this country is indeed astonishing. The Chicago licensors have banned newsreel films of Chicago policemen shooting at labor pickets and have ordered the deletion of a scene depicting the birth of a buffalo in Walt Disney's "Vanishing Prairie." . . . Before World War II, the Chicago censor denied licenses to a number of films portraying and criticizing life in Nazi Germany including the March of Time's "Inside Nazi Germany." . . . Recently, Chicago refused to issue a permit for the exhibition of the motion picture "Anatomy of a Murder" based upon the best-selling novel of the same title, because it found the use of the words "rape" and "contraceptive" to be objectionable. . . . The Chicago censor bureau excised a scene in "Street With No Name" in which a girl was slapped because this was thought to be a "too violent" episode. . . . "It Happened in Europe" was severely cut by the Ohio censors who deleted scenes of war orphans resorting to violence. The moral theme of the picture was that such children could even then be saved by love, affection and satisfaction of their basic needs for food. . . . The Memphis censors banned "The Southerner" which dealt with poverty among tenant farmers because "it reflects on the south." "Brewster's Millions," an innocuous comedy of fifty years ago, was recently forbidden in Memphis because the radio and film character Rochester, a Negro, was deemed "too familiar." . . . Maryland censors restricted a Polish documentary film on the basis that it failed to present a true picture of modern Poland. . . . "No Way Out," the story of a Negro doctor's struggle against race prejudice, was banned by the Chicago censor on the ground that "there's a possibility it could cause trouble." The principal objection to the film was that the conclusion showed no reconciliation between blacks and whites. The ban was lifted after a storm of protest and later deletion of a scene showing Negroes and whites arming for a gang fight. . . . Memphis banned "Curley" because it contained scenes of white and Negro children in school together. . . . Atlanta barred "Lost Boundaries," the story of a Negro physician and his family who "passed" for white, on the ground that the exhibition of said picture "will adversely affect the peace, morals and good order" in the city. . . . "Witchcraft," a study of superstition through the ages, was suppressed for years because it depicted the devil as a genial rake with amorous leanings, and because it was feared that certain historical scenes, portraying the excesses of religious fanatics, might offend religion. "Scarface," thought by some as the best of the gangster films, was held up for months; then it was so badly mutilated that retakes costing a hundred thousand dollars were required to preserve continuity. The New York censors banned "Damaged Lives," a film dealing with venereal disease, although it treated a difficult theme with dignity and had the sponsorship of the American Social Hygiene Society. The picture of Lenin's tomb bearing the inscription "Religion is the opiate of the people" was excised from "Potemkin." From "Joan of Arc" the Maryland board eliminated Joan's exclamation as she stood at the stake: "Oh, God, why has thou forsaken me?" and from "Idiot's Delight," the sentence: "We, the workers of the world, will take care of that." "Professor Mamlock" was produced in Russia and portrayed the persecution of the Jews by Nazis. The Ohio censors condemned it as "harmful" and calculated to "stir up hatred and ill will and gain nothing." It was released only after substantial deletions were made. The police refused to permit its showing in Providence, Rhode Island, on the ground that it was communistic propaganda. "Millions of Us," a strong union propaganda film, encountered trouble in a number of jurisdictions. "Spanish Earth," a pro-Loyalist documentary picture, was banned by the board in Pennsylvania. . . . During the year ending June 30, 1938, the New York board censored, in one way or another, over five per cent of the moving pictures it reviewed. . . . Charlie Chaplin's satire on Hitler,

"The Great Dictator," was banned in Chicago, apparently out of deference to its large German population. . . . Ohio and Kansas banned newsreels considered pro-labor. Kansas ordered a speech by Senator Wheeler opposing the bill for enlarging the Supreme Court to be cut from the "March of Time" as "partisan and biased." . . . An early version of "Carmen" was condemned on several different grounds. The Ohio censor objected because cigarette-girls smoked cigarettes in public. The Pennsylvania censor disapproved the duration of a kiss. . . . The New York censors forbade the discussion in films of pregnancy, venereal disease, eugenics, birth control, abortion, illegitimacy, prostitution, miscegenation and divorce. . . . A member of the Chicago censor board explained that she rejected a film because "it was immoral, corrupt, indecent, against my . . . religious principles." . . . A police sergeant attached to the censor board explained, "Coarse language or anything that would be derogatory to the Government—propaganda" is ruled out of foreign films. "Nothing pink or red is allowed," he added. *Chicago Daily News*, Apr. 7, 1959, p. 3, cols. 7–8. The police sergeant in charge of the censor unit has said: "Children should be allowed to see any movie that plays in Chicago. If a picture is objectionable for a child, it is objectionable period." *Chicago Tribune*, May 24, 1959, p. 8, col. 3. And this is but a smattering produced from limited research. Perhaps the most powerful indictment of Chicago's licensing device is found in the fact that between the Court's decision in 1952 in *Joseph Burstyn, Inc. v. Wilson* and the filing of the petition for *certiorari* in 1960 in the present case, not once have the state courts upheld the censor when the exhibitor elected to appeal. Brief of American Civil Liberties Union as *amicus curiae*, pp. 13–14.

This is the regimen to which the Court holds that all films must be submitted. It officially unleashes the censor and permits him to roam at will, limited only by an ordinance which contains some standards that, although concededly not before us in this case, are patently imprecise. . . .

Moreover, more likely than not, the exhibitor will not pursue judicial remedies. His inclination may well be simply to capitulate rather than initiate a lengthy and costly litigation. In such case, the liberty of speech and press, and the public, which benefits from the shielding of that liberty, are, in effect, at the mercy of the censor's whim. This powerful tendency to restrict the free dissemination of ideas calls for reversal.

Freedom of speech and freedom of the press are further endangered by this "most effective" means for confinement of ideas. It is axiomatic that the stroke of the censor's pen or the cut of his scissors will be a less contemplated decision than will be the prosecutor's determination to prepare a criminal indictment. The standards of proof, the judicial safeguards afforded a criminal defendant and the consequences of bringing such charges will all provoke the mature deliberation of the prosecutor. None of these hinder the quick judgment of the censor, the speedy determination to suppress. Finally, the fear of the censor by the composer of ideas acts as a substantial deterrent to the creation of new thoughts. This is especially true of motion pictures due to the large financial burden that must be assumed by their producers. The censor's sword pierces deeply into the heart of free expression. . . .

. . . The Court, in no way, explains why moving pictures should be treated differently than any other form of expression, why moving pictures should be denied the protection against censorship—"a form of infringement upon freedom of expression to be *especially* condemned." *Joseph Burstyn, Inc. v. Wilson.* (Emphasis added.) When pressed during oral argument, counsel for the city could make no meaningful distinction between the censorship of newspapers and motion pictures. In fact, the percentage of motion pictures dealing with social and political issues is steadily rising. The Chicago ordinance makes no exception for newsreels, documentaries, instructional and educational films or the like. All must undergo the censor's inquisition. Nor may it be suggested that motion pictures may be treated differently from newspapers because many movies are produced essentially for purposes of entertainment. As the Court said in *Winters v. New York:*

> We do not accede to appellee's suggestion that the constitutional protection for a free press applies only to the exposition of ideas. The line between the informing and the entertaining is too elusive for the protection of that basic right. Everyone is familiar with instances of propaganda through fiction. What is one man's amusement, teaches another's doctrine. . . .

The Court, not the petitioner, makes the "broadside attack." I would reverse the decision below.

*   *   *

The first major response to the Times Film *precedent came three years later when the Supreme Court in* Jacobellis v. Ohio *suggested that the concept of "contemporary community standards" in dealing with obscenity (Roth) might be interpreted as "national standards" because of the application of a national constitution. The six Justices who voted for reversal, however, could not reach agreement for an opinion of the Court. Five separate opinions were expressed by the nine Justices in their 6–3 decision. At issue was the French film "The Lovers," in which there was a brief but explicit love scene. But any hope that a majority of Justices would soon agree on the national standards test suggested in* Jacobellis *were put aside when Chief Justice Burger, writing for a firm five-man majority in* Miller, *rejected the requirement that national standards necessarily be imposed on states and local communities and, further, rejected the "utterly without redeeming social value" test also suggested in the badly splintered* Jacobellis *decision. Perhaps, then, the most memorable outcome of* Jacobellis *is the line by Justice Stewart, who had "held out" for censorship only of "hard-core pornography" and who had decided that this film wasn't it. He issued his oft quoted definition of obscenity, "I know it when I see it."*

A major qualification of the Times Film *decision occurred in 1965 with* Freedman v. Maryland. *The Court unanimously reversed a conviction of Ronald Freedman, Baltimore theater owner, for showing the film "Revenge at Daybreak" without a license. This case was similar to* Times Film *in that the motion picture admittedly could have received a license if one had been sought. What makes this case of more than passing interest are two conditions set by the Court in dealing with film licensing and censorship. First, the Court said in a unanimous opinion delivered by Justice Brennan, the burden of proof lies with the censor rather than with the exhibitor, and second, the question of denial of a license to an exhibitor must move swiftly to the courts of law, which are to have the ultimate decision on questions of prior restraint. On the point of swift judicial review, Justice Brennan used as a model the Kingsley Books case. Still, the Court reaffirmed its view that motion pictures are a unique form of expression which require unique safeguards, i.e. pre-screening, censorship and licensing.*

FREEDMAN V. MARYLAND
380 U.S. 51 (1965)

JUSTICE BRENNAN *delivered the opinion of the Court.*

Appellant sought to challenge the constitutionality of the Maryland motion picture censorship statute . . . and exhibited the film "Revenge at Daybreak" at his Baltimore theatre without first submitting the picture to the State Board of Censors as required. . . . The State concedes that the picture does not violate the statutory standards and would have received a license if properly submitted, but the appellant was convicted . . . despite his contention that the statute in its entirety unconstitutionally impaired freedom of expression. . . .

In *Times Film Corp. v. City of Chicago*, we considered and upheld a requirement of submission of motion pictures in advance of exhibition. . . .

Unlike the petitioner in *Times Film*, appellant does not argue that sec. 2 (of the Maryland statute) is unconstitutional simply because it may prevent even the first showing of a film whose exhibition may legitimately be the subject of an obscenity prosecution. He presents a question quite distinct from that passed on in *Times Film*; accepting the rule in *Times Film*, he argues that sec. 2 constitutes an invalid prior restraint because, in the context of the remainder of the statute, it presents a danger of unduly suppressing protected expression. He focuses particularly on the procedure for an initial decision by the censorship board, which, without any judicial participation, effectively bars exhibition of any disapproved film, unless and until the exhibitor undertakes a time-consuming appeal to the Maryland courts and succeeds in having the Board's decision reversed. Under the statute, the exhibitor is required to submit the film to the Board for examination, but no time limit is imposed for completion of Board action, sec. 17. . . .

Thus there is no statutory provision for judicial participation in the procedure which bars a film, nor even assurance of prompt judicial review. Risk of delay is built into the Maryland procedure, as is borne out by experience; in the only reported case indicating the length of time required to complete an appeal, the initial judicial determination has taken four months and final vindication of the film on appellate review, six months. . . .

. . . In substance his argument is that, because the apparatus operates in a statutory context in which judicial review may be too little and too late, the Maryland statute lacks sufficient safeguards for confining the censor's action to judicially determined constitutional limits, and therefore contains the same vice as a statute delegating excessive administrative discretion.

Although the Court has said that motion pictures are not "necessarily subject to the precise rules governing any other particular method of expression," *Joseph Burstyn, Inc. v. Wilson*, it is as true here as of other forms of expression that "[a]ny system of prior restraints of expression comes to this Court bearing a heavy presumption against its constitutional validity." *Bantam Books, Inc. v. Sullivan.* ". . . [U]nder the Fourteenth Amendment, a State is not free to adopt whatever procedures it pleases for dealing with obscenity . . . without regard to the possible consequences for constitutionally protected speech." *Marcus v. Search Warrant.* The administration of a censorship system for motion pictures presents peculiar dangers to constitutionally protected speech. Unlike a prosecution for obscenity, a censorship proceeding puts the initial burden on the exhibitor or distributor. Because the censor's business is to censor, there inheres the danger that he may well be less responsive than a court—part of an independent branch of government—to the constitutionally protected interests in free expression. And if it is made unduly onerous, by reason of delay or otherwise, to seek judicial review, the censor's determination may in practice be final.

Applying the settled rule of our cases, we hold that a noncriminal process which requires the prior submission of a film to a censor avoids constitutional infirmity only if it takes place under procedural safeguards designed to obviate the dangers of a censorship system. First, the burden of proving that the film is unprotected expression must rest on the censor. As we said in *Speiser v. Randall*, "Where the transcendent value of speech is involved, due process certainly requires . . . that the State bear the burden of persuasion to show that the appellants engaged in criminal speech." Second, while the State may require advance submission of all films, in order to proceed effectively to bar all showings of unprotected films, the requirement cannot be administered in a manner which would lend an effect of finality to the censor's determination whether a film constitutes protected expression. . . . To this end, the exhibitor must be assured, by statute or authoritative judicial construction, that the censor will, within a specified brief period, either issue a license or go to court to restrain showing the film. Any restraint imposed in advance of a final judicial determination on the merits must similarly be limited to preservation of the status quo for the shortest fixed period compatible with sound judicial resolution. Moreover, we are well aware that, even after expiration of a temporary restraint, an administrative refusal to license, signifying the censor's view that the film is unprotected, may have a discouraging effect on the exhibitor. See *Bantam Books, Inc. v. Sullivan.* Therefore, the procedure must also assure a prompt final judicial decision, to minimize the deterrent effect of an interim and possibly erroneous denial of a license. . . .

It is readily apparent that the Maryland procedural scheme does not satisfy these criteria. First, once the censor disapproves the film, the exhibitor must assume the burden of instituting judicial proceedings and of persuading the courts that the film is protected expression. Second, once the Board has acted against a film, exhibition is prohibited pending judicial review, however protracted. Under the statute, appellant could have been convicted if he had shown the film after unsuccessfully seeking a license, even though no court had ever ruled on the obscenity of the film. Third, it is abundantly clear that the Maryland statute provides no assurance of prompt judicial determination. We hold, therefore, that the appellant's conviction must be reversed. The Maryland scheme fails to provide adequate safeguards against undue inhibition of protected expression, and this renders the sec. 2 requirement of prior submission of films to the Board an invalid previous restraint. . . .

*　　*　　*

In 1968 the Court for the first time faced the question of the constitutionality of motion picture classification. While tossing out a Dallas classification system as too vague, the Court nonetheless endorsed in Interstate Circuit, Inc. v. Dallas *the principle of movie classification relating to minors. After warning of the dangers inherent in a loosely drawn classification law, Justice Marshall, writing for the 8–1 majority, emphasized that a state "may regulate the dissemination to juveniles of, and their access to, material objectionable as to them, but which a state clearly could not regulate as to adults." This echoes the sentiments of the Court in relation to printed matter as expressed in* Ginsberg v. New York, *announced the same day and given in Chapter 7.*

In 1973 the Burger Court issued a major film obscenity decision involving the showing of so-called obscene movies in an adults-only theater. Paris Adult Theatre I v. Slaton. *The question involved an interesting extension of the earlier* Stanley *and* Interstate Circuit *decisions, i.e. if a state could not prohibit an adult from viewing obscene matter in the privacy of his or her own living room, could not that person be free to view that same matter "jointly" with other like-minded adults in a public theater? The Paris Adult Theatre I in Atlanta, Georgia, had posted no pictures outside which might be offensive to passersby, but did post signs warning potential ticket buyers, "Adults Only" and "If viewing the nude body offends you, Do Not Enter." No evidence was presented that minors were admitted. The question, then, was not one of offense to an unwilling citizen or a minor. It was simply a question of whether it was constitutional for a state to prohibit adults from viewing any type of film, even if it were obscene, if that viewing is voluntary and in the "privacy" of an adults-only theater.*

The Supreme Court handed down the Paris Adult Theatre I *decision on the same day as it did the* Miller *decision, which re-defined obscenity, and by an identical 5–4 vote. The Court reiterated the rule that obscene matter does not fall under First Amendment protection and that the states have a legitimate interest in regulating obscenity in public places, such as theaters. Also important in this case was the dissent of Justice Brennan, who acknowledged the failure of his majority opinion in* Roth *some 16 years earlier and who urged a total new look into the regulation of obscenity. But a majority of Justices Burger, Blackmun, Powell, Rehnquist, and White ruled, as they did in* Miller.

PARIS ADULT THEATRE I V. SLATON
413 U.S. 49 (1973)

CHIEF JUSTICE BURGER *delivered the opinion of the Court.*

Petitioners are two Atlanta, Georgia, movie theatres and their owners and managers, operating in the style of "adult" theatres. On December 28, 1970, respondents, the local state district attorney and the solicitor for the local state trial court, filed civil complaints in that court alleging that petitioners were exhibiting to the public for paid admission two allegedly obscene films, contrary to Georgia Code.

It should be clear from the outset that we do not undertake to tell the States what they must do, but rather to define the area in which they may chart their own course in dealing with obscene material. This Court has consistently held that obscene material is not protected by the First Amendment as a limitation on the state police power by virtue of the Fourteenth Amendment. . . .

We categorically disapprove the theory, apparently adopted by the trial judge, that obscene, pornographic films acquire constitutional immunity from state regulation simply because they are exhibited for consenting adults only. This holding was properly rejected by the Georgia Supreme Court. Although we have often pointedly recognized the high importance of the state interest in regulating the exposure of obscene materials to juveniles and unconsenting adults, this Court has never declared these to be the only legitimate state interests permitting regulation of obscene material. The States have a long-recognized legitimate interest in regulating the use of obscene material in local commerce and in all places of public accommodation. . . .

. . . The sum of experience, including that of the past two decades, affords an ample basis for legislatures to conclude that a sensitive, key relationship of human existence, central to family life, community welfare, and the development of human personality, can be debased and distorted by crass commercial exploitation of sex. Nothing in the Constitution prohibits a State from reaching such a conclusion and acting on it legislatively simply because there is no conclusive evidence or empirical data. . . .

. . . Even assuming that petitioners have vicarious standing to assert potential customers' rights, it is unavailing to compare a theatre, open to the public for a fee, with the private home of *Stanley v. Georgia* and the marital bedroom of *Griswold v. Connecticut*. This Court has, on numerous occasions, refused to hold that commercial ventures such as a motion-picture house are "private" for the purpose of civil rights litigation and civil rights statutes. The Civil Rights Act of 1964 specifi-

cally defines motion-picture houses and theatres as places of "public accommodation" covered by the Act as operations affecting commerce.

Our prior decisions recognizing a right to privacy guaranteed by the Fourteenth Amendment included "only those personal rights that can be deemed
'fundamental' or 'implicit in the concept of ordered liberty.' " *Palko v. Connecticut,
Roe v. Wade.* This privacy right encompasses and protects the personal intimacies
of the home, the family, marriage, motherhood, procreation, and child rearing.
Nothing, however, in this Court's decisions intimates that there is any "fundamental" privacy right "implicit in the concept of ordered liberty" to watch obscene
movies in places of public accommodation. . . .

JUSTICE DOUGLAS, *dissenting.*

. . . People are, of course, offended by many offerings made by merchants in
this area. They are offended by political pronouncements, sociological themes,
and by stories of official misconduct. The list of activities and publications and
pronouncements that offend someone is endless. Some of it goes on in private;
some of it is inescapably public, as when a government official generates crime,
becomes a blatant offender of the moral sensibilities of the people, engages in
burglary, or breaches the privacy of the telephone, the conference room, or the
home. Life in this crowded modern technological world creates many offensive
statements and many offensive deeds. There is no protection against offensive
ideas, only against offensive conduct.

"Obscenity" at most is the expression of offensive ideas. There are regimes in
the world where ideas "offensive" to the majority (or at least to those who control
the majority) are suppressed. There life proceeds at a monotonous speed. Most of
us would find that world offensive. One of the most offensive experiences in my life
was a visit to a nation where bookstalls were filled only with books on mathematics
and books on religion.

I am sure I would find offensive most of the books and movies charged with
being obscene. But in a life that has not been short, I have yet to be trapped into
seeing or reading something that would offend me. I never read or see the materials
coming to the Court under charges of "obscenity," because I have thought the First
Amendment made it unconstitutional for me to act as a censor. I see ads in
bookstores and neon lights over theatres that resemble bait for those who seek
vicarious exhilaration. As a parent or a priest or as a teacher I would have no
compulsion in edging my children or wards away from the books and movies that
did no more than excite man's base instincts. But I never supposed that government
was permitted to sit in judgment on one's tastes or beliefs—save as they involved
action within the reach of the police power of government. . . .

JUSTICE BRENNAN, *with whom Justice Stewart and Justice Marshall join,
dissenting.*

This case requires the Court to confront once again the vexing problem of
reconciling state efforts to suppress sexually oriented expression with the protec-

tions of the First Amendment, as applied to the States through the Fourteenth Amendment. No other aspect of the First Amendment has, in recent years, demanded so substantial a commitment of our time, generated such disharmony of views, and remained so resistant to the formulation of stable and manageable standards. I am convinced that the approach initiated 15 years ago in *Roth v. United States* and culminating in the Court's decision today, cannot bring stability to this area of the law without jeopardizing fundamental First Amendment values, and I have concluded that the time has come to make a significant departure from that approach. . . .

. . . I need hardly point out that the factors which must be taken into account are judgmental and can only be applied on "a case-by-case, sight-by-sight" basis. *Mishkin v. New York* (Black, J., dissenting). These considerations suggest that no one definition, no matter how precisely or narrowly drawn, can possibly suffice for all situations, or carve out fully suppressable expression from all media without also creating a substantial risk of encroachment upon the guarantees of the Due Process Clause and the First Amendment. . . .

As a result of our failure to define standards with predictable application to any given piece of material, there is no probability of regularity in obscenity decisions by state and lower federal courts. That is not to say that these courts have performed badly in this area or paid insufficient attention to the principles we have established. The problem is, rather, that one cannot say with certainty that material is obscene until at least five members of this Court, applying inevitably obscure standards, have pronounced it so. The number of obscenity cases on our docket gives ample testimony to the burden that has been placed upon this Court. . . .

*   *   *

One year after the Paris Adult Theatre and Miller decisions, the Supreme Court tried to disentangle itself from apparent contradictory positions. In Miller, the Court majority was firm in its support of local determination as to what constitutes patent offensiveness and obscenity. A jury in Albany, Georgia, did just that—it held that Mike Nichols' highly acclaimed film "Carnal Knowledge" was obscene. Jenkins v. Georgia. The Georgia Supreme Court affirmed the conviction of theater manager Billy Jenkins for violating the state's anti-obscenity laws. But the United States Supreme Court disagreed unanimously, Justice Rehnquist writing the opinion of the Court. In attempting to explain that the film really didn't fall under the Miller ruling, he noted that there was no pictorial focus on genitals, "lewd or otherwise," nor on the bodies of the actors when sexual acts were understood to be taking place. He wrote that it would be "a serious misreading of Miller to conclude that juries have unbridled discretion in determining what is 'patently offensive.'" Justice Brennan, in a concurring opinion, argued that his case illustrates the futility of the Miller decision. The film itself was released in 1971 and was listed among the best films of the year by several critics. Ann-Margret received an Academy Award nomination as best supporting actress for her role. The decision was another disappointment for publishers and film distributors who in friend-of-the-court briefs had argued for elimination of the Miller *"local standards" rule. But the Court's majority turned a deaf ear, leaving obscenity decisions up to local juries . . . at least for the most part . . . presumably.*

JENKINS V. GEORGIA
418 U.S. 153 (1974)

JUSTICE REHNQUIST *delivered the opinion of the Court.*

. . . Even though questions of appeal to the "prurient interest" or of patent offensiveness are "essentially questions of fact," it would be a serious misreading of *Miller* to conclude that juries have unbridled discretion in determining what is "patently offensive." Not only did we there say that "the First Amendment values applicable to the States through the Fourteenth Amendment are adequately protected by the ultimate power of appellate courts to conduct an independent review of constitutional claims when necessary," but we made it plain that under that holding "no one will be subject to prosecution for the sale or exposure of obscene materials unless these materials depict or describe patently offensive 'hard core' sexual conduct. . . ."

We also took pains in *Miller* to "give a few plain examples of what a state statute could define for regulation under . . ." the requirement of patent offensiveness. These examples included "representations or descriptions of ultimate sexual acts, normal or perverted, actual or simulated," and "representations or descriptions of masturbation, excretory functions, and lewd exhibition of the genitals." While this did not purport to be an exhaustive catalog of what juries might find patently offensive, it was certainly intended to fix substantive constitutional limitations, deriving from the First Amendment, on the type of material subject to such a determination. It would be wholly at odds with this aspect of *Miller* to uphold an obscenity conviction based upon a defendant's depiction of a woman with a bare midriff, even though a properly charged jury unanimously agreed on a verdict of guilty.

Our own view of the film satisfied us that "Carnal Knowledge" could not be found under the *Miller* standards to depict sexual conduct in a patently offensive way. Nothing in the movie falls within either of the two examples given in *Miller* of material which may constitutionally be found to meet the "patently offensive" element of those standards, nor is there anything sufficiently similar to such material to justify similar treatment. While the subject matter of the picture is, in a broader sense, sex, and there are scenes in which sexual conduct including "ultimate sexual acts" is to be understood to be taking place, the camera does not focus on the bodies of the actors at such times. There is no exhibition whatever of the actors' genitals, lewd or otherwise, during these scenes. There are occasional scenes of nudity, but nudity alone is not enough to make material legally obscene under the *Miller* standards.

Appellant's showing of the film "Carnal Knowledge" is simply not the "public portrayal of hard core sexual conduct for its own sake, and for ensuing commercial gain" which we said was punishable in *Miller*. . . .

*　　*　　*

The question of showing "R" or "X" rated films or nudity on drive-in movie screens was certain to come before the Court. It did in 1975, and the Supreme Court ruled that city ordinances which prohibit displays of nudity per se are unconstitutionally broad. Erznoznik v. Jacksonville. *Struck down was a Jacksonville, Florida, ordinance which prohibited such scenes if they could be viewed from the public streets. Justice Powell, writing for a 6–3 majority, noted that the ordinance in question was so broad that it would prohibit showing a picture of a baby's buttocks or a woman's breasts even where nudity might be accepted public behavior or might be indigenous to the story. The Court in the same term declined to hear a case that could have extended the* Stanley *"privacy" concept to motel rooms.* Antico v. California. *Involved was the conviction of a Los Angeles motel owner for showing obscene films to patrons over a closed circuit television screen.*

So, with Jenkins, Erznoznik *and* Vance, *which follows, the qualifications of* Miller *began. In all probability, they will continue through the 1990s as the Court is forced into the "traditional" case-by-case determination it had hoped to avoid by* Miller. *It is interesting to note that the decisions in these cases have been "passed around" among the Nixon appointees—Burger in* Miller *and Paris Adult Theatre, Rehnquist in* Jenkins, *and Powell in* Erznoznik. *There seems little doubt that the groping for a satisfactory definition will continue despite the past failures.*

ERZNOZNIK V. JACKSONVILLE
422 U.S. 205 (1975)

JUSTICE POWELL *delivered the opinion of the Court.*

This case presents a challenge to the facial validity of a Jacksonville, Fla., ordinance that prohibits showing films containing nudity by a drive-in movie theater when its screen is visible from a public street or place. . . .

Appellee concedes that its ordinance sweeps far beyond the permissible restraints on obscenity and thus applies to films that are protected by the First Amendment. Nevertheless, it maintains that any movie containing nudity which is visible from a public place may be suppressed as a nuisance. . . .

Although each case ultimately must depend on its own specific facts, some general principles have emerged. A State or municipality may protect individual privacy by enacting reasonable time, place, and manner regulations applicable to all speech irrespective of content. But when the government, acting as censor, undertakes selectively to shield the public from some kinds of speech on the ground that they are more offensive than others, the First Amendment strictly limits its power. Such selective restrictions have been upheld only when the speaker intrudes on the privacy of the home, see *Rowan v. Post Office Dept.*, or the degree of captivity makes it impractical for the unwilling viewer or auditor to avoid exposure. See *Lehman v. City of Shaker Heights*. . . .

The plain, if at times disquieting, truth is that in our pluralistic society, constantly proliferating new and ingenious forms of expression, "we are inescapably captive audiences for many purposes." *Rowan v. Post Office Dept.* Much that we encounter offends our esthetic, if not our political and moral, sensibilities. Nevertheless, the Constitution does not permit government to decide which types of otherwise protected speech are sufficiently offensive to require protection for the unwilling listener or viewer. Rather absent the narrow circumstances described above, the burden normally falls upon the viewer to "avoid further bombardment of [his] sensibilities simply by averting [his] eyes." *Cohen v. California*. . . .

Appellee also attempts to support the ordinance as an exercise of the city's undoubted police power to protect children. Appellee maintains that even though it cannot prohibit the display of films containing nudity to adults, the present ordinance is a reasonable means of protecting minors from this type of visual influence.

It is well settled that a State or municipality can adopt more stringent controls on communicative materials available to youths than on those available to adults. See *Ginsberg v. New York*. Nevertheless, minors are entitled to a significant measure of First Amendment protection, see *Tinker v. Des Moines School Dist.*, and only in relatively narrow and well-defined circumstances may government bar public dissemination of protected materials to them. See *e.g.*, *Interstate Circuit, Inc. v. City of Dallas*.

In this case, assuming the ordinance is aimed at prohibiting youths from viewing the films, the restriction is broader than permissible. The ordinance is not directed against sexually explicit nudity, nor is it otherwise limited. Rather, it sweepingly forbids display of all films containing *any* uncovered buttocks or breasts, irrespective of context or pervasiveness. Thus it would bar a film containing a picture of a baby's buttocks, the nude body of a war victim, or scenes from a culture in which nudity is indigenous. The ordinance also might prohibit newsreel scenes of the opening of an art exhibit as well as shots of bathers on a beach. Clearly all nudity cannot be deemed obscene even as to minors. See *Ginsberg v. New York*. . . .

CHIEF JUSTICE BURGER, *with whom Justice Rehnquist joins, dissenting.*

. . . A careful consideration of the diverse interests involved in this case illustrates, for me, the inadequacy of the Court's rigidly simplistic approach. In the first place, the conclusion that only a limited interest of persons on the public streets is at stake here can be supported only if one completely ignores the unique visual medium to which the Jacksonville ordinance is directed. . . . Such screens are invariably huge; indeed, photographs included in the record of this case show that the screen of petitioner's theater dominated the view from public places including nearby residences and adjacent highways. Moreover, when films are projected on such screens the combination of color and animation against a necessarily dark background is designed to, and results in, attracting and holding the attention of all observers. . . .

So here, the screen of a drive-in movie theater is a unique type of eye-catching display that can be highly intrusive and distracting. Public authorities have a legitimate interest in regulating such displays under the police power; for example, even though traffic safety may not have been the only target of the ordinance in issue here, I think it not unreasonable for lawmakers to believe that public nudity on a giant screen, visible at night to hundreds of drivers of automobiles, may have a tendency to divert attention from their task and cause accidents. . . .

On the other hand, assuming *arguendo* that there could be a play performed in a theater by nude actors involving genuine communication of ideas, the same conduct in a public park or street could be prosecuted under an ordinance prohibiting indecent exposure. This is so because the police power has long been interpreted to authorize the regulation of nudity in areas to which all members of the public have access, regardless of any incidental effect upon communication. A nudist colony, for example, cannot lawfully set up shop in Central Park or Lafayette Park, places established for the public generally. . . .

*   *   *

Two Supreme Court actions in the early 1980s responded to the continuing uncertainty over film censorship. The first was Vance v. Universal Amusement, *in which the Court in a brief, unsigned opinion struck down a Texas public nuisance law that was used to close movie theaters which showed allegedly obscene films. The vote was 5–4 that such laws were examples of unconstitutional prior restraint. States were still free to use criminal statutes to prosecute individual theater owners for showing obscene films, but only after such films had been exhibited. The closing of the movie houses themselves was held to be incompatible with the First Amendment, the majority said. Note the similarity of this view with the landmark prior restraint decision,* Near v. Minnesota, *covered in Chapter 2. Voting in the majority were Justices Brennan, Marshall, Stewart, Blackmun and Stevens.*

In 1981, the Court let stand a Memphis conviction of the producer and two distributors of the film "Deep Throat." Peraino v. U.S. *The Justices declined to review the film and judge its alleged obscenity, allowing the determination of the Memphis jury to stand without comment. Dissenting were Justices Brennan and Marshall, who no longer could count on support from Justice Stewart, who by this time had resigned. His replacement, Justice Sandra O'Connor, voted with the majority, signaling perhaps her alignment for the obscenity cases which are sure to continue to flow upward to the Supreme Court as the final arbiter of such intractable questions.*

MORALS AND THE CONSTITUTION

By Louis Henkin[*]

. . . If I am correct about the origins and purposes of obscenity legislation, much of the constitutional discussion about the control of obscenity seems out of focus. Concentration on whether obscenity may—or may not—incite to unlawful acts aims beside the mark. The question, rather, is whether the state may suppress expression it deems immoral, may protect adults as well as children from voluntary exposure to that which may "corrupt" them, may preserve the community from public, rampant "immorality." This different question may receive the same or a different answer; clearly, the path and the guideposts, the facts sought, the issues considered and the doctrine applied may be very different. Indeed, this inquiry might today command attention even to a question that must have appeared insubstantial earlier in the history of the Constitution: the authority of government under the Constitution to adopt "morals legislation," to suppress private, individual indulgence which does no harm to others, in the name of traditional notions of morality. . . .

. . . The accepted definition of obscenity, as that which "appeal[s] . . . to prurient interest," makes no assumption that it will incite to any action. The history of obscenity legislation points, rather, to origins in aspirations to holiness and propriety. Laws against obscenity have appeared conjoined and cognate to laws against sacrilege and blasphemy, suggesting concern for the spiritual welfare of the person exposed to it and for the moral well-being of the community. Metaphors of "poison" and "filth" also emphasize concern for the welfare of the one exposed and for the atmosphere of the community. A "decent" community does not tolerate obscenity. A "decent" man does not indulge himself with obscene materials.

The moral concern of the community may consist of several different strands frequently entangled beyond separation. Obscenity is immoral, an individual should not indulge it, and the community should not tolerate it. In addition, obscenity, like other immoral acts and expressions, has a deleterious effect on the individual from which the community should protect him. Obscenity is bad for a man, and the concern is not for his "psyche," his mental health. Obscenity is bad for character. It "corrupts" morals, it corrupts character. Character, of course, bears on behavior, but the corruption feared, it should be emphasized, has a very unclear, very remote, and problematic relation to a likelihood that he will commit

---

[*] From Louis Henkin. "Morals and the Constitution: The Sin of Obscenity." *Columbia Law Review*, Vol. 63 (March, 1963), p. 391. Used with permission of the *Columbia Law Review* and the author, a professor of law at Columbia University.

any particular unlawful act or indeed any unlawful act at all, immediately or in the future.

This concern of the state for the "character" and "morals" of the person exposed is particularly evident in the plethora of laws designed to prevent the "corruption of youth." Among other evil influences, obscenity, it is assumed, may "corrupt" a child. The state assists parents who seek to prevent this corruption, or may even act in loco of those parents who are remiss in protecting their own children. The Supreme Court built constitutional doctrine on these assumptions when it held that Michigan could not "reduce the adult population of Michigan to reading only what is fit for children." Again, the corruption of youth by obscenity is deemed to have some immeasurable effect on character and personality; it is not believed to "incite" to any particular actions now or in the future. While in regard to youth it has always been assumed that government has special responsibility and authority, laws adopted for their protection reflect assumptions and attitudes about obscenity not inapplicable to the regulation of obscenity for adults. . . .

If obscenity laws are seen primarily as "morals legislation," if a principal purpose of these laws is to protect, from himself, the person who wishes to indulge, and to maintain the moral "tone" of a community, constitutional discussion of such laws would seem to deserve emphasis different from that which has preoccupied the judges and the writers. . . .

As was perhaps inevitable, this preoccupation with the relation between speech, and action, and undeniably unlawful consequences, led lawyers as well as Justices carelessly to impose this context upon the problem of obscenity when it finally forced itself upon the Supreme Court's attention. If in fact the state's concern with obscenity has little to do with incitement to action, constitutional discussion based on the link between obscenity and unlawful action seems far beside the point. If unlawful action is not the evil at which the state aims, whether obscenity creates a "clear and present" danger of an unlawful action is not the relevant concern. The evils at which the state aims are not unlawful action, but indecency and corruption of morals. . . .

The need for facing the questions here suggested may be emphasized by reference to a unanimous decision of the Supreme Court that does not deal with obscenity at all. In *Kingsley Int'l Pictures Corp. v. Regents of the Univ. of the State of N.Y.*, the state had refused to license the film "Lady Chatterley's Lover" on the ground that it was "immoral," or "of such a character that its exhibition would tend to corrupt morals." The legislature had defined these terms to apply to any film "which portrays acts of sexual immorality . . . or which . . . presents such acts as desirable, acceptable or proper patterns of behavior." The New York courts affirmed the denial of a license for the film "because its subject matter is adultery presented as being right and desirable for certain people under certain circumstances."

The Supreme Court of the United States was agreed in reversing the state's judgment below, though hardly in the reasons for doing so. The majority recognized—as some writers have not—that this was not an obscenity case, that there was nothing in the film that appealed to prurient interests, that the case could not be decided on the basis of some special exception to the freedom of speech enjoyed by "obscenity laws." Yet the Court's opinion, too, did not wrestle with what, I believe, is the real issue. It did not consider that while this was not an obscenity case, it was a "morals" case. The Court stated that New York was censoring the advocacy of an idea, whereas the Constitution, the opinion said, guarantees freedom to advocate ideas. "It protects advocacy of the opinion that adultery may sometimes be proper, no less than advocacy of socialism or the single tax." But ideas promoting adultery—unlike those urging the single tax—impinge on traditional morality. The state, indeed, did not claim that the film incited to adultery; it found the film to be immoral and tending to corrupt morals. Incitement to action, one might urge, is as irrelevant here as it is to obscenity cases in which, in effect, the state bars the obscene because it is immoral and tends to corrupt morals.

Recognition that laws against "obscenity" and laws against "immorality" are equally "morals" legislation would have required a very different opinion from the Court, if not a different result. The Court would have had to recognize that legislation against the "immoral" had historical credentials similar to, if not better than, obscenity laws, that the common obscenity statute indeed also forbade the "immoral"; legislation against the "immoral," then, might have as good a claim as obscenity legislation to historical exception from the freedom of speech. The result in the case could have been reached only by distinguishing, in some relevant way, this "morals legislation" from obscenity laws. An acceptable distinction does not readily appear. Somehow, the Court seemed to be denying to the state the assumption that ideas can be immoral or can corrupt morals, even though it had permitted to the state, in effect, the assumption that obscenity is immoral or can corrupt morals. (Would the Court hold that a child also is deprived of his liberty without due process of law if the state keeps from him materials expressing ideas that may "corrupt morals" without inciting to action?) Or did the Court silently measure and conclude that freedom for "ideas," any ideas, inevitably outweighs the state's interest in preventing "immorality by idea" or corruption of morals by ideas?

The confusion remains. Nothing we have said suggests that any of the obscenity cases before the Court was wrongly decided, or that the dissenters, pursuing the analysis urged, could not again find themselves in dissent. The questions suggested may well reconfirm a majority in the conclusion that "obscenity is not within the area of constitutionally protected speech or press." Dissenting Justices may yet conclude that although a state may legislate against certain acts on the ground that they are immoral, it cannot constitutionally suppress expression on the ground that it is immoral or that it corrupts morals. On any view, the recognition of the moral foundations of obscenity laws may suggest that proper differentiation might bring different constitutional results in different cases. It may be that the Constitution regards state concern with private morality privately indulged differently from state protection of the sensibilities of others against offensive public display, or state prohibition of commercial exploitation and promotion of obscenity. It may be that however much one questions the authority of the state to impose morals, even on children, our society recognizes the authority of parents to educate their children, and the state may protect and support the right of parents to impose their morality on their children.

Courts and lawyers, it seems to me, must face the problem of obscenity on the terms in which society has framed it. Laws against obscenity are rooted in traditional notions of morality and decency; the moral foundations of these laws cannot be disregarded in re-assessing their constitutional validity today. It should not be assumed, without re-examination, that the morality of another day remains between the lines of the Constitution. Nor should it be assumed, without re-examination, that the morality of an older day remains a legitimate aim of government with social import outweighing growing claims of individual freedom.

It has been suggested that the Supreme Court has read obscenity out of the protection for expression in the First and Fourteenth Amendments without asking whether the "moral" character of obscenity laws continues to justify that historical exception today, or whether the moral aims of these laws may properly outweigh the freedoms suppressed. I venture now to suggest that the moral purpose and motive of obscenity legislation—and of other prevalent laws aimed at private indulgence in "immoral" activity—may invite inquiry of yet a different, fundamental order.

We lay aside now claims of freedom to communicate, even the obscene; we are concerned, instead, with claims of the "consumer" to freedom and privacy to indulge in what others may deem immoral. The authority of the state, under the Constitution, to enact "morals legislation"—laws reflecting some traditional morality having no authentic social purpose to protect other persons or property—has always been assumed; it has deep roots, and it has seemed obvious and beyond question. It may now be respectable to ask whether indeed the state may adopt any "morals legislation." And if it be concluded that morals legislation is not ipso facto beyond the state's power, can one avoid asking: what morality the state may enforce; what limitations there are on what the state may deem immoral; how these limitations are to be determined?

In doctrinal terms, one may present these as several constitutional questions, not wholly discrete. For the sake of clarity, I declare them as hypotheses to be examined:

First: even if the "freedom of speech" protected by the First and Fourteenth Amendments does not include a freedom to communicate obscene speech, suppression of obscenity is still a deprivation of liberty or property—of the person who would indulge in it, at least—which requires due process of law. Due process of law demands that legislation have a proper public purpose; only an apparent, rational, utilitarian social purpose satisfies due process. A state may not legislate merely to preserve some traditional or prevailing view of private morality.

Second: due process requires, as well, that means be reasonably related to proper public ends. Legislation cannot be based on unfounded hypotheses and assumptions about character and its corruption.

Third: morals legislation is a relic in the law of our religious heritage; the Constitution forbids such establishment of religion.

The inquiry urged can only be suggested here. I would attempt to state the principal issues. I would underscore the complexity of the questions involved. I would urge, too, that the questions suggested are not clearly insubstantial.

The relation of law to morals has been a favored preoccupation of legal philosophers for a thousand years; in the history of American law the relevance of that relation to constitutional limitations has lain unexamined behind discussions of the scope and the limits of government. That morals were the concern of government was assumed, not explored, in discussions of the reaches of the "police power" limited by substantive "due process of law."

May the state, under our Constitution, legislate in support of "morals"? The question may take us back to another: What are the purposes for which the state may legislate under the Constitution? That question, in other contexts, once deeply troubled the Supreme Court. Not too many years ago the Court seemed to assume that by the law of nature and by social contract government was given limited powers for limited purposes. Freedom was the rule; government had to justify itself, and the justifications had to satisfy the Constitution. . . .

Today, a court would probably not begin with the assumption that government has defined purposes and corresponding "inherent," "natural" limitations. The only limitations on the state, a court might say, are the prohibitions of the Constitution—specific, like those few in the original Constitution, or more general, like those in the Civil War amendments. If one would today examine embedded assumptions about morals legislation, the question, then, is not whether legislation for decency and morality is within the accepted powers of government; we must ask, rather, whether such legislation deprives one to whom it applies of "liberty or property" without due process of law. But if that question looks very different from the one that might have been asked in the nineteenth century, it may be less different than it looks. For some of the "inherent" limitations on the police power may still be with us in notions that the state may legislate only for a "public purpose." And "due process" still requires some link in reason between purpose and the means selected by the legislature to achieve that purpose. We may state the question, then, as whether morality legislation deprives one of liberty or property without due process of law. The subsidiary questions may still be: Is the state's purpose in "morality legislation" a proper public purpose? Are the means used to achieve it "reasonable"?

Emphasis on "public purpose" has usually been intended to exclude legislation for the special interest of some private person or group. Morals legislation presumably does not serve a strictly "private purpose," even if some groups seem more concerned about morals legislation than is the community at large. The beneficiaries of this legislation, it is assumed, are each citizen and the whole community. But is every "nonprivate" purpose a proper public purpose of government? Can the state legislate, not to protect the person or property of others or to promote general economic or social welfare, but to protect and promote "morals," particularly morals reflected—or violated—in private activity?

Perhaps the question can have no provable answer. Supporters of legislation like obscenity laws may urge that government has always legislated in support of accepted morality, and may challenge those who would deny the authority of government to find anything in the Constitution that would take it away. But supporters of the past do not have the only word. Others will stress that the due process clause has intervened, and that it requires government to be reasonable, in purpose as well as in means to achieve the purpose. One may even accept the right of the state to impose restrictions on the individual for his own good—by preventing his suicide, or forcing medical aid, or compelling education; in the context of society, these are "rational" ends, reasonably achieved. But how can "morals," a nonutilitarian, nonrational purpose, be "reasonable"? Could government conjure up some new (or old), nonsocial principle of morality and impose it by law? Could a state forbid me to go to an astrologer—or require me to go to one or abide by his conclusions? And if history is invoked, does the fact that some behavior has been deemed "immoral" in the past—by some, even a violation of "natural law"—render it forever a proper object of legislative prohibition? Is it sufficient to justify legislation that such acts continue to be regarded as "immoral," "sinful," "offensive" by large segments of the community? Or does the due process clause, in this context too, serve to protect individuals from the irrationalities of the majority and of its representatives?

One may ask, it is suggested, whether any nonutilitarian morality can be a reasonable public purpose of legislation. But purpose aside, due process requires also that the means to achieve that purpose be not unreasonable. Of course, means and purposes are not discrete categories, and purposes may themselves be means to other purposes. But assuming that the preservation of private morals continues to be a proper purpose of government, obscenity legislation, in particular, raises the further question whether suppression of obscenity is reasonably related to the morality that the state seeks to preserve.

The question may be clarified if one compares obscenity laws to other morals legislation, e.g., laws against incest. Incestual relations have indubitably been deemed "immoral," at least since Biblical times. If the state may suppress what is immoral, there can be no doubt about the validity of laws against incest. Exposure to obscenity, on the other hand, is at most a derivative, secondary "immorality." In itself, it has no ancient roots; presumably, it would have been condemned, or frowned on, as inconsistent with admonitions to be holy and to avoid pagan abominations. In modern times, obscenity has been condemned in large part because it corrupts morals or character. Since, I have said, corruption of morals or character has no clear relation to any unlawful acts, or even acts that could be made unlawful, what evidence is required of the state, or what assumptions permitted to it, to support the conclusion that obscenity corrupts morals? What are these "morals" and this "character," and what does their corruption mean? And if we accept the concept of "morals" as well as their corruption, how does one decide whether the state is reasonable in its conclusion that indulgence in obscenity does or does not effect this "corruption" of these "morals"?

The Constitution does not enact legal positivism; it does not enact natural law. Due process, I hypothesize, requires that the state deal with the area of the reasonable and deal with it reasonably. It is proper to ask whether the preservation of a nonsocial morality is within the realm of the reasonable, whether concepts like "private morality" and its corruption are subject to logic and proof inherent in reasonableness and rationality. These, of course, are not merely technical requirements of constitutional jurisprudence. They suggest that the Constitution renders unto government the rational governance of the affairs of man in relation to his neighbor; only if government is kept within this domain can it be limited government, subject to constitutional requirements of rational, reasonable action administered by an impartial judiciary. It is only by confining government to what is reasonable that the Constitution and the courts can protect the individual against the unreasonable. Private "morals," and their "corruption," and what "corrupts" them, as differently conceived, have profound significance in the life of a nation and of its citizens. But they are not in the realm of reason and cannot be judged by standards of reasonableness; they ought not, perhaps, to be in the domain of government.

Civilized societies, including ours, have increased the area of government responsibility to protect one against his neighbor. The authority of government to protect us from ourselves is less clearly recognized today, except when injury to ourselves may in turn have undesirable social consequences; although, we have suggested, one may justify—within the limits of the "rational"—governmental efforts to prevent suicide, or compel health measures, "for the individual's own good." When we deal not with physical injury to ourselves but with "sin," respectable and authoritative voices are increasingly heard that there exists "a realm of private morality and immorality which is, in brief and crude terms, not the law's business." Should not the Supreme Court today, or tomorrow, consider whether under the Constitution some morality, at least, may be not the law's business and not appropriate support for legislation consistent with due process of law? . . .

PUBLIC MORALITY AND FREE EXPRESSION

By Harry Clor*

. . . Can rational lines be drawn in this twilight zone? The rulings both in *Erznoznik* and *Young* accord with common sense. Perhaps they can be saved from the contradiction suggested by critics through a common sense consideration of the communal interests at stake in each case. There is no doubt that the protection of juveniles is a valid interest. But that hardly justifies the sweeping provisions of the *Erznoznik* ordinance. Rather, the *Erznoznik* ordinance looks to its justification primarily in the privacy interests of persons in the streets. These interests, however, are still weak, since the First Amendment seems to require us to see and hear much which may offend us.

In *Young*, however, the concern of the Detroit ordinance is the preservation of neighborhoods from deterioration. The ordinance was designed to protect against the congregation of prostitutes and their associates, drug traffic, and a general decline in the moral and aesthetic attractiveness of the city with the consequent departure of legitimate businesses and residents. The public interest at stake is arguably much more substantial in *Young* than it was in *Erznoznik*. The preservation of communities (and communal bonds and communal spirit) should be given considerable weight at a time when this vital ingredient of human well-being is undermined by so many forces of modern life, commercial, technological, and pluralistic. The atomistic view of man represented by the philosophy of John Stuart Mill was probably erroneous even when *On Liberty* was written. It is certainly erroneous now. While individual freedom is an important value, there are other values which are no less important, and the concept of community must be considered to be one of them. And there can be little doubt that one of the major elements contributing to or detracting from the sense of community is the moral and aesthetic atmosphere which prevails in public places. If we did not think that this were important, we would not spend so much effort and money on urban and public beautification. If we acknowledge that there are things which can make our cities more livable, then we must acknowledge that there are things which can make our cities more livable, then we must acknowledge that there are things which make our cities less livable. It is true that these considerations are not susceptible of scientific proof, but that does not mean that they can be ignored. It can be argued that the crucial problem of contemporary America

* From Harry Clor. "Public Morality and Free Expression: The Judicial Search for Principles of Reconciliation." *Hastings Law Journal*, Vol. 28 (July 1977), p. 1305 at p. 1311. Used with permission of the *Hastings Law Journal* and Dr. Clor, professor of political science at Kenyon College.

is more a declining sense of community than a decreasing amount of free speech. What I am suggesting, then, is that we recognize this communal interest as a valid interest, just as even the most vigorous opponents of obscenity laws have recognized valid interests in protection of children and protection of personal privacy. The interest in community is no less valid. In fact, I find the interests that Detroit is trying to protect considerably more important than the interest in preventing a fleeting glance at nudity which was the source of the ordinance in *Erznoznik*.

It cannot be denied that some suppression is inevitable in the economic results of the Detroit ordinance. And it is not suggested that there are no interests that would tend to weigh on the other side of community interests. But, as Mr. Justice Stevens points out in *Young*, "there is surely a less vital interest in the uninhibited exhibition of material that is on the borderline between pornography and artistic expression than in the free dissemination of ideas of social and political significance. . . ." This is content discrimination, but content discrimination is inherent in the general settlement of the obscenity problem represented by *Miller* and *Paris Adult Theatre*. It is inherent in the general settlement of the problems of libel and commercial speech as well. All that Mr. Justice Stevens has done is to make explicit what is implicit in the *Miller* interpretation of the First Amendment—that its essential concern is to protect the communication of ideas and works of "serious literary, artistic, political, or scientific value." This interpretation is thoroughly consistent with American constitutional and political tradition and more logical than an interpretation that would protect all words and all pictures at the expense of every other value in society. The concept of absolute equality is a simple but unrealistic and unworkable solution to the complexity of interests represented by modern life.

Essential to a proper balance among the interests involved is that diminished protection is not the same as absolute suppression. Freedom for serious literature and serious discussion requires a rather large zone of security. I do not deny the concept of the "chilling effect." Therefore, it seems inadvisable to completely suppress the worthless vulgarities purveyed by many adult establishments. But protection from suppression and protection of the purveyors from criminal penalties need not entail protection from all secondary regulations which may take account of the character and content of the materials. Such a secondary regulation cannot, of course, be permitted if it is covertly aimed at total suppression or if it would have the effect of actual suppression of protected speech or inhibition of the public's access to protected speech. Moreover, these secondary regulations ought to be permitted only if they promote a substantial public interest, something more than the mere rational basis accepted in other areas of constitutional adjudication. But none of these invalidating factors seem present in *Young*. Adult erotic establishments have been flourishing in our cities, and it is quite predictable that they will continue to flourish in Detroit and other cities which choose to adopt Detroit's strategy. Since there is little likelihood of any actual suppression, Detroit's rather mild and moderate approach promotes the interests in community without sacrific-ing those represented by the First Amendment.

We do not abandon the vital interests in free speech by giving this modest degree of recognition to another interest—the quality of communal life. Liberal democracy needs to recognize a basic proposition of political philosophy that communities, as well as individuals, have some right to maintain a way of life.

CHAPTER **9**

LIBEL

Concern over a good reputation is as old as society itself. On the tablets brought down from Mount Sinai by Moses was inscribed, "Thou shalt not bear false witness against thy neighbor." And Shakespeare in "Othello" wrote, "Who steals my purse steals trash . . . But he that filches from me my good name robs me of that which not enriches him, and makes me poor indeed."

The theory behind the laws of libel, then, is to protect a person's good name and reputation until such time as it comes under legitimate question. Libel most often is a civil action, i.e. a contest in which one party attempts to recover damages for alleged harm done him by the acts of another.

The person defamed, the plaintiff, must establish that the statement was published, was defamatory, was taken by the reader to refer to the plaintiff and that there was fault, i.e. malice or negligence, on the part of the medium. The defendant then is called upon to justify the use of the statement in question. Common law defenses include the truth of the statement, the right of fair comment and criticism on matters before the public, and the right to publish privileged material such as that found in legal and governmental documents and actions. The Warren Court gave increasingly wide latitude to the press in fulfilling its function as "watchdog" of the public's business and, consequently, has made it increasingly difficult for public figures to collect damages in libel suits against the media.

The Warren Court in a 1964 landmark decision held that debate on public issues should be "uninhibited" and "robust" and that with such free and wide open debate error would be inevitable. Thus, the Court sided with the New York Times in its defense against libel charges brought by Commissioner of Public Affairs L. B. Sullivan of Montgomery, Alabama. It held that a public official cannot collect damages for a defamatory falsehood relating to his official capacity unless he is able to prove actual malice, i.e. that the statement was made with knowledge of its falsity or with reckless disregard of its truth or falsity. Also, the fact that the

297

defamation might be contained in a paid advertisement did not exempt it from constitutional protection. The Court noted that public officials themselves enjoy immunity for their statements where no actual malice is shown. The unanimous opinion was read by Justice Brennan. Justices Goldberg, Black, and Douglas would have gone one step further by ruling out any suit by a public official, whether malice is proven or not. The case involved an advertisement, in which certain errors of fact appeared, placed in the New York Times *by civil rights advocates.*

NEW YORK TIMES CO. V. SULLIVAN
376 U.S. 254 (1964)

JUSTICE BRENNAN *delivered the opinion of the Court.*

We are required in this case to determine for the first time the extent to which the constitutional protections for speech and press limit a State's power to award damages in a libel action brought by a public official against critics of his official conduct.

Respondent L. B. Sullivan is one of the three elected Commissioners of the City of Montgomery, Alabama. He testified that he was "Commissioner of Public Affairs and the duties are supervision of the Police Department, Fire Department, Department of Cemetery and Department of Scales." He brought this civil libel action against the four individual petitioners, who are Negroes and Alabama clergymen, and against petitioner the New York Times Company, a New York corporation which publishes the *New York Times*, a daily newspaper. A jury in the Circuit Court of Montgomery County awarded him damages of $500,000, the full amount claimed, against all the petitioners, and the Supreme Court of Alabama affirmed.

Respondent's complaint alleged that he had been libeled by statements in a full-page advertisement that was carried in the *New York Times* on March 29, 1960. Entitled "Heed Their Rising Voices," the advertisement began by stating that "As the whole world knows by now, thousands of Southern Negro students are engaged in widespread non-violent demonstrations in positive affirmation of the right to live in human dignity as guaranteed by the U. S. Constitution and the Bill of Rights." It went on to charge that "in their efforts to uphold these guarantees, they are being met by an unprecedented wave of terror by those who would deny and negate that document which the whole world looks upon as setting the pattern for modern freedom. . . ." Succeeding paragraphs purported to illustrate the "wave of terror" by describing certain alleged events. The text concluded with an appeal for funds for three purposes: support of the student movement, "the struggle for the right-to-vote," and the legal defense of Dr. Martin Luther King, Jr., leader of the movement, against a perjury indictment then pending in Montgomery.

The text appeared over the names of 64 persons, many widely known for their activities in public affairs, religion, trade unions, and the performing arts. Below these names, and under a line reading "We in the south who are struggling daily for dignity and freedom warmly endorse this appeal," appeared the names of the four individual petitioners and of 16 other persons, all but two of whom were identified as clergymen in various Southern cities. The advertisement was signed at the bottom of the page by the "Committee to Defend Martin Luther King and the Struggle for Freedom in the South," and the officers of the Committee were listed.

Of the 10 paragraphs of text in the advertisement, the third and a portion of the sixth were the basis of respondent's claim of libel. They read as follows:

Third paragraph:
"In Montgomery, Alabama, after students sang 'My Country, 'Tis of Thee' on the State Capitol steps, their leaders were expelled from school, and truckloads of police armed with shotguns and tear-gas ringed the Alabama State College Campus. When the entire student body protested to state authorities by refusing to re-register, their dining hall was padlocked in an attempt to starve them into submission."

Sixth paragraph:
"Again and again the Southern violators have answered Dr. King's peaceful protests with intimidation and violence. They have bombed his home almost killing his wife and child. They have assaulted his person. They have arrested him seven times—for 'speeding,' 'loitering' and similar 'offenses.' And now they have charged him with 'perjury'—a *felony* under which they could imprison him for *ten years.* . . ."

Although neither of these statements mentions respondent by name, he contended that the word "police" in the third paragraph referred to him as the Montgomery Commissioner who supervised the Police Department, so that he was being accused of "ringing" the campus with police. He further claimed that the paragraph would be read as imputing to the police, and hence to him, the padlocking of the dining hall in order to starve the students into submission. As to the sixth paragraph, he contended that since arrests are ordinarily made by the police, the statement "They have arrested [Dr. King] seven times" would be read as referring to him; he further contended that the "They" who did the arresting would be equated with the "They" who committed the other described acts and with the "Southern violators." Thus, he argued, the paragraph would be read as accusing the Montgomery police, and hence him, of answering Dr. King's protests with "intimidation and violence," bombing his home, assaulting his person, and charging him with perjury. Respondent and six other Montgomery residents testified that they read some or all of the statements as referring to him in his capacity as Commissioner.

It is uncontroverted that some of the statements contained in the two paragraphs were not accurate descriptions of events which occurred in Montgomery. Although Negro students staged a demonstration on the State Capitol steps, they sang the National Anthem and not "My Country, 'Tis of Thee." Although nine students were expelled by the State Board of Education, this was not for leading the demonstration at the Capitol, but for demanding service at a lunch counter in the Montgomery County Courthouse on another day. Not the entire student body, but most of it, had protested the expulsion, not by refusing to register, but by boycotting classes on a single day; virtually all the students did register for the ensuing semester. The campus dining hall was not padlocked on any occasion, and the only students who may have been barred from eating there were the few who had neither signed a preregistration application nor requested temporary meal tickets. Although the police were deployed near the campus in large numbers on three occasions, they did not at any time "ring" the campus, and they were not called to the campus in connection with the demonstration on the State Capitol steps, as the third paragraph implied. Dr. King had not been arrested seven times, but only four; and although he claimed to have been assaulted some years earlier in connection with his arrest for loitering outside a courtroom, one of the officers who made the arrest denied that there was such an assault.

On the premise that the charges in the sixth paragraph could be read as referring to him, respondent was allowed to prove that he had not participated in the events described. Although Dr. King's home had in fact been bombed twice when his wife and child were there, both of these occasions antedated respondent's tenure as Commissioner, and the police were not only not implicated in the bombings, but had made every effort to apprehend those who were. Three of Dr. King's four arrests took place before respondent became Commissioner. Although Dr. King had in fact been indicted (he was subsequently acquitted) on two counts of perjury, each of which carried a possible five-year sentence, respondent had nothing to do with procuring the indictment.

Respondent made no effort to prove that he suffered actual pecuniary loss as a result of the alleged libel. One of his witnesses, a former employer, testified that if he had believed the statements, he doubted whether he "would want to be associated with anybody who would be a party to such things that are stated in that ad," and that he would not re-employ respondent if he believed "that he allowed the Police Department to do the things that the paper say he did." But neither this witness nor any of the others testified that he had actually believed the statements in their supposed reference to respondent.

The cost of the advertisement was approximately $4800, and it was published by the *Times* upon an order from a New York advertising agency acting for the signatory Committee. The agency submitted the advertisement with a letter from A. Philip Randolph, Chairman of the Committee, certifying that the persons whose names appeared on the advertisement had given their permission. Mr. Randolph was known to the *Times'* Advertising Acceptability Department as a responsible person, and in accepting the letter as sufficient proof of authorization it followed its established practice. . . .

The . . . contention is that the constitutional guarantees of freedom of speech and of the press are inapplicable here, at least so far as the *Times* is concerned, because the allegedly libelous statements were published as part of a paid, "commercial" advertisement. . . .

The publication here was not a "commercial" advertisement [because it] . . . communicated information, expressed opinion, recited grievances, protested claimed abuses, and sought financial support on behalf of a movement whose existence and objectives are matters of the highest public interest and concern. That the *Times* was paid for publishing the advertisement is as immaterial in this connection as is the fact that newspapers and books are sold. Any other conclusion would discourage newspapers from carrying "editorial advertisements" of this type, and so might shut off an important outlet for the promulgation of information and ideas by persons who do not themselves have access to publishing facilities—who wish to exercise their freedom of speech even though they are not members of the press. The effect would be to shackle the First Amendment in its attempt to secure "the widest possible dissemination of information from diverse and antagonistic sources." *Associated Press v. United States.* To avoid placing such a handicap upon the freedoms of expression, we hold that if the allegedly libelous statements would otherwise be constitutionally protected from the present judgment, they do not forfeit that protection because they were published in the form of a paid advertisement. . . .

The general proposition that freedom of expression upon public questions is secured by the First Amendment has long been settled by our decisions. The constitutional safeguard, we have said, "was fashioned to assure unfettered interchange of ideas for the bringing about of political and social changes desired by the people." *Roth v. United States.* . . .

Thus we consider this case against the background of a profound national commitment to the principle that debate on public issues should be uninhibited, robust, and wide-open, and that it may well include vehement, caustic, and sometimes unpleasantly sharp attacks on government and public officials. The present advertisement, as an expression of grievance and protest on one of the major public issues of our time, would seem clearly to qualify for the constitutional protection. The question is whether it forfeits that protection by the falsity of some of its factual statements and by its alleged defamation of respondent . . .

. . . Erroneous statement is inevitable in free debate, and . . . it must be protected if the freedoms of expression are to have the "breathing space" that they "need . . . to survive," *N.A.A.C.P. v. Button.* . . .

A rule compelling the critic of official conduct to guarantee the truth of all his factual assertions—and to do so on pain of libel judgments virtually unlimited in amount—leads to a comparable "self-censorship." Allowance of the defense of truth, with the burden of proving it on the defendant, does not mean that only false speech will be deterred. Even courts accepting this defense as an adequate safeguard have recognized the difficulties of adducing legal proofs that the alleged libel was true in all its factual particulars. . . . Under such a rule, would-be critics of official conduct may be deterred from voicing their criticism, even though it is believed to be true and even though it is in fact true, because of doubt whether it can be proved in court or fear of the expense of having to do so. They tend to make only statements which "steer far wider of the unlawful zone." *Speiser v. Randall.* The rule thus dampens the vigor and limits the variety of public debate. It is inconsistent with the First and Fourteenth Amendments.

The constitutional guarantees require, we think, a federal rule that prohibits a public official from recovering damages for a defamatory falsehood relating to his official conduct unless he proves that the statement was made with "actual malice"—that is, with knowledge that it was false or with reckless disregard of whether it was false or not. . . .

We hold today that the Constitution delimits a State's power to award damages for libel in actions brought by public officials against critics of their official conduct. Since this is such an action, the rule requiring proof of actual malice is applicable. While Alabama law apparently requires proof of actual malice for an award of punitive damages, where general damages are concerned malice is "presumed." Such a presumption is inconsistent with the federal rule. . . .

. . . The *Times'* failure to retract upon respondent's demand, although it later retracted upon the demand of Governor Patterson, is likewise not adequate evidence of malice for constitutional purposes. Whether or not a failure to retract may ever constitute such evidence, there are two reasons why it does not here. *First,* the letter written by the *Times* reflected a reasonable doubt on its part as to whether the advertisement could reasonably be taken to refer to respondent at all. *Second,* it was not a final refusal, since it asked for an explanation on this point—a request that respondent chose to ignore. . . .

Finally, there is evidence that the *Times* published the advertisement without checking its accuracy against the news stories in the *Times'* own files. The mere presence of the stories in the files does not, of course, establish that the *Times* "knew" the advertisement was false, since the state of mind required for actual malice would have to be brought home to the persons in the *Times'* organization having responsibility for the publication of the advertisement. With respect to the failure of those persons to make the check, the record shows that they relied upon their knowledge of the good reputation of many of those whose names were listed as sponsors of the advertisement, and upon the letter from A. Philip Randolph, known to them as a responsible individual, certifying that the use of the names was authorized. There was testimony that the persons handling the advertisement saw nothing in it that would render it unacceptable under the *Times'* policy of rejecting advertisements containing "attacks of a personal character"; their failure to reject it on this ground was not unreasonable. We think the evidence against the *Times* supports at most a finding of negligence in failing to discover the misstatements, and is constitutionally insufficient to show the recklessness that is required for a finding of actual malice.

We also think the evidence was constitutionally defective in another respect: it was incapable of supporting the jury's finding that the allegedly libelous statements were made "of and concerning" respondent. Respondent relies on the words of the advertisement and the testimony of six witnesses to establish a connection between it and himself. . . .

The judgment of the Supreme Court of Alabama is reversed and the case is remanded to that court for further proceedings not inconsistent with this opinion. . . .

JUSTICE GOLDBERG, *with whom Justice Douglas joins, concurring in the result.*

The Court today announces a constitutional standard which prohibits "a public official from recovering damages for a defamatory falsehood relating to his official conduct unless he proves that the statement was made with 'actual malice'—that is, with knowledge that it was false or with reckless disregard of whether it was false or not." The Court thus rules that the Constitution gives citizens and newspapers a "conditional privilege" immunizing nonmalicious misstatements of fact regarding the official conduct of a government officer. The impressive array of history and precedent marshaled by the Court, however, confirms my belief that the Constitution affords greater protection than that provided by the Court's standard to citizen and press in exercising the right of public criticism.

In my view, the First and Fourteenth Amendments to the Constitution afford to the citizen and to the press an absolute, unconditional privilege to criticize official conduct despite the harm which may flow from excesses and abuses. . . . The theory of our Constitution is that every citizen may speak his mind and every newspaper express its view on matters of public concern and may not be barred from speaking or publishing because those in control of government think that what is said or written is unwise, unfair, false or malicious. In a democratic society, one who assumes to act for the citizens in an executive, legislative, or judicial capacity must expect that his official acts will be commented upon and criticized. Such criticism cannot, in my opinion, be muzzled or deterred by the courts at the instance of public officials under the label of libel. . . .

This is not to say that the Constitution protects defamatory statements directed against the private conduct of a public official or private citizen. Freedom of press and of speech insures that government will respond to the will of the people and that changes may be obtained by peaceful means. Purely private defamation has little to do with the political ends of a self-governing society. . . .

*   *   *

Eight months after the 1964 New York Times *decision, Justice Brennan again spoke for the Court in a libel case,* Garrison v. Louisiana. *The significance of the* Garrison *decision is in its application of* New York Times *civil libel principles to cases of criminal libel, i.e. that actual malice must be proven in order to sustain criminal sanctions for a defamatory falsehood against a public official. As in the* New York Times *case, Justices Douglas, Black, and Goldberg, concurring with the results, argued that the Constitution prohibits prosecution for seditious libel, knowingly making falsehoods and reckless disregard for truth notwithstanding. The case revolved around a New Orleans district attorney who severely criticized the bench, charging laziness and inefficiency. The Supreme Court reversed his conviction without dissent.*

GARRISON V. LOUISIANA
379 U.S. 64 (1964)

JUSTICE BRENNAN *delivered the opinion of the Court.*

Appellant is the District Attorney of Orleans Parish, Louisiana. During a dispute with the eight judges of the Criminal District Court of the Parish, he held a press conference at which he issued a statement disparaging their judicial conduct. As a result he was tried without jury before a judge from another parish and convicted of criminal defamation under the Louisiana Criminal Defamation Statute. The principal charges alleged to be defamatory were his attribution of a large backlog of pending criminal cases to the inefficiency, laziness, and excessive vacation of the judges, and his accusation that, by refusing to authorize disbursements to cover the expenses of undercover investigations of vice in New Orleans, the judges had hampered his efforts to enforce the vice laws. In impugning their motives he said:

> The judges have now made it eloquently clear where their sympathies lie in regard to aggressive vice investigations by refusing to authorize use of the DA's funds to pay for the costs of closing down the Canal Street clip joints. . . .
> . . . This raises interesting questions about the racketeer influences on our eight vacation-minded judges.

The Supreme Court of Louisiana affirmed the conviction. The trial court and the State Supreme Court both rejected appellant's contention that the Statute unconstitutionally abridged his freedom of expression. . . .

In *New York Times Co. v. Sullivan* we held that the Constitution limits state power, in a civil action brought by a public official for criticism of his official conduct, to an award of damages for a false statement "made with 'actual malice'— that is, with knowledge that it was false or with reckless disregard of whether it was false or not." At the outset, we must decide whether, in view of the differing history and purposes of criminal libel, the *New York Times* rule also limits state power to impose criminal sanctions for criticism of the official conduct of public officials. We hold that it does.

Where criticism of public officials is concerned, we see no merit in the argument that criminal libel statutes serve interests distinct from those secured by civil libel laws, and therefore should not be subject to the same limitations. . . .

We . . . consider whether the historical limitation of the defense of truth in criminal libel to utterances published "with good motives and for justifiable ends" should be incorporated into the *New York Times* rule as it applies to criminal libel statutes; in particular, we must ask whether this history permits negating the truth defense, as the Louisiana statute does, on a showing of malice in the sense of ill-will. . . . [W]here the criticism is of public officials and their conduct of public business, the interest in private reputation is overborne by the larger public interest, secured by the Constitution, in the dissemination of truth. In short, we agree with the New Hampshire court in *State v. Burnham:*

> If upon a lawful occasion for making a publication, he has published the truth, and no more, there is no sound principle which can make him liable, even if he was actuated by express malice. . . .
>
> It has been said that it is lawful to publish truth from good motives, and for justifiable ends. But this rule is too narrow. If there is a lawful occasion—a legal right to make a publication—and the matter true, the end is justifiable, and that, in such case, must be sufficient.

Moreover, even where the utterance is false, the great principles of the Constitution which secure freedom of expression in this area preclude attaching adverse consequences to any except the knowing or reckless falsehood. Debate on public issues will not be uninhibited if the speaker must run the risk that it will be proved in court that he spoke out of hatred; even if he did speak out of hatred, utterances honestly believed contribute to the free interchange of ideas and the ascertainment of truth. . . .

We held in *New York Times* that a public official might be allowed the civil remedy only if he establishes that the utterance was false and that it was made with knowledge of its falsity or in reckless disregard of whether it was false or true. The reasons which led us so to hold in *New York Times* apply with no less force merely because the remedy is criminal. . . .

JUSTICE BLACK, *with whom Justice Douglas joins, concurring.*

For reasons stated at greater length in my opinions concurring in *New York Times Co. v. Sullivan*, and dissenting in *Beauharnais v. Illinois*, as well as in the opinion of Mr. Justice Douglas in this case, I concur in reversing the conviction of appellant Garrison, based as it is purely on his public discussion and criticism of public officials. I believe that the First Amendment, made applicable to the States by the Fourteenth, protects every person from having a State or the Federal Government fine, imprison, or assess damages against him when he has been guilty of no conduct other than expressing an opinion, even though others may believe that his views are unwholesome, unpatriotic, stupid or dangerous. . . . Fining men or sending them to jail for criticizing public officials not only jeopardizes the free, open public discussion which our Constitution guarantees, but can wholly stifle it. I would hold now and not wait to hold later, . . . that under our Constitution there is absolutely no place in this country for the old, discredited English Star Chamber law of seditious criminal libel. . . .

*   *   *

A second post-New York Times decision, Rosenblatt v. Baer, was handed down early in 1966. As with New York Times and Garrison, Justice Brennan wrote the opinion of the Court in the 8–1 decision. The lone dissent came from Justice Fortas, who noted that the Rosenblatt-Baer trial in 1960 was prior to the Court's 1964 New York Times decision. The majority, however, elaborated on the New York Times decision in overturning a libel judgment against Alfred D. Rosenblatt, a Laconia (N.H.) columnist. He was charged with libeling a former supervisor of a county recreation area. The major significance was an extension and further refinement of the New York Times' "public official" concept. The Court held that at least those who have substantial responsibility for the conduct of government affairs should be included. Disagreement erupted over the majority's view that the trial judge should make the first determination of whether one is a "public official" in the New York Times sense. In addition, Justice Douglas urged a wider interpretation of the "public official" concept.

A major extension of libel protection for the press was handed down by the Court in June 1967 as it applied the 1964 New York Times rule to "public figures" as well as "public officials." The Court, considering together two widely publicized libel cases, upheld 5–4 Wallace Butts' judgment against Curtis Publishing Co., but reversed unanimously Edwin Walker's judgment against the Associated Press. In reaching these decisions, the Court laid down the test of "accepted publishing standards." Unintentional error spawned by the need for immediacy in covering fast-breaking news stories, the Court ruled, cannot be the basis for libel judgments awarded to "public figures." The Walker suit was based upon the 1962 AP account of his role in the rioting which surrounded the entry of James Meredith, a black, into the University of Mississippi. The 1963 Saturday Evening Post story involving Wallace Butts, former director of athletics at the University of Georgia, was entitled "The Story of a Football Fix." The Court held that the urgency of the AP news account was missing from the Post "exposé" and that the Post ignored "elementary precautions" of good publication practice. Walker had sued AP and more than a dozen other publications for a total of $33 million. His suit against AP was for $2 million, which lower courts had reduced to $500,000. Butts had sued Curtis for $10 million, but eventually was awarded $460,000. The majority opinion, covering both cases, was written by Justice Harlan. Dissenters in the 5–4 Curtis case were Justices Black, Douglas, Brennan, and White. Justice Black, joined by Justice Douglas, warned the Court that it was "getting itself into the same quagmire" with libel as it had with obscenity. He reaffirmed his "absolutist" interpretation of the First Amendment and urged the Court to free the press altogether from the "harassment" of libel actions.

CURTIS PUBLISHING CO. V. BUTTS

ASSOCIATED PRESS V. WALKER
388 U.S. 130 (1967)

JUSTICE HARLAN *announced the judgment of the Court and delivered an opinion in which Justice Clark, Justice Stewart, and Justice Fortas join.*

In *New York Times Co. v. Sullivan,* this Court held that "[t]he constitutional guarantees [of freedom of speech and press] require . . . a federal rule that prohibits a public official from recovering damages for a defamatory falsehood relating to his official conduct unless he proves that the statement was made with 'actual malice'—that is, with knowledge that it was false or with reckless disregard of whether it was false or not." We brought these two cases here to consider the impact of that decision on libel actions instituted by persons who are not public officials, but who are "public figures" and involved in issues in which the public has a justified and important interest. . . .

I

Curtis Publishing Co. v. Butts stems from an article published in petitioner's *Saturday Evening Post* which accused respondent of conspiring to "fix" a football game between the University of Georgia and the University of Alabama, played in 1962. At the time of the article, Butts was the athletic director of the University of Georgia and had overall responsibility for the administration of its athletic program. Georgia is a state university, but Butts was employed by the Georgia Athletic Association, a private corporation, rather than by the State itself. Butts had previously served as head football coach of the University and was a well-known and respected figure in coaching ranks. He had maintained an interest in coaching and was negotiating for a position with a professional team at the time of publication.

The article was entitled "The Story of a College Football Fix" and prefaced by a note from the editors stating: "Not since the Chicago White Sox threw the 1919 World Series has there been a sports story as shocking as this one. . . . Before the University of Georgia played the University of Alabama . . . Wally Butts . . . gave [to its coach] . . . Georgia's plays, defensive patterns, all the significant secrets Georgia's football team possessed." The text revealed that one George Burnett, an Atlanta insurance salesman, had accidentally overheard, because of electronic error, a telephone conversation between Butts and the head coach of the University of Alabama, Paul Bryant, which took place approximately one week prior to the game. Burnett was said to have listened while "Butts outlined Georgia's offensive plays . . . and told . . . how Georgia planned to defend. . . . Butts mentioned both players and plays by name. "The readers were told that Burnett had made notes of the conversation, and specific examples of the divulged secrets were set out.

The article went on to discuss the game and the players' action to the game, concluding that "[t]he Georgia players, their moves analyzed, and forecast like those of rats in a maze, took a frightful physical beating," and said that the players, and other sideline observers, were aware that Alabama was privy to Georgia's secrets. It set out the series of events commencing with Burnett's later presentation of his notes to the Georgia head coach, Johnny Griffith, and culminating in Butts' resignation from the University's athletic affairs, for health and business reasons. The article's conclusion made clear its expected impact:

> The chances are that Wally Butts will never help any football team again. . . . The investigation by university and Southeastern Conference officials is continuing; motion pictures of other games are being scrutinized; where it will end no one so far can say. But careers will be ruined, that is sure.

Butts brought this diversity libel action in the federal courts in Georgia seeking $5,000,000 compensatory and $5,000,000 punitive damages. The complaint was filed, and the trial completed, before this Court handed down its decision in *New York Times*, and the only defense raised by petitioner Curtis was one of substantial truth. No constitutional defenses were interposed although Curtis' counsel were aware of the progress of the *New York Times* case, and although general constitutional defenses had been raised by Curtis in a libel action instituted by the Alabama coach who was a state employee.

Evidence at trial was directed both to the truth of the article and to its preparation. . . . The evidence showed that Burnett had indeed overheard a conversation between Butts and the Alabama coach, but the content of that conversation was hotly disputed. It was Butts' contention that the conversation had been general football talk and that nothing Burnett had overheard would have been of any particular value to an opposing coach. Expert witnesses supported Butts by analyzing Burnett's notes and the films of the game itself. The *Saturday Evening Post*'s version of the game and of the players' remarks about the game was severely contradicted.

The evidence on the preparation of the article . . . cast serious doubt on the adequacy of the investigation underlying the article. It was Butts' contention that the magazine had departed greatly from the standards of good investigation and reporting and that this was especially reprehensible, amounting to reckless and wanton conduct, in light of the devastating nature of the article's assertions. . . .

The jury returned a verdict for $60,000 in general damages and for $3,000,000 punitive damages. The trial court reduced the total to $460,000 by remittitur. Soon thereafter we handed down our decision in *New York Times* and Curtis immediately brought it to the attention of the trial court by a motion for new trial. The trial judge rejected Curtis' motion on two grounds. He first held that *New York Times* was inapplicable because Butts was not a public official. He also held that "there was ample evidence from which a jury could have concluded that there was reckless disregard by defendant of whether the article was false or not."

Curtis appealed to the Court of Appeals for the Fifth Circuit which affirmed the judgment of the District Court by a two-to-one vote. . . .

II

Associated Press v. Walker arose out of the distribution of a news dispatch giving an eyewitness account of events on the campus of the University of Mississippi on the night of September 30, 1962, when a massive riot erupted because of federal efforts to enforce a court decree ordering the enrollment of a Negro, James Meredith, as a student in the University. The dispatch stated that respondent Walker, who was present on the campus, had taken command of the violent crowd and had personally led a charge against federal marshals sent there to effectuate the court's decree and to assist in preserving order. It also described Walker as encouraging rioters to use violence and giving them technical advice combating the effects of tear gas.

Walker was a private citizen at the time of the riot and publication. He had pursued a long and honorable career in the United States Army before resigning to engage in political activity, and had, in fact, been in command of the federal troops during the school segregation confrontation at Little Rock, Arkansas, in 1957. He was acutely interested in the issue of physical federal intervention, and had made a number of strong statements against such action which had received wide publicity. Walker had his own following, the "Friends of Walker," and could fairly be deemed a man of some political prominence.

Walker initiated this libel action in the state courts of Texas, seeking a total of $2,000,000 in compensatory and punitive damages. Associated Press raised both the defense of truth and constitutional defenses. At trial both sides attempted to reconstruct the stormy events on the campus of the University of Mississippi. Walker admitted his presence on the campus and conceded that he had spoken to a group of rioters. He claimed, however, that he had counseled restraint and peaceful protest, and exercised no control whatever over the crowd which had rejected his plea. He denied categorically taking part in any charge against the federal marshals.

There was little evidence relating to the preparation of the news dispatch. It was clear, however, that the author of this dispatch, Van Savell, was actually present during the events described and had reported them almost immediately to the Associated Press office in Atlanta. A discrepancy was shown between an oral account given the office and a later written dispatch, but it related solely to whether Walker had spoken to the group before or after approaching the marshals. No other showing of improper preparation was attempted, nor was there any evidence of personal prejudice or incompetency on the part of Savell or the Associated Press. . . .

A verdict of $500,000 compensatory damages and $300,000 punitive damages was returned. The trial judge, however, found that there was "no evidence to support the jury's answers that there was actual malice" and refused to enter the punitive award. . . . The trial judge also noted that this lack of "malice" would require a verdict for the Associated Press if *New York Times* were applicable. But he rejected its applicability since there were "no compelling reasons of public policy requiring additional defenses to suits for libel. Truth alone should be an adequate defense."

Both sides appealed and the Texas Court of Civil Appeals affirmed both the award of compensatory damages and the striking of punitive damages. . . .

III

We thus turn to a consideration, on the merits, of the constitutional claims raised by Curtis in *Butts* and by the Associated Press in *Walker*. Powerful arguments are brought to bear for the extension of the *New York Times* rule in both cases. In *Butts* it is contended that the facts are on all fours with those of *Rosenblatt v. Baer*, since Butts was charged with the important responsibility of managing the athletic affairs of a state university. It is argued that while the Athletic Association is financially independent from the State and Butts was not technically a state employee, as was Baer, his role in state administration was so significant that this technical distinction from *Rosenblatt* should be ignored. Even if this factor is to be given some weight, we are told that the public interest in education in general, and in the conduct of the athletic affairs of educational institutions in particular, justifies constitutional protection of discussion of persons involved in it equivalent to the protection afforded discussion of public officials.

A similar argument is raised in the *Walker* case where the important public interest in being informed about the events and personalities involved in the Mississippi riot is pressed. In that case we are also urged to recognize that Walker's claims to the protection of libel laws are limited since he thrust himself into the "vortex" of the controversy. . . .

The law of libel has, of course, changed substantially since the early days of the Republic. . . . The emphasis has shifted from criminal to civil remedies, from the protection of absolute social values to the safe-guarding of valid personal interests. Truth has become an absolute defense in almost all cases, and privileges designed to foster free communication are almost universally recognized. . . .

In the cases we decide today none of the particular considerations involved in *New York Times* is present. These actions cannot be analogized to persecutions for seditious libel. Neither plaintiff has any position in government which would permit a recovery by him to be viewed as a vindication of governmental policy. Neither was entitled to a special privilege protecting his utterances against accountability in libel. We are prompted therefore, to seek guidance from the rules of liability which prevail in our society with respect to compensation of persons injured by the improper performance of a legitimate activity by another. . . . In defining these rules, and especially in formulating the standards for determining the degree of care to be expected in the circumstances, courts have consistently given much attention to the importance of defendants' activities. The courts have also, especially in libel cases, investigated the plaintiff's position to determine whether he has a legitimate call upon the court for protection in light of his prior activities and means of self-defense. We note that the public interest in the circulation of the materials here involved, and the publisher's interest in circulating them, is not less than that involved in *New York Times*. And both Butts and Walker commanded a substantial amount of independent public interest at the time of the publication; both, in our opinion, would have been labeled "public figures" under ordinary tort rules. See *Spahn v. Julian Messner, Inc.* . . .

These similarities and differences between libel actions involving persons who are public officials and libel actions involving those circumstanced as were Butts and Walker, viewed in light of the principles of liability which are of general applicability in our society, lead us to the conclusion that libel actions of the present kind cannot be left entirely to state libel laws, unlimited by any overriding constitutional safeguard, but that the rigorous federal requirements of *New York Times* are not the only appropriate accommodation of the conflicting interests at stake. We consider and would hold that a "public figure" who is not a public official may also recover damages for a defamatory falsehood whose substance makes substantial danger to reputation apparent, on a showing of highly unreasonable conduct constituting an extreme departure from the standards of investigation and reporting ordinarily adhered to by responsible publishers.

Nothing in this opinion is meant to affect the holdings in *New York Times* and its progeny, including our recent decision in *Time, Inc. v. Hill.*

IV

Having set forth the standard by which we believe the constitutionality of the damage awards in these cases must be judged, we turn now, as the Court did in *New York Times*, to the question whether the evidence and findings below meet that standard. We find the standard satisfied in *Butts*, and not satisfied by either the evidence or the findings in *Walker* . . .

The evidence showed that the Butts story was in no sense "hot news" and the editors of the magazine recognized the need for a thorough investigation of the serious charges. Elementary precautions were, nevertheless, ignored. The *Saturday Evening Post* knew that Burnett had been placed on probation in connection with bad check charges, but proceeded to publish the story on the basis of his affidavit without substantial independent support. Burnett's notes were not even viewed by any of the magazine's personnel prior to publication. John Carmichael who was supposed to have been with Burnett when the phone call was overheard was not interviewed. No attempt was made to screen the films of the game to see if Burnett's information was accurate, and no attempt was made to find out whether Alabama had adjusted its plans after the alleged divulgence of information.

The *Post* writer assigned to the story was not a football expert and no attempt was made to check the story with someone knowledgeable in the sport. At trial such experts indicated that the information in the Burnett notes was either such that it would be evident to any opposing coach from the game films regularly exchanged or valueless. Those assisting the *Post* writer in his investigation were already deeply involved in another libel action, based on a different article, brought against Curtis

Publishing Co. by the Alabama coach and unlikely to be the source of a complete and objective investigation. The *Saturday Evening Post* was anxious to change its image by instituting a policy of "sophisticated muckraking," and the pressure to produce a successful exposé might have induced a stretching of standards. In short, the evidence is ample to support a finding of highly unreasonable conduct constituting an extreme departure from the standards of investigation and reporting ordinarily adhered to by responsible publishers.

The situation in *Walker* is considerably different. There the trial court found the evidence insufficient to support more than a finding of even ordinary negligence and the Court of Civil Appeals supported the trial court's view of the evidence.

In contrast to the *Butts* article, the dispatch which concerns us in *Walker* was news which required immediate dissemination. The Associated Press received the information from a correspondent who was present at the scene of the events and gave every indication of being trustworthy and competent. His dispatches in this instance, with one minor exception, were internally consistent and would not have seemed unreasonable to one familiar with General Walker's prior publicized statements on the underlying controversy. Considering the necessity for rapid dissemination, nothing in this series of events gives the slightest hint of a severe departure from accepted publishing standards. We therefore conclude that General Walker should not be entitled to damages from the Associated Press.

V

We come finally to Curtis' contention that whether or not it can be required to compensate Butts for any injury it may have caused him, it cannot be subjected to an assessment for punitive damages limited only by the "enlightened conscience" of the community. Curtis . . . contends that an unlimited punitive award against a magazine publisher constitutes an effective prior restraint by giving the jury the power to destroy the publisher's business. We cannot accept this reasoning. Publishers like Curtis engage in a wide variety of activities which may lead to tort suits where punitive damages are a possibility. To exempt a publisher, because of the nature of his calling, from an imposition generally exacted from other members of the community, would be to extend a protection not required by the constitutional guarantee. We think the constitutional guarantee of freedom of speech and press is adequately served by judicial control over excessive jury verdicts, manifested in this instance by the trial court's remittitur, and by the general rule that a verdict based on jury prejudice cannot be sustained even when punitive damages are warranted. . . .

Where a publisher's departure from standards of press responsibility is severe enough to strip from him the constitutional protection our decision acknowledges, we think it entirely proper for the State to act not only for the protection of the individual injured but to safeguard all those similarly situated against like abuse. Moreover, punitive damages require a finding of "ill will" under general libel law and it is not unjust that a publisher be forced to pay for the "venting of his spleen" in a manner which does not meet even the minimum standards required for constitutional protection. . . . We would hold, therefore, that misconduct sufficient to justify the award of compensatory damages also justifies the imposition of a punitive award, subject of course to the limitation that such award is not demonstrated to be founded on the mere prejudice of the jury. . . .

CHIEF JUSTICE WARREN, *concurring in the result.*

While I agree with the results announced by Mr. Justice Harlan in both of these cases, I find myself in disagreement with his stated reasons for reaching those results. Our difference stems from his departure from the teaching of *New York Times v. Sullivan*, to which we both subscribed only three years ago. . . .

To me, differentiation between "public figures" and "public officials" and adoption of separate standards of proof for each has no basis in law, logic, or First Amendment policy. Increasingly in this country, the distinctions between governmental and private sectors are blurred. Since the depression of the 1930s and World War II there has been a rapid fusion of economic and political power, a merging of science, industry, and government, and a high degree of interaction between the intellectual, governmental, and business worlds. Depression, war, international tensions, national and international markets, and the surging growth of science and technology have precipitated national and international problems that demand national and international solutions. While these trends and events have occasioned a consolidation of governmental power, power has also become much more organized in what we have commonly considered to be the private sector. . . .

Viewed in this context then, it is plain that although they are not subject to the restraints of the political process, "public figures," like "public officials," often play an influential role in ordering society. And surely as a class these "public figures" have as ready access as "public officials" to mass media of communication, both to influence policy and to counter criticism of their views and activities. Our citizenry has a legitimate and substantial interest in the conduct of such persons, and freedom of the press to engage in uninhibited debate about their involvement in public issues and events is as crucial as it is in the case of "public officials." . . .

I therefore adhere to the *New York Times* standard in the case of "public figures" as well as "public officials." It is a manageable standard, readily stated and understood, which also balances to a proper degree the legitimate interests traditionally protected by the law of defamation. Its definition of "actual malice" is not so restrictive that recovery is limited to situations where there is "knowing falsehood" on the part of the publisher of false and defamatory matter. "Reckless disregard" for the truth or falsity, measured by the conduct of the publisher, will also expose him to liability for publishing false material which is injurious to reputation. More significantly, however, the *New York Times* standard is an important safeguard for the rights of the press and public to inform and be informed on matters of legitimate interest. Evenly applied to cases involving "public men"—

whether they be "public officials" or "public figures"—it will afford the necessary insulation for the fundamental interests which the First Amendment was designed to protect. . . .

JUSTICE BLACK, *with whom Justice Douglas concurs, dissenting.*

I would reverse this case [*Curtis*] first for the reasons given in my concurring opinion in *New York Times v. Sullivan* and my concurring and dissenting opinion in *Rosenblatt v. Baer,* but wish to add a few words.

This case illustrates, I think, the accuracy of my prior predictions that the *New York Times* constitutional rule concerning libel is wholly inadequate to save the press from being destroyed by libel judgments. Here the Court reverses the case of *Associated Press v. Walker,* but affirms the judgment of *Curtis Publishing Co. v. Butts.* The main reason for this quite contradictory action, so far as I can determine, is that the Court looks at the facts in both cases as though it were a jury and reaches the conclusion that the *Saturday Evening Post,* in writing about Butts, was so abusive that its article is more of a libel at the constitutional level than is the one by the Associated Press. That seems a strange way to erect a constitutional standard for libel cases. If this precedent is followed, it means that we must in all libel cases hereafter weigh the facts and hold that all papers and magazines guilty of gross writing or reporting are constitutionally liable, while they are not if the quality of the reporting is approved by a majority of us. In the final analysis, what we do in these circumstances is to review the factual questions in cases decided by juries—a review which is a flat violation of the Seventh Amendment.

It strikes me that the Court is getting itself in the same quagmire in the field of libel in which it is now helplessly struggling in the field of obscenity. No one, including this Court, can know what is and what is not constitutionally obscene or libelous under this Court's rulings. . . .

I think it is time for this Court to abandon *New York Times v. Sullivan* and adopt the rule to the effect that the First Amendment was intended to leave the press free from the harassment of libel judgments.

*   *   *

*In the last of the Warren Court's series of post-*New York Times *decisions, handed down in 1968, the Court continued to tighten the conditions under which a public official could collect damages for libel.* St. Amant v. Thompson. *The Court said if the attacker has good reason to believe the damaging statements to be true, mere failure to thoroughly investigate their veracity does not in itself constitute "reckless disregard" as defined in* Times. *"Reckless disregard," wrote Justice White for the 8–1 majority, "is not measured by whether a reasonably prudent man would have published, or would have investigated before publishing. There must be sufficient evidence to permit the conclusion that the defendant in fact entertained serious doubts as to the truth of his publication." Judge Fortas, the lone dissenter, decried the interpretation by noting that the First Amendment should not be a "shelter for the character assassinator" nor should it authorize "virtually unlimited* *open-season" on public servants. The* St. Amant *decision, however, emphasized the importance the Court places in public discussions of the public's business.*

The Supreme Court continued its commitment to "uninhibited, robust, and wide-open" debate on public issues following the retirement of Chief Justice Warren. In May of 1970 the Court unanimously reversed a $17,500 libel judgment won by Charles S. Bresler against the Greenbelt (Md.) News Review. Greenbelt Publishing Assn. v. Bresler. *The controversy centered around the use of the word "blackmail" in the news columns of the weekly newspaper. The term had been used in heated public debates before the city council. These debates had been covered by the* News Review. *Justice Stewart, writing the opinion of the Court, noted that the news stories were accurate accounts of the public debates and referred to* New York Times *and* Curtis *as precedents. He noted, however, that if the stories had been "truncated" or "distorted," different results might have been forthcoming.*

The Court in 1971 continued to restrict libel judgments involving public persons in three decisions handed down in 1971. The Court emphasized that libel actions dealing with public figures must be accompanied by evidence of actual malice, i.e. knowingly printing a falsehood or exhibiting reckless disregard for truth or falsity.

In the first of the three cases, Monitor Patriot Co. v. Roy, *a jury had awarded libel judgments of $10,000 against the* Concord (N.H.) Monitor *and the North American Newspaper Alliance syndicate because of a Drew Pearson column published in 1960. The column described Alphonse Roy, a former New Hampshire congressman who was running for the United States Senate, as a "former small-time bootlegger." Roy lost in the Democratic primary. It was argued that since the alleged criminal conduct had occurred in the 1920s and had involved the candidate's private life rather than his performance as a public servant, the newspaper and the syndicate were vulnerable to a possible libel judgment. The Supreme Court in a unanimous decision disagreed. Justices Black and Douglas concurred in the judgment, but dissented in part, arguing against sending the case back for a possible retrial.*

Justice Stewart also wrote the second libel opinion in Ocala Star-Banner Co. v. Damron. *The newspaper in 1966 had charged that the mayor of Ocala, Florida, Leonard Damron, who was a candidate for county tax assessor, had been charged in Federal Court with perjury in a civil rights case. It was, in fact, Damron's brother who had been accused of perjury. An editor who was unfamiliar with the background of the story had changed the first name in the story to that of the mayor. Damron lost the election, which was held two weeks after the story appeared.*

The trial judge had instructed the jury that the New York Times *rule did not apply since the error did not involve Damron's official conduct, that the story constituted libel* per se *and that the mayor could be awarded damages. The jury awarded Damron $22,000 in compensatory damages. The Supreme Court, as in* Monitor Patriot Co., *reached a unanimous decision supporting the newspaper, but with Justices Black and Douglas again dissenting in part. In his brief opinion, Justice Stewart noted the wide latitude of the* New York Times *rule and referred to the* Monitor Patriot *decision handed down earlier in the day.*

In the third libel decision that day, Time, Inc. v. Pape, the question was whether the failure of Time magazine to use the word "alleged" constituted actual malice. The magazine in 1961 carried a report of the findings of the U.S. Commission on Civil Rights in which charges of brutality were made against Chicago police. Detective Frank Pape was one of those involved. The allegations in the Commission's report were not proven and Time failed to make clear it was reporting mere allegations.

The opinion, reflecting the 8–1 decision, was again written by Justice Stewart. Much of the opinion reflected dissatisfaction with the Commission's report, but it did warn the media that the judgment in this case was not to be taken as authorizing careless reporting. Time's writer and researcher admitted at the trial that the wording of the report had been changed significantly, but that the changes did not alter the true meaning of the report. Justice Stewart noted that the Time article reflected, at worst, an error in judgment, but went on to say that media which maintain professional standards should not be subject to financial liability for nonmalicious errors in judgment.

In what appeared to be an extension of the landmark 1964 New York Times ruling, the Supreme Court in June of 1971 handed down a 5–3 judgment which held that no person—public or private—involved in an event of public interest could collect libel damages unless he could prove actual malice on the part of the publisher or broadcaster. Rosenbloom v. Metromedia. This decision made it appear almost impossible for any person to successfully sue a newspaper or news broadcaster for libel. Malice, extremely difficult to prove, was defined in New York Times as publishing a defamatory falsehood with knowledge of its falsity or with reckless disregard as to its truth or falsity. This broad media protection previously had applied only to "public officials" or "public figures." The Rosenbloom decision appeared to extend media immunity from libel suits to private citizens who are involved in an event of "general concern" and to firmly establish news broadcasters as falling under First Amendment protection. But there was no majority on the reasons for the decision, and the importance of Rosenbloom has diminished over the years.

George A. Rosenbloom, a Philadelphia magazine distributor, had filed libel action against radio station WIP, which in its accounts of the arrest of Rosenbloom on obscenity charges used the terms "smut distributor" and "girlie-book peddler." Rosenbloom was acquitted of the obscenity charges. In his suit against WIP he claimed he was neither a public official (under New York Times) nor a public figure (under Curtis Publishing Co.), but a private person conducting a private business when he was falsely defamed. The trial court agreed, awarding him $275,000 in damages. The Court of Appeals reversed the decision, and the Supreme Court upheld that reversal. Justice Brennan, in announcing the judgment of the Court, emphasized the hazy distinction today between public and private persons. "We honor," he wrote, "the commitment to robust debate on public issues, which is embodied in the First Amendment, by extending constitutional protection to all discussion and communication involving matters of public or general concern, without regard to whether the persons involved are famous or anonymous." He was joined by Chief Justice Burger and Justice Blackmun. Justices Black and White concurred in the judgment, but not in Justice Brennan's written opinion. Dissenting were Justices Harlan, Marshall and Stewart. Justice Douglas did not participate.

*   *   *

A decade of decisions which had given constitutionally favored status to news media when involved in libel actions reached an uncertain plateau in 1974 with a Supreme Court decision involving a defamation suit against American Opinion, a magazine of the John Birch Society. Gertz v. Robert Welch, Inc. By a 5–4 majority, the Court held that private citizens, even if involved in events of public interest, are entitled to recover damages without having to prove the stringent Times-Sullivan malice test. They need to establish only "negligence" on the part of the publisher or broadcaster. These private persons, however, have to show damages, a significant departure from the historic concept of the presumption of injury in questions of libel per se. Private persons, the Court said, are more vulnerable to injury, have less access to the media for rebuttal, and are more deserving of recovery because they had not voluntarily entered the public spotlight. Justices disagreed on the implications of these majority rulings, Justice Brennan predicting less "breathing space" for a free press and Justice White predicting that ordinary citizens would be "powerless to protect themselves" against irresponsible media. He also objected to what he termed as a "wholesale" elimination of the civil libel laws of the 50 states. This disagreement in interpretation by the Justices apparently results from uncertainty as to how trial judges and juries will define "private person," "negligence," and "damage," which the plaintiff apparently now must establish. The Times "knowledge or reckless disregard" rule will still apply for a plaintiff who seeks punitive damages. The decision, of course, mitigates the 1971 Rosenbloom stance, which had been given wide publicity even though the Justices could not reach agreement on a majority opinion. And despite a five-man majority opinion in Gertz, the decision can hardly be said to be "set in cement," for Justice Blackmun wrote that he voted with the five so as to allow the Court to reach a working majority. Voting with Blackmun were Justices Powell, Marshall, Rehnquist, and Stewart, leaving dissents by the unusual combination of Justices Burger, Brennan, Douglas, and White.

GERTZ V. ROBERT WELCH, INC.
418 U.S. 323 (1974)

JUSTICE POWELL delivered the opinion of the Court.

This Court has struggled for nearly a decade to define the proper accommodation between the law of defamation and the freedoms of speech and press protected by the First Amendment. With this decision we return to that effort. We granted certiorari to reconsider the extent of a publisher's constitutional privilege against liability for defamation of a private citizen.

In 1968 a Chicago policeman named Nuccio shot and killed a youth named Nelson. The state authorities prosecuted Nuccio for the homicide and ultimately obtained a conviction for murder in the second degree. The Nelson family retained petitioner Elmer Gertz, a reputable attorney, to represent them in civil litigation against Nuccio.

Respondent publishes *American Opinion*, a monthly outlet for the views of the John Birch Society. Early in the 1960s the magazine began to warn of a nationwide conspiracy to discredit local law enforcement agencies and create in their stead a national police force capable of supporting a communist dictatorship. As part of the continuing effort to alert the public to this assumed danger, the managing editor of *American Opinion* commissioned an article on the murder trial of officer Nuccio. . . .

. . . The article [in *American Opinion*] stated that petitioner had been an official of the "Marxist League for Industrial Democracy, originally known as the Inter-collegiate Socialist Society, which has advocated the violent seizure of our government." It labelled Gertz a "Leninist" and a "Communist-fronter." It also stated that Gertz had been an officer of the National Lawyers Guild, described as a communist organization that "probably did more than any other outfit to plan the Communist attack on the Chicago police during the 1968 Democratic convention."

These statements contained serious inaccuracies. The implication that petitioner had a criminal record was false. Petitioner had been a member and officer of the National Lawyers Guild some 15 years earlier, but there was no evidence that he or that organization had taken any part in planning the 1968 demonstrations in Chicago. There was also no basis for the charge that petitioner was a "Leninist" or a "Communist-fronter." And he had never been a member of the "Marxist League for Industrial Democracy" or the "Intercollegiate Socialist Society."

The managing editor of *American Opinion* made no effort to verify or substantiate the charges against petitioner. Instead, he appended an editorial introduction stating that the author had "concluded extensive research into the Richard Nuccio case." And he included in the article a photograph of petitioner and wrote the caption that appeared under it: "Elmer Gertz of the Red-Guild harasses Nuccio." Respondent placed the issue of *American Opinion* containing the article on sale at newsstands throughout the country and distributed reprints of the article on the streets of Chicago. . . .

The principal issue in this case is whether a newspaper or broadcaster that publishes defamatory falsehoods about an individual who is neither a public official nor a public figure may claim a constitutional privilege against liability for the injury inflicted by those statements. . . .

. . . The first remedy of any victim of defamation is self-help—using available opportunities to contradict the lie or correct the error and thereby to minimize its adverse impact on reputation. Public officials and public figures usually enjoy significantly greater access to the channels of effective communication and hence have a more realistic opportunity to counteract false statements than private individuals normally enjoy. Private individuals are therefore more vulnerable to injury, and the state interest in protecting them is correspondingly greater.

More important than the likelihood that private individuals will lack effective opportunities for rebuttal, there is a compelling normative consideration underlying the distinction between public and private defamation plaintiffs. An individual who decides to seek governmental office must accept certain necessary consequences of that involvement in public affairs. He runs the risk of closer public scrutiny than might otherwise be the case. And society's interest in the officers of government is not strictly limited to the formal discharge of official duties. . . .

Those classed as public figures stand in a similar position. Hypothetically, it may be possible for someone to become a public figure through no purposeful action of his own, but the instances of truly involuntary public figures must be exceedingly rare. For the most part those who attain this status have assumed roles of especial prominence in the affairs of society. Some occupy positions of such persuasive power and influence that they are deemed public figures for all purposes. More commonly, those classed as public figures have thrust themselves to the forefront of particular public controversies in order to influence the resolution of the issues involved. In either event, they invite attention and comment.

Even if the foregoing generalities do not obtain in every instance, the communications media are entitled to act on the assumption that public officials and public figures have voluntarily exposed themselves to increased risk of injury from defamatory falsehoods concerning them. No such assumption is justified with respect to a private individual. He has not accepted public office nor assumed an "influential role in ordering society." He has relinquished no part of his interest in the protection of his own good name, and consequently he has a more compelling call on the courts for redress of injury inflicted by defamatory falsehood. Thus, private individuals are not only more vulnerable to injury than public officials and public figures; they are also more deserving of recovery. . . .

The common law of defamation is an oddity of tort law, for it allows recovery of purportedly compensatory damages without evidence of actual loss. Under the traditional rules pertaining to actions for libel, the existence of injury is presumed from the fact of publication. . . .

. . . It is necessary to restrict defamation plaintiffs who do not prove knowledge of falsity or reckless disregard for the truth to compensation for actual injury. We need not define "actual injury," as trial courts have wide experience in framing appropriate jury instructions in tort action. Suffice it to say that actual injury is not limited to out-of-pocket loss. Indeed, the more customary types of actual harm inflicted by defamatory falsehood include impairment of reputation and standing in the community, personal humiliation, and mental anguish and suffering. . . .

We also find no justification for allowing awards of punitive damages against publishers and broadcasters held liable under state-defined standards of liability for defamation. In most jurisdictions jury discretion over the amounts awarded is limited only by the gentle rule that they not be excessive. Consequently, juries assess punitive damages in wholly unpredictable amounts bearing no necessary relation to the actual harm caused. And they remain free to use their discretion selectively to punish expressions of unpopular views. Like the doctrine of presumed damages, jury discretion to award punitive damages unnecessarily exacerbates the danger of media self-censorship, but, unlike the former rule, punitive damages are wholly irrelevant to the state interest that justifies a negligence standard for private defamation actions. They are not compensation for injury. Instead, they are private fines levied by civil juries to punish reprehensible conduct and to deter its future occurrence. In short, the private defamation plaintiff who establishes liability under a less demanding standard than that stated by *New York Times* may recover only such damages as are sufficient to compensate him for actual injury.

JUSTICE BLACKMUN, *concurring.*

The Court today refuses to apply *New York Times* to the private individual, as contrasted with the public official and the public figure. It thus withdraws to the factual limits of the pre-*Rosenbloom* cases. It thereby fixes the outer boundary of the *New York Times* doctrine and says that beyond that boundary, a State is free to define for itself the appropriate standard of a media's liability so long as it does not impose liability without fault. As my joinder in *Rosenbloom's* plurality opinion would intimate, I sense some illogic in this.

The Court, however, seeks today to strike a balance between competing values where necessarily uncertain assumptions about human behavior color the result. Although the Court's opinion in the present case departs from the rationale of the *Rosenbloom* plurality, in that the Court now conditions a libel action by a private person upon a showing of negligence, as contrasted with a showing of willful or reckless disregard, I am willing to join, and do join, the Court's opinion and its judgment for two reasons:

1. By removing the spectres of presumed and punitive damages in the absence of *New York Times* malice, the Court eliminates significant and powerful motives for self-censorship that otherwise are present in the traditional libel action. By so doing, the Court leaves what should prove to be sufficient and adequate breathing space for a vigorous press. What the Court has done, I believe, will have little, if any, practical effect on the functioning of responsible journalism.

2. The Court was sadly fractionated in *Rosenbloom*. A result of that kind inevitably leads to uncertainty. I feel that it is of profound importance for the Court to come to rest in the defamation area and to have a clearly defined majority position that eliminates the unsureness engendered by *Rosenbloom's* diversity. If my vote were not needed to create a majority, I would adhere to my prior view. A definitive ruling, however, is paramount. . . .

JUSTICE BRENNAN, *dissenting.*

. . . The teaching to be distilled from our prior cases is that, while public interest in events may at times be influenced by the notoriety of the individuals involved, "[t]he public's primary interest is in the event[,] . . . the conduct of the participant and the content, effect, and significance of the conduct. . . ." *Rosenbloom.* Matters of public or general interest do not "suddenly become less so merely because a private individual is involved, or because in some sense the individual did not 'voluntarily' choose to become involved."

. . . The Court's holding . . . simply den[ies] free expression its "breathing space." Today's decision will exacerbate the rule of self-censorship of legitimate utterances as publishers "steer far wider of the unlawful zone." . . .

The Court does not discount altogether the danger that jurors will punish for the expression of unpopular opinions. This probability accounts for the Court's limitation that "the States may not permit recovery of presumed, or punitive damages, at least when liability is not based on a showing of knowledge of falsity or reckless disregard for the truth." But plainly a jury's latitude to impose liability for want of due care poses a far greater threat of suppressing unpopular views than does a possible recovery of presumed or punitive damages. Moreover, the Court's broad-ranging examples of "actual injury," including impairment of reputation and standing in the community, as well as personal humiliation, and mental anguish and suffering, inevitably allow a jury bent on punishing expression of unpopular views a formidable weapon for doing so. Finally, even a limitation of recovery to "actual injury"—however much it reduces the size or frequency of recoveries—will not provide the necessary elbow room for First Amendment expression. . . .

JUSTICE WHITE, *dissenting.*

. . . [T]he Court, in a few printed pages, has federalized major aspects of libel law by declaring unconstitutional in important respects the prevailing defamation law in all or most of the 50 States. That result is accomplished by requiring the plaintiff in each and every defamation action to prove not only the defendant's culpability beyond his act of publishing defamatory material but also actual damage to reputation resulting from the publication. Moreover, punitive damages may not be recovered by showing malice in the traditional sense of ill will; knowing falsehood or reckless disregard of the truth will now be required.

I assume these sweeping changes will be popular with the press, but this is not the road to salvation for a court of law. As I see it, there are wholly insufficient grounds for scuttling the libel laws of the States in such wholesale fashion, to say nothing of deprecating the reputation interest of ordinary citizens and rendering them powerless to protect themselves. I do not suggest that the decision is illegitimate or beyond the bounds of judicial review, but it is an ill-considered exercise of the power entrusted to this Court, particularly when the Court has not had the benefit of briefs and argument addressed to most of the major issues which the Court now decides. I respectfully dissent.

Lest there be any mistake about it, the changes wrought by the Court's decision cut very deeply. . . .

The impact of today's decision on the traditional law of libel is immediately obvious and indisputable. No longer will the plaintiff be able to rest his case with proof of a libel defamatory on its face or proof of a slander historically actionable *per se.* In addition, he must prove some further degree of culpable conduct on the part of the publisher, such as intentional or reckless falsehood or negligence. And if he succeeds in this respect, he faces still another obstacle: recovery for loss of reputation will be conditioned upon "competent" proof of actual injury to his standing in the community. This will be true regardless of the nature of the defamation and even though it is one of those particularly reprehensible statements that have traditionally made slanderous words actionable without proof of fault by the publisher or of the damaging impact of his publication. The Court rejects the judgment of experience that some publications are so inherently capable of injury, and actual injury so difficult to prove, that the risk of falsehood should be borne by the publisher, not the victim. Plainly, with the additional burden on the plaintiff of proving negligence or other fault, it will be exceedingly difficult, perhaps impossible, for him to vindicate his reputation interest by securing a judgment for nominal damages, the practical effect of such a judgment being a judicial declaration that the publication was indeed false. Under the new rule the plaintiff can lose, not because the statement is true, but because it was not negligently made.

So too, the requirement of proving special injury to reputation before general damages may be awarded will clearly eliminate the prevailing rule, worked out over a very long period of time, that, in the case of defamations not actionable *per se,* the recovery of general damages for injury to reputation may also be had if some form of material of pecuniary loss is proved. Finally, an inflexible federal standard is imposed for the award of punitive damages. No longer will it be enough to prove ill will and an attempt to injure.

These are radical changes in the law and severe invasions of the prerogatives of the States. They should at least be shown to be required by the First Amendment or necessitated by our present circumstances. Neither has been demonstrated. . . .

          *   *   *

Two years after Gertz, *in* 1976, *the Court narrowed the definition of "public figures" by excluding those persons who do not have a significant role to play in the resolution of public policies or controversies.* Time, Inc. v. Firestone. *On a vote of 5–3, the Court ruled that publishers could be held liable for inaccurate reporting of legal proceedings even though the story for some might be a "rational interpretation of an ambiguous document." Justice Rehnquist delivered the majority opinion. Justices Brennan, Marshall, and White dissented. Newly appointed Justice Stevens did not participate.*

At issue was a divorce involving Mary Alice Firestone, a Palm Beach, Florida, socialite. The article claimed that adultery was a part of the judge's findings. Such was not the case. Adultery was charged during the litigation, but it was not ruled upon by the judge. The Florida Supreme Court claimed that since alimony was awarded, the reporter should have known that adultery was not part of the finding because Florida law denies alimony to those who are found to have committed adultery. Supreme Court Justices Powell and Stewart, in a concurring opinion, suggested, however, that this might be too much to expect of the average reporter. They said the court record "invited misunderstanding." Still, the story was erroneous as it stood, and the jury found that Mrs. Firestone had suffered damages as a result of its publication. If Mrs. Firestone had been ruled a "public person" under Times-Sullivan and Gertz, she would have had to establish actual malice in order to collect damages. But since she was considered a "private person" by this Supreme Court ruling, she was required to show only negligence plus damages in order to win a judgment. Negligence is usually considered far less difficult to prove than is malice.

The major significance of the Firestone decision, then, appeared to be fivefold: (1) It narrowed the definition of "public persons" in libel actions by presumably excluding socialites, entertainers, and similar persons, thereby making it easier for such persons to bring libel suits; (2) it limited the "public person" definition to only those who have roles to play in the resolution of public issues; (3) it reinforced the Gertz concept that damages need not be limited to actual pecuniary loss; (4) it rejected the argument that the Times-Sullivan rule should apply to all judicial proceedings, making new, more rigorous demands for media accuracy when covering complex legal questions; and (5) it stood as a warning to all news media that the Burger Court had accepted a new, more restricted definition of the First Amendment—at least in dealing with questions of libel—than that which was held during the Warren years.

TIME, INC. V. FIRESTONE
424 U.S. 448 (1976)

JUSTICE REHNQUIST delivered the opinion of the Court.

. . . Time's editorial staff, headquartered in New York, was alerted to the fact that a judgment had been rendered in the Firestone divorce proceeding by a wire service report and an account in a New York newspaper. The staff subsequently received further information regarding the Florida decision from Time's Miami bureau chief and from a "stringer" working on a special assignment basis in the Palm Beach area. On the basis of these four sources, Time's staff composed the following item, which appeared in the magazine's "Milestones" section the following week:

> "DIVORCED. By Russell A. Firestone Jr., heir to the tire fortune: Mary Alice Sullivan Firestone, 32, his third wife; a onetime Palm Beach schoolteacher; on grounds of extreme cruelty and adultery; after six years of marriage, one son; in West Palm Beach, Fla. The 17-month intermittent trial produced enough testimony of extra-marital adventures on both sides, said the judge, 'to make Dr. Freud's hair curl.' "

Within a few weeks of the publication of this article respondent demanded in writing a retraction from petitioner, alleging that a portion of the article was "false, malicious and defamatory." Petitioner declined to issue the requested retraction.

Respondent then filed this libel action against petitioner in the Florida Circuit Court. Based on a jury verdict for respondent, that court entered judgment against petitioner for $100,000, and after review in both the Florida District Court of Appeal and the Supreme Court of Florida the judgment was ultimately affirmed. . . .

[Mrs. Firestone] did not assume any role of especial prominence in the affairs of society, other than perhaps Palm Beach society, and she did not thrust herself to the forefront of any particular public controversy in order to influence the resolution of the issues involved in it.

Petitioner contends that because the Firestone divorce was characterized by the Florida Supreme Court as a *cause célèbre*, it must have been a public controversy and respondent must be considered a public figure. But in so doing petitioner seeks to equate "public controversy" with all controversies of interest to the public. . . .

Dissolution of a marriage through judicial proceedings is not the sort of "public controversy" referred to in *Gertz*, even though the marital difficulties of extremely wealthy individuals may be of interest to some portion of the reading public. Nor did respondent freely choose to publicize issues as to the propriety of her married life. She was compelled to go to court by the State in order to obtain legal release from the bonds of matrimony. We have said that in such an instance "[r]esort to the judicial process . . . is no more voluntary in a realistic sense than that of the defendant called upon to defend his interests in court." *Boddie v. Connecticut*. Her actions, both in instituting the litigation and in its conduct, were quite different from those of General Walker in *Curtis Publishing Co*. She assumed no "special prominence in the resolution of public questions." *Gertz*. We hold respondent was not a "public figure" for the purpose of determining the constitutional protection afforded petitioner's report of the factual and legal basis for her divorce.

For similar reasons we likewise reject petitioner's claim for automatic extension of the *New York Times* privilege to all reports of judicial proceedings. It is argued that information concerning proceedings in our Nation's courts may have such importance to all citizens as to justify extending special First Amendment protection to the press when reporting on such events. We have recently accepted a significantly more confined version of this argument by holding that the Constitution precludes States from imposing civil liability based upon the publication of truthful information contained in official court records open to public inspection. *Cox Broadcasting Corp. v. Cohn*. . . .

Petitioner has urged throughout this litigation that it could not be held liable for publication of the "Milestones" item because its report of respondent's divorce was factually correct. . . .

For petitioner's report to have been accurate, the divorce granted Russell Firestone must have been based on a finding by the divorce court that his wife had committed extreme cruelty toward him *and* that she had been guilty of adultery. This is indisputably what petitioner reported in its "Milestones" item, but it is equally indisputable that these were not the facts. Russell Firestone alleged in his counterclaim that respondent had been guilty of adultery, but the divorce court never made any such finding. Its judgment provided that Russell Firestone's "counterclaim for divorce be and the same is hereby granted," but did not specify that the basis for the judgment was either of the two grounds alleged in the counterclaim. The Supreme Court of Florida on appeal concluded that the ground actually relied upon by the divorce court was "lack of domestication of the parties," a ground not theretofore recognized by Florida law. The Supreme Court nonetheless affirmed the judgment dissolving the bonds of matrimony because the record contained sufficient evidence to establish the ground of extreme cruelty.

Petitioner may well argue that the meaning of the trial court's decree was unclear, but this does not license it to choose from among several conceivable interpretations the one most damaging to respondent. Having chosen to follow this tack, petitioner must be able to establish not merely that the item reported was a conceivable or plausible interpretation of the decree, but that the item was factually correct. . . .

The trial court charged, consistently with *Gertz*, that the jury should award respondent compensatory damages in "an amount of money that will fairly and adequately compensate her for such damages," and further cautioned that "It is only damages which are a direct and natural result of the alleged libel which may be recovered." There was competent evidence introduced to permit the jury to assess the amount of injury. Several witnesses testified to the extent of respondent's anxiety and concern over *Time* inaccurately reporting that she had been found guilty of adultery, and she herself took the stand to elaborate on her fears that her young son would be adversely affected by this falsehood when he grew older. The jury decided these injuries should be compensated by an award of $100,000. We have no warrant for re-examining this determination. . . .

JUSTICE BRENNAN, *dissenting.*

. . . At stake in the present case is the ability of the press to report to the citizenry the events transpiring in the Nation's judicial systems. There is simply no meaningful or constitutionally adequate way to report such events without reference to those persons and transactions that form the subject matter in controversy. . . .

Also no less true than in other areas of government, error in reporting and debate concerning the judicial process is inevitable. Indeed, in view of the complexities of that process and its unfamiliarity to the laymen who report it, the probability of inadvertent error may be substantially greater. . . .

JUSTICE MARSHALL, *dissenting.*

. . . Mrs. Firestone brought suit for separate maintenance, with reason to know of the likely public interest in the proceedings. As the Supreme Court of Florida noted, Mr. and Mrs. Firestone's "marital difficulties were . . . well-known," and the lawsuit became "a veritable *cause célèbre* in social circles across

the country." The 17-month trial and related events attracted national news coverage, and elicited no fewer than 43 articles in the *Miami Herald* and 45 articles in
the *Palm Beach Post* and *Palm Beach Times*. Far from shunning the publicity, Mrs.
Firestone held several press conferences in the course of the proceedings.

These facts are sufficient to warrant the conclusion that Mary Alice Firestone
was a "public figure" for purposes of reports on the judicial proceedings she
initiated. . . .

We must assume that it was by choice that Mrs. Firestone became an active
member of the "sporting set"—a social group with "especial prominence in the
affairs of society," whose lives receive constant media attention. Certainly there is
nothing in the record to indicate otherwise, and Mrs. Firestone's subscription to a
press clipping service suggests that she was not altogether uninterested in the
publicity she received. Having placed herself in a position in which her activities
were of interest to a significant segment of the public, Mrs. Firestone chose to
initiate a lawsuit for separate maintenance, and most significantly, held several
press conferences in the course of that lawsuit. If these actions for some reason fail
to establish as a certainty that Mrs. Firestone "voluntarily exposed [herself] to
increased risk of injury from defamatory falsehood," surely they are sufficient to
entitle the press to act on the assumption that she did. . . .

*   *   *

The years following Firestone *focused on refining the definition of "public
figure." What was becoming clear was* (1) *that the Supreme Court was narrowing its
definition of "public figure," thereby making it more difficult for media defendants
to turn back libel challenges;* (2) *that libel actions against the media were proliferating significantly, as were verdicts unfavorable to them; and* (3) *that it was becoming
more crucial for media defendants to establish that the persons bringing libel actions
against them were "public figures" rather than "private persons." "Public figures"
under* Gertz *and* Firestone *were limited to persons in three groups:* (1) *those who
occupy positions of such pervasive power and influence that they were public figures
for all purposes,* (2) *those who are intimately involved in the resolution of a
particular important public question, and* (3) *those who voluntarily thrust themselves into the vortex of a significant public controversy in order to influence the
resolution of that particular issue. Those persons must establish malice as defined in*
New York Times v. Sullivan. *All others need establish only that the press acted
negligently in publishing the defamatory falsehood, a much easier test for a plaintiff
to establish than that of malice.*

In 1979, three years following Firestone, *three important libel decisions came
down from the Supreme Court:* Herbert v. Lando, Hutchinson v. Proxmire *and*
Wolston v. Reader's Digest. *The first was brought against Barry Lando and others of
the CBS program "60 Minutes" by Col. Anthony Herbert, a retired Army officer. He
had accused his superiors of covering up war crimes charges, but he claimed when
the program was aired he was depicted as a liar. He claimed that because he was a*

public figure the only way he could establish the malice necessary for him to win his case was by questioning the "state of mind" of those putting the program together. The Supreme Court agreed. Even though this was a libel action, the Court's opinion is given in Chapter 3 because the decision appears to have the greatest impact on the gathering and preparation of news for publication.

The Hutchinson *and* Wolston *decisions were handed down the same day in 1979. Both narrowed the definition of "public figure," and, as such, have adverse implications for the media. Senator William Proxmire had received national press coverage through his "Golden Fleece Awards" presented monthly to those whom he considered wasteful of public funds. One such recipient was Ronald R. Hutchinson, a scientist who had received a public grant to study monkey reaction to stress. The Court held by an 8–1 vote that (1) the receipt of a research grant or past professional positions did not make Hutchinson a "public figure" and (2) Proxmire lost his senatorial immunity from suit when he chose to convey his ridicule of the Hutchinson research off the floor of the Senate and through such means as press releases and newsletters. Justice Brennan was the lone dissenter, calling Proxmire's actions part of the public debate on public issues.*

HUTCHINSON V. PROXMIRE
443 U.S. 111 (1979)

CHIEF JUSTICE BURGER *delivered the opinion of the Court.*

We granted certiorari to resolve three issues: (1) Whether a Member of Congress is protected by the Speech or Debate Clause of the Constitution, Art. I, Sec. 6, against suits for allegedly defamatory statements made by the Member in press releases and newsletters; (2) Whether petitioner Hutchinson is either a "public figure" or a "public official," thereby making applicable the "actual malice" standard of *New York Times v. Sullivan*; and (3) Whether respondents were entitled to summary judgment.

Ronald Hutchinson, a research behavioral scientist, sued respondents, William Proxmire, a United States Senator, and his legislative assistant, Morton Schwartz, for defamation arising out of Proxmire's giving what he called his "Golden Fleece" award. The "award" went to federal agencies that had sponsored Hutchinson's research. Hutchinson alleged that in making the award and publicizing it nationwide, respondents had libeled him, damaging him in his professional and academic standing, and had interfered with his contractual relations. The District Court granted summary judgment for respondents and the Court of Appeals affirmed.

We reverse and remand to the Court of Appeals for further proceedings consistent with this opinion.

Respondent Proxmire is a United States Senator from Wisconsin. In March

1975 he initiated the "Golden Fleece of the Month Award" to publicize what he perceived to be the most egregious examples of wasteful governmental spending. The second such award, in April 1975, went to the National Science Foundation, the National Aeronautics and Space Administration, and the Office of Naval Research, for spending almost half a million dollars during the preceding seven years to fund Hutchinson's research.

At the time of the award, Hutchinson was director of research at the Kalamazoo State Mental Hospital. Before that he had held a similar position at the Ft. Custer State Home. Both the hospital and the home are operated by the Michigan State Department of Mental Health; he was therefore a state employee in both positions. During most of the period in question he was also an adjunct professor at Western Michigan University. When the research department at Kalamazoo State Mental Hospital was closed in June 1975, Hutchinson became research director of the Foundation for Behavioral Research, a nonprofit organization. The research funding was transferred from the hospital to the foundation.

The bulk of Hutchinson's research was devoted to the study of emotional behavior. In particular, he sought an objective measure of aggression, concentrating upon the behavior patterns of certain animals, such as the clenching of jaws when they were exposed to various aggravating stressful stimuli. The National Aeronautics and Space Agency and the Navy were interested in the potential of this research for resolving problems associated with confining humans in close quarters for extended periods of time in space and undersea exploration.

The Golden Fleece Award to the agencies that had sponsored Hutchinson's research was based upon research done for Proxmire by Schwartz. While seeking evidence of wasteful governmental spending, Schwartz read copies of reports that Hutchinson had prepared under grants from NASA. Those reports revealed that Hutchinson had received grants from the Office of Naval Research, the National Science Foundation, and the Michigan State Department of Mental Health. Schwartz also learned that other federal agencies had funded Hutchinson's research. After contacting a number of federal and state agencies, Schwartz helped to prepare a speech for Proxmire to present in the Senate on April 18, 1975; the text was then incorporated into an advance press release, with only the addition of introductory and concluding sentences. Copies were sent to a mailing list of 275 members of the news media throughout the United States and abroad.

Schwartz telephoned Hutchinson before releasing the speech to tell him of the award; Hutchinson protested that the release contained an inaccurate and incomplete summary of his research. Schwartz replied that he thought the summary was fair.

In the speech Proxmire described the federal grants for Hutchinson's research, concluding with the following comment:

> The funding of this nonsense makes me almost angry enough to scream and kick or even clench my jaws. It seems to me it is outrageous.

Dr. Hutchinson's studies should make the taxpayers as well as his monkeys grind their teeth. In fact, the good doctor has made a fortune from his monkeys and in the process made a monkey out of the American taxpayer.

It is time for the Federal Government to get out of this 'monkey business.' In view of the transparent worthlessness of Hutchinson's study of jaw-grinding and biting by angry or hard-drinking monkeys, it is time we put a stop to the bite Hutchinson and the bureaucrats who fund him have been taking of the taxpayer.

In May 1975, Proxmire referred to his Golden Fleece Awards in a newsletter sent to about 100,000 people whose names were on a mailing list that included constituents in Wisconsin as well as persons in other states. The newsletter repeated the essence of the speech and the press release. Later in 1975, Proxmire appeared on a television interview program where he referred to Hutchinson's research, though he did not mention Hutchinson by name. . . .

On April 16, 1976, Hutchinson filed this suit in United States District Court in Wisconsin. In Count I he alleges that as a result of the actions of Proxmire and Schwartz he has "suffered a loss of respect in his profession, has suffered injury to his feelings, has been humiliated, held up to public scorn, suffered extreme mental anguish and physical illness and pain to his person. Further, he has suffered a loss of income and ability to earn income in the future." Count II alleges that the respondents' conduct has interfered with Hutchinson's contractual relationships with supporters of his research. He later amended the complaint to add an allegation that his rights of privacy and peace and tranquility have been infringed. . . .

We reach a similar conclusion here. A speech by Proxmire in the Senate would be wholly immune and would be available to other Members of Congress and the public in the Congressional Record. But neither the newsletters nor the press release was "essential to the deliberations of the Senate" and neither was part of the deliberative process. . . .

. . . Valuable and desirable as it may be in broad terms, the transmittal of such information by individual Members in order to inform the public and other Members is not a part of the legislative function or the deliberations that make up the legislative process. As a result, transmittal of such information by press releases and newsletters is not protected by the Speech or Debate Clause. . . .

It is not contended that Hutchinson attained such prominence that he is a public figure for all purposes. Instead, respondents have argued that the District Court and the Court of Appeals were correct in holding that Hutchinson is a public figure for the limited purpose of comment on his receipt of federal funds for research projects. That conclusion was based upon two factors: first, Hutchinson's successful application for federal funds and the reports in local newspapers of the federal grants; second, Hutchinson's access to the media, as demonstrated by the fact that some newspapers and wire services reported his response to the announce ment of the Golden Fleece Award. Neither of those factors demonstrates that Hutchinson was a public figure prior to the controversy engendered by the Golden Fleece Award; his access, such as it was, came after the alleged libel.

On this record Hutchinson's activities and public profile are much like those of countless members of his profession. His published writings reach a relatively small category of professionals concerned with research in human behavior. To the extent the subject of his published writings became a matter of controversy it was a consequence of the Golden Fleece Award. Clearly those charged with defamation cannot, by their own conduct, create their own defense by making the claimant a public figure.

Hutchinson did not thrust himself or his views into public controversy to influence others. Respondents have not identified such a particular controversy; at most, they point to concern about general public expenditures. But that concern is shared by most and relates to most public expenditures; it is not sufficient to make Hutchinson a public figure. If it were, everyone who received or benefited from the myriad public grants for research could be classified as a public figure—a conclusion that our previous opinions have rejected. The "use of such subject-matter classifications to determine the extent of constitutional protection afforded defamatory falsehoods may too often result in an improper balance between the competing interests in this area." *Time, Inc. v. Firestone.* . . .

Finally, we cannot agree that Hutchinson had such access to the media that he should be classified as a public figure. Hutchinson's access was limited to responding to the announcement of the Golden Fleece Award. He did not have the regular and continuing access to the media that is one of the accouterments of having become a public figure.

We therefore reverse the judgment of the Court of Appeals and remand the case to the Court of Appeals for further proceedings consistent with this opinion.

Reversed and remanded.

*   *   *

The same day the Hutchinson *decision came down, another setback for the media—but a victory for private persons claiming to have been defamed by the media—came in the form of* Wolston v. Reader's Digest. *Ilya Wolston had been alleged to be a Soviet agent in a book published in 1974 by the* Digest. *Wolston some 15 years earlier had been held in contempt for failing to respond to a subpoena by a grand jury investigating Soviet espionage. No other indictments or criminal charges were filed against him. The lower courts held that Wolston was a "limited public figure" both at the time of his failure to respond and at the time of publication of the book. The Supreme Court reversed, however. Wolston's conviction on failure to respond did not result in his becoming a "public figure" for purposes of libel, Justice Rehnquist wrote for the 8–1 majority. It was noted that following the initial media attention, Wolston was able to return to the private life he enjoyed prior to the subpoena. Justice Brennan, as in* Hutchinson, *was alone in dissent.*

WOLSTON V. READER'S DIGEST
443 U.S. 157 (1979)

JUSTICE REHNQUIST *delivered the opinion of the Court.*

. . . We explained in *Gertz* that the rationale for extending the *New York Times* rule to public figures was two-fold. First, we recognized that public figures are less vulnerable to injury from defamatory statements because of their ability to resort to effective "self-help." They usually enjoy significantly greater access than private individuals to channels of effective communication, which enable them through discussion to counter criticism and expose the falsehood and fallacies of defamatory statements. Second, and more importantly, was a normative consideration that public figures are less deserving of protection than private persons because public figures, like public officials, have "voluntarily exposed themselves to increased risk of injury from defamatory falsehood concerning them." . . .

. . . The District Court concluded that by failing to appear before the grand jury and subjecting himself to a citation for contempt, petitioner "became involved in a controversy of a decidedly public nature in a way that invited attention and comment, and thereby created in the public an interest in knowing about his connection with espionage. . . ." Similarly, the Court of Appeals stated that by refusing to comply with the subpoena, petitioner "stepped center front into the spotlight focused on the investigation of Soviet espionage. In short, by his voluntary action he invited attention and comment in connection with the public questions involved in the investigation of espionage."

We do not agree with respondents and the lower courts that petitioner can be classed as such a limited-purpose public figure. First, the undisputed facts do not justify the conclusion of the District Court and Court of Appeals that petitioner "voluntarily thrust" or "injected" himself into the forefront of the public controversy surrounding the investigation of Soviet espionage in the United States. It would be more accurate to say that petitioner was dragged unwillingly into the controversy. The government pursued him in its investigation. Petitioner did fail to respond to a grand jury subpoena, and this failure, as well as his subsequent citation for contempt, did attract media attention. But the mere fact that petitioner voluntarily chose not to appear before the grand jury, knowing that his action might be attended by publicity, is not decisive on the question of public figure status. . . .

. . . Similarly, petitioner never discussed this matter with the press and limited his involvement to that necessary to defend himself of the contempt charge. It is clear that petitioner played only a minor role in whatever public controversy there may have been concerning the investigation of Soviet espionage. We decline to hold that his mere citation for contempt rendered him a public figure for purposes of comment on the investigation of Soviet espionage.

Petitioner's failure to appear before the grand jury and citation for contempt no doubt were "newsworthy," but the simple fact that these events attracted media attention also is not conclusive of the public figure issue. A private individual is not automatically transformed into a public figure just by becoming involved in or associated with a matter that attracts public attention. . . .

Nor do we think that petitioner engaged the attention of the public in an attempt to influence the resolution of the issues involved. Petitioner assumed no "special prominence in the resolution of public questions." *Gertz v. Robert Welch.* His failure to respond to the grand jury's subpoena was in no way calculated to draw attention to himself in order to invite public comment or influence the public with respect to any issue. He did not in any way seek to arouse public sentiment in his favor and against the investigation. Thus, this is not a case where a defendant invites a citation for contempt in order to use the contempt citation as a fulcrum to create public discussion about the methods being used in connection with an investigation or prosecution. To the contrary, petitioner's failure to appear before the grand jury appears simply to have been the result of his poor health. He then promptly communicated his desire to testify and when the offer was rejected, passively accepted his punishment. . . .

This reasoning leads us to reject the further contention of respondents that any person who engages in criminal conduct automatically becomes a public figure for purposes of comment on a limited range of issues relating to his conviction. . . .

Accordingly, the judgment of the Court of Appeals is

Reversed.

*   *   *

In 1984, two years before what was to be the end of the Burger era, four libel decisions of note were forthcoming. One, Bose v. Consumers Union, *was of particular significance. The first two, involving questions of jurisdiction, were decided the same day and gave plaintiffs greater latitude in bringing their suits against the press. In* Keeton v. Hustler *the Supreme Court held that publishers could be sued in a state by a nonresident even though a relatively small number of copies of the publication in question were circulated in that state. The opinion would appear to encourage "forum shopping" in libel actions. Kathy Keeton, a resident of New York and colleague of Penthouse publisher Bob Guccione, sought out New Hampshire as the location for her libel suit against* Hustler *magazine, an Ohio corporation, because New Hampshire had a six-year statute of limitations for libel actions and, as such, was the only state in which her suit still could be filed. Most states' limitations range from one to three years. It was estimated that* Hustler *sold fewer than 15,000 copies per month in New Hampshire, a sufficient number to cause damage and to bring suit, the Court held. Justice Rehnquist, writing for a unanimous Court, admitted that most of the damage would be done outside of the state, but wrote nonetheless that "there was no justification for restricting libel actions to the plaintiff's home forum."*

The second case that day involved entertainer Shirley Jones. Calder v. Jones.

She had brought suit in California against the National Enquirer, *published in Florida, and editor Iain Calder and writer John South. The headline, "Husband's Bizarre Behavior Is Driving Shirley Jones to Drink," resulted in a $20 million action. The* Enquirer *did not challenge the jurisdictional question and settled out of court. Of the more than 5 million copies sold each week, more than 600,000 were sold in California, causing significant injury in the home state of Jones and her husband, Marty Ingels. The fact that defendants Calder and South live in Florida and would have incurred significant additional costs defending themselves in California should not prevent Shirley Jones—or other plaintiff in a similar case— from bringing libel action where she lives, works, and where she was allegedly damaged most severely, Justice Rehnquist wrote for a unanimous Court.*

Later that year, in another decision that went against the press, the Court ruled that newspapers have no First Amendment right to publish material obtained from a plaintiff through court-ordered pretrial discovery procedures. Seattle Times v. Rhinehart. *A trial judge had ordered the* Seattle Times *and the* Walla Walla Union-Bulletin *not to publish information they obtained as part of a libel suit brought by Keith Rhinehart, leader of a small spiritual group called the Aquarian Foundation, which had been the subject of several critical stories published over the years by the newspapers. The Supreme Court in recent years had been firm in its view that the press was free under the Constitution to publish information which it had in its possession, if such material was obtained legally and published accurately (see Chapters 2 and 3). This, in effect, was an exception to that rule. While there might not be an absolute First Amendment right to publish information obtained through discovery—information which, after all, is "forced" from the plaintiff under an order of the court—a trial judge nonetheless could allow publication of such information by denying the protective order request of the litigant. Also, the media are free to publish the identical information if they obtain it independently from outside sources, Justice Powell wrote for the unanimous Supreme Court.*

The most important defamation decision of that year—and some say of the past decade—came in Bose. *In it, the Court held 6–3 that appellant judges must independently review findings of actual malice in cases governed by the* Sullivan *rules.* Consumer Reports, *published by the Consumers Union, had run a review critical of certain Bose stereo loudspeakers. Bose sued for product disparagement. The magazine lost a $210,000 judgment at the trial stage when the judge ruled that the article was false, damaging and published with actual malice, as required by* Sullivan. *His decision was overturned on appeal. Bose took the case to the Supreme Court, arguing that the appeals court should not have looked at the factual matters of the case, but only at the legal rulings. Justice Stevens wrote for the Supreme Court majority, which sustained the ruling of the Circuit Court of Appeals. Dissenting were Justices Rehnquist, O'Connor and White.*

The press waited nervously for the decision, because the Court could have significantly watered down Sullivan, *but instead reinforced it and made it even more advantageous to the media. In addition to allowing appeals courts to make independent judgments of fact because of the importance of First Amendment considerations, the decision also would seem to strengthen the principle of "fair comment" as a defense against libel actions. The importance can be seen also by the fact that recent research indicates that about 80 percent of libel decisions made by juries go against the press, while about 70 percent of those decisions are reversed on appeal. Any limitation imposed upon the appeals process, then, would tend to be troublesome to the media. Below are excerpts which focus on the factual matters under consideration in* Bose.

BOSE CORP. V. CONSUMERS UNION
466 U.S. 485 (1984)

JUSTICE STEVENS *delivered the opinion of the Court.*

. . . In the May 1970 issue of its magazine, *Consumer Reports*, respondent published a seven-page article evaluating the quality of numerous brands of medium priced loudspeakers. In a boxed-off section occupying most of two pages, respondent commented on "some loudspeakers of special interest," one of which was the Bose 901—an admittedly "unique and unconventional" system that had recently been placed on the market by petitioner. After describing the system and some of its virtues, and after noting that a listener "could pinpoint the location of various instruments much more easily with a standard speaker than with the *Bose* system," respondent's article made the following statements:

> "Worse, individual instruments heard through the Bose system seemed to grow to gigantic proportions and tended to wander about the room. For instance, a violin appeared to be 10 feet wide and a piano stretched from wall to wall. With orchestral music, such effects seemed inconsequential. But we think they might become annoying when listening to soloists."

After stating opinions concerning the overall sound quality, the article concluded: "We think the *Bose* system is so unusual that a prospective buyer must listen to it and judge it for himself. We would suggest delaying so big an investment until you were sure the system would please you after the novelty value had worn off."

Petitioner took exception to numerous statements made in the article, and when respondent refused to publish a retraction, petitioner commenced this product disparagement action. . . .

The statement that instruments tended to wander "about the room" was found false because what the listeners in the test actually perceived was an apparent movement back and forth along the wall in front of them and between the two speakers. Because an apparent movement "about the room"—rather than back and forth—would be so different from what the average listener has learned to expect, the District Court concluded "that the location of the movement of the apparent sound source is just as critical to a reader as the fact that movement occurred.". . .

. . . [The engineer's] initial in-house report contained this sentence: " 'Instruments not only could not be placed with precision but appeared to suffer from giganticism and a tendency to wander around the room; a violin seemed about 10 ft. wide, a piano stretched from wall to wall, etc.' " Since the editorial revision from "around the room" to "about the room" did not change the meaning of the false statement, and since there was no evidence that the editors were aware of the inaccuracy in the original report, the actual malice determination rests entirely on an evaluation of [the engineer's] state of mind when he wrote his initial report, or when he checked the article against that report. . . .

The Court of Appeals was correct in its conclusions (1) that there is a significant difference between proof of actual malice and mere proof of falsity, and (2) that such additional proof is lacking in this case. . . .

JUSTICE REHNQUIST, *with whom Justice O'Connor joins, dissenting:*

There is more than one irony in this "Case of the Wandering Instruments," which subject matter makes it sound more like a candidate for inclusion in the "Adventures of Sherlock Holmes" than in a casebook on constitutional law. It is ironic in the first place that a constitutional principle which originated in *New York Times v. Sullivan,* because of the need for freedom to criticize the conduct of public officials is applied here to a magazine's false statements about a commercial loudspeaker system.

In this case the District Court concluded by what it found to be clear and convincing evidence that respondent's engineer Arnold Seligson had written the defamatory statement about Bose's product with actual knowledge that it was false. It reached that conclusion expressly relying on its determination about the credibility of Seligson's testimony. . . .

. . . But to me, the only shortcoming here is an appellate court's inability to make the determination which the Court mandates today—the *de novo* determination about the state of mind of a particular author at a particular time. Although there well may be cases where the "actual malice" determination can be made on the basis of objectively reviewable facts in the record, it seems to me that just as often it is made, as here, on the basis of an evaluation of the credibility of the testimony of the author of the defamatory statement. I am at a loss to see how appellate courts can even begin to make such determinations. In any event, surely such determinations are best left to the trial judge.

*   *   *

Two years later, as Chief Justice Burger was about to step down, the Supreme Court issued two rulings that were highly favorable to the press by placing a heavy burden on a private individual who wishes to sue for libel. The Court picked up where Bose *left off and reverted, as it were, to the Warren Court position of encouraging "uninhibited, robust and wide open" discussion of public issues, a line from* Sullivan *which had become a hallmark of the Warren Court insofar as press freedom was concerned. The rulings again made clear the "preferred status" of the First Amendment.*

In the first case, Philadelphia Newspapers v. Hepps, the Court ruled that even private person plaintiffs bringing libel actions against the press in which public issues are involved must prove—not just claim—that the published statements in question were false, thereby relieving media defendants from having to prove that the statements were true. The decision may have been narrow (5–4), but it was a significant expansion of First Amendment rights for the press. Public officials and public figures already carried the burden of proving the falsity of alleged libelous statements, but this decision expanded that requirement to include private persons involved in public issues. The Philadelphia Inquirer had published a series of articles seeking to tie Maurice S. Hepps to organized crime. Hepps was neither a public official nor a public figure, but an owner of beer and soft drink companies. At the trial, the judge instructed the jury that Hepps had the burden of proving that the alleged libelous statements in the articles were false. The jury ruled for the newspaper. On appeal, the Pennsylvania Supreme Court set aside the jury's decision and held that it was the newspaper which had the burden of proving that the statements in question were true. The United States Supreme Court reversed that decision, Justices O'Connor, Blackmun, Brennan, Powell and Marshall making up the majority. A strong dissent was issued by Justice Stevens, with whom Justices Burger, Rehnquist and White joined.

Various states had taken different positions on the burden of proof question, but the Supreme Court's action in Hepps sets a national constitutional standard, as it did in Sullivan. There was no change in the requirement that private persons must establish only negligence rather than malice (see Gertz), but the need to prove the falsity of the statements would seem to give a decided advantage to the press, an advantage the majority said was required because of the potential "chilling effect" libel actions have on freedom to discuss public issues. The decision reinforced and expanded the position the Court took in Sullivan, handed down 22 years earlier. One could argue that, by definition, news media publish only items of public concern, thereby requiring every plaintiff who brings a libel action against a news organization to carry the heavy burden of proof established in Hepps, but whether that interpretation is acceptable to the Court will have to wait for another day.

PHILADELPHIA NEWSPAPERS V. HEPPS
475 U.S. 767 (1986)

JUSTICE O'CONNOR delivered the opinion of the Court.

This case requires us once more to "struggl[e] . . . to define the proper accommodation between the law of defamation and the freedoms of speech and press protected by the First Amendment." Gertz v. Robert Welch, Inc. In Gertz, the Court held that a private figure who brings a suit for defamation cannot recover without some showing that the media defendant was at fault in publishing the statements at issue. Here, we hold that, at least where a newspaper publishes speech of public concern, a private-figure plaintiff cannot recover damages without also showing that the statements at issue are false. . . .

. . . Pennsylvania follows the common law's presumption that an individual's reputation is a good one. Statements defaming that person are therefore presumptively false, although a publisher who bears the burden of proving the truth of the statements has an absolute defense. . . .

Here, as in *Gertz*, the plaintiff is a private figure and the newspaper articles are of public concern. In *Gertz*, as in *New York Times*, the common-law rule was superseded by a constitutional rule. We believe that the common law's rule on falsity—that the defendant must bear the burden of proving truth—must similarly fall here to a constitutional requirement that the plaintiff bear the burden of showing falsity, as well as fault, before recovering damages. . . .

. . . Because . . . a "chilling" effect would be antithetical to the First Amendment's protection of true speech on matters of public concern, we believe that a private-figure plaintiff must bear the burden of showing that the speech at issue is false before recovering damages for defamation from a media defendant. To do otherwise could "only result in a deterrence of speech which the Constitution makes free." *Speiser.*

We recognize that requiring the plaintiff to show falsity will insulate from liability some speech that is false, but unprovably so. Nonetheless, the Court's previous decisions on the restrictions that the First Amendment places upon the common law of defamation firmly support our conclusion here with respect to the allocation of the burden of proof. In attempting to resolve related issues in the defamation context, the Court has affirmed that "[t]he First Amendment requires we protect some falsehood in order to protect speech that matters." *Gertz.* Here the speech concerns the legitimacy of the political process, and therefore clearly "matters." . . . To provide " 'breathing space,' " *New York Times*, for true speech on matters of public concern, the Court has been willing to insulate even *demonstrably* false speech from liability, and has imposed additional requirements of fault upon the plaintiff in a suit for defamation. . . . We therefore do not break new ground here in insulating speech that is not even demonstrably false.

We note that our decision adds only marginally to the burdens that the plaintiff must already bear as a result of our earlier decisions in the law of defamation. The plaintiff must show fault. A jury is obviously more likely to accept a plaintiff's contention that the defendant was at fault in publishing the statements at issue if convinced that the relevant statements were false. As a practical matter, then, evidence offered by plaintiffs on the publisher's fault in adequately investigating the truth of the published statements will generally encompass evidence of the falsity of the matters asserted. . . .

JUSTICE STEVENS, *with whom Chief Justice Burger, Justice White, and Justice Rehnquist join, dissenting.*

The issue the Court resolves today will make a difference in only one category of cases—those in which a private individual can prove that he was libeled by a defendant who was at least negligent. For unless such a plaintiff can overcome the burden imposed by *Gertz v. Robert Welch*, he cannot recover regardless of how the burden of proof on the issue of truth or falsity is allocated. By definition, therefore, the only litigants—and the only publishers—who will benefit from today's decision are those who act negligently or maliciously. . . .

While deliberate or inadvertent libels villify private personages, they contribute little to the marketplace of ideas. . . .

In my opinion deliberate, malicious character assassination is not protected by the First Amendment to the United States Constitution. That Amendment does require the target of a defamatory statement to prove that his assailant was at fault, and I agree that it provides a constitutional shield for truthful statements. I simply do not understand, however, why a character assassin should be given an absolute license to defame by means of statements that can be neither verified nor disproven. The danger of deliberate defamation by reference to unprovable facts is not a merely speculative or hypothetical concern. Lack of knowledge about third parties, the loss of critical records, an uncertain recollection about events that occurred long ago, perhaps during a period of special stress, the absence of eyewitnesses—a host of factors—may make it impossible for an honorable person to disprove malicious gossip about his past conduct, his relatives, his friends, or his business associates. . . .

In my view, as long as publishers are protected by the requirement that the plaintiff has the burden of proving fault, there can be little, if any, basis for a concern that a significant amount of true speech will be deterred unless the private person victimized by a malicious libel can also carry the burden of proving falsity. The Court's decision trades on the good names of private individuals with little First Amendment coin to show for it.

I respectfully dissent.

*   *   *

In June 1986, as the Court was about to take its summer recess and after Chief Justice Burger had announced his resignation, another important press victory in the area of libel was handed down. In a 6–3 decision, the Court ruled that the potential "chilling effect" of libel actions requires that cases brought by public figures show "clear and convincing" evidence that their claims against the media have validity before their cases go forward to trial. Summary judgments, which dismiss cases before a trial, are important to media defendants because they allow judges to immediately terminate libel actions that do not have merit, thereby saving considerable time and money for the defendant press. Also, since about 80 percent of all jury decisions in libel cases go against the press, most trial results would be appealed, thereby requiring additional time and money. The question, then, focused on just how much evidence of actual malice under the Sullivan *rule a public figure must show before a trial is ordered. Little guidance was given to trial judges on how to apply this "clear and convincing" standard, bringing a warning from the three dissenting Justices that the opinion of the Court would result in confusion and inconsistency. Justice White wrote for the majority. Dissenting were Justices Burger, Rehnquist and, in an interesting departure from his usual pro-press stance, Brennan. The significance of the decision is that public figures bringing libel suits against the media now know they will have to meet a tough test before their cases will be heard by a jury. It is hoped that the ruling will reduce frivolous suits by public figures.*

The case involved the Liberty Lobby, a conservative citizen's group, which filed a libel action against columnist Jack Anderson, who had described the group in articles as neo-Nazi, anti-Semitic, racist and fascist. A federal trial court had upheld Anderson's motion for summary judgment, dismissing the case, noting that the plaintiffs were public figures and that the evidence presented by them was not sufficient to win at the trial stage. That ruling, however, was overturned by a 2–1 vote of a Circuit Court of Appeals, which said that to require "clear and convincing" evidence of malice was too high a standard to require of a plaintiff before the trial itself began. The author of the Circuit Court opinion, interestingly, was Judge Antonin Scalia, who was to join the Supreme Court the following October with Justice Burger's departure. Media lawyers pondered whether this view was to be a forerunner of a long string of anti-media positions to come from the newest justice.

ANDERSON V. LIBERTY LOBBY
477 U.S. 242 (1986)

JUSTICE WHITE *delivered the opinion of the Court.*

. . . [W]e are convinced that the inquiry involved in a ruling on a motion for summary judgment or for a directed verdict necessarily implicates the substantive evidentiary standard of proof that would apply at the trial on the merits. If the defendant in a run-of-the-mill civil case moves for summary judgment or for a directed verdict based on the lack of proof of a material fact, the judge must ask himself not whether he thinks the evidence unmistakably favors one side or the other but whether a fair-minded jury could return a verdict for the plaintiff on the evidence presented. The mere existence of a scintilla of evidence in support of the plaintiff's position will be insufficient; there must be evidence on which the jury could reasonably find for the plaintiff. . . .

In terms of the nature of the inquiry, this is no different from the consideration of a motion for acquittal in a criminal case, where the beyond-a-reasonable-doubt standard applies and where the trial judge asks whether a reasonable jury could find guilt beyond a reasonable doubt. . . . Similarly, where the First Amendment mandates a "clear and convincing" standard, the trial judge in disposing of a directed verdict motion should consider whether a reasonable fact finder could conclude, for example, that the plaintiff had shown actual malice with convincing clarity. . . .

Our holding that the clear-and-convincing standard of proof should be taken into account in ruling on summary judgment motions does not denigrate the role of the jury. It by no means authorizes trial on affidavits. Credibility determinations, the weighing of the evidence, and the drawing of legitimate inferences from the facts are jury functions, not those of a judge, whether he is ruling on a motion for summary judgment or for a directed verdict. . . .

. . . [We] conclude that the determination of whether a given factual dispute requires submission to a jury must be guided by the substantive evidentiary standards that apply to the case. This is true at both the directed verdict and summary judgment stages. Consequently, where the New York Times "clear and convincing" evidence requirement applies, the trial judge's summary judgment inquiry as to whether a genuine issue exists will be whether the evidence presented is such that a jury applying that evidentiary standard could reasonably find for either the plaintiff or the defendant. Thus, where the factual dispute concerns actual malice, clearly a material issue in a New York Times case, the appropriate summary judgment question will be whether the evidence in the record could support a reasonable jury finding either that the plaintiff has shown actual malice by clear and convincing evidence or that the plaintiff has not.

In sum, a court ruling on a motion for summary judgment must be guided by the New York Times "clear and convincing" evidentiary standard in determining whether a genuine issue of actual malice exists—that is, whether the evidence presented is such that a reasonable jury might find that actual malice had been shown with convincing clarity. Because the Court of Appeals did not apply the correct standard in reviewing the District Court's grant of summary judgment, we vacate its decision and remand the case for further proceedings consistent with this opinion.

It is so ordered.

JUSTICE BRENNAN, *dissenting.*

. . . I cannot agree that the authority cited by the Court supports its position. In my view, the Court's result is the product of an exercise akin to the child's game of "telephone," in which a message is repeated from one person to another and then another; after some time, the message bears little resemblance to what was originally spoken. In the present case, the Court purports to restate the summary judgment test, but with each repetition, the original understanding is increasingly distorted.

But my concern is not only that the Court's decision is unsupported; after all, unsupported views may nonetheless be supportable. I am more troubled by the fact that the Court's opinion sends conflicting signals to trial courts and reviewing courts which must deal with summary judgment motions on a day to day basis. This case is about a trial court's responsibility when considering a motion for summary judgment, but in my view, the Court, while instructing the trial judge to "consider" heightened evidentiary standards, fails to explain what that means. In other words, how does a judge assess how one-sided evidence is, or what a "fair minded" jury could "reasonably" decide? The Court provides conflicting clues to these mysteries, which I fear can lead only to increased confusion in the district and appellate courts. . . .

JUSTICE REHNQUIST, *with whom Chief Justice Burger joins, dissenting.*

. . . The Court, I believe, makes an even greater mistake in failing to apply its newly announced rule to the facts of this case. Instead of thus illustrating how the rule works, it contents itself with abstractions and paraphrases of abstractions, so that its opinion sounds much like a treatise about cooking by someone who has never cooked before and has no intention of starting now. . . .

*   *   *

As the decisions above suggest, it was becoming increasingly difficult for public figures to win libel suits against the press. The actual malice test was almost impossible for public-person plaintiffs to meet. But in 1983, a series of events began to unfold that caused great concern among the media. Hustler *magazine publisher Larry Flynt ran a parody involving the Rev. Jerry Falwell, who sued for libel, invasion of privacy and intentional infliction of emotional distress. And it was the latter which was the major concern.* Hustler Magazine v. Falwell. *The trial judge dismissed the invasion of privacy suit, and the jury rejected the libel claim. But jurors did award Falwell $200,000 for intentional infliction of emotional distress. A unanimous three-person Court of Appeals upheld the jury's findings, but in 1988 a unanimous Supreme Court reversed, holding for* Hustler. *Flynt had indicated that his ultimate goal was to symbolically "assassinate" Falwell. And the conservative minister, for his part, chose to distribute the tasteless parody around the country in a fund-raising campaign that raised hundreds of thousands of dollars.*

It is important to note that if the finding had favored Falwell and the concept of intentional infliction of emotional distress, a door would have been open to circumvent the limitations imposed by the Court on libel actions. No requirement of actual malice, for example, would be needed by public figures, as it is in libel suits. And, presumably, private persons in emotional distress actions would not have to show negligence or damages. The chilling effect this might have had on parody, satire, editorial cartoons, theater reviews—even stage performances—can only be imagined. The nation's media sighed deeply when the Supreme Court handed down its unanimous Hustler *decision.*

HUSTLER MAGAZINE V. FALWELL
108 S. Ct. 876 (1988)

CHIEF JUSTICE REHNQUIST *delivered the opinion of the Court, in which Justices Brennan, Marshall, Blackmun, Stevens, O'Connor, and Scalia join.*

Petitioner *Hustler* Magazine, Inc., is a magazine of nationwide circulation. Respondent Jerry Falwell, a nationally known minister who has been active as a commentator on politics and public affairs, sued petitioner and its publisher, petitioner Larry Flynt, to recover damages for invasion of privacy, libel, and intentional infliction of emotional distress. . . .

The inside front cover of the November 1983 issue of *Hustler* Magazine featured a "parody" of an advertisement for Campari Liqueur that contained the name and picture of respondent and was entitled "Jerry Falwell talks about his first time." This parody was modeled after actual Campari ads that included interviews with various celebrities about their "first times." Although it was apparent by the end of each interview that this meant the first time they sampled Campari, the ads clearly played on the sexual double entendre of the general subject of "first times." Copying the form and layout of these Campari ads, *Hustler's* editors chose respondent as the featured celebrity and drafted an alleged "interview" with him in which he states that his "first time" was during a drunken incestuous rendezvous with his mother in an outhouse. The *Hustler* parody portrays respondent and his mother as drunk and immoral, and suggests that respondent is a hypocrite who preaches only when he is drunk. In small print at the bottom of the page, the ad contains the disclaimer, "ad parody—not to be taken seriously." The magazine's table of contents also lists the ad as "Fiction; Ad and Personality Parody." . . .

This case presents us with a novel question involving First Amendment limitations upon a State's authority to protect its citizens from the intentional infliction of emotional distress. We must decide whether a public figure may recover damages for emotional harm caused by the publication of an ad parody offensive to him, and doubtless gross and repugnant in the eyes of most. . . .

. . . [W]e think the First Amendment prohibits such a result in the area of public debate about public figures.

Were we to hold otherwise, there can be little doubt that political cartoonists and satirists would be subjected to damages awarded without any showing that their work falsely defamed its subject. Webster's defines a caricature as "the deliberately distorted picturing or imitating of a person, literary style, etc. by exaggerating features or mannerisms for satirical effect." *Webster's New Unabridged Twentieth Century Dictionary of the English Language* 275 (2d ed. 1979). The appeal of the political cartoon or caricature is often based on exploration of unfortunate physical traits or politically embarrassing events—an exploration often calculated to injure the feelings of the subject of the portrayal. The art of the cartoonist is often not reasoned or even-handed, but slashing and one-sided. One cartoonist expressed the nature of the art in these words:

> "The political cartoon is a weapon of attack, of scorn and ridicule and satire; it is least effective when it tries to pat some politician on the back. It is usually as welcome as a bee sting and is always controversial in some quarters." Long, *The Political Cartoon: Journalism's Strongest Weapon*, The Quill, 56, 57 (Nov. 1962).

Several famous examples of this type of intentionally injurious speech were drawn by Thomas Nast, probably the greatest American cartoonist to date, who was associated for many years during the post-Civil War era with *Harper's Weekly*. In the pages of that publication Nast conducted a graphic vendetta against William M. "Boss" Tweed and his corrupt associates in New York City's "Tweed Ring." It has been described by one historian of the subject as "a sustained attack which in its passion and effectiveness stands alone in the history of American graphic art." M. Keller, *The Art and Politics of Thomas Nast* 177 (1968). . . .

Respondent contends, however, that the caricature in question here was so "outrageous" as to distinguish it from more traditional political cartoons. There is no doubt that the caricature of respondent and his mother published in *Hustler* is at best a distant cousin of the political cartoons described above, and a rather poor relation at that. If it were possible by laying down a principled standard to separate the one from the other, public discourse would probably suffer little or no harm. But we doubt that there is any such standard, and we are quite sure that the pejorative description "outrageous" does not supply one. "Outrageousness" in the area of political and social discourse has an inherent subjectiveness about it which would allow a jury to impose liability on the basis of the jurors' tastes or views, or perhaps on the basis of their dislike of a particular expression. An "outrageousness" standard thus runs afoul of our longstanding refusal to allow damages to be awarded because the speech in question may have an adverse emotional impact on the audience. . . .

Admittedly, these oft-repeated First Amendment principles, like other principles, are subject to limitations. We recognized in *Pacifica Foundation*, that speech that is " 'vulgar,' 'offensive,' and 'shocking' " is "not entitled to absolute constitutional protection under all circumstances." In *Chaplinsky v. New Hampshire* we held that a state could lawfully punish an individual for the use of insulting " 'fighting' words—those which by their very utterance inflict injury or tend to incite an immediate breach of the peace." These limitations are but recognition of the observation in *Dun & Bradstreet, Inc. v. Greenmoss* that this Court has "long recognized that not all speech is of equal first Amendment importance." But the sort of expression involved in this case does not seem to us to be governed by any exception to the general First Amendment principles stated above.

We conclude that public figures and public officials may not recover for the tort of intentional infliction of emotional distress by reason of publications such as the one here at issue without showing in addition that the publication contains a false statement of fact which was made with "actual malice," i.e., with knowledge that the statement was false or with reckless disregard as to whether or not it was true. This is not merely a "blind application" of the *New York Times* standard, it reflects our considered judgment that such a standard is necessary to give adequate "breathing space" to the freedoms protected by the First Amendment. . . .

LIBEL AND THE SUPREME COURT

By Jerome Lawrence Merin*

. . . The proposition that "[w]hatever is added to the field of libel is taken from the field of free debate" is not necessarily true. Free debate is not a simple phenomenon but is the result of many interrelated factors; it should not be an absolute end; it should be a means toward the end of a free and democratic society. Free debate may aid in achieving and maintaining a democratic society; but freedom cannot be equated with anarchy, since anarchy results in freedom only for the strongest, the richest, the loudest, or the most numerous. Freedom flourishes when it is limited by the boundaries of self-restraint and the rights of others. Free debate cannot be achieved merely by removing all barriers to public speech and writings because true debate also depends on the willingness of men to enter the public arena, on the presence of, and belief in, the presence of credible statements, and on a responsive, educated, and unintimidated populace.

Zechariah Chafee, Jr. wrote that

> [o]ne of the most important purposes of society and government is the discovery and spread of truth on subjects of general concern. This is possible only through absolutely unlimited discussion, for, as Bagehot points out, once force is thrown into the argument, it becomes a matter of chance whether it is thrown on the false side or the true, and truth loses all its natural advantage in the contest.

This is the Holmesian "marketplace of ideas" view derived, in large measure, from the philosophy of John Stuart Mill. The concept of a clash of conflicting ideas resulting in the truth, however, depends upon a prior assumption that all ideas will be presented in good faith and in a straightforward manner without the use of force or guile. If truth is to emerge from a free clash of ideas, all ideas must reach all citizens, and each citizen must be both interested in weighing the ideas presented and educated enough to evaluate them. The "marketplace of ideas" theory is a philosophic equivalent of the economic theory of laissez-faire which also developed in the nineteenth century. Like a laissez-faire economic marketplace, the "marketplace of ideas" theory is postulated upon an ideological abstraction—a perfect, frictionless society where all entrants in the market are equally powerful and honest and are dealing with a citizenry that will behave in an intelligent, rational manner. It is ironic that the very people who have rejected the theory of

* From Jerome Lawrence Merin. "Libel and the Supreme Court," *William and Mary Law Review*, Vol. 11 (1969), p. 371, at p. 415. Used with permission of the *William and Mary Law Review*. The author received his J.D. from Harvard Law School in 1969.

laissez-faire economics have feverishly embraced the theory of laissez-faire civil liberties.

Chafee did not, however, view a free press and free speech as unlimited; he believed that though the spread of truth was important,

> there are other purposes of government, such as order, the training of the young, protection against external aggression. Unlimited discussion some-times interferes with these purposes, which must then be balanced against freedom of speech, but freedom of speech ought to weigh heavily in the scales.

Beginning values and rights requires a prior determination of what the conflicting interests are and the importance of those interests. Fixed abstract doctrines and popular clichés are injurious to consideration of even everyday problems; but they are disastrous when used to deal with problems of civil rights. Doctrinaire formulas lead to a substitution of words for thought and of easy platitudes for the difficult solutions and unsatisfying compromises that allow democracies to function.

The value of free expression, according to one authority, is that it assures individual self-fulfillment, provides a means of attaining the truth, creates a method of securing the participation of the members of a society in political and social decision-making, and serves as a means of maintaining the balance between stability and change in a society. Limiting ourselves to the area of libel and freedom of the press, let us weigh these functions against the interest of the individual in his good name and sound reputation. Granting that man's ability to reason, to feel, and to think in abstract terms distinguishes him from other animals, it does not follow that *any* limitation on the public expression of a man's opinions and beliefs is a denial of his humanity. A statement which jeopardizes others' lives or property or quality of living carries the ideal of individual self-fulfillment beyond the individual by affecting other individuals. In doing so, it also limits other individuals' right to self-fulfillment. A verbal trespass, to use a term from torts, can be just as injurious as a physical trespass. Indeed, it injures one more if he loses his job because someone falsely accused him of theft than if that person physically injures him and thus keeps him away from work for a week. Limitation of free speech becomes harmful only when it is broadly and thoughtlessly applied.

Having considered the ideal of free expression as a means to arrive at truth in the discussion of Holmes' marketplace theory, let us consider the role free expression plays in bringing people into the decision-making process. A lack of free expression will either turn people against a government or, as is more often the case, make citizens apathetic and docile in their dealings with the government. In a system where free expression is not allowed, decisions are made by the few and obeyed by the masses. Unlimited freedom of expression, however, may well result in the same situation if it allows the powerful, the unscrupulous, or the careless to defame those they oppose, shout into silence those who disagree, distort the truth to a guileless population, and make an interested citizenry cynical and jaded. Under such circumstances, unlimited debate may become the province of the few and potential debaters representing different points of view can be discouraged or intimidated from entering the decision-making process. One of the functions of the First Amendment is to protect the press, but the First Amendment must also protect the weak, the unpopular, and the isolated. The society's needs in the abstract ought not to preempt the individual's actual needs.

Freedom of expression is an agent of peaceful change. Expression is also an agent of violence. Both of these statements have a bearing on the establishment of certain limits of expression, but the allowance of libel suits is not tantamount to foreclosure of freedom of expression. The same reasons advanced to justify safeguarding individual reputations and preventing verbal mudslinging and journalistic carelessness also apply here. A person who is afraid to express himself publicly because he may be defamed or ridiculed is as much the victim of suppression as the person who avoids proposing a reform because he fears the secret police. . . .

Having raised the fair comment rule to the level of a constitutional right, and having broadened it to protect not only opinions but also facts, the Court has cut loose the fair comment privilege from libel law and allowed it to float into the rarified heights of "free communication." Disregarding the conflicts which created the need for protection against defamation, Justices Brennan, White, Black, and Douglas, and Chief Justice Warren . . . viewed libelous comments in the light of principles that were formulated by Justices Holmes and Brandeis to deal with prosecutions for seditious speech or writings. . . .

. . . Society's valuation of free speech cannot utterly disregard the needs of the sum of the individuals who make up that society. An individual's good name and reputation determine, in large part, where that individual will live, where he will work, and whether or not he will be accepted as a member in good standing in the community. . . .

The Supreme Court would not deny redress to a man against whom a newspaper arranged a boycott, nor would it consider it legal for a mob to drive a man from his home or from his town. Yet, if the same results are accomplished by the use of speech or newspapers or radio and television, they are considered privileged. This result is both unjust and unsound. There is undoubtedly a great interest and necessity for public comment about and public scrutiny of government officials and the heads of public institutions, as well as of the institutions themselves since they greatly affect the public. Likewise, certain private corporations and institutions deserve public scrutiny because they too play a great role in shaping public life. Being a public servant, however, should not mean that a man's private and public life is fair game for the vicious, the ignorant, and the self-interested. The malice test in the original *New York Times* rule recognized this and provided some limitation on the press, but this check has been all but removed. Whatever the reasons for subjecting public officials to uncontrolled abuse, there is no reason not to provide some remedy to a "public figure" since his prominence generally does not affect the public, even though he may be of public interest.

The Court speaks of the need for "breathing space" for First Amendment rights, but "breathing space," like "Lebensraum," is a limitless concept. The term "breathing space" is meaningless. If the Court fears that a deterrent effect on expression might result from either vague or Draconian laws, it is difficult to see how a clearly defined and liberally interpreted fair comment rule would have that effect on newspapers today. A much harsher rule failed to stifle comment prior to 1964.

The *New York Times* rule, it seems, is unwieldy and unsound because it results in legal overkill. The rule fails even to ask the questions: why is debate necessary, and, what kind of debate is useful? The Court confuses debate with cacophony. We live in a democracy, yet the Court has failed to ask what the needs of democratic government are and how free expression meets these needs. Is completely free expression necessary or even desirable? Does free expression conflict with and jeopardize other values? If so, what are the other values and how important are they in furthering the ideal of a democracy of individuals, for individuals, and by individuals? What harms can result from free expression? What harms can result from the allowance of civil libel suits? The Court has not answered these questions; it has apparently not even considered them. Granting that the public must be able to criticize and scrutinize those persons controlling public or quasi-public institutions which affect the public's life, who are these persons and how far ought the public scrutiny go? Is there a strong social benefit in dissecting a public official's past, his private life, or the past of his associates and family? How vital is such exposure if it is accurate, and how damaging will it be if it is reckless? The Supreme Court seems to adopt the position that exposures of public officials are positive blessings no matter how recklessly inaccurate, and stops there. What about public figures and persons who have not chosen to enter the public arena? How relevant to the public welfare is the private life of an artist? Is there a public interest in allowing critics to make broad charges about an author's life if such charges are inaccurate? How vital are such exposures to the workings of a democracy? How harmful is such publicity to the individual? These questions have been ignored. The Court has likewise failed to ask whether its goals can be accomplished within the law of libel. . . .

The law of libel is an imperfect tool designed to protect individuals. Practically, libel law offers less protection to the average person than he needs. A libel suit is a long and difficult process which revitalizes old lies and reopens old wounds and often ends with only minimal damage awards. It does, however, allow men to redress their injuries in the courts and not in the alleys or the dueling fields. The press may be restrained by the threat of a libel suit, but this restraint will only prompt more thorough investigation. Society has no interest in protecting lies or sheltering the character assassin or the printer who is grossly negligent. The question of whether or not libel law has a valid function cannot turn on the prejudices and ideals of one era but must be adapted to allow the greatest flexibility in dealing with future threats to the individual and the society. Indeed, a press that is in the vanguard of reform today may be in the last rank of reaction tomorrow.

We are living in an era in which newspapers and communications media are vast corporations which are unlikely to be snuffed out by a libel suit. News media have advanced far beyond the hand-press of Madison's day, and can obliterate a man's reputation within five minutes by telling the story in every state. Unlike the small, rural society of the nineteenth century, more people read or listen to the mass media and fewer people are acquainted with the person who is being discussed. The revolution in communications and the vast day-to-day power of the news media, which, in many cases, have a monopoly on the facts available because of time and space limitations, have created new problems in our mass society. In the decisions expanding the *New York Times* rule the Supreme Court . . . failed to recognize or to deal with these problems.

CHAPTER 10

RIGHT OF PRIVACY

The second half of the nineteenth century saw the press of America become big business. The mass appeal of Pulitzer and Hearst, the growing importance of advertising, the introduction of photojournalism, and the increasing reliance on sensationalism brought with them a new problem—the invasion of privacy. The "right to be let alone" had not been seriously challenged prior to this time.

Two Boston attorneys, Louis Brandeis (later to be appointed to the Supreme Court) and Samuel Warren, took the first significant step in recognizing this growing "invasion" by publishing in 1890 an article on the right of privacy in the Harvard Law Review. They appealed for legal remedies for what they saw as a deterioration of one of man's basic freedoms. The article received widespread comment, but the prevailing feeling at the turn of the century was that protection from unwanted and unwarranted intrusion should come from the various state legislatures rather than from the courts.

The New York Court of Appeals in 1902 rejected in a 4–3 decision the claim of a woman who sought redress for the use of her picture in the advertising and merchandising of baking flour. But in its rejection, the court suggested that action might be taken by the legislature to solve such invasions of privacy, noting that the right of privacy had "not yet found an abiding place in our jurisprudence." Roberson v. Rochester Folding Box Co. The following year the New York legislature forbade the use of a person's name or likeness for commercial purposes without consent. More than two-thirds of the states by the end of the Warren era had recognized right of privacy either through legislation or common law proceedings, though the scope of such protection varies with each jurisdiction.

Three years after the Roberson decision, a Georgia court did recognize the right of privacy by ruling in favor of a man who sought damages from an insurance company which had used his picture in its advertising. The man, in fact, did not even carry insurance from the firm in question. Pavesich v. New England Life

Insurance Co. *The California Constitution was used as a basis for a 1931 decision for a plaintiff who sought redress after her maiden name was used in advertising a motion picture, "The Red Kimono." The woman was a former prostitute who later had led a "normal" life. The picture was advertised as a "true story" taken from accounts of the trial. The court ruled that it was the use of the woman's name in the advertising that invaded her privacy, not the facts of the story, which were taken from public court records.* Melvin v. Reid.

By the early 1940s the question concerned newsworthy figures. The courts have generally held that when a person thrusts himself—or is thrust—into the public eye he gives up much of his right of privacy. A former child prodigy who was graduated from Harvard at 16 had been featured in a New Yorker *article as not fulfilling his earlier promise and living in shabby surroundings. His suit was dismissed as the court ruled that the account was substantially true and that the public had a legitimate interest in the later life of a prodigy. Certiorari was denied by the Supreme Court.* Sidis v. F-R Publishing Co. *There are, however, limits as to the extent of the public's right to know even when the story might be of great reader interest. A woman who had an insatiable appetite was photographed without her consent in a hospital bed. The picture was used in* Time *magazine accompanied by a caption entitled "Starving Glutton" and an article on the unusual medical problem. The court held for the woman.* Barber v. Time, Inc.

Accidental reference to a private person was judged not to excuse an invasion of privacy in a 1942 decision in California. Hal Roach Studios, in publicizing a coming motion picture, sent through the mails 1,000 copies of a "suggestive" letter handwritten on pink stationery. The "letter" was signed "Marion Kerby." A real Marion Kerby sued for invasion of privacy and won. Innocent mistake, the court ruled, was no excuse. Kerby v. Hal Roach Studios.

The question of a "fictionalized" account of a person's biography was raised by baseball pitcher Warren Spahn in 1966. He sought and won an injunction and damages against an unauthorized publication of his life. The court found in the story a great many "factual errors, distortions and fanciful passages" and that, as such, it was proscribed by New York law dealing with right of privacy. The Court of Appeals drew a line between his actions as a public figure and the alleged "fictionalized" accounts of his private life used in a commercial venture. Spahn v. Julian Messner, Inc.

The California Supreme Court in 1971 ruled unanimously that a rehabilitated felon has the right to sue for invasion of privacy if a publication exposes his criminal record "years after the crime." He has a right to be let alone, the Court said, once he again enters the anonymity of the community and has not acted to reattract public attention. Briscoe v. Reader's Digest.

The Supreme Court actively entered the debate over right of privacy with a decision involving a $30,000 judgment against Time, Inc. In the decision the Court held that the First Amendment shields the press from invasion of privacy suits involving the public lives of newsworthy persons unless there is proof of malice, deliberate falsehood, or "reckless disregard of the truth." This philosophy had been *applied earlier to libel actions by the Court in the 1964 New York Times case. In the present suit, James J. Hill had instituted legal action after Life had published a feature article based upon the play "The Desperate Hours," which, in turn, was based upon Hill's experience as a 1952 kidnap victim. He charged serious falsehood and commercial use of his name and story. The Supreme Court decision places the burden of proof upon the citizen if he is a newsworthy figure and sues on the basis of misstatement of fact.*

TIME, INC. V. HILL
385 U.S. 374 (1967)

JUSTICE BRENNAN *delivered the opinion of the Court.*

The question in this case is whether appellant, publisher of *Life Magazine*, was denied constitutional protections for speech and press by the application by the New York courts of sec. 50–51 of the New York Civil Rights Law to award appellee damages on allegations that *Life* falsely reported that a new play portrayed an experience suffered by appellee and his family.

The article appeared in *Life* in February 1955. It was entitled "True Crime Inspires Tense Play," with the subtitle, "The ordeal of a family trapped by convicts gives Broadway a new thriller, 'The Desperate Hours.' " The text of the article reads as follows:

> Three years ago Americans all over the country read about the desperate ordeal of the James Hill family, who were held prisoners in their home outside Philadelphia by three escaped convicts. Later they read about it in Joseph Hayes' novel, *The Desperate Hours*, inspired by the family's experience. Now they can see the story re-enacted in Hayes' Broadway play based on the book, and next year will see it in his movie, which has been filmed but is being held up until the play has a chance to pay off.
>
> The play, directed by Robert Montgomery and expertly acted, is a heart-stopping account of how a family rose to heroism in a crisis. *Life* photographed the play during its Philadelphia tryout, transported some of the actors to the actual house where the Hills were besieged. On the next page scenes from the play are re-enacted on the site of the crime.

The pictures on the ensuing two pages included an enactment of the son being "roughed up" by one of the convicts, entitled "brutish convict," a picture of the daughter biting the hand of a convict to make him drop a gun, entitled "daring daughter," and one of the father throwing his gun through the door after a "brave try" to save his family is foiled.

The James Hill referred to in the article is the appellee. He and his wife and five children involuntarily became a front-page news story after being held hostage by three escaped convicts in their suburban, Whitemarsh, Pennsylvania, home for

19 hours on September 11–12, 1952. The family was released unharmed. In an interview with newsmen after the convicts departed, appellee stressed that the convicts had treated the family courteously, had not molested them, and had not been at all violent. The convicts were thereafter apprehended in a widely publicized encounter with the police which resulted in the killing of two of the convicts. Shortly thereafter the family moved to Connecticut. The appellee discouraged all efforts to keep them in the public spotlight through magazine articles or appearances on television.

In the spring of 1953, Joseph Hayes' novel, *The Desperate Hours*, was published. The story depicted the experience of a family of four held hostage by three escaped convicts in the family's suburban home. But unlike Hill's experience, the family of the story suffer violence at the hands of the convicts; the father and son are beaten and the daughter subjected to a verbal sexual insult.

The book was made into a play, also entitled "The Desperate Hours," and it is *Life's* article about the play which is the subject of appellee's action. The complaint sought damages under sec. 50–51 on allegations that the *Life* article was intended to, and did, give the impression that the play mirrored the Hill family's experience, which, to the knowledge of defendant, ". . . was false and untrue." Appellant's defense was that the subject of the article was "a subject of legitimate news interest," "a subject of general interest and of value and concern to the public" at the time of publication, and that it was "published in good faith without any malice whatsoever. . . ." A motion to dismiss the complaint for substantially these reasons was made at the close of the case and was denied by the trial judge on the ground that the proofs presented a jury question as to the truth of the article.

The jury awarded appellee $50,000 compensatory and $25,000 punitive damages. On appeal the Appellate Division of the Supreme Court ordered a new trial as to damages but sustained the jury verdict of liability. The court said as to liability:

> "Although the play was fictionalized, *Life's* article portrayed it as a reenactment of the Hills' experience. It is an inescapable conclusion that this was done to advertise and attract further attention to the play, and to increase present and future magazine circulations as well. It is evident that the article cannot be characterized as a mere dissemination of news, nor even an effort to supply legitimate newsworthy information in which the public had, or might have a proper interest."

At the trial on damages, a jury was waived and the court awarded $30,000 compensatory damages without punitive damages. . . .

The guarantees for speech and press are not the preserve of political expression or comment upon public affairs, essential as those are to healthy government. One need only pick up any newspaper or magazine to comprehend the vast range of published matter which exposes persons to public view, both private citizens and public officials. Exposure of the self to others in varying degrees is a concomitant of life in a civilized community. The risk of this exposure is an essential incident of life in a society which places a primary value on freedom of speech and of press. "Freedom of discussion, if it would fulfill its historic function in this nation, must embrace all issues about which information is needed or appropriate to enable the members of society to cope with the exigencies of their period." *Thornhill v. Alabama.* "No suggestion can be found in the Constitution that the freedom there guaranteed for speech and the press bears an inverse ratio to the timeliness and importance of the ideas seeking expression." *Bridges v. California.* We have no doubt that the subject of the *Life* article, the opening of a new play linked to an actual incident, is a matter of public interest. "The line between the informing and entertaining is too elusive for the protection of . . . [freedom of the press]. *Winters v. New York.* Erroneous statement is no less inevitable in such case than in the case of comment upon public affairs, and in both, if innocent or merely negligent, ". . . it must be protected if the freedoms of expression are to have the 'breathing space' that they 'need to survive.' . . ." *New York Times Co. v. Sullivan.* As James Madison said, "Some degree of abuse is inseparable from the proper use of everything and in no instance is this more true than of the press." We create grave risk of serious impairment of the indispensable service of a free press in a free society if we saddle the press with the impossible burden of verifying to a certainty the facts associated in news articles with a person's name, picture or portrait, particularly as related to nondefamatory matter. Even negligence would be a most elusive standard, especially when the content of the speech itself affords no warning of prospective harm to another through falsity. A negligence test would place on the press the intolerable burden of guessing how a jury might assess the reasonableness of steps taken by it to verify the accuracy of every reference to a name, picture or portrait. . . .

We find applicable here the standard of knowing or reckless falsehood not through blind application of *New York Times Co. v. Sullivan,* relating solely to libel actions by public officials, but only upon consideration of the factors which arise in the particular context of the application of the New York statute in cases involving private individuals. This is neither a libel action by a private individual nor a statutory action by a public official. Therefore, although the First Amendment principles pronounced in *New York Times* guide our conclusion, we reach that conclusion only by applying these principles in this discrete context. . . .

The requirement that the jury . . . find that the article was published "for trade purposes," as defined in the charge, cannot save the charge from constitutional infirmity. "That books, newspapers and magazines are published and sold for profit does not prevent them from being a form of expression whose liberty is safeguarded by the First Amendment." *Joseph Burstyn, Inc. v. Wilson.*

The judgment of the Court of Appeals is set aside and the case is remanded for further proceedings not inconsistent with this opinion.

JUSTICE BLACK, *with whom Justice Douglas joins, concurring.*

I concur in reversal of the judgment in this case based on the grounds and reasons stated in the Court's opinion. I do this, however, in order for the Court to be able at this time to agree on an opinion in this important case based on the prevailing constitutional doctrine expressed in *New York Times v. Sullivan.* The Court's opinion decides the case in accordance with this doctrine, to which the majority adhere. In agreeing to the Court's opinion, I do not recede from any of the views I have previously expressed about the much wider press and speech freedoms I think the First and Fourteenth Amendments were designed to grant to the people of the Nation. . . .

I think it not inappropriate to add that it would be difficult, if not impossible, for the Court ever to sustain a judgment against *Time* in this case without using the recently popularized weighing and balancing formula. Some of us have pointed out from time to time that the First Amendment freedoms could not possibly live with the adoption of that Constitution ignoring and destroying technique, when there are, as here, palpable penalties imposed on speech or press specifically because of the views that are spoken or printed. The prohibitions of the Constitution were written to prohibit certain specific things, and one of the specific things prohibited is a law which abridges freedom of the press. That freedom was written into the Constitution and that Constitution is or should be binding on judges as well as other officers. The "weighing" doctrine plainly encourages and actually invites judges to choose for themselves between conflicting values, even where, as in the First Amendment, the Founders made a choice of values, one of which is a free press. . . .

JUSTICE FORTAS, *with whom the Chief Justice and Justice Clark join, dissenting.*

The Court's holding here is exceedingly narrow. It declines to hold that the New York "Right of Privacy" statute is unconstitutional. I agree. The Court concludes, however, that the instructions to the jury in this case were fatally defective because they failed to advise the jury that a verdict for the plaintiff could be predicated only on a finding of knowing or reckless falsity in the publication of the *Life* article. Presumably, the plaintiff is entitled to a new trial. If he can stand the emotional and financial burden, there is reason to hope that he will recover damages for the reckless and irresponsible assault upon himself and his family which this article represents. But he has litigated this case for 11 years. He should not be subjected to the burden of a new trial without significant cause. . . .

The Court today does not repeat the ringing words of so many of its members on so many occasions in exaltation of the right of privacy. Instead, it reverses a decision under the New York "Right of Privacy" statute because of the "failure of the trial judge to instruct the jury that a verdict of liability could be predicated only on a finding of knowing or reckless falsity in the publication of the *Life* article." In my opinion, the jury instructions, although they were not a textbook model, satisfied this standard. . . .

The courts may not and must not permit either public or private action that censors or inhibits the press. But part of this responsibility is to preserve values and procedures which assure the ordinary citizen that the press is not above the reach of the law—that its special prerogatives, granted because of its special and vital functions, are reasonably equated with its needs in the performance of these functions. For this Court totally to immunize the press—whether forthrightly or by the subtle indirection—in areas far beyond the needs of news, comment on public persons and events, discussion of public issues and the like would be no service to freedom of the press, but an invitation to public hostility to that freedom. This Court cannot and should not refuse to permit under state law the private citizen who is aggrieved by the type of assault which we have here and which is not within the specially protected core of the First Amendment to recover compensatory damages for recklessly inflicted invasions of his rights. . . .

*   *   *

If Time, Inc. v. Hill *muddied the legal waters of privacy, as many believe, the silt began to settle by the middle 1970s, and what was becoming visible should be of some concern to the media. Two important decisions handed down in the 1974–75 term dealt with questions of invasion of privacy by major news media, the* Cleveland Plain Dealer *in one case and* Cox Broadcasting and WSB-TV *of Atlanta, covered in Chapter 2, in the other. The* Plain Dealer *decision,* Cantrell v. Forest City Publishing Co., *was the first invasion of privacy decision against a newspaper to be sustained by the Supreme Court. It sustained a jury finding that the paper had held Mrs. Margaret Mae Cantrell and her son in a "false light" through publication of a news feature in its* Sunday Magazine. *"False light" is one of four principles of privacy enunciated by William C. Prosser, who argued that the law of privacy should not be considered a single law, but rather is made up of four separable concepts. In addition to the "false light" theory, Prosser listed intrusion upon a person's solitude, disclosure of embarrassing private information which violates common decency, and the use of one's name or likeness for commercial gain. Of particular interest in the* Cantrell *decision is the one-sided vote, 8–1. The single dissent was by Justice Douglas, who renewed his appeal for an "absolute" interpretation of the First Amendment. This decision, coupled with earlier recent decisions in libel, obscenity, and access cases, indicate a growing interest by the Court in this relatively new area of law. It should encourage greater care by the media when publishing items about private persons, just as the* Gertz *decision did relative to libel. Also, it might be noted here that the line between libel and privacy appears to be becoming less distinct. For example, a similarity can be found between* Cantrell *and* Curtis v. Butts, *in which the Court also dealt with what it considered to be a violation of "professional publishing standards." (See Chapter 9.) Prosser's "intrusion" theory also has been given authenticity by the Court. In* Lehman v. The City of Shaker Heights, *the Supreme Court ruled that the city was not required to sell political advertising space on public transportation vehicles because of, among other things, possible intrusion upon unwilling patrons who must use the transit lines.* Rowan v. Post Office, *while dealing with obscene matter, also focused on the intrusion idea. And* Stanley v. Georgia *is now considered to be more important to privacy law than to obscenity. The Court also has been moving to protect one's privacy from unwanted and unwarranted intrusion in non-media cases, for example in* United States v. U.S. District Court, *in which a unanimous Court in 1972 rejected the Justice Department's right to engage in domestic wire tapping at will, and the 1973 Roe v.* Wade *decision, setting down complex privacy and abortion guidelines. All of these, then, touch upon the increasingly sensitive area of privacy of the individual and the Court's eagerness to protect that privacy. An exception might be* Cox Broadcasting Corp. v. Cohn, *which involved privacy and matters on the public record. (See Chapter 2.) The* Cantrell *decision, which follows, has particular interest not only to the major media, but also to freelance writers and the so-called alternative or advocacy journals.*

CANTRELL V. FOREST CITY PUBLISHING CO.
419 U.S. 245 (1974)

JUSTICE STEWART *delivered the opinion of the Court.*

Margaret Cantrell and four of her minor children brought this diversity action in a federal district court for invasion of privacy against the Forest City Publishing Company, publisher of a Cleveland newspaper, *The Plain Dealer,* and against Joseph Eszterhas, a reporter formerly employed by *The Plain Dealer,* and Richard Conway, a *Plain Dealer* photographer. The Cantrells alleged that an article published in *The Plain Dealer Sunday Magazine* unreasonably placed their family in a false light before the public through its many inaccuracies and untruths. The District Judge struck the claims relating to punitive damages as to all the plaintiffs and dismissed the actions of three of the Cantrell children in their entirety, but allowed the case to go to the jury as to Mrs. Cantrell and her oldest son, William. The jury returned a verdict against all three of the respondents for compensatory money damages in favor of these two plaintiffs.

The Court of Appeals for the Sixth Circuit reversed, holding that, in the light of the First and Fourteenth Amendments, the District Judge should have granted the respondents' motion for a directed verdict as to all the Cantrells.

In December 1967, Margaret Cantrell's husband Melvin was killed along with 43 other people when the Silver Bridge across the Ohio River at Point Pleasant, West Virginia, collapsed. The respondent Eszterhas was assigned by *The Plain Dealer* to cover the story of the disaster. He wrote a "news feature" story focusing on the funeral of Melvin Cantrell and the impact of his death on the Cantrell family.

Five months later, after conferring with the *Sunday Magazine* editor of *The Plain Dealer,* Eszterhas and photographer Conway returned to the Point Pleasant area to write a follow-up feature. The two men went to the Cantrell residence, where Eszterhas talked with the children and Conway took 50 pictures. Mrs. Cantrell was not at home at any time during the 60 to 90 minutes that the men were at the Cantrell residence.

Eszterhas' story appeared as the lead feature in the August 4, 1968, edition of *The Plain Dealer Sunday Magazine*. The article stressed the family's abject poverty; the children's old, ill-fitting clothes and the deteriorating conditions of their home were detailed in both the text and accompanying photographs. As he had done in his original, prize-winning article on the Silver Bridge disaster, Eszterhas used the Cantrell family to illustrate the impact of the bridge collapse on the lives of the people in the Point Pleasant area.

It is conceded that the story contained a number of inaccuracies and false statements. Most conspicuously, although Mrs. Cantrell was not present at any time during the reporter's visit to her home, Eszterhas wrote, "Margaret Cantrell will talk neither about what happened nor about how they are doing. She wears the same mask of non-expression she wore at the funeral. She is a proud woman. She says that after it happened, the people in town offered to help them out with money and they refused to take it." Other significant misrepresentations were contained in details of Eszterhas' descriptions of the poverty in which the Cantrells were living and the dirty and dilapidated conditions of the Cantrell home.

The case went to the jury on a so-called "false light" theory of invasion of privacy. In essence, the theory of the case was that by publishing the false feature story about the Cantrells and thereby making them objects of pity and ridicule, the respondents damaged Mrs. Cantrell and her son William by causing them to suffer outrage, mental distress, shame, and humiliation. . . .

. . . [T]he sole question that we need decide is whether the Court of Appeals erred in setting aside the jury's verdict. . . .

The Court of Appeals appears to have assumed that the District Judge's finding of no malice "within the legal definition of that term" was a finding based on the definition of "actual malice" established by this Court in *New York Times Co. v. Sullivan* "with knowledge that [a defamatory statement] was false or with reckless disregard of whether it was false or not." As so defined, of course, "actual malice" is a term of art, created to provide a convenient shorthand for the standard of liability that must be established before a State may constitutionally permit public officials to recover for libel in actions brought against publishers. As such, it is quite different from the common-law standard of "malice" generally required under state tort law to support an award of punitive damages. In a false-light case, common-law malice—frequently expressed in terms of either personal ill will toward the plaintiff or reckless or wanton disregard of the plaintiff's rights—would focus on the defendant's attitude toward the plaintiff's privacy, not towards the truth or falsity of the material published. See *Time, Inc. v. Hill*. See generally W. Prosser, *Law of Torts* 9–10 (4th ed.).

Although the verbal record of the District Court proceedings is not entirely unambiguous, the conclusion is inescapable that the District Judge was referring to the common-law standard of malice rather than to the *New York Times* "actual malice" standard when he dismissed the punitive damages claims. . . .

Moreover, the District Judge was clearly correct in believing that the evidence introduced at trial was sufficient to support a jury finding that the respondents

Joseph Eszterhas and Forest City Publishing Company had published knowing or reckless falsehoods about the Cantrells. There was no dispute during the trial that Eszterhas, who did not testify, must have known that a number of the statements in the feature story were untrue. In particular, his article plainly implied that Mrs. Cantrell had been present during his visit to her home and that Eszterhas had observed her "wear[ing] the same mask of non-expression she wore [at her husband's] funeral." These were "calculated falsehoods," and the jury was plainly justified in finding that Eszterhas had portrayed the Cantrells in a false light through knowing or reckless untruth.

The Court of Appeals concluded that there was no evidence that Forest City Publishing Company had knowledge of any of the inaccuracies contained in Eszterhas' article. However, there was sufficient evidence for the jury to find that Eszterhas' writing of the feature was within the scope of his employment at *The Plain Dealer* and that Forest City Publishing Company was therefore liable under traditional doctrines of *respondeat superior.* Although Eszterhas was not regularly assigned by *The Plain Dealer* to write for the *Sunday Magazine,* the editor of the magazine testified that as a staff writer for *The Plain Dealer* Eszterhas frequently suggested stories he would like to write for the magazine. When Eszterhas suggested the follow-up article on the Silver Bridge disaster, the editor approved the idea and told Eszterhas the magazine would publish the feature if it was good. From this evidence, the jury could reasonably conclude that Forest City Publishing Company, publisher of *The Plain Dealer,* should be held vicariously liable for the damage caused by the knowing falsehoods contained in Eszterhas' story.

For the foregoing reasons, the judgment of the Court of Appeals is reversed and the case is remanded to that court with directions to enter a judgment affirming the judgment of the District Court as to the respondents Forest City Publishing Company and Joseph Eszterhas.

It is so ordered.

JUSTICE DOUGLAS, *dissenting.*

I adhere to the views which I expressed in *Time, Inc. v. Hill* and to those of Justice Black in which I concurred, *id.* Freedom of the press is "abridged" in violation of the First and Fourteenth Amendments by what we do today. This line of cases, which of course includes *New York Times Co. v. Sullivan,* seems to me to place First Amendment rights of the press at a midway point similar to what our ill-fated *Betts v. Brady* did to the right to counsel. The press will be "free" in the First Amendment sense when the judge-made qualifications of that freedom are withdrawn and the substance of the First Amendment restored to what I believe was the purpose of its enactment.

An accident with a bridge catapulted the Cantrells into the public eye and their disaster became newsworthy. To make the First Amendment freedom to report the news turn on subtle differences between common-law malice and actual malice is to stand the Amendment on its head. Those who write the current news seldom have the objective, dispassionate point of view—or the time—of scientific analysts. They deal in fast moving events and the need for "spot" reporting. The jury under today's formula sits as a censor with broad powers—not to impose a prior restraint but to lay heavy damages on the press. The press is "free" only if the jury is sufficiently disenchanted with the Cantrells to let the press be free of this damage claim. That regime is thought by some to be a way of supervising the press which is better than not supervising it at all. But the installation of the Court's regime would require a constitutional amendment. Whatever might be the ultimate reach of the doctrine Justice Black and I have embraced, it seems clear that in matters of public import such as the present news reporting, there must be freedom from damages lest the press be frightened into playing a more ignoble role than the Framers visualized.

I would affirm the judgment of the Court of Appeals.

*　　*　　*

The question of maintaining a right of publicity came before the Supreme Court in an interesting case involving the "Human Cannonball," Hugo Zacchini. Zacchini v. Scripps-Howard Broadcasting. A Cleveland television crew had filmed the carnival performer's entire 15-second ride through the air after his ejection from a cannon. The episode was shown on the evening news. The Ohio court said that any right to protect his performance must bow to the newsworthiness of the event and the First Amendment rights of the press. The Supreme Court, however, reversed 5–4. It is important to note that the fact that the film was shown on a news program did not protect the station from possible damages. None of the traditional privacy tests— appropriation, intrusion, private facts or false light—seemed to apply in this case. Indeed, several conditions made this a unique case. First, Zacchini's entire performance was shown, not mere excerpts, as one might expect in normal news coverage. Second, Zacchini had asked the film crew not to shoot the act, but the request was disregarded. Third, the showing of the entire act lessened Zacchini's chances of making a livelihood since it would be unlikely that people would pay admission to see his 15-second act if they could see it free at home. Fourth, Zacchini, on the other hand, was in a business which depended upon publicity and recognition. Finally, there was no specific monetary gain by the station in running the performance. The decision adds a new dimension—and further confusion—to the emerging muddle of one's right of privacy. Still, it is clear that the Burger Court was concerned with media invasion of privacy, an important fact to keep in mind, especially when tempted by the new technology, such as fast film, miniaturization and electronic news gathering, which allow greater access to formerly inaccessible or private situations.

ZACCHINI V. SCRIPPS-HOWARD
BROADCASTING CO.
433 U.S. 562 (1977)

JUSTICE WHITE *delivered the opinion of the Court.*

Petitioner, Hugo Zacchini, is an entertainer. He performs a "human cannon-ball" act in which he is shot from a cannon into a net some 200 feet away. Each performance occupies some 15 seconds. In August and September, 1972, petitioner was engaged to perform his act on a regular basis at the Geauga County Fair in Burton, Ohio. He performed in a fenced area, surrounded by grandstands, at the fairgrounds. Members of the public attending the fair were not charged a separate admission fee to observe his act.

On August 30, a freelance reporter for Scripps-Howard Broadcasting Company, the operator of a television broadcasting station and respondent in this case, attended the fair. He carried a small movie camera. Petitioner noticed the reporter and asked him not to film the performance. The reporter did not do so on that day; but on the instructions of the producer of respondent's daily newscast, he returned the following day and videotaped the entire act. This film clip, approximately 15 seconds in length, was shown on the 11 o'clock news program that night, together with favorable commentary.

Petitioner then brought this action for damages, alleging that he is "engaged in the entertainment business," that the act he performs is one "invented by his father and . . . performed only by his family for the last fifty years," that respondent "showed and commercialized the film of his act without his consent," and that such conduct was an "unlawful appropriation of plaintiff's professional property." . . .

We granted certiorari to consider an issue unresolved by this Court: whether the First and Fourteenth Amendments immunized respondent from damages for its alleged infringement of petitioner's state law "right of publicity." . . .

The differences between [*Time, Inc. v. Hill* and this case] are important. First, the State's interests in providing a cause of action in each instance are different. "The interest protected" in permitting recovery for placing the plaintiff in a false light "is clearly that of reputation, with the same overtones of mental distress as in defamation." Prosser. By contrast, the State's interest in permitting a "right of publicity" is in protecting the proprietary interest of the individual in his act in part to encourage such entertainment. As we later note, the State's interest is closely analogous to the goals of patent and copyright law, focusing on the right of the individual to reap the reward of his endeavors and having little to do with protecting feelings or reputation. Second, the two torts differ in the degree to which they intrude on dissemination of information to the public. In "false light" cases the only way to protect the interests involved is to attempt to minimize publication of the damaging matter, while in "right of publicity" cases the only question is who gets to do the publishing. An entertainer such as petitioner usually has no objection to the widespread publication of his act as long as he gets the commercial benefit of such publication. Indeed, in the present case petitioner did not seek to enjoin the broadcast of his act; he simply sought compensation for the broadcast in the form of damages. . . .

Moreover, *Time, Inc. v. Hill, New York Times, Metromedia, Gertz,* and *Firestone* all involved the reporting of events; in none of them was there an attempt to broadcast or publish an entire act for which the performer ordinarily gets paid. It is evident, and there is no claim here to the contrary, that petitioner's state-law right of publicity would not serve to prevent respondent from reporting the newsworthy facts about petitioner's act. Wherever the line in particular situations is to be drawn between media reports that are protected and those that are not, we are quite sure that the First and Fourteenth Amendments do not immunize the media when they broadcast a performer's entire act without his consent. The Constitution no more prevents a State from requiring respondent to compensate petitioner for broadcasting his act on television than it would privilege respondent to film and broadcast a copyrighted dramatic work without liability to the copyright owner. . . .

The broadcast of a film of petitioner's entire act poses a substantial threat to the economic value of that performance. As the Ohio court recognized, this act is the product of petitioner's own talents and energy, the end result of much time, effort and expense. Much of its economic value lies in the "right of exclusive control over the publicity given to his performance"; if the public can see the act for free on television, they will be less willing to pay to see it at the fair. The effect of a public broadcast of the performance is similar to preventing petitioner from charging an admission fee. "The rationale for [protecting the right of publicity] is the straightforward one of preventing unjust enrichment by the theft of good will. No social purpose is served by having the defendant get for free some aspect of the plaintiff that would have market value and for which he would normally pay." Kalven, Privacy in Tort Law—Were Warren and Brandeis Wrong? Moreover, the broadcast of petitioner's entire performance, unlike the unauthorized use of another's name for purposes of trade or the incidental use of a name or picture by the press, goes to the heart of petitioner's ability to earn a living as an entertainer. Thus in this case, Ohio has recognized what may be the strongest case for a "right of publicity"— involving not the appropriation of an entertainer's reputation to enhance the attractiveness of a commercial product, but the appropriation of the very activity by which the entertainer acquired his reputation in the first place. . . .

There is no doubt that entertainment, as well as news, enjoys First Amendment protection. It is also true that entertainment itself can be important news. *Time, Inc. v. Hill.* But it is important to note that neither the public nor respondent will be deprived of the benefit of petitioner's performance as long as his commercial stake in his act is appropriately recognized. Petitioner does not seek to enjoin the broadcast of his performance; he simply wants to be paid for it. Nor do we think that a state-law damages remedy against respondent would represent a species of liability without fault contrary to the letter or spirit of *Gertz*. Respondent knew exactly that petitioner objected to televising his act, but nevertheless displayed the entire film.

JUSTICE POWELL, *with whom Justice Brennan and Justice Marshall join, dissenting.*

. . . The Court's holding that the station's ordinary news report may give rise to substantial liability has disturbing implications, for the decision could lead to a degree of media self-censorship. Hereafter, whenever a television news editor is unsure whether certain film footage received from a camera crew might be held to portray an "entire act," he may decline coverage—even of clearly newsworthy events—or confine the broadcast to watered-down verbal reporting, perhaps with an occasional still picture. The public is then the loser. This is hardly the kind of news reportage that the First Amendment is meant to foster.

In my view the First Amendment commands a different analytical starting point from the one selected by the Court. Rather than begin with a quantitative analysis of the performer's behavior—is this or is this not his entire act?—we should direct initial attention to the actions of the news media: what use did the station make of the film footage? When a film is used, as here, for a routine portion of a regular news program, I would hold that the First Amendment protects the station from a "right of publicity" or "appropriation" suit, absent a strong showing by the plaintiff that the news broadcast was a subterfuge or cover for private or commercial exploitation. . . .

Since the film clip here was undeniably treated as news and since there is no claim that the use was subterfuge, respondent's actions were constitutionally privileged. I would affirm.

*　　*　　*

The Court in June of 1989 returned to the question of publishing private or embarrassing facts, which it had debated in the Cox *and* Daily Mail *decisions a decade earlier. The* Cox *case dealt with publishing the name of a rape victim obtained in open court. The question in 1989 also dealt with a state law that prohibited publishing names of victims of a sexual attack, but this time the identification was obtained inadvertently from the Sheriff's Department rather than from open court.* Florida Star v. B.J.F. *A Florida jury awarded the plaintiff, B.J.F., $100,000 for invasion of privacy based on the Florida law. The reporter-trainee submitted the news item, which ran inadvertently in the small weekly publication, despite the paper's policy against publishing such names. The reporter obtained the victim's name from copies of the crime report placed in the Sheriff Department's press room. The victim sued both the paper and the Sheriff's Department, which settled out of court. A state Court of Appeal upheld the jury's finding, but the United States Supreme Court reversed in a 6-3 decision.*

Justice Marshall, in his opinion of the court, did not go as far as many in the media would have preferred, i.e. to see a court ruling that would constitutionally protect any publication of truthful information obtained legally. Justice Marshall emphasized that there could be times when the publication of truthful information might result in penalties against the press, but plaintiffs in such cases would be required to show that such sanctions were "overwhelming necessary." This was not one of those times.

FLORIDA STAR V. B.J.F.
109 S. Ct. 2603 (1989)

JUSTICE MARSHALL *delivered the opinion of the Court.*

Florida [law] makes it unlawful to "print, publish, or broadcast . . . in any instrument of mass communication" the name of the victim of a sexual offense. Pursuant to this statute, appellant *The Florida Star* was found civilly liable for publishing the name of a rape victim which it had obtained from a publicly released police report. The issue presented here is whether this result comports with the First Amendment. We hold that it does not. . . .

The tension between the right which the First Amendment accords to a free press, on the one hand, and the protections which various statutes and common-law doctrines accord to personal privacy against the publication of truthful information, on the other, is a subject we have addressed several times in recent years. Our decisions in cases involving government attempts to sanction the accurate dissemination of information as invasive of privacy, have not, however, exhaustively considered this conflict. On the contrary, although our decisions have without exception upheld the press' right to publish, we have emphasized each time that we were resolving this conflict only as it arose in a discrete factual context. . . .

We conclude that imposing damages on appellant for publishing B.J.F.'s name violates the First Amendment, although not for either of the reasons appellant urges. . . .

Applied to the instant case, the *Daily Mail* principle clearly commands reversal. The first inquiry is whether the newspaper "lawfully obtain[ed] truthful information about a matter of public significance." It is undisputed that the news article describing the assault on B.J.F. was accurate. In addition, appellant lawfully obtained B.J.F.'s name. Appellee's argument to the contrary is based on the fact that under Florida law, police reports which reveal the identity of the victim of a sexual offense are not among the matters of "public record" which the public, by law, is entitled to inspect. But the fact that state officials are not required to disclose such reports does not make it unlawful for a newspaper to receive them when furnished by the government. . . .

At a time in which we are daily reminded of the tragic reality of rape, it is undeniable that these are highly significant interests, a fact underscored by the Florida Legislature's explicit attempt to protect these interests by enacting a criminal statute prohibiting much dissemination of victim identities. We accordingly do not rule out the possibility that, in a proper case, imposing civil sanctions for publication of the name of a rape victim might be so overwhelmingly necessary to advance these interests as to satisfy the *Daily Mail* standard. . . .

. . . B.J.F.'s identity would never have come to light were it not for the erroneous, if inadvertent, inclusion by the department of her full name in an incident report made available in a press room open to the public. Florida's policy against disclosure of rape victims' identities . . . was undercut by the Department's failure to abide by this policy. Where, as here, the government has failed to police itself in disseminating information, it is clear under *Cox Broadcasting, Oklahoma Publishing*, and *Landmark Communications* that the imposition of damages against the press for its subsequent publication can hardly be said to be a narrowly tailored means of safeguarding anonymity. Once the government has placed such information in the public domain, "reliance must rest upon the judgment of those who decide what to publish or broadcast," *Cox Broadcasting*, and hopes for restitution must rest upon the willingness of the government to compensate victims for their loss of privacy, and to protect them from the other consequences of its mishandling of the information which these victims provided in confidence.

That appellant gained access to the information in question through a government news release makes it especially likely that, if liability were to be imposed, self-censorship would result. Reliance on a news release is a paradigmatically "routine newspaper reporting techniqu[e]." *Daily Mail*. The government's issuance of such a release, without qualification, can only convey to recipients that the government considered dissemination lawful, and indeed expected the recipients to disseminate the information further. Had appellant merely reproduced the news release prepared and released by the Department, imposing civil damages would surely violate the First Amendment. The fact that appellant converted the police report into a news story by adding the linguistic connecting tissue necessary to transform the report's facts into full sentences cannot change this result.

Our holding today is limited. We do not hold that truthful publication is automatically constitutionally protected, or that there is no zone of personal privacy within which the State may protect the individual from intrusion by the press, or even that a State may never punish publication of the name of a victim of a sexual offense. We hold only that where a newspaper publishes truthful information which it has lawfully obtained, punishment may lawfully be imposed, if at all, only when narrowly tailored to a state interest of the highest order, and that no such interest is satisfactorily served by imposing liability . . . to appellant under the facts of this case. . . .

JUSTICE WHITE, *with whom the Chief Justice and Justice O'Connor join, dissenting.*

"Short of homicide, [rape] is the 'ultimate violation of self.' " *Coker v. Georgia.* For B.J.F., however, the violation she suffered at a rapist's knife point marked only the beginning of her ordeal. A week later, while her assailant was still at large, an account of this assault—identifying by name B.J.F. as the victim—was published by *The Florida Star.* As a result, B.J.F. received harassing phone calls, required mental health counseling, was forced to move from her home, and was even threatened with being raped again. Yet today, the court holds that a jury award of $75,000 to compensate B.J.F. for the harm she suffered due to the *Star's* negligence is at odds with the First Amendment. I do not accept this result.

At issue in this case is whether there is any information about people, which—though true—may not be published in the press. By holding that only "a state interest of the highest order" permits the State to penalize the publication of truthful information, and by holding that protecting a rape victim's right to privacy is not among those state interests of the highest order, the Court accepts appellant's invitation to obliterate one of the most noteworthy legal inventions of the 20th century: the tort of the publication of private facts. Even if the Court's opinion does not say as much today, such obliteration will follow inevitably from the Court's conclusion here. If the First Amendment prohibits wholly private persons (such as B.J.F.) from recovering for the publication of the fact that she was raped, I doubt that there remain any "private facts" which persons may assume will not be published in the newspapers, or broadcast on television. . . .

PRIVACY: THE RIGHT THAT FAILED

By Donald L. Smith*

In a sense, the right of privacy is like Miniver Cheevy, who "wept that he was ever born, and he had his reasons." It seemed like a good idea at the time it was introduced into tort law, a concept filled with great promise for soothing abrasions caused by friction between the sensibilities of many citizens and the probings of a press becoming more pervasive through industrialization. But its development has been so uneven and its performance so unsatisfactory that, if torts had tear ducts, it might weep that it was ever born.

The right, as is well known, grew out of an article by Samuel D. Warren and Louis D. Brandeis published in the *Harvard Law Review* in 1890. Writing as an era of yellow journalism dawned, they wanted the law to afford relief to people who were victims of unwanted or embarrassing publicity. The influence of the article has been enormous. It is "the outstanding example of the influence of legal periodicals upon the American law," according to William L. Prosser, and it did "nothing less than add a chapter to our law," according to Roscoe Pound.

Some experts wish that that chapter had never been written. Others, disagreeing as to just what privacy involves, wish that it had turned out better. Still others, believing that it was basically well executed, wish that the United States Supreme Court had not recently found a new meaning in its pages.

Among those who think tort law could do without a right of privacy are Frederick Davis and Harry Kalven, Jr., both professors of law. Davis has complained that "one can logically argue that the concept of a right to privacy was never required in the first place." And Kalven, although he says "privacy is for me a great and important value," has called it "a mistake" and a "petty" tort.

Some other commentators have trouble agreeing on just what the right encompasses. The leading modern article on privacy, by Prosser, appeared in the August, 1960, issue of the *California Law Review*. After surveying a slew of privacy cases (he said some 300 were on the books at the time), Prosser concluded that privacy "is not one tort, but a complex of four." A major challenge to this interpretation has been issued by Edward J. Bloustein, who complains that Prosser has in effect repudiated Warren and Brandeis "by suggesting that privacy is not an independent value at all but a composite of the interests of reputation, emotional tranquillity and intangible property." For Bloustein, privacy is a dignitary tort; that is, the interest protected concerns individual dignity.

---

* From Donald L. Smith. "Privacy: The Right That Failed." *Columbia Journalism Review*, Vol. 8, No. 1 (Spring 1969), p. 18. Used with permission of the *Columbia Journalism Review* and the author, an associate professor of journalism at Pennsylvania State University.

Although Prosser's analysis has not gone unchallenged, it has been very influential and will serve nicely here as a summary of the kinds of cases involving the mass media that arise in privacy law. The four torts he distinguishes are:

• Intrusion upon a plaintiff's seclusion or solitude, or into his private affairs. The main risk for the media lies in such acts as photographing people without their consent in their home or in a hospital bed.

• Public disclosure of embarrassing private facts about a plaintiff. This is what chiefly concerned Warren and Brandeis. But suits for such invasions generally fail, because the law recognizes a broad privilege to report news.

• Publicity that places a plaintiff in a false light in the public eye. False-light invasion has two main consequences for the media. First, it is important as an independent principle. Examples of cases involving it are: pictures of people used to illustrate books or articles about things with which they have no reasonable connection; books and articles, or ideas expressed in either, spuriously attributed to people; and fictitious testimonials used in advertising and attributed to real people. Second, it has often been used to defeat the media's privilege to report news and matters of public interest.

There has been a rather widespread overlapping with defamation in the false-light cases, and this has worried some authorities. For example, in his 1960 article, Prosser wondered if this branch of privacy might not be capable of "swallowing up and engulfing" the whole law of public defamation and if there were any false libel that might not be redressed on false-light grounds.

• Appropriation, for a defendant's advantage, of a plaintiff's name or likeness. Many cases on the books concern appropriation; the number is large partly because the nation's oldest privacy law deals mainly with this tort. It was enacted by the New York legislature in 1903. Similar statutes have been approved in Oklahoma, Virginia, and Utah. Some thirty other states have recognized a right of privacy at common law. . . .

One criticism of *Hill*, made by several dissenting justices as well as by other persons, is that the court has cavalierly undercut a basic right—an action especially disturbing to many observers because it comes at a time when privacy is being increasingly threatened in a "naked society." Such complaints usually point out that the court itself as recently as 1965 had found a right of privacy in "penumbras" of five amendments to the Constitution. (The case was *Griswold v. Connecticut*; the court voided a state law against disseminating information about birth control.) But this overlooks an important point made by Dana Bullen, then Supreme Court reporter for the *Washington Star*, in an interpretive story printed shortly after *Hill* was decided. He wrote:

> Recognizing the toughness of the [actual malice] test, three of the four dissenting justices accused the majority of giving only "lip service" to rights of privacy that the court has backed in other types of cases.

The difference, of course, is that the other situations involved contests between an individual and a government agency [as in *Griswold*] or between an individual and the police.

Although he did not spell it out, the difference referred to by Bullen concerns the fact that the tort of privacy does not enjoy constitutional status. "It is statutes and the law of torts—not constitutional guarantees—which forbid invasions of privacy by private individuals," Bernard Schwartz recently wrote in his monumental commentary on the Constitution. "The constitutional guarantees, from which a constitutional right of privacy may be derived, are directed against government action alone. To the extent that the Constitution does confer a right of privacy, it is a right against governmental invasions."

Some critics of *Hill* assert that the court's extension of the actual malice rule from libel to privacy was an illogical leap. They seem to assume that libel and privacy are very distinct torts—from which it follows that a defense originated in libel cannot be legitimately used in privacy as well. If the court's "leap" is not completely defensible, it may at least be seen as an understandable one.

First, libel and privacy are not always readily distinguishable. Although libel concerns one's reputation and privacy concerns one's peace of mind, the two have always overlapped somewhat. And increasingly, as noted earlier, there has been a tendency for defamations to be absorbed into false-light privacy, where newsworthiness, a broad defense to many privacy actions, has no privileged status. The decided cases, wrote John W. Wade in the October, 1962, issue of the *Vanderbilt Law Review*, indicate that "the 'privilege' of publishing matters of public interest does not extend to false statements, so that even a public personage or a person connected with a newsworthy event can maintain an action if the false statement is one which would offend a person of ordinary sensibilities."

Second, it is clear that in a string of decisions going back to *Times* in 1964, the Supreme Court has been reducing the threat to the media of defamation actions in an effort to encourage "debate on public issues" that is "uninhibited, robust, and wide open." And it is also clear that the creation of the actual malice test in *Times* was partly related to the Court's commitment to the Negro rights movement. At a time when the nation is experiencing the worst crises in a century, the Court understandably wishes to facilitate peaceful social change by encouraging wide discussion of controversial questions. (Of course, the Court is undoubtedly naïve to suppose that the media will indulge in robust discussion now that the threat of lawsuits has been reduced; it seems unaware of the fact that their status as businesses appealing to mass audiences often softens the media's spines.)

Third, in its efforts to facilitate peaceful change by promoting public debate, the Court has been greatly influenced by the First Amendment theory of the late Alexander Meiklejohn. His key ideas are that the people are both the governors and the governed, and that the intent of the First Amendment is to prohibit all subordinate agencies from abridging the freedom of the electoral power of the people. Speech is free not because an individual desires to speak, but because the people as governors need to hear.

When *Hill* is judged against this background, one can imagine that the Court saw that its efforts to foster debate could be frustrated if there was any chance that people no longer able to sue for libel without proof of actual malice could collect for false-light invasion of privacy. And any tendency for the Court to think this way may have been reinforced by a long-held interest in protecting expression for the civil rights movement.

That some such link connected the *Times* test to *Hill* was divined by Dana Bullen. In the story mentioned earlier, he noted that some recent Supreme Court decisions bolstering the constitutional guarantees of expression had occurred in the context of the civil rights movement. Then he concluded in regard to *Hill*: "In most purely private lawsuits, it seems, the developing remedy for invasion of privacy simply lost out. It may be yet another unintended victim of the civil rights struggle." Also important to note is the influence of Meiklejohn (whose ideas were relied on by counsel for Time Inc. in their brief for reargument), an influence made clear by striking parallels in language between Justice William J. Brennan's opinion and Meiklejohn's writings. . . .

Meantime, one should not conclude that the Court has destroyed the tort of privacy. It has simply ruled that damages will not be awarded for false-light actions unless plaintiffs prove knowing or reckless falsehood. Nor should one conclude that much has been lost, or will have been lost in the future if the Court undercuts privacy still more.

For regardless of how noble the interest may be that the right seeks to protect, the tort of privacy has not been a notable success. This seems especially true of the kind of interests Warren and Brandeis wished to see protected because, as Harry Kalven has said, the "generous privilege to serve the public interest in news" is so great as to virtually swallow the public-disclosure tort. And even the tort aimed at affording relief in instances of commercial appropriation—a tort that most experts agree makes sense—leaves much to be desired. As Frederick Davis has said of the New York statute, it "excludes almost as many deserving plaintiffs as it covers."

Given the slowness of the law to change, it is hard to believe that privacy will soon vanish from the tort scene. But given the checkered history of the right, it is easy to agree with Zechariah Chafee, Jr. He said:

> Times have changed since Brandeis wrote in 1890. Seeing how society dames and damsels sell their faces for cash in connection with cosmetics, cameras, and cars, one suspects that the right to publicity is more highly valued than any right to privacy. . . . *So I recommend that respect for privacy be left to public opinion and the conscience of owners and editors.*

REPORTERS HAVE A RIGHT TO KNOW, BUT THE PUBLIC HAS A RIGHT OF PRIVACY

By Arthur R. Miller*

During the past few years, Americans have become increasingly sensitive to the right of individual privacy. Popular concern over the computerization of personal information, governmental surveillance of citizens, the excessive zeal of the FBI and CIA and the abuses of Watergate has led to a remarkable series of statutes, administrative regulations and judicial decisions designed to limit data collection, to extend the rights of those on whom files are kept and prevent access to dossiers by those with no legitimate need to know their contents.

The nation's press has begun to argue that it needs immunity from these new rules. But I believe the media have it backward; it is the public's right to privacy that needs increased protection against the press.

Although I appreciate that the nation's journalists have served as a bastion against abuse of governmental power, as in the case of Watergate, I reject the suggestion that the media have such a paramount status that the judgment of editors as to what is newsworthy need not be balanced against other social considerations.

After all, as Justice William O. Douglas once observed, "The right to be let alone is indeed the beginning of all freedom." The U.S. Supreme Court has protected the privacy of personal association, ideology, the home, the marital relationship and the body. Similarly, an individual's desire to control the dissemination of information about himself is a natural part of personal autonomy and should not be dismissed as some kind of eccentric Greta Garbo-Howard Hughes syndrome.

Many people feel embarrassed or demeaned when information about them is disclosed or exchanged, even though it may be accurate and not professionally or socially damaging. To some, loss of privacy equals loss of dignity. Lewis Carroll put it well in "Alice's Adventures in Wonderland": "Oh, 'tis love, 'tis love, that makes the world go 'round!" the Duchess remarks, prompting Alice to whisper, "It's done by everybody minding their own business!"

We live in a crowded, complex world, one in which a host of decisions affecting our daily lives—whether we are insurable, credit-worthy, employable or eligible for government benefits—are made by people we never see, using informa-

---

* From Arthur R. Miller. "Reporters Have a Right to Know, But the Public Has a Right of Privacy," *Los Angeles Times* (April 16, 1978). Used with permission of the *Los Angeles Times* and the author, professor of law at Harvard University.

tion over which we have no control. The individual is increasingly at the mercy of information brokers who covet, collect and abuse personal information on other people.

Ironically, while the media decry these developments, they assert their right to investigate our private lives—an act which surely contributes to the erosion of privacy and emphasizes the need for protection. An excessively zealous newspaper, television network or radio station poses a significant threat to our right to be let alone. Indeed, disclosures in the public press about one's private life can be more devastating than dissemination of the same information by a credit bureau.

With the help of the courts, we must protect our right of privacy by balancing it against the legitimate needs and First Amendment rights of America's media. The courts, after all, have accorded extraordinary protection to journalists in recent years, thereby creating the contemporary imbalance between individual rights and press prerogatives. The media's liability for defamation has been limited, the scope of executive privilege has been contained and publication restrictions based on national security have been overcome. The courts have done these things by expansively interpreting the First Amendment and striking down countless attempts to intimidate journalists by repressive agency regulations or governmental practices.

Despite these court victories, the press now claims that it is threatened by America's growing social sensitivity to privacy. Journalists apparently think they are engaged in a never-ending series of life-and-death cliffhangers. Challenged by one Goliath after another, media Davids must repeatedly sally forth to slay the enemy. This strikes me as a highly distorted and egocentric view of the universe. Spiro Agnew notwithstanding, not everyone is out to get the media.

I am not persuaded that press freedom will come tumbling down like a house of cards unless every competing social interest is subordinated to this one right. However fragile the condition of newspapers at the time of the American Revolution, the present economic power of the broadcast networks and publishing giants casts serious doubt on any suggestion of media vulnerability.

Why do journalists insist on pressing their prerogatives to the limits? Why is it that the press reacts like a terrified hemophiliac to the slightest pinprick of criticism? Apparently, it fears that recognizing the importance of any other public interest may inhibit news gathering and is the first step toward erosion of the media's special status. But the nation's press can remain vibrant without a license to intrude on our privacy. The law already affords the media so much protection that tempering journalistic zeal by requiring a modicum of respect for people's privacy poses no real risk that anything of news value will be lost.

Moreover, other, profound human values are at stake. People involuntarily thrust into the glare of publicity pay a terrible price when they lose their right to be let alone. Oliver Sipple, who lunged at Sara Jane Moore and deflected her revolver as she fired at President Ford, paid that price in 1975, when the media revealed his membership in San Francisco's gay community.

Unless reporters are deterred from excessive and unwarranted curiosity, many of us may be inhibited from participating in society's affairs. Any risk of dampening press enthusiasm for newsgathering must be measured against creating a public fear, what George Orwell called "the assumption that every sound you made was overheard, and, except in darkness, every move was scrutinized."

Despite this specter, the press begrudges us some of the measures recently taken to protect our privacy. For example, it demands immunity from laws that deny unfettered access to certain criminal records—typically those of juveniles and of people who have been rehabilitated.

Vigorous and diligent reporters can effectively monitor the criminal-justice system without examining the records of individuals who have paid their debt to society, who have met the stringent prerequisites for having their record sealed and who deserve a second chance. Why should society not draw a protective curtain over the record of a youthful peccadillo that has never been repeated? It is inexcusably self-serving for the press to say that those who are protected by such curtains must be sacrificed on the altar of the First Amendment's absolute primacy.

The media ask for prerogatives unavailable to anyone else. For example, some journalists argue that a reporter who trespasses or uses false pretenses to enter someone's home should not be accountable if the resulting story "benefited the public." In short, where the press is concerned, the end justifies the means. Yet if a police officer entered a private home without a lawful warrant, we would be outraged by his violations of the rules against intruding on a citizen's private domain—even if the officer believed his entry would "benefit the public."

To permit the press to justify intrusive conduct because it "benefited the public" is an open-ended invitation to arbitrary and capricious actions. It could encourage certain elements of the press to invade the privacy of people and institutions with whom it disagrees. The media understand this risk, having reacted with shock to the revelation that various governmental intelligence organizations have spied on political dissidents and infiltrated various liberal organizations.

Should we not react with comparable shock if ultraconservative and right-wing journalists engage in similar conduct? And how could we condone violation of the privacy and associational freedoms of the members of the American Independent Party, the John Birch Society or even the American Nazi Party, by liberal elements of America's press?

Accepting the notion that the end justifies the means compromises the rule of law. Higher "justification" was precisely the defense employed by the Nixon administration. The press argues that there is a difference between surveillance by a governmental agent and by a reporter. True, but it happens to be one of degree, not principle. Our fear of official surveillance reflects a healthy apprehension about the oppressive use of governmental power. But in mid-20th century America, the power of media institutions has become such that, as a practical matter, the ramifications of intrusive behavior by the government, the media—or any other powerful social institution—are much the same.

Insisting on increased media sensitivity to privacy may be a modest incursion on editors. But the First Amendment does not give the press unfettered discretion. In various contexts, courts have decided that certain other values are worth protecting, even if it means second-guessing the journalist. The Supreme Court's recent conclusion that the Constitution does not give a television station immunity to broadcast the Human Cannonball's entire theatrical performance shows that our respect for property rights allows people to exploit their talents without fear of appropriation by the media. In the libel field, the courts have tried to achieve a principled accommodation between free speech and the integrity of an individual's reputation. And under certain circumstances, the law gives a rape victim's name a privacy-type protection.

To be sure, the courts are extremely reluctant to substitute their judgment for that of the media in determining what is "newsworthy." But, by exercising this restraint, judges have made journalists unaccountable and, in some cases, have abandoned the lambs to the wolves. In some contexts, particularly in gossip and "where are they now" columns, the media rationale underlying a decision of newsworthiness is circular: "When we publish it, people read and find it interesting; that makes it newsworthy and gives us the right to acquire and print it."

"Interesting" is not synonymous with "newsworthy." What is "newsworthy" about the activities of someone unconnected with the events of the day, especially a person who has been seeking anonymity for years? Even our "interest" in Jacqueline Kennedy Onassis doesn't make her every movement "newsworthy" and justify photographers following her day in and day out. Nor does our "interest" in the drug difficulties of a teen-age child of a senator or governor make it "newsworthy." The drug problem can be reported upon without identifying individuals; their relation to prominent citizens is irrelevant.

The apparently unauthorized entry into the locked apartment of David R. Berkowitz, accused of the "Son of Sam" murders, shows how far some journalists may go in quest of "a story," a real problem during this post-Watergate period of media euphoria and muscle-flexing.

The press claims that it is accountable to its readership. I doubt that. Americans are captivated by gossip. We revel in the latest pratfalls of celebrities of every description and derive vicarious pleasure from the intimate discussions of Dear Abby and the like.

No one disputes the public's "right to know." But like any platitude, it is only a generalization. The deeper questions are: "Know what?" and "What practices may the press employ to gather information?" As things now stand:

• The press may publish demonstrable falsehoods, subject only to remote threat of liability.

• The media claim the right to publish *any* "truth," no matter how private it may be or how prurient the interest to which it caters.

• Some journalists justify using improper and intrusive techniques in terms of the "benefit" produced by their stories.

In our complex society, rights frequently collide. Thus, it is imperative that no institution press its special prerogatives to the utmost. I believe that the press would further its own long-term interests if it more equitably balanced individual privacy against the public's right to know, and if it developed principles that would stay the typesetter's hands when the former seem paramount.

CHAPTER 11

TRIAL BY NEWSPAPER

Under the law there is no priority listing among the first ten amendments, the Bill of Rights. Freedom of the press, as guaranteed in the First Amendment, is no more or no less important than the guarantee of a fair trial, covered by the Sixth Amendment. Indeed, these human rights protected by the first ten amendments are closely entwined and often interdependent. But this closeness also brings entanglements, and this is the present state of the First and Sixth Amendments—the present debate over "fair trial vs. free press," or "trial by newspaper."

Interest was focused on this apparent conflict first by the 1954 murder trial of Dr. Sam Sheppard and later by the report of the Warren Commission following the 1963 assassination of President Kennedy, the confusion that followed in Dallas and the murder of the accused assassin, Lee Harvey Oswald. The fundamental question can be simply stated: "Had he lived to face trial, could Lee Harvey Oswald have received a fair trial?"

The broad implications of "trial by newspaper" are not easily answered. Three solutions have been widely discussed since the tragedies of November 1963. The first calls for voluntary adherence by the news media to a code which would demand restrained treatment of criminal trial coverage. The press would agree to turn to the more significant aspects of American justice and away from the sensational aspects which normally are used to boost circulation or which are "knee-jerk" reactions of overenthusiasm.

Only a few members of the news media, however, have announced such voluntary restraints. There has been much serious discussion within the media, but most of it has centered on opposition to lawyers who have argued for firm control of trial news. Also, voluntary media codes of restraint have not been particularly successful in the past. The Motion Picture Production Code is an example. Finally, a voluntary code is only as effective as the members of the media want it to be, and the news profession has not seen fit to censure its members who are guilty of "trial by newspaper." Nor is there a unanimous view among editors and publishers that such a code would be desirable.

A second proposal has been to follow the lead of England by laying a heavy hand on the press through the contempt powers of the court. The Supreme Court, in this regard, has given the American press a generally free hand in discussing cases before the bar since the landmark Bridges decision of 1941. Critics of strong contempt powers also point to the shortcomings of the English system—which is far from foolproof—and to the differences between our legal systems, such as the election of judges in this country and the presence of a Constitution which protects press freedom. Also, public prosecutors are responsible to the electorate, who must be kept informed as to the condition of law enforcement and justice. It is more than mere curiosity, therefore, that motivates the press to cover and comment upon American justice and those who seek to enforce it.

Finally, a third method of controlling pre-trial publicity is to govern the flow of information at the source, i.e. at those legally under the jurisdiction of the court. This was the method approved by the House of Delegates of the American Bar Association in 1968 with the adoption of the ABA's Reardon Report. The judge, if the Reardon recommendations are followed, would limit the information available to the press from the prosecutor, the defense attorney, the police, and all others directly within his control. Principals, under threat of contempt, would be prohibited from discussing alleged confessions, prior criminal records, potential witnesses, potential pleas or other comments as to guilt or innocence of the accused.

The success of the Reardon suggestions, however, must await the test of time and trial. The press, it should be noted, is not being restrained directly. Still, members of the media generally have been opposed to the Reardon recommendations. Some point to the lack of evidence surrounding media coverage and juror reaction. Not all members of the Bar support the Reardon Report either. Nor have they been without fault in trying to win cases for their clients. Both prosecutors and defense attorneys have long "courted" the media openly when it was to their advantage to do so. Neither the Bar nor the press, in truth, is without fault in this most delicate of human considerations. One thing is clear, however, and that is the fact that "gag" orders and contempt citations against the press have increased dramatically in recent years. See Fred P. Graham, " 'Gag' Orders Leave a Quagmire," this chapter.

The Court in 1941 turned a significant corner in dealing with out-of-court contempt with its opinion in the California cases of Bridges v. California and Times-Mirror v. Superior Court, handed down together. In a 5-4 decision, the Court formally rejected the Toledo "reasonable tendency" guide and substituted the more restrictive concept of "clear and present danger," which Justice Holmes had first proposed for seditious utterances in his 1919 Schenck v. United States opinion. The Bridges decision meant that a clear and present danger to the administration of justice—not just a possible threat—would have to be established in order for a court to substantiate out-of-court contempt. Also, comment was authorized in cases still pending, especially if they have great public interest.

The debate, of course, was between two fundamental principles that continue to this day to be in apparent philosophic and real conflict—freedom of the press to comment on public affairs and the right to administer justice without undue interference. The Bridges case resulted from a telegram attacking the judgment of the court. The Los Angeles Times contempt was based on editorials run after verdicts were announced but before sentencing, application for probation, or appeal. Both contempts were set aside by the Supreme Court. The press heralded the decisions as significant to First Amendment guarantees. The Los Angeles Times was awarded a Pulitzer Prize for Public Service in 1942 for its pursuance of the principles involved.

BRIDGES V. CALIFORNIA

TIMES-MIRROR CO. V. SUPERIOR COURT
314 U.S. 252 (1941)

JUSTICE BLACK *delivered the opinion of the Court.*

These two cases, while growing out of different circumstances and concerning different parties, both relate to the scope of our national constitutional policy safeguarding free speech and a free press. All of the petitioners were adjudged guilty and fined for contempt of court by the Superior Court of Los Angeles County. Their conviction rested upon comments pertaining to pending litigation which were published in newspapers. In the Superior Court and later in the California Supreme Court, petitioners challenged the state's action as an abridgment, prohibited by the Federal Constitution, of freedom of speech and of the press, but the Superior Court overruled this contention, and the Supreme Court affirmed. The importance of the constitutional question prompted us to grant *certiorari*. . . .

We may appropriately begin our discussion of the judgments below by considering how much, as a practical matter, they would affect liberty of expression. It must be recognized that public interest is much more likely to be kindled by a controversial event of the day than by a generalization, however penetrating, of the historian or scientist. Since they punish utterances made during the pendency of a case, the judgments below therefore produce their restrictive results at the precise time when public interest in the matters discussed would naturally be at its height. Moreover, the ban is likely to fall not only at a crucial time but upon the most important topics of discussion. Here, for example, labor controversies were the topics of some of the publications. Experience shows that the more acute labor controversies are, the more likely it is that in some aspect they will get into court. It is therefore the controversies that command most interest that the decisions below would remove from the arena of public discussion. . . .

The Los Angeles Times Editorials. The Times-Mirror Company, publisher of the *Los Angeles Times,* and L. D. Hotchkiss, its managing editor, were cited for contempt for the publication of three editorials. Both found by the trial court to be responsible for one of the editorials, the company and Hotchkiss were each fined $100. The company alone was held responsible for the other two, and was fined $100 more on account of one, and $300 more on account of the other.

The $300 fine presumably marks the most serious offense. The editorial thus distinguished was entitled "Probation for Gorillas?" After vigorously denouncing two members of a labor union who had previously been found guilty of assaulting nonunion truck drivers, it closes with observation: "Judge A. A. Scott will make a serious mistake if he grants probation to Matthew Shannon and Kennan Holmes. This community needs the example of their assignment to the jute mill." Judge Scott had previously set a day (about a month after the publication) for passing upon the application of Shannon and Holmes for probation and for pronouncing sentence.

The basis for punishing the publication as contempt was by the trial court said to be its "inherent tendency" and by the Supreme Court its "reasonable tendency" to interfere with the orderly administration of justice in an action then before a court for consideration. In accordance with what we have said on the "clear and present danger" cases, neither "inherent tendency" nor "reasonable tendency" is enough to justify a restriction of free expression. But even if they were appropriate measures, we should find exaggeration in the use of those phrases to describe the facts here.

From the indications in the record of the position taken by the *Los Angeles Times* on labor controversies in the past, there could have been little doubt of its attitude toward the probation of Shannon and Holmes. In view of the paper's long-continued militancy in this field, it is inconceivable that any judge in Los Angeles would expect anything but adverse criticism from it in the event probation were granted. Yet such criticism after final disposition of the proceedings would clearly have been privileged. Hence, this editorial, given the most intimidating construction it will bear, did no more than threaten future adverse criticism which was reasonably to be expected anyway in the event of a lenient disposition of the pending case. To regard it, therefore, as in itself of substantial influence upon the course of justice would be to impute to judges a lack of firmness, wisdom, or honor, which we cannot accept as a major premise. . . .

JUSTICE FRANKFURTER, *with whom concurred the Chief Justice, Justice Roberts and Justice Byrnes, dissenting.*

Our whole history repels the view that it is an exercise of one of the civil liberties secured by the Bill of Rights for a leader of a large following or for a powerful metropolitan newspaper to attempt to over-awe a judge in a matter immediately pending before him. The view of the majority deprives California of means for securing to its citizens justice according to law—means which, since the Union was founded, have been the possession, hitherto unchallenged, of all the states. This sudden break with the uninterrupted course of constitutional history has no constitutional warrant. To find justification for such deprivation of the historic powers of the states is to misconceive the idea of freedom of thought and speech as guaranteed by the Constitution. . . .

We turn to the specific cases before us:

The earliest [*Times*] editorial . . . "Sit-strikers Convicted," commented upon a case the day after a jury had returned a verdict and the day before the trial judge was to pronounce sentence and hear motions for a new trial and applications for probation. On its face the editorial merely expressed exulting approval of the verdict, a completed action of the court, and there is nothing in the record to give it additional significance. The same is true of the second editorial, "Fall of an Ex-Queen," which luridly draws a moral from a verdict of guilty in a sordid trial and which was published eight days prior to the day set for imposing sentence. In both instances imposition of sentences was immediately pending at the time of publication, but in neither case was there any declaration, direct or sly, in regard to this. As the special guardian of the Bill of Rights this Court is under the heaviest responsibility to safeguard the liberties guaranteed from any encroachment, however astutely disguised. The Due Process Clause of the Fourteenth Amendment protects the right to comment on a judicial proceeding, so long as this is not done in a manner interfering with the impartial disposition of litigation. There is no indication that more was done in these editorials; they were not close threats to the judicial function which a state should be able to restrain. We agree that the judgment of the state court in this regard should not stand.

"Probation for Gorillas?", the third editorial, is a different matter. On April 22, 1938, a Los Angeles jury found two defendants guilty of assault with a deadly weapon and of a conspiracy to violate another section of the penal code. On May 2d, the defendants applied for probation and the trial judge on the same day set June 7th as the day for disposing of this application and for sentencing the defendants. In the *Los Angeles Times* for May 5th appeared the following editorial entitled "Probation for Gorillas?":

> Two members of Dave Beck's wrecking crew, entertainment committee, goon squad or gorillas, having been convicted in Superior Court of assaulting nonunion truck drivers, have asked for probation. Presumably they will say they are 'first offenders,' or plead that they were merely indulging a playful exuberance when, with slingshots, they fired steel missiles at men whose only offense was wishing to work for a living without paying tribute to the erstwhile boss of Seattle.
>
> Sluggers for pay, like murderers for profit, are in a slightly different category from ordinary criminals. Men who commit mayhem for wages are not merely violators of the peace and dignity of the State; they are also conspirators against it. The man who burgles because his children are hungry may have some claim on public sympathy. He whose crime is one of impulse may be entitled to lenity. But he who hires out his muscles for the creation of disorder and in aid of a racket is a deliberate foe of organized society and should be penalized accordingly.

It will teach no lesson to other thugs to put these men on good behavior for a limited time. Their 'duty' would simply be taken over by others like them. If Beck's thugs, however, are made to realize that they face San Quentin when they are caught, it will tend to make their disreputable occupation unpopular. Judge A. A. Scott will make a serious mistake if he grants probation to Matthew Shannon and Kennan Holmes. This community needs the example of their assignment to the jute mill.

This editorial was published three days after the trial judge had fixed the time for sentencing and for passing on an application for probation, and a month prior to the date set. It consisted of a sustained attack on the defendants, with an explicit demand of the judge that they be denied probation and be sent "to the jute mill." This meant, in California idiom, that in the exercise of his discretion the judge should treat the offense as a felony, with all its dire consequences, and not as a misdemeanor. Under the California Penal Code the trial judge had wide discretion in sentencing the defendants: he could sentence them to the county jail for one year or less, or to the state penitentiary for two years. The editorial demanded that he take the latter alternative and send the defendants to the "jute mill" of the state penitentiary. A powerful newspaper admonished a judge, who within a year would have to secure popular approval if he desired continuance in office, that failure to comply with its demands would be "a serious mistake." Clearly, the state court was justified in treating this as a threat to impartial adjudication. It is too naive to suggest that the editorial was written with a feeling of impotence and an intention to utter idle words. The publication of the editorial was hardly an exercise in futility. . . . Here there was a real and substantial manifestation of an endeavor to exert outside influence. A powerful newspaper brought its full coercive power to bear in demanding a particular sentence. If such sentence had been imposed readers might assume that the court had been influenced in its action; if lesser punishment had been imposed at least a portion of the community might be stirred to resentment. It cannot be denied that even a judge may be affected by such a quandary. We cannot say that the state court was out of bounds in concluding that such conduct offends the free course of justice. . . .

*   *   *

The Warren Court in 1961 was the first to reverse a state criminal conviction on grounds of adverse pre-trial publicity. Leslie "Mad Dog" Irvin, as he was popularly identified, was arrested in Indiana on suspicion of burglary and passing bad checks, but subsequently was connected with several murders. He was tried, convicted, and sentenced to death. He claimed—and the Supreme Court agreed—that he was denied a fair trial because of the extremely prejudicial nature of the press coverage. For example, 370 of the 430 prospective jurors admitted under voir dire they believed Irvin to be guilty. The Irvin decision acted as a prelude to the free press and fair trial argument and was followed by three additional reversals—Sheppard,

Rideau, *and* Estes—*which allowed the Justices in the final Warren years to speak out forcefully on questions of pretrial publicity.*

IRVIN V. DOWD
366 U.S. 717 (1961)

JUSTICE CLARK *delivered the opinion of the Court.*

. . . It is not required . . . that the jurors be totally ignorant of the facts and issues involved. In these days of swift, wide-spread and diverse methods of communication, an important case can be expected to arouse the interest of the public in the vicinity, and scarcely any of those best qualified to serve as jurors will not have found some impression or opinion as to the merits of the case. . . . It is sufficient if the juror can lay aside his impression or opinion and render a verdict based on the evidence presented in court. . . .

Here the build-up of prejudice is clear and convincing. An examination of the then current community pattern of thought as indicated by the popular news media is singularly revealing. For example, petitioner's first motion for a change of venue from Gibson County alleged that the awaited trial of petitioner had become the *cause célèbre* of this small community—so much so that curbstone opinions, not only as to petitioner's guilt but even as to what punishment he should receive, were solicited and recorded on the public streets by a roving reporter, and later were broadcast over the local stations. A reading of the 46 exhibits which petitioner attached to his motion indicates that a barrage of newspaper headlines, articles, cartoons and pictures was unleashed against him during the six or seven months preceding his trial. The motion further alleged that the newspapers in which the stories appeared were delivered regularly to approximately 95% of the dwellings in Gibson County and that, in addition, the Evansville radio and TV stations, which likewise blanketed that county, also carried extensive newscasts covering the same incidents. These stories revealed the details of his background, including a reference to crimes committed when a juvenile, his convictions for arson almost 20 years previously, for burglary and by a court-martial on AWOL charges during the war. He was accused of being a parole violator. The headlines announced his police line-up identification, that he faced a lie detector test, had been placed at the scene of the crime and that the six murders were solved but the petitioner refused to confess. Finally, they announced his confession to the six murders and the fact of his indictment for four of them in Indiana. They reported petitioner's offer to plead guilty if promised a 99-year sentence, but also the determination, on the other hand, of the prosecutor to secure the death penalty, and that petitioner had confessed to 24 burglaries (the *modus operandi* of these robberies was compared to that of the murders and the similarity noted). One story dramatically relayed the promise of a sheriff to devote his life to securing petitioner's execution by the State of Kentucky, where petitioner is alleged to have committed one of the six murders, if Indiana failed to do so. Another characterized petitioner as remorseless and without conscience but also having been found sane by a court-appointed panel of doctors. In many of the stories petitioner was described as the "confessed slayer of six," a parole violator and fraudulent-check artist. Petitioner's court-appointed counsel was quoted as having received "much criticism over being Irvin's counsel" and it was pointed out by way of excusing the attorney, that he would be subject to disbarment should he refuse to represent Irvin. . . .

Finally, and with remarkable understatement, the headlines reported that "impartial jurors are hard to find.". . .

*   *   *

The classic case in the debate over "trial by newspaper" involved the 1954 murder conviction of Dr. Sam Sheppard. The Supreme Court denied certiorari on the original appeal, but a decade later accepted the question of pre-trial publicity and decided 8–1 that Sheppard did not get a fair trial because of the sensational press coverage. The Court reversed the murder judgment against him and ordered him freed until such time as a new trial was sought by the prosecution. The majority opinion by Justice Clark recounts in detail the events leading to Sheppard's conviction. The Court was critical of press coverage, reporting independently discovered "evidence" and gossip, and assumptions of guilt. Still, the opinion appeared to be aimed more at the court for allowing the "massive, pervasive and prejudicial publicity" than directly at the media which published it. The case was given banner headline treatment not only in Cleveland, where the drama unfolded, but in media across the nation. The significance of the Sheppard decision and its influence upon press-court relations still is being felt. Sheppard, in a second trial in 1966, was acquitted. The significant and readable opinion of Justice Clark follows in its entirety except for case reference numbers.

SHEPPARD V. MAXWELL
384 U.S. 333 (1966)

JUSTICE CLARK *delivered the opinion of the Court.*

This federal *habeas corpus* application involves the question whether Sheppard was deprived of a fair trial in his state conviction for the second-degree murder of his wife because of the trial judge's failure to protect Sheppard sufficiently from the massive, pervasive and prejudicial publicity that attended his prosecution. The United States District Court held that he was not afforded a fair trial and granted the writ subject to the State's right to put Sheppard to trial again, 231 F. Supp. 37 (D.C.S.D. Ohio 1964). The Court of Appeals for the Sixth Circuit reversed by a divided vote, 346 F. 2d 707 (1965). We granted *certiorari*, 382 U.S. 916 (1966). We have concluded that Sheppard did not receive a fair trial consistent with the Due Process Clause of the Fourteenth Amendment and, therefore, reverse the judgment.

I

Marilyn Sheppard, petitioner's pregnant wife, was bludgeoned to death in the upstairs bedroom of their lakeshore home in Bay Village, Ohio, a suburb of Cleveland. On the day of the tragedy, July 4, 1954, Sheppard pieced together for several local officials the following story: He and his wife had entertained neighborhood friends, the Aherns, on the previous evening at their home. After dinner they watched television in the living room. Sheppard became drowsy and dozed off to sleep on a couch. Later, Marilyn partially awoke him saying that she was going to bed. The next thing he remembers was hearing his wife cry out in the early morning hours. He hurried upstairs and in the dim light from the hall saw a "form" standing next to his wife's bed. As he struggled with the "form" he was struck on the back of the neck and rendered unconscious. On regaining his senses he found himself on the floor next to his wife's bed. He raised up, looked at her, took her pulse and "felt that she was gone." He then went to his son's room and found him unmolested. Hearing a noise he hurried downstairs. He saw a "form" running out the door and pursued it to the lake shore. He grappled with it on the beach and again lost consciousness. Upon his recovery he was lying face down with the lower portion of his body in the water. He returned to his home, checked the pulse of his wife's neck, and "determined or thought that she was gone." He then went downstairs and called a neighbor, Mayor Houk of Bay Village. The Mayor and his wife came over at once, found Sheppard slumped in an easy chair downstairs and asked, "What happened?" Sheppard replied: "I don't know but somebody ought to try to do something for Marilyn." Mrs. Houk immediately went up to the bedroom. The Mayor told Sheppard, "Get hold of yourself. Can you tell me what happened?" Sheppard then related the above-outlined events. After Mrs. Houk discovered the body, the Mayor called the local police, Dr. Richard Sheppard, petitioner's brother, and Aherns. The local police were the first to arrive. They in turn notified the Coroner and Cleveland police. Richard Sheppard then arrived, determined that Marilyn was dead, examined his brother's injuries, and removed him to the nearby clinic operated by the Sheppard family. When the Coroner, the Cleveland police and other officials arrived, the house and surrounding area were thoroughly searched, the rooms of the house were photographed, and many persons, including the Houks and the Aherns, were interrogated. The Sheppard home and premises were taken into "protective custody" and remained so until after the trial.

From the outset officials focused suspicion on Sheppard. After a search of the house and premises on the morning of the tragedy, Dr. Gerber, the Coroner, is reported—and it is undenied—to have told his men, "Well, it is evident the doctor did this, so let's go get the confession out of him." He proceeded to interrogate and examine Sheppard while the latter was under sedation in his hospital room. On the same occasion, the Coroner was given the clothes Sheppard wore at the time of the tragedy together with the personal items in them. Later that afternoon Chief Eaton and two Cleveland police officers interrogated Sheppard at some length, confronting him with evidence and demanding explanations. Asked by Officer Shotke to take a lie detector test, Sheppard said he would if it were reliable. Shotke replied that it was "infallible" and "you might as well tell us all about it now." At the end of the interrogation Shotke told Sheppard: "I think you killed your wife." Still later in the same afternoon a physician sent by the Coroner was permitted to make a detailed examination of Sheppard. Until the Coroner's inquest on July 22, at which time he was subpoenaed, Sheppard made himself available for frequent and extended questioning without the presence of an attorney.

On July 7, the day of Marilyn Sheppard's funeral, a newspaper story appeared in which Assistant County Attorney Mahon—later the chief prosecutor of Sheppard—sharply criticized the refusal of the Sheppard family to permit his immediate questioning. From there on headline stories repeatedly stressed Sheppard's lack of cooperation with the police and other officials. Under the headline "Testify Now In Death, Bay Doctor Is Ordered," one story described a visit by Coroner Gerber and four police officers to the hospital on July 8. When Sheppard insisted that his lawyer be present, the Coroner wrote out a subpoena and served it on him. Sheppard then agreed to submit to questioning without counsel and the subpoena was torn up. The officers questioned him for several hours. On July 9, Sheppard, at the request of the Coroner, reenacted the tragedy at his home before the Coroner, police officers, and a group of newsmen, who apparently were invited by the Coroner. The home was locked so that Sheppard was obliged to wait outside until the Coroner arrived. Sheppard's performance was reported in detail by the news media along with photographs. The newspapers also played up Sheppard's refusal to take a lie detector test and "the protective ring" thrown up by his family. Front-page newspaper headlines announced on the same day that "Doctor Balks At Lie Test; Retells Story." A column opposite that story contained an "exclusive" interview with Sheppard headlined: " 'Loved My Wife, She Loved Me,' Sheppard Tells News Reporters." The next day, another headline story disclosed that Sheppard had "again late yesterday refused to take a lie detector test" and quoted an Assistant County Attorney as saying that "at the end of a nine-hour questioning of Dr. Sheppard, I felt he was now ruling [a test] out completely." But subsequent newspaper articles reported that the Coroner was still pushing Sheppard for a lie detector test. More stories appeared when Sheppard would not allow authorities to inject him with "truth serum."

On the 20th, the "editorial artillery" opened fire with a front-page charge that somebody is "getting away with murder." The editorial attributed the ineptness of the investigation to "friendships, relationships, hired lawyers, a husband who ought to have been subjected instantly to the same third degree to which any person under similar circumstances is subjected. . . ." The following day, July 21, another page-one editorial was headed: "Why No Inquest? Do It Now, Dr. Gerber." The Coroner called an inquest the same day and subpoenaed Sheppard. It was staged the next day in a school gymnasium; the Coroner presided with the County Prosecutor as his advisor and two detectives as bailiffs. In the front of the room was a long table occupied by reporters, television and radio personnel, and broadcasting equipment. The hearing was broadcast with live microphones placed at the Coroner's seat and the witness stand. A swarm of reporters and photographers attended. Sheppard was brought into the room by police who searched him in full view of several hundred spectators. Sheppard's counsel were present during the three-day inquest but were not permitted to participate. When Sheppard's chief counsel attempted to place some documents in the record, he was forcibly ejected from the room by the Coroner, who received cheers, hugs, and kisses from ladies in the audience. Sheppard was questioned for five and one-half hours about his actions on the night of the murder, his married life, and a love affair with Susan Hayes. At the end of the hearing the Coroner announced that he "could" order Sheppard held for the grand jury, but did not do so.

Throughout this period the newspapers emphasized evidence that tended to incriminate Sheppard and pointed out discrepancies in his statements to authorities. At the same time, Sheppard made many public statements to the press and wrote feature articles asserting his innocence. During the inquest on July 26, a headline in large type stated: "Kerr [Captain of the Cleveland Police] Urges Sheppard's Arrest." In the story, Detective McArthur "disclosed that scientific tests at the Sheppard home have definitely established that the killer washed off a trail of blood from the murder bedroom to the downstairs section," a circumstance casting doubt on Sheppard's accounts of the murder. No such evidence was produced at trial. The newspapers also delved into Sheppard's personal life. Articles stressed his extra-marital love affairs as a motive for the crime. The newspapers portrayed Sheppard as a Lothario, fully explored his relationship with Susan Hayes, and named a number of other women who were allegedly involved with him. The testimony at trial never showed that Sheppard had any illicit relationships besides the one with Susan Hayes.

On July 28, an editorial entitled "Why Don't Police Quiz Top Suspect" demanded that Sheppard be taken to police headquarters. It described him in the following language:

> "Now proved under oath to be a liar, still free to go about his business, shielded by his family, protected by a smart lawyer who has made monkeys of the police and authorities, carrying a gun part of the time, left free to do whatever he pleases. . . ."

A front-page editorial on July 30 asked: "Why Isn't Sam Sheppard in Jail?" It was later titled "Quit Stalling—Bring Him In." After calling Sheppard "the most unusual murder suspect ever seen around these parts" the article said that "[e]xcept for some superficial questioning during Coroner Sam Gerber's inquest he has been scot-free of any official grilling. . . ." It asserted that he was "surrounded by an iron curtain of protection [and] concealment."

That night at 10 o'clock Sheppard was arrested at his father's home on a charge of murder. He was taken to the Bay Village City Hall where hundreds of people, newscasters, photographers and reporters were awaiting his arrival. He was immediately arraigned—having been denied a temporary delay to secure the presence of counsel—and bound over to the grand jury.

The publicity then grew in intensity until his indictment on August 17. Typical of the coverage during this period is a front-page interview entitled: "Dr. Sam: 'I Wish There Was Something I Could Get Off My Chest—but There Isn't.'" Unfavorable publicity included items such as a cartoon of the body of a sphinx with Sheppard's head and the legend below: "'I Will Do Everything In My Power to Help Solve This Terrible Murder.'—Dr. Sam Sheppard." Headlines announced, *inter alia*, that: "Doctor Evidence is Ready for Jury," "Corrigan Tactics Stall Quizzing," "Sheppard 'Gay Set' Is Revealed By Houk," "Blood Is Found In Garage," "New Murder Evidence Is Found, Police Claim," "Dr. Sam Faces Quiz At Jail On Marilyn's Fear Of Him." On August 18, an article appeared under the headline "Dr. Sam Writes His Own Story." And reproduced across the entire front page was a portion of typed statement signed by Sheppard: "I am not guilty of the murder of my wife, Marilyn. How could I, who have been trained to help people and devote my life to saving life, commit such a terrible and revolting crime?" We do not detail the coverage further. There are five volumes filled with similar clippings from each of the three Cleveland newspapers covering the period from the murder until Sheppard's conviction in December 1954. The record includes no excerpts from newscasts on radio and television but since space was reserved in the courtroom for these media we assume that their coverage was equally large.

II

With this background the case came on for trial two weeks before the November general election at which the chief prosecutor was a candidate for municipal judge and the presiding judge, Judge Blythin, was a candidate to succeed himself. Twenty-five days before the case was set, a list of 75 veniremen were called as prospective jurors. This list, including the addresses of each venireman, was published in all three Cleveland newspapers. As a consequence, anonymous letters and telephone calls, as well as calls from friends, regarding the impending prosecution were received by all of the prospective jurors. The selection of the jury began on October 18, 1954.

The courtroom in which the trial was held measured 26 by 48 feet. A long temporary table was set up inside the bar, in back of the single counsel table. It ran the width of the courtroom, parallel to the bar railing, with one end less than three feet from the jury box. Approximately 20 representatives of newspapers and wire services were assigned seats at this table by the court. Behind the bar railing there were four rows of benches. These seats were likewise assigned by the court for the entire trial. The first row was occupied by representatives of television and radio stations, and the second and third rows by reporters from out-of-town newspapers and magazines. One side of the last row, which accommodated 14 people, was assigned to Sheppard's family and the other to Marilyn's. The public was permitted to fill vacancies in this row on special passes only. Representatives of the news media also used all the rooms on the courtroom floor, including the room where cases were ordinarily called and assigned for trial. Private telephone lines and telegraphic equipment were installed in these rooms so that reports from the trial could be speeded to the papers. Station WSRS was permitted to set up broadcasting facilities on the third floor of the courthouse next door to the jury room, where the jury rested during recesses in the trial and deliberated. Newscasts were made from this room throughout the trial, and while the jury reached its verdict.

On the sidewalk and steps in front of the courthouse, television and newsreel cameras were occasionally used to take motion pictures of the participants in the trial, including the jury and the judge. Indeed, one television broadcast carried a staged interview of the judge as he entered the courthouse. In the corridors outside the courtroom there was a host of photographers and television personnel with flash cameras, portable lights and motion picture cameras. This group photographed the prospective jurors during selection of the jury. After the trial opened, the witnesses, counsel, and jurors were photographed and televised whenever they entered or left the courtroom. Sheppard was brought to the courtroom about 10 minutes before each session began; he was surrounded by reporters and extensively photographed for the newspapers and television. A rule of court prohibited picture-taking in the courtroom during the actual sessions of the court, but no restraints were put on photographers during recesses, which were taken once each morning and after-noon, with a longer period for lunch.

All of these arrangements with the news media and their massive coverage of the trial continued during the entire nine weeks of the trial. The courtroom remained crowded to capacity with representatives of news media. Their move-ment in and out of the courtroom often caused so much confusion that, despite the loud speaker system installed in the courtroom, it was difficult for the witnesses and counsel to be heard. Furthermore, the reporters clustered within the bar of the small courtroom made confidential talk among Sheppard and his counsel almost impossible during the proceedings. They frequently had to leave the courtroom to obtain privacy. And many times when counsel wished to raise a point with the judge out of the hearing of the jury it was necessary to move to the judge's chambers. Even then, news media representatives so packed the judge's anteroom that counsel could hardly return from the chambers to the courtroom. The reporters vied with each other to find out what counsel and the judge had dis-cussed, and often these matters later appeared in newspapers accessible to the jury.

The daily record of the proceedings was made available to the newspapers and the testimony of each witness was printed *verbatim* in the local editions, along with objections of counsel, and rulings by the judge. Pictures of Sheppard, the judge, counsel, pertinent witnesses, and the jury often accompanied the daily newspaper and television accounts. At times the newspapers published photographs of exhibits introduced at the trial, and the rooms of Sheppard's house were featured along with relevant testimony.

The jurors themselves were constantly exposed to the news media. Every juror, except one, testified at *voir dire* to reading about the case in the Cleveland papers or to having heard broadcasts about it. Seven of the 12 jurors who rendered the verdict had one or more Cleveland papers delivered in their homes; the remaining jurors were not interrogated on the point. Nor were there questions as to radios or television sets in the talesmen's homes, but we must assume that most of them owned such conveniences. As the selection of the jury progressed, individual pictures of prospective members appeared daily. During the trial, pictures of the jury appeared over 40 times in the Cleveland papers alone. The court permitted photographers to take pictures of the jury in the box, and individual pictures of the members in the jury room. One newspaper ran pictures of the jurors at the Sheppard home when they went there to view the scene of the murder. Another paper featured the home life of an alternate juror. The day before the verdict was rendered—while the jurors were at lunch and sequestered by two bailiffs—the jury was separated into two groups to pose for photographs which appeared in the newspapers.

III

We now reach the conduct of the trial. While the intense publicity continued unabated, it is sufficient to relate only the more flagrant episodes:

1. On October 9, 1954, nine days before the case went to trial, an editorial in one of the newspapers criticized defense counsel's random poll of people on the streets as to their opinion of Sheppard's guilt or innocence in an effort to use the resulting statistics to show the necessity for change of *venue*. The article said the survey "smacks of mass jury tampering," called on defense counsel to drop it, and stated that the bar association should do something about it. It characterized the poll as "non-judicial, non-legal, and nonsense." The article was called to the attention of the court but no action was taken.

2. On the second day of *voir dire* examination a debate was staged and broadcast live over WHK radio. The participants, newspaper reporters, accused Sheppard's counsel of throwing roadblocks in the way of the prosecution and asserted that Sheppard conceded his guilt by hiring a prominent criminal lawyer. Sheppard's counsel objected to this broadcast and requested a continuance, but the judge denied the motion. When counsel asked the court to give some protection from such events, the judge replied that "WHK doesn't have much coverage," and that "[a]fter all, we are not trying this case by radio or in newspapers or any other means. We confine ourselves seriously to it in this courtroom and do the very best we can."

3. While the jury was being selected, a two-inch headline asked: "But Who Will Speak for Marilyn?" The front-page story spoke of the "perfect face" of the accused. "Study that face as long as you want. Never will you get from it a hint of what might be the answer. . . ." The two brothers of the accused were described as "Prosperous, poised. His two sisters-in-law. Smart, chic, well-groomed. His elderly father. Courtly, reserved. A perfect type for the patriarch of a staunch clan." The author then noted Marilyn Sheppard was "still off stage," and that she was an only child whose mother died when she was very young and whose father had no interest in the case. But the author—through quotes from Detective Chief James

McArthur—assured readers that the prosecution's exhibits would speak for Marilyn. "Her story," McArthur stated, "will come into this courtroom through our witnesses.". . .

4. As has been mentioned, the jury viewed the scene of the murder on the first day of the trial. Hundreds of reporters, cameramen and onlookers were there, and one representative of the news media was permitted to accompany the jury while they inspected the Sheppard home. The time of the jury's visit was revealed so far in advance that one of the newspapers was able to rent a helicopter and fly over the house taking pictures of the jurors on their tour.

5. On November 19, a Cleveland police officer gave testimony that tended to contradict details in the written statement Sheppard made to the Cleveland police. Two days later, in a broadcast heard over Station WHK in Cleveland, Robert Considine likened Sheppard to a perjuror and compared the episode to Alger Hiss' confrontation with Whittaker Chambers. Though defense counsel asked the judge to question the jury to ascertain how many heard the broadcast, the court refused to do so. The judge also overruled the motion for continuance based on the same ground, saying:

> Well, I don't know, we can't stop people, in any event, listening to it. It is a matter of free speech, and the court can't control everybody. . . . We are not going to harass the jury every morning. . . . It is getting to the point where if we do it every morning, we are suspecting the jury. I have confidence in this jury. . . .

6. On November 24, a story appeared under an eight-column headline: "Sam Called a 'Jekyll-Hyde' By Marilyn, Cousin To Testify." It related that Marilyn had recently told friends that Sheppard was a "Dr. Jekyll and Mr. Hyde" character. No such testimony was ever produced at the trial. The story went on to announce: "The prosecution has a 'bombshell witness' on tap who will testify to Dr. Sam's display of fiery temper—countering the defense claim that the defendant is a gentle physician with an even disposition." Defense counsel made motions for change of venue, continuance and mistrial, but they were denied. No action was taken by the court.

7. When the trial was in its seventh week, Walter Winchell broadcasted over WXEL television and WJW radio that Carole Beasley, who was under arrest in New York City for robbery, had stated that, as Sheppard's mistress, she had borne him a child. The defense asked that the jury be queried on the broadcast. Two jurors admitted in open court that they had heard it. The judge asked each: "Would that have any effect upon your judgment?" Both replied, "No." This was accepted by the judge as sufficient; he merely asked the jury to "pay no attention whatever to that type of scavenging. . . . Let's confine ourselves to this courtroom, if you please." In answer to the motion for mistrial, the judge said:

> Well, even so, Mr. Corrigan, how are you ever going to prevent those things, in any event? I don't justify them at all. I think it is outrageous, but in

a sense, it is outrageous even if there were no trial here. The trial has nothing to do with it in the Court's mind, as far as its outrage is concerned, but—

Mr. Corrigan: I don't know what effect it had on the mind of any of these jurors, and I can't find out unless inquiry is made.

The Court: How would you ever, in any jury, avoid that kind of a thing?

8. On December 9, while Sheppard was on the witness stand he testified that he had been mistreated by Cleveland detectives after his arrest. Although he was not at the trial, Captain Kerr of the Homicide Bureau issued a press statement denying Sheppard's allegations which appeared under the headline: " 'Bare-faced Liar,' Kerr Says of Sam." Captain Kerr never appeared as a witness at the trial.

9. After the case was submitted to the jury, it was sequestered for its deliberations, which took five days and four nights. After the verdict, defense counsel ascertained that the jurors had been allowed to make telephone calls to their homes every day while they were sequestered at the hotel. Although the telephones had been removed from the juror's rooms, the jurors were permitted to use the phones in the bailiffs rooms. The calls were placed by the jurors themselves; no record was kept of the jurors who made calls, the telephone numbers or the parties called. The bailiffs sat in the room where they could hear only the juror's end of the conversation. The court had not instructed the bailiffs to prevent such calls. By a subsequent motion, defense counsel urged that this ground alone warranted a new trial, but the motion was overruled and no evidence was taken on the question.

IV

The principle that justice cannot survive behind walls of silence has long been reflected in the "Anglo-American distrust for secret trials." *In re Oliver.* A responsible press has always been regarded as the handmaiden of effective judicial administration, especially in the criminal field. Its function in this regard is documented by an impressive record of service over several centuries. The press does not simply publish information about trials but guards against the miscarriage of justice by subjecting the police, prosecutors, and judicial processes to extensive public scrutiny and criticism. This Court has, therefore, been unwilling to place any direct limitations on the freedom traditionally exercised by the news media for "[w]hat transpires in the court room is public property." *Craig v. Harney.* The "unqualified prohibitions laid down by the framers were intended to give to liberty of the press . . . the broadest scope that could be countenanced in an orderly society." *Bridges v. California.* And where there was "no threat or menace to the integrity of the trial," *Craig v. Harney,* we have consistently required that the press have a free hand, even though we sometimes deplored its sensationalism.

But the Court has also pointed out that "[l]egal trials are not like elections, to be won through the use of the meeting-hall, the radio, and the newspaper." *Bridges v. California.* And the Court has insisted that no one be punished for a crime without "a charge fairly made and fairly tried in a public tribunal free of prejudice, passion, excitement, and tyrannical power." *Chambers v. Florida.* "Freedom of

discussion should be given the widest range compatible with the essential requirement of the fair and orderly administration of justice." *Pennekamp v. Florida*. But
it must not be allowed to divert the trial from the "very purpose of a court system
. . . to adjudicate controversies, both criminal and civil, in the calmness and
solemnity of the courtroom according to legal procedures." *Cox v. Louisiana*
(Black, J., dissenting). Among these "legal procedures" is the requirement that the
jury's verdict be based on evidence received in open court, not from outside
sources. Thus, in *Marshall v. United States*, we set aside a federal conviction where
the jurors were exposed "through news accounts" to information that was not
admitted at trial. We held that the prejudice from such material "may indeed be
greater" than when it is part of the prosecution's evidence "for it is then not
tempered by protective procedures." At the same time, we did not consider
dispositive the statement of each juror "that he would not be influenced by the news
articles, that he could decide the case only on the evidence of record, and that he
felt no prejudice against petitioner as a result of the articles." Likewise, in *Irvin v.
Dowd*, even though each juror indicated that he could render an impartial verdict
despite exposure to prejudicial newspaper articles, we set aside the conviction
holding:

> With his life at stake, it is not requiring too much that petitioner be tried
> in an atmosphere undisturbed by so huge a wave of public passion. . . .

The undeviating rule of this Court was expressed by Mr. Justice Holmes over a
half a century ago in *Patterson v. Colorado:*

> The theory of our system is that the conclusions to be reached in a case
> will be induced only by evidence and argument in open court, and not by any
> outside influence, whether of private talk or public print.

Moreover, "the burden of showing essential unfairness . . . as a demonstrable
reality," *Adams v. United States ex rel. McCann*, need not be undertaken when
television has exposed the community "repeatedly and in depth to the spectacle of
[the accused] personally confessing in detail to the crimes with which he was later
to be charged." *Rideau v. Louisiana*. In *Turner v. Louisiana* two key witnesses were
deputy sheriffs who doubled as jury shepherds during the trial. The deputies swore
that they had not talked to the jurors about the case, but the Court nonetheless held
that,

> even if it could be assumed that the deputies never did discuss the case
> directly with any members of the jury, it would be blinking reality not to
> recognize the extreme prejudice inherent in this continual association. . . .

Only last Term in *Estes v. Texas*, we set aside a conviction despite the absence
of any showing of prejudice. We said there:

> It is true that in most cases involving claims of due process deprivations
> we require a showing of identifiable prejudice to the accused. Nevertheless, at

times a procedure employed by the State involves such a probability that prejudice will result that it is deemed inherently lacking in due process.

And we cited with approval the language of Mr. Justice Black for the Court in *In re Murchison* that "our system of law has always endeavored to prevent even the probability of unfairness."

V

It is clear that the totality of circumstances in this case also warrant such an approach. Unlike Estes, Sheppard was not granted a change of venue to a locale away from where the publicity originated; nor was his jury sequestered. The *Estes* jury saw none of the television broadcasts from the courtroom. On the contrary, the Sheppard jurors were subjected to newspaper, radio and television coverage of the trial while not taking part in the proceedings. They were allowed to go their separate ways outside of the courtroom, without adequate directions not to read or listen to anything concerning the case. The judge's "admonitions" at the beginning of the trial are representative:

> I would suggest to you and caution you that you do not read any newspapers during the progress of this trial, that you do not listen to radio comments nor watch or listen to television comments, insofar as this case is concerned. You will feel very much better as the trial proceeds. . . . I am sure that we shall all feel very much better if we do not indulge in any newspaper reading or listening to any comments whatever about the matter while the case is in progress. After it is all over, you can read it all to your heart's content. . . .

At intervals during the trial, the judge simply repeated his "suggestions" and "requests" that the jury not expose themselves to comment upon the case. Moreover, the jurors were thrust into the role of celebrities by the judge's failure to insulate them from reporters and photographers. The numerous pictures of the jurors, with their addresses, which appeared in the newspapers before and during the trial itself exposed them to expressions of opinion from both cranks and friends. The fact that anonymous letters had been received by prospective jurors should have made the judge aware that this publicity seriously threatened the jurors' privacy.

The press coverage of the Estes trial was not nearly as massive and pervasive as the attention given by the Cleveland newspapers and broadcasting stations to Sheppard's prosecution. Sheppard stood indicted for the murder of his wife; the State was demanding the death penalty. For months the virulent publicity about Sheppard and the murder had made the case notorious. Charges and counter-charges were aired in the news media besides those for which Sheppard was called to trial. In addition, only three months before trial, Sheppard was examined for more than five hours without counsel during a three-day inquest which ended in a public brawl. The inquest was televised live from a high school gymnasium seating hundreds of people. Furthermore, the trial began two weeks before a hotly contested election at which both Chief Prosecutor Mahon and Judge Blythin were candidates for judgeships.

While we cannot say that Sheppard was denied due process by the judge's refusal to take precautions against the influence of pretrial publicity alone, the court's later rulings must be considered against the setting in which the trial was held. In light of this background, we believe that the arrangements made by the judge with the news media caused Sheppard to be deprived of that "judicial serenity and calm to which [he] was entitled." *Estes v. Texas*. The fact is that bedlam reigned at the courthouse during the trial and newsmen took over practically the entire courtroom, hounding most of the participants in the trial, especially Sheppard. At a temporary table within a few feet of the jury box and counsel table sat some 20 reporters staring at Sheppard and taking notes. The erection of a press table for reporters inside the bar is unprecedented. The bar of the court is reserved for counsel, providing them a safe place in which to keep papers and exhibits, and to confer privately with client and co-counsel. It is designed to protect the witness and the jury from any distractions, intrusions or influences, and to permit bench discussions of the judge's rulings away from the hearing of the public and the jury. Having assigned almost all of the available seats in the courtroom to the news media the judge lost his ability to supervise that environment. The movement of the reporters in and out of the courtroom caused frequent confusion and disruption of the trial. And the record reveals constant commotion within the bar. Moreover, the judge gave the throng of newsmen gathered in the corridors of the courthouse absolute free rein. Participants in the trial, including the jury, were forced to run a gauntlet of reporters and photographers each time they entered or left the courtroom. The total lack of consideration for the privacy of the jury was demonstrated by the assignment to a broadcasting station of space next to the jury room on the floor above the courtroom, as well as the fact that jurors were allowed to make telephone calls during their five-day deliberation.

VI

There can be no question about the nature of the publicity which surrounded Sheppard's trial. We agree, as did the Court of Appeals, with the findings in Judge Bell's opinion for the Ohio Supreme Court:

> Murder and mystery, society, sex and suspense were combined in this case in such a manner as to intrigue and captivate the public fancy to a degree perhaps unparalleled in recent annals. Throughout the preindictment investigation, the subsequent legal skirmishes and the nine-week trial, circulation-conscious editors catered to the insatiable interest of the American public in the bizarre. . . . In this atmosphere of a "Roman holiday" for the news media, Sam Sheppard stood trial for his life.

Indeed, every court that has considered this case, save the court that tried it, has deplored the manner in which the news media inflamed and prejudiced the public.

Much of the material printed or broadcast during the trial was never heard from the witness stand, such as the charges that Sheppard had purposely impeded the murder investigation and must be guilty since he had hired a prominent criminal lawyer; that Sheppard was a perjurer; that he had sexual relations with numerous women; that his slain wife had characterized him as "Jekyll-Hyde"; that he was "a bare-faced liar" because of his testimony as to police treatment; and, finally, that a woman convict claimed Sheppard to be the father of her illegitimate child. As the trial progressed, the newspapers summarized and interpreted the evidence, devoting particular attention to the material that incriminated Sheppard, and often drew unwarranted inferences from testimony. At one point, a front-page picture of Mrs. Sheppard's blood-stained pillow was published after being "doctored" to show more clearly an alleged imprint of a surgical instrument.

Nor is there doubt that this deluge of publicity reached at least some of the jury. On the only occasion that the jury was queried, two jurors admitted in open court to hearing the highly inflammatory charge that a prison inmate claimed Sheppard as the father of her illegitimate child. Despite the extent and nature of the publicity to which the jury was exposed during trial, the judge refused defense counsel's other requests that the jury be asked whether they had read or heard specific prejudicial comment about the case, including the incidents we have previously summarized. In these circumstances, we can assume that some of this material reached members of the jury.

VII

The court's fundamental error is compounded by the holding that it lacked power to control the publicity about the trial. From the very inception of the proceedings the judge announced that neither he nor anyone else could restrict prejudicial news accounts. And he reiterated this view on numerous occasions. Since he viewed the news media as his target, the judge never considered other means that are often utilized to reduce the appearance of prejudicial material and to protect the jury from outside influence. We conclude that these procedures would have been sufficient to guarantee Sheppard a fair trial and so do not consider what sanctions might be available against a recalcitrant press nor the charges of bias now made against the state trial judge.

The carnival atmosphere at trial could easily have been avoided since the courtroom and courthouse premises are subject to the control of the court. As we stressed in *Estes*, the presence of the press at judicial proceedings must be limited when it is apparent that the accused might otherwise be prejudiced or disadvantaged. Bearing in mind the massive pretrial publicity, the judge should have adopted stricter rules governing the use of the courtroom by newsmen, as Sheppard's counsel requested. The number of reporters in the courtroom itself could have been limited at the first sign that their presence would disrupt the trial. They certainly should not have been placed inside the bar. Furthermore, the judge should have more closely regulated the conduct of newsmen in the courtroom. For instance, the judge belatedly asked them not to handle and photograph trial exhibits lying on the counsel table during recesses.

Secondly, the court should have insulated the witnesses. All of the newspapers and radio stations apparently interviewed prospective witnesses at will, and in many instances disclosed their testimony. A typical example was the publication of numerous statements by Susan Hayes, before her appearance in court, regarding her love affair with Sheppard. Although the witnesses were barred from the courtroom during the trial the full *verbatim* testimony was available to them in the press. This completely nullified the judge's imposition of the rule.

Thirdly, the court should have made some effort to control the release of leads, information, and gossip to the press by police officers, witnesses, and the counsel for both sides. Much of the information thus disclosed was inaccurate, leading to groundless rumors and confusion. That the judge was aware of his responsibility in this respect may be seen from his warning to Steve Sheppard, the accused's brother, who had apparently made public statements in an attempt to discredit testimony for the prosecution. The judge made this statement in the presence of the jury:

> Now, the court wants to say a word. That he was told—he was not read anything about it at all—but he was informed that Dr. Steve Sheppard, who has been granted the privilege of remaining in the courtroom during the trial, has been trying the case in the newspapers and making rather uncomplimentary comments about the testimony of the witnesses for the State.
>
> Let it be now understood that if Dr. Steve Sheppard wishes to use the newspapers to try his case while we are trying it here, he will be barred from remaining in the courtroom during the progress of the trial if he is to be a witness in the case.
>
> The Court appreciates he cannot deny Steve Sheppard the right of free speech, but he can deny him the . . . privilege of being in the courtroom, if he wants to avail himself of that method during the progress of the trial.

Defense counsel immediately brought to the court's attention the tremendous amount of publicity in the Cleveland press that "misrepresented entirely the testimony" in the case. Under such circumstances, the judge should have at least warned the newspapers to check the accuracy of their accounts. And it is obvious that the judge should have further sought to alleviate this problem by imposing control over the statements made to the news media by counsel, witnesses, and especially the Coroner and police officers. The prosecution repeatedly made evidence available to the news media which was never offered in the trial. Much of the "evidence" disseminated in this fashion was clearly inadmissible. The exclusion of such evidence in court is rendered meaningless when a news medium makes it available to the public. For example, the publicity about Sheppard's refusal to take a lie detector test came directly from police officers and the Coroner. The story that Sheppard had been called a "Jekyll-Hyde" personality by his wife was attributed to a prosecution witness. No such testimony was given. The further report that there was "a 'bombshell witness' on tap" who would testify as to Sheppard's "fiery temper" could only have emanated from the prosecution. Moreover, the newspapers described in detail clues that had been found by the police, but not put into the record.

The fact that many of the prejudicial news items can be traced to the prosecution, as well as the defense, aggravates the judge's failure to take any action. Effective control of these sources—concededly within the court's power—might well have prevented the divulgence of inaccurate information, rumors, and accusations that made up much of the inflammatory publicity, at least after Sheppard's indictment.

More specifically, the trial court might well have proscribed extrajudicial statements by any lawyer, party, witness, or court official which divulged prejudicial matters, such as the refusal of Sheppard to submit to interrogation or take any lie detector tests; any statement made by Sheppard to officials; the identity of prospective witnesses or their probable testimony; any belief in guilt or innocence; or like statements concerning the merits of the case. See *State v. Van Duyne*, in which the court interpreted Canon 20 of the American Bar Association's Canons of Professional Ethics to prohibit such statements. Being advised of the great public interest in the case, the mass coverage of the press, and the potential prejudicial impact of publicity, the court could also have requested the appropriate city and county officials to promulgate a regulation with respect to dissemination of information about the case by their employees. In addition, reporters who wrote or broadcasted prejudicial stories, could have been warned as to the impropriety of publishing material not introduced in the proceedings. The judge was put on notice of such events by defense counsel's complaint about the WHK broadcast on the second day of trial. In this manner, Sheppard's right to a trial free from outside interference would have been given added protection without corresponding curtailment of the news media. Had the judge, the other officers of the court, and the police placed the interest of justice first, the news media would have soon learned to be content with the task of reporting the case as it unfolded in the courtroom—not pieced together from extra-judicial statements.

From the cases coming here we note that unfair and prejudicial news comment on pending trials has become increasingly prevalent. Due process requires that the accused receive a trial by an impartial jury free from outside influences. Given the pervasiveness of modern communications and the difficulty of effacing prejudicial publicity from the minds of the jurors, the trial courts must take strong measures to ensure that the balance is never weighed against the accused. And appellate tribunals have the duty to make an independent evaluation of the circumstances. Of course, there is nothing that proscribes the press from reporting events that transpire in the courtroom. But where there is a reasonable likelihood that prejudicial news prior to trial will prevent a fair trial, the judge should continue the case until the threat abates, or transfer it to another county not so permeated with publicity. In addition, sequestration of the jury was something the judge should have raised *sua sponte* with counsel. If publicity during the proceedings threatens the fairness of the trial, a new trial should be ordered. But we must remember that reversals are but palliatives; the cure lies in those remedial measures that will prevent the prejudice at its inception. The courts must take such steps by rule and regulation that will protect their processes from prejudicial outside interferences. Neither prosecutors, counsel for defense, the accused, witnesses, court staff nor enforcement officers coming under the jurisdiction of the court should be permitted to frustrate its function. Collaboration between counsel and the press as to information affecting the fairness of a criminal trial is not only subject to regulation, but is highly censurable and worthy of disciplinary measures.

Since the state trial judge did not fulfill his duty to protect Sheppard from the inherently prejudicial publicity which saturated the community and to control disruptive influences in the courtroom, we must reverse the denial of the *habeas* petition. The case is remanded to the District Court with instructions to issue the writ and order that Sheppard be released from custody unless the State puts him to its charges again within a reasonable time.

It is so ordered.

* * *

One year to the day after the Gannett *ruling, which allowed judges to close pretrial hearings and suggested the same for trials themselves (see Chapter 3), the Court handed down* Richmond Newspapers v. Virginia, *an eagerly awaited decision, though the wait was not without some trepidation on the part of the press. The Court held 7–1 that the Constitution allowed for the closing of trials only in the most extraordinary circumstances. While the ruling did not guarantee that all trials be open, as the press would have preferred, it did place a heavy burden on any judge who might order a closed trial. Only Justice Rehnquist dissented. Justice Powell took no part in the case. But, to add to the already confused state created by* Gannett, *there was no majority opinion. The seven Justices in the majority wrote six different opinions, apparently not being able to agree on any one as an opinion of the Court. Still, the size of the majority was a relief to the press, as were the several strong statements favoring open trials voiced by the Justices.*

RICHMOND NEWSPAPERS V. VIRGINIA
448 U.S. 555 (1980)

CHIEF JUSTICE BURGER *announced the judgment of the Court and delivered an opinion in which Justice White and Justice Stevens joined.*

The narrow question presented in this case is whether the right of the public and press to attend criminal trials is guaranteed under the United States Constitution. . . .

We begin consideration of this case by noting that the precise issue presented here has not previously been before this Court for decision. In *Gannett Co., Inc. v. DePasquale,* the Court was not required to decide whether a right of access to trials, as distinguished from hearings on *pretrial* motions, was constitutionally guaranteed. . . .

. . . [T]he historical evidence demonstrates conclusively that at the time when our organic laws were adopted, criminal trials both here and in England had long been presumptively open. This is no quirk of history; rather, it has long been recognized as an indispensible attribute of an Anglo-American trial. Both Hale in the 17th century and Blackstone in the 18th saw the importance of openness to the proper functioning of a trial; it gave assurance that the proceedings were conducted fairly to all concerned, and it discouraged perjury, the misconduct of participants, and decisions based on secret bias or partiality. . . .

The Bill of Rights was enacted against the backdrop of the long history of trials being presumptively open. Public access to trials was then regarded as an important aspect of the process itself; the conduct of trials "before as many of the people as chuse to attend" was regarded as one of "the inestimable advantages of a free English constitution of government." Journals of the Continental Congress. In guaranteeing freedoms such as those of speech and press, the First Amendment can be read as protecting the right of everyone to attend trials so as to give meaning to those explicit guarantees. . . . What this means in the context of trials is that the First Amendment guarantees of speech and press, standing alone, prohibit government from summarily closing courtroom doors which had long been open to the public at the time that amendment was adopted. "For the First Amendment does not speak equivocally. . . . It must be taken as a command of the broadest scope that explicit language, read in the context of a liberty-loving society, will allow." *Bridges v. California.* . . .

We hold that the right to attend criminal trials is implicit in the guarantees of the First Amendment; without the freedom to attend such trials, which people have exercised for centuries, important aspects of freedom of speech and "of the press could be eviscerated." *Branzburg.* . . .

The Court in *Gannett* made clear that although the Sixth Amendment guarantees the accused a right to a public trial, it does not give a right to a private trial. Despite the fact that this was the fourth trial of the accused, the trial judge made no findings to support closure; no inquiry was made as to whether alternative solutions would have met the need to ensure fairness; there was no recognition of any right under the Constitution for the public or press to attend the trial. In contrast to the pretrial proceeding dealt with in *Gannett*, there exist in the context of the trial itself various tested alternatives to satisfy the constitutional demands of fairness. There was no suggestion that any problems with witnesses could not have been dealt with by their exclusion from the courtroom or their sequestration during the trial. Nor is there anything to indicate that sequestration of the jurors would not have guarded against their being subjected to any improper information. All of the alternatives admittedly present difficulties for trial courts, but none of the factors relied on here was beyond the realm of the manageable. Absent an overriding interest articulated in findings, the trial of a criminal case must be open to the public. Accordingly, the judgment under review is reversed.

JUSTICE WHITE, *concurring.*

This case would have been unnecessary had *Gannett Co. v. DePasquale* construed the Sixth Amendment to forbid excluding the public from criminal proceedings except in narrowly defined circumstances. But the Court there rejected the submission of four of us to this effect, thus requiring that the First Amendment issue involved here be addressed. On this issue, I concur in the opinion of The Chief Justice.

JUSTICE STEVENS, *concurring.*

This is a watershed case. Until today the Court has accorded virtually absolute protection to the dissemination of information or ideas, but never before has it squarely held that the acquisition of newsworthy matter is entitled to any constitutional protection whatsoever. . . .

Twice before, the Court has implied that any governmental restriction on access to information, no matter how severe and no matter how unjustified, would be constitutionally acceptable so long as it did not single out the press for special disabilities not applicable to the public at large. . . . Today, however, for the first time, the Court unequivocally holds that an arbitrary interference with access to important information is an abridgment of the freedoms of speech and of the press protected by the First Amendment.

It is somewhat ironic that the Court should find more reason to recognize a right of access today than it did in *Houchins.* For *Houchins* involved the plight of a segment of society least able to protect itself, an attack on a long-standing policy of concealment, and an absence of any legitimate justification for abridging public access to information about how government operates. . . .

JUSTICE BLACKMUN, *concurring in the judgment.*

. . . The decision in this case is gratifying for me for two reasons:

It is gratifying, first, to see the Court now looking to and relying upon legal history in determining the fundamental public character of the criminal trial. The partial dissent in *Gannett* took great pains in assembling—I believe adequately— the historical material and in stressing its importance to this area of the law. Although the Court in *Gannett* gave a modicum of lip service to legal history, it denied its obvious application when the defense and the prosecution, with no resistance by the trial judge, agreed that the proceeding should be closed.

The Court's return to history is a welcome change in direction.

It is gratifying, second, to see the Court wash away at least some of the graffiti that marred the prevailing opinions in *Gannett*. No less than 12 times in the primary opinion in that case, the Court (albeit in what seems now to have become clear dicta) observed that its Sixth Amendment closure ruling applied to the *trial* itself. The author of the first concurring opinion was fully aware of this and would have restricted the Court's observations and ruling to the suppression hearing. Nonetheless, he *joined* the Court's opinion with its multiple references to the trial itself; the opinion was not a mere concurrence in the Court's judgment. And Mr. Justice Rehnquist, in his separate concurring opinion, quite understandably observed, as a consequence, that the Court was holding "without qualification," that " 'members of the public have no constitutional right under the Sixth and Fourteenth Amendments to attend criminal trials,' " quoting from the primary opinion. The resulting confusion among commentators and journalists was not surprising.

The Court's ultimate ruling in *Gannett*, with such clarification as is provided by the opinions in this case today, apparently is now to the effect that there is no *Sixth* Amendment right on the part of the public—or the press—to an open hearing on a motion to suppress. I, of course, continue to believe that *Gannett* was in error, both in its interpretation of the Sixth Amendment generally, and in its application to the suppression hearing, for I remain convinced that the right to a public trial is to be found where the Constitution explicitly placed it—in the Sixth Amendment. . . .

Having said all this, and with the Sixth Amendment set to one side in this case, I am driven to conclude, as a secondary position, that the First Amendment must provide some measure of protection for public access to the trial. The opinion in partial dissent in *Gannett* explained that the public has an intense need and a deserved right to know about the administration of justice in general; about the prosecution of local crimes in particular; about the conduct of the judge, the prosecutor, defense counsel, police officers, other public servants, and all the actors in the judicial arena; and about the trial itself. . . .

JUSTICE REHNQUIST, *dissenting*.

In the Gilbert & Sullivan operetta *Iolanthe*, the Lord Chancellor recites:

"The Law is the true embodiment
of everything that's excellent,

It has no king of fault or flaw,
And I, my lords, embody the law."

It is difficult not to derive more than a little of this flavor from the various opinions supporting the judgment in this case. . . .

We have at present 50 state judicial systems and one federal judicial system in the United States, and our authority to reverse a decision by the highest court of the State is limited to only those occasions when the state decision violates some provision of the United States Constitution. And that authority should be exercised with a full sense that the judges whose decisions we review are making the same effort as we to uphold the Constitution. . . .

The proper administration of justice in any nation is bound to be a matter of the highest concern to all thinking citizens. But to gradually rein in, as this Court has done over the past generation, all of the ultimate decision-making power over how justice shall be administered, not merely in the federal system but in each of the 50 States, is a task that no Court consisting of nine persons, however gifted, is equal to. Nor is it desirable that such authority be exercised by such a tiny numerical fragment of the 200 million people who compose the population of this country. . . .

However high minded the impulses which originally spawned this trend may have been, and which impulses have been accentuated since the time Justice Jackson wrote, it is basically unhealthy to have so much authority concentrated in a small group of lawyers who have been appointed to the Supreme Court and enjoy virtual life tenure.

The issue here is not whether the "right" to freedom of the press conferred by the First Amendment to the Constitution overrides the defendant's "right" to a fair trial conferred by other amendments to the Constitution; it is instead whether any provision in the Constitution may fairly be read to prohibit what the trial judge in the Virginia state court system did in this case. Being unable to find any such prohibition in the First, Sixth, Ninth, or any other Amendments to the United States Constitution, or in the Constitution itself, I dissent.

"GAG" ORDERS LEAVE A QUAGMIRE

BY FRED P. GRAHAM*

Aggie Whelan is understandably puzzled. As a courtroom artist for CBS news, she illustrated two trials recently for television. For her sketches of the Mitchell-Stans trial, the National Academy of Television Arts and Sciences awarded her an Emmy. For her sketches of the trial of the Gainesville 8, U.S. District Judge Winston Arnow awarded CBS a conviction for contempt of court.

Whelan's puzzlement, unhappily, is not all that unusual in journalism these days. She is one of a growing list of victims of a legal quagmire called "fair trial-free press," the lawyers' tidy term for the chaotic relationship that has developed between the news media and a judicial system that is groping for a partial exemption from free journalistic scrutiny.

It has now been a decade since the issue was brought forward by the Warren Commission's criticism of the press coverage of the Kennedy assassination; Aggie Whelan is typical enough to be a starting point in taking stock of where things seem to be heading after those 10 years.

The Gainesville 8 were members of the Vietnam Veterans Against the War (VVAW), one of America's most non-newsworthy organizations until the Justice Department accused them of conspiring to disrupt the 1972 Republican convention in Miami by ingenious forms of violence, including firecrackers and wrist slingshots. They were arrested and hustled out of Miami for the duration of the convention and, when they were finally brought to trial in Gainesville before Judge Arnow, they were ready to tell anyone who would listen that they thought it was a political frame-up.

But Judge Arnow, apparently not wanting any nonlegal factors to intrude into the case, issued a "gag order"—a type of order that was virtually unknown 10 years ago but which now has become the focal point of the fair trial-free press issue. Among other things, this one barred the defendants and all their supporters (apparently the entire membership of the VVAW) from communicating with the press, and it prohibited any sketches of courtroom scenes.

The trial resulted in a conviction—not of the defendants, who were quickly acquitted, but of CBS. Whelan had returned to her hotel room one day and had sketched, from memory, courtroom scenes that later appeared on television. Judge Arnow fined CBS $500 for contempt of court.

* Published originally in the *Washington Post* and reprinted in the *Los Angeles Times* November 11, 1974. Used with permission of Benjamin C. Bradlee, Executive Editor of the *Washington Post*, and the author, former legal correspondent for CBS News.

After enough hearings and appeals to convict a Godfather, the U.S. Court of Appeals for the Fifth Circuit unreeled a dizzying chain of logic that zigged and zagged as follows: (a) It held that Judge Arnow's attempt to control the media's reporting of events in open court violated the First Amendment and was therefore invalid; but, (b) a contempt conviction could be imposed for violating that order anyway because even unconstitutional orders by judges must be obeyed until overturned by higher courts; but, (c) because contempt of Judge Arnow's own order was at stake, CBS is entitled to a new trial before another judge.

The thing that keeps this incident from being funny is that it is too typical of other bizarre judicial conduct that has occurred recently in the name of "fair trial-free press."

● A San Francisco judge ordered all public officials—including Mayor Joseph Alioto—to stop discussing the defendants in the "zebra" murders, and forbade the news media from making public the criminal records or reputations of the arrested suspects.

● A judge in New Orleans ordered the press not to report the open court testimony in a pretrial hearing of a rape-murder case or any editorial comment that might tend to affect the case.

● When a suspect was arrested in the "alphabet" bombings in Los Angeles, a judge "gagged" everyone—including the defendant, who had been so silent anyway that some people thought he was a deaf-mute.

This is only a sampling of the gag orders that have been issued recently in the name of fair trial-free press. Some were overturned on appeal, some were not.

But they do indicate that the use of gag orders and secrecy in efforts to head off prejudicial publicity can produce erratic judicial behavior and can impede free discussion of matters of public importance and interest.

Yet the very sensitivity and importance of those matters, which should call for the greatest possible news coverage, appear instead to be influencing judges to resort to gag orders and secrecy in the name of fair trial-free press.

In doing this, the trial judges seem to be cutting against the grain of the approach suggested by the Supreme Court. The court [had not] ruled on the gag order question [at this writing. But see *Nebraska Press Assn.*, Chapter 2.] But when the court . . . ruled on . . . *Sheppard v. Maxwell* [in 1966], it instructed judges to deal with publicity by directing its efforts inward, toward the system of justice, not outward toward public officials and the press. Justice Tom Clark's opinion for the majority catalogued all of the internal measures that should be considered, without mentioning external measures.

"Of course, there is nothing that proscribes the press from reporting events that transpire in the courtroom. But where there is a reasonable likelihood that prejudicial news prior to trial will prevent a fair trial, the judge should continue the case until the threat abates, or transfer it to another county not so permeated with publicity. In addition, sequestration of the jury was something the judge should have raised *suasponte* with counsel. If publicity during the proceedings threatens the fairness of the trial, a new trial should be ordered."

The problem with that heavy hint about continuances and changes of venue is that trial judges relish playing center stage in highly publicized cases; once a newsworthy case is assigned to them, they tend to find reasons why it can be tried promptly in their courts—if only stern steps are taken to muzzle all that publicity.

Of the Watergate cases that have been tried so far, trial delays or changes of venue out of the District of Columbia were requested by defendants in each case. Not only were all these motions denied, but the lawyers and sometimes the defendants were subsequently gagged as the judges sought to dampen the publicity surrounding the trials.

In cases not involving gag orders, it's frequently easier to tell when the cure is clearly worse than the disease—such as when Judge John Sirica suggested postponing the impeachment proceedings to ease publicity problems at the coverup trial, or when Judge Walter Hoffman considered calling off the grand jury investigation of Vice President Agnew because there had been news leaks.

But it is much more difficult to show that a gag order has done more damage to the First Amendment (guarantee of press freedom) than is justified by the threat of prejudicial publicity. As a result, the pressures of free press-fair trial have produced an outpouring of gag orders that seems to be steadily increasing, both in numbers and in the breadth of the limits they place on free expression. And, in addition, judicial proceedings, which used to be automatically held in the open for all to see, are increasingly conducted in secret.

Nobody knows how far this has gone because gag orders so rarely turn up in case reports.

So, to measure the trend, I have made an informal, unscientific sampling composed of all the reported cases I could find; all the additional unreported cases cited in the few law review articles published on this subject; and newspaper indexes and clipping services. All these suggest that the gag order problem is a phenomenon of the past decade—and that the problem is growing steadily.

This sampling turned up no gag orders until 1966—two years after the Warren Commission report, and the same year as the report of the American Bar Association's Advisory Committee on Fair Trials and Free Press and the Supreme Court's reversal of a murder conviction because of prejudicial publicity in *Sheppard v. Maxwell*. But in 1966, there were two known cases in which gag orders were issued. In 1967, there were 4; in 1968, 15; in 1969, 5; in 1970, 9; in 1971, 13; in 1972, 10; in 1973, 22; So far in 1974, there have been 20.

It is impossible to say how huge an iceberg lurks below this visible tip, but whatever the total is in numbers, gag orders are affecting a high percentage of the cases that the national press is interested in covering. I have not covered a trial in the past two years where the judge didn't issue a gag order, and I don't know of any other CBS correspondent who did.

In theory, a judge shouldn't issue an order curbing anyone's absolute freedom of expression unless there's a proven "clear and present danger" that publicity threatens the fairness of the trial. But in California, gag orders are now issued routinely in newsworthy cases.

These orders fall into three general categories: orders that seek to limit the statements that may be made to the press by lawyers' parties, witnesses and, sometimes, outsiders; orders that purport to tell the press directly what it may or may not publish; and orders sealing court records and proceedings from the press and public.

They are listed in that order because a pattern seems to be developing in which judges try to dampen publicity by gagging those most obviously under the judicial thumb—the lawyers, defendants and witnesses. When that fails, there's a tendency to try direct action against the press, or—increasingly—to employ secret proceedings.

As a result, there are currently about a half-dozen major confrontations each year between judges and newsmen. Into that fractious atmosphere has been injected a new doctrine known as the Dickinson rule. [*Dickinson v. United States*]

It got its name from a case in Baton Rouge, La. in 1972, when a judge ordered the press not to report a hearing in open court and then convicted two reporters for contempt after they wrote stories. The U.S. Fifth Circuit Court of Appeals said the order was unconstitutional, but upheld the conviction, saying the reporters should have obeyed the order and appealed it.

It was the first time in the history of this country that newsmen had been held in contempt for reporting a public hearing in the face of an admittedly unconstitutional order. But when the Supreme Court was asked to review the case, it declined, leaving other judges free, at least for the present, to invoke the Dickinson rule against the press.

It is not difficult to imagine that, when some future Watergate occurs somewhere, lawyers for those hoping to cover it up will manage to persuade a judge that it will be necessary to order the local Woodwards and Bernsteins not to publish any more stories about the case in the name of fair trial and free press. And even though that order may be unconstitutional, those reporters will have to obey for as long as it takes to win an appeal—and this time the coverup may succeed.

The problems would be minimal if the judges would confine themselves to the internal measures of trial delays, change of venue and careful jury selection as prescribed by the Supreme Court. But once they undertake to control the publicity, there's a tendency to escalate their efforts, which, in the long run, seems detrimental to everyone concerned.

Exhibit A is the Watergate coverup trial. Watergate had been so much in the news that the public was growing sick of it when, last March, Judge Sirica issued an order forbidding all attorneys, defendants and subpoenaed witnesses from "making extrajudicial statements concerning any aspect of this case that are likely to interfere with the rights of the accused or the public to a trial by an impartial jury."

But the publicity about the trial continued and Judge Sirica responded with increasing secrecy.

The result is that the Watergate coverup trial has become a secret trial in some respects. It is an ominous example of how contagious secrecy can be, once it is injected into the judicial system in the name of fair trial-free press.

Several days ago, in desperation, George Lardner of the *Washington Post* and I wrote a letter to Judge Sirica, protesting the growing secrecy and requesting that the records be unsealed. He refused, and—you guessed it—sealed our letter.

THE LAWYER'S ADVERSARY SYSTEM
IS ADVERSE TO A JOURNALIST'S THINKING

By Reuven Frank*

Freedom of the press is threatened by lawyers. You have heard Professor Kingsfield tell his young law students that they have come to him with their skulls full of mush, and if they survive they will leave thinking like lawyers.

Believing in the adversary system is what thinking like lawyers means. The adversary system postulates that truth, and therefore justice, is best derived through controversy and debate, that each side—that is, each side of two—will marshal its best evidence and argument, and that a judge or jury can then determine truth and separate right from wrong.

I think the adversary system is the reason the law business and the news business in this country are on a collision course.

Lawyers do not understand what we do, because they do not think as we do. Their thinking is organized, ritualized and bipolar. Ours is disorganized, individual and multipolar. When a reporter goes forth on a story he has no idea of what he will find, and only a general idea of what he is looking for. He does not—or at least he should not—be seeking only such information as buttresses a conclusion he has already reached. Within limitations of reason and budget he will go anywhere and talk to anyone for information of any kind. You can see the difference when you realize that if his story becomes part of a trial, his notes may be subpoenaed by both sides, each looking for something else. This difference between lawyers and journalists is crucial because journalists are under the power of lawyers, not vice versa.

The best example I know governs broadcasting. Broadcasting operates under the fairness doctrine, the obligation to present different sides of an issue. This is a lawyer's formulation, sensible only to those who think in terms of adversary and advocate.

One news program I was associated with was ordered to present a rebuttal even though neither we nor the people who ordered it could find anyone willing to offer an opposing view. But if you believe the public is well-served if extreme and irrational statements are made on both sides, without reporters checking facts, if truth becomes manifest when Lavrenti Beria debates Paul Joseph Goebbels, then

* From Reuven Frank. "The Lawyer's Adversary System is Adverse to a Journalist's Thinking." *The Quill*, Vol. 67, No. 8 (September 1979), p. 42. Used with permission of *The Quill*, published by the Society of Professional Journalists, and the author, former president of NBC News.

rebuttal is always in order. If you believe there is no such thing as simple curiosity, nothing is worth reporting unless it can be debated.

In the same light, fair trial will always win over free press, not because it is nobler in concept, or more central to the workings of democracy, but because whenever the choice has to be made it will be made by a judge. And, don't forget, a judge was first a lawyer.

During the trial of Dr. Mario Jascalevich, when the notes of *New York Times* reporter Myron Farber were being subpoenaed, I met two New Jersey judges of middle-level status at social occasions. None of us had anything to do with the case, but all of us were following it hungrily. You may remember how complicated the case became when it was learned that Farber had contracted for a book and that his editor knew more than Farber was willing to tell in court. Both judges were gleeful. So much for reporters' confidentiality, they crowed. Farber was just out for money. Farber, meanwhile, was already in jail for contempt of court. I know enough about the Bergen County jail to believe that no intelligent human being goes there for money. But here was a judge of a fairly high court of the state of New Jersey doubting and ridiculing the constitutional reasons Farber gave for refusing to let lawyers paw through his notes.

A lot of newsmen around town who stopped their intense support were reacting to the public relations aspects of the case, and not to the case itself. They, of all people, should have known better. Farber's notes, if they were like yours or mine, were full of things that were nobody's business but his. They were not adversary material because his sources were not forewarned that they were supplying adversary material. He went to jail because the notes were his business. The lawyers wanted him in jail for reasons of their business. It's not the same business.

Theodore H. White wrote on the Farber case: "A good reporter is a cross between a beggar and a detective, a wheedler and a prosecutor. This is how he collects facts. But the essence of his trade is to know how to sift out of rumor, gossip and hearsay the essential facts and then to arrange those facts so that a story comes out as close to the truth as he can make it. . . . Recently I have had the experience of trying to weave some of my old reporter's notes into a book. I found in those notes so many falsehoods, so many wild conversations, so many confidences of people who trusted me, that I am appalled by how much harm could be squeezed out of them by a smart lawyer, a smart politician, a smart propagandist."

All the frontiers of reporting news touch the legal system these days. And the lawyers and judges who control our future increasingly think of us as a species of nuisance. Journalists are supposed to be outsiders—strangers, in the sense that Camus used the word. We operate best when we operate outside systems, not against them. The reporter is the last existential man. What seems new to me is a conflict between two methods of thinking. The conflict is not ideological. A lawyer for the civil liberties union has as much trouble understanding what we do as a lawyer who has become a bank president. And that is why Farber went to jail.

In the history of this republic, many judges have gone to jail, but I know of none who went there on a matter of principle.

CHAPTER 12

TRIAL BY TELEVISION

The presence of cameras in the courtroom has been debated since the 1935 trial of Richard Bruno Hauptmann on charges of kidnapping the baby of Charles A. Lindbergh. Judges historically have forbidden the use of cameras, following the guidance of the American Bar Association's Canon 35, adopted soon after the Hauptmann trial and recently renumbered Canon 3A(7). The ABA argues that cameras tend to lessen the essential dignity of the court and its deliberations.

Arguments in favor of allowing cameras to record the courtroom scene include: 1) the public's right to know, 2) the constitutional guarantees of a free press, 3) the camera and resulting pictures are merely extensions of the courtroom's walls, 4) the defendant's right to a public trial, 5) the several experiments which have shown no loss of courtroom decorum when cameras have been used surreptitiously, 6) the technical improvements including miniaturization of equipment and fast film which uses natural light and 7) the lack of firm evidence that the presence of cameras is harmful to the administration of justice.

Those who argue for continuation and strengthening of a ban on cameras point to the unknown effects, including: 1) the subconscious effect on witnesses or potential witnesses, 2) the possibility of attorney theatrics, 3) the question of the distraction of jury members, 4) the microscopic probe of the camera which tends to focus on an instant out of context and in closeup, 5) the tendency for the photographer to focus on the unusual, 6) the temptation to play up the sensational rather than the significant, 7) the possibility with television of commercial interjections and 8) the general lessening of the basic dignity of the proceedings.

The fundamental question, of course, is whether justice tends to blur on film and on the screen. And this essential question has not been adequately answered, though the prohibitive view of the ABA generally has been opposed by professional journalism organizations. Still, there has been serious doubt expressed over the ability to secure a fair trial for Lee Harvey Oswald, the accused assassin of President

Kennedy, who in turn was slain before live television cameras as millions watched. . . .

The role of a pre-trial television confession first came under Supreme Court scrutiny with the appeal of Wilbert Rideau, charged in 1961 with armed robbery, kidnapping and murder. Justice Stewart, in his majority opinion, details the facts leading to the Court's findings. It was held that Rideau was denied due process of law because the trial court failed to grant a change of venue. The pre-trial televised "interview," which was given repeated exposure to a substantial segment of the community, contained a personal confession of the crimes with which Rideau was later to be charged. Justice Clark, who was joined by Justice Harlan, dissented by claiming there was no evidence that the televised confession did in fact result in an unfair trial for the defendant.

RIDEAU V. LOUISIANA
373 U.S. 723 (1963)

JUSTICE STEWART *delivered the opinion of the Court.*

On the evening of February 16, 1961, a man robbed a bank in Lake Charles, Louisiana, kidnapped three of the bank's employees, and killed one of them. A few hours later the petitioner, Wilbert Rideau, was apprehended by the police and lodged in the Calcasieu Parish jail in Lake Charles. The next morning a moving picture film with a sound track was made of an "interview" in the jail between Rideau and the Sheriff of Calcasieu Parish. This "interview" lasted approximately 20 minutes. It consisted of interrogation by the sheriff and admissions by Rideau that he had perpetrated the bank robbery, kidnapping, and murder. Later the same day the filmed "interview" was broadcast over a television station in Lake Charles, and some 24,000 people in the community saw and heard it on television. The sound film was again shown on television the next day to an estimated audience of 53,000 people. The following day the film was again broadcast by the same television station, and this time approximately 29,000 people saw and heard the "interview" on their television sets. Calcasieu Parish has a population of approximately 150,000 people.

Some two weeks later, Rideau was arraigned on charges of armed robbery, kidnapping, and murder, and two lawyers were appointed to represent him. His lawyers promptly filed a motion for a change of venue, on the ground that it would deprive Rideau of rights guaranteed to him by the United States Constitution to force him to trial in Calcasieu Parish after the three television broadcasts there of his "interview" with the sheriff. After a hearing, the motion for change of venue was denied, and Rideau was accordingly convicted and sentenced to death on the murder charge in the Calcasieu Parish trial court.

Three members of the jury which convicted him had stated on *voir dire* that they had seen and heard Rideau's televised "interview" with the sheriff on at least one occasion. Two members of the jury were deputy sheriffs of Calcasieu Parish. Rideau's counsel had requested that these jurors be excused for cause, having exhausted all of their peremptory challenges, but these challenges for cause had been denied by the trial judge. The judgment of conviction was affirmed by the Supreme Court of Louisiana. . . .

The record in this case contains as an exhibit the sound film which was broadcast. What the people of Calcasieu Parish saw on their television sets was Rideau, in jail, flanked by the sheriff and two state troopers, admitting in detail the commission of the robbery, kidnapping, and murder, in response to leading questions by the sheriff. The record fails to show whose idea it was to make the sound film, and broadcast it over the local television station, but we know from the conceded circumstances that the plan was carried out with the active cooperation and participation of the local law enforcement officers. And certainly no one has suggested that it was Rideau's idea, or even that he was aware of what was going on when the sound film was being made. . . .

The case now before us does not involve physical brutality. The kangaroo court proceedings in this case involved a more subtle but no less real deprivation of due process of law. Under our Constitution's guarantee of due process, a person accused of committing a crime is vouchsafed basic minimal rights. Among these are the right to counsel, the right to plead not guilty, and the right to be tried in a courtroom presided over by a judge. Yet in this case the people of Calcasieu Parish saw and heard, not once but three times, a "trial" of Rideau in a jail, presided over by a sheriff, where there was no lawyer to advise Rideau of his right to stand mute. . . .

*   *   *

The question of courtroom television was inevitably to come before the Supreme Court. In June of 1965 the Court handed down its first such decision on appeal by Billie Sol Estes, a much publicized Texas financier who was closely associated with Washington politics. He claimed he did not get a fair trial because of the televising and broadcasting of portions of his judicial proceedings. Justice Clark wrote the opinion of the 5–4 majority, which agreed. He was joined by Justices Warren, Douglas, Goldberg, and Harlan. But the broader question of courtroom television in general would have to wait until 1981, for Justice Harlan was specific in pointing out in his concurrence that his agreement with the 5–4 majority applied to the Estes case only (because of Estes' nation-wide prominence) and that he did not rule out the possibility of televising proceedings of lesser notoriety. Interestingly enough, Justice Brennan, issuing a salvo foretelling future discussions, pointed out in a separate dissent that only four of the nine justices favored an outright ban on courtroom television. However, Chief Justice Warren in a strongly worded concurrence to the majority opinion argued that courtroom television in a criminal trial did indeed violate the Sixth Amendment for federal courts and the Fourteenth Amendment for state courts. He was joined in this concurrence by Justices Douglas and Goldberg. Estes was convicted in the District Court for the Seventh Judicial

District of Texas of swindling. The judgment was affirmed by the Texas Court of Criminal Appeals. Both before and during his trial, he voiced objections to the telecasting and broadcasting of courtroom proceedings. Texas courts did not adhere to Canon 35 of the American Bar Association, which recommended a ban on cameras in the courtroom.

ESTES V. TEXAS
381 U.S. 532 (1965)

JUSTICE CLARK *delivered the opinion of the Court.*

The question presented here is whether the petitioner, who stands convicted in the District Court for the Seventh Judicial District of Texas at Tyler for swindling, was deprived of his right under the Fourteenth Amendment to due process by the televising and broadcasting of his trial. Both the trial court and the Texas Court of Criminal Appeals found against the petitioner. We hold to the contrary and reverse his conviction.

While petitioner recites his claim in the framework of Canon 35 of the Judicial Canons of the American Bar Association he does not contend that we should enshrine Canon 35 in the Fourteenth Amendment, but only that the time-honored principles of a fair trial were not followed in his case and that he was thus convicted without due process of law. Canon 35, of course, has of itself no binding effect on the courts but merely expresses the view of the Association in opposition to the broadcasting, televising and photographing of court proceedings. Likewise, Judicial Canon 28 of the Integrated State Bar of Texas, which leaves to the trial judge's sound discretion the telecasting and photographing of court proceedings, is of itself not law. In short, the question here is not the validity of either Canon 35 of the American Bar Association or Canon 28 of the State Bar of Texas, but only whether petitioner was tried in a manner which comports with the due process requirement of the Fourteenth Amendment.

Petitioner's case was originally called for trial on September 24, 1962, in Smith County after a change of venue from Reeves County, some 500 miles west. Massive pretrial publicity totaling 11 volumes of press clippings, which are on file with the Clerk, had given it national notoriety. All available seats in the courtroom were taken and some 30 persons stood in the aisles. However, at that time a defense motion to prevent telecasting, broadcasting by radio and news photography and a defense motion for continuance were presented, and after a two-day hearing the former was denied and the latter granted.

These initial hearings were carried live by both radio and television, and news photography was permitted throughout. The videotapes of these hearings clearly illustrate that the picture presented was not one of that judicial serenity and calm to which petitioner was entitled. Indeed, at least 12 cameramen were engaged in the courtroom throughout the hearing taking motion and still pictures and televising the proceedings. Cables and wires were snaked across the courtroom floor, three microphones were on the judge's bench and others were beamed at the jury box and the counsel table. It is conceded that the activities of the television crews and news photographers led to considerable disruption of the hearings. . . .

When the case was called for trial on October 22 the scene had been altered. A booth had been constructed at the back of the courtroom which was painted to blend with the permanent structure of the room. It had an aperture to allow the lens of the cameras an unrestricted view of the courtroom. All television cameras and newsreel photographers were restricted to the area of the booth when shooting film or telecasting.

Because of continual objection, the rules governing live telecasting, as well as radio and still photos, were changed as the exigencies of the situation seemed to require. As a result, live telecasting was prohibited during a great portion of the actual trial. Only the opening and closing arguments of the State, the return of the jury's verdict and its receipt by the trial judge were carried live with sound. Although the order allowed videotapes of the entire proceeding without sound, the cameras operated only intermittently, recording various portions of the trial for broadcast on regularly scheduled newscasts later in the day and evening. At the request of the petitioner, the trial judge prohibited coverage of any kind, still or television, of the defense counsel during their summations to the jury.

Because of the varying restrictions placed on sound and live telecasting the telecasts of the trail were confined largely to film clips shown on the stations' regularly scheduled news programs. The news commentators would use the film of a particular part of the day's trial activities as a backdrop for their reports. Their commentary included excerpts from testimony and the usual reportorial remarks. On one occasion the videotapes of the September hearings were rebroadcast in place of the "late movie.". . .

We start with the proposition that it is a "public trial" that the Sixth Amendment guarantees to the "accused." The purpose of the requirement of a public trial was to guarantee that the accused would be fairly dealt with and not unjustly condemned. History had proven that secret tribunals were effective instruments of oppression. . . .

The free press has been a mighty catalyst in awakening public interest in governmental affairs, exposing corruption among public officers and employees and generally informing the citizenry of public events and occurrences, including court proceedings. While maximum freedom must be allowed the press in carrying on this important function in a democratic society its exercise must necessarily be subject to the maintenance of absolute fairness in the judicial process. While the state and federal courts have differed over what spectators may be excluded from a criminal trial, the *amici curiae* brief of the National Association of Broadcasters and the Radio Television News Directors Association, says, as indeed it must, that "neither of these two amendments [First and Sixth] speaks of an unlimited right of access to the courtroom on the part of the broadcasting media. . . ." Moreover, they recognize that the "primary concern of all must be the proper administration of justice"; that "the life or liberty of any individual in this land should not be put in jeopardy because of actions of any news media"; and that "the due process requirements in both the Fifth and Fourteenth Amendments and the provisions of the Sixth Amendment require a procedure that will assure a fair trial. . . ."

Nor can the courts be said to discriminate where they permit the newspaper reporter access to the courtroom. The television and radio reporter has the same privilege. All are entitled to the same rights as the general public. The news reporter is not permitted to bring his typewriter or printing press. When the advances in these arts permit reporting by printing press or by television without their present hazards to a fair trial we will have another case. . . .

As has been said, the chief function of our judicial machinery is to ascertain the truth. The use of television, however, cannot be said to contribute materially to this objective. Rather its use amounts to the injection of an irrelevant factor into court proceedings. In addition experience teaches that there are numerous situations in which it might cause actual unfairness—some so subtle as to defy detection by the accused or control by the judge. We enumerate some in summary:

1. The potential impact of television on the jurors is perhaps of the greatest significance. They are the nerve center of the fact-finding process. It is true that in States like Texas where they are required to be sequestered in trials of this nature the jurors will probably not see any of the proceedings as televised from the courtroom. But the inquiry cannot end there. From the moment the trial judge announces that a case will be televised it becomes a *cause célèbre*. The whole community, including prospective jurors, becomes interested in all the morbid details surrounding it. The approaching trial immediately assumes an important status in the public press and the accused is highly publicized along with the offense with which he is charged. . . .

Moreover, while it is practically impossible to assess the effect of television on jury attentiveness, those of us who know juries realize the problem of jury "distraction." The State argues this is *de minimis* since the physical disturbances have been eliminated. But we know that distractions are not caused solely by the physical presence of the camera and its telltale red lights. It is the awareness of the fact of telecasting that is felt by the juror throughout the trial. . . .

Furthermore, in many States the jurors serving in the trial may see the broadcasts of the trial proceedings. . . . [J]urors would return home and turn on the TV if only to see how they appeared upon it. They would also be subjected to re-enactment and emphasis of the selected parts of the proceedings which the requirements of the broadcasters determined would be telecast and would be subconsciously influenced the more by that testimony. Moreover, they would be subjected to the broadcast commentary and criticism and perhaps the well-meant advice of friends, relatives and inquiring strangers who recognized them on the streets. . . .

2. The quality of the testimony in criminal trials will often be impaired. The impact upon a witness of the knowledge that he is being viewed by a vast audience is simply incalculable. Some may be demoralized and frightened, some cocky and

given to overstatement; memories may falter, as with anyone speaking publicly, and accuracy of statement may be severely undermined. Embarrassment may impede the search for the truth, as may a natural tendency toward overdramatization. Furthermore, inquisitive strangers and "cranks" might approach witnesses on the street with jibes, advice or demands for explanation of testimony. . . .

While some of the dangers mentioned above are present as well in newspaper coverage of any important trial, the circumstances and extraneous influences intruding upon the solemn decorum of court procedure in the televised trial are far more serious than in cases involving only newspaper coverage.

3. A major aspect of the problem is the additional responsibilities the presence of television places on the trial judge. His job is to make certain that the accused receives a fair trial. This most difficult task requires his undivided attention. Still when television comes into the courtroom he must also supervise it. . . .

But this is not all. There is the initial decision that must be made as to whether the use of television will be permitted. This is perhaps an even more crucial consideration. Our judges are high-minded men and women. But it is difficult to remain oblivious to the pressures that the news media can bring to bear on them both directly and through the shaping of public opinion. Moreover, where one judge in a district or even in a State permits telecasting, the requirement that the others do the same is almost mandatory. Especially is this true where the judge is selected at the ballot box.

4. Finally, we cannot ignore the impact of courtroom television on the defendant. Its presence is a form of mental—if not physical—harassment, resembling a police line-up or the third degree. The inevitable closeups of his gestures and expressions during the ordeal of his trial might well transgress his personal sensibilities, his dignity, and his ability to concentrate on the proceedings before him—sometimes the difference between life and death—dispassionately, freely and without the distraction of wide public surveillance. A defendant on trial for a specific crime is entitled to his day in court, not in a stadium, or a city or nationwide arena. . . .

It is said that the ever-advancing techniques of public communication and the adjustment of the public to its presence may bring about a change in the effect of telecasting upon the fairness of criminal trials. But we are not dealing here with future developments in the field of electronics. Our judgment cannot be rested on the hypothesis of tomorrow but must take the facts as they are presented today.

The judgment is therefore reversed.

CHIEF JUSTICE WARREN, *whom Justice Douglas and Justice Goldberg join, concurring.*

While I join the Court's opinion and agree that the televising of criminal trials is inherently a denial of due process, I desire to express additional views on why this is so. In doing this, I wish to emphasize that our condemnation of televised criminal trials is not based on generalities or abstract fears. The record in this case presents a vivid illustration of the inherent prejudice of televised criminal trials and supports our conclusion that this is the appropriate time to make a definitive appraisal of television in the courtroom. . . .

On September 24, a hearing was held to consider petitioner's motion to prohibit television, motion pictures, and still photography at the trial. The courtroom was filled with newspaper reporters and cameramen, television cameramen and spectators. At least 12 cameramen with their equipment were seen by one observer, and there were 30 or more people standing in the aisles. . . .

With photographers roaming at will through the courtroom, petitioner's counsel made his motion that all cameras be excluded. As he spoke, a cameraman wandered behind the judge's bench and snapped his picture. . . .

The televising of trials would cause the public to equate the trial process with the forms of entertainment regularly seen on television and with the commercial objectives of the television industry. In the present case, tapes of the September 24 hearing were run in place of the "Tonight Show" by one station and in place of the late night movie by another. Commercials for soft drinks, soups, eyedrops and seatcovers were inserted when there was a pause in the proceedings. In addition, if trials were televised there would be a natural tendency on the part of broadcasters to develop the personalities of the trial participants, so as to give the proceedings more of an element of drama. This tendency was noticeable in the present case. Television commentators gave the viewing audience a homey, flattering sketch about the trial judge, obviously to add an extra element of viewer appeal to the trial. . . .

The television industry might also decide that the bareboned trial itself does not contain sufficient drama to sustain an audience. It might provide expert commentary on the proceedings and hire persons with legal backgrounds to anticipate possible trial strategy, as the football expert anticipates plays for his audience. . . .

Moreover, should television become an accepted part of the courtroom, greater sacrifices would be made for the benefit of broadcasters. In the present case construction of a television booth in the courtroom made it necessary to alter the physical layout of the courtroom and to move from their accustomed position two benches reserved for spectators. If this can be done in order better to accommodate the television industry, I see no reason why another court might not move a trial to a theater, if such a move would provide improved television coverage. Our memories are short indeed if we have already forgotten the wave of horror that swept over this country when Premier Fidel Castro conducted his prosecutions before 18,000 people in Havana Stadium. . . .

. . . The next logical step in this partnership might be to schedule the trial for a time that would permit the maximum number of viewers to watch and to schedule recesses to coincide with the need for station breaks. Should the television industry become an integral part of our system of criminal justice, it would not be unnatural for the public to attribute the shortcomings of the industry to the trial process itself. The public is aware of the television industry's consuming interest in ratings, and it is also aware of the steps that have been taken in the past to maintain viewer interest in television programs. Memories still recall vividly the scandal caused by the disclosure that quiz programs had been corrupted in order to heighten their dramatic appeal. Can we be sure that similar efforts would not be made to heighten the dramatic appeal of televised trials? Can we be sure that the public would not inherently distrust our system of justice because of its intimate association with a commercial enterprise? . . .

It is argued that television not only entertains but also educates the public. But the function of a trial is not to provide an educational experience; and there is a serious danger that any attempt to use a trial as an educational tool will both divert it from its proper purpose and lead to suspicions concerning the integrity of the trial process. . . .

Finally, if the televising of criminal proceedings were approved, trials would be selected for television coverage for reasons having nothing to do with the purpose of trial. A trial might be televised because a particular judge has gained the fancy of the public by his unorthodox approach; or because the district attorney has decided to run for another office and it is believed his appearance would attract a large audience; or simply because a particular courtroom has a layout that best accommodates television coverage. For the most part, however, the important factor that would draw television to the courtroom would be the nature of the case. The alleged perpetrator of the sensational murder, the fallen idol, or some other person who, like petitioner, has attracted the public interest would find his trial turned into a vehicle for television. Yet, these are the very persons who encounter the greatest difficulty in securing an impartial trial, even without the presence of television. . . .

JUSTICE HARLAN, *concurring*.

I concur in the opinion of the Court, subject, however, to the reservations and only to the extent indicated in this opinion. . . .

The probable impact of courtroom television on the fairness of a trial may vary according to the particular kind of case involved. The impact of television on a trial exciting wide popular interest may be one thing; the impact on a run-of-the-mill case may be quite another. Furthermore, the propriety of closed circuit television for the purpose of making a court recording or for limited use in educational institutions obviously presents markedly different considerations. The *Estes* trial was a heavily publicized and highly sensational affair. I therefore put aside all other types of cases; in so doing, however, I wish to make it perfectly clear that I am by no means prepared to say that the constitutional issue should ultimately turn upon the nature of the particular case involved. When the issue of television in a non-notorious trial is presented it may appear that no workable distinction can be drawn based on the type of case involved, or that the possibilities for prejudice, though less severe, are nonetheless of constitutional proportions. . . . The resolution of those further questions should await an appropriate case; the Court should proceed only step by step in this unplowed field. The opinion of the Court necessarily goes no farther, for only the four members of the majority who unreservedly join the Court's opinion would resolve those questions now. . . .

*   *   *

The question of whether the physical presence of cameras in the courtroom, as well as other "extended media," including audio tape recorders, denies a person a fair trial was undertaken by the Supreme Court in Chandler v. Florida *in 1981. The Southeastern state was among the earliest to experiment with televised trials. The question here was quite simple: did cameras and other equipment, allowed by the judge over the objections of the defendants, deny* per se *their rights under the Sixth and Fourteenth Amendments to the Constitution? The accused were two Miami Beach police officers who were convicted of burglary and sentenced to jail.*

It should be emphasized that the unanimous decision (with Justice Stevens taking no part in the case) did not require cameras and other equipment to be admitted, but merely that there was nothing in the Constitution which prohibited the entry of such equipment. It was another illustration of the Court's approach to federalism, i.e. letting the states decide their own policies so long as those policies do not conflict with the Constitution. More than half the states at the time were allowing extended media into their courtrooms. It also should be noted that the Chandler *decision does not overturn* Estes, *decided sixteen years earlier. Justice Harlan in* Estes *had noted that his deciding vote to overturn Billie Sol Estes' conviction applied to that case only because of the widespread notoriety of the accused. Justices Stewart and White in the present case, however, argued that the* Chandler *decision did, in fact, overturn* Estes *and that the Supreme Court ought to acknowledge it. The American Bar Association had continued its four-decade objection to cameras in the courtroom, but to no avail. Much of the concern about cameras, of course, is not merely the presence of the physical equipment, but focuses on the editing process the film undergoes in the newsroom and on the impact those brief, fleeting images have on the viewers at home. The pro and con arguments are well presented in the two articles which follow the* Chandler *excerpts.*

CHANDLER V. FLORIDA
449 U.S. 560 (1981)

CHIEF JUSTICE BURGER *delivered the opinion of the Court.*

The question presented on this appeal is whether, consistent with constitutional guarantees, a state may provide for radio, television, and still photographic coverage of a criminal trial for public broadcast, notwithstanding the objection of the accused.

Background. Over the past 50 years, some criminal cases characterized as "sensational" have been subjected to extensive coverage by news media, sometimes seriously interfering with the conduct of the proceedings and creating a setting wholly inappropriate for the administration of justice. Judges, lawyers, and others soon became concerned, and in 1937, after study, the American Bar Association House of Delegates adopted Judicial Canon 35, declaring that all photographic and broadcast coverage of courtroom proceedings should be prohibited. In 1952, the House of Delegates amended Canon 35 to proscribe television coverage as well. The Canon's proscription was reaffirmed in 1972 when the Code of Judicial Conduct replaced the Canons of Judicial Ethics and Canon 3A (7) superseded Canon 35. A majority of the states, including Florida, adopted the substance of the ABA provision and its amendments. In Florida, the rule was embodied in Canon 3A (7) of the Florida Code of Judicial Conduct. . . .

. . . The Florida Supreme Court then supplemented its order and established a new one-year pilot program during which the electronic media were permitted to cover all judicial proceedings in Florida without reference to the consent of participants, subject to detailed standards with respect to technology and the conduct of operators. The experiment began in July 1977 and continued through June 1978.

When the pilot program ended, the Florida Supreme Court received and reviewed briefs, reports, letters of comment, and studies. It conducted its own survey of attorneys, witnesses, jurors, and court personnel through the Office of the State Court Coordinator. A separate survey was taken of judges by the Florida Conference of Circuit Judges. The court also studied the experience of six states that had, by 1979, adopted rules relating to electronic coverage of trials, as well as that of the 10 other states that, like Florida, were experimenting with such coverage. . . .

Appellants rely chiefly on *Estes v. Texas*, and Chief Justice Warren's separate concurring opinion in that case. They argue that the televising of criminal trials is inherently a denial of due process, and they read *Estes* as announcing a *per se* constitutional rule to that effect.

Chief Justice Warren's concurring opinion, in which he was joined by Justices Douglas and Goldberg, indeed provides some support for the appellants' position. . . . If appellants' reading of *Estes* were correct, we would be obliged to apply that holding and reverse the judgment under review.

The six separate opinions in *Estes* must be examined carefully to evaluate the claim that it represents a *per se* constitutional rule forbidding all electronic coverage. Chief Justice Warren and Justices Douglas and Goldberg joined Justice Clark's opinion announcing the judgment, thereby creating only a plurality. . . .

Since we are satisfied that *Estes* did not announce a constitutional rule that all photographic or broadcast coverage of criminal trials is inherently a denial of due process, we turn to consideration, as a matter of first impression, of the petitioner's suggestion that we now promulgate such a *per se* rule.

Any criminal case that generates a great deal of publicity presents some risks that the publicity may compromise the right of the defendant to a fair trial. Trial courts must be especially vigilant to guard against any impairment of the defendant's right to a verdict based solely upon the evidence and the relevant law. Over the years, courts have developed a range of curative devices to prevent publicity about a trial from infecting jury deliberations.

An absolute constitutional ban on broadcast coverage of trials cannot be justified simply because there is a danger that, in some cases, prejudicial broadcast accounts of pretrial and trial events may impair the ability of jurors to decide the issue of guilt or innocence uninfluenced by extraneous matter. The risk of juror prejudice in some cases does not justify an absolute ban on news coverage of trials by the printed media; so also the risk of such prejudice does not warrant an absolute constitutional ban on all broadcast coverage. . . .

In confronting the difficult and sensitive question of the potential psychological prejudice associated with broadcast coverage of trials, we have been aided by *amicus* briefs submitted by various state officers involved in law enforcement, the Conference of Chief Justices, and the Attorneys General of 17 states in support of continuing experimentation such as that embarked upon by Florida, and by the American Bar Association, the American College of Trial Lawyers, and various members of the defense bar representing essentially the views expressed by the concurring Justices in *Estes*.

Not unimportant to the position asserted by Florida and other states is the change in television technology since 1962, when Estes was tried. It is urged, and some empirical data are presented, that many of the negative factors found in *Estes*—cumbersome equipment, cables, distracting lighting, numerous camera technicians—are less substantial factors today than they were at that time.

It is also significant that safeguards have been built into the experimental programs in state courts, and into the Florida program, to avoid some of the most egregious problems envisioned by the six opinions in the *Estes* case. Florida admonishes its courts to take special pains to protect certain witnesses—for example, children, victims of sex crimes, some informants, and even the very timid witness or party—from the glare of publicity and the tensions of being "on camera.". . .

Nonetheless, it is clear that the general issue of the psychological impact of broadcast coverage upon the participants in a trial, and particularly upon the defendant, is still a subject of sharp debate—as the *Amicus* Briefs of the American Bar Association, the American College of Trial Lawyers, and others of the trial bar in opposition to Florida's experiment demonstrate. . . .

. . . Selection of which trials, or parts of trials, to broadcast will inevitably be made not by judges but by the media, and will be governed by such factors as the nature of the crime and the status and position of the accused—or of the victim; the effect may be to titillate rather than to educate and inform. The unanswered question is whether electronic coverage will bring public humiliation upon the accused with such randomness that it will evoke due process concerns by being "unusual in the same way that being struck by lightning" is "unusual." Societies and political systems, that, from time to time, have put on "Yankee Stadium" "show trials" tell more about the power of the state than about its concern for the decent administration of justice—with every citizen receiving the same kind of justice. . . .

. . . Dangers lurk in this, as in most, experiments, but unless we were to conclude that television coverage under all conditions is prohibited by the Constitution, the states must be free to experiment. We are not empowered by the Constitution to oversee or harness state procedural experimentation; only when the state action infringes fundamental guarantees are we authorized to intervene. We must assume state courts will be alert to any factors that impair the fundamental rights of the accused.

The Florida program is inherently evolutional in nature; the initial project has provided guidance for the new canons which can be changed at will, and application of which is subject to control by the trial judge. The risk of prejudice to particular defendants is ever present and must be examined carefully as cases arise. Nothing of the "Roman circus" or "Yankee Stadium" atmosphere, as in *Estes*, prevailed here. . . .

In this setting, because this Court has no supervisory authority over state courts, our review is confined to whether there is a constitutional violation. We hold that the Constitution does not prohibit a state from experimenting with the program authorized by revised Canon 3A (7).

Affirmed.

LET THE SUNSHINE IN

By Talbot D'Alemberte*

On a recent visit to Williamsburg, restored capital of colonial Virginia, I was particularly impressed by the colonial courtroom. Besides the necessary furniture, it contained ample viewing room for interested members of the public. The balconies were for distinguished observers and, at floor level, there was a standing room area about 35 feet square. Some trials attracted so much interest that people would lean in through the two windows to the right.

Our tour guide attested to the vast public interest in colonial courts, and what she said fit my understanding of rural America as I knew it. In the North Florida area where I grew up, large, fan-cooled courtrooms still serve as a place where citizens come to learn about their courts. There, important trials are attended by enough jurors, witnesses and observers to pass on information by word of mouth to a significant number of the people.

Most Americans, however, do not learn about the courts over the cracker barrel or by the fireside but in the same way as they get their other news—television, radio and newspapers. Modern courts are not and should not be like colonial courts or even rural courts, but the fact that most citizens have never seen a court in action may be a cause of public distrust that ten thousand Law Day speeches and countless lawyers' public relations committees cannot overcome.

Public opinion polls tell us that courts are among our less respected institutions, and every lawyer knows that the legal profession is often mistrusted by the public. Of course, the judiciary is not the only institution suffering from a credibility gap. But the judiciary is unique in that there are no reform movements to make it accessible. Common Cause is not outraged about judicial secrecy as it is about cloistered proceedings of the legislative and executive branches. The reform movements for "sunshine laws" and public access to information largely ignore this branch of government.

Our judicial institutions must be de-mystified, and lawyers should take the lead in this movement. . . .

A recent article on the Op-Ed page of the *New York Times* was entitled, "Smile—You're on Candid Courtroom." The article, written by the political editor of WCBS-TV in New York, accuses lawyers and judges of imposing unrealistic restrictions on television and even hints that the legal profession may be substituting unctuous conclusions for analysis in development of these rules.

* From Talbot D'Alemberte. "Let the Sunshine In: The Case for an Open Judicial System." *Judicature*, Vol. 59, No. 2 (August–September, 1974), p. 60. Used with permission of *Judicature*. The author, a former legislator, is Dean of the College of Law at Florida State University.

I agree.

Lawyers have long feared that broadcasting of trials would destroy courtroom dignity and decorum and deprive a criminal defendant of the right to a fair trial. The American Bar Association raised this fear to official dogma in 1937 by adopting Canon 35 which forbids photographs and broadcasting of court proceedings.

The dogma became a constitutional principle in 1965 when the Supreme Court voted 5–4 to reverse the conviction of Billie Sol Estes, a conviction which came out of a televised trial. Six opinions were filed in that case, making it difficult to analyze, but the case has come to stand for the principle that a criminal defendant has a constitutional right to a trial without broadcast.

This does not foreclose all broadcasting. There is no constitutional barrier to broadcast of civil cases, appeals, or criminal cases where the defendant does not object.

The fact is that *Estes*, as applied, and the ABA rule . . . are not rooted in reality. People who enter public places expect to see television cameras and broadcast apparatus, for they have seen them elsewhere in their daily lives—at athletic events, in the schools (including law schools), and in serious councils of government: city councils, school boards, legislative chambers and administrative agencies. There is no evidence that people would find television cameras more frightening than the court reporter's unfamiliar stenotype machine, and radio broadcast equipment does not differ significantly from the recording devices now used in many courtrooms.

Indeed, two days after the *Times* article, UPI reported the development of a "courtroom of the future" by a California law school. It featured sophisticated electronic equipment including television screens for the jurors to view videotaped evidence. Several weeks later, a Vermont jury considered a negligence case solely on videotape evidence presented. In Alaska, sound recordings are typically used to report trial testimony, and videotape has been in courtroom use in Florida, California, Massachusetts, Nebraska, Pennsylvania and Ohio. The ABA rule contained in its Code of Judicial Ethics recognizes that television cameras can enter the courtroom for educational purposes and for ceremonial occasions.

The irony is that the same courts which benefit from modern technology are denying the news media the use of the same technology. Journalists are forbidden to carry tape recorders into courtrooms, yet many courtrooms are equipped with visible microphones and recording devices. Photographic equipment is not permitted, yet motion pictures are shown to juries. Broadcasting is not permitted, yet microphones and sound systems are found in many courts.

The rule outlawing electronic media should be changed because it has been made an anachronism by current technology. The *Estes* opinion of reversal emphasized the physical distractions: twelve cameramen, cables and wires snaked across the courtroom floor, microphones on the judge's bench, the jury box and counsel tables. The opinion concludes that "Television *in its present state* and by its very nature, reaches into a variety of areas in which it may cause prejudice to an accused." (Emphasis added.)

The opinion seems to concede that there would come a time of low light level cameras and an end to the massive equipment and glaring lights of early television. This is now the case. Manufacturers of television camera equipment are delivering compact, noiseless color cameras which operate on ten footcandles of light, well within the normal lighting available in virtually all courtrooms.

The Court, conceding that "one can not put his finger on its specific mischief" went on to suggest some ways in which televised trials "might" cause unfairness, and mentioned the potential impact on jurors as being of the greatest significance. This is so, the Court concluded, because of the fact that only the "notorious" trial will be broadcast because of the necessity of "paid sponsorship" and that this "may" have a conscious or unconscious effect on the juror's judgment. The Court, without experience, states that "experience" indicates that it is not only possible but highly probable that it will have a direct bearing on his vote as to guilt or innocence.

The simple answer to this is to prevent televising of a juror where the juror objects for fear that his friends and neighbors, hostile to the defendant, have their eyes on the juror through television.

Second, the opinion suggests that the quality of testimony will be impaired by broadcasting—yet a basic rationale for a defendant's right to a public trial has been that the quality of testimony is improved. Again, the witness who objects to being televised need not be televised where there is a basis for the objection.

All the other arguments of the *Estes* opinion are similar. The Court points out that the judge has to supervise the television reporters (doesn't he have to supervise all courtroom spectators?), that the defendant might be nervous (certainly) and, finally, that only the newsworthy trial is covered by the news media. The *Estes* opinion is founded on assumptions which never have been tested.

Moreover, all these arguments are equally applicable to the print media reporters who, by their very presence, make a trial a special event, need supervision, and may make jurors, lawyers and defendants nervous.

The 1968 ABA study on Fair Trial and Free Press pointed to the importance of media coverage to make the system work, yet we will not have truly public trials in today's urban society until we come to grips with the realities of electronic journalism and allow cameras in the courtroom.

But if television and radio are allowed in the courtroom, electronic journalists must be able to answer these important questions:

1. Can television journalists agree to pooling arrangements for courtroom cameras so that the mere numbers of cameras do not create distraction?

2. Can cameras be provided which will not distract from the courtroom proceedings?

3. Can reasonable agreements be made concerning privacy of counsel tables, bench conferences, and other courtroom events which deserve protection?

If these questions can be answered, electronic journalists should be allowed inside the courtroom using cameras and electronic devices for recording and broadcasting. . . .

[And], the appellate process should allow coverage by the electronic media. None of the reasons expressed in *Estes* apply to appellate procedure, unless it is the thought that judges and lawyers will somehow alter their conduct in the presence of cameras. This thought is too speculative and non-specific to warrant sacrificing the benefit to the public understanding which will flow from electronic reporting. Indeed, it is entirely possible that the alteration of behavior would be pleasing to the judges who must listen to oral arguments. Lawyers might be better prepared and more alert. . . .

The courts are, after all, dominated by a single profession, functioning largely out of public view. The public, kept in ignorance of courts and their functioning, is asked to respect courts, honor judges and believe in "judicial supremacy." In another era, faith in the unknown might be reasonably expected, but today's skeptical public will not allow the courts to hide behind a veil of mystery without regarding that secrecy with distrust.

ARE WE AT THE POINT OF NO RETURN?

By George Gerbner*

Television is moving into the American courtroom. The sudden rush seems to fly in the face of the known risks of prejudice, the certainty of endless litigation, a decision of the Supreme Court, resistance on the federal level, and a vote last year by the American Bar Association to uphold its advisory ban on cameras in the courtroom.

Some speakers called the ABA stand "a rear guard action long after the dawn of the electronic age." Since television made its claims on behalf of the public's right to know, resistant delegates appeared to be in a last-ditch defense against the inevitable march of freedom. In the most widely reported comment, former FCC Commissioner and Washington attorney Lee Loevinger told the ABA delegates: "You're fooling yourselves. I don't think we have any choice. We'll continue to get television coverage whether we like it or not."

Events may prove Loevinger right. Television has already entered courtrooms in the majority of states or is about to do so for "experiments" whose long-range effects no one is prepared to evaluate seriously. No meaningful research has yet demonstrated the validity of arguments for television trials or the benefits from trials already televised. No one has yet investigated the potentially far-reaching social impact and institutional consequences of plugging the administration of criminal justice into a system geared to entertainment and sales.

Our organs of public discussion, the mass media, are hardly disinterested parties in the debate. They are not motivated, to say the least, to expose their own blindspots and limitations. As a result, the public debate has been conducted on narrow, obsolete, and at times misleading grounds.

● Freedom to report is not the issue. Journalists—both broadcast and print—are free to cover most trials. The fact that they choose to report only a few of the most dramatic ones already warps public understanding of the judicial process. Television trials would not help that. They would only add audiovisual spectacle and further dramatic diversion to the reporting.

● Obtrusive equipment and courtroom decorum are no longer issues. Video technology can be unobtrusive and can even reduce the movement of reporters during the trial by providing monitors for them outside the courtroom.

● Even video recording is not the issue. Canon 3A(7) of the Code of Judicial

* From "Trial by Television: Are We at the Point of No Return?" *Judicature*, Vol. 63, No. 9 (April, 1980), p. 416. Used with permission of Dr. Gerbner, Dean of the Annenberg School of Communications at the University of Pennsylvania.

Conduct already permits recording of trials for educational purposes, so long as the tapes are shown after the trial and all appeals have been exhausted.

The only remaining issue is whether the addition of video spectacle to the already existing press and broadcast coverage would reduce or increase the risk of prejudice and whether it would correct or further extend the viewers' already distorted image of the court. That issue has been addressed—and then ignored. The Supreme Court has said that the sudden notoriety of judges, jurors, attorneys, and defendants and "heightened public clamor" would "inevitably result in prejudice." [*Estes v. Texas*] And prejudice could extend far beyond the courtroom since television profoundly affects the social and political climate and the institutional setting in which courts work.

Trials by television are likely to alter the historic relationship between two institutions that have largely divergent and partially conflicting functions. Popular entertainment and news via mass media represent the conventional cultural pressures of the social order. The judicial process, however, represents an effort to adjudicate individual cases according to law. That distinction is crucial to this whole discussion.

In criminal cases, the most likely to be televised, a fair trial means determination of guilt of the specific offense charged, and not, as in general entertainment and news, whether a person has done something bad for which he or she should be punished. In fact, a trial must proceed as independently as possible from conventional moral pressures and the popular clamor of the moment. Televising trials may erode independence of judges to do justice in each case; it would do nothing to ensure greater fairness that existing media scrutiny could not do.

The erosion of independence will be hard to track and difficult to measure. It will occur as television trials, despite any safeguards within the court, are selected and edited to fit the existing patterns of television. We may be on the verge of drifting into a major institutional transformation while assuming that we are only making a few public-spirited adjustments.

A review of research on the impact of television on American institutions shows that it has reshaped politics, changed the nature of sports and business, transformed family life and the socialization of children, and affected public security and the enforcement of laws. The debate over cameras in the courts may be our last opportunity to consider the evidence already available on the influence of television on public images of law and the courts, and to halt the rush toward televised trials until we can take a fresh look at the problem.

Television is our common and constant learning environment. Our children are born into it. In the typical home, the family watches more than six hours of TV a day in a ritual most people perform with little selectivity or deviation.

Television demands no mobility, literacy, or concentrated attention. Its repetitive patterns come into the home and show as well as tell about people and society. Presidents, policemen, judges, spies and celebrities are familiar parts of a selective, synthetic, symbolic environment of entertainment and news in which we grow up and learn most of what we know in common.

Different kinds of programs serve the same basic formula: they assemble viewers and sell them at the least cost. The classifications of the print era—the relatively sharp differentiation between news, drama, documentary, etc.—do not apply to television. Heavy viewers watch more of everything. Different programs complement and reinforce each other as they entertain the same audiences and repeat the same propositions about life and society. Most program formulas present different aspects of the same symbolic world made to the same specifications of television and its sponsors.

The process of socialization via entertainment is an exercise in social typing. It sets the norms of society by showing their frequent violations. Offenders and their victims cast for most dramatic attention (or selected as "newsworthy") tend to be those who fit established preconceptions. . . .

Entertainment is the cultivation of conventional morality. It "entertains" the basic values and norms of the community and cultivates conformity to those norms. An important part of that process is the exploitation of popular prejudices and the cultivation of public support for the suppression of threats and challenges to the social order.

From the arenas of the Roman empire to this very day, show trials, highly publicized confessions, public tribunals and executions have helped to reaffirm the legitimacy of contemporary values. The most widely frequented shows in London just emerging from the Middle Ages were public executions. . . .

The great show trials and public confessions of the twentieth century occurred under dictatorships and during periods of witchhunt in democracies. They were a part of the entertainment mainstream, now joined by much of what we call news, compelling attention, exposing deviation, spreading fear, and cultivating conformity.

The struggle to remove trials from the public arena paralleled the fight against secret proceedings, the Star Chamber. In fact, the two are sides of the same coin. Arbitrary power wants no public witness to its private deliberations but needs all the hoopla it can get to legitimize its actions.

The integrity and independence of judicial proceedings serve to protect the accused from both arbitrary power and public prejudice. The purpose of open trials is to help assure observance of these protections, not to entertain or even to educate. . . .

The drawing power of the Watergate impeachment hearings and the lure of sensational trials has lately led to mounting media pressures to open the courts to cameras. But look at what has happened so far.

• In an Ohio case, the defendant, charged with the rape and murder of a nine-year-old girl, was allowed to be hypnotized during the examination, creating high viewer interest in the trial.

• *Hustler* magazine owner Larry Flynt was shot during a recess of the televised trial in which he was charged with distributing obscene material.

• The murder-robbery trial of 17-year-old Ronny Zamora, televised during a one-year "experiment" in the state of Florida, became a national media sensation because television was "on trial"; in a novel defense, Zamora's attorney charged that TV had induced his insanity through "involuntary subliminal intoxication." Ratings reportedly exceeded those of the Johnny Carson Show.

In an effort to limit some of the adverse effects of broadcasting, several states—including Florida, Wisconsin and now Iowa—give their judges the power to decide whether to turn off the cameras for a particular witness or a particular case. Florida, for example, allows a judge to exclude electronic media if he finds that such coverage will affect a particular person much differently than it affects other people—and differently from the ways in which print media affect him or her. Iowa allows the judge to refuse media coverage if a witness can show "good cause." But how can a witness or defendant possibly know, let alone show, such a thing? . . .

Television presents a coherent world of images and messages serving its own institutional interests. The question is whether the judiciary should be enlisted to add further credibility to media mythology. Plugging courtrooms into the television system can make them appendages of that system. Once televised trials attract a large national following, the process will be irresistible, cumulative, and probably irreversible.

The scenario unfolding now is what Chief Justice Warren warned against when, agreeing with the majority in *Estes v. Texas* that "the televising of criminal trials is inherently a denial of due process," expressed the additional view that the case at hand was only "a vivid illustration of the inherent prejudice of televised criminal trials." Therefore, Warren wished to "make a definitive appraisal of television in the courtroom."

In doing so, he predicted with uncanny foresight the entertainment pressures upon the selection and treatment of trials; the impact of notoriety upon participants, including jurors returning to their communities; the problem of impartially retrying a case after wide national exposure; and the likelihood that defendants who have attracted public interest and find their "trial turned into a vehicle for television . . . are the very persons who encounter the greatest difficulty in securing an impartial trial even without the presence of television.". . .

Without a doubt television has enriched the horizons of many who have been out of the cultural mainstream since the coming of print-oriented culture. It sometimes offers superb insight and enlightenment. Indeed, it has even provided dramatic reenactments of great moments in judicial history, going behind the scenes to illuminate the invisible but all-important principles of justice in a calmer historical perspective. But telecasting of live trials—television at its spontaneous best—would not encourage that kind of dispassionate analysis.

The political opportunities inherent in the shifting balance of powers will become more and more compelling. About 10 per cent of the electorate can now identify any judicial candidate during an election. A television trial can easily multiply that recognition factor for a candidate. (Will others ask for equal television trial time?) As a system of mutual accommodations and pay-offs develops, controls and inhibitions are likely to fall by the wayside.

Neither history nor existing research support the contention that television coverage of courts would enhance fairness, protect freedom, increase public understanding, or promote needed court reform. Only an immediate moratorium on televising trials can give us the time and the opportunity we need for responsible action.

In the face of demonstrated conflicts and incalculable risks, the burden of proof must shift from the potential victims to the proponents of trials by television. An independent scientific investigation is what we need now, both to analyze a representative sample of televised trials and segments of trials and to assess conceptions of the judicial process that television trials cultivate in the minds of the viewers, as well as the minds of participants. Until we undertake such research and until it disproves reasonable expectations about TV's effects, we should prevent television from remaking our system of justice in its own image.

RESPONSIBILITY OF NEWS MEDIA

THE WARREN COMMISSION*

. . . If Oswald had been tried for his murders of November 22, the effects of the news policy pursued by the Dallas authorities would have proven harmful both to the prosecution and the defense. The misinformation reported after the shootings might have been used by the defense to cast doubt on the reliability of the State's entire case. Though each inaccuracy can be explained without great difficulty, the number and variety of misstatements issued by the police shortly after the assassination would have greatly assisted a skillful defense attorney attempting to influence the attitudes of jurors.

A fundamental objection to the news policy pursued by the Dallas police, however, is the extent to which it endangered Oswald's constitutional right to a trial by an impartial jury. Because of the nature of the crime, the widespread attention which it necessarily received, and the intense public feelings which it aroused, it would have been a most difficult task to select an unprejudiced jury, either in Dallas or elsewhere. But the difficulty was markedly increased by the divulgence of the specific items of evidence with which the police linked Oswald to the two killings. The disclosure of evidence encouraged the public, from which a jury would ultimately be impaneled, to prejudge the very questions that would be raised at trial.

Moreover, rules of law might have prevented the prosecution from presenting portions of this evidence to the jury. For example, though expressly recognizing that Oswald's wife could not be compelled to testify against him, District Attorney Wade revealed to the Nation that Marina Oswald had affirmed her husband's ownership of a rifle like that found on the sixth floor of the Texas School Book Depository. Curry stated that Oswald had refused to take a lie detector test, although such a statement would have been inadmissible in a trial. The exclusion of such evidence, however, would have been meaningless if jurors were already familiar with the same facts from previous television or newspaper reports. Wade might have influenced prospective jurors by his mistaken statement that the paraffin test showed that Oswald had fired a gun. The tests merely showed that he had nitrate traces on his hands, which did not necessarily mean that he had fired either a rifle or a pistol.

The disclosure of evidence was seriously aggravated by the statements of

---

* From the *Report of the President's Commission on the Assassination of President John F. Kennedy.* Washington, D.C.: Government Printing Office (1964) at p. 238.

numerous responsible officials that they were certain of Oswald's guilt. Captain Fritz said that the case against Oswald was "cinched." Curry reported on Saturday that "we are sure of our case." Curry announced that he considered Oswald sane, and Wade told the public that he would ask for the death penalty.

The American Bar Association declared in December 1963 that "widespread publicizing of Oswald's alleged guilt, involving statements by officials and public disclosures of the details of 'evidence,' would have made it extremely difficult to impanel an unprejudiced jury and afford the accused a fair trial." Local bar associations expressed similar feelings. The Commission agrees that Lee Harvey Oswald's opportunity for a trial by 12 jurors free of preconception as to his guilt or innocence would have been seriously jeopardized by the premature disclosure and weighing of the evidence against him.

The problem of disclosure of information and its effect on trials is, of course, further complicated by the independent activities of the press in developing information on its own from sources other than law enforcement agencies. Had the police not released the specific items of evidence against Oswald, it is still possible that the other information presented on television and in the newspapers, chiefly of a biographical nature, would itself have had a prejudicial effect on the public.

In explanation of the news policy adopted by the Dallas authorities, Chief Curry observed that "it seemed like there was a great demand by the general public to know what was going on." In a prepared statement, Captain King wrote:

> At that time we felt a necessity for permitting the newsmen as much latitude as possible. We realized the magnitude of the incident the newsmen were there to cover. We realized that not only the nation but the world would be greatly interested in what occurred in Dallas. We believed that we had an obligation to make as widely known as possible everything we could regarding the investigation of the assassination and the manner in which we undertook that investigation.

The Commission recognizes that the people of the United States, and indeed the world, had a deep-felt interest in learning of the events surrounding the death of President Kennedy, including the development of the investigation in Dallas. An informed public provided the ultimate guarantee that adequate steps would be taken to apprehend those responsible for the assassination and that all necessary precautions would be taken to protect the national security. It was therefore proper and desirable that the public know which agencies were participating in the investigation and the rate at which their work was progressing. The public was also entitled to know that Lee Harvey Oswald had been apprehended and that the State had gathered sufficient evidence to arraign him for the murders of the President and Patrolman Tippit, that he was being held pending action of the grand jury, that the investigation was continuing, and that the law enforcement agencies had discovered no evidence which tended to show that any other person was involved in either slaying.

However, neither the press nor the public had a right to be contemporaneously informed by the police or prosecuting authorities of the details of the evidence being accumulated against Oswald. Undoubtedly the public was interested in these disclosures, but its curiosity should not have been satisfied at the expense of the accused's right to a trial by an impartial jury. The courtroom, not the newspaper or television screen, is the appropriate forum in our system for the trial of a man accused of a crime.

If the evidence in the possession of the authorities had not been disclosed, it is true that the public would not have been in a position to assess the adequacy of the investigation or to apply pressures for further official undertakings. But a major consequence of the hasty and at times inaccurate divulgence of evidence after the assassination was simply to give rise to groundless rumors and public confusion. Moreover, without learning the details of the case, the public could have been informed by the responsible authority of the general scope of the investigation and the extent to which State and Federal agencies were assisting in the police work.

While appreciating the heavy and unique pressures with which the Dallas Police Department was confronted by reason of the assassination of President Kennedy, primary responsibility for having failed to control the press and to check the flow of undigested evidence to the public must be borne by the police department. It was the only agency that could have established orderly and sound operating procedures to control the multitude of newsmen gathered in the police building after the assassination.

The Commission believes, however, that a part of the responsibility for the unfortunate circumstances following the President's death must be borne by the news media. The crowd of newsmen generally failed to respond properly to the demands of the police. Frequently without permission, news representatives used police offices on the third floor, tying up facilities and interfering with normal police operations. Police efforts to preserve order and to clear passageways in the corridor were usually unsuccessful. On Friday night the reporters completely ignored Curry's injunction against asking Oswald questions in the assembly room and crowding in on him. On Sunday morning, the newsmen were instructed to direct no questions at Oswald; nevertheless, several reporters shouted questions at him when he appeared in the basement.

Moreover, by constantly pursuing public officials, the news representatives placed an insistent pressure upon them to disclose information. And this pressure was not without effect, since the police attitude toward the press was affected by the desire to maintain satisfactory relations with the news representatives and to create a favorable image of themselves. Chief Curry frankly told the Commission that

I didn't order them out of the building, which if I had it to do over I would. In the past like I say, we had always maintained very good relations with our press, and they had always respected us.

Curry refused Fritz' request to put Oswald behind the screen in the assembly room at the Friday night press conference because this might have hindered the taking of pictures. Curry's subordinates had the impression that an unannounced transfer of Oswald to the county jail was unacceptable because Curry did not want to disappoint the newsmen; he had promised that they could witness the transfer. It seemed clear enough that any attempt to exclude the press from the building or to place limits on the information disclosed to them would have been resented and disputed by the newsmen, who were constantly and aggressively demanding all possible information about anything related to the assassination.

Although the Commission has found no corroboration in the video and audio tapes, police officials recall that one or two representatives of the press reinforced their demands to see Oswald by suggesting that the police had been guilty of brutalizing him. They intimated that unless they were given the opportunity to see him, these suggestions would be passed on to the public. Captain King testified that he had been told that

> A short time after Oswald's arrest one newsman held up a photograph and said, "This is what the man charged with the assassination of the President looks like. Or at least this is what he did look like. We don't know what he looks like after an hour in the custody of the Dallas Police Department."

City Manager Elgin Crull stated that when he visited Chief Curry in his office on the morning of November 23, Curry told him that he "felt it was necessary to cooperate with the news media representatives, in order to avoid being accused of using Gestapo tactics in connection with the handling of Oswald." Crull agreed with Curry. The Commission deems any such veiled threats to be absolutely without justification.

The general disorder in the Police and Courts Building during November 22–24 reveals a regrettable lack of self-discipline by the newsmen. The Commission believes that the news media, as well as the police authorities, who failed to impose conditions more in keeping with the orderly process of justice, must share responsibility for the failure of law enforcement which occurred in connection with the death of Oswald. On previous occasions, public bodies have voiced the need for the exercise of self-restraint by the news media in periods when the demand for information must be tempered by other fundamental requirements of our society.

At its annual meeting in Washington in April 1964, the American Society of Newspaper Editors discussed the role of the press in Dallas immediately after President Kennedy's assassination. The discussion revealed the strong misgivings among the editors themselves about the role that the press had played and their desire that the press display more self-discipline and adhere to higher standards of conduct in the future. To prevent a recurrence of the unfortunate events which followed the assassination, however, more than general concern will be needed. The promulgation of a code of professional conduct governing representatives of all news media would be welcome evidence that the press had profited by the lesson of Dallas.

The burden of insuring that appropriate action is taken to establish ethical standards of conduct for the news media must also be borne, however, by State and local governments, by the bar, and ultimately by the public. The experience in Dallas during November 22–24 is a dramatic affirmation of the need for steps to bring about a proper balance between the right of the public to be kept informed and the right of the individual to a fair and impartial trial.

APPENDIX I

AMENDMENTS
TO THE CONSTITUTION
OF THE UNITED STATES
RELEVANT TO FREEDOM OF EXPRESSION

ARTICLE I

Congress shall make no law respecting an establishment of religion, or prohibiting the free exercise thereof; or abridging the freedom of speech, or of the press; or the right of the people peaceably to assemble, and to petition the government for a redress of grievances.

ARTICLE IV

The right of the people to be secure in their persons, houses, papers, and effects, against unreasonable searches and seizures, shall not be violated, and no warrants shall issue, but upon probable cause, supported by oath or affirmation, and particularly describing the place to be searched, and the persons or things to be seized.

ARTICLE V

No person shall be held to answer for a capital, or otherwise infamous crime, unless on a presentment or indictment of a grand jury, except in cases arising in the land or naval forces, or in the militia, when in actual service in time of war or public danger; nor shall any person be subject for the same offense to be twice put in jeopardy of life or limb; nor shall be compelled in any criminal case to be a witness against himself, nor be deprived of life, liberty, or property, without due process of law; nor shall private property be taken for public use without just compensation.

ARTICLE VI

In all criminal prosecutions, the accused shall enjoy the right to a speedy and public trial, by an impartial jury of the State and district wherein the crime shall have been committed, which district shall have been previously ascertained by law, and to be informed of the nature and cause of the accusations; to be confronted with the witnesses against him; to have compulsory process for obtaining witnesses in his favor, and to have the assistance of counsel for his defense.

ARTICLE VII

In suits at common law, where the value in controversy shall exceed twenty dollars, the right of trial by jury shall be preserved, and no fact tried by a jury shall be otherwise reexamined in any court of the United States, than according to the rules of the common law.

ARTICLE VIII

Excessive bail shall not be required, nor excessive fines imposed, nor cruel and unusual punishments inflicted.

ARTICLE X

The powers not delegated to the United States by the Constitution, nor prohibited by it to the States, are reserved to the States respectively, or to the people.

ARTICLE XIV

SECTION 1. All persons born or naturalized in the United States, and subject to the jurisdiction thereof, are citizens of the United States and of the State wherein they reside. No State shall make or enforce any law which shall abridge the privileges or immunities of citizens of the United States; nor shall any State deprive any person of life, liberty, or property, without due process of law; nor deny to any person within its jurisdiction the equal protection of the laws.

APPENDIX II

JUSTICES OF THE
UNITED STATES SUPREME COURT

JUSTICE	TERM	YRS.
* Jay, John	1789–1795	5
Rutledge, John	1789–1791	1
Cushing, William	1789–1810	20
Wilson, James	1789–1798	8
Blair, John	1789–1796	6
Harrison, Robert H.	1789–1790	—
Iredell, James	1790–1799	9
Johnson, Thomas	1791–1793	1
Paterson, William	1793–1806	13
* Rutledge, John	1795–1795	—
Chase, Samuel	1796–1811	15
* Ellsworth, Oliver	1796–1799	4
Washington, Bushrod	1798–1829	31
Moore, Alfred	1799–1804	4
* Marshall, John	1801–1835	34
Johnson, William	1804–1834	30
Livingston, Brockholst	1806–1823	16
Todd, Thomas	1807–1826	18
Story, Joseph	1811–1845	33
Duval, Gabriel	1812–1835	22
Thompson, Smith	1823–1843	20
Trimble, Robert	1826–1828	2
McLean, John	1829–1861	32
Baldwin, Henry	1830–1844	14
Wayne, James M.	1835–1867	32
* Taney, Roger B.	1836–1864	28
Barbour, Philip P.	1836–1841	4
Catron, John	1837–1865	28
McKinley, John	1837–1852	15
Daniel, Peter V.	1841–1860	19
Nelson, Samuel	1845–1872	27
Woodbury, Levi	1845–1851	5
Grier, Robert C.	1846–1870	23
Curtis, Benjamin R.	1851–1857	6
Campbell, John A.	1853–1861	8
Clifford, Nathan	1858–1881	23
Swayne, Noah H.	1862–1881	18
Miller, Samuel F.	1862–1890	28
Davis, David	1862–1877	14
Field, Stephen J.	1863–1897	34
* Chase, Salmon P.	1864–1873	8
Strong, William	1870–1880	10
Bradley, Joseph P.	1870–1892	21
Hunt, Ward	1873–1882	9
* Waite, Morrison R.	1874–1888	14
Harlan, John M.	1877–1911	34
Woods, William B.	1881–1887	6
Matthews, Stanley	1881–1889	7
Gray, Horace	1882–1902	20
Blatchford, Samuel	1882–1893	11
Lamar, Lucius	1888–1893	5
* Fuller, Melville W.	1888–1910	21
Brewer, David J.	1890–1910	20
Brown, Henry B.	1891–1906	15
Shiras, George, Jr.	1892–1903	10
Jackson, Howell E.	1893–1895	2
White, Edward D.	1894–1910	16
Peckham, Rufus W.	1896–1909	13
McKenna, Joseph	1898–1925	26
Holmes, Oliver W.	1902–1932	29
Day, William R.	1903–1922	19
Moody, William H.	1906–1910	3
Lurton, Horace H.	1910–1914	4
Hughes, Charles E.	1910–1916	5
Van Devanter, Willis	1911–1937	26
Lamar, Joseph R.	1911–1916	5
* White, Edward D.	1910–1921	10
Pitney, Mahlon	1912–1922	10
McReynolds, James C.	1914–1941	26
Brandeis, Louis D.	1916–1939	22
Clarke, John H.	1916–1922	5
* Taft, William H.	1921–1930	8
Sutherland, George	1922–1938	15
Butler, Pierce	1922–1939	16

Sanford, Edward T.	1923–1930	7	* Warren, Earl	1953–1969	16
Stone, Harlan F.	1925–1941	16	Harlan, John M.	1955–1971	16
* Hughes, Charles E.	1930–1941	11	Brennan, Wm. J., Jr.	1956–	
Roberts, Owen J.	1930–1945	15	Whittaker, Charles E.	1957–1962	5
Cardozo, Benjamin N.	1932–1938	6	Stewart, Potter	1958–1981	23
Black, Hugo L.	1937–1971	34	White, Byron R.	1962–	
Reed, Stanley F.	1938–1957	19	Goldberg, Arthur J.	1962–1965	3
Frankfurter, Felix	1939–1962	23	Fortas, Abe	1965–1969	4
Douglas, Wm. O.	1939–1975	36	Marshall, Thurgood	1967–	
Murphy, Frank	1940–1949	9	* Burger, Warren	1969–1986	17
* Stone, Harlan	1941–1946	5	Blackmun, Harry	1970–	
Byrnes, James F.	1941–1942	1	Powell, Lewis F., Jr.	1972–1987	
Jackson, Robert H.	1941–1954	12	* Rehnquist, Wm. H.	1972–	
Rutledge, Wiley B.	1943–1949	6	Stevens, John Paul	1976–	
Burton, Harold H.	1945–1958	13	O'Connor, Sandra Day	1981–	
* Vinson, Fred M.	1946–1953	7	Scalia, Antonin	1986–	
Clark, Tom C.	1949–1967	18	Kennedy, Anthony M.	1988–	
Minton, Sherman	1949–1956	7			

* Indicates Chief Justice.

APPENDIX III

GLOSSARY OF MAJOR LEGAL TERMS
USED IN THE PRECEDING CASES

Acquittal. Being set free or exonerated of a criminal charge through a verdict of not guilty.

Affirm. To sustain the decision or ruling of a lower court.

Amicus curiae. A friend of the court who offers advice.

Appellant. A party who brings an appeal. Also called plaintiff-in-error.

Appellee. A party against whom an appeal is brought (usually the winner in the lower court action). Also called respondent-in-error.

Cause. Grounds for legal action.

Certiorari, writ of. A request by a higher court for the lower court to forward the record of the case in review. Also called writ of error or writ of review.

Claimant. One who makes a claim.

Complaint. A specific charge against an individual which leads to legal action.

Concur. To agree or to be in accord with, such as to share a legal opinion.

Continuance. A postponement of an action pending.

Defame. To hold a party up to public ridicule, hatred or contempt. A libel.

Defendant. The party against whom a legal action is brought.

Demurrer. A pleading by a defendant that even if the charge is true, it constitutes insufficient grounds for legal action.

De novo. From the beginning. Once more. Anew.

Dissent. To differ or to disagree.

Due process. The normal and proper administration of law.

Enjoin. To forbid or restrain through an injunction.

Error, writ of. A request by a higher court for the lower court to forward the record of the case in review. Also called writ of certiorari or writ of review.

Ex parte. In the interest of or on behalf of one party.

Ex rel. In the interest of or at the instigation of one party after which the state assumes responsibility for the case.

Habeas corpus, writ of. A requirement that the prisoner be brought before the court, which then is to determine the legality of his detention.

Indictment. A formal charge against an individual made by a grand jury.

Information. A formal charge against an individual made by a public officer, usually a district attorney.

Infra. Below.

Injunction. A court order restraining a party from committing certain acts.

In re. Concerning or in the matter of.

Inter alia. Among other things.

Judgment. A decision of the court as to the outcome of the case before it.

Jurisprudence. The science of law.

Libel. To hold a party up to public hatred, ridicule or contempt. To defame.

Litigation. A legal action.

Malfeasance. Wrongdoing or misconduct.

Malice. Intent to commit a wrongful act.

Mandamus. A court order requiring a party to fulfill some act or duty.

Memorandum case. One involving usually a brief, informal statement noting the findings of the court.

Mistrial. Termination without decision of a trial because of some legal error or because the jury could not reach agreement.

Nonfeasance. Failure to fulfill some act required by law.

Opinion. A formal statement by a court as to the outcome of the case before it.

Per curiam. An opinion delivered by the court as a whole and without reference to opinions of individual jurists.

Per quod, libel. A defamation which can be ascertained only after additional information is known.

Per se, libel. A defamation on its surface and without the need of any additional background information.

Petition. A formal written request in which specific legal action is requested.

Plaintiff. A party which brings charges in a civil action.

Plaintiff-in-error. A party appealing a lower court decision to a higher court. Also called appellant.

Remand. To send back to a lower court for specific action.

Remit. To send back to a lower court for further action.

Res judicata. A legal principle which has been settled by court action.

Respondent. A party against whom an appeal has been sought. A defendant. Also called respondent-in-error.

Reverse. To set aside or annul a decision of a lower court.

Review, writ of. A request by a higher court for the lower court to forward the record of the case in review. Also called writ of certiorari or writ of error.

Sequester. To temporarily remove property from the possession of the owner until certain legal questions are answered. Also to remove the jury from public exposure.

Show cause. To substantiate legally why a certain judgment should not take effect.

Summary judgment. A statement by the court giving the legal questions and rendering a decision without a formal trial.

Supra. Above.

Sustain. To uphold, support or confirm.

Tort. A civil wrong (or personal injury) for which damages may be recovered.

Veniremen. Those called to jury service.

Venue. The locality of the criminal act or cause of legal action, or the place where the jury is called or the trial is held.

Voir dire. The preliminary questioning of a prospective juror or witness by the court.

Writ. A formal document ordering or prohibiting some act.

INDEX